For Alix

PHILIP HOARE

NOËL
COWARD

A Biography

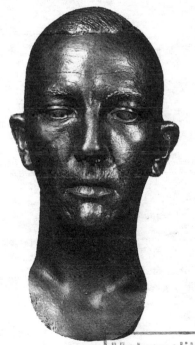

SINCLAIR-STEVENSON

First published in Great Britain in 1995
by Sinclair-Stevenson
an imprint of Reed Books Ltd
Michelin House, 81 Fulham Road, London SW3 6RB
and Auckland, Melbourne, Singapore and Toronto

A CIP catalogue record for this book
is available at the British Library
ISBN 1 85619 265 2 (hardback)
ISBN 1 85619 672 5 (paperback)

Typeset by CentraCet Limited, Cambridge
Printed and bound in Great Britain
by Clays Ltd, St Ives plc

Contents

Contents

List of Illustrations

First black and white plate section

'Captain' Henry Gordon Veitch (*Noel Coward Estate*)
Mary Kathleen Veitch (*Noel Coward Estate*)
Arthur Sabin Coward (*Noel Coward Estate*)
Violet Agnes Coward (*Noel Coward Estate*)
Noel aged five years (*Noel Coward Estate*)
5 Waldegrave Road (now No. 131), Teddington (*The author*)
Noel sketched by Philip Streatfeild, 1914 (*Noel Coward Estate*)
Noel at Charlestown (*Private collection*)
Noel and Philip Streatfeild in Cornwall (*Jon Wynne-Tyson*)
The Great Name: Noel, Lydia Bilbrooke, Charles Hawtrey
Noel and Philip Tonge in *Where the Rainbow Ends* (*Noel Coward Estate*)
Noel and Lillian Gish in *Hearts of the World* (*British Film Institute*)
John Ekins, Esme Wynne and Noel (*Noel Coward Estate*)
Noel in *The Knight of the Burning Pestle* (*Noel Coward Estate*)
Mrs Astley Cooper with Noel (*Private collection*)
Noel in the Med (*Bobbie Andrews album*)
Coney Island, 1921: Teddie Gerrard, Noel, Jeffrey Amherst and Napier
   Alington (*Private collection*)
Davos, Christmas 1922 (*Private collection*)
Benita Hume, Ivor Novello, Mabel Poulton and Francis Doble on location
   for *The Constant Nymph* (*Bobbie Andrews album*)
Noel at Ivor Novello's Red Roofs (*Bobbie Andrews album*)
Douglas Fairbanks, Mary Pickford and Noel (*Private collection*)
Coney Island, 1925: Gladys Calthrop, Noel, Bobbie Andrews
   (*Bobbie Andrews album*)
Noel and Lilian Braithwaite in *The Vortex* (*Noel Coward Estate*)
'Noel the fortunate': the front page of the *Sketch*, 1925
Noel and Edna Best in *The Constant Nymph* (*Private collection*)

List of Illustrations

Noel and Violet at the French production of *Present Laughter*
   (*Noel Coward Estate*)
With Marlene Dietrich at the Globe Theatre, June 1954
   (*Timothy Morgan-Owen*)
At the Desert Inn, Las Vegas (*Noel Coward Estate*)
Our Man in Havana (*British Film Institute*)
Bunny Lake is Missing (*British Film Institute*)
The Midnight Matinee, Phoenix Theatre (*Timothy Morgan-Owen*)
Gladys Calthrop, Sir Noel and Joyce Carey, April 1970
   (*Timothy Morgan-Owen*)
Final bow, March 1970 (*Timothy Morgan-Owen*)

Colour plates

Easter greetings to Violet (*Noel Coward Estate*)
'Poj, Lynton, June 1918' (*Jon Wynne-Tyson*)
Bathers on the Rocks, Philip Streatfeild (*Christie's Images*)
Graham Payn at Blue Harbour (*Private collection*)
Noel in the pool (*Private collection*)
An island exile (*Private collection*)
Lorn Loraine at Blue Harbour (*Private collection*)
The view from Firefly Hill, watercolour by Beaton (*Hugo Vickers*)
Firefly (*The author*)
On the veranda of the Old Lookout (*Private collection*)
Dust jacket for *Pomp and Circumstance*
Noel, unidentified artist, Cole Lesley, Gladys Calthrop, Blanche Blackwell
   and Clemence Dane (*Private collection*)
Two Nuns, Noel Coward (*Christie's Images*)
Noel, Graham Payn, Charles Russell and Cole Lesley (*Private collection*)
Lorn Loraine, Noel and Joyce Carey arrive in California (*Private collection*)
Bill Traylor (*Private collection*)
Noel on the set of *Nude with Violin* (*Private collection*)
Cole Lesley at Les Avants (*Private collection*)
Joyce Carey and Alan Webb (*Private collection*)
Being photographed by Richard Avedon (*Private collection*)
At Goldenhurst in favourite Nehru jacket (*Private collection*)
Blue Harbour, 1993 (*The author*)
Noel Coward's grave, Firefly Hill, 1993 (*The author*)
Poster for *Brief Encounter* (*British Film Institute*)
Programme for *Sail Away* (*Private collection*)
Album covers, 1955

List of Illustrations

Illustrations in the text

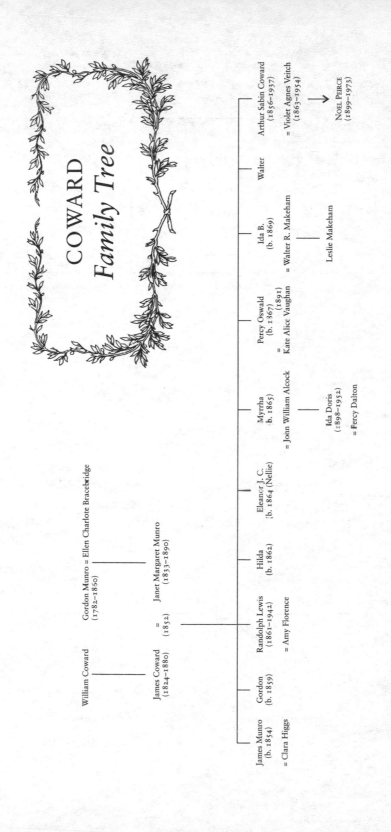

COWARD
Family Tree

William Coward ——— Gordon Munro = Ellen Charlotte Bracebridge
(1782–1850)

James Coward ——— = ——— Janet Margaret Munro
(1824–1880)   (1852)   (1833–1890)

James Munro (b. 1854) = Clara Higgs

Gordon (b. 1859)

Randolph Lewis (1861–1942) = Amy Florence

Hilda (b. 1862)

Eleanor J. C. (b. 1864) (Nellie)

Myrrha (b. 1865) = Joan William Alcock

Ida Doris (1898–1952) = Percy Dalton

Percy Oswald (b. 1867) = (1891) Kate Alice Vaughan

Ida B. (b. 1869) = Walter R. Makeham

Leslie Makeham

Walter

Arthur Sabin Coward (1856–1937) = Violet Agnes Veitch (1863–1954)

→ NOEL PEIRCE (1899–1973)

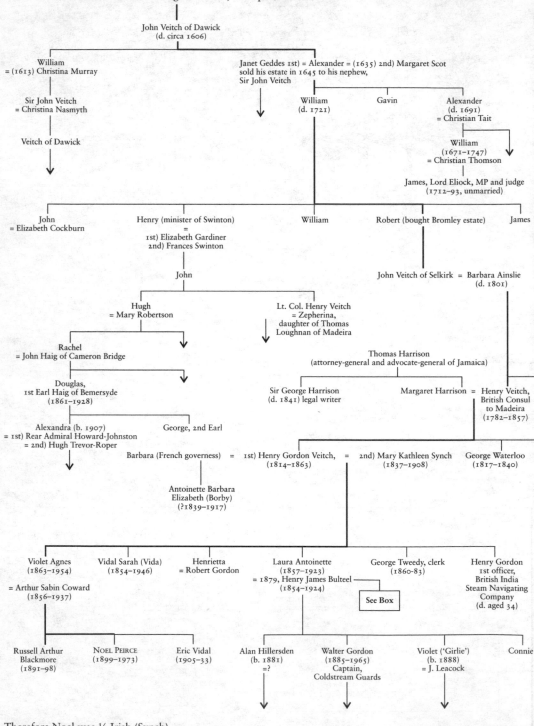

Gailard – came from Normandy during the reign of Robert Bruce, who gave him the lands of Dawyk upon the Tweed, and a coat of arms bearing three cow's heads, hence the name change to Vache, corrupted to Veitch.

John Veitch of Dawick
(d. circa 1606)

William
= (1613) Christina Murray

Janet Geddes 1st) = Alexander = (1635) 2nd) Margaret Scot
sold his estate in 1645 to his nephew,
Sir John Veitch

William
(d. 1721)

Gavin

Alexander
(d. 1691)
= Christian Tait

Sir John Veitch
= Christina Nasmyth

William
(1671–1747)
= Christian Thomson

Veitch of Dawick

James, Lord Eliock, MP and judge
(1712–93, unmarried)

John
= Elizabeth Cockburn

Henry (minister of Swinton)
=
1st) Elizabeth Gardiner
2nd) Frances Swinton

William

Robert (bought Bromley estate)

James

John

John Veitch of Selkirk = Barbara Ainslie
(d. 1801)

Hugh
= Mary Robertson

Lt. Col. Henry Veitch
= Zepherina,
daughter of Thomas
Loughnan of Madeira

Rachel
= John Haig of Cameron Bridge

Thomas Harrison
(attorney-general and advocate-general of Jamaica)

Douglas,
1st Earl Haig of Bemersyde
(1861–1928)

Sir George Harrison
(d. 1841) legal writer

Margaret Harrison =

Henry Veitch,
British Consul
to Madeira
(1782–1857)

Alexandra (b. 1907)
= 1st) Rear Admiral Howard-Johnston
= 2nd) Hugh Trevor-Roper

George, 2nd Earl

Barbara (French governess) =

1st) Henry Gordon Veitch,
(1814–1863)

= 2nd) Mary Kathleen Synch
(1837–1908)

George Waterloo
(1817–1840)

Antoinette Barbara
Elizabeth (Borby)
(?1839–1917)

Violet Agnes
(1863–1954)

= Arthur Sabin Coward
(1856–1937)

Vidal Sarah (Vida)
(1854–1946)

Henrietta
= Robert Gordon

Laura Antoinette
(1857–1923)
= 1879, Henry James Bulteel
(1854–1924)

George Tweedy, clerk
(1860–83)

Henry Gordon
1st officer,
British India
Steam Navigating
Company
(d. aged 34)

See Box

Russell Arthur
Blackmore
(1891–98)

NOEL PEIRCE
(1899–1973)

Eric Vidal
(1905–33)

Alan Hillersden
(b. 1881)
=?

Walter Gordon
(1885–1965)
Captain,
Coldstream Guards

Violet ('Girlie')
(b. 1888)
= J. Leacock

Connie

Therefore Noel was ¼ Irish (Synch)
½ Scottish (Veitch/Munro)
and ¼ English (Coward)

VEITCH
Family Tree

Mungo Park of Selkirk

Ann
(b. 1792)
= Brydene
(Edinburgh lawyer)

Violet of Bromley House
(b. 1787)
= Col. Robert Tweedy

Robert   James   Mary
=
Alexander Park

Mungo Park (1771–1806)
African explorer

Sarah Antoinette
(d. 1818)
= (1839) Captain Alexander
(later Admiral) Vidal

Henrietta
= (1850)
Alexander of Oliveira
of Funchal

Barbara m. 2nd 1839
= Sir Robert Torrens
1st premier of South Australia

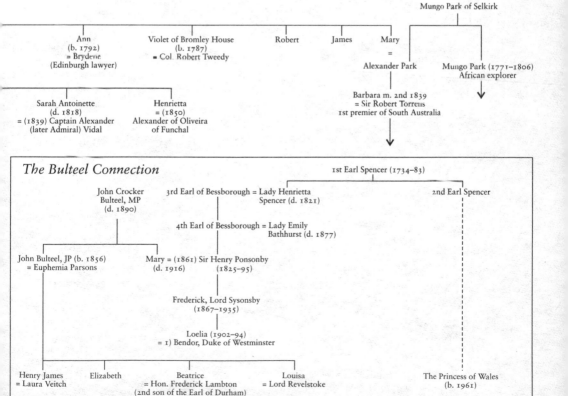

The Bulteel Connection

1st Earl Spencer (1734–83)

John Crocker
Bulteel, MP
(d. 1890)

3rd Earl of Bessborough = Lady Henrietta
Spencer (d. 1821)

2nd Earl Spencer

4th Earl of Bessborough = Lady Emily
Bathurst (d. 1877)

John Bulteel, JP (b. 1856)
= Euphemia Parsons

Mary = (1861) Sir Henry Ponsonby
(d. 1916)   (1825–95)

Frederick, Lord Sysonsby
(1867–1935)

Loelia (1902–94)
= 1) Bendor, Duke of Westminster

Henry James
= Laura Veitch

Elizabeth

Beatrice
= Hon. Frederick Lambton
(2nd son of the Earl of Durham)

Louisa
= Lord Revelstoke

The Princess of Wales
(b. 1961)

Family Album

Oh how fortunate I was to have been born poor ... Had my
formative years been passed in more assured circumstances I might
easily have slipped into precociousness; as it was I merely had to
slip *out* of precociousness and bring home the bacon.

Noel Coward's diary, 21 December 1967

WITH impeccable timing Noel Coward was born on 16
December 1899, just in time to catch the fleeting grandeur of
the old century. This seemed to endow him with a vital sense
of his country's past. When a cartoon was published around the time of
the hugely successful *Cavalcade*, depicting a baby Noel taking notes in
his pram, the cartoonist was nearer to the truth than he knew.

Even from his birth, Coward's life was defined by myth. The future
genius of the stage is supposed to have sprung from the anonymity
of suburbia and an unremarkable family background: the effect was
to make the legend of Noel Coward – the self-created celebrity – all
the more extraordinary. The truth is rather different. Behind the
bland redbrick of his birthplace is a story more interesting than he
intimated: a tale of fallen fortunes which would perceptibly influence
his life and work. Coward's obsession with class and status – so
resonant in his dramas – can be traced to an awareness of his own
ancestry. Far from being merely the son of an impoverished south
London family, Coward's forebears included high-ranking naval
officers and public servants, literary and musical noteworthies – he
could even claim royal and aristocratic connections. It was partly his
mother's knowledge of this antecedence that would fire Coward's social
climb; and in order to understand the sometimes tenuous nature of the
position he achieved, it is necessary to recall the accomplishments of his
ancestors.

Coward wrote of his mother, Violet, that she came from 'good family
... brought up in the tradition of being a gentlewoman'. Her family
were of Scottish descent and definite, if somewhat eroded, gentility: the
Veitches of later years were to evince the snobbery of a line formerly
grand, now diminished – a concern with 'good families' inherited by
both Coward and his mother. In 1922 Violet and her sister Vida wrote
to the office of the Lord Lygon King of Arms, enquiring about the
Veitch family crest and whether Noel could use it. He could not, but
the existence of a crest practically ennobled the family in his mother's
eyes. She boasted of other notable connections: a cousin, Rachel Veitch,
had married John Haig of Bemersyde, being described as 'daughter of a
family who thought themselves socially superior to the Haigs but were
too poor to endow their daughter'. Rachel's fifth son was Douglas, later
Field Marshal Earl Haig; and the Veitches' familial home at Dawyck
(pronounced Doick), near Peebles, featured in John Buchan's *John
Burnett of Barns*, a Veitch of Dawyck as its heroine. Examining his
literary provenance, Coward noted, 'I believe that a certain Miss Veitch,
a far-flung-back ancestress of my mother's, who lived in Dawick House,
Moffat, near the Scottish border, wrote a number of spirited novels at
the beginning of the nineteenth century.' Other notable members of this
border gentry family included the nurseryman John Veitch, the classical
scholar William Veitch, the professor of philosophy John Veitch; and
through marriage the family could claim kinship with Sir Robert
Torrens, the first premier of Australia, and the explorer Mungo Park.

But of Coward's immediate maternal ancestors, it was his great-
grandfather, Henry Veitch, who was famous, even infamous. Born in
Selkirk, he was appointed consul-general to Madeira by George III in
1809, a post which paid him a substantial £800 per annum. He was an
ambitious man, wealthy and handsome, owning five *quintas* and large
tracts of land, and well liked by the locals. When HMS *Northumberland*
anchored at Funchal harbour on 23 August 1815, carrying the defeated
Emperor Napoleon to his exile in St Helena, Veitch erred in addressing
the prisoner as 'Your Majesty' rather than 'General', a mistake said to
have cost him his post; but the real reason was his meddling in island
politics. He secretly sided with the constitutionalists who sought independence from Portugal, and the foreign secretary, Lord Aberdeen,
ordered his return to England. However, the locals demanded his
reinstatement, and Veitch was reappointed by Lord Palmerston, remaining consul until he was dismissed for the second and final time in 1835.

Veitch had again become embroiled in politics, and during a constitutional crisis, had virtually appointed himself acting governor. His private life was also called into question; he had married Margaret Harrison (sister of Sir George Harrison, Secretary to the Treasury) in 1808, but was known to have sired many illegitimate children by various mistresses in Madeira, and had the reputation of being 'one of the greatest sinners on the island'.* He was frowned upon for not attending church, preferring to spend the weekends at his country house promoting weekly balls; Henry Veitch was a committed socialite. When he began to interfere in clerical matters, it was the last straw. A keen amateur architect, he had designed and built the English Church (complete with a masonic all-seeing eye), and his lordly behaviour to its cleric brought a formal complaint from the Bishop of London. Palmerston, weary of the trouble Veitch was causing, dismissed him in December 1835.

By now Veitch had a legitimate family to support. His eldest son, Coward's grandfather, Henry Gordon Veitch, had been born in Madeira on 29 July 1814. After schooling in Switzerland, Henry Gordon entered the Royal Naval College at Dartmouth in 1828, where he won prizes for his drawing (Violet Coward recalled that her asthmatic father 'was never really fond of the sea but always wanted to be an artist'). As a child Coward remembered seeing his grandfather's water-colours in a leather-bound album. 'He was good at mountains and clouds and ships, and reflections in the sea, but consciously bad at figures, so he frequently cut these out from coloured prints and stuck them . . . on to his blue mountains, to give them life.' Henry Gordon Veitch spent twenty years in the navy as a surveyor, rising in rank to lieutenant (not captain or commander as the family later claimed), and married his sister's governess, 'a lovely French girl'; a daughter, Barbara, was born in Madeira.† But Henry's first wife died young, and he had been a widower for some years when he was posted to the west coast of Ireland, where he met Mary Kathleen Synch, a pretty Irish girl with blonde hair and blue eyes only two years older than his daughter. They

---

* Coward's interest in his great-grandfather was stimulated by Rupert Croft-Cooke, who wrote a history of Madeira in 1961, and to whom Noel wrote, 'In what way was he notorious? I *long* to know. Can it be what I think? He was *very* handsome. I have a miniature of him somewhere. Do let me know all.'
† 'She was a lovely dark girl', recalled Violet of her stepsister, 'rather French looking'. In his memoirs, Coward refers to 'an extra relation called Barbara, or "Borby," who had fallen out of a port-hole on her head at the age of two, and was consequently a little peculiar', but his mother does not mention any such disability.

were married at Sneem, a fishing village in County Kerry, and had two daughters.

Henry's asthma had worsened, and on 15 April 1848 he was discharged from HMS *Powerful*. He retired to England and settled in London. Violet romanticised the life of her parents before her birth: 'After a round of gaiety, they left England for Madeira . . . My father of course entertained a great deal, when any of the fleet arrived.' On one such occasion the Duke of Edinburgh (Queen Victoria's second son) was at a ball, 'and asked for Barbara to be presented to him, and danced with her'. In August 1862, the family arrived in London, settling in Westbourne Park Road, a quiet, respectable middle-class district. Violet found it odd that they should have gone there, considering her father's health, but noted, with her customary preening tone, 'their great friends the Count and Countess Irme Bella were living in London, otherwise I can see no reason . . .' The following January her father's asthma, accentuated by a severe attack of bronchitis, killed him,* leaving Mary, his twenty-six-year-old wife, pregnant with Noel Coward's mother.

Veitch had neglected to make a will, and all his money – some £3,000 – went to probate. Count Irme Bella and Henry's solicitors tried to sort matters out, but a number of debts had to be paid off by Henry's brother George, and the family were left with little to live on; what money was left from Henry's estate was supplemented by his naval pension, which Mary was entitled to draw. It was the beginning of the fall from grace of the Veitch family.

Mary Veitch's fourth daughter, Noel's mother, Violet Agnes, was born on 20 April 1863 at 6 Cornwall Terrace, her mother's address being 31 Nutford Place, off the Edgware Road, where they had moved, presumably due to financial constraints. A time of transience had begun; although the family now consisted of four girls and two boys, Mary had to move to a smaller house in St John's Wood. Here Violet spent the first six years of her life, until a further removal was necessary, this time to the country, where it was cheaper to live. They settled in Chobham, Surrey, then pure countryside. Her elder siblings went to school, while Violet stayed at home with her sister Laura, taught by a governess. Violet was growing up, and had become aware of her

---

* Coward wrote that 'Captain' Veitch died in Madeira 'comparatively young', and his wife and children returned to England, but records show that Henry Gordon Veitch, 'formerly of the island of Madeira', died in London on 9 January 1863 at 6 Cornwall Terrace, Regent's Park, presumably a nursing home.

appearance; she thought herself rather plain, with fair hair scraped back 'off my very high forehead'. She was a clever child, and quite solitary.

Noel's adolescent friend, Esme Wynne, later described Violet as 'an extraordinary woman ... [she] was, in a way, a preparation for Noel ... She looked like a little parrot, and so did her sister. They both had little beaky noses...' Violet developed a talent for music, and before the family left London could play barrel-organ tunes on the piano; a family friend would give her a penny to sing, and Violet always made sure she was paid in advance for her efforts.

Perhaps the absence of a father encouraged the Veitch children to be particularly naughty. Violet's brother Henry was expelled from the Royal Naval College at Dartmouth for refusing to salute a captain, and at eight Violet ran off to London with the family housemaid, Ellen, although she returned the same day. When she was implicated as a go-between in a romance of Laura's, their mother decided to send her two younger daughters to be 'finished' at a bleak nunnery outside Brussels. Here Violet became ill; she was delirious for days and no one did much about it. After the fever subsided, Violet found she had become slightly deaf. 'That illness really spoilt my life', she wrote bitterly, laying at least part of the blame on the nuns. It provoked a distrust of religion which her son inherited. It also indirectly bequeathed another legacy to Coward: precise enunciation, his speech clipped for her benefit.

Violet returned to a new home, the family having moved from Maidenhead to South Norwood, close to well-to-do Aunt Henrietta and her husband, Alexander Oliveira. Mary Veitch was also proud of her acquaintance with the Bulteels, whom she met when she collected her pension from the Admiralty, and with whom Violet and Laura would often stay. The Bulteels were a 'good family' from Devon with a strong naval tradition and royal connections, and when their son Henry married Laura in 1879, Mary Veitch found it a satisfactory match.

But Violet had her share of suitors, and she was engaged for three weeks to a William Glanville Richards. Years later, Coward would draw on such tales of his mother's early affairs; a figure as strong and as close to him as she was would naturally emerge in his work. In his Ruritanian romance, *The Queen was in the Parlour*, a duchess, colourful representative of an older generation, tells the young lovers, 'it's easier to follow other people's machinations than your own heart'; to which the heroine replies, 'No! Follow your heart always – if possible!' 'That sounds very fine in theory,' says the duchess, 'but in practice it's often *dismally* unsuccessful. I've done it several times with the most *devastating* results.'

The family moved again, to a yet smaller house, in Harlesden, north-west London. Her brother George supported the family by working as a clerk, but, like their Uncle George, developed tuberculosis, and died at the age of twenty-three. Two years later, in 1885, the family made its final move, this time to a quieter, almost rural area, recalling happier days at Chobham. Teddington-on-Thames was little changed since Alexander Pope and Horace Walpole had chosen it for their out-of-town retreats in the eighteenth century. The Veitches settled in Udney Park Road, in a villa which Mary named 'Dawick' in echo of former Veitch grandeur. Here the family lived 'a trifle sadly, making over last year's dresses and keeping up social appearances'. And here, where the river Thames flowed lazily by before it reached London, Noel Peirce Coward was born.

Like the Veitches, whom they met soon after they arrived in Teddington, the Coward family too had aspired to greater things, hopes frustrated by the loss of the head of their household.

Noel's paternal great-grandfather, William Coward, had been a surveyor (as had Henry Gordon Veitch), living at Heston in Middlesex, where his son James Coward was born on 25 January 1824. There was already musical talent in the family; as a young boy, James was admitted into the Westminster Abbey choir, distinguishing himself in solo per-formances. His first job was as organist to the parish church of Lambeth, and there he met and married Janet Margaret Munro in 1852. Janet was the daughter of Gordon Munro, who worked for the Board of Ordnance at the War Office in Pall Mall, and lived in Charles Street, off St James's Square. She was just eighteen when she married James Coward, and the marriage appears to have been a happy one. It was certainly fruitful: Janet gave birth to six sons and four daughters, the family lived in Pimlico, at 176 Cambridge Street, later moving to 38 Lupus Street, with three servants – a cook, a housemaid, and a nurse. It was at Cambridge Street that Arthur Sabin Coward was born, on 20 November 1856. The second of James's and Janet's sons, he owed his middle name to the vicar, Reverend John Edward Sabin, who had married his parents at St James's Church in Westminster.

James Coward became resident organist at the Crystal Palace, where he gave recitals on gala evenings; a programme for one such evening reads: 'After the Display, the Palace will be brilliantly Illuminated for Promenade until 10.30, during which Mr James Coward will perform on the Handel Festival Organ.' He also became the conductor of glee clubs at Westminster Abbey and in the City, and organist to St George's Church, Bloomsbury, the Sacred Harmonic Society, and the Grand Lodge of Freemasons. His membership of the freemasons (of which Henry Veitch was also a member) facilitated such valued appointments, but James had talent too. His substantial entry in the *Dictionary of National Biography* notes that 'his compositions are not numerous, but they show considerable refinement and musical knowledge, as well as an earnestness of aim for which he was scarcely given credit by those who were accustomed to hear his operatic selections or transcriptions for the organ'. It adds rather sniffily, 'it is to be regretted that so great a power of improvisation as he possessed should so often have been turned to account to provide musical accompaniment for acrobatic displays'.

But James Coward was another victim of tuberculosis. After three years of suffering, he died on 22 January 1880, aged fifty-five, leaving his wife, like Mary Veitch, to care for a large family. Unlike Henry Gordon Veitch, however, James had made a will, leaving just under £600 to his wife. Later that year, the Cowards moved to a more modest house at 4 Amyand Park Road, Twickenham, along the river from Teddington. Of the fate of Noel's paternal uncles and aunts, so numerous in number, little is known. James's musical career was marred by heavy drinking; Randulph married and lived close to the family home. Walter was the grandest, a Gentleman-in-Ordinary of the Chapel Royal at St James's Palace, where he also held the office of Librarian of the Chapel Royal's music. The most interesting uncle was Percy, the black sheep of the family, who was said to have married a 'professional pianist', had a daughter, deserted both, and was never heard of again, 'with the exception of a few vague rumours from Australia'. In fact, he had married the daughter of a civil servant in Islington in 1891; Aunt Kitty was a pianist, however, and joined in the Coward family's Twickenham concerts. Like his father, Percy sang alto in the Westminster Abbey choir, and a tenor from the Chapel Royal recalled that his voice 'excelled any woman I ever heard . . . he could interpret many arias by Handel and other early composers neglected by most singers'. After touring Canada with a group of Westminster Abbey singers, Percy settled in Toronto as a singing teacher. But like his nephew, he had a restless spirit, and deserting Kitty (who returned to London), Percy left for Australia where he died shortly afterwards. Of Noel's paternal aunts, only Ida and Myrrha featured in his life. Ida married W. R. Makeham, and ran a boarding house in Ebury Street; their son became a great friend of Noel's brother Eric. Myrrha married John William Alcock, a civil servant at the Office of Works; her daughter, Ida Doris, born in 1898, was Noel's favourite cousin.

The one great unifying joy for the Coward family and their father's greatest legacy was their love of music. Since his early teens, when he was at Kings College School in London (where he won prizes for his drawing), Arthur had earned an early living as a 'choral exhibitor'; like his son, he came young to professional entertainment. He and his siblings swelled the ranks of the Twickenham Choral Society; Randulph organised evenings of entertainment with the Teddington Glee Club, in which he, Arthur and Walter Makeham all sang. But the great Mecca of all musical ambition in that part of London was further up the river, on the banks of Teddington Lock. Teddington society – a shade grander than its downstream counterpart – centred on the new parish church of St Albans, dubbed 'the Cathedral of the Thames Valley' by John Betjeman, who described it as looking like a little piece of Westminster Abbey stranded up-river. Built in 1887 by a local architect, William Niven (father of David Niven and a neighbour of the Veitches at Udney Park), this grandiose Victorian gothic pile rose above the river at the lock. Its vicar was Francis Leith Boyd, who was given to 'furious outbursts' from the pulpit; he was popular enough to fill the church to overflowing when he delivered his fiery sermons.

In the late 1880s the Cowards moved to Teddington and a house at Coleshill Road. Their musical talents assured them of a major role in the parish life of the new church: Arthur's elder brother James became responsible for the 'highly ambitious character' of the church's programme of music, creating 'on the musical side a tradition which could compare with any leading London church'. James presided at St Albans all year, except during August, when he went to Paris to relieve Guilmant as organist at Notre-Dame.

It was in the St Albans church choir that Violet Veitch met Arthur Coward. Arthur, in his early thirties, worked as a correspondence clerk in the warehouse of Metzler's, the music publishers whose head office was in Great Marlborough Street, where he travelled daily by train from Teddington station. He graduated to salesman, and Sir Henry Wood, conductor of the promenade concerts, recalled 'very enjoyable times in Metzler's going through the marvellous Mustel organs that they used to sell, and no one ever displayed them with such a wonderful technique as did Arthur Coward'. Arthur was quite handsome, described by his son as 'very spruce', often with a blue cornflower in his buttonhole, proud of the cold baths he took both in summer and in winter. From his childhood, Coward recalled a framed photograph of his father 'looking tenacious and distinctly grim'. The grimness came from his brows, which pinched together, a feature inherited by his son – a mark of determination in Noel, but not apparently in his father. Arthur led an ordinary life, the model of a dapper office worker commuting to London; regular in his habits, with certain passions, most evidently for music. Esme Wynne remembered 'a very shadowy person, but even there Noel seemed to inherit a little of his real fondness for music . . . He could play rather charming things by heart, he composed them as he went along.'

In photographs Arthur Coward appears a slight figure, perceptibly stooped. But he was quite as tall as his son in maturity, and shared his sense of humour. Noel recalled him at one of his early theatrical parties at Ebury Street: 'Have a tongue sandwich,' Arthur said to Jane Cowl, the leopardskin-clad temptress then starring in *Easy Virtue*, 'that'll make you talk.' He also had a certain affability: Cole Lesley remembered him using what he thought 'unnecessary charm' on the grocer's boy. If this amounted to flirtation, it worked on Violet Veitch; there was little else about Arthur which would make him an irresistible consort. Few of Noel Coward's friends could remember much about him, let alone anything remarkable. It was said that, like his elder brother James, he drank too much and in later years became an alcoholic; but in 1890, he seemed a good catch to Violet.*

The courtship was conducted at church services, and at amateur theatricals such as *The Gondoliers*, staged at the Town Hall, with the family Coward out in strength in the principal parts, Violet demure in the chorus. Comparatively old in Victorian terms (Arthur was thirty-four, Violet twenty-seven), they were married on 8 October 1890 at St Albans, and rented 'Helmsdale', 5 Waldegrave Road, a typical late Victorian semi-detached, with three floors of modest-sized rooms. It was a respectable neighbourhood; at the end of the road was Horace Walpole's gothick villa, Strawberry Hill, then occupied by Elizabeth Waldegrave, society hostess and rumoured mistress of Edward, Prince of Wales. Teddington High Street was close, as was the Thames, along whose pleasant tree-lined banks they would walk, crossing the river by a narrow iron footbridge. 'I remember the smell of rotting leaves',

---

* In Coward's 1932 revue, *Words and Music*, a mother sings, 'Then I married your father,/ Gay and handsome and frank,/ But it shattered me rather/ When I found he drank.'

Coward later wrote; 'In the autumn quietness of suburban roads/ And seeing the winter river flooding/ And swirling over the tow-path by the lock.'

For Violet, matrimony was no great adventure. Indeed, in her pencilled memoirs, written in the early 1930s, Arthur receives barely a mention; one would hardly know he had existed. Far more important for Violet was the birth of their first son, Russell Arthur Blackmore Coward on 1 August 1891, named after his godfather, R. D. Blackmore, author of *Lorna Doone* and one of Teddington's celebrities. Blackmore was 'fond of young ladies especially if modest and gentle', and Violet visited his home, Gomer House, to talk and take tea; Blackmore's wife had died in 1888, and Violet was a consolation to the novelist. After Violet's marriage the friendship persisted, Blackmore liking Arthur whom he regarded as 'an accomplished musician and genial friend'; he went so far as to break with his usual custom and call upon the Cowards at Waldegrave Road. 'What a peaceful and delightful baby!' wrote Blackmore. 'I shall be proud to have such a little godson; who deserves, and (I trust) will have a very happy life . . .'

Russell was the focus of his parents' attentions, 'so lovely and so clever, too clever', recalled Violet, who noted that her first son developed musical talent at a much earlier age than did her second (raising the possibility that the great man of music and theatre might have been named Russell Coward). Blackmore doted on Russell, and sent his pony carriage to take the boy driving, promising to give Russell the white pony for his own when he was old enough. He even ordered a saddle to be made for his godson. 'Our lives were wrapped up in his, and those six years were so happy', wrote Violet. But aged six and a half, Russell developed spinal meningitis. It killed him within days.

Violet became seriously ill, 'and longed and longed to die'. And yet she had recovered enough, nine months later, to conceive another son. 'Everyone was amazed when it became known that I was to have another baby,' she recalled, 'and though my feelings were mixed, I did so long to feel baby arms round my neck again.' Having lost her first, Violet's second child would be that much more precious, and that much more important. She would not let go of him easily.

On the afternoon of 15 December 1899, Violet was standing at the window of 'our cosy little home'. Outside it was beginning to snow. The time seemed right for her new child, and she suddenly felt the first contractions. By two-thirty the next morning, she was delivered of a baby boy, weighing a healthy seven and a half pounds, with golden brown hair. 'He was a fine big baby, and oh the joy of him!'

The boy was named Noel, it being so close to Christmas; and Peirce, after friends whom the Veitches had known in Harlesden. Jessie ('Flower') Peirce was his godmother and the cause of a second name which Coward despised almost as soon as he could pronounce it. Emma Adams, who had nursed Russell, took charge in the nursery as Violet's ill-health, exacerbated by the birth, meant that once more she took to her bed. Christmas was a quiet affair at Helmsdale, subdued because of illness in the family: on Boxing Day, Arthur's mother Janet died of cancer. Violet was still ill and unable to organise Noel's first social engagement until 11 February 1900, when he was christened at St Albans by the Bishop of Kingston, with the Reverend Boyd's family in attendance. The reception was held at Waldegrave Road, where baby Noel was brought down from the nursery wearing his fine Madeira-worked gown, to be admired by family and friends.

With the new year came a new century, and a changing world. The relief of Mafeking was announced, restoring British supremacy in South Africa and heralding a brief period of glory that would shape Coward's view of the world. Street barrel-organs played patriotic songs such as 'Goodbye, Dolly, I Must Leave You' and 'We Are the Soldiers of the Queen'; these lodged as early memories, resurfacing in Coward's work to evoke the past. Queen Victoria's death in 1901 was a breakpoint; even after *Cavalcade*, Noel was embroidering on the scene in free verse:

> When Queen Victoria died
> And was buried and the gun-carriage was dragged empty away again
> The shops re-opened and so did the theatres
> Although business was none too good . . .
> And it looked as if nothing much had happened
> And perhaps nothing much had really
> Except that an era, an epoch, an attitude of mind, was ended.

The gay Edwardian era replaced the dourness of the previous century, and the theatre flourished under the reign of the actor-managers. New technology evolved – gramophone, telephone, wireless and the first tabloid newspapers – all important to the propagation of the future dramatist's career.

Eighteen months after Noel's birth the family took a larger house, shared with Grandmother Mary and Aunt Vida. At the top of the new house, Violet and Arthur had two rooms knocked into one, so that Baba (as baby Noel called himself) could run about, dressed in the skirts habitually worn by unhousetrained children, gripping his inseparable companion, a toy monkey. He was 'very forward and amusing', cooed Violet. As she admitted, 'I am sadly afraid he was very much spoilt', a consequence of Russell's early death; when an innocuous lump appeared on the baby's tongue, Violet immediately sent for the doctor. Noel was already demanding more than his share of attention. A bell had been fixed up in the nursery, and during Violet's At Homes, Baba was dressed and ready to make an appearance should he be summoned by the bell. No ring, and there would be a ruction in the nursery; but if it did sound all was sweetness and light, as Baba was brought down to shake hands with everyone. Violet played the piano, while the infant phenomenon held up his silk frock delicately and danced for the general amusement of all.

Songs seemed important even in his earliest days. Coward noted that he was 'born into a generation that still took light music seriously. The lyrics and melodies of Gilbert and Sullivan' – which he later professed to dislike, and yet which appeared to be a discernible influence on his work – were 'hummed and strummed into my consciousness at an early age ... By the time I was four years old "Take a Pair of Sparkling Eyes", "Tit Willow", "We're Very Wide Awake, the Moon and I", and "I Have a Song to Sing-O" had been fairly inculcated into my bloodstream.'

It comes as no surprise to learn that the child was 'highly strung', and when a visiting doctor friend witnessed Baba's antics he pronounced that the boy's brain was too far in advance of his body, that his curls should be shorn and all further social invitations summarily refused. By Christmas 1903 he had grown 'big and strong' enough to be taken to his first theatre at Kingston to see *Aladdin*. The boy sat 'quite quietly all the time, watching, watching!'

The following year, when Noel was four years old, the Cowards left Teddington for good (Coward recalled that 'economy forced us to leave in rather a hurry'), with a vague idea of emigrating to Australia. Their furniture in store, they spent six months at the seaside, first at Bognor, then at Brighton, where Noel's theatre visits resumed, going to matinees 'whenever there was anything suitable on, like a revue, or a musical show'. It was a happy time for Violet and her son, and she seemed reluctant to move again; but the imminence of another baby made more permanent accommodation necessary. There were other changes in

family circumstances too: Arthur Coward had joined a newly established piano firm, Payne's, as a traveller. He was away from home a
great deal, and once went as far as Naples. His absence from the family
strengthened his wife's matriarchal control, and intensified her relationship with her son. Soon after their arrival at Lenham Road in Sutton,
Violet gave birth to her third son. Eric Vidal Coward was born on 13
July 1905, 'bright red and singularly unattractive', as Noel recalled, 'but
everyone else was delighted with him'. He gave no hint of jealousy, nor
should he have done, for Violet's affections, energies and love were
always his; the rest of the family was subordinate to that fact.

Noel had his first taste of formal education at a small local primary
school in Sutton. Violet had been unsuccessful in teaching her son to tie
his laces, and the teachers at the school refused to perform this function.
His outraged mother promptly took him away. At six he was sent to St
Margaret's, a girls' day school whose headmistress was a Miss Willington, a prim figure in puffed sleeves and pinned-up hair. Noel did not
care for her, or her school, and was 'really very naughty'. Emma used
to take Noel to the school in the morning, but he would escape and run
home again. One day Miss Willington caught him and pulled him back.
He kicked out furiously and bit his schoolmistress's arm down to the
bone; 'an action', recalled the adult Coward, 'which I have never for an
instant regretted'. The wilfulness of the young Coward's act was an
indication of the headstrong and demanding adult-to-be. Demure in
sailor suit or stern in a succession of outsize Eton collars, early
photographs show decidedly determined features; from grinning baby
to smiling young boy, there was a self-assurance, as if he knew what he
was and what he was going to be.

Miss Willington, against all expectations, liked Noel, and was proud
of his obvious cleverness, 'for he was beginning to develop musical
talent, and had a sweet voice'. The schoolmistress, herself of a theatrical
disposition, arranged for Coward to sing at a school concert, to which
she had invited two or three 'London artists' to make it more interesting.
His first public appearance came at the school's end-of-term prize-giving
on 23 July 1907. Clad in a spotless white sailor suit, he sang 'Coo' from
Lionel Monckton's *A Country Girl*, with its plaintive refrain:

> Hark to the sound of 'coo-oo-oo!'
> Calling for me and you-ou-ou,
> For me and you-ou,
> Whether through darkest storm we go,

Or under sky of blue,
Nothing shall sever
I will be ever
True to my 'Coo-oo-oo!'

This was followed by a winsome song on the subject of spring for which Noel accompanied himself on the piano. The resultant applause demanded an encore, but Coward was to learn early that public approbation does not always bring official rewards. Despite his rapturous reception, he watched as all the prizes disappeared from the top table, and Violet took him home quite unaware that her son had expected one too. Back at Lenham Road he ran inside and threw himself down on the sofa, yelling and crying. Violet, rather than reprimanding him, felt sorry for Noel; had she been harsher, such scenes might not have been repeated (as they were) even in middle age.

The person responsible for introducing Coward formally to music was Gwen Kelly, a school friend of his mother's, who often came to stay. Kelly, with her 'large mournful Irish eyes' and smart tailormade clothes, was a good singer and musician (Esme Wynne later noted that Kelly 'played well and looked hideous'). However, Coward could remember no piano lessons as a boy, 'except occasionally from my mother who tried once or twice, with singular lack of success, to teach me my notes. I could, however, from the age of about seven onwards, play on the piano in the pitch dark any tune I had heard.' Even in adult life, Coward's piano-playing was limited to three keys: E flat, B flat and A flat. 'The sight of two sharps frightens me to death', he confessed, and recalled that 'dear George Gershwin used to moan ... and try to force my fingers on to the right notes'. Coward would play down such early encouragement in the arts, as if to enhance the uniqueness of his own genius. He later remarked of his mother that 'the sad thing was that she knew little about the theatre, but she used to take me to it on my birthday'. In fact Violet had been an avid fan since before her marriage. Their visits were formative experiences for the young playwright-to-be, waiting in the pit queue at the Hippodrome to see a 'Spectacle', or in Croydon for a pantomime: as impressive were the 'Panoramas' at Earls Court, long vistas painted in narrow strips to reproduce famous battles or foreign lands.

At seven Noel was packed off to spend the summer with his Aunt Laura at Charlestown, near St Austell in Cornwall. Violet's sister was 'kind, pretty, and vain', and, according to her descendants, 'certainly very unpopular in the village of Charlestown', where she was seen as 'domineering and autocratic . . . and thoroughly stand-offish'. The Bulteels' house was grand in comparison with the Cowards' Sutton villa, with Georgian furniture, fine china and silverware, and walls decorated with Chinese paintings on mirrors. In the large grounds there was a deep lake, with an unstable blue punt used to reach an island in its middle. With its hidden paths and dark green water, it was a secret playground for the young boy. Cousin Walter, his daughter recalls, 'didn't much like Noel (several years his junior) and used to palm him off on his sister Violet . . .' The young Coward preferred to play with Violet Bulteel, and on later visits he wrote home, telling his mother that his cousin was teaching him to row, and that 'I had some little boys over yesterday afternoon to tea and I dressed up in a short dress and danced to them and sung to them and we all went round the lake and on it to[o].'

Noel returned to London to find further family upheaval. Payne's Pianos had gone bust, and Arthur had lost his job (a possible reason for Noel's Cornish sojourn, as the Cowards sought to defray family expenses). 'No money', Violet recalled, 'anxious times'. They moved again, this time to 70 Prince of Wales Mansions, facing Battersea Park. Their flat was at the top of the redbrick block, with a small balcony overlooking the park and the Thames beyond. Despite their decreasing fortunes and living space, there was one major bonus; they were within the boundaries of London, an important step for a young boy whose waking thoughts were already centred on the theatre. His favourite toy was a miniature auditorium, in which Noel re-enacted *Cinderella* and *Black-eyed Susan* with cardboard cut-outs; Victorian-style penny pantomime sheets supplied an augmented cast and decor. Later he acquired a larger model, for which Arthur painted scenery and helped Noel to make different sets, on which dolls danced instead of pasteboard figures. These Noel dressed in 'long chiffon draperies of different colours', fixing them on to a wire circle which he worked from the top, so that the dolls seemed to dance a ballet. 'He never cared to put on a whole play, but was always trying effects, lighting with electric torches and candles', recostuming his china cast for tableaux.

But Coward also showed that he had inherited the rebellious streak of the Veitches. He made friends with children in neighbouring flats, and with Noel as ringleader they would tie prams to doorknobs, ring the bells and run. Outdoors, Battersea Park provided ample space for misbehaviour: Noel was often found annoying the park-keepers by roller-skating on the pavements. If Violet's disciplinary grip on her son was slack, it may have been because financial crises continued to beset the family; with Arthur's small income and two growing boys to clothe and feed, it was difficult to maintain even a modicum of lower middle-class respectability. A desperate situation demanded a drastic solution and, like her sister-in-law, Ida, Violet took it upon herself to rent rooms. Noel enjoyed the change in arrangements, largely because it involved dressing for dinner in his high Eton collar and Norfolk jacket. But living with strangers in cramped conditions could cause fraught tempers, bickering which would resurface in Coward's dramas as echoes of family rows. To these he contributed in the clipped speech he had adopted, not only for his mother's benefit but to overcome a slight lisp.

There was still the problem of his education. Uncle Walter encouraged Violet to apply to Claude Selfe's Chapel Royal School, sited in a large house in Clapham. This was a new adventure for Noel, exciting because the journey involved two tram rides to reach his destination, 385 Clapham Road. Arriving at school, he hoped not to see the mortar-boards of the choirboys proper on the pegs in the hall; for three days a week, they did not attend school, which meant that not only would Mr Selfe be in a better mood but there would be no bullying. Life at the school was 'pretty rough', recalled Sir Thomas Armstrong, who joined in January 1908, 'There were brutal and coarse "initiation ceremonies": and if I were to describe in details the things that were done to us I should hardly be believed . . .' As a dayboy, Noel could avoid the worst of the abuse, but when caught he resorted to his dramatic talents: 'Once during one of these boyish pranks I pretended to faint, having kicked one of them in the fork, an unmanly performance which frightened everyone very much indeed.'

On the day Noel's voice was to be tested for the Chapel Royal choir, he appeared before the organist, Dr Walter Alcock, in a higher-than-ever Eton collar, his hair plastered down. Alcock, formerly organist at Twickenham, was a lofty figure, made yet more remote by his contact with the royal family, 'as well as the Almighty, [which] faintly upset his balance as a human being'. Undaunted, Coward sang Gounod's 'There is a Green Hill Far Away'. He sang well, albeit dramatically, later telling Judy Garland, 'I did the whole crucifixion bit – with expression. The organist, poor man, fell back in horror.' Noel and his mother were ushered out, Dr Alcock informing Mrs Coward that not only was her son too young but there was no vacancy. Violet decided that this was a good thing, as Dr Alcock obviously didn't know what he was talking about, and they all looked rather common – including Uncle Walter.

Violet did, however, consider her son's master, Claude Selfe, a benevolent figure. He was fervently interested in the theatre (he had formed the New Stagers Operatic Society, which wrote and performed its own operas, as well as those of Gilbert and Sullivan), and was willing to tutor Coward later when he began to get theatre work. This in itself proved a hazard to Noel's formal education; as Thomas Armstrong noted, '[Coward] didn't make the grade because he was always being taken out of school for dancing lessons or to play a juvenile part in some show, and his time at the Chapel Royal School was a period of his life that in later years he didn't wish to remember or to be reminded of.' In this Noel was vindicated; soon afterwards, two boys ran away from the school to escape the abuse. The allegations must have been serious, the police were called, and an enquiry set up; in consequence the school was closed, and Claude Selfe disappeared.

Soon after the Chapel Royal audition débâcle, Mrs Coward's paying guests left, and she decided to let the flat for six months and move to the country. 'Small poverty is a greater strain in a town than in a village', her son wrote, 'and Mother was country-bred, and weary of whining Cockney tradesmen and crowded buses and genteel make-shifts.' A Miss Davis rented the flat, and the Cowards left to stay with grandmother and Aunts Borby and Vida at Southsea, the pretty Georgian seaside town nestling next to its saltier neighbour, naval Portsmouth. While their parents looked for a suitable cottage, Noel and Eric enjoyed trips around the harbour and to the Isle of Wight. It was early April, and the winds whipped up the waves which crashed on to the stone-studded slopes of the breakwaters by Southsea Castle: here Noel would sit for hours, watching the grey-green sea of the Solent. The 'romantic desolation' Coward saw in Southsea stirred his feelings for the sea, a love which would remain. In his short story 'Ashes of Roses', the young Leonora is brought up with her uncle and aunt in a seaside boarding house (whose tenants exhibit 'aggressive gentility'). Out of season, Leonora stays in the 'second floor front' bedroom, where she could 'kneel on clear winter nights, with the window wide open and an eiderdown wrapped around her, and look out over the dark sea ... Here, with the smell of the sea, the sound of the waves pounding the shingle and the sharp wind blowing the curtains out into the room, she could make plans for the future.'

There were other attractions: the masculine charm of the naval uniforms so plentiful around Southsea, with Portsmouth just next door, and sailors represented the excitement of adventure, of travel, and of sex. That this image of tradition should also represent unconventional desires seemed a metaphor for the tensions that existed in Coward's life; passion and patriotism, desire and duty. The English sailor, with his bell-bottoms and jaunty cap, embodied cheerful masculinity, the ocean roll in his step. It was a romantic, theatrical, and irresistible image, from Lord Mountbatten – the real thing – to Graham Payn as the stage *matelot*.

The Cowards moved to Meon, a hamlet a mile or so inland from the eastern borders of the Solent. Meon Cottage, just off the country lane that led eventually to the shore, was a farmworker's modest thatched cottage, set among the fruit smallholdings of the flat countryside. Arthur and Violet leased it from a Mrs Spurgin, who lived in the large house at the end of the drive. Tiny inside, with a spiral staircase to an even smaller upper floor, it had a country quaintness which the city dwellers appreciated. 'We lived there for six months completely happily', Coward recalled, although the quaintness palled somewhat when the goat got into the outside lavatory. Poor as they were – 'at times I believe there wasn't quite enough food' – they were content; a bucolic existence out of the books of Mary Webb or Sheila Kaye-Smith. On the beach, they watched the yachts parade; for Violet, a reminder of her family's past. During the Cowes Week regatta, they charted the royal arrivals, and saw the Kaiser saluted by the Fleet. That evening they had a moonlight picnic on the edge of the low sandy cliff, with Arthur Coward letting off some fireworks bought in nearby Fareham.

Noel later professed to have learned a lot about country ways, claiming to be adept in tree-climbing, but Mrs Spurgin's sons declared their new neighbour 'a milk sop', and useless at such activities. They would send Noel to climb a tree at the end of the Spurgins' drive, keeping him aloft 'by aiming air gun bullets at his behind'. Noel took his revenge subtly, stealing from their landlady's plum trees in an after-dark raid in which the conspiratorial Violet also took part. When they thought they had been discovered, they had to lie in a ditch, giggling, for half an hour.

Coward's childhood was marked by a series of dramatic accidents. In Teddington, a horse lunged at his head; in Sutton a terrier attacked him in the street, leaving him with a permanent scar on his leg. Barely had he recovered when a boy on a bicycle knocked him down, and in Bognor a horse ran at him as they were walking on the green, taking a bite from behind Noel's ear. But the most serious mishap came at Meon, when he trod on a broken bottle in the sea. Violet heard violent screams, and found the water turning red: Noel had severed an artery between his toes. Laid up with a stitched foot, he recuperated in the garden, reading and writing. It was in those lazy summer afternoons in a Hampshire orchard that he wrote his first dramas. He decided to put them into production, and cast the three Spurgin sisters and his cousin Winnie in a tragedy. Extorting the girls' pocket-money, he cycled into Titchfield for props (as much ribbon as he could buy for sixpence), and an army bell tent was set up for the performance. However, his cast's lack of seriousness – they giggled and forgot their lines, an indiscipline which would ever after vex the dramatist – drove Noel to smite the eldest over the head with a wooden spade, thus ending the drama with real tears and a nasty quarrel between their respective mothers.

When their summer lease expired, the family returned to Southsea for six weeks, as Miss Davis was still at Prince of Wales Mansions. But Grandmother Veitch, now seventy-two, was increasingly ill, and when the Cowards returned to Battersea, she moved into a flat at 81 Prince of Wales Mansions, where she died on 27 November 1908. Mary Veitch, unlike her husband, was respectably solvent and left £1,519 19s 8d, a considerable sum, to be divided among her surviving children, Vida, Laura, Violet and Etta. New funds may have prompted the decision, after Christmas 1908, to resume Noel's education at the Chapel Royal School; he was to stay with Uncle Randulph and Aunt Amy in nearby Pimlico. 1909 was a miserable year for Coward, 'mother-sick' and bullied: 'I am still very unhappy and I shan't get over it till I see you again . . . oh Mother do send me some money to come down to you please do I am not very happy here without you . . .'

However, Coward the performer was developing apace. Noel's voice gained strength, 'more full-blooded than the usual boyish treble' and soon he was performing at the church garden party at St Albans in Teddington. Violet Coward now decided that attention should focus on her son's terpsichorean talents, and he was sent to Miss Janet Thomas's Dancing Academy in Hanover Square for a six-week course early in 1910. The self-sufficient ten-year-old again made his way across London every Thursday and Friday afternoon. Violet's way of instilling independence worked a little too well: Noel amused himself en route in conversations with strangers, in which he reported an appalling home life of a drunken father, squalid tenements and malnourished siblings. 'It was also a pleasant game to be discovered sobbing wretchedly in the corners of railway carriages or buses in the hope that someone would take pity on me and perhaps give me tea at Fuller's', a ploy successful on just two occasions, both Samaritans being of the cloth. One clergyman gave Noel a lecture on trusting in the Almighty; the other gave him sixpence and pinched his knee. 'Of the two, I preferred the latter.'*

* Incidents remembered, perhaps, in the words of a 1925 Coward song:

> When our thoughts are most volcanic
> We remember in our panic
> Even clergymen are naughty
> Now and then.

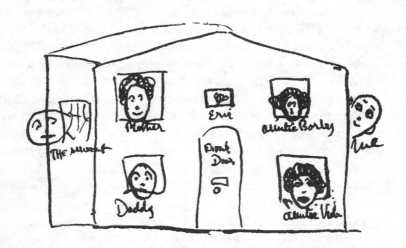

2

A Talented Boy

CAST OF CHILDREN – Young Actors in Charming Play Chosen from Applicants to *Daily Mirror*. Before a delighted audience at the Little Theatre yesterday Miss Lila Field's company of child actors ... made their first bow to the public in 'The Goldfish' ... Great success was scored by Master Noel Coward as Prince Mussel ...

Daily Mirror, 28 January 1911

TOWARDS the end of his dancing classes Noel's career took a professional turn. The *Daily Mirror* of 7 September 1910 reported Miss Lila Field's plan to set up a children's theatre (none of the actors to be over fourteen years old) and noted that she had found it difficult to find suitable boys for her project.

Coward romanticised the origins of his first West End appearance when he wrote in *Present Indicative* of an advertisement in the paper, which 'stated that a talented boy of attractive appearance was required by a Miss Lila Field to appear in her production of an all-child fairy play: *The Goldfish*. This seemed to dispose of all argument. I was a talented boy, God knows, and when washed and smarmed down a bit, passably attractive.' Violet wrote informing Miss Field of the eminent suitability of her son for the job, and soon after mother and son, in grey satin and feather boa and new Norfolk suit and Eton collar respectively, arrived at the audition in a state of trepidation. They were greeted by the colourful Peruvian-born Miss Field (also an amateur aviator and clothes designer), who asked Noel to recite. According to Violet, tears came to her eyes; her sister Bertha arrived in time to hear 'There is a Green Hill Far Away', Noel's heart-tugging audition standard: it was too much for the Misses Fields, who both 'passed out'. Terms were quickly agreed. 'It will be a guinea and a half a week', pronounced Lila Field, which Violet thought beyond her means. 'He will *receive* that', said Miss Field.

Two other children in that Little Theatre production made their names on the stage: Ninette de Valois, prima ballerina and choreographer; and Alfred Willmore, better known as the actor, writer and producer Michael MacLiammoir. He played King Goldfish, she the queen. Both were older than Noel, yet to MacLiammoir, Coward 'seemed, with his straight, neatly arranged hair, his pale complexion, his small humorous almond eyes, and his clipped way of speaking, far more sophisticated and self-possessed'. He asked what Noel would like to be when he grew up. 'An actor of course. That's why I'm here . . . There's nothing as good as the theatre', Noel said with conviction. 'That is, if you're made for it. I should think you were you know, same as me . . .'

The engagement seemed to set Coward's career on course, but after only four days of performances illness struck, as it would do throughout his working life. Noel had severe earache, and the doctor forbade any exertion. Violet wrapped Noel in a blanket and took him to the theatre to show Miss Field his condition: 'She said that as Noel was the success of the play, it could not possibly go on', wrote Violet, although she realised that it gave Miss Field an excuse to close the failing show. Lila Field revived *The Goldfish* later that year, at the Royal Court Theatre, and then at the Crystal Palace for two matinees. For his efforts, Noel received the sum of one guinea; hardly a fortune. But he had had his first taste of theatrical success, and Miss Field's efforts had been noticed; when the Cowards returned to Prince of Wales Mansions after another summer at Meon, they found a letter from Charles Hawtrey, the great actor-manager, summoning Noel to the Prince of Wales Theatre, where rehearsals for the comedy *The Great Name* had begun. After Noel's elaborate audition, Hawtrey turned to his stage-manager and said, 'Tarver, never let me see that boy again.' Tarver persuaded him otherwise however, and Noel secured the part – just one spoken line – at two pounds a week. Slight as the role was, it had a greater significance, by virtue of the director who auditioned him.

Hawtrey, then fifty-three, was famous for his adaptation of a German play, *The Private Secretary*, which became as popular a revival as *Charley's Aunt*. A fine light comedy actor, he exemplified the English gentleman-about-town. Coward remembered him vividly: a strong scent of eau-de-cologne, expensive striped shirts from Paris, and 'a twinkle in his eye'. In unabashed hero-worship, Coward followed him about, chattering shrilly and asking him to sign his autograph book (which Hawtrey did, seventeen times). He was once so distracting that Hawtrey missed an entrance. 'Go away, boy,' sighed the suffering director, 'for God's sake leave me alone.'

As a child actor under the age of fourteen, Noel had to acquire a licence to perform; this involved a 'tortured' trip to Bow Street magistrates' court, where a dyspeptic magistrate, believing that such children were forced on to the stage to keep their ne'er-do-well parents, regulated young careers. When the licence was refused Violet leapt to her feet, protesting that her son would decline into sickness and end up in hospital as a result of the decision. She then sat down quickly, blushing, her hat askew. The elderly magistrate granted the licence. Mother and son left the court in tears, with dignified bows to all present.

The Great Name was not a great success, running for just two months. But Coward once more found himself in the right place at the right time; as that contract ended another presented itself in Hawtrey's production of *Where the Rainbow Ends*. This was the first staging of what became as much a children's standard as *Peter Pan*, playing every Christmas for the next forty years. It was a morality tale of the dragon Slitherslime which lazy boys became; the Slacker was just such an idle, wicked boy, 'who has given up all idea of work, and has even lost the saving love for his country, and, above all, love for his parents'. The play featured two eminent young thespians, Miss Esme Wynne and Philip Tonge. Tonge was one of the most successful boy actors of the time, and with his ruddy schoolboy complexion, oversized overcoat and hat with ear-flaps, he was a romantic figure, the object of a youthful crush by Noel.

Where the Rainbow Ends was lavishly financed to rival *Peter Pan*, and staged just before Christmas 1911 at the Savoy Theatre, the first public building to be electrically lit, festively decorated with holly wreaths. Violet and Arthur Coward watched the last dress rehearsal from the stalls until four in the morning. Italia Conti was ballet mistress, delivering shrill Joyce Grenfell-like commands from the dress circle, ' "Dorothy, do your *coupé* again" or "Grace, how many times have I told you never to push Phyllis in your pirouette?" ' She singled Coward out for special treatment, suggesting he double as a hyena and a dog after his part in the first act was over; but Violet disapproved of her son spreading himself so thinly. Hermione Gingold was understudy to Esme Wynne's Rosamund, and recalled Coward's performance as 'quite fantastic. People used to stand and gape in astonishment ... Charles Hawtrey was always threatening Noel with the sack but never carried out his threat because even Noel's scene-stealing had a ring of genius about it.' This involved kicking the hapless actor who played the Lion.

Coward basked in the glory. When the *Daily Graphic* printed photographs of the young stars of *Where the Rainbow Ends*, he managed not only to feature with Philip and Esme but added his already distinctive 'Noel Coward' autograph, writ large across the studio shot, thus establishing his name as a virtual trademark. At twelve, he assumed the stance of a star, and his was not the picture of a fresh-faced young boy. Coward always looked worldly, and his features conveyed preoccupations greater than those of a child.

By 1912 the Cowards had moved again, to 'Ben Lomond', 50 Southside, Clapham Common. Clapham, centred on its expansive park and ponds, had peaked in bourgeois fashion in the previous century, and was now known for its schools, of which the Chapel Royal was just one. Even the Cowards' landlady, the grandly named Madame Charles Hunt, who lived downstairs, was a teacher of singing; her peripheral involvement in 'the business' may have been a deciding factor in the Cowards' tenancy. They lived in the top two floors. Noel had an attic bedroom, next to the kitchen in which the family ate their meals. The Cowards could no longer afford a servant, but Violet made the housework look like fun, to encourage Noel and Eric who might have been upset by the sight of their mother skivvying. Arthur made toy yachts and sailed them on the pond across the road. Noel was already assuming family responsibilities beyond his age; Mrs Astley Cooper, who befriended Coward a year or so later, noted that 'when he was about twelve, his father was very ill, and he went to a well-known doctor, and said, "You must come to see my father, we are very poor and can't pay you, but I am going to be famous and I'll pay you then." Many years later he sent him a large cheque.'

Southside was a busy street, the first in Clapham to boast an electric tramway. Beyond the Plough Inn, down Clapham Road, 'the atmosphere became palpably commoner', but it was lively on Saturday nights, when the shops stayed open until midnight. At Christmas 'the poulterers' and butchers' and greengrocers' were glaring yellow caves of light, with the slow-moving crowds on the shining pavements silhouetted against them'. To get into town, there was the number 88 bus, or the Underground. Memories of the tube evoked the world of his youth for Coward. 'I went through every sort of emotion in the City and South London Railway', he remembered, from 'exaltation, having been sent for by some agent', to 'utter despair, returning home in the evening having failed to get the job'. Transpontine London made a lasting impression, appearing as a location in many of his short stories: Battersea, the Oval, Kennington, and Clapham, the territory of his youth. Now, as he approached adolescence, it was a starting-point for his adult life.

With the end of *Where the Rainbow Ends* came a lull in Coward's early career. The spring of 1912 was spent in a weary two-day-a-week tour of the agencies – Blackmore's, Denton's and Bellew and Stock. Violet was criticised for the time her son was taking off school, and she too began to have doubts. But such persistence was bound to triumph, and Coward was engaged for a ballet called 'An Autumn Idyll' at the Savoy Theatre, arranged to a mélange of Chopin melodies. Noel was to play a mushroom, clad in tights with a frill round his middle. After a high-kicking entrance and a *pas de deux* with Joan Carroll as a toadstool, he exited to lukewarm applause. *The Times* noted that 'Miss Joan Carroll and Master Coward, as the Toadstool and the Mushroom, headed delightfully a little troupe of small but engaging fungi.' His brother Eric, who was one of the fungi, was forgotten; little importance was attached to the possibility of a stage career for him.

On his return from a holiday at Charlestown with Aunt Laura, Noel was engaged for another Hawtrey production, *A Little Fowl Play*, a sketch by Harold Owen. But Coward's keen anticipation was blunted when a less amenable magistrate at Bow Street refused him a licence to perform in the evening. However, Hawtrey insisted on paying him his full salary and, from the wings, close observation of professionals like George Robey provided valuable experience. Noel was also concentrating on tentative literary efforts, after the success of Esme Wynne's youthful effort, *The Prince's Bride*, which had been produced as a matinee during the run of *Where the Rainbow Ends*. Inspired by *Drake*, a production at His Majesty's Theatre, he wrote a burlesque on the same subject, *Sir Francis Drake*. This was Noel's first proper written play, and according to Violet it was hilarious. Hawtrey 'and some others read it, and laughed till they nearly cried', although it came to nothing.

The year 1912 marked another vital step in Coward's development. Walking with his hero Philip Tonge to Tonge's house in Baker Street, Noel received his first lesson in sex education. By the time he got home, 'immersed in a sea of pornographic misinformation', an appalling sense of guilt overtook him and he burst in on his worried mother exclaiming, 'Mother, I have lost my innocence!' According to his account, he was put to bed with a cup of cocoa and assured that every good actor needed to know about life as early as possible. But Tonge's lessons became more practical, and Coward did lose his innocence when the two young actors went on a picnic in the woods together. In matters of sex, as in everything else, Noel was precocious.

During his second appearance in *Where the Rainbow Ends* early in 1913, Violet had recourse to unusual means to justify the path he was following; the family was growing ever more disapproving of the life the boy was leading. Appearing at the London Coliseum was a mind-reading act, a Miss Anna Eva Fay from America. A special note printed in the programme warned that Miss Fay was 'not infallible ... and there are times when she becomes over fatigued. Her answers at such times frequently go astray. The purpose is ... bright, amusing, pictur-esque, and mysterious entertainment, without fraud, deceit, or impro-priety ...' A friend of Violet's, whose husband was an electrical engineer, suggested Violet accompany her to a session. Her husband had had some copper wire stolen, and he wanted his wife to ask Miss Fay its whereabouts; she had been twice already, and got no reply. As they sat in the crowded balcony, slips of paper were distributed for their questions. Violet wrote carefully in pencil on one of the slips, 'Do you advise me to keep my son Noel Coward on the stage? Violet Coward.' Miss Fay came onstage, accompanied by her male assistant, who draped a sheet over her as she sat down. 'She held out her arms like a ghost, and answered one or two questions, and then called out, "Mrs Coward, Mrs Coward." Violet stood up. Miss Fay shouted, "You ask me about your son Noel Coward. Keep him where he is, keep him where he is, he has great talent and will have a wonderful career!"'

Violet was 'entirely flabbergasted' and wrote down what Miss Fay had said, 'so as not to forget a word of it'. Divining a future genius proved too much for Miss Fay; after answering only one or two other questions, she fainted away and was led off by her assistant, leaving Violet's friend to report a third disappointment to her wire-less spouse.

In March 1913 Italia Conti approached Violet with a proposal for Noel to appear in *Hannele*, a play by Gerhart Hauptmann which Basil Dean was to produce with the Liverpool Repertory Company. Noel aud-itioned for Dean, and was offered the part of an angel, a three-week engagement, at two pounds a week.

Violet saw Noel off for Liverpool and Manchester from Euston Station. He travelled with a company of ten other children, among them a 'vivacious child with ringlets to whom I took an instant fancy. She wore a black satin coat and a black velvet hat with a peak, her face was far from pretty, but tremendously alive.' This 'very *mondaine*' actress confided that her name was Gertrude Lawrence, but he should call her Gert. Just fourteen, she was a veteran of Max Reinhardt's spectacle, *The Miracle*, at Olympia. She gave Noel an orange, and told him some 'mildly dirty stories . . . I loved her from then onwards'.

Harold French, a boy actor two years Coward's senior, was on the same train. Like Noel, he was to play an angel, a part for which he was well suited; his blond good looks ensured a sensational adult debut when he appeared half-naked in *The Blue Lagoon* in 1920. French remembered Coward as having 'noticeable ears and a smile that brought an engaging tilt to his eyes . . .' They played cards on the journey up; another boy, Roy Royston, taught them nap on Noel's suitcase. French was equivocal about Coward's adolescent charms. 'I did like him,' he recalls, 'but I think I was rather in awe of him, even then. He already had his wit, his direct approach. He was the master of the four of us – he bossed us around a bit.'

Arriving at their Liverpool boarding-house, Noel was already home-sick, and Miss Conti's doses of Epsom salts as a cure-all did not help matters. They began rehearsals. Hauptmann's *Hannele*, a fantasy set in a German mountain village, was full of theatrical effects, draped scenery and ghostly lighting, and Coward and French played schoolboys who became angels of light and materialised in 'heaven', where their school-master (played by Balliol Holloway) had become 'the stranger', a Christlike figure. Gertrude Lawrence was one of the angelic chorus, and Noel was soon playing practical jokes and giggling incontinently with her; it was only a matter of time before his first confrontation with the redoubtable Basil Dean.

Dean had trained as an analytical scientist, and was now director of the Liverpool Repertory Theatre. Harold French recalled that he 'knew what he wanted and no nonsense. He gave us . . . every gesture, every intonation, and we were all scared to death of him.' They had been rehearsing for a week 'when a strange terrifying thing happened'. Noel was delivering his speech, which began 'The wealth of the gold-laden cornfields', when Basil Dean interrupted: 'No, no. You – whatever your name is – I want a slight emphasis on the word gold.' He ordered the boy to start again. The director was walking back to his chair when French heard Coward's voice: ' "Are you sure you're right about that?" Mr Dean stopped walking. The rest of us stopped breathing. Slowly he turned. "What was that you said?" "Are you sure you're right about that, Mr Dean?"' His smile was 'tolerant, his tone enquiring' as he explained that '"a cornfield could hardly be silver-laden could it?" A smile spread across Mr Dean's face. "I take your point, my boy, it's just possible I was wrong." He returned to his chair. "And now, ladies and gentlemen, with that young man's permission we'll get on with the rehearsal."'

The play opened on 31 March, and was a success. They moved to Manchester and were lodged in a gloomy rooming-house, where Noel and Gertrude Lawrence talked long into the night, their acquaintance becoming intimate friendship. Given the maturity of both teenagers, rumours of less innocent nocturnal encounters arose. According to Cole Lesley, Coward once confessed that Lawrence had taken him to the bedroom and introduced him to 'the facts of life'. It may have been Coward's only heterosexual experience, but Graham Payn thinks it unlikely, reasoning that Coward would have told him if the juvenile relationship had been 'consummated'. (When Coward denied ever having slept with a woman, Gore Vidal asked, 'Not even with Gertie Lawrence?' 'Particularly *not* with Miss Lawrence', Noel replied.) But the two certainly saw in each other like minds, not least in a propensity for mischief. During their time off Coward, Lawrence and French used to idle away the hours in town. 'We used to go to the Lyons Corner House and sit all afternoon over a cup of tea, waiting for the band to begin. I remember there were paintings of bare-chested ladies on the walls down the stairs, and Gertie got out her lipstick and painted their nipples pink – it was Noel's suggestion, of course . . .'

Important though Gertrude Lawrence might be to Coward's future career, another girl in his life proved valuable to his dramatic and literary career: Esme Wynne, the successful child actor whose 'faintly bleating voice' Noel had first heard in *Where the Rainbow Ends*. Her strong, passionate character influenced his work and mental development, as well as providing a model for many of his early female roles.

Wynne had attended Noel's birthday party in 1911, when the Cowards still lived at Battersea. She remembered what she called 'the only sentimental incident of our whole career . . . we played hide-and-seek, and he elected to hide in the same place as me . . . and dared to peck at my cheek . . . And when he had done so, instead of becoming my devoted slave, we both shrieked with laughter, and that was the end of any sentiment between Noel and me . . .' It is a typical Cowardian scene: a theatrically heterosexual flirtation followed by the shriek of ironic laughter.

Noel wrote that when he first made Esme's acquaintance, he found her 'pompous, podgy, and slightly superior'. This annoyed Wynne. 'I was *never* a podgy child', she asserted. 'When we met I was slim and he was like a spotted suet pudding in shape and colour. I called him Podge, and he, resenting my interest . . . in religious matters, retorted by calling me Stodge. 'What wonderful *enemies* we would have made', Coward later said, as their friendship 'alternated between childishness and strange maturity'. When Wynne was sent off to a convent school in Belgium, the two friends exchanged enthusiastic letters. 'Can't we arrange it so that we can be together lots?' wrote Noel. 'Please go on with all your wicked ways at the Convent and get expelled and come home! DO!!!!!!!!!! I am longing for you . . . N.B. You got Some Romantic in your last letter.'

Coward's devotion seemed that of 'a perfectly normal young man in a state of adolescent calf-love', says Esme's son, Jon Wynne-Tyson. Wynne said she doubted that she could have 'borne the convent without Noel's letters, which were screamingly funny, and all the funnier when I thought that the nuns had to read them first'. Wynne had a mature attitude towards sex (and a lively practical interest in it), and was reluctant to discuss 'what went on in friends' bedrooms'. But she accepted Coward's emergent homosexuality, and observed that they would compare notes on attractive young men. She wrote, 'I adored his sense of humour . . . and his complete sexlessness (as far as females were concerned).'

Coward acknowledged that it was Wynne who 'egged him on to write', and his mother remarked that Noel and Esme were writing together as early as 1912, on a typewriter given to Coward by Walter Bulteel. A fierce competitive spirit existed between them: when Esme wrote romantic verse, Noel saw it as a challenge and set it to music. Coward graduated to writing prose, 'beastly little whimsies' much in the Kate Greenaway–Arthur Rackham fashion of the day.

Esme lived in nearby Stockwell, and the two went on expeditions to Woolworth's or Bon Marché in Brixton, cycled into the country, or played gramophone records in each other's bedrooms. Running fast down the steep stone steps of Ben Lomond and across the road to the Common, they were free to pursue adventure, not always of an orthodox nature. They decided it would be fun to swap clothes, and thus attired, paraded up and down the West End, apparently unnoticed.

Esme recalled Noel running across the Common, the hat and dress he had borrowed from her flying in the wind.

Meanwhile Noel had been offered two pounds ten shillings a week to play 'the prologue' in an American-written spectacle, *War in the Air*, at the London Palladium. His role was that of an infant aviator, Tommy, with a model aeroplane, transformed into a fighter pilot in subsequent scenes. 'It had its moments', Coward recalled, 'usually when I climbed into a prop airplane which was supposed to fly magnificently off into the wings . . . Nine times out of ten it flew into the stalls and I had to be retrieved from under old ladies' feet and from among their shopping bundles. Finally one day it flew quite out into the auditorium and I hung for two hours before they could cut me down from the railing around the edge of the dress circle. That finished that show.'

There was, however, one production to which all child actors aspired, J. M. Barrie's *Peter Pan*. To appear in it, on a West End stage, was confirmation that the under-age thespian had truly 'arrived'. During the summer, while the family were staying at Lee-on-Solent with aunts Vida and Borby, Violet had written to Dion Boucicault, the producer, to ask for a part for her son in that season's production of the play. He replied with a date for an audition. Boucicault, in the stalls, waited to hear Coward sing. He called out to the boy, insisting on just one verse. 'Noel sang one, and the accompanist stopped, but Boucicault called, "Go on, go on". So he sang to the end of the song, and they could hear him right up in the room where the children were waiting.' Boucicault asked Violet what part Noel wanted. They had set their sights on Slightly, one of the Lost Boys; Boucicault told them to return in an hour, when he gave Noel the part, and a princely wage of four pounds a week.

Peter Pan – with Noel in shaggy fur coat and silk top hat – opened at the Duke of York's Theatre on 23 December, and ended with Coward 'dizzy with triumph'. On the last night, 'people went mad', with crowds waiting outside the stage door. As Noel came out, they shouted 'good old Slightly', and shook his hand vigorously. They bundled into a taxi, piled high with chocolates and flowers, and got home to snatch a few hours' sleep, before starting on a four-week tour. This time Violet went too, unwilling to subject her son to another bout of homesickness. They travelled by chartered trains to Glasgow, Edinburgh, Newcastle and Birmingham, returning to London dates at Wimbledon, Hammersmith and Kennington. Coward was pleased to have the company of his *Goldfish* co-star, Alfred Willmore, who had the part of John Darling. He thought Coward quite unsuitable for the part of Slightly, usually played by an older man, but considered his friend's performance a 'clear foreshadowing of that brilliant crispness that was to be his own style and manner forever. In fact he was far too brilliant and too crisp for poor, stupid Slightly.' Noel said, 'It really is unbelievably difficult to act like a moron when one isn't a moron. And I have very little sympathy, darling, with morons.' He was already using an endearment to both sexes which even ten years later was shocking to the greater world.

After the excitement of *Peter Pan*, Coward found himself out of work again. 'I couldn't have been very happy really,' he recalled, 'because I was never completely happy when I wasn't working. But there was another reason for his inactivity; he had developed a cough he could not shake, and his concerned mother was glad when Noel met Dr Etlanger, a family friend, who ran a sanatorium, Pinewood, near Stroud in Gloucestershire. Etlanger took Coward there for tests; he was X-rayed and found to have tubercular glands in his neck. Violet's concern grew. Tuberculosis had killed Noel's uncle and grandfather, and could manifest itself in many organs besides the lungs. But the tubercular gland was easily cured, said Dr Etlanger, by country air and avoidance of smoky theatres.

Coward remained at Pinewood, where he stayed in Dr Etlanger's private house in the grounds. 'It is simply perfect down here,' he told Violet, 'it's a dear little cottage on the side of a very steep hill, woods at the back and woods at the side and a lovely valley in front with a lake, a cow, a horse, two puppies, and a good many snakes! ... Mrs E is so nice so is the Doctor. There is a lovely pony I ride.' On this he processed, dressed as 'an Arab' with 'two very jolly girls, friends of the Doctor', into the village 'throwing flowers at everyone and telling their fortunes. It *was* fun.'

But Pinewood also introduced him to disease and death. For much of his life, Coward was fascinated by medical matters, and this often morbid interest may have begun at the sanatorium, where he could observe the effects of TB. Many patients were army officers, and they seemed remarkably cheerful – a consequence of the heightened sensations TB induces. Noel watched the men playing sports on the lawns, clad in bathing trunks, sunburned and apparently healthy, 'talking so gaily of the future'.

He returned to Clapham much improved, although Violet was afraid that the London air would not be good for him. So when a new friend of Noel's suggested a holiday in Cornwall, she readily agreed. This new friend was not a young actor or actress, but an artist, and member of a perceptibly decadent society. James Philip Sydney Streatfeild* worked from a studio at 53 Glebe Place, just off Chelsea's King's Road, where he had lived on and off, since 1907. It was a fashionably Bohemian locale: the painter Glyn Philpot lived at 52; while the fashion photographer Baron de Meyer lived at 58.† Both were homosexual, as was Streatfeild.

Streatfeild was born on 5 November 1879 at 23 Grafton Square, Clapham. His father, Arthur Ogle Streatfeild, worked as a clerk at the Bank of England, and was related to the Streatfeilds of Chiddingstone, Kent, who were ancient landed gentry. Philip had studied at art college (possibly the Chelsea School of Art), and by 1914 was a proficient and talented artist, making a living from his portraits, still lifes and landscapes, exhibited from 1901 at such prestigious galleries as the Royal Academy and the Royal Society of Portrait Painters. When he met Coward, Streatfeild's most lucrative work was portraiture; his sitters had included the speaker of the House of Commons, Gerald du Maurier, and various members of the peerage. His was a peripatetic existence – he had changed his London address three times in the past ten years, moving up and down Manresa Road and Glebe Place, either side of the King's Road. He was also leading 'a fairly wild life', according to his sister, Monica, who recalled 'parties attended by society figures especially the stage and artistic set'. His friends included the remnants of the decadent Nineties, among them Robbie Ross, patron of the arts and Wilde's first male lover.

In his memoirs, Coward is unclear about his first meeting with Philip, possibly because he sought to spare his mother; Streatfeild family legend had it that Violet Coward was working as a charlady to make ends meet, and met Streatfeild when she was cleaning his studio in Glebe Place. One day she brought her son with her, and Philip asked Noel to sit for him. Coward's published recollection is that Streatfeild was painting a portrait of the actress Phyllis Monkman, then appearing as

---

* Not Streatfield, as Coward's memoirs misspelt it.
† Glyn Philpot was an accomplished society portraitist, who also painted working-class white boys and American negroes. Like many of that post-Wilde set, he was a Catholic convert. De Meyer's wife, Olga, was the illegitimate daughter of Edward VII, and a lesbian. Both were fond of cocaine, as were their friends. After the baroness's death, Princess Murat and her girlfriend were visiting the widowed de Meyer when they found a box of white powder, which they immediately began sniffing. De Meyer informed them too late that the box contained not cocaine but his wife's ashes.

principal dancer at the Alhambra Theatre. She wore a pink velvet dress; another model, named Doris, 'posed casually in the nude and made tea afterwards'. Esme Wynne remembered going to the studio with Noel, who sang his standard, 'There is a Green Hill Far Away', leaning nonchalantly against a grand piano. It was a heady introduction to artistic Bohemia for a young boy, and Streatfeild must have swayed Coward's emotions at an impressionable age. Rather short, Philip had mousy-blond hair and very English features, with a touch of loucheness about the eyes and lips. At thirty-five, he was twenty-one years older than Coward.

That May Philip Streatfeild and a friend, Sydney Lomer (a captain in the Sherwood Foresters), took Noel off to Cornwall, where the painter was a regular visitor. It apparently did not seem odd to Violet Coward that two grown men should want her fourteen-year-old son as a companion. She was either innocent of the implications or she felt their class made the association advantageous. Noel bounced 'blissfully' in the back of Lomer's fast car for two weeks, while they stopped at farms and inns along the way, with Streatfeild setting up his easel to work in quaint fishing villages. They dropped him off at Charlestown with his Aunt Laura, and Coward stayed on there, pillion-riding on Walter Bulteel's motorbike ('It certainly beats motoring for thrills!' Noel told Esme) and entertaining by dressing up in drag again. Wearing one of Connie's dresses and made up, Noel ensnared one young guest, Aldwyn Smith, as they walked in the garden. Coward struck coquettish poses, given a racy tinge by the cigarette holder he/she sported. The besotted young man appeared the next morning, only to be told by the Bulteel cousins that the mysterious young lady had left. They promised to forward his letter. Addressed to 'My Dear Little Flapper', it said that Aldwyn was 'fearfully sick' at having missed her, and asked for a photo. Coward and his cousins 'laughed their heads off'. Despite the protestation of Coward's future secretary, Cole Lesley, that 'there were in those days no Freudian implications' to such behaviour, it is difficult not to read some sexual challenge in Noel's pantomime.

Esme Wynne denied any suggestion of physical homosexuality in Coward at that age, telling her son in 1967 that 'Noel was never homosexual', meaning that he did not, as far as she knew, take part in homosexual acts. 'I do know that while he was friendly with me he never did anything that was criminally wrong, I mean that would have been punishable . . . he didn't indulge in homosexualism.' She did note that as a boy, Coward was 'terribly afraid of illness . . . he had said to me, I'd never do anything – well the disgusting thing they do – because I know I could get something wrong with me'. According to other friends, it was a revulsion against penetrative sex which remained with Coward all his life.

Streatfeild remains a shadowy figure, and nothing is known of what he thought about Noel.* However, visual evidence supports a certain attraction. A recently discovered painting by Streatfeild, entitled 'Bathers on the Rocks' and painted in 1914, depicts four naked boys on a rocky shoreline, gazing Narcissus-like into the water. The subject leaves little doubt as to the painter's proclivities. The style is similar to that of Henry Scott Tuke, RA, whose paintings of boys bathing were popular in the 1890s, and who worked at Falmouth in Cornwall, where he found his swimming and sunbathing young models. It is certain that Streatfeild knew Tuke there, and Streatfeild may have been a student of his. Tuke's pictures were an expression of the desires of the Uranians, late nineteenth-century enthusiasts of boy-love; writers, artists and Catholic converts inclined to intellectual paedophilia, among them Wilde, Frederick Rolfe, Sholto Douglas and Lord Alfred Douglas.† Streatfeild's connexion with the Uranians is confirmed by his friendship with Sydney Lomer, who that year had privately published *The Greek Anthology*, under the pseudonym 'Sydney Oswald'. Bound in red cloth, this was his English translation of 'Epigrams from Anthologia Palatina XII', an explicit paederastic text. Lomer was also a friend of Tuke's, who was commissioned to paint a nude portrait of the officer's 'extremely attractive' batman, Leo Marshall.

What is additionally intriguing about Streatfeild's picture is the apparent similarity between the boy on the far right of the group and photographs of Coward naked on the beach taken by Esme Wynne around that time. Philip Streatfeild's brother, William, possessed a portrait said to be of Noel, depicting 'a young boy, standing on a rocky

---

* But there is a hint of what the Streatfeilds thought about Philip's new friend. His great-niece recalls that when he brought Noel home with him, his mother later referred to Coward as 'a common little boy'.

† Timothy d'Arch Smith writes, 'What that particular area of the Cornish coast had to offer boy-lovers apart from being the home of Tuke seems indiscernible, but Fox [another Uranian] was not the only participant in the illicit sexual *mores* of those parts. The owner of a boys' training-ship was also regularly abusing his position of authority and the bodies of the boys under his charge at about this time. Photographs of the orgies held on the ship, a little dulled by time and persistent copying, still circulate in some coteries.' In his survey of the Uranian poets, *Love in Earnest*, d'Arch Smith observes that Wilde's *The Importance of Being Earnest* was a double pun, 'Earnest' being another euphemism for 'Uranian'.

path naked except for a very short, crumpled white shirt' – a painting which William's daughter recalls as a favourite of hers. (The picture disappeared when William Streatfeild died in 1957.) The only extant and positively identified Streatfeild portrait of Noel, a pencil drawing, also done in 1914, was proudly kept by Violet; resembling an innocent choirboy, it indicates how young Philip's new friend was.

Back in London in June, Noel wrote to Esme, still at 'finishing school' outside Brussels. In purple ink, he reported that the family would be staying at Lee-on-the-Solent for six weeks at the beginning of August 'and I don't know what I am going to do without my Stodge because there won't be any room at Lee when we are all down there'. He also detailed a string of engagements, concerts and At Homes, and another trip 'avec Philip – it will be ripping will it not?'

Streatfeild and Coward returned to Cornwall on 1 July, as that idyllic pre-war summer stretched on, 'hot and placid'. Streatfeild had taken a house on the south coast at Polperro, where they were joined by another London friend of Philip's, Donald Bain. Their house was 'beautifully furnished', he wrote, and 'about 300 feet above the sea', directly over a sandy cove. Here they swam and sunbathed, Coward initially turning a bright lobster colour (a sunlover all his life, he learned early that exposing one's entire body to the sun produced the best results). Noel had no inhibitions about nudity, as Philip's painting bore witness. Streatfeild had bought Noel a net, with which he caught 'le denizens de la deep (Bow-wow!)', and they had a boat in which they went as far as the harbour mouth, 'and then we came back because Philip said it was too rough'. When war was declared on 4 August, they saw three warships steaming by, 'they looked proud and invulnerable and almost smug'.

For Streatfeild, king and country called. He prepared to join Sydney Lomer's regiment, and sent Noel back to London by train on 6 August. By chance, a friend and former neighbour of his, the writer Hugh Walpole,* who also had a house at Polperro, was returning to London, and Noel was put in the writer's charge for the journey. According to Rupert Hart-Davis, Walpole was impressed with Coward, for he 'stood the boy lunch on the train and tipped him half-a-crown when they separated in London'. In town, Noel spent a night in an

---

* Hugh Walpole (1884–1941) had lived at 20 Glebe Place from 1909 to 1911. Writer and critic, he too was associated with the Uranians.

hotel, presumably alone, before going south to Lee to be with the Cowards.

Noel spent the early autumn dividing his favours between Esme and Philip. Streatfeild enlisted on 10 November 1914, joining Lomer in the 6th Battalion of the Sherwood Foresters as a second lieutenant. Coward wrote to his mother from 53 Glebe Place announcing, 'Philip is now a Soldier! (cheers) and I am going to stay to-night with him too as I shan't see very much of him when he is drilling all day. I took him to the "Little Minster" last night . . . I am going to see Captain Charlton this morning and Captain Lomer is going to take Philip and Captain C and Yours Truly to a box at a Music Hall to-night, no evening dress required . . .'

As news from the Western Front grew grimmer, officers and men sought desperate pleasures, and theatre people, even as young as Noel, were natural outlets for their exuberance. The theatre was a social arena where class barriers were flexible; as Captain Charlton noted, 'it was so ridiculously easy, during the war, to hob-nob with women, and men too for that matter, whose names and faces were continually advertised in the dreary photographic pages of society weeklies'. Leo Charlton was a romantic figure, having served in the Boer War and across the Empire. In 1914 he had joined the Royal Flying Corps, and was wounded in action the following year. An aristocratic Catholic, homosexual and later socialist, Charlton was altogether an atypical officer. He lived in Chelsea, with the then highly unusual convenience for a town house of an indoor swimming-pool. Here Charlton would entertain 'young officers of the Flying Corps in whom he was interested' and 'one or two of the West Indian boys, his gymnastic pupils', he later wrote. 'It cannot be claimed that the scenes which were enacted late at night were uniformly decorous. Much licence was allowed, especially to those who had just come from, or were immediately returning to, the agony of life at the war.'

Both Charlton and Lomer were representative of a hidden vein of homosexuality in the forces, which war served to intensify. Not only was the imminence of death a factor but, as Paul Fussell points out in his book *The Great War and Modern Memory*, the levelling of class in the army enabled upper- and middle-class homosexuals to come into contact with working-class men to whom they were sexually attracted. Noel's involvement in this closeted world was important. Not only would the connections with high-ranking members of the armed forces stand him in good stead for his later social uprise but they provided an introduction to the emotional tensions of homosexual society, disguised and subterranean, which would inform his work.

Even at that tender age, Noel had learned how to infiltrate the services. Esme Wynne recalled that Philip made his friend a mascot of the regiment while they were training in Essex (Sydney Lomer had a house in the barrack town of Colchester), and Noel accompanied the regiment on exercises in Hertfordshire. He wrote to tell Violet that he was 'having the time of my life . . . I have just come back from a long day with Lomer's division and I've marched 10 miles! and I'm "John tired" all the officers are so nice to me and all wanted to share their lunch with me You've got a fascinating youth for your son my dear.' Streatfeild 'loathed military life', recalled Esme, 'and to have a little boy there who could keep them in fits of laughter from morning into evening was a great relief'. Wynne found homosexual men witty and entertaining, with none of the pressures of heterosexuality to get in the way of friendship. 'It was amusing,' she recalled, 'it was so lovely to have people talking to you sensibly, and the people he knew were all very intelligent. As a young girl you don't visualise any physical side to it, and . . . as far as I know, no physical side was indulged in, beyond the odd kiss and whatnot.'

Back in town, it was the period of 'Darkest London', when the streets of the metropolis were cast into blackout and the first German air raid on the city began in late December. That Christmas Noel tried for *Peter Pan* again, but A. W. Baskcomb had been cast as Slightly, and the production started without him on Christmas Eve. A few days later, to Coward's joy, Baskcomb fell ill and Noel squeezed back into the previous year's furs and pink-and-black striped boots. 'It was heaven to be back in the theatre again', and he relished the accolades of the audience, who often threw bunches of violets, tied to thimbles, on stage (Wendy's thimble symbolising a kiss for Peter Pan). He also enjoyed a memorable corridor greeting from Peter Pan herself, Madge Titheradge: 'My name's Madge, what's yours?' She would do well to remember the reply.

3

Podge and Stodge

Isn't it gorgeous? He is going back to Hawtrey today to say that he
has perfect confidence in me and that I am throughly natural and
unaffected etc: oh I am a star!!

Noel Coward, undated letter to Violet Coward

O N 7 March 1915, 'entirely to please Mother', Coward was
confirmed at Holy Trinity Church, the imposing Georgian
edifice on the northern edge of Clapham Common. He later
told Robin Maugham that the clergyman instructing him for confirmation had 'groped' him. Noel had firmly removed his hand. 'There's a
time and place for everything', said Coward. 'And if I ever want a bit of
fun I'll let you know.' He added, 'I've despised the Cloth ever since.'*

Coward, remarked Esme Wynne, was 'dead from the neck up' as far
as religion was concerned. The issue became such a source of contention
that Noel and Esme agreed to draw up a 'Palship Contract', one clause
of which forbade any discussion of religion. Coward's attitude hardened
as he grew older. He often took the opportunity, in his plays and prose,
to snipe at its practitioners and its hypocrisy; perhaps it was the early
loss of beloved friends that induced this lack of faith. Philip Streatfeild
had contracted a virulent form of pulmonary tuberculosis and, like his
fellow officers at Pinewood, was facing death. Unable to complete his
training, getting progressively worse during the spring of 1915, he had
been sent to a nursing home in Croydon, coughing blood. Yet even
from his sickbed, Streatfeild could do his friend a favour. The previous

---

* In Coward's story 'Me and the Girls', the protagonist, a dying homosexual actor, recalls
his childhood: 'I shall never forget those jovial wet-handed clergymen queuing up outside the
stage-door to take us out to tea and stroke our knees under the table . . . I once got a box of
Fuller's soft-centres and a gramophone record of *Casse Noisette* for no more than a quick
grope in a taxi.'

year, when Noel and Philip had been holidaying in Cornwall, they had met an interesting family in Polperro. Mrs Astley Cooper had taken her son, Stephen, and his friend, Peter Ward, on holiday there: the two boys had met Philip and Noel, and become good friends. Stephen and Philip took to patrolling the cliffs, and fishing with Noel and Peter, while Mrs Astley Cooper, an amateur artist and a patron of the arts, took a lively interest in Streatfeild's work. After the party had dispersed under the cloud of war, they had kept in touch and Mrs Astley Cooper visited the Croydon nursing home where Streatfeild was in the last stages of consumption. Thinking to help her young friend, she 'made that senseless observation, though I saw he was dying "Is there anything I can do for you?" He said, "Will you take Noel Coward home with you, he is delicate and wants taking care of."'

It was thus because of a promise to Streatfeild – but also because she found his fifteen-year-old friend interesting – that Mrs Astley Cooper invited Noel to stay with her at Hambleton, her large estate near Oakham in Rutlandshire. Violet Coward saved up for a return ticket, but when she took Noel to St Pancras she left her handbag on the tube, and with it the money. She rushed to a nearby pawnshop with her diamond ring to pay for the journey. Her son appreciated the gesture, for this was an introduction to an entirely new society. Deep in the heart of the English shires, Hambleton Hall stood high on a hill, a self-important late Victorian stone mansion in parkland grazed by decorative sheep. Yet the war touched even this pastoral idyll, as the hall was soon to be taken over as a military hospital. In anticipation of this, Mrs Astley Cooper was living in the manor house in the grounds, a smaller building but still possessing twelve bedrooms.

The country-house routine had hardly changed since the nineteenth century. Early-morning tea arrived with thin slices of bread and butter, eaten while the maid made up the fire. At breakfast proper, a huge selection of fish, meat and fruit greeted the guests, and the morning might be spent following the hunt. This was Cottesmore country, packed with stately homes, and dominated by Belvoir Castle, home of the Dukes of Rutland (whose glamorous daughter, Lady Diana Manners, would become a friend of Noel's). After a picnic lunch and more hunting, they returned for high tea, then retired to their rooms, where there were log fires and their evening clothes were laid out. Cocktails and dinner followed, a custom which required stamina to retain consciousness to the end, such was the consumption of alcohol. Noel, no great drinker later, appreciated its social function here. Descending the polished staircase in evening clothes and new patent leather shoes, as if coming on stage, Noel revelled in the luxury. It was a realisation of another life altogether; Mrs Astley Cooper recalled Noel's particular surprise at 'the brass hot water cans'. She felt maternal towards this waif: 'Some weeks in the country, good food, and a fixed determination on my part to keep him out of doors the whole time (it was early spring) restored his health.'

Philip had recommended the trip, not just for Noel's physical health, but so that he could 'profit by the astringent wisdom' of his hostess. Evangeline Julia Astley Cooper was an eccentric and colourful character, as was her brother, Walter Marshall, the builder of Hambleton, whose motto was 'Do As You Please'. Marshall had died suddenly in 1899, leaving Hambleton to his younger sister because she shared his independent way of thinking. Although a Catholic convert, Mrs Astley Cooper was 'totally unshockable, and rather like a man in her interest in matters intellectual', says the current owner of Hambleton Hall, Tim Hart. She collected 'rather weird friends', recalls her granddaughter, 'I remember my father asking her why she bothered with "all these pansies from London"' – many of whom were also Catholic. Among the friends she invited were C. K. Scott Moncrieff,* translator of Proust; and the conductor Malcolm Sargent. James Lees-Milne was a later visitor; he thought Mrs Astley Cooper not 'particularly intellectual . . . essentially a country woman, well read . . . and kind to the young whom she cherished if they responded to her particular wry, no-nonsense kind of humour . . . She was just a tyrant with a heart of gold.'

Scott Moncrieff worked on his Proust translation at Hambleton, with Mrs Astley Cooper's help, and wrote a poem to her which he published as a dedication in *Swann's Way*; he added a handwritten stanza in her own copy, 'Five years have passed, and I am come/ To bask once more beneath your lime –/ A sense of duty keeps me dumb/ I may return another time.' Scott Moncrieff was a complex character, also caught up in Wilde's set. A Catholic and a dedicated spiritualist, he was Scottish-born, dark and handsome with a moustache; he was also impecunious and quarrelsome. As a poet and writer, Scott Moncrieff was closely associated with the Uranians and was known as the author of *Evensong and Morewesong*, 'a bravely obscene story of adolescent fellation'.

---

* Charles Keoch Scott Moncrieff, writer and journalist, an army captain during the war. In his *Who's Who* entry he listed under recreation 'nepotism'. He also translated the work of Pirandello, another perceptible influence on Coward.

Badly wounded in the war, Scott Moncrieff was rumoured to have seduced the poet Wilfred Owen while on leave.

Coward was already reading Wilde, Laurence Hope and Omar Khayyam, a result of his acquaintance with Philip Streatfeild and Sydney Lomer; through Mrs Astley Cooper and Scott Moncrieff he learned of Proust, although he did not read the author until much later. But it was a smart name to drop, and Coward used it as a barometer of intellectual and unconventional tastes (he also later named his cat after him); Act Two of *Easy Virtue* opens with its 'scarlet woman' heroine reading *Sodom and Gomorrah* by Proust. However, Noel encountered the works of another author at Hambleton who was to be of greater influence: Hector Hugh Munro, better known as Saki. Coward found a copy of Saki's new book *Beasts and Super-Beasts* on a hall table, and stayed awake into the early hours reading it.

The writer's elegantly tailored short stories, sometimes just a page in length, were society-set vignettes or more sinister tales, but usually featuring brilliant, cynical and well-dressed young men, a world already threatened by the changes of the war. Coward later wrote in appreciation of his literary hero: 'His articulate duchesses sipping China tea on their impeccable lawns, his witty, effete young heroes Reginald, Clovis Sangrail, Comus Bassington, with their gaily irreverent persiflage and their preoccupation with oysters, caviar and personal adornment, finally disappeared in the gunsmoke of 1914.' His *métier* was pre-Wodehousian high comedy of an epicene Edwardian style; he was famous for sayings such as 'She was a good cook as good cooks go, and as good cooks go she went.'

Coward never met his hero. Munro was killed on the Western Front in November 1916, and *Beasts and Super-Beasts* was the last collection of stories published in his lifetime. Like Streatfeild and Scott Moncrieff, Saki celebrated a cult of youth: Martin Green writes in *Children of the Sun* that his fiction was 'full of both insolent scorn for the mature figures of English civilization and a romantic-ironical fondness for its young and beautiful boys. "There is one thing I care for, and that is youth," Munro said.' Such themes – the predominance, almost arrogance of youth – would inform Coward's dramas, and Saki's style permeated his comic work, in short stories, verse, and plays from *I'll Leave It to You* onwards; the echo of the older writer's sardonic humour is heard over and over again in his successor's quips. Saki's few plays seem maquettes for Coward's (particularly his country-house drama, *The Watched Pot*). More specifically, the novel *When William*

Came, a fantasy of Britain under German occupation published in 1914 (when fears of invasion induced a crop of such stories), was 'shamelessly borrowed' for Coward's own Occupied Britain play, *'Peace in Our Time'* (1946).

Saki became a role model for the young Coward; it was as though he had inherited the elder writer's mantle. The homosexual but very English sensibility of Saki's fiction, with its decorative young men fencing words with colonels, archdeacons' wives, society ladies and their daughters, and the clash of generations and sensibilities (highlighted at Hambleton, where the aesthetes met the hunting hearties) provided dramatic and comic dynamic for both writers. In Coward's early comedy *The Young Idea*, country orthodoxy is satirised in Saki style. Noel willingly admitted his influence, extolling Saki's virtues when his works were republished posthumously: 'His stories and novels appear as delightful and, to use a much abused word, sophisticated, as they did when he first published them ... High comedy was undoubtedly his greatest gift.'

Mrs Astley Cooper was a Saki figure come to life. She had given up her first love, hunting, because of her obesity. 'A massive, shapeless lump of a woman', she was too fat to get in and out of her bath without the aid of her butler, Fred, and 'draped scarves over all mirrors', Coward recalled, 'because she said she could find no charm in her own appearance'. Instead 'she took up the chase of conversation, as it were, the thrills and spills of talk, finding her excitement in a more cerebral way'. She was 'very witty and acerbic', recalls her granddaughter, able to put anyone down with a sharp retort. She ruled Hambleton; her husband Clem was 'dotty', and lived in the dining room where the children would tie a rag lead to him and pretend he was a hunting dog.

It was an unconventional household, and could well have been the inspiration for Coward's 1924 play *Hay Fever*, as Mrs Astley Cooper maintained. Her family 'enjoyed a sort of amateur Follies', which were performed for the benefit of house guests. Her children's similarity to Sorel and Simon Bliss of *Hay Fever* (Stephen Astley Cooper was, like Simon, an artist), or Sholto and Gerda Brent of *The Young Idea*, reinforces her claims as a model for Coward's comedies. 'I have gone to see most of his plays', she wrote in 1938, 'because it amuses me to hear my remarks put into the mouths of the actors. He used, when staying with me, to carry a little black notebook in which he put down everything I said. I told him he would never reproduce it in any play, but he did more or less, and I think that his best plays, such as *Hay Fever*, were those in which the conversation of Hambleton predominated . . . somebody once said, "The play was very amusing, but no one ever talked like that." A companion said: "On the contrary, I know the family from whom it was all taken down."'

Hers is a vivid image – that of the young boy following his hostess about the house, scribbling her bon mots in his notebook. It was not an entirely one-sided affair, however: Coward, as a clever, even presumptuous young boy of fifteen, seemed far in advance of his years. His talent, and the ease with which he fell into gracious living, made him an amusing and desirable guest. He sang for his supper, and received return invitations as a result. Noel often revisited Hambleton Hall, and when the house became a convalescent hospital later in the war, was summoned by Mrs Cooper to entertain her recuperating troops. Her granddaughter remembers Noel's performance on the flat roof of a farm building, for the benefit of local village children. However, Mrs Astley Cooper hints that the young Coward sometimes outstayed his welcome; he 'came perpetually down afterwards, and always behaved as though he were the son of the house, rather to the annoyance of my husband'.

Whatever its dramatic influence, Hambleton was pivotal to Coward's progress. It identified a social goal, a standard to which he could aspire now that he knew what life among his 'betters' was like. He could, and would, live among these people, accepted by virtue of where he was going rather than where he had come from. He knew that this was the life for which he was destined, and achieved it by hard work and application of the talent he possessed. But respect was another matter. The rarefied strata he aspired to remained equivocal about such ambition, which was seen as slightly vulgar: 'A gentleman disguised his abilities as much as he disguised his emotions,' wrote Noel Annan, 'not to do so was to show side and drop one's guard.' These were engrained notions that Coward would have to deal with for much of his life.

To Esme Wynne, Coward was 'frightfully ambitious', even then. 'He was full of determination and willpower, and made his name through that determination . . . He knew he could get there and would get there.' She recalled that Coward was 'rightfully annoyed' when people said of him, '"He's clever – and knows it." He always logically commented "How do they think I could be clever and *not* know it?"'

*

43

Back in the real world the war was progressing at a rate of inches, with death the only advance. At least death came quickly on the Western Front; it took five months for Philip Streatfeild to die of tuberculosis of the lungs. His father was with him when he died, on 3 June 1915, at the nursing home in Croydon.* Coward deals with the event in one sentence in his autobiography, having described his visit to Hambleton: 'He died the following year without ever realising to the full the great kindness he had done me.' It is a brief epitaph; perhaps he was too hurt, even twenty years later, by the memory.

In his will dated 2 November 1914 (eight days before he enlisted) Streatfeild directed his executor, his brother William, to pay 'my friend Noel Coward of 50 Southside Clapham Common SW the sum of £50 free of legacy duty'. However, in a codicil dated 16 April 1915, he instructed, 'I hereby revoke the legacy of fifty pounds bequeathed to my friend Noel Coward', whether because he and Coward had fallen out or because Streatfeild had 'advanced' his friend the money is not clear. Tuberculosis could induce great changes of temper, as Noel's later friend, G. B. Stern, wrote of her tubercular hero, Giles Goddard, 'overwrought, in a sort of spiritually unreasonable state'. Another possibility is that Streatfeild's homosexual proclivities had been uncovered by Coward's family, and that Noel had been dissuaded from the association (as he was not yet sixteen years of age, it was a potentially scandalous situation).

On 4 October 1915 Coward returned from Lee-on-Solent where he had been staying with his Aunt Vida. He was met by Esme Wynne; keen to hear each other's news and gossip, they went off to tea. That autumn and winter Noel and Esme were practically inseparable, more especially now that Coward was bereft of Streatfeild's company. It was an enjoyable routine. Esme called for Noel, or vice versa, and they took the tube to town to eat lunch at Frascati's and take tea at the Elysée, if solvent (at Maison Lyons, if not), with theatre in the afternoon or evening. Alternatively, they stayed at Noel's, working on their latest co-production, a dance or a drama, which occasionally saw public performance in charity concerts. One such was on 30 October 1915, when they appeared on a varied bill designed to enhance patriotic feelings,

* The younger Streatfeild family believed that Philip died of typhoid, contracted while in a French camp, but his death certificate indicates otherwise. If the contraction of tuberculosis was blamed on Coward, the family may have sought to disguise or dismiss the fact of their son's death.

although the Coward–Wynne collaboration, a duet and dance entitled 'Monkeys', seemed unlikely to fire notions of king and country.

The war was beginning to affect the theatre, and not for the worse. Entertainment, both for troops on leave and civilians seeking escape, was at a premium; by 1915 unemployment among actors had been cut by nearly fifty per cent. For both Coward and Wynne it was a period of relatively full employment; the productions staged had become increasingly escapist, and the fairy play was more popular than ever. On 14 December Noel and Esme began rehearsing together for the fourth season of *Where the Rainbow Ends* at the Garrick. Coward, too old for his original part of page boy, was engaged as the dragon-man, the Slacker, a 'short but showy' part which involved much blue and yellow make-up and some green sequins stuck on his eyelids. The dress rehearsal on Christmas Eve 'went off beautifully', Esme noted. The theatre was a hard taskmaster; both teenagers had to rehearse on Christmas afternoon, and the play opened with a matinee performance on 27 December.

Another old friend was in the cast: Harold French was playing Crispian, and his voice was breaking. Noel had been through this trauma earlier that year and, although upset by the change, had come to accept it. (Unlike his mother: 'One of the saddest things in life', she wrote, 'is when a boy who has a beautiful voice loses it for good and all! I shall never forget how unhappy I was when he cracked on a high note and never sang as a boy again', a telling indication of her wish to keep him a boy.) Noel consoled his friend, 'You may never sing "Oh for the Wings of a Dove" again, but think how impressive you'll be when you have a go at "Rocked in the Cradle of the Deep".' At sixteen, he was already dispensing advice with the voice of authority. 'Now that your ... er ... voice has dropped, you'll have to try and get juvenile parts and you'll need a decent wardrobe', Noel advised. 'Go to my man', he said airily, giving French the address of a tailor off the Strand, 'mention my name'. When Harold protested at the cost, Noel told him to pay in monthly instalments: 'You don't have to say which month. But no hanky-panky, he's got to be paid sometime.' French did as he was told.

Despite food shortages and the precarious blackout, life in wartime London was fun for Noel and Esme, enjoying the freedom of the city and being in a successful production. On New Year's Day 1916, the cast of *Where the Rainbow Ends* celebrated with a harlequinade after the matinee. The following week Noel and Esme went to the Golders

Green Empire to see Charles Hawtrey in *The Compleat Angler*. Coward and Wynne were not the best-behaved theatre-goers, 'the rest of the programme was awful, and we giggled lots'. Nor were they forgiving in their criticisms – *The Peddler of Dreams* at the Vaudeville was 'a terrible amateurish performance, *so* boring – we could hardly sit through it . . . the Principal was as camp as Hell'.

In early January the pair were offered auditions for a touring production of Brandon Thomas's well-worn favourite, *Charley's Aunt*, due to begin soon after *Where the Rainbow Ends* closed. Cecil Barth was responsible for the production, and they both went to see him on 11 January. Esme thought Barth 'rather swinish', but they accepted his invitation to see *Charley's Aunt* that evening. 'Were *so* bored . . .' noted Esme tartly. They went back to Barth ('more swinish than ever') the next day, to read their parts. It was arranged that they should see Mrs Brandon Thomas (widow of the play's author) at her house in Gordon Square. Unlike the swinish Mr Barth, Mrs Thomas was 'charming and quite approved of us', and terms were arranged.

Coward and Wynne celebrated with tea at the Criterion, assured of two pounds a week, every week, for the near future. The following evening they went to see Sydney Lomer: now a major, he entertained Noel and Esme in his 'wonderful' house, filled with 'gorgeous books'. Lomer was particularly charming to Esme, and asked to keep a book of her poetry to read later. The following week Wynne wrote to him, and Lomer invited them both to lunch at the Royal Automobile Club, to discuss their work.

The *Charley's Aunt* tour began at Southampton. Noel, Esme and her mother had digs at West Marland Terrace, close to the Grand Theatre. The Brandon Thomas Company 'had been going the rounds for about twenty years . . . They were all old, old men who had grown into their part, and elderly ladies.' Wynne was to play Amy; Noel, the eponymous Charley. This was not a lavish production. Both had to supply their own clothes, and Noel was taken aback to discover that his flannels had shrunk to the length of cycling knickers. In Southampton they loitered on the pier, reading 'nonsense novels' to each other (Esme bought Noel '*un petit livre d'amour*'); and explored the Common where they trespassed on an army camp, 'were rude to two soldiers and retired with dignity'. Nearby, on the shores of Southampton Water at Netley, was the huge military Royal Victoria Hospital, full of casualties from the war. The cast of *Charley's Aunt* was to entertain the troops, and drove there, crossing the Itchen by the Floating Bridge. Noel and Esme performed 'Nonsense Rhymes' and the second act of *Charley's Aunt*; afterwards they took tea in the officers' quarters, 'overlooking the waters and long stretches of lawn and dark pine trees. The sky was grey and pink and a big splodge of gold showing between the pines.'

Such outings were a bonus of a tour. The New Forest was close by, and Coward and Wynne rambled in Lyndhurst, lunching hungrily in the Crown Hotel. They admired the huge yew tree on the green at Bolton's Bench, 'and then we went into the forest and heard the stillness of it all and rubbed our faces on the soft moss and I picked ferns and red and green ivy and baby leaves. The smell was earthy and good.' It is odd to imagine Noel communing with nature, but such was the influence of Esme. The next week they returned to London, to open in Croydon. They travelled by bus, sitting on the open top deck, talking endlessly; quite often their discussions would over-heat: 'He behaved like a fool', Esme wrote in her diary. She was undergoing the stress of a love affair with one of the cast, nicknamed Babs, while 'poor Noel had a dreadful disappointment as S. L. [Sydney Lomer] wrote to say he couldn't put him up . . . Podge very depressed on bus'. A few days later Noel arrived at the theatre 'in new suit and intense state of depression – had a row with him – made it up and we came back together on top of a car philosophising on love and life sitting perched on our make-up boxes on a snow covered seat – then we saw how funny it was and shrieked . . .' Such arguments, born of fervent adolescent emotion, were minor dramas in themselves, their mutable relationship a rehearsal for future Coward productions.

On the Hammersmith leg of the tour, which began on 28 February, Wynne first mentions John Ekins, whom Noel had introduced to her. Ekins was the handsome, fresh-faced son of the rector of Rame in Cornwall, the same age as Coward, with whom he had appeared in the 1915–16 production of *Where the Rainbow Ends*. He was currently playing in *Anthony in Wonderland*, a Hawtrey production at the Prince of Wales's Theatre. Sharing a mutual ambition and sense of humour, he and Coward had become close, as did Wynne and Ekins; Esme later confessed to a 'little *tendresse* . . . we might just have married one another', she admitted, acknowledging that this created a certain tension between the two older friends: 'Noel was inclined to be jealous especially of John Ekins's good looks and popularity.'

If envious of Ekins's looks or talent, Noel did not allow this to stand in the way of their relationship, which probably thrived on healthy competition, as did his friendship with Esme. When Ekins eventually persuaded his parents to let him live in London to pursue a stage career, the friendship intensified, despite John's rapid success in getting parts for which Noel had tried. The three friends indulged in a great deal of ragging, throwing stinkbombs and generally annoying the populace. But Coward and Ekins were also up to other tricks: they had taken to petty theft. Shoplifting is a daredevil game many adolescents play, but for Noel, who never did things by halves, the targets were the luxury goods he could not afford to buy but felt like owning. He and John strolled into Hawes and Curtis, the Savile Row tailors, and casually walked out with a selection of shirts and ties.

Coward later admitted to Robin Maugham that he had been 'an almost compulsive thief' as a teenager, his brazenness utterly lacking shame. He once went to Fortnum & Mason's, picked up a suitcase, and took it along Piccadilly to Hatchards the bookshop, where he filled it up. On another raid, he found himself being watched by a shop assistant. 'Really!' said Noel. 'Look how badly this store is run. I could have made off with a dozen books and no one would have noticed.' Such behaviour terrified the law-fearing Wynne, especially when, on her way with Coward and her mother to see her father in the City, they stopped at a bookstall, 'and suddenly saw him take a book and fly, with the bookman after him . . . my mother nearly had a fit'. Coward seemed not to care about getting caught. 'Noel had no fear of anything. I expect he knew in his heart of hearts that he would say something funny, and make the policeman laugh, you know? He was so assured.' His lightfingeredness made shopping trips painful for Esme, although he did pay for the 'futurist pyjamas' they acquired one Saturday together with some matching tulle, costumes for their *Shadow Dance*, which they auditioned (with Gwen Kelly as chaperone) at the Hippodrome for the producer of a new show. 'Both dressed in same room – were so amused', Esme noted.

The *Charley's Aunt* tour continued in the Midlands, interrupted occasionally by the 'Zepp hooter' announcing Zeppelin bombing raids. In Chester there was a minor crisis when they were told that they were staying in a 'bad house', as Esme put it, 'and Mr Barth made me write a note to say I was not returning'. Coward maintained it was a brothel, although Wynne denied it. Whatever the truth, they were swiftly moved out the following morning, and went to spend the rest of the day sculling on the river. There they saw 'two lovely young boys in black and white sweaters' who kept their canoes in the woods. In a phrase reminiscent of Philip Streatfeild's Uranian tributes to radiant young boys, Coward and Wynne dubbed the pair 'Golden Youth', and went back the next day, discovering that they lived in a tent on top of a hill. Whether either pursued this acquaintance further is not known, but their intimacy was greater because of such shared desires. They seemed unable to spend time away from each other, even sharing digs after Noel had argued with his housemate, Arnold Raynor, the juvenile lead. Coward 'hated being on his own. He had to be on his own at first, then in the end we thought, well, bother the thing, if we can't talk with our friends and have any sort of life outside the theatre then we must give notice.' They got their own way. 'I don't mean we shared bedrooms or anything,' added Esme hastily, 'we had two bedrooms and a sitter, which you want on tour, you see. But we *could* go on talking. Whereas when we were segregated poor Noel sat in his horrible rooms and I sat in my horrible rooms with no one to talk to.' 'We even had baths together,' Noel recalled, 'it seemed affected to stop short in the middle of some vital discussion for such a paltry reason as conventional modesty.'

Both had their share of admirers, usually men in uniform. In Nottingham, they received a note from 'two subs in front' – the ever-present sub-lieutenants, who had a reputation as 'stage door johnnies'. 'Noel interviewed them. We refused to see them but they were in the front row of the stalls and looked rather pets'; while on the train back to London from Blackpool, 'officers began trying to talk and we allowed two Military and one Naval to do so'. So deigned the haughty stars, neither yet eighteen.

When the tour reconvened in Torquay, they found a secluded cove on Babbacombe beach and took all their clothes off 'and sat on a rock and let the water run over us, then we raced about the rocks and danced on the cliffs in the nude – it was so lovely and our figures looked so pretty against the green and blue'. Only later would Noel note that 'their aesthetic eyes' were blind to the fact that Esme's hair went unbecomingly straight when wet, and that his back was covered in spots. Then in Bristol Noel underwent a strange and sudden religious enlightenment when a storm sent him into 'black nostalgia for Mother and the dear familiarity of my bedroom at Clapham Common'. This was taken seriously by the ethereal Esme, who saw it as an epiphany of sorts. She reminded Noel of it in later years, 'I wonder if you remember us standing in a field during that awful *Charley's Aunt* tour, realizing (as I see it was, now) *Power*. We admitted to each other that we felt within us the power to achieve *anything*, and your integrated wish was to have the world at your feet, theatrically speaking . . .' This near-supernatural revelation (as Wynne saw it) seemed to prove that Coward's ambition could not be contained.

The tour proceeded with pitifully small audiences and various rows. In Wolverhampton Coward had a stand-up fight with Arnold Raynor, who had become exasperated by his fellow actor's sometimes vexing behaviour. 'He knocked Noel about horribly . . . great hulking cad', wrote Esme accusingly. Noel, 'poor child, came home covered with bumps', and the next day felt 'very feverish and sleepy'. It was a great deal livelier than what went on onstage, where Coward's performances were less impressive, accordingly to Wynne. 'He was a very bad actor in his youth; it took a long time to make Noel a good actor . . .'

Charley's Aunt gave up the ghost on 3 June, leaving Coward and Wynne thankful but jobless. In the search for employment, Noel felt he lacked facility at auditions, even when accompanied at the piano by Aunt Kitty (who had returned from Toronto, deserted by Uncle Percy). However, soon after Esme was recommended for a part in *A Pair of Silk Stockings*, he was able to announce – as they lay out in a hammock Noel had fixed on the tiny balcony at 50 Southside – his new role in *The Light Blues*. He had secured it only after a certain persistence, as Coward's friend Lord Amherst remembered: 'He went to a call for people to join a musical run by Cicely Courtneidge and her husband [Jack Hulbert], and they were rehearsing and put Noel in the chorus. Noel said "Oh no, I've got to have a part" and stamped his foot and went off. Sure enough they gave him a small part.'

The Light Blues was a two-act musical comedy by Mark Ambient and Jack Hulbert concerning 'the excruciating adventures of a jolly actress called Topsy Devigne'. Noel played an Edwardian 'dude' in morning clothes, top hat and false moustache, with Cicely Courtneidge as Topsy, in an extravagant pink dress. Coward enjoyed the three-week tour, but was crushed when Robert Courtneidge, Cicely's father, flew at him when he discovered the boy doing 'saucy' imitations for the amusement of the cast. Cicely Courtneidge consoled him with a pat on the back and 'you mustn't mind father'. To Miss Courtneidge, Noel appeared to be 'very tall, skinny not good-looking and rather spotty, wasn't the sort of bloke you'd take to at all, but my goodness, was he clever!'

The Light Blues opened at the Shaftesbury Theatre on 16 September 'with the mark of death emblazoned upon it'. The phrase had a certain macabre aptness, as the Zeppelin raids on London began that night and were an obvious disincentive to audiences to negotiate blacked-out streets as dangerous as falling bombs. It ran for just two weeks, leaving Noel to seek his first and last engagement as a professional dancer, an occupation with definite gigolo overtones. But as Cicely Courtneidge had observed, Noel at sixteen was not a seductive figure, 'too gangling and coltish to promote evil desire in even the most debauched night-club habitues'. With a girl named Eileen Dennis, he sashayed across the floor of the Elysée Restaurant (later the Café de Paris) performing a slow waltz, a tango, and 'a rather untidy onestep'. It was a decidedly disappointing introduction to decadent nightlife.

His next role combined his singing and dancing skills; he was engaged as a Sandhurst cadet for Cecil Aldin's and Adrian Ross's *The Happy Family*. The play also featured Fabia Drake, cast in the lead role of Babs; Noel was to play her 'young man'. She recalled that Coward 'had rather "stuck-out" ears and ... extraordinary powers of application'; it was Drake who gave Noel an inappropriate nickname which nonetheless stuck: 'Cowardy Custard'. A critic wrote that Coward 'combined the grace and movement of a Russian dancer with the looks and manner of an English schoolboy'; Noel kept the cutting until it yellowed with age. Esme, back from her latest tour, judged it a 'topping show'. The trium-virate of Coward, Wynne and Ekins resumed their old routine, seeing *Chu Chin Chow*, 'that gorgeous spectacle ... a riot of colours' but a 'paltry plot'; and its burlesque by Alice Delysia and Leon Morton in *Pell Mell*. They might have forgotten that there was a war going on, had they not been regularly woken by air raids, and had Noel not turned up to tea with 'a nice sub [lieutenant] called Herbert Edward Clark'.

Ten days later Coward finished in *The Happy Family*, leaving him free to concentrate on writing with Wynne. Although Esme was reading Walt Whitman and Nietzsche, their first literary collaboration was a book of light sketches and stories which they called *Parachutes*, parachutes being an innovation of the war. So assured of its quality were they that the manuscript was sent to John Lane, who invited the co-authors to tea. According to Wynne, 'quite an illustrious company were assembled; he introduced us as a young couple with a promising future [the pair were often mistaken for boyfriend and girlfriend] ... We were told, however, that ... *Parachutes* suggested ... we would do better work in a short time and that the Bodley Head would rather wait for more mature work from our pens.' Such professional encouragement prompted Noel and Esme to begin writing curtain-raisers under the unattractive joint *nom de plume* of Esnomel. The initial idea came from

Wynne, but Coward took it up avidly, and they were soon swapping ideas in his room at Clapham.

Noel had meanwhile been to stay with the Ekins family in Cornwall, where he and John went to the Theatre Royal in Plymouth, 'very casual and grand in our carefully pressed navy blue suits and coloured silk socks'. The Ekins household was 'one of the nicest ... I have ever known', Coward remarked. Their contentment seemed idyllic: Mr and Mrs Ekins, John, and his two sisters, Christine and Audrey – the picture of a happy family, to which he perhaps unfavourably compared his own. But even here were intimations of mortality; Audrey was tubercular, and the boys used to have tea parties in her bedroom to cheer her up. It was not the only sadness the family were to suffer. John Ekins joined the Royal Flying Corps as an air mechanic and on 20 April Noel received a letter from him; he had a day's leave, could they meet for a matinee? But in the same post was a letter from Mrs Ekins saying that John had died on 17 April at the Military Isolation Hospital in Aldershot, from spinal meningitis.

It was a profound shock to Coward, his second experience of the death of a close friend in as many years. He went to the matinee alone, but began to cry and had to leave. The tube ride home was interminable as he conjured up memories of his friend. 'It took a long while for my unhappiness to disperse', he recalled twenty years later, 'and even now I feel a shadow of it when I think of him.' The loss of two of his closest friends subjected Coward to the grief which affected most families in England during that war. Esme, a serious believer, had her faith to sustain her. Noel, cynical before his time, had none, and was perhaps insensitive to that of others. The Ekins family suffered further loss. 'Tragedy certainly descended swiftly on that gentle, harmless rectory. Within a year or so Christine, the healthy elder daughter, had married and died in childbirth, and there was only Audrey left to linger on for a few months. Mr and Mrs Ekins live there still and Christine's daughter is with them, but even so the house must feel empty.'

Coward's pessimism seemed to manifest itself in a youthful disregard for authority; not only did he not believe in the law, or in God, but he had no faith in country either. Esme maintained that she and Noel were 'terrifically pacifist, in the First War – not pacifist as I afterwards became through understanding, but the sheer unintelligence of it. We used to go with our ... nice young men to the Carlton hotel, and then the next minute that nice young man is blown up sky-high, and everything gone ... And we lost our darling John Ekins ...'

In their reaction to all this destruction, Coward and Wynne were driven by the arrogance of adolescence. Esme thought they were 'horribly stridently detestably young!', making a cult of their youth. Later they conceived a magazine 'which was to be by youth for youth and about youth and its name, quite simply, would be Youth – and we its editors'. They even got as far as choosing paper, type and printer for the venture, but money prevented their going further. 'We were as rebellious, defiant and disillusioned as intelligent youth is in any age, but I think we had more justification for our cynicism, bitterness and intolerance ... Not for a moment were Noel and I deceived by the claptrap and jargon of patriotic fervour that was doled out from press, pulpit and stage.' She recalled a heated discussion they had with the novelist Coningsby Dawson, 'then a patriotic young officer', whom they had met at John Lane's. He took them to eat at a restaurant, the Rendezvous. Their awe at lunching with a novelist 'turned to indignation when we realised that he was on the side of the war mongers; we had imagined him more intelligent then it occurred to us that he could not be far off thirty, the age we hated only less than we hated war'.

Coward and Wynne continued to work on the book for John Lane. Another manuscript had been returned 'from the ungrateful editor of "Smart Set"', noted Wynne, but they persevered with burlesques, and 'arrangements' for their joint literary effort. They also saw a new film from the United States which caused a sensation when it opened in London. As they left the theatre on 11 May, having seen D. W. Griffith's epic *Intolerance*, neither could have known that by the summer Noel would be working for that exalted director.

Griffith's *Hearts of the World* was the story of a French village as it changed hands in the course of the war, a propaganda film to persuade the United States to come in on the Allied side, the director having been invited to England by Lord Beaverbrook, then minister of information. Although America had entered the war the day before the premiere of *Intolerance*, Griffith went ahead with *Hearts of the World*. Lillian and Dorothy Gish came over from the States, and in London casting began for minor roles: Coward's ubiquitous presence in agents' offices around town secured him a role, for the respectable sum of one pound a day.

Coward was summoned to Staunton in Worcestershire on location, to make his film debut. There was a disturbingly early morning call, and the application of a layer of bright yellow make-up for the benefit of the black and white cameras. It was a brief appearance. Miss Gish recalled, 'In one scene the French girl I was playing packed her possessions and left home just a few minutes ahead of the approaching Germans. This young actor was supposed to help me by pushing the loaded wheelbarrow toward the camera instead of away from it. I am sure that if Mr Griffith had not been so preoccupied with such a responsible assignment, he would have perceived the boy's extraordinary talent.' Coward got on well with the Gish girls and, characteristically, with their mother (also appearing in the film), who used to wait for her girls in a carriage and pair at lunch, and Noel was invited to join them. (He later referred to his film experience in *I'll Leave It to You*, in which Sylvia becomes a movie actress, and talks of 'that day in the middle of the village street, when I had to do three "close ups" on top of one another'. 'It all sounds vaguely immoral to me', comments her mother.)

Cinematic success was followed by another Manchester appearance in Dorothy Brandon's *Wild Heather*. The indications were that the engagement would not be exciting: minced haddock on toast and a throat infection confirmed Coward's opinion that Manchester was 'a beastly hole'. There were also worries about home; Noel asked Violet to wire him if the air raids went 'anywhere near our delectable residence ... I shall probably hear that Clapham has been razed to the ground.' However, free after the second act of *Wild Heather*, he would run round to the Palace Theatre to catch Ivy St Helier and Clara Evelyn playing their piano duets. The two women gave him useful tips on 'the value of "authority" in a piano entertainer', and 'some good striking chords to play as introduction to almost any song'; Noel 'profited a lot from that afternoon'. The advice allowed him to develop musical techniques for gaining his audience's attention in the same way that Hawtrey's tuition had directed his acting abilities.

His career was accelerating rapidly. Gilbert Miller, the producer, appeared in Manchester, having been advised by Hawtrey to see Noel's performance. Coward was flattered by the attentions of this 'dark enthusiastic American' who sent for him at the Midland Hotel. 'My Dear he had come down *specially* to see me in Wild Heather', Noel told Violet, 'and he said I was *really splendid* and that I hadn't half enough to do!' Miller offered him a part in a new production at the Garrick, *The Saving Grace*, in which he was 'absolutely certain I should make my name! ... He says it is a Terrific part and I have to play with Marie Lohr! Isn't it gorgeous?' he gushed. 'He is going back to Hawtrey to-day to say that he has perfect confidence in me and that I am throughly natural and unaffected etc: oh I am a star!!' It was, he wrote later, 'the real start of my name being known'.

Manchester also introduced Noel to Ivor Novello, the handsome idol of many a female – and male – theatre-goer. Novello's career was in the ascendant, and as singer, actor, film star, composer and playwright, he and Coward would later be seen as rival talents. The Welsh-born Novello (his real name was the more prosaic David Davies) was six years older than Coward, and his first success, *Theodore & Co.*, written by himself, had opened at the Gaiety Theatre in September 1916 and run for eighteen months; his patriotic 'Keep the Home Fires Burning', a plantive war song, became a huge hit with soldiers and their sweethearts everywhere.

Coward was eager to meet this handsome new star, and had a mutual friend in Bobbie Andrews, who had rivalled Philip Tonge for the status of best-known boy actor. Andrews was a good-looking young man, who became Novello's lover and eventually his heir. Coward persuaded Andrews to effect an introduction, but found the reality of meeting a hero disappointing. They met on the pavement outside the Midland Hotel, where Noel's 'illusion of this romantic handsome youth ... drooped and died and lay in the gutter'. Novello's face was yellow and unshaven, he was dressed in a shabby overcoat with an astrakhan collar and wore a battered brown hat; Noel could as easily have mistaken him for a busker and thrown him some coins. Novello invited him to see his musical *Arlette*, and afterwards they took tea in his rooms at the Midland. As Novello shaved and changed for dinner Coward watched him transformed into the matinee idol. He experienced a serious pang of envy: 'I just felt suddenly conscious of the long way I had to go before I could break into the magic atmosphere in which he moved and breathed with such nonchalance.'

But further advancement arrived in Manchester in the shape of the composer and impresario Max Darewski. 'Nearly mad with excitement', Coward wrote, telling his mother that he was collaborating with Darewski on a new song. The lessons of Clara Evelyn and Ivy St Helier were being put to good use. 'I wrote the lyric yesterday after breakfast, I hummed it to him in the Midland lounge at 12 o'clock, we at once rushed up to his private room, and he put harmonies to it, there were some other people there, when they sung it once or twice, Max leapt off the piano stool and danced for joy and said it was going to take London by storm! We are putting the verse to music this morning', reported Noel, who said the song – 'When You Come Home on Leave' – a patriotic number which sought to capitalise on Novello's hit – was to be published the following week, and in all probability sung by Lee White or Phyllis Dare. 'I shall probably make a lot of money out of it', he maintained airily. Another number, 'Bertha from Balham', was to be placed with Margaret Cooper, a performer he much admired.

'You see he is one of the most influential men in town,' Noel said of Darewski, 'he owns three theatres, at least I am beginning to make my way, really Manchester has been astonishingly lucky for me . . .' More than ever, Coward was determined to become a truly brilliant star.

4

Rising Star

Ever since a child of tender age
The world has been a stage
For me to dance upon;
Wedding bells would never ring for me,
The only thing for me
Was 'Getting On'

Noel Coward, *Operette*

O NE of the greatest saving graces about *The Saving Grace* – 'a gentle, witty and delightful comedy' – was that Charles Hawtrey introduced Coward on the opening night with a short biographical sketch of the young performer, thus conferring the status of a star-to-be. With that facile theatrical emotion of which he was later critical, Coward cried ('but imperceptibly'). His ascendance seemed assured. *Talk of the Town* printed a profile photograph, and under the headline, VERSATILITY, noted, 'The part of the young lover ... is played by Noel Coward ... He has a difficult job, and manages it with considerable skill and tact. But Noel Coward is not only an actor, [he] has written, in collaboration with Miss Esme Wynne, some one-act plays, one of which has been produced as a curtain-raiser ... He is a composer, too, and Margaret Cooper is now singing one of his songs, many of which have been published.'

During the production Coward learned much from Hawtrey, in particular technical points of comedy acting which he used thereafter. 'I was eager to learn and he knew it', Coward recalled. Noel learnt by example, watching the great actor's technique, quickly picking up the tricks and nuances of his performance. Hawtrey showed Coward how to laugh, for instance, beginning with a low exhaling of breath, 'Ho-ho-ho', then with a smile, and finally releasing to produce a stage laugh which was entirely technical. He also taught Noel never to put his hands in his pockets, but to use them as part of his performance – Coward's gesticulatory finesse would become an art in itself. But perhaps Hawtrey's most valuable lesson was how to inhabit a stage and fix the attention of the audience so that eyes were on him, and him alone. It was an ability which, along with his other talents, made Coward one of the most charismatic performers of his time.

Coward's onstage tuition continued, despite regular air raids in which Hawtrey advised the audience to leave, yet continued with the performance: empirical evidence of the British phlegm which Coward was both to eulogise and to parody. (Hawtrey was rewarded for his insolence when, during the run of *This Saving Grace*, a bomb from the infamous 'Silent Raid' fell outside in Piccadilly Circus, creating a twelve-foot crater and blasting the actor through the door of the Trocadero.) Violet said that Hawtrey was 'always so very much interested in Noel, and appreciated his charms and humour, and often repeated his remarks . . .' She was prouder than ever of her son: 'Noel was now a tall well set-up young man, very very popular. He was always witty and amusing [and] made wonderful friends, who always wanted him to be with them.' She felt that the upbringing she had given him was justified: 'He was wrapped up in the theatre, and everything connected with it, and when people used to be so shocked to think he had had no real education, I always said and felt that he [was] having his education [from] his career.'

As *Talk of the Town* had noted, Noel and Esme co-operated in writing a curtain-raiser. *The Last Chapter* (later known as *Ida Collaborates*) was presented on 20 August 1917 at the Theatre Royal, Aldershot. A successful young writer, Arthur, asks his cleaning lady, Ida (first in a long line of Cockney caricatures, all dropped aitches and dusters), for her advice on his new plot; she thinks he is referring to her when he speaks, in the third person, of a young man in love with a girl. Enter Cecilia, the real object of his affections, and passionate kisses follow. When they leave, Ida returns to see Cecila's photograph on the table. She 'savagely goes to tear it up' but, looking 'at her own dress and hands . . . her face crumples up into a sad grimace and she sinks on to a chair weeping into her apron'. The sentiment of the piece says something about the co-author's attitude to the working classes, but contains few lines worthy of the mature Coward. Yet the brisk wit of the exchanges between the lovers was a hint of what was to come: 'Oh Cecilia, do please listen properly', implores Arthur. 'I'm all ears', she says. 'You're not', replies Arthur. 'You've only got two and they're very tiny and shell pink . . .'

As a follow-up, Coward and Wynne wrote *Women and Whisky*, performed at the Wimbledon Theatre in November, again as a curtain-raiser to *A Pair of Silk Stockings*. A more substantial piece than *The Last Chapter*, it is set in the 'lounge' of a large house during a dance. Major Curtis, a 'middle-aged, somewhat bronzed man' escaping the hubbub, is making for the whisky decanter when Mrs Grace appears. Also middle aged, she too is escaping. They bemoan the Modern Woman, 'men expect their wives to be their mistresses as well now-adays', says Mrs Grace. In comes Norah Chalmers, seventeen, a girl-next-door type, fleeing 'all those silly boys. Why do they always want to make love to one?' The three chat flippantly, and flashes of future Coward shine through, in light, Sakiesque references to moral indis-cretions; Mrs Grace interjects about a mutual friend, recalling 'fearful scandal about him and the Colonel's dear wife when they were at Bombay – I never knew whether it was a riding boy or an indiscreet hair-pin, but *everyone* knew about it'.

As was necessary with all public performances, the play had to be submitted to the Lord Chamberlain's office,* where typescripts would be rigorously examined by official readers, often dramatists themselves. 'The Major, while "sitting out" a dance and longing to start a whisky-and-soda, is attacked in his secluded nook by an enterprising widow and equally enterprising young flirt whom he stalls off by pretending that he has a wife at Brighton and is thus not eligible', wrote Ernest A. Bendall. 'The talk of which the little Play consists is rather bright if occasionally too bookish, and is wholly void of offence, so the com-edietta is Recommended for Licence.'

Drama was not Noel's only literary outlet at that time: he was writing fiction too. 'There are indeed a great number of prose exercises of my own written between the ages of eleven and seventeen which are locked away in trunks and strong boxes and which I am determined will never see the light of day in my lifetime', he wrote in later years. 'After I am dead is quite another matter . . .'

From those dusty archives (actually his mother's suitcase) comes a compact notebook, dated 1 October 1917. It contains a short story, 'Sleuth Hounds', written in pencil, a juvenile pastiche of detective

---

* The Lord Chamberlain was Lord Sandhurst, succeeded in 1921 by the Duke of Atholl, who in turn was succeeded a year later by Lord Cromer.

fiction, while a later 'Plot for Novel' involves a dark, good-looking woman sporting large earrings and 'fond of bright colours . . . trying to be Pshycic [sic]', her career threatened by a 'madly jealous' and drunken husband. The 'pshycic' idea is particularly fascinating in the light of his use of spirits and ghosts in later plays: *Blithe Spirit* most obviously, but predated by *Weatherwise*, written in 1923, in which Lady Warple falls into a trance at a séance and behaves like a dog whenever the weather is mentioned. Coward's interest in matters supernatural may have stemmed from an experience at Hambleton (where Scott Moncrieff espoused spiritualist beliefs), when he woke during the night to find his bed shaking, and was told the next morning he had been mistakenly put in a 'haunted' room. The worn notebook also includes improbable but hilarious songs such as 'Annie the Auctioneer':

> On a box she'd take her stand
> With hammer in her hand
> And a firm resolve to keep from skidding
> We don't think that she fell
> She went most awfully well
> With the men who came to do her bidding
> Annie was an Auctioneer
> Tho' what she sold is not quite clear
> And as a business woman she may never have shone
> She discovered young men's choice was
> I hear how well her voice was
> Going, Going, Gone!

a precursor of many Coward comic numbers which employed sexual innuendo to poke gentle fun at middle-aged ladies.

Back in South London there were new developments in the Coward household. Violet, tired of penury and the cramped life of a flat, had decided, after consultations with Aunt Ida, to set up a boarding house. Acquiring the lease and 'good will' of a Mrs Cleaver's business at 111 Ebury Street, opposite Ida's at 112, Violet moved her family, Aunt Vida and all, into the narrow house.

What could Coward, so prone to snobbery in later years, have thought of this descent of the social ladder? He did not attempt to conceal the facts when writing of that time, nor did Violet Coward consider her new calling beneath her; she just got on with advertising her select accommodation, suitable for genteel travelling salesmen or discerning widows. 111 Ebury Street was well suited to the purpose. A tall Georgian terraced house engrained with years of soot, it had a wooden extension at the back, known as 'The Bungalow', where the Coward family spent most of their time; Noel had a tiny bedroom under the eaves of the roof. Ebury Street was a busy thoroughfare, caught between Victoria Station to the south and the upmarket area of Belgravia to the north; the street seemed to be straining to break away from the tawdriness of Pimlico, aspiring to the gentility of its neighbour. Despite his mother's new occupation, the move saw Coward edging closer to the confines of the wealthy West End; his eventual stake at Gerald Road was just across the street, but on the crucial 'right' side.

The atmosphere of Ebury Street was slightly gone-to-seed. Apart from the fact that the young Mozart had stayed there, it was known as the residence of George Moore, the novelist and playwright, whose *Conversations in Ebury Street* was published in 1924; while next door to the Cowards, at 109, were the Evans family, whose daughter, Edith, would also pursue a stage career. Mrs Evans, like Violet Coward, was a landlady, and both carefully preserved the 'thin dividing line between a "lodging house" and a home where carefully scrutinised guests were given accommodation'. The transitory nature of the street seemed to attract such interesting characters as Irene Dean Paul, Polish-born wife of the baronet, Sir Aubrey Dean Paul, a polyglot and lesbian whose daughter Brenda was yet more wayward (dying from a heroin overdose in 1959). Lady Dean Paul recalled that the Cowards were great friends; both families were poor, and Noel often had to run across the street in his dressing gown to borrow a shilling for the gas meter.

Violet inherited a full complement of lodgers, and worked hard, and harder when two domestics were found to be too expensive and the staff was reduced to one. Arthur Coward's job had 'evaporated into an inconclusive mist of failure' when the war had proved disastrous for Payne's Pianos, and he now spent his time sailing his model yachts on various park ponds. Noel, who cherished his mother to the point of jealousy, perhaps relished becoming the male provider. Violet was determined to help her son's career, as Esme Wynne recalled, 'She was a brave little woman . . . she took on this Ebury Street apartment house and worked like a slave in order to keep Podge in London, and not to send him on tour' – thereby making him available for better jobs.

His mother's sacrifice ensured that Noel's fortunes continued to rise; he was recognised by strangers in the street and allotted his own dressing-room in the theatre. Of this he was over-proud, and when he discovered the stage manager was using it for auditions while he was on stage, he flew into a petulant tantrum, and told Hawtrey he would not go on with the show. Hawtrey gave the stage manager a ticking-off, and Noel a whack on the behind for his 'appalling impertinence'. But that year a ruling force was about to crush his spirit more efficiently than the temporary loss of a dressing-room: his country needed Noel Coward.

Noel had been turned down for active service by a medical board in January 1918, ostensibly because of his tubercular history. Esme maintained that he had resorted to drinking tea leaves, which he had been told induced symptoms that would disqualify him on health grounds; he 'simply didn't want to get killed'. This understandable reluctance was underlined by a new part in the offing, for which Noel was to receive £15 a week. There was every reason not to take the king's shilling.

Esme stoked her friend's rebellious nature. 'We were rooted and grounded in Bernard Shaw who said that the majority were always wrong ... so we didn't smoke and we didn't drink and we were violently pacifist. And we used to say to any young men who took us out "Look here, you simply go and object. Say 'I will not go to the Front'." Of course, we didn't know anything about sedition in those days, but sedition it was.' Coward's reading of Siegfried Sassoon's *Counter-Attack* that year might reinforce Wynne's assertions, but his reaction probably lay in an instinct for self-preservation. Whatever tricks he employed to postpone military service, he was aware that it was a temporary escape. One morning the dreaded grey card came through the letter-box, requiring him to report to Camberwell swimming baths for a medical board. Here he was subjected to 'several hours of beastliness', indecorously prodded by various medics. He was then told to dress, and with a group of fifty men 'in various states of physical and mental decay', was marched to Whitehall and thence across Waterloo Bridge in a public display perhaps calculated to shame these suspected malingerers. Coward hoped none of his matinee-going friends would see him as the rag-tag procession paraded through Aldwych.

At Waterloo, they entrained for Hounslow, where they were deposited in a hut with bread and margarine, cups of 'greasy cocoa', and three blankets each. Coward's neighbour was covered in sores and was led away; Noel declined the offer of the man's extra blanket. A miserable night dawned to parade-ground horror, by which time 'despair had given place to a still, determined rage'; he could not spend another night in this place. After drill, Noel went up to a sergeant and handing him a ten-shilling note, asked to be shown to the commanding officer. The bribe worked, and Noel was taken to the officer, to whom he insisted that he needed a day to settle his affairs, having been so peremptorily plucked from civilian life. Clutching a day pass, he went home for a tearful reunion with his mother, and set off in civvies to visit every contact he had who might help him. Having exhausted his list of army officers, he came at last to an air force captain whom he had met 'casually at one or two parties' (probably those of Leo Charlton). This angel of the War Office telephoned Hounslow and in 'a sharp official voice' said 'there had been a disgraceful muddle of N. Coward who was perfectly fit and had no earthly right to be in a Labour corps'. Thanking his saviour, Noel left, never to see the man again; months later he heard a rumour that he had been killed.

Coward was attached to the Artists' Rifles OTC at Gidea Park, Essex, a train ride east from London, with leave on alternate weekends. This was a more civilised arrangement, although Coward's basic unsuitability as officer material was obvious: on his first day, his puttees refused to stay up (a reprise of his bootlace ineptitude at school) and he dropped his cane seventeen times. But far from being a humorous scenario worthy of British farce, Noel recalled his army career as 'one long series of sad little disasters. First of all I hated it. I hated making my bed out of boards, and having made my bed out of boards, I hated sleeping on them.'

'My stage life had ill-prepared me for any discipline other than that of the theatre, and that discipline is peculiar to itself', he observed. Without the experience of school, and its enforced intimacy and team spirit, Coward found it impossible to conform, or to participate wholeheartedly in bayonet practice, stabbing straw sacks while a corporal shouted 'They're bellies, they're bellies, they're all German bellies!' Such ferocity was hard to summon up, even for a young man practised in the pretence of the stage. Noel was tormented with the idea that he was wasting time; that his career was hampered by the 'unimportant' needs of his country. 'It was a matter of pressing urgency ... that I should become rich and successful as soon as possible', he argued, both for his sake, and for his mother's, to pluck her out of domestic servitude. Later he would admit the selfishness of such thoughts, while 'millions of young men with far graver responsibilities than mine ... were sacrificing their lives daily', but then he felt 'resentful and rebellious and profoundly wretched'.

It was not long before Coward's health began to be affected. The 'cracking headaches' and insomnia may have been psychosomatic, but the discomfort was no less the real for that. Unable to sleep in a hut of thirty men, after lights out Noel developed a nervous habit of winding string around his finger until it cut into his flesh, to stop himself from 'giving way to nerves and yelling the place down'. When returning from drill, he stumbled and struck his head on a wooden stake, and was concussed for three days, his only memory being a recollection of Novello's *Arlette* score being played incessantly – a camp image evoked almost as an out-take from one of his own plays. But it is clear he had suffered a nervous breakdown – not the last for a man who lived on the edge of his nerves.

Coward was sent to the First London General Hospital in Camberwell, where he spent six weeks in a ward inhabited mostly by shellshock patients. Violet arrived weeping, 'a little bit overdoing it she was because she knew it wasn't really serious'; perhaps she hoped to convince the doctors of her son's unsuitability for further service. Esme Wynne visited and 'knew it was an act put on. He didn't want to conscientiously object, because that would cause attention . . . There was no conviction.' He was examined thoroughly by a succession of doctors, and any suspicion of malingering was dispelled by a temperature chart 'which resembled an outline of the Rocky Mountains drawn by a drunken child'. Noel's condition – the mysterious nature of which subjected him to severe questioning on the grounds that it might be a hoax – finally began to improve.

He gradually achieved stability, and Violet, making daily visits, brought him books, among them novels by Sheila Kaye-Smith and her sometime collaborator, G. B. Stern. The escapism of fiction preserved Coward's sanity, and out of gratitude he began to write to both authors – he never blushed at composing a fan letter. An admiring correspondence with Kaye-Smith and Stern ensued, to be followed by meetings and eventual friendship.

The writer Ethel Mannin described Sheila Kaye-Smith as 'a little woman of small build and no particular age. She reminded me, somehow, of a little brown withered apple. She was very quiet in manner and speech and wore tweeds and brogues.' A prolific writer, her rustic romances, such as *Joanna Godden*, with their country dialects provided the target for Stella Gibbons's satire, *Cold Comfort Farm*. Coward later met her for dinner in London, but of the two writers, Stern assumed particular importance within the close-knit group of Coward's friends. With flame-red hair and vivid blue eyes, she rejoiced

in a Bohemian dress sense and admitted to 'a strong pierrotic tendency
... influenced by the fashion of the period'. This manifested itself in her
writing, 'curling and uncurling all over my first novels, stories and
poems'. Best known for her *Rakonitz Chronicles* (a kind of Jewish
Forsyte Saga), she was a lesbian, as was Kaye-Smith, and had a
passionate temperament.

By the time he had recovered enough to leave his bed, and was put to
sweeping the ward and taking meals to the bedridden, Coward had
made a valuable ally of a good-looking young New Zealander with
curly blond hair named Geoffrey Holdsworth. He endeared himself to
Noel 'by sitting wide-eyed by the rickety upright piano and imploring
me to play him the "Lilac Domino" waltz'. This 'paved the way to
mutual confidences', and a supply of officer-quality meals from a friend
in the kitchens; it is evident that there was what Esme might have called
'a little *tendresse*' between the two. Coward introduced Holdsworth to
the novels and letters of G. B. Stern; the New Zealander also began to
write to Stern, and a few months later, married her. It was a brief
alliance, due to the couple's homosexual orientations (although Stern
did experience a phantom pregnancy, her stomach swelling to the size
of a balloon, which Coward dubbed 'the Melon'). Most of Stern's male
friends were homosexual, just as many of Coward's female friends were
lesbian.

Holdsworth also showed Coward a hole in the hospital perimeter
wall through which they could escape to the civilian world; the risk of
arrest by the military police served only to heighten the excitement.
Noel went straight home to change and, clad in the coloured silk shirt
and tie of a man-about-town, set off for theatreland once more. He
ascended in its most famous lift, to Ivor Novello's Aldwych flat, there
to relish a 'delicious atmosphere of slight quarrels. Everyone drank a lot
of tea and discussed what Charlot had said and what Fay (Compton)
had said and how Eddie (Marsh) thought it was marvellous anyhow.'
The contrast between the decorative artificiality of theatre society and
the grimness of army and hospital life could not have been greater.

In June 1918 Noel was discharged from hospital, but remained in the
army. He spent a week's leave in Devon with Esme Wynne and her
fiancé, Lyndon Tyson, a dashing officer in the Royal Flying Corps;
although Esme had fallen in love with Tyson, neither she nor Noel
seemed to let this new relationship affect their old one. As Tyson was
due to go away after their wedding, there was to be a 'pre-honeymoon',

although not a 'physical one', she stressed: 'We were so terrified of having babies that my husband and I didn't have sexual connections for eighteen months after we married.' Coward's presence as chaperon was an odd arrangement which Tyson thought even odder when he found Noel and Esme coming out of the bathroom together. 'We often followed each other in and out just as two girls would ... I was horrified to find out how shocked Lyndon was.' Tyson 'was getting a bit jealous of Master Noel. I mean he spent most of the time with my fiancée and when one morning I saw both of them coming out of the loo together – I don't know who pulled the plug but one of them did – that, to me, was the end.' It led to an enormous row, and only after tears and hysterics (a dramatic scene in which Coward seemed to revel) was Tyson convinced of the platonic nature of the relationship and persuaded not to return to London on the next train.

Although neither Coward nor Wynne seemed to want it, the marriage effectively ended their intimate relationship. Esme was gradually moving away from the sort of life Noel was intent on living. To her the theatre was changing – the pre-war graciousness, when 'we were all shamefully spoiled, inundated with chocolates, flowers and beautiful presents', was gone, and she had become a more serious person. In 1926 she boasted that 'neither my husband nor I have danced since we married'. Such puritanism could find no common ground with her old friend.

Back at the Artists' Light Rifles in Essex, Noel was put on 'Light Duties', which included cleaning out the latrines. Under such conditions, his 'black melancholia' was bound to return, and Coward sought the solace of the tin-hut church, the only peaceful place in camp, an ironic retreat for a non-believer. On the eve of the Theatrical Garden Party, the acting charity event for which he had obtained leave, he woke with a headache so intense he could not stand up. He was taken to the General Military Hospital at Colchester in an ambulance, convinced that he was suffering from a brain tumour. The nurse refused him an aspirin, as his malady had yet to be diagnosed; he was then moved to a ward for epileptics which aggravated what Coward later defined as 'acute neurasthenia'. But his medical curiosity got the better of him, and he was soon helping the nurses with his fitting neighbours, squeezing tongues back into mouths while being assailed by saliva. Many of the victims had no idea that they were epileptic, and it occurred to Noel that he was in the ward because he too might be a sufferer, so he stayed awake for forty-eight hours, checking off ten-minute periods in an exercise book to prove that he was not having unconscious fits.

Days dragged into weeks, and it seemed that no serious consideration was being given to his case. He spent July and August in bed, passing the time by writing 'a bad novel', although he did manage to obtain leave to visit Sydney Lomer at his house in Colchester. And when Major-General Ashmore came on an official visit, Noel surprised everyone by chatting intimately with 'Splash' Ashmore (a comrade of Leo Charlton's, they had met when Noel was appearing in *The Saving Grace* and was invited to one of Ashmore's 'musical parties'). Eventually the time came for his medical board, and it was recommended that he should be discharged; his value as a soldier was minimal, and the sooner he left the service the better. It is clear that the powers-that-be saw in Coward not exactly dereliction of duty, but passive resistance. After six days of 'feverish anticipation of freedom', Noel went before the board, only to be sent back for full duty with the Artists' Rifles. His medical officer fulminated against these 'bloody fools', and pledged that not only would Coward be discharged within a week, but that he would receive a thirteen-week war pension for his pains.

Noel left the hospital and the army, with his pension, a suit, an overcoat and a medal to commemorate his discharge. Violet was astonished, 'for I am afraid he was more trouble than he was worth in the army, and did not help the war along very much'. That hot August noon, Coward arrived back in town, passing the theatres: the Gaiety, the Vaudeville, the Savoy and the Adelphi; imagining the familiar scenes inside, he 'almost wept with sentimental love for it all'. He was free to pursue his career once more.

Released from military duties, Coward set about finding work, but the optimistic, not to say arrogant, offer of his services met with a lack of enthusiasm. This disheartened the erstwhile star of *The Saving Grace*, particularly as he was singing his own compositions at auditions – numbers such as 'Forbidden Fruit', his first complete lyric already exhibiting 'that unfortunate taint of worldly cynicism'. It was certainly risqué, as well as being early evidence of his love of the internal rhyme: 'For the brute loves the fruit that's forbidden/ And I'll bet you half a crown/ He'll appreciate the flavour of it much, much more/ If he has to climb a bit to shake it down.'

It was the kind of song Coward might have written for his new friend Beatrice Lillie. Lillie, Canadian-born with an Irish father, had come to

England in 1912 to begin a career in the music halls. Noel admired her comic talent and 'naughty' appeal (although she later achieved social respectability when she married Sir Robert Peel, the fifth baronet). Lillie arranged an audition for him with André Charlot, the inspired creator of revues with whom she was working. Unfortunately for Noel, Charlot was unimpressed; he told Lillie not to waste his time again with 'young composers who played the piano badly and sang worse'. Nonetheless, that June Coward's name was credited in Charlot's revue, *Tails-Up*, with writing 'Peter Pan', sung by Phyllis Titmus (lyrics by Noel Coward, music by Doris Joel).

Noel was not dismayed by dispiriting auditions: he only supposed that his 'cold-blooded realism' was too much. Experience had taught him that preparation was all, and he developed an approach akin to the military tasks he had assuredly not learned in the past few months. Assembling a uniform of navy-blue suit, with a coloured shirt, tie, socks and handkerchief to match, he assumed a steely psychological shield, 'a blend of assurance and professional vivacity; the fact that my bowels were as water I hope was not apparent to anybody'. Striding onstage to address the company with a loud 'Good morning', he dismissed the accompanist, played his own introduction, and launched into his audition number before anyone had time to stop him. When he auditioned for the American musical *Oh, Boy* and found Grossmith and Laurillard chatting between themselves, he informed the illustrious producers that he saw no point in wasting his time singing if they continued to waste their time not listening. George Grossmith invited him to start again, and Coward was engaged, at twelve pounds a week.

Waiting for rehearsals to begin, Noel took up an invitation from G. B. Stern to join her at St Merryn in Cornwall, where she was staying with her friends, the Dawson-Scotts. Mrs Dawson-Scott, a novelist who used the pen-name Sappho, was the founder of PEN (initially the Tomorrow Club). Her daughter Marjorie recalled that Stern, with her hair 'plaited in a pigtail, brownish make-up on her already dark and sun-tanned face, vivid clothes and a gypsy bandana handkerchief round her head', seemed 'very affected and . . . quite useless on the cliffs or in the sea'. When Miss Stern, known to her friends as 'Peter', announced that she wanted to invite two young men to stay, 'we were *not* pleased', recalled Marjorie Dawson-Scott. Holdsworth was acceptable, but the other sent a telegram which damned him from the first: ARRIVING PADSTOW 5.30. TALL AND DIVINELY HANDSOME IN GREY.

Marjorie Dawson-Scott recalled that 'it is not surprising that Coward felt himself to be unwelcome, which is just what he was'. They had been told that their visitor was a 'pansy', and Mrs Dawson-Scott was alarmed on behalf of her fourteen-year-old son Toby. 'She had . . . a horror of any kind of "perversion".' Sappho (apparently unaware of the associations of her pen-name) told her 'to keep a protecting eye on Toby . . . Undoubtedly Sappho and I both behaved badly . . . to Noel, but in 1918 it was perhaps understandable, just as it is understandable that Noel did not forgive us.'

It was a measure of Coward's charm that despite such antipathy the family 'listened spellbound to the endless game of repartee that he and Peter played'. Coward and Stern went for long walks together, but Noel also went out with the younger Dawson-Scotts. On one walk, they discussed future careers: 'What are you going to be, Noel?' they asked. 'A success', he said, 'and wrote on the sand in big letters, "Read 'Cats and Dogs' by Noel Coward"'. Marjorie took Noel out digging for sand eels by moonlight, and as they dug he suddenly turned and asked why she disliked him so much; she admitted the suspicions of the family. 'Noel stopped short in the brilliant light of the full moon and looked at me with his mischievous faun's eyes. Then he threw back his head and laughed – and no more was said.'

If the Dawson-Scotts' *froideur* was predicated on snobbery and homophobia, a potential *faux pas* on his part indicated how his wit enabled him to rise above social transgressions. At a Tomorrow Club meeting organised by Sappho, Coward arrived attired in full evening dress, only to find everyone else in day clothes. He paused long enough for the assembled intelligentsia to take in the full effect, then said, 'Now I don't want *anybody* to feel embarrassed.' It was at the Tomorrow Club that Coward met some of the great names of contemporary literature, including Somerset Maugham, whose greeting, Coward later told a friend, was unconventional: 'Maugham gave him a large kiss, which surprised him very much.' Other eminent authors included John Galsworthy, H. G. Wells, Rose Macaulay, Arnold Bennett and E. F. Benson. Through Stern, Noel also met Wells's then lover, Rebecca West, another friend-to-be.

But for Coward, life was frustrating. His achievements – a few stage appearances and performances of his work – seemed insignificant compared to the company he was now keeping. The years 1917 to 1919 had launched him into friendship with Ivor Novello, Charles Hawtrey, Fay Compton and Beatrice Lillie; and set him on 'pleasant, if not intimate terms' with Ronald Colman, Gladys Cooper, Gerald du

Maurier and Viola Tree. Noel collected names almost superstitiously, as if by association he would acquire celebrity. But fame, for the moment, remained elusive.

Oh, Boy (rechristened *Oh, Joy* lest the American slang offend British audiences) was a shaky step up the ladder. An American musical written by Jerome Kern, Guy Bolton and P. G. Wodehouse, it had been successful on Broadway, and the producers, Grossmith and Laurillard, hoped to repeat that success in the West End with Beatrice Lillie. Noel had been engaged for what he thought would be a good role, and returned from Cornwall ready for the fray, only to contract influenza (then a pandemic, killing more people than did the First World War). Nonetheless he spurned his sickbed to attend rehearsals, where he discovered his name on the chorus list. Slighted, Noel stormed out and, after a neat brandy in a nearby pub, confronted the producers in their Golden Square offices. Laurillard calmed him by applying the balm of praise to Coward's wounded pride, telling him he was too good an actor to waste his time in such a trivial musical comedy, and instead promised him a part in *Scandal*, a new play by Cosmo Hamilton which would open in two months' time.

To occupy himself in the meantime, Coward began a 'lush' novel called *Cherry Pan*, 'dealing in a whimsical vein with the adventures of a daughter of Pan' in the modern world, who 'contrived to be arch, and elfin, and altogether nauseating, for nearly thirty thousand words'. But Cherry's winsome ways were to be the death of her, and 'she finally petered out, owing to lack of enthusiasm on my part, and lack of stamina on hers'. He did better by selling some short stories to magazines, and was introduced by Esme Wynne-Tyson to Ethel Mannin, then editing the *Blue Magazine*.

Mannin, an early feminist and socialist, recalled that Esme ('who had written a number of pleasant poems for *The Pelican*') 'brought with her a tall pale young man whom I took to be her husband. They were both intensely amused when they discovered this, and she repeated his name to me, more clearly this time, to correct my error . . . All Noel's friends gushed and raved about his "genius", but nobody outside of that inner circle knew or cared about him at that time.' She thought Coward 'the most electric person' she had ever met. When she encountered him later, she found that success had not changed him; he exhibited 'the same gushing manner; everyone is "darling", and he used it a great deal years before it became fashionable; the same droll way of saying "My deah!"

when he is amused or pained; the same impression that he only stays still by force of will, and if he lets himself go he would be doing a step-dance over the room the whole time, chanting amusing couplets, rhyming flagellation with adulation, and things like that. When he is being droll, or maliciously amusing, he looks like a satyr, one of the early Roman satyrs who suggest mischievousness rather than wickedness, uncontrollable high spirits rather than viciousness.

'I shall always carry in my mind a picture of Noel Coward in George Doran's sitting-room at the Savoy one night after a party. "The distinguished American publisher" had just made a remark about being 'ware of woman with loose hips, because it generally went with loose lips. Noel leapt up and did a *pas seul* round the room, with his coat-tails flying, chanting like a revue catch number, "Loose about the hips,/ Loose about the lips". He said what "marvellous" words they would make for a fox-trot song or a revue number.' Mannin recalled Rebecca West there, 'vivid and vivacious as always, and as usual being amusing at someone else's expense . . . G. B. Stern seems to me a similar type'. She recalled Noel taking her, Esme, Sheila Kaye-Smith 'and a dark exotic-looking young woman who had divorce complications' (possibly Gladys Calthrop) to see Epstein's sensational Christ sculptures at the Leicester Galleries, Noel marching them across Leicester Square in single file. 'He appeared determined not to take the exhibition seriously. Sheila was womanly about the babies' heads. Esme and the young divorcee appeared to take their cue from Noel.' Coward had found a new extended family, retailing 'intimate gossip' about each and using nicknames which amused Mannin: '. . . Peter and Gug [Holdsworth], Stoj and Poj . . . and Panther [West] . . . Well, well.'

As Coward manoeuvred in London's literary circles, he dallied with those the respectable public would have regarded as more suspicious figures. On 3 October, Scott Moncrieff, wounded from the war and elsewhere preoccupied with Wilfred Owen, took him to see Robbie Ross, who was about to leave the country for the post of curator of the Melbourne Art Gallery. The wartime climate was difficult for homosexuals; that May, Ross had been implicated as one of the 47,000 'perverts' in British society.

Noel Pemberton Billing, a flamboyant right-wing MP and owner of the *Imperialist* newspaper, had published an article by a Captain Harold Spencer in January 1918 in which Spencer alleged that he had seen a 'black book' at the Bavarian castle of Prince William of Wied. In April, Billing printed a paragraph written by Spencer entitled 'The Cult of the

Clitoris'. Prompted by a letter from novelist Marie Corelli (a fanatical upholder of moral decency, although probably a lesbian herself), it suggested that subscribers to a private performance of Wilde's *Salome*, given by actress Maud Allan, constituted many of the 47,000. Allan sued Pemberton Billing for libel on the grounds that the article portrayed her as a lesbian.

The trial was presided over by Lord Justice Darling (himself cited as one of the 47,000), who tried to keep the proceedings from becoming a display of patriotic prejudice in which misconduct of the war and hatred of the Germans was caught up with anti-homosexual abuse. It was in effect a reprise of the Wilde trial. 'Massage houses' were said to be the province of blackmailing German spies; other establishments 'being conducted for practising unnatural vice' were identified (such as one at 11a Duke Street, off Manchester Square, managed by a Lally Highfield); and Wilde was spoken of as being an 'extraordinary perverted genius'. Lord Alfred Douglas (now an enemy of Ross's) was called as a defence witness and identified Ross as 'the leader of all the sodomites in London'. The outcome of the trial was a salutary lesson for Noel in British justice and prejudice. Pemberton Billing won the case on a wave of popular hysteria, carried on the shoulders of cheering crowds outside the Old Bailey; Robbie Ross died of a heart attack on 5 October (just two days after the meeting with Coward), as much a victim of hate as Wilde had been before him. Captain Harold Spencer was certified insane later that year.

The other guest in Ross's rooms at 40 Half Moon Street that afternoon was Siegfried Sassoon, who had just published *Counter-Attack*. He had hoped to have 'a nice quiet talk' with Ross, who was suffering from the publicity of the trial and Alfred Douglas's vicious attacks. Sassoon recalled Scott Moncrieff's entrance 'with a tall thin youth whose name meant nothing to me . . . The "boy actor" – for such he had announced himself, was being almost excessively appreciative to me about my war poems, telling me that he had quite lately read them aloud to a lady novelist while lying on the rocks in Cornwall.' Sassoon found Noel's behaviour 'gushing', and noted that he also had a negative effect on Ross, 'who, for once, lacked his usual liveliness as host . . . But the youthful stranger rattled brightly on, making smart remarks, which I considered cheap. There were several copies of *Counter-Attack* on Robbie's table, one of which I sourly inscribed for him at his request.'*

---

* When he and Sassoon met later, Coward admitted that he 'must have been pretty shattering'

Although his social manner irritated, Coward sought the company of writers for good reason: he was serious about writing. His song-writing talents were already being exploited by a three-year contract with Herman Darewski (brother of Max) at Francis, Day and Hunter. For sums of £50, £75 and £100 for each subsequent year, Noel delivered lyrics which no one seemed interested in, although he received his money without fail; he was not surprised to learn that the publishing firm later went bust. But Darewski liked Noel, and enlisted his and Esme's talents for a two-act opera set in Sicily, with Doris Joel as librettist. The *Sketch* announced that the opera 'may possibly have a first production in America', but such hopes were not fulfilled, and *Crissa* withered quietly away.

While Coward was busy trying to establish his place in society, the war ground to a halt. This meant little to the young man who spent Armistice Day 'in a tail coat, a Rolls-Royce, and obviously aristocratic company' – that of Tony and Juanita Gandarillas, whom he had met at one of Splash Ashmore's parties. Señor Don José Antonio Gandarillas, a wealthy Chilean diplomat, was an epicene figure, darkly handsome and definitely glamorous. He was also bisexual, and like his friends Napier Alington and Christopher Wood, leader of an emerging Bohemian set which would dominate the avant-garde reaches of society in the post-war years. Noel's acquaintance with Gandarillas showed just how far the eighteen-year-old had climbed; it also indicated an acquaintance with a darker side, for Gandarillas was an opium addict.

London was alive again, its lights turned up for the first time in four years. Pushing through a packed Trafalgar Square full of crowds celebrating peace, the group arrived at the Savoy, where champagne flowed and Alice Delysia sang the 'Marseillaise' standing on a table. 'It was a thrilling night, and I regret to say that the tragic significance of it was almost entirely lost on me', said Noel (it was telling that he tried to recreate it in *Cavalcade* and elsewhere, as if to capture an experience he'd never had). For him, the end of the war merely meant that 'life would probably be a good deal more enjoyable without it'. But significantly, at that Victory Ball was a young actress whose death that night

---

on that first encounter. The poet's impression of Noel's darting attendance on literary alumni was reinforced by a conversation with Edmund Gosse. 'Certainly I know him', said Gosse. 'I met him at dinner at James Barrie's.' 'Was he nice to you?' asked Sassoon. 'Nice to me! Why he fluttered round me like a butterfly round an oak.'

would provide Noel with material for a play which propelled him into the national consciousness. Had it not been for the careless demise of Miss Billie Carleton – a starlet whom Coward had met through Beatrice Lillie – *The Vortex* might never have been written.

In newspaper reports lurid enough to rival those of the Pemberton Billing trial, Noel and his friends read the sordid sequence of events: Carleton had fallen in with bad friends, sniffing cocaine and heroin, and attending opium dens in the East End and in Dover Street. The inquest (attended by 'a large number of actors and actresses') heard evidence from Carleton's maid that her mistress had gone to the ball with a little gold jewel box full of white powder in her Dorothy bag. A young actor friend of Carleton's told the court that it was 'rather public property' that Billie took drugs, 'several people had mentioned it'. The inquest established that drug abuse was widespread in the theatrical world, and Noel's friends seemed dangerously involved; Beatrice Lillie was mentioned by the maid as being a frequent visitor to Carleton's rooms at Savoy Court.

The inquest heard that friends saw Carleton home after the ball. The maid let her mistress sleep until the afternoon. 'She snored until 3.30. A little later she (the maid) went into the room and said "Wake up", but got no answer. The doctor was then telephoned for.' It was then that the maid discovered the cocaine. The doctor found Carleton dead, her pupils widely dilated, and a stain on the side of her mouth, 'as if of something trickling out . . . The fingernails of the left hand were blue . . . The signs of asphyxia were slight. The signs pointed to a narcotic poison as being the probable cause . . .'

Ada Song Ping You, thirty-eight, of Limehouse (in London's docklands, where a large Asian community lived), was charged with supplying prepared opium and cocaine to Billie Carleton, and also with supplying Mr and Mrs De Vellue with the drugs for 'disgusting orgies [which] took place extending from Saturday night until early in the Sunday afternoon' at their flat at 16 Dover Street. 'After dinner the party adjourned, at about 10 o'clock, to the drawing room of the flat and provided themselves with cushions and pillows, placed these on the floor, and sat themselves in a circle. The men divested themselves of their clothing and got into pyjamas, and the women into chiffon nightdresses . . . Miss Carleton arived later at the flat from the theatre, and she, after disrobing, took her place in this circle of degenerates.' Mrs Ping You sat in the middle, preparing the pipes of opium, and 'the party remained, apparently in a comatose state until about 3 o'clock on the following afternoon, Sunday'.

The case prompted the usual public discussion of the evils of drug addiction and the suppliers of the drugs, and *The Times* called for more effective means of control. Coward's contemporaries bear witness to the drug use of the time. Sir Anthony Havelock-Allan, then a young theatre fan, spoke of cocaine as being 'the drug of the period', useful in social circumstances where it was not easily detected by the uninitiated. The fast-speaking euphoria induced by the drug suited the frenzied *Zeitgeist* perfectly; although Coward's machine-gun delivery needed no chemical stimulants, it might have taken its speed from this unnatural conversational pace. Narcotics had been over-produced for the First World War, and there was now a ready market for that surplus, easily exploited by pushers. It was a facet of café and theatrical society Coward could not have escaped, and it is certain that many of his close friends, if not Noel himself, dabbled in drugs.

Here was material to store away for use later, in Coward's dramatic *tour de force* of 1924, *The Vortex*. But his would not be the first play to deal with drug addiction: following the Carleton case, there were at least three productions on the London stage in 1919 which used it as a central theme: *Dope* by Frank Price; *Drug Fiends* by Owen Jones; and *The Girl Who Took Drugs* (aka *Soiled*) by Aimée Grattan-Clyndes. Nor was *The Vortex* his first attempt at the subject: in 1918 he wrote a three-act play, untitled and unfinished, in which a post-prandial scene has the dinner guests discussing China:

> Alice: But do go on telling us about the opium den, Mr Saville. It's frightfully thrilling.
> Katt: There's really nothing more to tell. The temporary satisfaction given by the drug doesn't last long, then one once more becomes normal and generally the victim of horrible depression.
> Elvira: But really it's worth it. Think how glorious it must be to merge one's personality into a fantastic world of sensuous dreams.

Another guest, Hilary, comments, 'Doping is quite a hobby among society women in Paris', and Iris says, 'I knew a girl who used to drug a lot. Her descriptions of the sensation were most interesting.' 'What happened to her eventually?' asks Katt. 'She went into a convent and now spends her time in penitence and prayer', replies Iris. Coward's light-hearted approach to a fashionable but dangerous theme was evidence of the flippancy with which he would later be charged.

Such conversations were drawn from real life, as Coward's friends dabbled in recreational drugs. His friend Iris Tree, daughter of Herbert Beerbohm Tree, and her husband Curtis Moffat entertained guests at their Hampstead home with sardines, wine and hashish; even Mrs Astley Cooper had a close friend who took drugs and woke one morning to find he had gone blind. 'He had been the great interest and amusement of my early married life', she recalled, declining to name the man. 'He was musical and witty', and she claimed that 'many of his sayings have adorned the plays of Noel Coward'. Coward's interest in the phenomenon is understandable, even though his attitude to it, as with all forms of excess (save that of success), was puritanical; for him self-control was paramount. His fear of loss of control accorded with the tight rein he kept on himself. He admitted to using marijuana only once, in New York, when he had bought a joint and smoked it in his hotel room. He felt so strange that he called a doctor, who put him to bed and promptly lit up the remainder of the cigarette as he said it would be a shame to waste it.

It was perhaps appropriate, in the light of recent events, that in December Coward secured his first serious part in a melodrama entitled *Scandal*, starring Arthur Bourchier and Kyrle Bellew. Noel got on well with his fellow actors, Nora Swinburne and Mary Robson, but 'apart from these pleasant contacts, my stock was low in the company'.

'Noel was engaged to play the young man, and it was my first straight part – I was about seventeen or eighteen', Swinburne recalled. 'We all met at rehearsals, and Noel was always very spruce and well-dressed – he made a great deal of himself – and also very amusing and very witty. Not handsome, but tall and elegant, and had a good figure. And the voice was distinctive – not quite so elaborate, though, then. That was in his favour, because he didn't have much education.

'Anyway, we opened the play, and at rehearsals we were always laughing and joking and everybody was very jolly. I had a love scene with him on a chaise longue, and he had his back to the audience, facing me. I had to face him, upstage, looking down. And he used to say awful things – you see, he could say things to me without the audience seeing – awful things to make me laugh. "Have you seen the woman in the second row with that hat?" – that sort of thing. Then he would move about the stage and pop up in an unexpected place. It was absolutely impossible not to laugh, and I used to get the most dreadful giggles, and I'm a very serious actor ... Not only that, but he used to make all the others laugh. Mary [Robson] used to laugh terribly, and every night, Arthur Bourchier would send for us, and say, "Really, this is going to ruin the play. You must stop it. You must not laugh at him." He said, "I do it myself – I can't help it, but we must all . . ." And then Noel would go in and he'd say, "I'm sorry, Noel, but you've *got* to stop this, my boy, you're ruining the play. And if you don't you'll have to go."

'Well, we tried. We struggled. But after the first week . . . everybody was taken over the coals for laughing again, and Noel was threatened. I don't know what was the matter with him, but he just couldn't help it. He was terribly witty. And after two weeks, he got the sack!' Coward recalled that Bourchier told him the management were about to give him his notice; perhaps he could save himself the humiliation, and resign? Noel composed a letter to Grossmith and Laurillard: 'I explained with dignity that owing to the peculiar behaviour of the old ladies in the cast, I felt myself compelled to tender my resignation.' Having said goodbye to Nora and Mary, he 'rattled blithely on all the old ladies' doors' and drove off in a taxi.

To Nora Swinburne, Noel seemed 'bubbling over with energy . . . writing madly'. His latest effort was *The Last Trick*, a melodrama in four acts which took him a week to complete. 'The first and second acts were quite amusing, the third act good, and the the last act weak and amateurish', wrote Coward, adding that 'the plot hinged on the "revenge" motif and wasn't particularly original, but the dialogue was effective, and showed a marked improvement on my other work'. Gilbert Miller promised to take it with him to New York and check possibilities for producing it. Encouraged, Noel went on to write 'two bad plays and one better one. The first two are not worthy of discussion, but the third, *The Rat Trap*, was my first really serious attempt at psychological conflict.' He felt, 'for the first time with genuine conviction', that he could write drama.

The Rat Trap sets out the youthful writer's opinions on modern relationships and social issues, informed by themes of free love and adultery (a result of the war), which were to permeate the rest of his creative career. Olive Lloyd-Kennedy (a G. B. Stern figure) represents mannered modernity and her creator's youthful scepticism: 'Marriage nowadays is nothing but a temporary refuge for those who are uncomfortable at home.' Sheila and Keld are sexual beings whose love may not outlive their marriage. They are a modern couple, dismissive of previous generations' ideas of gender: 'If you were a proper girlish bride,' says Keld, 'you'd like me to reek of tobacco and tweed, and you could call me your "big brown husband" . . .' They are blurred mirror images of Noel and Esme – always arguing but always making up. Permanent friction combined with deep regard was another theme which found anchor in Coward's dramatic repertoire.

Keld has an affair with a former chorus girl, Ruby Raymond, who retains the vague sluttishness of her original calling ('. . . the fuss she made about dressing-rooms, not that I minded being put up on the second floor, but it was hard luck on the Guards having to tramp up all those stairs after they'd been fighting for us and everything'). If Gertrude Lawrence provided the carefree, loose-living model for Ruby, Esme's serious-minded proto-feminism lay behind Sheila's character. She comments that Keld's claim to be able to write about women is 'like standing outside Buckingham Palace and trying to make an inventory of the furniture . . . I merely say that your women aren't good. No man, unless he's abnormal, can ever really get a grip on the feminine mind, and you're not a bit abnormal' – an advertisement of Noel's own 'abnormality'.

Characteristically, Coward disclaimed the seriousness of the play, saying that the dialogue was 'excruciatingly sophisticated', its construction 'not very good', and the last act 'an inconclusive shambles . . . based on the sentimental and inaccurate assumption that the warring egos of the man and wife will simmer down into domestic bliss merely because the wife is about to have a dear little baby. I suppose that I was sincere about this at the time but I find it very hard to believe.' Yet for all his self-deprecation, *The Rat Trap* was an intimation of the successes to come.

Noel busied himself throughout 1919 writing magazine stories for Ethel Mannin, relentlessly modern in conception, after the style of *The Rat Trap*. 'I flung aside all bastard whimsies and concentrated on realism', he wrote. 'I dealt, almost exclusively, with the most lurid types; tarts, pimps, sinister courtesans, and cynical adulterers whirled across my pages in great confusion.' The stories met with a 'withering lack of response' from editors, but Coward judged the phase useful, and did not regret it.

Among his new society friends was Betty Chester (whose real name, Grundtvig, explained her pseudonym), a diminutive, charming girl who lived with her parents in Chester Square. Here Coward met Meggie Albanesi, a young actress whom he admired, writing to her after the first night of Maugham's *East of Suez* (another play with a drug theme), saying her performance was 'the best anyone has done for years!! ... Your opium bit, coming at the end of all that emotion in the previous acts, was exquisite...' Albanesi was 'one of two understanding companions' (Gertrude Lawrence being the other), recalled Cole Lesley, 'whom he could take dancing at Murray's or Rector's'. If it were Noel's turn to pay, he would tell his guest to feign indisposition and decline to order; his dish was shared between them.

Another friend of Albanesi and Chester's was Lorn Macnaughtan, whose wry acceptance of her more wealthy friends' patronage indicated a worldly outlook. Her authoritative manner was a legacy of her Scottish ancestry, and Coward found it hard to reconcile this with her pursuit of a stage career, in the chorus at the Empire Theatre. He discovered that Lorn's stage career was as much a surprise to her as to everyone else.

As with his own family, the Macnaughtans, allied to the Scottish Campbells, were formerly somewhat grand but had fallen on hard times. Edith Lorn Macnaughtan was born in 1894 in Chelsea; her father, Malcolm, was a ne'er-do-well who left Lorn's writer aunt to pay for her to go to school, where she met Betty Grundtvig. The Macnaughtans were now living in a modest house off the King's Road, and Lorn was scraping a living in the theatre. A fellow club member of her father's, Sir Seymour Hicks, had found Lorn a place on the tour of *Bluebell in Fairyland*, and she later appeared in *Irene*, a long-running musical at the Empire, in 1921.

Five years Noel's senior, she had large feet and an unlovely figure, and her face seldom saw more than a touch of powder, but her personality was magnetic. Bawdy chorus-girl jargon sprung from her lips at the most unexpected moments: she told of a fellow performer who was absent because she was having an abortion, and how she relished the comment of the girl's friend, 'Oh, what a silly girl – fancy letting him put it *there*!' Lorn's imperiousness and infectious laughter mixed breeding with stage slang to produce the perfect woman for a difficult role, that of Coward's secretary (a service she was already performing for Meggie's mother, the novelist E. Maria Albanesi). Lorn served the man she called (with a characteristic twist of irony) 'the Master' until her own death, more than forty years later.

5

The Young Idea

If one wants to be, so to speak, in at the birth of a considerable dramatic talent it is worthwhile going to *I'll Leave It to You*.

Rebecca West, *Time and Tide*, 30 July 1920

COWARD'S status as a writer proper was reflected in his move from the attic at 111 Ebury Street to a room on the floor below. Able now to return hospitality, he gave tea parties, to which Gertrude Lawrence brought the succession of Guards officers for whom, like Ruby in *The Rat Trap*, she had a well-known penchant; they had also a certain attraction for Coward. These stage-door johnnies sat about 'puzzled by the theatrical conversation, but securely wrapped in regimental poise'. Other guests included the Wynne-Tysons, Mrs Astley Cooper, Lorn Macnaughtan, Betty Chester, G. B. Stern and Sheila Kaye-Smith. On the housemaid's afternoon off, Arthur was drafted into service, 'waltzing into the room with the tea-tray'. Some found the idea of one's father serving tea odd; with 'Bohemian geniality' Noel 'tried not to intercept the ironic glances that any strangers present exchanged with each other'.

One particular young Guardsman, a lieutenant in the Coldstreams, appealed to Coward. Stewart Forster had a 'deceptively guileless personality, and a timid butter-coloured moustache'; soon Noel was invited to dine with Forster on guard at St James's Palace. The rank of officer in the Brigade of Guards was strictly the pursuit of a gentleman, and the elaborate uniform – close-fitting scarlet tunic, highly polished brass and silver, patent leather straps and belt – bespoke undeniable glamour to Noel, as well as imparting a sexual attraction. In London, the other ranks of the Guards were regarded as free with their favours, and Ebury Street, as Michael Davidson noted, was known as 'guardsmen's country' where 'a bit of scarlet' might be had. Charles Dalmon, relic of the decadent Nineties and resident of Noel's road, told David-son, 'My *dear*, my ambition is to be *crushed* to death between the thighs of a guardsman!'

To Coward, who loved men in uniform, the invitation was thus a direct appeal to both his snobbish and his emotional side. He arrived in hired tails from Moss Brothers, regretting that the only decoration he had was his army discharge medal. After a sybaritic dinner, Noel left 'no longer oppressed by military tradition, but quite definitely part of it'. Forster became a close friend – presumably a lover – and Noel spent part of the summer at Rumwood, the family home, a large Tudor country house at Langley in Kent. Here Stewart lived with his widowed mother Grace, whom Noel evoked as 'smelling slyly of amber' and 'wrapped in gallant vanity', romantically 'swishing across shady lawns and night clubs'. Grace Forster inspired the character of Florence Lancaster in *The Vortex*; perhaps her son – handsome, fair-faced and innocent-looking – provided that of Nicky Lancaster. A faded snapshot in Coward's album shows a Rumwood family group seated on those lawns, the men (among them the golden-haired Stewart, in striped blazer and cricket flannels) standing behind the sun-hatted women, one lost late summer day in September 1920: stilled, distant faces which beg a dramatic story.

In August 1919, Coward played Ralph in *The Knight of the Burning Pestle* at Birmingham Repertory Theatre, a comedy by Beaumont and Fletcher, 'two of the dullest Elizabethan writers ever known', Noel claimed. 'I had a very very long part. But I was very very bad at it.' Sixteenth-century drama and its phraseology was far removed from Coward's world. 'I played that poor apprentice with a stubborn Mayfair distinction which threw the whole thing out of key', he confessed, at the same time unfairly blaming the director, Nigel Playfair, for lacking seriousness.

The memory was quickly extinguished by a new and unexpected piece of good news which arrived in a cable from Gilbert Miller in New York: someone called Al Woods was willing, eager even, to pay him $500 for a year's option on *The Last Trick*. The incredulous playwright accepted, and was duly paid one hundred pounds sterling, an extravagant sum. Coward went on a tailor's spending spree, paid off the family rent and bought a second-hand grand piano from Harrods 'which contributed richness and joy to my room, and considerable pain to the lodgers immediately above and below it'. A celebration meal was arranged at the Ivy, the fashionable theatrical restaurant wedged in a narrow street off Shaftesbury Avenue. Here Coward could confidently dine and dance in his new tails and backless waistcoat (copied from Michael Arlen's), 'feeling smart and *soigné*, and very, very smooth'.

Harold French, then appearing in C. B. Cochran's production of *Cyrano de Bergerac* at the Garrick, recalled meeting his old friend at Martin's, a dance club which later became the Embassy. French was there with an actress in the same production. 'I quite fancied myself as a dancer, until . . . Noel Coward and a very chic and grown-up "Gertie" Lawrence glided on to the floor. Then I knew I had been wasting my time. Whereas I had hopped, bounced and jigged through a fox-trot, they covered the floor . . . as though on skates . . . As Noel and I were waiting for the girls who had gone to pick up their coats, Noel asked me, "Who is she, cock, your Mother?" "She's only a year older than I am," I protested. "*Et ta soeur*," said Noel with a grin.' A similar remark, made of Grace Forster, seen in a nightclub with a young man, inspired *The Vortex* and its pertinent post-war theme of older women in pursuit of younger men.

As a follow-up to *The Last Trick* Gilbert Miller commissioned Coward to work up an idea for a comedy Miller had into a fully fledged play. Reluctant to write to order, Noel nonetheless came up with *I'll Leave It to You*, in which he created Bobbie, the young son, with himself in mind. A 'slim, bright-looking youth of twenty', narcissistic and fey, he is partly drawn from Saki's clever protagonists, all mannered epigrams and gesture. Bobbie accuses his sister of reading Maeterlinck as a pose. 'Try not to be so irritating, Bobbie dear,' she says, 'just because *you* don't happen to appreciate good literature, it's very small and narrow to laugh at people who do.' 'Oh, don't betray your jealousy of my looks, Evangeline', parries Bobbie. 'It's so degrading.'

Depending on a slim plot (Uncle Daniel's promise to leave his money to whichever of his nieces or nephews makes good in the world) *I'll Leave It to You* is self-consciously clever. Full of effects and 'brilliant' ripostes, the play resembles Bobbie: bright, witty and effusive, but ultimately without definition or intent. Noel remarked that he 'at least had the sense to write a part in the play for myself, in which I should undoubtedly, when the moment came, score an overwhelming personal triumph'. There was also a part for Esme, as Faith Crombie, Bobbie's gold-digging girlfriend. Miller approved the play, then left for the States, promising to arrange for its production on his return.

At a loose end, Coward took a holiday in Paris with Stewart Forster. Complete tourists (neither had left Britain before), they visited the

sights, drank in street cafés, and danced 'round the cabarets of Mont-
martre with metallic tarts, who persisted in mistaking us for Americans'.
They even quarrelled over the attentions of a 'young lady from
Cincinnati' who displayed 'that fine line of conduct which separated
racy conversation from staunch moral integrity'. Coward's stance seems
contrived in the light of his real passions – very much towards Forster
rather than the opposite sex.* Novello's (and later Coward's) lover
Bobbie Andrews appeared in Paris, too, the city being a refuge for
English homosexuals ever since Wilde had adopted the Parisian code of
a green carnation. Andrews was struck by Coward's comment that he
was glad that (unlike Forster) he had no private income; if he had, his
ambition would have been compromised. In keeping such upper-class
company, Coward's thoughts of his position in society were never far
away.

Back home, Noel barely had time to unpack his bags before society –
in the shape of Mrs Astley Cooper – issued another invitation to foreign
travel. She was to spend the winter in Alassio, and enlisted her young
friend as travelling companion. It was a magical journey, breathlessly
described in *The Young Idea*, in which the characters board the Orient
Express in Paris: 'We get into it about seven-thirty, and have dinner as
we whizz through the suburbs ... Then we come back and find our
wagon-lits have been made up, so we sit in rather strained positions and
play games ...' They wake 'in the middle of the night, because of the
Swiss customs'; at dawn 'you peep out, and it's all mountains and
valleys and rushing torrents and white, white snow as far as you can
see'. Mrs Astley Cooper and Noel shared a sleeping compartment, and
talked endlessly as they steamed through Switzerland, his hostess
amused by Noel's excited reaction to the Alps. They changed at Milan,
then 'down to the Lombardy plains with my nose pressed against the
railway carriage window', he recalled. At Alassio, they booked into the
Grand Hotel, which 'wasn't very grand', according to Mrs Astley
Cooper, who found herself among 'the English colony of unenjoyed
ladies'. But to Coward, the pastel houses covered in wisteria and
bougainvillea, the dusty palms hanging over a brilliant blue sea and the
olive groves and cypresses rising to a decorative backdrop of snow-
topped mountains were indelibly romantic, and he was delighted to
discover sunbathing in February.

---

* Forster later married and had a family, and apparently did not keep in touch with Coward
thereafter. He rose to the rank of brigadier in the Coldstream Guards, and died in 1965.

He reluctantly left this Mediterranean idyll for England, where *I'll Leave It to You* was to be produced by Robert Oswald at the Gaiety Theatre in Manchester. After a minor crisis (the Lord Chamberlain, Sandhurst, demanded the removal of 'damn' from the script), rehearsals went well. On the first night (3 May 1920) Noel made a curtain speech which despite its boyish modesty had been rehearsed in his rooms beforehand. 'I had seen too many authors hauled on to the stage on first nights, trembling and confused, with goggling eyes, to make the mistake of being caught unprepared.' It was a measure of his confidence that he also seemed to have anticipated the 'gallery girls' who mobbed him for autographs at the stage door.

The *Sketch* printed a photograph of Coward, Wynne and Lois Stuart in one scene, and the *Daily News* reported on a 'double triumph of Youth': 'One has not far to seek for a reason for the great success at the Gaiety Theatre, Manchester, last night of Mr Noel Coward's new comedy, "I'll leave it to you". It is simply that the author, himself not yet 21, has endowed everybody in it with the spirit and freshness of youth.' The paper considered that youthfulness did not mean immaturity, 'for an author so young the creator shows a skill that is almost uncanny . . .'

During the play's first week, Mrs Charles Hawtrey and Mrs Gilbert Miller came to see it. Coward expected a London run, but the two women shook their heads, sympathising; they would have to cable their husbands and tell them the play couldn't possibly 'go in'. Noel, fuming, appeared cool, and told them that *I'll Leave It to You* would be entertaining the capital's audiences sooner than they thought. Two and a half months later, the play opened at the New Theatre in London, presented by Mary Moore (Lady Wyndham, the influential actress and manager). The first night was a triumph, and Coward gave another 'boyish' speech. However, Ivor Novello and Bobbie Andrews, who were in the audience, did not come to see him backstage. 'When I eventually tackled them about this, Ivor replied that the play, in the intervals of irritating him excessively, had bored him stiff.' Novello's concurrence with Mrs Miller and Mrs Hawtrey confirmed Noel's intermittent suspicion of Novello.

The play received more than its fair share of press. The *Daily Mail* thought it 'freshly written and brightly acted', although guilty of 'a certain striving after comic effect', and the *Sportsman* noted that 'the author, of an age and ability so to do, takes the part of Bobbie, making it gay and natural, as well as spirited'. Noel's personal publicity was notable; in the *Daily Dispatch*, Geoffrey Holdsworth supplied a profile in which he compared his friend to 'one of the late Saki's characters . . . There is something freakish, Puck-like, about the narrow slant of his grey-green eyes, the tilt of his eyebrows, the sleek backward rush of his hair . . . Noel has many virtues and one supreme fault; he never forgets an injury, and takes the keenest delight in planning some fiendishly brilliant revenge. "I'll tell you what I'll do to him . . ." and then his eyes kindle while he unfolds a plot that is always neat but never gaudy, for his victim's discomfiture.' Despite the enthusiastic notices, *I'll Leave It to You* ran for just five weeks. But Noel was able to sell the rights to Samuel French for a respectable fee, and began to work 'with renewed vigour' on his next play, *Barriers Down*, 'which was awful'.

In November, Coward was again engaged as Ralph in *The Knight of the Burning Pestle* at the Kingsway Theatre. A review in the *London News* said, 'One should have liked an apprentice with a more humorous physiognomy than Mr Noel Coward's, and a keener sense of fun . . . but the young actor does his best.' A month later, Coward fell ill but declined doctor's advice and went on, exposing sixteen of the company to his mumps, not a popular disease among its male members. This, and generally bad business, closed the play, leaving Noel free for Gilbert Miller's production of *Polly with a Past* at the St James's Theatre, with rehearsals to start in February.

He promptly set off for Rapallo, to renew his romantic Italian experiences of the previous year. But he also discovered an insurmountable problem: he could not speak Italian. So he retreated to Mrs Astley Cooper and the Grand Hotel at Alassio, where Noel was prevailed upon to sing at the English Club, an engagement notable because the smart young woman sitting in the front row – 'who appeared to be fighting an attack of convulsive giggles with singular lack of success' – was Gladys Calthrop. Mrs Astley Cooper introduced the pair. When Noel had forgiven Gladys for her ill-timed laughter, he decided she was worth knowing, not least because she had a cure for 'Mediterranean stomach'.

Calthrop was born in 1897 in Ashton, Devon, daughter of Frederick and Mabel Treeby. Product of a good county family, she was educated at Grassendale in Southbourne, although she showed an early rebelliousness by running away from school. She was then sent to Paris to be 'finished', and on her return had married Everard Calthrop, 'a landed gentleman from Norfolk'. Calthrop, six years her senior, was an army captain, who had served in the Royal Engineers in the war. But it was a marriage largely to spite her father, an autocratic figure with whom

Gladys clashed: her friend Patrick Woodcock recalled her tales of throwing plates at Mr Treeby. While disliking her father, Gladys had been emotionally attached to her brother, who died in an aeroplane crash during the war; she later took flying lessons, and bought her own plane, as if to maintain some spiritual connection with her brother.

Wilfully independent, Gladys Calthrop had studied art at the Slade, and was now separated from her husband. She was a true English amateur – she wrote poetry ('surprisingly good', according to Woodcock) and dabbled in clothes design, once hosting a fashion show in her London house and making all the clothes herself. 'She was rather like Vita Sackville-West in her amateurism', recalled Woodcock, and, like Sackville-West, her sexual desires were predominantly for her own sex, but like many lesbians of the time, she had found it difficult to avoid traditional marriage and children. Calthrop had come to the South of France with her baby, Hugo, whose care she later entrusted to her mother. 'She was terribly neglectful of her son', to whom she seemed 'incapable of love . . . not exactly cold, but knowing, and glamorous'. Jeffrey Amherst, another new friend of Noel's, remembered her as 'small of stature but strikingly handsome, with an unmistakable chic all her own. You would see Gladys at West End first nights striding down the centre aisle . . . with Noel to their house seats in Row E in the stalls. Her head was held so high one wondered if she might be in danger of falling over backwards.' Her dark wavy hair, grey eyes, aristocratic profile and stylish dress sense contributed to her chic appearance, and she sported 'barbaric' jewellery which emphasised her mannishness, in the way of the intelligent fashion-conscious young woman of the period. It was fateful that Calthrop was seemingly casting about for a new role in life, and the liaison was encouraged by Mrs Astley Cooper, who might have had thoughts of romance for these two brilliant young people. She supervised painting trips for them, and they often spent the mornings painting 'in a lovely studio on the sea shore', and afternoons sketching in the Andorra Valley.

According to Mrs Astley Cooper, Gladys was vexed that she could not sketch as well as her hostess: 'I pointed out she had another and probably far better talent, and on her return [to England] I tried to help her to find it . . . She spent much time . . . painting glass bottles which washed off! Later she took a course of theatre designing, and then with the help of Noel Coward went in for theatre decor, where she has made a name and money, and incidentally carried on my work with Noel, and taken the place I could no longer fill.' As with all of Noel's close friends, Gladys received her nickname, 'Blackheart', usually abbreviated to 'Blackie'. It was 'a strange relationship', noted Patrick Woodcock. 'She must have driven him mad in many ways. She wasn't a nice warm person – not like Noel . . . Noel used to say "Gladys has a genius for discomfort," and she did . . . But she did really understand Noel; they were part of the Beautiful People. When they first met, he adored her as a sort of Amanda [the heroine of *Private Lives*]. She was extremely beautiful. She had great presence . . .'

In Alassio, the pair attended a *festa* at the Combattente Club. They found the English presence restricting and, having feigned leaving with the others, returned later to enjoy the party. It was to be the setting of Coward's play *Sirocco*, with 'much tawdry glamour . . . contributed by sweet champagne, an electric piano, paper streamers, and the usual paraphernalia of Latin carnival'. Coward found a model for the romantic, fiery Sirio in an attractive local boy who caught his eye. Noel would encounter the unnamed object of desire again in Berlin in December 1922: 'I've just re-met the boy from whom I wrote the hero in *Sirocco*. I haven't seen him since Alassio two years ago – my French has suddenly become *really* fluent in a miraculous manner so I could talk to him comfortably', he told Violet.

Noel encouraged the naughtier side of Gladys. One 'particularly rowdy night' they wrecked the English Club by smearing black paint over its walls, and were not welcome there again. He had a propensity for irritation; also staying at the hotel was a friend of Mrs Astley Cooper's who 'resented Noel Coward's presence, and was disagreeable to him'. He should have known that Coward had the ultimate power of revenge. 'Noel called him "Auntie Egerton" and introduced him in one of his plays. He breathed again when Noel left!'

Polly with a Past was another Guy Bolton work, an American farce written with George Middleton. Gilbert Miller hoped to replicate its Broadway success in London, with Edna Best, Henry Kendall and Edith Evans in the cast. Coward, as Clay Collins, was the 'feed' for the main male roles. 'By the end of the run, however, I was embroidering and overacting to such an extent that they had to fight like steers to get their lines over at all.' A photograph from the production shows Noel grinning broadly in character, his hand held tight by Henry Kendall.

During the run of the play Coward received another Guards officer in his dressing-room, a short, blond, blue-eyed young man with a Military Cross: Jeffrey Holmesdale, the future Earl Amherst. A captain in the Coldstream Guards, Amherst appeared 'gay and a trifle strained' to Coward, with a 'certain quality of secrecy ... It was as though he knew too many things too closely, and was consequently over-wary', a combination perhaps of his war experience and natural reticence.

Jeffrey (Noel habitually misspelt his friend's name as Jeffery) was the scion of an esteemed family; his forebear and namesake, Sir Jeffrey Amherst, had been commander-in-chief of the British army during the American War of Independence; and the 1st Earl Amherst was ambassador to China, whose refusal to perform the *ko-tou* ceremony to the emperor gave the expression 'kow-tow' to the English language. Jeffrey's immediate origins were a little less grand; he was born in a modest house in Paddington, the son of a junior army captain who was soon to retire. Educated at Eton, Amherst's upbringing did not offer common ground between the two, but their interests and sensibilities did. A schoolfriend of the theatrically inclined Lord Lathom, it was at the latter's lavish Park Lane apartment that Amherst met Coward (rather than in Noel's fourth-floor dressing-room, as he records). Their second meeting was, however, at a certain altitude – Ivor Novello's Aldwych flat: 'It was a large party, with all the people like Phyl [Phyllis] Monkman and that lot ... Ivor was busy on the piano and everybody else was pushing around.' Coward and Amherst left the party together. 'We walked back to the house which my father had rented in Princes Gate where there was a piano. Noel played and sang until it was time to stop and get some sleep. I remember two songs which I do not think he ever subsequently used either in a show or as single numbers. From the first came, "I thought you might be lonely/ So I came along to see/ It's only me/ It's only me." And from the second, "I saw him fish/ the Sisters Gish/ from out of a glassy sea,/ He took them riding in his Rolls-Royce/ Saying death or dishonour/ Take your choice,/ But he never did that to me/ Oh! no/ He never did that to me."'

Amherst's quoting of these lines gives some clue to the nature of his friendship with Coward. His attractions were strong – a refined, aristocratic face, characteristically English; tousled blond hair falling over his forehead; a slight figure elegantly dressed, with a hint of feyness. Most of all, there was an impenetrable quality about Amherst: he remained enigmatic, and therefore yet more attractive, to Coward: 'I watched him twinkling and giggling through several noisy theatrical parties, but it took a long while for even me to begin to know him.' Amherst recognised Coward's talent for observation quickly enough: 'He had a very quick brain – he was frightfully quick to pick up accents, the mood of people. A great observer of people. I asked him about it. He told me "I keep my eyes open, my ears open, and my mouth shut."'

They became close friends, dining together when Amherst was 'on guard', or with his family at their town house. 'I suppose it could have been thought odd that such a friendship ... developed between two people of such different origins and upbringing', said Amherst. He admitted that 'it was quite likely that my youthful military experience help[ed] to feed an emotion in Noel which amongst other things much later urged him to write *Cavalcade*'. These were much the same feelings Stewart Forster had stirred in Coward; like his love of sailors and the sea, military tradition and masculine appeal conflated into a desirable image.

The relationship was, according to Amherst, a 'sort of two pronged mutual admiration'. According to other friends, it was love. Patricia Frere acknowledged that Coward 'loved ... him. When Jeffrey Amherst made it clear that he didn't want to do anything about it, Noel was perfectly distracted ... that was a big drama.' In later life Amherst remained reticent about the friendship, speaking movingly of their attachment but declining to delve deeper; their relationship remains shadowy, essentially private. Unrequited love caused Coward pain throughout his life, and the assertion of discipline and self-control typified his reaction to emotional adversity. Such defensive mechanisms were born of necessity, to deal with desires not allowed the full expression of more conventional passions. Most often, work was the antidote, and Coward was busy writing – plays, songs, and sketches 'bursting out ... far too quickly, and without nearly enough critical discrimination'. Looking back, Noel thought *The Young Idea* the best of that period.

Coward unashamedly based the boy and girl of that play on the smart-talking sophisticates of Shaw's *You Never Can Tell* (which had been revived at the Everyman Theatre, Hampstead, in September 1919). Fearing accusations of plagiarism (and unaware that Shaw conceded his own plots to be less than original), Coward sent the manuscript to him for comment. It was returned, with a long letter in which Shaw wrote that the author 'showed every indication of becoming a good play-wright, providing that I never again in my life read another word that he, Shaw, had written'. Noel was impressed as much by the gesture as by the content of the letter, and 'in the trouble that that great man had taken in going minutely over the work of a comparatively unknown writer'. His script was 'covered with corrections and awful crossings-out and "No you don't, young author" underlined and an entire idea for the end of the second act. This was to an unknown playwright aged twenty-two', Coward marvelled. 'The idea for the second act completely saved the play.' It was the same kindness Coward would thereafter demonstrate to his own importuning correspondents, to the surprise of less patient fellow professionals.

Despite its admitted plagiarism, in *The Young Idea* Coward's characteristic voice began to emerge, dealing with a familiar plot in a more mature manner than he had with *I'll Leave It to You*. Just as that play owed its genesis to another's inspiration, so the new work owed much not only to Shaw but to Mrs Astley Cooper. Set partly at 'George Brent's house in the hunting country', and partly at a villa in Alassio, the plot concerns attempts by Brent's children by his former marriage – Sholto and Gerda – to reunite their parents. 'Beautifully dressed', and eighteen and twenty-one years of age respectively, they arrive from Alassio where they live with their writer mother, to whom George is still attracted (they parted because 'they were too temperamental').

Beyond the obvious comparisons with Shaw's clever young Dolly and Philip Clandon of *You Never Can Tell* (whose mother is also a writer living in Madeira), Sholto and Gerda resemble nothing so much as the author and his new friend, Gladys (with vestiges of Esme): sharp, smart, elegant and witty, *mondaine* beyond their years, they are perfect Coward youths, exemplars of an entire generation. Boy-child and girl-child and yet sexually knowing, they are the anarchic antithesis of the pompous county set ('They're all against us just because we're not narrow and horsey like them'). Sholto and Gerda are the acid drops in this bag of marshmallows.

Jennifer Brent, 'chic, golden-haired . . . dressed in a scarlet overall', is another pristine Coward creation: 'I have never been able to take anything seriously after eleven o'clock in the morning.' Of her maid, she observes, 'Isn't Maria attractive? She has no morals and many more children than are usual for a single woman.' Sholto and Gerda smuggle George to Alassio, and seeing off an American suitor by telling him their father is mad,* they leave their parents to circle, bickering, towards an inevitable reunion which might have been a rehearsal for *Private Lives*. George accuses Jennifer of revelling in the tease of

---

* They tell him 'he eats the buttons off padded chairs', an odd obsession of Coward's. In *A Withered Nosegay*, 'Madcap Moll, the Duchess of Wapping' designs a machine 'exclusively for the fixing of leather buttons in church hassocks'; and in *South Sea Bubble*, a character complains that the abolition of classes on the island boat service has caused havoc, with 'buttons gouged out of cushions'.

argument, in a speech worthy of Elyot Chase, 'You've wanted me all these years as much as I have wanted you. The sight of you has completely annihilated the time we've been parted. The only thing that matters in the world is Youth. And I've got it back . . .' It was the cry for immortality which pervaded Coward's work – an image as gilded and artificial as Sholto and Gerda, prototypes to populate his plays for the next two decades.

Coward was now fully integrated into theatrical society, an habitué of its glamorous nights, but he had yet greater aspirations. Ever since Mary Robson, his *Scandal* colleague, had described the Waldorf Astoria, the Flat Iron Building, Central Park, Wall Street and Broadway by night, New York had caught Coward's imagination, and its lights his ambition. 'Its gigantic sky-signs dazzled my dreams, flashing . . . with unfailing regularity, the two words "Noel Coward".' Coward became convinced that his talents would find full scope there. In the post-war world, America promised fame and fortune and romance (the aesthete Harold Acton saw it as the 'home of sexual energy') and Coward hoped to experience all three.

Jeffrey Amherst was going to New York to work as a journalist, and 'as *Polly with a Past* was to close shortly, Noel decided to come too', he wrote. One obstacle to Coward's conquest of the New World was, however, unresolved: how to pay for the trip? Violet had no significant funds, and Noel's savings were not enough for an impressive arrival, or indeed, to share a transatlantic cabin with his new friend. The wealthy theatre patron Ned Lathom came to the rescue by buying two of Coward's songs, and with other borrowings this provided the £100 needed for a one-way fare on the *Aquitania*. Having obtained permission from Gilbert Miller to leave the cast of *Polly with a Past*, Coward joined Amherst en route for New York.

On Saturday, 14 May 1921, they found themselves in adjoining inside cabins of the Cunard Line's *Aquitania*. Such ships, even then, were floating hotels, with lavish interior decoration, restaurants, bars and ballrooms; a Savoy away from home. The effect was marred, however, by a stewards' and cooks' strike, which meant that volunteer retired naval officers – including Sir Percy Bates, a director of the Cunard Lines – had rallied around to wait upon the 2600 passengers. But standards were not allowed to slip; saloons were laid with starched white tablecloths and blood-red tulips. Passengers included Lady Meredith, Countess of Suffolk and Berkshire, Commander V. S. Jackson, the last of the American War Staff to leave Britain, and thirteen British babies being adopted by 'prominent New York families'.

Also on board was a Mrs Maxwell, a member of one of those Social Register families. A clergyman friend of the Amhersts had asked her to keep an eye on Jeffrey, so he and Noel shared her table, together with her niece, Grace. When Coward 'casually mentioned that he was an actor and had just ended a successful run at the St James's Theatre', Mrs Maxwell 'looked pained'. She took Jeffrey aside and explained that 'in the social circle in which she moved in New York the stage and its people were not received. In fact she and her friends did not live or visit on the West Side . . .' A few days after their arrival, Jeffrey was walking along Fifth Avenue when a limousine drew up and someone called his name. 'There was Mrs Maxwell, niece Grace *and* Noel Coward. They were on their way sightseeing to Chinatown . . .' The incident showed 'the power of Noel's personality. When he wanted, he could charm even the most reluctant bird off its perch.'

The *Aquitania* brought the two friends smoothly and elegantly across the Atlantic, and nudged into the Hudson River from the expanse of New York Bay. Coward saw Manhattan for the first time on a 'breathless June morning'. They were met by Napier Alington, Teddie Gerrard, Gabrielle Enthoven and Cecile Sartoris – a colourful, Bohemian group, all with a marked preference for their own sex. George Plimpton, chairman of the Board of Trustees of Amherst College and publisher of fine books, was also there to meet the two travellers. The respectable Mr Plimpton was introduced by Jeffrey Amherst to the others, who were 'in high spirits and certainly giving a distinct impression of having a drop taken'; Mr Plimpton 'soon hurried away', leaving Coward and Amherst to be hustled off to the Algonquin Hotel.

In the rising heat of Manhattan in summer, the improbable brick and concrete canyons and the die-straight streets and avenues, the shock of the new was tangible, and audible. On every side was motion: trains, trams, trucks and people. The elevated railway shuttled along remorselessly; nothing stood still. They crossed Times Square, not a square at all, but a stretch of theatreland, 'the very hub of Broadway. It was just at the time in the early evening when the famous lights were being switched on. It took what breath we had left . . .' The huge blown-up photographs of stars and their names spelt out in electric bulbs represented overwhelming glamour. For Coward, the dream of seeing his own name up there was suddenly attainable, such was the enabling power of Manhattan.

They checked into the Algonquin, whose wood-panelled public rooms were the legendary meeting-place for New York's literati. Here gathered at its Round Table such people as Robert Benchley, Edna Ferber, Dorothy Parker and Alexander Woollcott, their brand of wit one with which Coward would find himself very much at home.

Arranging to meet Amherst later, Coward went off to the theatre, determined to savour the city alone. On Broadway he gazed up at illuminated advertisements, jostled by crowds, 'The sky was not yet dark and the million lights flamed against it, changing from rich blue to deep purple'; it was 'a slightly tawdry beauty, detached, impersonal, and a little scarifying'. He settled on *Nice People*, in which Katherine Cornell and Tallulah Bankhead were playing small parts. The play was unremarkable; what impressed Noel was its speed: 'It took me a good ten minutes of the first act to understand what anyone was saying. They all seemed to be talking at once.' This accelerated tempo was a vital lesson. American acting relied on 'the technique of realising, first, which lines in the script are superflous, and second, knowing when, and how, to throw them away'; Noel would quicken his productions accordingly, injecting them with 42nd Street speed. By allying English humour to American pace, Coward would create his own successful style.

After the performance, he took a cab downtown to Washington Square, then a palatial residential area in Greenwich Village, where he found Teddie Gerrard's party in full swing. Gerrard, star of Ziegfeld revues and a friend of Lorn Macnaughtan's, was a vampish 'male impersonator' who dressed in elegant Edwardian men's suits for her West End shows in the 1910s and 1920s; Michael Davidson recalled seeing her then, 'as naughty as *La Vie Parisienne*'. The lesbian painter Gluck portrayed her as a raven-haired, fine-featured woman of boyish appearance, and claimed that she was famed for her rich lovers of either sex.

The pace of her party also bewildered Noel, with its 'haze of chatter, piano-playing, and cigarette smoke'. He recognised 'a dark, attractive woman, whose eyes slanted up at the corners, and who seemed unable to carry on a connected conversation in one language for more than three minutes'. Lady Dean Paul, his Ebury Street neighbour and Cecile Sartoris's girlfriend, had come to the States 'with an urgent determination to make money', and had left her husband and children in England to do so. Also there was Napier Alington, whom Coward knew from London. 'Naps' was an Etonian friend of Amherst's, in whose opinion he 'completely lacked any kind of discipline in respect of himself, his family, or even workwise'. Jeffrey laid the blame with Alington's mother, Lady Feodorovna Alington; she and his father owned large sections of Hoxton slums in London's East End, where their tenants celebrated Bonfire Night by burning effigies of their landlords.

Alington was 'a strange Faun, an almost Pan-like creature, surely a drawing for one of the Diaghilev Ballets', wrote Amherst, 'a near caricature but of considerable magnetism and charm'. He was employed in New York with the Guaranty Trust Company on Wall Street, but did little work there, partly because he seldom got to bed before two or three in the morning, having been drinking gin at Teddie Gerrard's apartment. 'He would struggle into the subway in a fairly dazed condition in time to get to his office just about opening time', Amherst recalled. A friend of the Vanderbilts, Alington once asked Amherst to the theatre with him and 'two sailor friends', and was anguished to spot Mrs Cornelius Vanderbilt, with whom he was supposed to be dining that evening, in a box. Alington slunk out when the lights went down, leaving his guests to meet him later.

Exhausted by such a frenetic introduction to New York life, Coward fell asleep with the soundtrack of Manhattan traffic in his ears. But not only was the Algonquin's antiquated accommodation oppressive without air-conditioning, it was expensive, so Noel moved downtown to the Brevoort Hotel on 5th Avenue, while Jeffrey went to stay with Naps on 8th Street.

Coward's first week in New York was enthralling. Alington provided loosely guided tours: Wall Street's bustle, views from the Woolworth Building, Harlem cabarets. Noel learned to distinguish between expresses and local subway trains, and with Amherst, Alington and Gerrard, rode out to join the crowds at Coney Island, where the funfair's huge ferris wheel and roller-coaster stood like iron skeletons on the broad Atlantic seafront. They were snapped play-acting at a beachside studio, the three men in their city-smart suits on their knees to a haughty Gerrard; although why each is gesturing to her with two fingers is unclear. Noel had already taken lessons in style from America: a snappy bow-tie, tight-waisted sports coat, trim grey pants, and a floppy driving cap in his hand – the image of a Scott Fitzgerald character. It was all terribly exciting, until the novelty and his money began to run out. Coward had delivered letters of introduction to Al Woods, David Belasco and Charles Dillingham, all influential theatre people; and, unfortunately, all three out of town. This, and his dwindling finances, forced another move, this time upwards, to a smaller room in the eaves of the Brevoort.

Amherst also deserted, on a trip upstate to Amherst College, leaving Coward to fend for himself. Luckily, he was offered a room in the apartment shared by Gabrielle Enthoven* and Cecile Sartoris on Washington Square, rent-free, at least until he made some money. This was generous, as neither was affluent. In the small flat with its dark wood furniture and whitewashed walls, the three friends stayed in on evenings when they could not afford to go to the movies. Wearing pyjamas and drinking red wine from the local Italian deli, they dined by the light of candles in sconces, flames fluttering in a rare breeze on hot airless nights.

Coward's new friends led erratic lives. Sartoris and Irene Dean Paul earned money giving recitals of Verlaine's poems, set to music, in the houses of the wealthy; Cecile reciting in a 'rhythmic monotone', Irene singing 'in her husky, attractive "musician's voice"'. The Polish Dean Paul was prone to sudden histrionic rages – 'vitriolic tirades against American houses, American culture, and American hostesses in particular' – and once tore up the cheque of a benefactor, throwing the pieces in her face, much to her partner's resentment. She lived on West 70th Street in a pitch-pine panelled apartment serviced by a stoic maid who was cashier to her impecunious mistress. Sometimes, 'when things looked especially black', Noel and Irene dressed up to dine and dance at Delmonico's, or on the Ritz roof, employing his illness-feigning tactic to avoid buying two meals. A luxurious respite from such stylised penury came with a weekend invitation from Florence Magee in Mount Kisco, when the lack of change to tip the servants was rectified by his luck at cards on the Sunday evening, providing him with a fortune of six dollars and fifty cents.

Coward was dancing on the edge of Broadway, moving in with persistence, and one new friendship proved important on every level when Noel met two young actors, Alfred Lunt and Lynn Fontanne. Fontanne was known for her supporting roles to Laurette Taylor, and she and Alfred Lunt – a dark and good-looking man from Milwaukee who had originally trained as an architect – were in the throes of early passion. Noel found Alfred, six years his senior, especially attractive; a

---

* Gabrielle Enthoven, widow of Charles H. Enthoven, was an actress, playwright and theatre historian whose collection provided the basis for the Theatre Museum in Covent Garden. Her adaptation of D'Annunzio's *Le Chèvrefeuille* was produced at the Lyceum in New York that year.

contemporary observes that Lunt was 'a bit of a freelancer' sexually. The couple lived at a boarding-house on West 70th Street named 'Doctor Rounds' after its proprietor, a fearsome woman with 'wary eyes', whose gruesome medical tales Coward loved. Here plans of world domination were hatched by the trio, a design for living which required Lynn and Alfred to marry and become theatrical idols; Noel would return to complete the successful triumvirate. Fontanne recalled Coward showing her his work, 'He'd hand me sheets and sheets of his writing and I knew he had something very special. Arrogant, but very special.' He showed her *The Young Idea*; 'I introduced him to Helen Hayes who would have been good casting for it', but Hayes 'wouldn't touch it'.

Coward's ambitions knew no bounds, and would indeed reach fruition in the States, partly with the help of this glamorous couple. For the moment, however, they contented themselves with walks in the park, and bus trips to Chinatown. Free theatre tickets meant a night out, taking the subway there and, if no supper invitation was forthcoming, walking home. But invitations to dine were often forthcoming, for Noel's primary asset was his ability to entertain his hosts. In early adulthood he was becoming a charismatic figure. His physical presence helped: lean (weighing less than 140 pounds), tall (just under six feet) and elegant, this well-tailored young man doggedly infiltrated New York society by his presence and will power. His highly polished foot was in the door, and he hoped his guests – the targets of his charm – would not notice that the shoe leather was wearing a little thin.

Despite claims of extreme poverty, Noel was earning some money: cables to Violet indicate that on 5 August 1921 he sold one story for £85 ('very bright'); another on 12 August for £100 ('brighter still'); and apparently a third for a similar sum. In late August he also sold parts of his book *A Withered Nosegay* to *Vanity Fair*. (Lynn Fontanne claimed credit for this, calling Frank Crowninshield, *Vanity Fair*'s editor, who agreed to a fee of $400.) This collection of very short stories had been the result of a collaboration with Lorn Macnaughtan, who illustrated them. They were pastiches of obscure nineteenth-century biographies, with such fictitious figures as Madcap Moll, Eighth Duchess of Wapping, Fürstin Liebewurst zu Schweinen-Kalber, and Julie de Poopinac. 'Who are we to criticise these frail, lovely, yet withal earthly creatures – who are we to condemn their occasionally slightly irritating behaviour – who are we, anyhow?' Dedicated, 'with affection', to Esme Wynne-Tyson, the book was quirky, whimsical and at times archly camp, recalling Saki, or perhaps Firbank: 'What vice! What intrigue! What corruption!' cried the narrator.

'Some of it was funny', Coward wrote later, 'and the basic idea was good, but it was written with too much ... personal enjoyment, and ... fell a long way short of success. Burlesque at any time is dangerous ground and for young and inexperienced writers usually disastrous. In this particular book there was a lot that was crude and careless' (including Macnaughtan's charming but amateur illustrations). Nonetheless *Vanity Fair* published three extracts – 'Brief Biographies of Some Famous Beauties of the Past, Written in the Inevitable Manner' – on a two-page spread: Madcap Moll, Maggie McWhistle and La Bibi, together with a flattering photograph of Noel.

Cash flow remained a major problem. Fontanne's appearance in George Kaufman's and Marc Connelly's *Dulcy*, which opened on Broadway on 13 August, brought acclaim, and Coward borrowed twenty dollars from his friend. This depressed him: in spite of his grey suit, blue shirt, tie and polished shoes, he felt 'vaguely bedraggled, as though my spirit hadn't been pressed properly and was shabby and creased'. When he interrupted Fontanne to make his request 'in the middle of a detailed description of a new bit of business she had inserted in the second act', she replied, 'Darling, of course, don't be so silly', gave him the money, and went on talking.

As Coward's luck would have it, the following morning he received a letter from James Whigham, editor of *Metropolitan Magazine*, asking him to lunch. He had been staying with the Magees, and while there had read *I'll Leave It to You* (sent by Coward as a thank-you present after his first visit). Whigham suggested that the author turn it into a short story, for the sum of five hundred dollars; Noel reflected that for $500 he would consider turning *War and Peace* into a music-hall sketch. The next day he paid his debts to Fontanne, his Italian deli and his maid, and sent £40 to his mother in compensation for the loss of revenue from the lodger, Mrs Herriot, who had 'inconsiderately abandoned our drawing-room suite early in June in favour of the grave'.

When Cecile and Gabrielle left town at the end of August, Noel stayed in their apartment, with their black maid, Gertrude. Most of the people he knew were on vacation, and meal tickets were few and far between. Theatres had closed, and scripts he had placed with the Theatre Guild 'had been consigned to some secret vault ... from which it was impossible to extricate, or even hear news of how they were faring'. In his reduced state, Noel walked the streets in search of cheap diversion. He found Battery Park, where the city's heat was cooled by trees and sea breezes, the best place to do nothing but watch the traffic in New York harbour. The sight of Europe-bound ships, next stop Southampton, induced homesickness, and Coward had to 'do a little honest, manly fist-clenching and shoulder-squaring'. There was no running home to Mother now.

For sustenance, he acquired bacon on tick from the Italian deli in McDougal Street, although luckily the weather reduced his appetite. It also accounted for the fact that he used to cook stark naked, and was observed doing so through the window of the kitchenette by a policeman. Noel disarmed the angry caller with the offer of some red wine, of which the officer drank three glasses. 'I offered him some bacon, which he refused, but at parting kindly lent me his revolver because, he said, it was a dangerous neighbourhood . . .' It is not the sort of scene one can imagine with a contemporary precinct cop; even then, a policeman lending his gun to a stranger seems odd, and the suspicious might sense a subtext to the tale. However, the idea of lurking danger had a fearful Coward lying awake, 'restraining the impulse to shoot at every shadow cast by the street lamp on to the white studio wall'; he felt less of a fool when he learnt that his laundryman had been murdered in the next street.

Matters improved when he received a modest advance for *A Withered Nosegay* from the publishers Boni and Liveright, and made new friends, among them Tallulah Bankhead. Daughter of a US senator, this tempestuous vamp had set her seductive eyes on Napier Alington, whom she chased round Manhattan. 'When she was first running around New York she was wearing a black dress, one of the only dresses she had', Jeffrey Amherst recalled. 'She was invited sometimes to those luncheon parties at the Algonquin, and had to take a mouthful out of everybody's plate because "poor Tallulah" hasn't got a job.' Bankhead was incorrigible; she took a summer cottage in England, 'at Datchet, next to Eton. Eventually one of the Eton authorities came to her and said, "We don't mind you taking some of the senior boys over for a smoke or a drink or a little sex on a Sunday afternoon. That doesn't upset us. What does upset us is your giving them cocaine before chapel."'

Noel also met up with an old friend, Ronald Colman, then appearing in a less than successful play. The two encouraged each other 'by formulating brave ambitions': Colman's to get into movies, Coward's not to leave New York until one of his plays had been accepted. The meeting stimulated him to begin writing *Sirocco*, imagining Eva Le Gallienne and Joseph Schildkraut, then playing in Molnar's *Liliom*, as the main characters, and inspired by his Italian trips and – perhaps – the heatwave. He finished the play quickly, 'and had no particular cause to regret it until several years later'.

Further dramatic inspiration was provided when Lunt and Fontanne took Coward to a party on the chic Upper East Side. Laurette Taylor and Hartley Manners, together with their children Dwight and Marguerite, were back at their redbrick gothic pile on Riverside Drive, facing the East River. They were a silent-screen parody of coupledom; the wide-eyed come-hither prettiness of Taylor matched by Manners's music-hall good looks. Laurette was 'frequently blunt to the point of embarrassment ... naive, intolerant, lovable and entirely devoid of tact', in Noel's opinion (her bluntness was due in part to a propensity to alcoholism which exacerbated her sometimes abusive manner). She was however a consummate actress, as Helen Hayes observed, 'Whatever she was doing seemed utterly spontaneous, as if it had just occurred to her ... I always especially loved her exits. There's a temptation among actors to make an exit a momentous happening in order to bring a round of applause. Laurette simply walked out of the room.'

Coward attended their famous Sunday evening suppers at Riverside Drive, with 'rather acrimonious games', played with 'a ferocity which appalled the more timid ... "In the manner of the word" was her favourite. An adverb was chosen, then each guest was asked to perform some particular action, recite or sing "in the manner of the word".' In this tyrannical atmosphere (Leslie Howard, another frequent visitor, referred to 'The Hardly-any-Manners atmosphere'), there were 'shrill arguments' over the rules 'waged entirely among the family, and frequently ended in all four of them leaving the room and retiring upstairs, where, later on, they might be discovered by any guest bold enough to go in search of them amicably drinking tea in the kitchen'.

Coward's experiences there would result in one of his best early plays. 'It was inevitable that someone should eventually utilise portions of this eccentricity in a play, and I am only grateful to Fate that no guest of the Hartley Manners thought of writing *Hay Fever* before I did.' Laurette Taylor enjoyed his company. 'Noel had a great deal of leisure that winter and not much else, and he spent a good deal of it at our house', she wrote. 'The sound of the piano ... meant that Noel was in the living room ... He was a great favorite with the family. Each member in turn would stop on the way upstairs, lean over the balcony, and invite him to stay for dinner. "Thank you, darling, I'd love to," Noel would reply, smiling up at each, the melody never ceasing beneath his roving fingers.' When Laurette bobbed her hair to be in fashion, a self-administered coiffure with a degree of spirited improvisation, she asked Noel what he thought. 'Darling', he exclaimed, 'you look like a lousy Shelley.'

Despite such honesty, the portrayal of her family and herself in *Hay Fever* came as a shock to Taylor. She was hurt by the news of it that 'drifted across the Atlantic ... After seeing the play in New York she found it hard to forgive him; the addle-pated group of rugged individualists whom he depicted were not her family at all. "None of us," she declared emphatically, "is ever unintentionally rude."'

Autumn brought cooler temperatures and serious business back to the theatre, and the return of all Noel's manuscripts, which, like old friends, he professed to be delighted to see again. However, he did sell *The Young Idea* as a second short story for a further $500 to the *Metropolitan Magazine*. With such financial security, and the imminent abandonment by Sartoris and Enthoven of their studio, Coward decamped to the Brevoort.

At one first night of the new season,* he made the acquaintance of Alexander Woollcott. Born in Phalanx, New Jersey, into a strange pseudo-religious communal sect of which his grandfather was a founder member, Woollcott had risen to prominence in New York as a critic of renown, dubbed 'The First Grave Digger'. He also gave his name to the cocktail Brandy Alexander. A sometime actor, his interest in the theatre was avid and consummate. He was an anglophile, and his appreciation of Coward's talents was immediate. Corpulent, bespectacled and possessed of an often destructive wit, Woollcott had as many enemies as friends, and Noel was pleased to count himself as one of the latter; Alec, as friends called him, was not without influence in the important offices of Broadway.

Another friend during Coward's last weeks in New York was Lester Donahue, a Brooklyn-born pianist with a 'pink, cherubic face', whom he had met in London. Donahue moved into the Brevoort, and his room had a piano at which Noel could practise. Together they went to parties

---

* *The Easiest Way* with Francis Starr, the climactic speech of which gave Coward his camp *cri de coeur* when faced with the prospect of a reluctant evening out: 'Doll me up, Annie! Dress up my body and paint my face – I am going to the rector's to make a hit, and to hell with the rest!'

and performances, including 'one of the first entirely coloured revues', *Shuffle Along*, in which Florence Mills moved 'like a streak of quicksilver'; and another at which they met a childhood friend of Donahue's, the singer Peggy Wood. There were encounters, too, with Fred and Adele Astaire, whose 'rhythm and taste' were another lesson for Noel. But New York had, for the present, outlived its usefulness. It was time to go home, with just £7 more than he had when he arrived, but with new friends, a play (*Sirocco*) and ideas for another (*Hay Fever*). He had not achieved the success he had imagined, but he had prepared the ground for the future.

6

Lord of a Day

They want me to play in this new comedy here in February – *such*
a good gesture to refuse it for my *own* play, altogether I'm a *riot*!
Noel Coward to Violet Coward, Paris, 1922

COWARD'S ticket home was generously provided by another of
his New York friends, Gladys Barbour, whose husband
arranged for a free cabin on the SS *Cedric*. On a snowy October
day in 1921 the ship docked in Liverpool; Noel's homecoming was
'unspoiled by anticlimax', he recalled, the Ebury Street bungalow *en
fête*, and Violet elated, although her son detected strain behind her joy.
Coward had to readjust to the old tensions of fragile family fortunes
and constant job-searching, as well as coping with the low spirits which
followed his exciting sojourn in the New World. It was not a happy
time: 1922 began with financial complications, involving 'borrowings,
mortgages on my beloved piano, pawnshops, black moments of distress,
brokers' men', and, for Noel, 'worst of all, days when even Mother's
invincible spirit came near to being broken'.

The family were near penury. John Dempsey, later a masseur on the
Cunard Line, recalled that Coward had become friendly with a deck
steward, Jimmy Wallace ('we called him Nellie Wallace'). 'In the early
Twenties, when Noel Coward was on the rocks, when he was really
struggling, Jimmy Wallace used to go round to his house with coal for
his fire.' Seemingly, Noel's luck had deserted him. There were no takers
for his own plays or for his performance in others', although he was
commissioned to adapt a French play for Dennis Eadie for £100. 'I was
in the awkward situation of being too well known to be able to accept
little jobs, and not well known enough to be able to command big ones.'
But what worried him most of all was that his mother might become
seriously ill. Her fortunes were intimately tied in with his – emotionally,

as well as financially – and desperation sent Coward back to Ned Lathom for help. He handed over £200 without demur, giving it rather than lending it: 'it was too dangerous a commodity . . . to pass between friends'. £150 paid off immediate debts; with the rest Coward whisked his mother off to the country. Gladys Calthrop and he discovered a suitable cottage at St Mary-in-the-Marsh in Kent, where they were soon installed, together with a black mongrel from Battersea Dogs' Home.

Coward had fallen in love with the countryside during the two weeks they had spent searching for Violet's holiday home. Cycling within a twenty-five-mile radius of Dymchurch, they discovered the beauty of Romney Marsh – wetlands under expansive skies, the colour of the landscape ever-changing: grey-green sea, silver-green watermeadows, gunmetal skies turning vivid amber in the sunset. ('Too red. Very affected', Coward quipped.) St Mary-in-the-Marsh looked across the marshes to the sea wall, where Napoleonic martello towers studded the coast; to the west was New Romney, its square church tower rising out of a clutch of trees. On evening rides Noel and Violet paused in the twilight and watched the narrow band of the sea fade into the marsh mist that rose from the dykes. This 'darkening country . . . lamps twinkling in cottage windows, bats swooping down from the high trees, and the lighthouses flashing all along the coast' was an echo of the land around Meon where Coward had spent his boyhood holidays.

Another link with his youthful past came in the shape of Coward's heroine, E. Nesbit, whose fantasies of Edwardian children and their magical adventures he reread throughout his life. Nesbit was a Bohemian figure with a history of younger lovers (among them Richard Le Gallienne, lover of Wilde) and a prodigiously unfaithful first husband, Hubert Bland. She had remarried T. T. Tucker, 'The Skipper', and they lived nearby in a couple of brick huts named The Long Boat and The Jolly Boat. Coward showed her his plays, which she discussed seriously. He later told Nesbit's biographer, Noel Streatfeild (a distant relation of Philip Streatfeild), that Edith was 'absolutely charming, with greyish-white hair and a rather sharp sense of humour'. But she was no 'sweet old lady', recorded a subsequent biographer. One day Coward was late for tea, and she was 'throughly annoyed' with him; on another occasion, Nesbit took a dislike to Violet. According to another biographer, Coward 'thought all the more of her for showing her feelings so openly', but Cole Lesley records that 'from then on [Noel] referred to Miss Nesbit as stuck-up'.

It was a part of England thick with literary and eccentric figures.

Nearby, in the quaint medieval town of Rye, lived another writer with whom Noel had been on 'nodding terms' since 1919: E. F. Benson, author of the sensational *Dodo* (a society skit on Margot Asquith), who had published his first Mapp and Lucia saga that year, 1921, tales of parochial snobbery much to Coward's taste, with their mannish women and effeminate men. (In the 1950s, when the books were out of print, Coward lent his name to a petition which included the names of Nancy Mitford, W. H. Auden, Michael MacLiammoir and Gertrude Lawrence, claiming, 'We will pay anything for Lucia books'.) Benson, later mayor of Rye, lived in Henry James's former abode, Lamb House, where he wrote in a Georgian 'garden room', and took his telephone calls in a special panelled room.

A more eccentric pair of writers also moved to Rye: the lesbian couple Miss Radclyffe Hall (whose scandalous Sapphic novel, *The Well of Loneliness*, was published in 1928) and Una, Lady Troubridge (widow of Admiral Troubridge), whom Noel probably met through their mutual friend, Teddie Gerrard.* Hall sported a cropped hairstyle and men's suits, and liked to be addressed as John by her more feminine girlfriend. As figures out of Benson's fiction, the pair maintained a spiky relationship with him partly because as campaigning lesbians they did not approve of Benson's undeclared homosexuality, considering it a disservice to 'the cause'.

Noel relished this exaggerated band, whose cliques and feuds informed his skittish prose satires of *A Withered Nosegay*, *Chelsea Buns* and *Spangled Unicorn*; but as a friend, he was closer to Sheila Kaye-Smith, who lived nearby, and whose novels set in rural Sussex inspired Noel's love of the area. Coward spent most of the spring of 1922 there; their cottage, propped up against the village pub with views of 'unlimited sheep' from its bedrooms, lay across the road from the church. There, in the churchyard, leaning on a tombstone, Noel wrote *The Queen Was in the Parlour*, whose 'passionate love-scenes and Ruritanian splendours' were a far remove from the surroundings which nurtured it.

In May, the Kentish lull was broken by an upswing in Coward's

---

* Una Troubridge notes in her 1923 diary, '30 Oct ... Teddie and Jo Carstairs arrived at 11.30 [p.m.] – without Etheline [Teddie's girlfriend] and stayed til 1.30 when we were glad to see the last of them.' The Canadian-born Jo 'Toughie' Carstairs (1900–93) was a famous lesbian of her time, a millionaire motor-boat racer sporting tattoos and a blonde crew-cut. She settled at Whale Cay, a Bahamian island where she hoped to install her then lover, Marlene Dietrich.

fortunes when Nelson Keys and George Grossmith performed one of his numbers, 'Bottles and Bones', at a Newspaper Press Fund matinee at Drury Lane. Another was used in *The Co-Optimists*, 'A Pierrotic Entertainment' at the Palace Theatre. Noel's skit 'The Co-Communists' reflected more revolutionary sentiments in a witty song, 'Down with the Whole Damn Lot!', sung by (among others) Stanley Holloway:

> Down with the idle rich!
> The bloated upper classes.
> They drive to Lord's
> In expensive Fords
> With their jewelled op'ra glasses.

A contemporary list of social ills is sarcastically challenged: the daily press, 'the bold Sinn Fein', 'the modern dance' and the Garrick Club.

Matters continued to improve with the Little Theatre's production of Coward's one-act comedy *The Better Half*. As usual, the playscript had to be sent to the Lord Chamberlain for licensing; the reader was George Street – drama critic and author of *The Autobiography of a Boy* – who was typical of the writers used by the Lord Chamberlain's office. He considered it 'a very bitter little comedy, a clever, one-sided and exaggerated litle satire . . .' In luxurious Mayfair, Alice is sick of her husband's priggishness and wants to provoke him 'to a little human brutality'. When she succeeds, she calls him a bully, and leaves him 'with a woman as aspiring as herself', going in search of a more 'human' husband. The cynical manipulation of and by lovers became a rich vein for Coward, although the play's inclusion in a Grand Guignol season had the *Clarion* hoping that the 'little play will not breed a little tribe of Rochesters'. Noel thought the play 'too flippant' to compete with the terrors which preceded it on the bill, but 'it . . . served the purpose . . . of keeping my name before the public'.

With theatrical success, Coward's social life improved. One weekend was spent with Lady Colefax at Oxford, where she was entertaining 'young people', her son, Peter, having just graduated. Sibyl Colefax, one of the most successful hostesses of the day, was unashamed in collecting celebrities, although the 'bouncing Michelin figure' of Elsa Maxwell, who arrived in gales of laughter, became a yet more egregious wooer of society. Maxwell was certainly noticeable, with a large, bovine face supported by an equally oversized body. As she sang her song, 'Tango Dream', 'a young man with an unusual, almost Mongolian countenance' watched her intently. Noel introduced himself; the fact that he knew her song (already ten years old) impressed Elsa: 'the youngster obviously had gone to the trouble of learning something about me'.

'I loved her at once', Coward wrote, '... all her boastfulness and noise and shrill assertiveness ...' The outcome of his encounter with Elsa was an extended if uneven friendship that lasted for more than thirty years; the short-term prospect was a party the following Tuesday. Here he found 'social and Bohemian graces tactfully mixed', and a tall, elegant woman with jet-black hair, Dorothy Fellowes-Gordon, known as Dickie. She had met the San Francisco-born Maxwell in Durban (where Elsa was playing the piano at the Edward Hotel), and brought her back to London in 1912. They had spent much of the war in New York, helping the English war effort and socialising. Elsa liked to mix in high society; Dickie was born to it. She came from a wealthy Scottish family* (she was a cousin of socialite Daisy Fellowes) and her father had died young, leaving her the family fortune. Fellowes-Gordon held the purse-strings for her profligate friend, and provided her with good counsel. Herself a singer (she had trained with Caruso, although her ambition did not match her talent), Dickie recalled that Elsa 'could have made a fortune from her songs, but she didn't have the sense to do that'.

Their friendship was a mystery to some: contemporary rumour had it that the pair were lovers, but the idea of Fellowes-Gordon – whose heterosexual lovers included Napier Alington and the Duke of Alba – as a sexual partner of Maxwell's remained contentious. 'A tall, stunning girl', Maxwell described her, 'the best and most helpful friend I have ever known ... Dickie ... had the beauty and sharp wit that were to make her one of Europe's *femmes fatales*, a role she attained without half trying'.

It was from hostesses like Sibyl Colefax that Maxwell learned the art of throwing parties, and the usefulness of clever young men like Coward. She began modestly in her two-roomed apartment in a converted stable, with a party which cost thirteen shillings and sixpence for twelve guests. Maxwell and Fellowes-Gordon had sought Coward's help with the guest list, inviting Diana Cooper, Viola Tree and 'a faun-like young man', Oliver Messel, the designer. The royal attraction (always one ingredient) was Princess Helena Victoria, granddaughter of

---

* She was born two days after Russell Coward, her birth being announced in the same edition of *The Times* in 1892.

Queen Victoria, escorted by Napier Alington. She 'sat on the floor . . . ate hard-boiled eggs and sausages and had the time of her life laughing at the antics of . . . Noel Coward, Bea Lillie, Gertrude Lawrence, and Ivor Novello'.

Both women were impressed by Coward, although Dickie was not convinced of his talents: 'He danced quite well, he sang a song fairly well, he played the piano very badly indeed – plink, plonk, plink! But he was very entertaining.' She and Maxwell decided to take their new friend with them to Italy, where Elsa was already rallying society to the Venetian Lido, and was to organise a party for the Duke of Spoleto. When Coward pleaded poverty, Maxwell said he would go as their guest. Not that Elsa was footing the bill; as she observed, 'Dickie was so open-handed with money that I knew she would not object to an added starter on the excursion.'

As a Mecca for the *beau monde*, Coward found Venice much to his liking. In this fantasy setting, frivolity prevailed; Fellowes-Gordon recalled Oliver Messel's speciality was a creative mime show. 'He did an Italian tart with an English colonel, behind a screen. You would have absolutely sworn they were two people. And then he'd do a child being given an enema, and you'd've sworn that was true too!' Hugo Rumbold was another acquaintance, fond of cross-dressing. One night he had Dickie turn out her entire wardrobe ('including my underwear, he was that particular') – in his search for the perfect costume as an 'eccentric Spanish authoress'.

Noel also discovered the 'myriads of feuds and scandals and small social rumpuses' of Venetian society. When Elsa Maxwell sent her guest list for the Spoleto party to the duke's equerry, it was returned with Noel's name crossed off. Elsa blamed an Italian socialite, Dorothy di Frasso, who had been worsted by Coward's wit at another gathering. Enraged, Maxwell informed the equerry that there would be no party without Mr Coward, and 'within the hour, my original list was returned without an omission'. On the night of the dinner, Maxwell met di Frasso. It was an uneven match of weights. 'I told her to take a flying jump in the Grand Canal and tried to implement the suggestion by grabbing her hair. We were separated before we set a new style in coiffures.'

Notwithstanding Maxwell's spirited defence, the incident pointed up Coward's precarious position. His clever comments did not always amuse, and he was not always accepted as an equal, or even as an amusing diversion. In later years, he was the centre of attention, but was he an equal, or merely a toy? Coward relied on hostesses such as Elsa Maxwell, Sibyl Colefax and Mrs Astley Cooper for introductions; without them, he would never have been on first-name terms with royalty and heads of state. Even so, he trod a fine wire with the ease of an adept social acrobat. Later, as a celebrity in his own right, such upper-class resorts as Venice became the meeting places for Noel and his chums. Freed from the restrictions of home (where his sexual desires were proscribed), Venice was the stage for wild hedonism. But for the moment, a burgeoning career, London and *The Young Idea* beckoned.

Coward had cast himself as Sholto in the production, much against producer Robert Courtneidge's will. Noel's argument was that he had not written such a good part for anyone else to play; Courtneidge's that, at twenty-two, he was too old for it, and far too sophisticated in profile. 'What he really meant, of course, was that I was not a good enough actor for it.' But Noel got his way.

However, the play's fate depended on the Lord Chamberlain's office. George Street considered it 'a clever and amusing comedy, but the atmosphere of it is more or less vicious and some of it in bad taste . . . Cicely has a lover, Rodney . . . It is not quite clear how far they have gone, but the atmosphere of the house and its guests is of the "fastest" sort . . . As a satire on that sort of English society which is immoral as well as stupid and rather vulgar Acts I and II are quite good. But the taste . . . is certainly bad and unpleasant.' Coward waited with bated breath: could he stage his play or not? 'The censorship', ruled Street loftily, 'is not an arbiter of taste, except when bad taste amounts to indecency, and there is nothing of that sort . . .' The play was licensed on 7 September 1922.

The Young Idea opened in Bristol on 25 September and toured for six weeks. Awaiting a London theatre, Coward cabled Ned Lathom in Davos, where he was recovering from a bout of tuberculosis. Lathom's reply summoned his young friend to consolidate plans for a new Noel Coward venture. The 3rd Earl of Lathom, Edward Bootle-Wilbraham, whose generosity had already helped Coward out of difficulties, was a colourful character. His grandfather had been Lord Chamberlain to Queen Victoria, and the Lathom fortune was largely associated with charitable works. This pale and willowy earl changed all that. He deserted the Lancashire family mansion for the dower house, Blyth, which he rebuilt, complete with a swimming pool and steps crowned with crystal banisters; guests were greeted by scented oil burnt on heated spoons, massed banks of luxuriant flowers, and the best food and wine money could buy. Extravagance was the keynote for this Firbankian figure, who would hire a railway carriage to send a footman to London for a box of chocolate almonds from Charbonnel & Walker, and dictate long letters which were then sent as telegrams. His love of perfume often took him to Floris in Jermyn Street, to buy 'Tantivy' or 'Mimosa', and he once told the manager that Paris had created a new scent called 'Suivez Moi, Jeune Homme' – 'a dangerous phrase, on his lips', remarked Beverley Nichols.

Lathom was irrevocably stage-struck, and spent a fortune financing masques in which his friends appeared lavishly and fancifully dressed at his expense. He invested professionally in the theatre too, on private productions of plays banned by the Lord Chamberlain, and wrote three dramatic works of his own. John Gielgud, who recollected him as 'a delightful friend', said that Lathom's own efforts were often staged as Sunday evening performances, but did not make the commercial theatre 'except on one occasion when the play failed'. (*Fear*, produced in 1927.) Gielgud was a frequent guest at Lathom's London home in Cumberland Place, 'a dream of decadent luxury', where he first met stars such as Marie Tempest and Gladys Cooper. Indeed, it was at one of Lathom's parties that Jeffrey Amherst had first met Noel.

The ingenuity of his extravagances rivalled the Bright Young Things' antics of the later Twenties: a fancy-dress party at the Tower of London; a 'come-as-the-person-you'd-most-like-to-sleep-with' party at Cliveden; a nursery party, where guests dressed as babies and were wheeled in prams. But for all his outrageous frivolity, Lathom provided promising and attractive young men like Coward with important support early in their careers, by social connexion and creative encouragement. Sadly, Lathom would have an unhappy end: 'he squandered his entire fortune by his generous habits', Gielgud recalls. He married Marie Xenia Tunzelman in 1927, but the couple lived apart; Lathom died from consumption in 1930, aged thirty-four, alone in a St John's Wood flat, attended by a valet to whom to owed money.

It was by courtesy of this ever-obliging aristocrat that Coward set off for Europe again. On 28 November he arrived at the Hotel de Londres in Paris, and wrote to Violet, assuring her of his safe crossing and a 'divine lunch' at the Ritz. There were plenty of friends to look after him: Elsa and Dickie took him on a tour of Parisian nightlife, and introduced him to the Irish-born couturier Edward Molyneux. Noel dined with him the following night after dancing at Claridges. Captain

Molyneux had been wounded in the war, losing the sight of his left eye; tall and elegant, he would turn his 'good side' to the camera, seldom looking at it face on. Like his designs, he was not extrovert in character; his work relied on subtle tailoring and simple shapes. 'Clothes must avoid the overdressed, the obvious, the showy,' he observed, 'also they must wear well.'

Fashion was not Molyneux's only venture; in partnership with Elsa Maxwell, he opened a pair of nightclubs. Maxwell had persuaded the designer he would help to sell his clothes by attracting a chic clientele to the nightspot (Poiret was already operating a similiar club). The first, at 7 rue des Acacias, was called the Acacia; here the young American dancer Clifton Webb was a star of the floor show. The second club, Le Jardin de ma Soeur, featured Josephine Baker and was described by Anita Loos as 'the most elegant place in which to greet the Paris dawn'.

Parisian life was exciting. Elsa and Dickie also introduced Noel to three eminent French dramatists, all apparently eager to have him play in a new production, an offer Coward grandly turned down: '*such* a good gesture to refuse it for my *own* play,' he told his mother, 'altogether I'm a *riot*!' Coward arrived in Davos-Platz on 2 December, to 'thick snow, glorious mountains and bright sunshine'. He spent three weeks alone with Lathom and his sister, Barbara, before other guests arrived. 'Ned looked better,' he recorded, 'but he still had coughing-fits from time to time'; it cannot have been pleasant to witness Lathom's state of health, recalling as it did, Philip Streatfeild's death.

Davos – the model for Thomas Mann's *Magic Mountain* – was a last resort of hope for TB victims, but among the dying Coward got on with the business of living. 'I am to do all the music for the new Charlot revue,' he told Violet on his first day in Davos, 'with a few extra songs interpolated, also all the words – isn't it thrilling – It will probably open in March at the Prince of Wales's, with Maisie Gay and Gertrude Lawrence!' Lathom's largesse attracted many influential people of the theatre, including André Charlot, the impresario and presenter of revues whose displeasure Coward had incurred back in 1918; it must have been satisfying for Noel to be reintroduced to Charlot under such circumstances. Lathom had financed his previous production, A to Z, and now decided on a new revue combining their talents. '*It's his solely and entirely*', Coward told his mother. 'Charlot is on salary as Director and Producer! My music will cause a stir I hope . . .'

Charlot was summoned, and Coward played his music to the impresario, who was '*delighted* – he sat without a smile and then took me aside and said they were *all* good – so that's that. I now quite definitely enter the Ranks of British Composers! I am excited as the music *is* good . . .' He set to work, rising early and working all morning, submitting the fruits of his labours to Lathom and Charlot in the afternoon, when, in 'a series of cigar-laden conferences', *London Calling* was born. Noel realised the size of the task, and agreed that Charlot could call in another writer if necessary (Ronald Jeans was eventually brought in to write the book for the revue). Charlot was keen for Coward to play the lead, if Courtneidge would release him from *The Young Idea*; and £30 a week was promised 'to *start* with and so much more as the New Editions are produced'.

Coward chose a choreographer, Laddie Cliff, and Molyneux had already begun designs for the costumes.* Molyneux would always dress Coward's leading ladies: 'It is a promise [he] made to me when he first started in haute couture', Noel maintained years later, and he particularly looked forward to stunning the audience in 'The Russian Blues' 'with the most marvellous Molyneux Russian Ballet costumes coming on in a sort of a dream Parade!'

For Maisie Gay, there would be 'a divine burlesque musical comedy song – very vivacious, with full chorus. She is to wear a full wig and very "bitty" clothes and look *quite* 55'; followed by her parasol dance 'with the male chorus – falling once or twice on her fanny – it's one of the *wittiest* burlesques I've ever done', he claimed modestly. Gertrude Lawrence was to sing 'Pretty Garde Lisette', 'Tamarisk Town' and 'Carrie Was a Careful Girl', 'with full chorus in lovely Victorian dresses, all very demure', and 'two duets with me'. The production, which Coward estimated would cost £7000, would open in April; before then, Charlot would pay for Noel to travel with him to New York for two weeks 'in search of new ideas'. The business side of all of this Noel left to his agents, Curtis Brown, 'because I know *nothing* about Revue Terms' – an ignorance which would cause problems later.

With so much uncertainty (and much riding on Courtneidge's good-will), Coward was nervous. Molyneux would not arrive at Davos until Christmas Eve, and Noel had to stay on to see him. A painful letter to England told Violet her son would not be back for Christmas, his first away from home: '*please* write and say you won't be disappointed – it

---

* Violet had recommended Edith Nesbit's daughter as costume designer, but Noel replied, 'I'm *sure* no daughter of Nesbit could make anything in the least "chic" and one can't jeopardise one's chances of success by promiscuous charity . . .'

really is only a matter of sentiment and you really will be sensible about it. I *know* you will . . .' (This letter also made clear how far Coward's earnings were supporting his family: 'Let me know how much Daddy wants for the Laura debt. I can manage Ten Pounds and at a *frightful* pinch fifteen . . .')

On 8 December they set off for Berlin. 'German is a terribly funny language to listen to – I get weak at moments and laugh in people's faces!' he wrote. He found Berlin 'gayer than anywhere – even Paris'; raging inflation meant that an English half-crown would buy dinner with champagne 'at any of the *best* hotels . . . I've *never* felt so rich'. He saw Fritzi Massary ('the greatest living German musical comedy artiste') in *Madame Pompadour*, and had his chance encounter with his *Sirocco* model. He enjoyed the risqué entertainments of the nightclubs: raucous jazz, satirical cabaret and overt homosexuality were commonplace in smoky dives. One such club provided the inspiration for his song 'Parisian Pierrot', written after Noel saw a cabaret number by a 'frowsy blonde, wearing a sequin chest-protector and a divided skirt . . . with a rag pierrot doll dressed in black velvet . . .' The performance of this sub-Dietrich diva was 'unimpressive but the doll fascinated me. The title "Parisian Pierrot" slipped into my mind, and in the taxi on the way back to the hotel the song began.' It was not the last Coward number to be born in the back of a cab.

The party left Berlin on 18 December to return to Davos, where a trainload of glamorous guests arrived from Paris: Elsa and Dickie; Edward Molyneux; Clifton Webb,* star of the Acacia Club who became a close friend of Coward's; Maxine Elliott, the American actress famous for having been Edward VII's mistress; Dick Wyndham, painter, writer and *bon viveur*; and the beautiful actress Gladys Cooper.

'I'm sunburnt and healthy', Noel reported, 'and I've never felt so well – I never wear a vest during the day a shirt and coat are enough . . . Yesterday I went driving with a German Baroness right up the mountain opposite . . . I've just come in from skating at which I'm becoming quite roguish, doing figure eights *mostly* on my fanny but then vive le sport! Ned is perfectly sweet – he suddenly bought me the most lovely tortoiseshell cigarette-case the other day. The leading men in the revue will be Clifton Webb and Morris Harvey (if possible) . . . Morris is very

---

* Clifton Webb (Webb Parmlee Hollenbeck) (1893–1966), Indiana-born actor, singer and dancer who had come to London in 1920 to appear at the Pavilion. Charlot wanted him in the revue: 'I said of course, providing that I was *indisputably* in the superior position! Aren't I a *deal*!' Coward told his mother.

amusing and anyhow the best dancer in the world. The hotel is full of Spaniards who teach me marvellous Spanish rythms [sic] on the Piano – and shriek and gesticulate wildly! . . . Ned and I have bread sauce with everything . . .'

Noel did not charm everyone, however: Gladys Cooper accused him of overweening conceit when he compared himself to Shaw and Maugham. That was like comparing herself to Bernhardt or Duse, she said; to which Noel riposted that 'the difference was not quite as fantastic as that'. But with the arrival of this crowd, the hotel became, 'with abrupt thoroughness, a resort', and 'Ned's Christmas guests, it is unnecessary to remark, were far and away the star turn'. None more so, he might have added, than their youngest member.

7

Bright Young Thing

Mr Noel Coward calls his brilliant little farce a 'comedy of youth' and so it is.

The Times, 2 February 1923

THE opening night of *The Young Idea* at the Savoy Theatre on 1 February 1923 gave one of the first intimations that Coward would become one of the great stage stars of his time. Coward made his 'usual self-deprecatory speech with a modesty which was rapidly becoming metallic, but which had the desired effect of lashing the audience to further ecstasies'.The *Evening Standard* recorded the emergence of a new trendsetter, the fashionable young Noel Coward fan. FIRST NIGHT LIKE A PARTY, it announced, adding that among the appreciative but undemonstrative majority, 'there were others who shouted "Noel! Noel! Noel!" ... When some bright remark in the classic way of English comedy was made, somebody behind me said ecstatically "Another Noelism".* After somebody else on stage had worn a jazz kind of scarf, a party of people in a box whose horn spectacles set off their youth, hung quantities of the same material over the ledge.'

To have captured his peer group was an essential step in Coward's rise to fame. Sholto and Gerda, those archetypal bright young things, were irresistible models for a generation ready to accept their values: nearly amoral, certainly modern, always smart. The flapper craze – born of female liberation and the German *backfisch*, 'a compromise between pederasty and normal sex', and the post-war boy – cynical, smart-

---

* Fifty years later, Kenneth Tynan wrote that *The Young Idea* 'contains the first line that distinguished Coward from all his predecessors in English comedy: "I lent that woman the top of my thermos flask and she never returned it. She's shallow, that's what she is, shallow."'

talking and effeminate – were the extremes of type to which Coward's pop culture aspired. It was a time of emancipation: birth control and sexual liberation; drink, drugs and dance-crazy clubs; divorce and adultery. Here, his fans thought, was the playwright for their time: no fusty Edwardian dramatist, but a man to inherit the mantle of Oscar Wilde. His languid urbanity, his elegant witticisms and his innate understanding and experience of the turbulent era in which he had grown up made Noel a perfect anti-hero of his time – even if his grounding in pre-war life would eventually lead him and his fellow rebels back to the reactionary values of their parents' generation.

It was all the more surprising, then, that *The Young Idea* failed to excite mass appeal, and closed within two months. But critics like James Agate – the homosexual writer who was to closely follow Coward's career – saw the promise of better things, even if he thought the dialogue unreal: 'There is something in the make-up of this young playwright beyond the mere *farceur*', he observed. 'I look to him not for "heart interest" but for the gentle castigation of manners. Let Mr Coward go on to give us closely observed people babbling matters of general interest and not, sempiternally, of their green passions.'

'The play is going quite well', Noel wrote to Violet in Kent. 'I've had several more ecstatic letters, Maxine Elliott *adored* it and has written to America post haste and hey presto about it!' He was very much in demand. In February there was a dinner with Jeffrey and Betty Chester at the Carisbrookes'* 'just us and them . . . They love us dearly and it was all very dainty. I shall come down on Sunday week . . . either with Gertie and Philip Astley [her lover] or else with Jeffery after the show on Saturday night. This next Sunday I'm going to Oxford then back in time for Irene Vanbrugh's† farewell dinner . . . Daddy's straining every nerve to make me comfortable – did you go for him?'

Arthur Coward was successfully running the houseful of lodgers and, as Noel noted (perhaps a little condescendingly), was deriving 'a great deal of personal gratification from it'. Chatting with the guests 'and hopping in and out of their rooms with breakfast trays', Arthur was

---

* The 1st Marquess (1886–1960) and Marchioness of Carisbrooke (1890–1956). He was brother of Queen Ena of Spain, and grandson of Queen Victoria. James Lees-Milne later described him 'immaculately dressed in a well-pressed check suit, padded shoulders, and jangling with gold bracelets and rings . . . really, a typical old queen'.
† Irene Vanbrugh (née Barnes) (1872–1949) was the immensely successful actress who appeared memorably in plays by Wilde and Pinero. She was the younger sister of the actress Violet Vanbrugh (wife of Arthur Bouchier). In February 1923 she went to South Africa with her husband, Dion Boucicault.

more willing to be sociable than Violet and had become popular with clientele and tradesmen alike, employing the Coward charm to full effect. His son was doing the same. 'London is outraged at the play coming off', he wrote from Ebury Street to St Mary's, 'everyone is talking about it and it's doing me a *lot* of good. I haven't written before because I've been working hard at the Vortex . . . Just off to dine with Ned.'

The Young Idea was 'one more step ahead achieved', with the added bonus of the income from the sale of publishing and performance rights to Samuel French, hopes of its sale to an American management, 'and a letter of the most generous praise' from C. B. Cochran, who took him to lunch at the Berkeley Hotel – confirmation that Noel had made his professional mark. This heady sense of having arrived was underlined that year when Coward engaged Lorn Loraine as his secretary. His mother had been acting as her son's organiser, sending out plays as and when requested, but the workload now required a more professional approach.

Lorn Macnaughtan's recent life had not been easy. She had married Rupert Loraine, a lieutenant-commander of submarines, but he was made redundant. Lorn had her friend Monica move into the house to help with expenses, but shortly after Rupert Loraine developed Parkinson's disease, and died later in the Twenties. Lorn's close friend and erstwhile employer (Loraine acted as her secretary), Meggie Albanesi, had died on 9 December 1923. Albanesi's mother said she had 'smoked far too much and lived on her nerves', but her death certificate confirms the rumour that she died from the effects of a botched abortion.

Taking up her secretarial role again, Loraine was soon installed at Ebury Street, dealing with the increasing volume of business. Her qualifications for the task were not obvious: she could neither type nor take shorthand. Instead, her duties were, according to Leslie Smith (later Noel's lawyer), more like those of a housewife. 'She used to mother him a bit – darn his socks and that sort of thing . . . She had a lot of commonsense, and she absolutely adored the Master.' Coward paid tribute to her skills by recreating her as Monica Reed (perhaps named after her house-sharing girlfriend), long-suffering secretary to the egotistical actor-dramatist, Garry Essendine, in *Present Laughter*. One of Garry's starstruck girlfriends says, 'I expect you know him better than anybody'; 'Less intimately than some,' replies Monica, 'better than most.' Such was Loraine's place in the scheme of things: privy to Coward's most intimate affairs, a silent witness to the drama of her master's personal life. 'I do envy you Monica,' says Garry, 'you're so unruffled and efficient. You go churning through life like some frightening old warship.' 'Thank you dear,' replies Monica, 'that sounds most attractive.'

After the London run of *The Young Idea*, which remained at the Savoy for sixty performances, Coward and Calthrop holidayed in Cap Ferrat (with Mrs Astley Cooper), and in Devon and Cornwall; Noel retained happy memories of the West Country, and had weekended there recently with Jeffrey. Stopping at Charlestown for lunch, Noel found his cousins 'detestable, gauche and rude', although Uncle Harry 'was charming and talked intelligently'. Vida was also there, 'very sweet and inclined to giggle' at Laura's deafness. Noel's aunt was undergoing a sad transformation; she had aged greatly, and looked ill. Shortly after Coward's visit she had a bad fall, backwards down the stone cellar steps, hitting her head. According to her family, the blow precipitated a mental illness, and Laura was admitted to the County Lunatic Asylum at Bodmin, where she died that July of a cerebral haemorrhage. Coward made no reference to this in his memoirs, perhaps out of deference to his mother's feelings about Aunt Laura's sad end.

London Calling – a reference to the call sign of the new radio station, 2LO London – was ready to go into production, with one exception: Coward himself. Discovering that some of the cast were being paid more than his £30 a week, Noel announced that appearing in a revue would damage his profile as a serious actor. Charlot called his bluff, but Coward used his veto on other nominations for the part until 'I allowed myself to be persuaded to change my mind' by Charlot's agreement to pay Coward £40 a week. His contract was for sixteen weeks, with a fortnight's notice after that.

Coward took lessons from Fred Astaire to polish up his footwork, and 'a small sharp-eyed woman' named Elsie April to tighten up his musical arrangements. April became pivotal to Noel's progress as a composer and song-writer. She had worked for Charlot until his rival, Cochran, poached her; to Cochran, she was 'chorus mistress, musical adviser and controller of the musical arrangement', notes his biographer Sam Heppner, with exceptional musical knowledge which was governed by the most refined perception and taste.' Five feet two, with an eccentric taste in clothes and hats, April was nonetheless able to notate, harmonise and transcribe a tune hummed to her even amid the noise of a rehearsal room, and she had perfect pitch. '"STOP! dear," she would roar, giving her hat an exasperated shove, "you didn't quite make that high G."' Invaluable to composers, she 'bubbled over with suggestions that immeasurably improved their original efforts. "Soling and heeling" was what she called it.'

Heppner noted that 'the long interval and winsome harmonic sequences; the unusual key changes and poignant angularities of phrase to be found in much of Coward's music owe a great deal to Elsie April, and her influence on his composition has clearly survived her death'. Another biographer records a possibly apocryphal tale of the genesis of one of Coward's most successful songs. April 'sat doodling at her piano and hit on a pleasing motif that went from F to B flat, down to F again and on to E flat ending up after a few bars on A flat. Coward . . . was immediately captivated . . . and used it as the theme of "I'll See You Again".' Noel once asked her why she never composed herself. 'Well, dear, I never seem to have any time' was her 'evasive' reply. He was sensitive about April's role in his musical *oeuvre*. Judy Campbell, who worked with Coward later in his career, remembered talking about a song in *Family Album* (from *Tonight at 8.30*) 'which has some of the most extraordinary shifts of key . . . I said something about Elsie April, did she do the orchestration? And he was quite suddenly a bit huffy. I thought, oh, this is a tiny Achilles heel.'

London Calling epitomised the 1920s revue: glamorous costumes and lavish scenery competing with bright pop songs and effective choreography in a fashionable evening's entertainment. Variety and pace were all; and Coward's talents suited the form admirably. The art of revue, he thought, was 'a very tricky and technical business' altogether; writing it required a certain formula, 'Everything has to be condensed to an appalling brevity. The biggest laugh must be on the last line before the black out. No scene or number should play for more than a few minutes at most, and, above all, the audience must never be kept waiting . . .' The success of his revues depended on brevity and a razor-sharp sense of timing – lessons learned in New York – as well as an awareness of contemporary culture. Ever able to tap the spirit of the times, Coward presented a spectacular which made his name, and his songs, more famous still.

Even Mr Street at the Lord Chamberlain's office approved. 'There is a good deal more talent (as was to be expected) in this than in the ordinary revue', he wrote, adding with satisfaction that it was 'mostly free from vulgarity and when it is daring it is in a cynical, not a coarse fashion . . . There are also burlesques of one of the (stupid) entertainments given recently by Miss Sitwell and her brothers . . .' However, he did object to a hint of sexual relations in 'Rain Before Sun', a sketch which prefigured *Private Lives*, with Coward and Lawrence portraying a honeymoon couple who have agreed to be 'only comrades for a year'. They have separate rooms, but quarrel, and the husband locks his wife's door 'obviously to remedy their unsatisfactory platonic relation . . . the atmosphere of a revue does seem to make it suggestive in a wrong way (for a revue audience) and the end is crude . . . Mr Noel Coward . . . is a promising playwright', lectured Street, 'and should understand that the atmosphere of a revue is not that of a serious play.'

But it was the perfect showcase for Coward's numbers. 'Parisian Pierrot', sung by Gertrude Lawrence in the fashionable fancy-dress of a pierrot – 'divinely forlorn/ with exquisite scorn', in acid yellow and green satin pantaloons and tulle ruff – was a wry glance at 'society's hero'. It was an immediate hit, as was Maisie Gay's 'What Love Means to Girls Like Me'. 'Sentiment', which Noel performed solo, was the only failure: critics agreed the revue was stupendous, but that Coward 'should never have been allowed to appear in it'. Noel did not care: his name was in lights outside a theatre, his music played in restaurants, and queues of fans waited at the stage door.

These were tangible signs of success. Gertrude Lawrence recalled, in a characteristically airy anecdote, 'Noel and I did a dance together in which we imitated Fred and Adele Astaire. When we danced off stage the applause was terrific. Noel made no attempt to take an encore at first. He caught my hand and just stood there in the wings. "That's for us, Gertie", he said, grinning. "That's for us – the two kids from the suburbs. We've definitely arrived. Let's stand here and see how long they keep it up." I wanted to go right out with him and take a bow, but he perversely insisted that we "hold it", and we did until what I suppose must have been the critical moment. Then he pushed me out in front of him and we took our bows.' Coward disputed this. 'Typical of Gertie's florid imagination – no number we did ever went that well! Of course, she may have been thinking of the time she tripped and fell during the dance – first time I ever had a chance to do a solo, while Gertie was on stage!'

The more caustic side of Coward's wit could cause trouble, however, as the 'Swiss Family Whittlebot' proved. The Sitwells' public profile as intellectual Bohemians was ripe for lampooning, and his sketch presented a barely disguised eccentric family of angular features and odd dress. It was clearly based on a performance of *Façade*, which Noel,

Elsa and Dickie had seen: to a jaunty musical score by William Walton, Edith and her brothers declaimed her breathless alliterative prose through a megaphone or from behind a curtain. The effect was whimsically avant-garde, but Noel told Dickie he thought it risible and marched out ostentatiously, mid-performance.

The eldest and perhaps the most sensitive of the three was Osbert Sitwell, whom Coward had known since the war (Scott Moncrieff was Osbert's implacable enemy), and who had invited him to *Façade*, suggesting it might give him 'a few ideas'. Sitwell was outraged by Coward's campaign, as he disseminated his 'Hernia Whittlebot' jokes in the gossip columns: 'Hernia is busy preparing for publication of her new books, *Gilded Sluts and Garbage*. She breakfasts on onions and Vichy water', and broadcasted his readings of her poems on 2LO. Most offensive of all were imputations that Edith Sitwell was lesbian. She wrote later, 'In 1923, Mr Coward began on me in a "sketch" of the utmost indecency – *really filthy*. I couldn't have him up, as I had no money and didn't know how to set about it. Nobody helped me, and I had to put up with having *filthy* verses about vice imputed to me and recited every night and three afternoons weekly for *nine months* . . . The woman who recited them went so far in her persecution . . . as to have a photograph of me in her dressing room.'

Osbert Sitwell wrote Coward a letter so angry that its recipient thought it was a joke. It was not, and another followed, 'even crosser than the first'. The feud lasted for twenty years and Edith thereafter considered Coward her 'major demon'. Coward professed puzzlement, but he had deliberately baited the Sitwells, for comic and public effect. For this publicity-conscious trio, the hardest part was that for a few painful weeks the family Whittlebot was more famous than the family Sitwell.

Despite its positive reception, the fate of Coward's first revue was less than happy. Charlot put on a New York revue which included three Coward numbers, Gertrude Lawrence and various other members of the cast, leaving *London Calling* to deteriorate visibly after three months; Coward wondered with ill-concealed and justified anger at 'this strange managerial juggling with success'. Perhaps Charlot regarded his paid employment, with Lord Lathom as patron, as a less serious venture than his other productions. The promised second edition of the revue reconstructed it entirely and Coward, his patience exhausted, took the opportunity to get out. It was time to move on, across the Atlantic, where at least he could hear his work on Broadway, and the possibility beckoned of writing a new musical with Jerome Kern.

Noel sailed for New York on the SS *Majestic* on 17 September 1924, in club comfort, having experienced the media accolade of a photograph at Waterloo Station and an interview at Southampton Docks. He left Violet in a rented cottage at Dockenfield in Surrey, and with two new plays under his belt. One would accelerate his rise to fame to such a degree that the press at the station and docks would have done well to sell their products to a reputable agency, for by the end of the year, *The Vortex* would draw enough attention to Coward to last any young playwright a lifetime; the other, *Fallen Angels*, would follow scandal with outrage.

Also on board were Basil Dean, Eugene Goossens (on his way to become conductor of the Eastman Orchestra), William Somerset Maugham and Gerald Haxton. Maugham was the most successful writer of his day, producing best-selling fiction and record-breaking plays. In future years, Coward and Maugham would vie for the title of 'the Master': in Coward's case, it was only a half-serious aspiration; in Maugham's, it was an assumption. Maugham's influence on Coward was detectable not only in style but in content; they shared an ability to write drawing-room dramas which transcended the genre, and Coward's later attempts at prose-writing directly mirrored Maugham's, specifically in the allure each felt for tropical themes. Maugham's journeys in the South Seas resulted, for example, in his short story and successful play *Rain*, set in Samoa; Coward used his travel experiences in his plays and prose (inventing the fictitious tropical territory of Samola). Both sought escape, subconsciously pursued by the morality of their homeland. Maugham, from his hugely popular and autobiographical novel *Of Human Bondage*, to his anti-war play *For Services Rendered*, rejected constricting English values. Coward questioned them too; *The Vortex* would be compared to Maugham's *Our Betters* (written in 1915 but not produced until 1923). But shared creative ground is no recipe for good relations, and the two writers spent their careers 'like two panthers prowling cautiously around each other'.

Coward had known Maugham since he had bestowed a kiss on the teenage prodigy; now he got to know him better. He found a somewhat cynical man, hardened and withdrawn, very much a closet homosexual, although most who knew him knew that Haxton, the alcoholic American adventurer, was his lover. Maugham was nonetheless congenial, and interested in Coward and his work; he was, after all, a charming young man. Goossens bore testament to Noel's wit when he said he laughed so much at the dinner table that he arrived in the United States with chronic indigestion.

New York promised other excitements too. A fashionable destination that year, it offered enjoyment beyond the restrictive English laws of the Hicks legislation. Indeed the Prince of Wales, who was partying on Long Island and in Manhattan that summer, was criticised at home for his excessive nocturnal activities, attending three parties a night and seldom getting out of bed before ten. His cousin and close friend, Dickie Mountbatten, was with him, with his glamorous wife, Edwina, famous among her friends for her promiscuity; in her set, moral laxity was not uncommon. Her husband was said to have homosexual tendencies; and Prince George, the Prince of Wales's brother whom Noel had met during the run of *London Calling* (when Gertrude Lawrence recalled finding him in her dressing-room, 'seated before my mirror, trying on a wig of long, false curls'), was rumoured to be particular debauched. His interest in black women, hard drugs and young men was widely whispered; it was even said that he and the Prince of Wales had imported a good-looking Italian boy whom they had installed at a London hotel.*

According to one writer, Prince George's 'appetite for sexual adventure was voracious ... as much with men as with women, with aristocrats, show business personalities or with strangers ... Of his homosexual lovers Noel Coward, then in his mid-twenties, was undoubtedly among the most famous. In later life [Coward] described his relationship with Prince George as "a little dalliance ..." Rumours of a liaison between Noel and the prince were common currency at the time. Peter Williams, the ballet designer, recalls, 'I heard a lot about it ... It was just one of those things one heard about.' The singer and female impersonator Douglas Byng – who also claimed to have 'dallied' with the prince – likewise maintained that 'Noel and Prince George were a big item ...'

Coward did not deny an affair between him and the king's son; partly out of mischief perhaps, and partly because it was a flattering idea. Later he became a close friend of Prince George's beautiful wife, Princess Marina, which in turn would produce rumours of their 'affair'. Such

---

* Prince George, later Duke of Kent (1902–42), was introduced to cocaine and morphine by one of his lovers, Kiki Whitney Preston, 'the girl with the silver syringe', one of the Happy Valley set. He was rescued by his brother David (the Prince of Wales) and Frieda Dudley Ward.

gossip galvanised the court and beyond; Coward was ever the subject of intrigue. By the 1940s, the affair with Prince George had passed into theatrical legend; his agent Charles Russell recalled that Coward 'used to tell me ... how, during the abdication crisis, there was grave misgiving about the Duke of York's capacity for kingship, and how the Duke of Kent was almost preferred because he already had a son to succeed him, and was married to a beautiful European princess – Marina. I am afraid I used to send him up rather over this. "You were almost a king's mistress, weren't you?"' A persistent rumour in later years was that the prince's love letters to Coward had been put up for auction but were mysteriously withdrawn before the sale.

Whatever the truth of the matter, New York certainly provided ample opportunity for amorous adventure. The photographer and theatre designer Cecil Beaton, who followed Coward's career with interest and a degree of envy, was shocked on his first visit to New York in 1928 to hear what Noel and friends got up to in that wicked city, and elsewhere. Beaton had not realised what active and often promiscuous sex lives people like Coward, Oliver Messel and Somerset Maugham lived, and listened with incredulity to Beverley Nichols's accounts of male brothels and rough trade pick-ups, and where to go 'to pick up sailors, marines, guardsmen'.

Beaton's remarks are a telling comment on sexual mores within Noel's peer group; and indeed on the young playwright's equivocal position in society as a whole. In October of the previous year, Beaton's Cambridge tutor, Billie Bullivant, had promised to introduce him to Coward. Cecil noted in his diary, 'I've heard so much about Noel Coward – rather nasty things about his mother being a charwoman & he being very naughty. But he's clever and well known since *London Calling* ...' The meeting was postponed but talk of Coward remained intense between Beaton and his tutor, who thought 'Noel is the coming youth & I ought to do his ballets & lighting & Ivor Novello & Boltie would help ...' But Beaton 'half-wondered later if I wanted to get into the Ivor/Noel naughty set ...' He had no desire to be 'a terrible homosexualist ... it's so much nicer just to be affectionate & ... sleep in the same bed but that's all. Everything else is repulsive to me & yet it's awfully difficult. That's why I think it's rather dangerous for me to get in with the Ivor–Noel crowd ...'

André Charlot's Revue of 1924 had opened at the Times Square Theatre that January, with Gertrude Lawrence, Beatrice Lillie and Jack Buchanan, among others, performing three of Coward's songs; he had arrived on Broadway. Noel's new status demanded that he be installed in the plush pink-and-gold luxury of the Ritz Carlton Hotel on Madison Avenue, but the pleasure was alloyed by the size of the week's bill, so he decamped to Lester Donahue's flat at East 32nd Street, and made use of his sofa. 'We had great fun in that flat, and gave several select cocktail parties', although for form's sake he kept the Ritz as his address.

He looked up all his old contacts, and a few new ones. Jeffrey Amherst was now working as a journalist on the *New York World*, and after a show they dined at the Algonquin. Jeffrey had been covering particularly gruesome crimes, and Noel had to 'tactfully . . . erase some of the bloodstains' from the conversation to make supper edible. The Lunts were now married and lived off Lexington Avenue in a 'comfortable greenish apartment'; Lynn had just finished a successful run in *In Love with Love*, while Alfred was playing in *Outward Bound*. Lunt refused to accept praise for his performance, saying he had overacted. It was part of the ritual both Lunts went through in their search for perfection. Lynn was 'unmoved by his despair. She said: "Never mind, darling, you gave a lovely performance last Thursday matinee," and went on with her scrambled eggs.'

The Jerome Kern project evaporated, but new friends stepped in to fill the space, among them Eva Le Gallienne, the actress and theatre director, lesbian lover of the Russian actress Alla Nazimova, and daughter of Richard Le Gallienne. Another new acquaintance was the artist Neysa McMein. 'Beautiful, untidy, casual', Marjorie Moran McMein changed her name on the advice of a fortune-teller. A portrait-painter, she was a key figure in the Algonquin Round Table set, 'endowed with a facile artistic talent, a quick wit, and a brilliant personality'. Alexander Woollcott had wanted to marry her, and described his inamorata as 'grave, and slightly soiled', but before Woollcott could press his suit, McMein had married John G. Baragwan-ath, a handsome mining engineer. Noel enjoyed her ability to tell hilarious stories against herself, such as arriving for a fancy-dress party attired as a cave-woman, only to discover a drawing-room full of people in formal evening wear.

The culmination of Coward's social progress in New York came at a party Laurette Taylor threw for the new film *Happiness*, where he met Douglas Fairbanks and Mary Pickford. Superstars of their time, they epitomised Hollywood glamour – she with long blonde curls and tiny features, he with a broad grin and handsome swarthiness. For Coward, the occasion was 'a big thrill, particularly as they were both charming to me'. During the evening Noel discovered that the Fairbankses' world tour, encompassing Europe, Russia and Japan, was to start with an Atlantic crossing on the SS *Olympic*, the same ship he was booked on. He schemed to become better acquainted; an unashamed lion-hunter, his technique was 'a careless indifference, so studied and practised that it could leave no doubt whatever in anybody's mind as to my easy intimacy of the object of the crowd's admiration'.

Alexander Woollcott, whose anglophile sensibilities supplied much good publicity for theatrical Britons, obliged with a puff for Coward in a New York paper: 'It ought to be fairly easy to get up an endurable ship's concert during the next voyage of the Olympic', he wrote, noting among the 747 passengers such luminaries as D. W. Griffith, the opera singer Mary Garden, and the Fairbankses, complete with their eight-year-old daughter Charlot, named after the impresario. 'Then, if the luckless wight on whom pressure is brought to manage the concert is really bright, he will be careful to exhume from his cabin one Noel Coward, a young and sprightly English comedian who wrote the words and music of three of the best numbers in the "Charlot Revue". Coward seems to have been born into the world just to write songs for Beatrice Lillie . . .'

Embarking on the *Olympic*, Coward relished the reflected glory of the fans who thronged to see the Fairbankses off. The Prince of Wales's set were also on board, among them the Mountbattens; by the time Coward arrived back in London, he was on first name terms with Dickie and Edwina. Atlantic hopping was always good for the social climber, and by travelling first class, Noel made connexions which he was at pains to maintain at home. They disembarked at Southampton, where eager fans attempted to outrun the train as it drew off for Waterloo; Coward made no secret of his enjoyment of the occasion. The glamour continued in town, where Richard and Jean Norton, who had also been on board, threw a party for Pickford and Fairbanks, to which both Noel and the Prince of Wales were invited. The prince threw Coward 'into a frenzy' when he asked him to play a tune which the young playwright, unusually, could not remember. Coward's relationship with the future king was not easy: Noel was irritated by the high public profile of the prince, of whom he later wrote, 'he had the charm of the world, with nothing whatever to back it up'. The prince could be high-handed, and Noel was displeased when the heir to the throne cut him at Hawes and Curtis, the Savile Row tailors, despite the fact that the previous evening Coward had been kept up to 'all hours' on the piano accompanying the prince on his ukelele. John Pringle, equerry to the prince (then the Duke of Windsor) during the war, said, 'I think he's the only person I've ever met who hated Noel. I don't know why. I remember Noel telling me he was with HRH, and the Duke was looking at a point over Noel's left shoulder, as royalty do, and he asked Noel, "So tell me about the theatre, Noel." Noel answered, "Well, where shall I begin, sir?"'

Despite glittering parties and friends, London paled in the shadow of New York, and Coward felt he had 'toiled . . . too long' in the city. An impression of dreariness and inefficiency (and a bad cold) overcame him. Illness and depression being excellent spurs to creativity, Noel took off for the cottage in Dockenfield in a new red sports car (bought at the Earls Court Motor Show), and promptly wrote *Hay Fever*. The play was perhaps his first mature work: his dialogue was 'becoming more natural and less elaborate', and he was starting to concentrate 'more on the comedy values of situation rather than . . . of actual lines'. He considered it a good vehicle for Marie Tempest, but the actress and her husband thought it 'too light and plotless and generally lacking', so he returned to Dockenfield and wrote *Easy Virtue*, just as quickly. Meanwhile, two other plays were 'voyaging disconsolately in and out of the London manager's offices': *The Vortex* had interest from Harold Harwood, the lessee of the Ambassadors Theatre, while Gladys Cooper wanted to play in *Fallen Angels* with Madge Titheradge. But outstanding contracts intervened, and Coward's dramatic career hung in abeyance – for the moment.

In July he escaped to Deauville. Its casinos were beyond his shallow pockets (although he enjoyed gambling, he had only £30 in the bank), but he derived a vicarious thrill from watching the upper classes spend their money. The millionaire financier Sir James Dunn arrived on his yacht, as did the Duff Coopers and other notables. Noel rode horseback, thinking he might cut a fine figure for the press – 'Noel Coward enjoying a brisk morning canter on the beach at Deauville' – but lacked style, and dismounted for his aperitif with his seat sagging 'like the elephant's child'.

On 23 July Coward wrote his customary away-from-home weekly letter to his mother (signed, as always, 'Snoopie'): '. . . I *think* it's going to prove a very lucky trip – but I'll explain why later – I'm full of quite surprisingly dashing plans which look like materialising . . .' His secrecy concealed a generous offer Sir James Dunn had made: Dunn had declared Coward a genius, and offered to finance his career for the next five years. To Noel, who was already considering another trip to America, this was a tempting proposal. It was also an indication of how far he had come that Dunn should consider him a sound investment; he might just have sought Sir James's company with such a scheme in mind. But back in London, he realised the wisdom of Gladys Calthrop's argument: patronage such as Dunn's would be 'an abysmal admission of defeat'. Noel turned down the offer, which was anyway not as handsome as it seemed: the canny businessman's contract would have reclaimed twenty per cent of Noel's earnings.

Coward looked back on the late summer of 1924 as a 'definite end to a chapter' in his life, 'the closing of a phase'. His position in the theatre world was equivocal, with many plays in dramatic limbo, although he was thought to be 'well known and moderately popular'. He was to rise above such doubtful fame, and become the most talked-about young man of his day.

8

The Vortex

During the era when strange fevers alternated with a lethargy that found nothing worth doing ... the bored, horribly bored set, who had been too young to do anything but look on and see too much sorrow, too much waste ... did not achieve much ... Literally, they had been in at the death. It was not worth while to be ambitious. War hung about in the air even after war was over, and they could not properly get started; and then everything was too late; they were suffering not from shell-shock, but from the echo of shell-shock.

G. B. Stern, *Monogram*

COWARD'S play shocked the theatre world of the 1920s into life, an antidote to the fantasies, base comedies and anodyne drawing-room dramas which were the legacy of the Great War. It was as though he had planned for this moment, and had designed a scenario to garner the maximum amount of publicity. It was a gamble: if he went too near the limit of what was acceptable, his play would not pass the censor; if he were too tame, the effect would be lost. With *The Vortex*, he seemed to have judged his moment exactly. But the often bizarre events that surrounded its production could not have been predicted, and the play's astonishing success owed as much to chance as a triumph ever did.

Coward's growing group of fans would have recognised the theme of the play, although rather more serious issues now preoccupied the playwright: the older woman (emblematic of the war widow) who takes a younger man for her lover, and her son, who takes drugs – both situations endemic to the period. In *The Vortex*, Coward characterises the prototypes of his world; the women are languid temptresses, 'brilliantly dressed ... to the point of being "outré"'; the men 'divinely selfish', if amusing. Exercise is equated with stupidity. Tom Veryan is the good-looking Guards officer and athlete, 'good at games and extremely bad at everything else'. He is lover to Florence Lancaster, a middle-aged woman whose face retains 'the remnants of great beauty'; Helen Saville is her friend, dispenser of good advice. Minor characters include Pawnie (Pauncefort), an effeminate older man who uses the perfume 'Narcisse Noir'; and Clara, 'an emaciated soprano . . . affected, but quite well dressed'. The accent is on superficiality and artifice born of a young man's obsession with fashion and appearance. In Coward's world, first impressions count; it is part of the two-dimensional, almost parabolic nature of his plays. Cocktails hover on silver trays borne by mute servants – only later did Coward exploit their dramatic potential. Into this world Florence's fey and feckless twenty-nine-year-old son Nicky returns from Paris, 'extremely well-dressed in travelling clothes'; he is 'tall and pale with thin, nervous hands', evidently a product of his time.

Nicky Lancaster's drug-taking has been seen by critics as a synonym for homosexuality; he is the first of many figures of unconventional sexuality in Coward's work, gaining in emphasis as his career progressed, self-portraits to a degree. 'Noel Coward put his sexuality in a little silver box and sniffed it', wrote the film-maker Derek Jarman, years later; to Jarman, the play was 'confession as innuendo'. The combination of Lancaster's habit and the illicitness of his implied sexuality gives the play its radical edge. There are clues to his bisexuality: his intimate friendship with John Bagot, and his lacklustre engagement to Bunty Mainwaring, whose cumbersome name alone marks her out as a 'beard', a guise of heterosexuality. Florence remarks, 'What a silly name! . . . Is she pretty?' 'I haven't really noticed', replies Nicky. Bunty too is ambisexual, 'more attractive than pretty in a boyish sort of way'. Her 'love scene' with Nicky is written in the clear clipped repartee which passes for a love scene in Coward's plays, as if he is too clever to write it 'straight':

Nicky: We're all so hectic and nervy . . .
Bunty: It doesn't matter – it probably only means we shan't live so long . . .

For the younger generation, the 1920s was a period of neurosis; they saw a foreshortened future, and the search for new sensation – whether through dancing (as new and faster steps succeeded one another), alcohol (ever more sophisticated cocktails) or drugs – induced a frenzied hedonism in poor little rich girls and boys for whom 'the craze for pleasure' steadily grew. *The Vortex* is more than a nod at this culture; it defined it. Even the title of the play asserts Twenties modernity, evoking the Vorticists, stylised interiors and art deco; or, more intellectually but equally fashionable, Freudian theory and psychoanalysis in a play which seeks to plumb human desperation.

Rebecca West was later to write that Coward 'took a serious historic interest in the social changes of the time. He's never been interested in causes but he had a better grasp of what was going wrong in our society than Shaw.' In the world of *The Vortex*, values have become inverted. In a party scene, Bruce Fairlight, a 'serious dramatist', is mocked by Coward, seen as useless at anything useful, useful in this context being either dancing or playing mah-jong. As Helen remarks, 'The great thing in this world is not to be obvious, Nicky – over *anything*!'

Nicky blames his mother for his problems, and it is tempting to wonder if Noel felt the same about Violet – a classic Freudian scenario. (Also, it must be admitted, a time-honoured dramatic device. When asked if the mother–son relationship in the play might have been inspired by Shakespeare, Coward replied, 'I doubt it. I've never seen *Hamlet*.') Nicky also accuses Florence of being responsible for his father's 'crushed' spirit. In an era when wanton behaviour was blamed on the lack of mature male role models, Coward's ineffectual father represented the lack of a guiding – and restraining – masculine figure.

The Vortex's climax is Florence's discovery of her son's addiction (in an alternate reading, the realisation of his true sexual nature), and as she flings his box of cocaine out of the window, she falls to her knees, begging him to give it up. 'It's only just the beginning –', he tells her, cynically, and implies that she cannot assume any moral high ground given her recent behaviour. 'I'm trying to control myself, but you won't let me – you're an awfully rotten woman, really.' Roles are thus reversed, in this topsy-turvy play, and we leave the pair on a bleak, almost anticlimactic note. 'Promise me you'll be different', says Nicky; 'Yes, yes – I'll try –', says Florence. 'We'll both try', he replies. 'Yes, dear. Oh, my dear – !' The Victorian melodrama is counterpointed by Coward's final stage direction, which returns the scene to its nervous edge: '[*She sits quite still, staring in front of her – the tears are rolling down her cheeks, and she is stroking Nicky's hair mechanically in an effort to calm him.*]'

The Vortex is simplistic, naive and shallow, but it is also entertaining and well-written, albeit with the facility and brilliance of effect which often disguise a slight work. Sensational scenes speed the play along, leaving no time for audience fatigue – something Coward could not forgive. The play also evinced his increasing economy of language which, as with *Hay Fever*, he had come to recognise as essential. It was a reaction, whether conscious or not, against the flowery, polysyllabic language of the previous generation. Verbose Edwardian and Victorian speech and prose had been replaced by short sharp abbreviations. 1920s slang worked on such principles (the dialect of youth, to confuse the elders), and Coward assimilated it; the result was a dramatic language, drawing on Wilde, Pinero and Shaw, but his own. Noel had found his voice, one which became recognisable as 'Cowardian'.

The venue chosen for Coward's *succès de scandale* was far removed from the West End sophistication of its setting. The Everyman Theatre in leafy Hampstead was a former drill hall managed by Norman Macdermott, who had launched many West End successes there. There was an artistic worthiness to the place which contrasted with Coward's ambitions: coconut matting and draughty dressing-rooms were not quite what he had anticipated as the site of his first big success. Macdermott had been a businessman before going into the theatre as a producer in 1918; two years later he had opened the Everyman, and claimed credit for reviving Shaw's plays in a series of seasons. He had read Coward's two most recent efforts and, although the businessman in him would have preferred to stage *Hay Fever*, the author persuaded his producer that *The Vortex* would be preferable; it had a better part for its creator.

The rest of the cast might not have been so easily appointed, for the Everyman paid only £5 per week as a fixed salary. With a great deal of persuasion, Kate Cutler (who had played Jennifer in *The Young Idea*) was engaged as leading lady, with a handful of moderately well-known supporting actors. Coward also persuaded Macdermott to pay Gladys Calthrop to do the costumes and scenery. But the whole project was put in jeopardy even before it had begun; as soon as the contracts were signed, the manager had a crisis of confidence and announced there was no money to pay for the play, and £200 had to be found immediately if it was to proceed. Noel was at a loss as to whom he could tap for this sum; the Coward address book was consulted, and the name of Michael Arlen leapt out.

As much as Coward became the archetypal dandy of the 1920s, Michael Arlen was already established as a notable exponent. Author of *The Green Hat*, the quintessentially 'decadent' Twenties novel, he was an Armenian who had perhaps wisely changed his name from Dikran Kouyoumdjian in his bid for fame. As his son notes, 'the celebrity business hadn't been around very long. The 1920s more or less invented it. Channel swimmers. Movie stars. Even writers.' Arlen, in jewelled stick-pin, astrakhan overcoat and large fedora, was as much of the period as was his heroine, Iris March, in her green cloche. 'Mr Arlen, what do you think of yourself as an artist?' asked a reporter. 'Per ardua ad astrakhan', he replied in a phrase Coward himself might have used. As one of the richest men Coward knew, Arlen was a logical source of finance. Over cocktails at the Embassy Club, he obliged by writing out a cheque for the requisite amount; after which 'the evening seemed even more charming than it had been in the beginning'.

Rehearsals proceeded and all seemed well until Kate Cutler suddenly refused to carry on. Coward maintained that he knew not what 'strange devil' had got into her, but her discontent might have had something to do with Noel's rewriting of the too-short last act, enlarging his part in the process. To the author-director, it was a 'painful and . . . unreasonable quarrel'; he cited 'literary integrity', but Cutler was adamant and left the production.* *The Vortex* was two weeks from opening.

'A grotesque ballet of middle-aged actresses whirled through my dreams', Coward wrote. He decided to look for someone entirely unlike Florence, and chose Lilian Braithwaite, the antithesis of Mrs Lancaster in that 'her moral position was clearly defined, and her virtue unassailable'. Undaunted, Noel rang her up, and within the hour was reading the play in Braithwaite's Pelham Crescent drawing-room. The actress 'wore a far-away expression', but by her nods Coward knew he had won: she agreed to take the part, for £5 a week. It was a good morning's work, and a major contribution to the success of his play. Braithwaite learned her part in two days, while Gladys Calthrop sweated over the costumes in the cramped basement, painting flats in the street during a foggy, icy November. Coward felt insecure about his performance; he looked to his leading lady for support, and they thrashed out the problems, wrapped in coats on an empty stage.

But a much more serious threat to curtain-up came from the Lord Chamberlain's office. *The Vortex* addressed contentious issues, and Coward must have expected trouble. The most obvious cause for complaint was Nicky's drug addiction, yet the stage portrayal of drug-taking was, as plays written after Billie Carleton's death indicate,

* She did, however, rejoin it on tour in April 1925, once the play had proved successful.

nothing new; Coward could have cited many precedents in his defence. But it was not Nicky's coke habit that aroused the ire of the righteous. George Street's report on the play did not at first suggest any real problems: 'Mr Coward has been known so far as a writer of light comedy and revue, but the theme of this play is grimly serious – and painful in an extreme degree. Until the end, however, the atmosphere is that of frivolous people who speak in a tiresome jargon – everything is "too divine", etc – and attempt wit with rather poor results . . . A scene in which a son upbraids a mother with her unchastity cannot be other than painful and in a way shocking, but I do not think it is of a nature to make it necessary to ban the play. The author might plead *Hamlet* as an example. The son is in deadly earnest to save them both and I think this tides one over the unpleasantness. The motive of the play is a good one and there are certainly people like Florence Lancaster whom it would do good to see how they look to an observer . . . Apart from this more serious question there are a couple of trifles in the dialogue which I have marked. 1) Act I . . . a sentence which suggests Lesbianism; it has nothing to do with the play, however; and 2) Act II, page 13 "Byes" apparently means bed and the sentence, if so, is too frank . . .'*

Apart from these minor alterations, Street saw no reason why the play should not be licensed. But the Lord Chamberlain, Lord Cromer, wrote in reply that 'this sort of play is unfortunately the inevitable sequence to a play like *Our Betters*† by which it is evidently inspired. This picture of a frivolous and degenerate set of people gives a wholly false impression of Society life and to my mind the time has come to put a stop to the harmful influence of such pictures on the stage.'

The powers of the period took their moral duties seriously; later, the government made propaganda films for screening at cinemas, salutary lessons in the evils of extra-marital love. The Lord Chamberlain wrote, 'The scene in Act III of the drug-taking son upbraiding his mother for

---

* In the censor's playscript, red pencil [italicised here] underscores Florence's speech in which she answers a telephone call from a friend: '*Inez* don't be angry, if you only knew how I longed for the sound of your wonderful wonderful voice . . . darling . . . *in my heart better than anyone else* . . . .Oh that's Tom Veryan, he's only a boy . . . Inez don't be cruel, of course I love you . . . tomorrow then . . .' The disputed line in Act Two was also underlined in red: 'Nicky: I think I am really but it's strange, *I don't want to "Byes" with Bunty a bit*, it's not that sort of being in love.'

† Maugham's play ran from September 1923 until January 1925. It was suggested by stories his wife Syrie had told him about her affairs, and about the American store magnate Gordon Selfridge, who had offered to settle £5000 a year on her. The play caused a great scandal, although it got past the censors.

the immoral conduct of her life is revolting in the last degree and it is no palliation to the story that the play ends with both mother and son making vows to give up their evil habits ... I am inclined to ban this play entirely, but before definite decision I should be grateful for the opinions of the Advisory Board.'

That Board included Sir Douglas Dawson, a long-serving comptroller with highly conservative views, in whose opinion *The Vortex* was 'a piece calculated to convey the worst possible impression of the social conditions under which we live today'. But another member, H. H. Higgins, a solicitor, while disliking the play, wrote, 'I cannot help feeling that if its surroundings were those of squalid poverty – if it were an "East End" – there would be no question of refusing it a licence'; thereby raising questions of hypocrisy. A third member of the Board, Lord Buckmaster, wrote on the subject of censorship of plays in general, which was, 'apart from the criminal law, the last control that remains over the liberty of free publication. It is I think a valuable right but its exercise must be capable of justification on ascertained principles.' Buckmaster agreed that Mayfair society could not 'claim immunity against the publication of even extreme views of their conduct unless the same immunity is granted to all classes. No one has ever protested against plays disclosing brutalised behaviour on the part of the poor ...'

Dawson maintained 'that no matter whether a scene is laid in Mayfair or Whitechapel, objection would, or certainly *should*, be taken to 1) a son upbraiding his mother for her adulterous past, or 2) a stepdaughter reciprocating the filthy advances of her stepfather ...' Not only did *The Vortex* assail the moral welfare of the nation, it posed a threat to its peaceable existence. 'Lord B considers the Board entitled to recommend refusal of licence to a play calculated to "promote public disorder" – I hold that any play liable to foster class hatred comes within the scope of his contention.'

So, rather than drugs, it was sex and class which aroused opposition to *The Vortex*; Coward was playing with issues close to the Establishment, whose rules could not lightly be flouted. The idea of an older woman taking a younger man as a lover was a pertinent contemporary social issue. Many women had lost husbands and lovers in the war, and there was a shortage of men; it was natural that men of Coward's age, just too young to have been killed in the trenches, should become the focus of amatory attention. This was a problem of which the great and the good were well aware, and it was their duty to see that Coward did not make matters worse.

With such powerful opposition from St James's Palace, it would have been understandable if Noel had conceded defeat. But this was a challenge he had to meet, and he decided to see Lord Cromer and argue his case in person. It was an extraordinary meeting, that of impetuous youth and sage lord: Coward acted out extracts of the play to show that *The Vortex* was 'little more than a moral tract'; that the opinions of Buckmaster and Higgins were justified. Silver-tongued as ever, Noel converted Cromer ('charming and sympathetic' as he turned out to be) and on 21 November – four days before it was due to open – *The Vortex* was granted its licence.*

As opening night drew near, excitement and anticipation rose; even the last-minute hitches, the threat of censorship and the limitations of resources seemed to indicate that something important was happening. On the night, despite the 'sickening silence' that greeted curtain-up, there was 'a certain feeling of expectancy in the air, an acceptance almost that the play would be a success'. Almost unconscious of what was going on around him, Coward gave 'one of [his] most effective, nerve-strung, *tour-de-force* performances, technically unstable, but vital enough to sweep people into enthusiasm'.

This spirit communicated itself to the audience. Enthralled by the applause, Coward ignored the slit vein in his wrist, cut when he swept the dressing-table clean of its bottles in the last act. Heroically bound, he took his bows as his friends stood to cheer his play, and came offstage to be greeted by Michael Arlen: 'I'd be so proud, so *very* proud if I had written it.' Coward recalled driving south into town that night and turning to Gladys to say, 'And now what?' Adulation, perhaps. Sibyl Colefax and Syrie Maugham, rival hostesses, both claimed to have thrown the after-play party; indeed, so many claimed to have been at the legendary first performance that there could hardly have been anyone left to go to the second night. *The Vortex* became, overnight, the most sought-after ticket in town.

Crucially, it had succeeded in interpreting the *Zeitgeist*. As the Lord Chamberlain's correspondence pointed out, the play held a mirror to contemporary society, the same society which now flocked to the Everyman Theatre. Sir Anthony Havelock-Allan saw *The Vortex*, and

---

* It was a narrow escape. A day or so previous, the correspondence had been sent to the king. Lord Stamfordham, the king's private secretary, wrote, 'The King has read the papers and says evidently it is a disgusting play but, unfortunately, cannot be prohibited.'

found it 'very exciting', as well as accurate: 'Among the smart rich people, the café society, everybody took drugs . . . it was very prevalent in the theatre. It was an English version of what happened in Paris after the war, when very rich American women came to find the gay life, and many had boyfriends young enough to be their sons . . . That was the world after the horror of the First World War, frenetic gaiety, stimulated and hopped-up with drink and drugs . . . They were part of his world, those people. I don't think for a moment that he indulged in any of those things, because he was far too certain where he was going to go. But he certainly had friends who did . . .' Jeffrey Amherst recalled 'cocaine on the table' in clubs and at Tallulah Bankhead's parties in Chelsea, at which one of her friends complained, 'I'm sick and tired of Tallulah's parties. Every morning they run out of cocaine, and it's me who's sent down to Limehouse to get some more!'

Critical reaction obliged by focusing on the 'cocktail-drinking, decadence and general smart-settishness of the play', which was excellent news for the box office. On cue, the ire of the older generation arose, and Gerald du Maurier exploded. 'The public are asking for filth . . . the younger generation are knocking at the door of the dustbin . . . if life is worse than the stage, should the stage hold up the mirror to such distorted nature? If so, where shall we be – without reticence or reverence?'

It was an argument to be rehearsed throughout the history of twentieth-century drama. Coward replied without equivocation, 'Sir Gerald du Maurier, having – if he will forgive me saying so – enthusiastically showered the English stage with second-rate drama for many years, now rises up with incredible violence and has a nice slap all round at the earnest and perspiring dramatists. This is awful; it is also a little unwise. Art demands reverence much more than life does – and Sir Gerald's reverence so far seems to have been entirely devoted to the box-office.'

The actor-manager had a suspiciously violent dislike of homosexuals. Robert Flemyng recalled that 'when I was young, there were John [Gielgud] and Ivor and Noel leading the theatre, all of them gay, and the old boys, like du Maurier, who probably should have been gay – he was a very effeminate man – but of course he wasn't and was consequently violently anti-gay . . . Du Maurier sent for Charles Laughton and asked if he was a bugger, and Laughton said no. Du Maurier wouldn't have had him in the theatre if he'd known the truth.' Mrs Astley Cooper also knew du Maurier: 'I suggested, before Noel Coward was famous, that Gerald should be nice to him, he did not respond to my suggestion, but I heard in later years that he wished so much he could act in one of Noel's plays. Gerald seldom had good plays latterly . . .'

Such furore contributed to the legendary status the play would achieve, and Coward did little to explode the myth. He seized the chance to propel himself to the heights of celebrity, an ascent which the growing media readily facilitated. The effect *The Vortex* had on the privileged youth of the time is found in many contemporary accounts. Cecil Beaton went to see the play (noting 'that flashy Godfrey Winn' in the audience), and wrote his diary on New Year's Eve 1924 with youthful acerbity: 'Even tho' I knew I had to pay 12/- for a seat – it's the one play I want to see . . . I enjoyed [it] tremendously. I thought that the first act was amusing but very ordinary – it's so easy to write those flashy remarks that are not absolutely brilliant.' Lilian Braithwaite was 'extraordinarily good. Generally I loathe her quiet reserved manner but in this she takes the part of a middle-aged woman whose pose is very modern & says that everything is "just too marvellous" & "too too *marvellous*" . . . the last act is very good. It is clever of Noel Coward to write a play like that. I didn't think it was as brilliant as most people said but it is very good . . .'

Another young witness was Braithwaite's daughter, the young actress Joyce Carey. She had gone to a dress rehearsal, and was 'literally shaking with excitement' afterwards. 'I wasn't encouraged as a rule to give my ideas on things', she recalled, 'but I flew down and, very articulate, I did the opposite of Cassandra and said, "It's all wonderful, and you'll have a huge success. You'll move at once to the West End and run for ever," which indeed it did.' Just a year older than Coward, Carey became, like Lorn and Gladys, an integral member of his 'family'. She had worked regularly on the West End stage since 1916, in Shakespeare and Shaw, and proved a perfect interpreter of Coward's work, appearing in *Easy Virtue* in 1925 (although she did not appear in another until Alison Leggatt fell ill during the run of *Tonight at 8.30* in 1936). Joyce's twinkling eyes indicated mischief and a passionate nature. Her tremulous, aristocratic voice – her mother's legacy – and her hauteur could take a swift dive into well-chosen four-letter words, once enquiring of the elegant Margaret Lockwood during their favourite charade game, 'Darling, could it by any chance be "Take a flying fuck at a galloping mule?"' Coward appreciated her no-nonsense approach. She was a talented actress and writer, although her successes were never as great as they might have been; she submitted to what she regarded as the greater talents of others, Coward's most especially. Their relationship was lifelong, born of devotion, perhaps even love, as his portrait of Carey as Liz Essendine, the playwright's estranged but devoted wife in *Present Laughter*, bore witness.

Carey's presumptuous prediction came true; *The Vortex* was Coward's first 'big moment . . . We were all right, more than all right. We were a smash hit.' The play transferred to the West End, opening at the Royalty on his birthday, 16 December 1924. John Gielgud was suggested as a suitable understudy because of his ability at the piano, and he was introduced to Coward backstage: '[His] room looked very glittering, with large bottles of eau-de-cologne on the wash-stand and an array of dressing-gowns hanging in the wardrobe. Noel was charming . . . He said it was a great relief to him to have someone reliable in the theatre, and that he would help me in any way he could . . .' Gielgud recalled that Coward used to arrive late at the theatre 'as his entrance . . . [was only] forty minutes after the rise of the curtain . . . I used to stand at the stage-door looking down the street with a stick of greasepaint in my hand, ready to rush off . . . and make up if he should fail to appear.'

The Vortex settled into its run, and Coward took to patronising the newly opened Gargoyle Club, close by in Meard Street, Soho. Run by David Tennant, it was the smart evening nightspot for the literary, artistic and aristocratic crowd with Bohemian tendencies: Nancy Cunard, Dick Wyndham and Iris Tree were all members. Its walls were decorated with mirrored tiles and Matisses, and its roof-top garden looked out over London's theatreland. It was the sort of place where rules were made to be broken, and every passion was indulged. After his performance, Coward and his crowd would drink and eat sausages and bacon, and listen to the dance band. Nearby was the Fifty-Fifty Club, run by Constance Collier and Ivor Novello, and catering 'exclusively to "Us"', meaning the theatre clique (although, given their prevalence, he could as easily have referred to its homosexual clientele).

Noel was everywhere in demand. Syrie Maugham announced in her high-pitched voice that the young Mr Coward would one day be spoken of in the same reverential tones as Wilde and Congreve. Acquaintances 'gummed strong affection to me like fly-paper and assumed tacit proprietary rights. "How does it feel", they cried, "to be a genius?"' An immodest reply was impossible, and Noel's customary self-deprecation, and a 'permanent blush' came into play. Yet he knew it was not due to luck; he had worked for it. 'The legend of my modesty grew and grew, I became extraordinarily unspoiled by my great success', he wrote in 1936. 'As a matter of fact, I still am.'

The success of *The Vortex* brought a notable improvement in Coward's material fortunes. At Ebury Street, as his star ascended, so he descended from attic to second and first floors. He had his sitting-room refurbished in chintz, and his bedroom painted scarlet, a modernist gesture he subsequently regretted. His rooms resembled a studio flat, newly fashionable as a residence for the town-dweller, a symbol of independence for the young. Gladys Calthrop (herself a studio dweller) added vivid murals 'out of the goodness of her heart and the deeps of her erotic imagination'.

Here Coward was photographed 'in bed wearing a Chinese dressing-gown and an expression of advanced degeneracy'. By his side were cigarettes and mysterious bottles; silk wraps were draped over the bed, and the playwright's head rested on a plump and voluptuous cushion. The apparently drug-induced stupor (he had blinked at the flashlight) was emblazoned across the *Sketch* with the caption, 'Noel the fortunate: the young playwright, actor, and composer, Mr Noel Coward, busy at breakfast', and produced protests from retired military men that these were the decadent poseurs who would be the downfall of the British Empire.

It was perfect publicity, stage-managed by Coward himself. 'I am never out of opium dens, cocaine dens, and other evil places', he told the *Evening Standard*. 'My mind is a mass of corruption.' It was true that he had taken to starting the day's business in bed, as Lorn Loraine brought him his breakfast every morning, with papers and the post. After his levee, Coward and Loraine reconvened in a room designated as their office, full of shelves and books. The filing system consisted of two files, marked 'Poppy' and 'Queen Anne' (the origin of these camp nicknames was not disclosed, although in *Present Laughter* a similar 'limbo' file is named 'Mount Pleasant', a reference to the sorting office of the Royal Mail in London). Another was labelled 'Shortly', into which they stuffed unanswered correspondence; after a month or so, three-quarters of the letters no longer needed reply.

Noel had defined himself within his immediate social group; in the greater world, his image also became familiar. *The Vortex* saw the debut of the dressing-gowned Noel Coward, symbol of the Jazz Age. The loose attire of a dressing gown – a Coward trademark – suggested loose living, but the actor-playwright insisted it was purely functional. 'If the part requires one, you couldn't keep me out of it, they're wonderful things to play in because they fall and because they're so comfortable to act in. And they've got swing...' The rest of his wardrobe also attracted attention. 'I took to wearing coloured turtle-necked jerseys ... more for comfort than for effect, and soon I was informed by my evening paper that I had started a fashion ... During the ensuing months I noticed more and more of our seedier West-End chorus boys parading about London in them.' Coward's taste for turtle-necks was paralleled by Oxbridge aesthetes, who wore flannel bags and high-necked jumpers. Like them, he also coveted silk shirts, pyjamas and underwear, and opened tailors' accounts accordingly, admitting later that such youthful exuberance left him 'still inclined to ruin a correct ensemble by some flashy error of taste'. In affecting anything other than the normal mode of masculine dress, Noel was opening himself to criticism. Those who knew about such matters whispered about his sexuality; those who did not, excused it as the garb of theatrical folk, who were 'different'. To the homosexual enclave within the theatre (and without), Noel became an icon. But his influence was not confined to those who shared his sexual tastes; as Cecil Beaton noted, 'all sorts of men suddenly wanted to look like Noel Coward – sleek and satiny, clipped and well groomed, with a cigarette, a tele-phone, or a cocktail at hand'.

Countless publications reproduced photographs from *The Vortex*, and Coward's seal-sleek head and well-tailored body began to acquire its own commercial value, an image diffused through the media; popular culture ensured that the Coward style was as well known in Manchester as it was in Mayfair. He was used, as much as he used; for the first time since Oscar Wilde, a writer's appearance seemed as important as what he wrote. Those fans who had followed him since *The Young Idea* now affected the silk socks and polo necks of their idol, still behaving noisily and relishing each new 'Noelism', which then became *de rigueur* slang. A later friend, Ginette Spanier, recalled that *The Vortex* 'started a whole new form of conversation – until November 1924 nobody called anyone "Darling" except as a declaration of love'.

But the precise, bullet-like delivery turned effeminate utterances into aural offensives; a Gatling gun of verbal rounds. Coward's clipped speech was a chic new dialect. His voice became as identifiable as his face, and imitators of his fluting, chopped-up stutter tried to reproduce his tones; the speech pattern went with the times. It became smart to say 'madly' and 'divine', and to 'clip one's speech as one turned one's toes in'.

The Coward persona was actually subversive. 'In ... the whole new spirit of affectation and frivolity', wrote Cecil Beaton, 'the influence of the theatre was far from negligible ... It became a fad to talk with equal authority on specialised subjects as well as on frivolous ones, to mingle cocktail chatter about great personages and events in history with jazz slang ... Men enjoyed imitating the exaggerated, clipped manner of certain leading actors and adopted the confident manner of those who are aware of their charms ... Noel Coward's influence spread even to the outposts of Rickmansworth and Poona. Hearty naval commanders or jolly colonels acquired the "camp" manners of calling everything from Joan of Arc to Merlin "lots of fun", and the adjective "terribly" peppered every sentence.'

But Coward's stance remained one of critical equivocation. He had been through a rebellious period when Esme and he were in their late teens, and it was due to his experience of earlier years that Coward could become a spokesman for a generation. He seized the chance: that Noel Coward became 'Noel Coward' overnight was as much an invention as was the idea that *The Vortex* broke dramatic taboos. By making it appear so, Coward had created himself.

9

Society's Hero

And then, there was the sound of laughter outside, and in walked
Noel Coward, and whenever Noel walks into a room the spotlights
automatically switch towards him.

Beverley Nichols, *A Case of Human Bondage*

ONE showman encapsulated the great rush of modernity within
the theatrical world of the 1920s: C. B. Cochran. His revues
combined the influences of the Russian Ballet, jazz and Holly-
wood-style glamour to dazzling effect. Always willing to take risks with
new talent, Cochran had been following Coward's career, and after
seeing him in *The Knight of the Burning Pestle* and *The Young Idea*,
had asked Noel to contribute to a revue on which Ronald Jeans was
working, only to discover that Coward was working for his rival,
Charlot.

At the height of *The Vortex*'s success, Cochran invited Coward to his
Old Bond Street office to discuss the idea of a revue. Cochran wanted
Noel to write the book, but Coward demanded that he be allowed to
write the score too; Cochran usually played writers against each other,
partly as insurance of good material. According to Cochran, Noel
pleaded to be allowed to do the revue, but he had his doubts about
Coward's ability to compose music. 'Don't try to do too much', he
advised. 'Your dialogue is good and you write excellent sketches. Stick
to what you know.' Telling Noel that he would engage Philip Braham
as composer, Cochran sent him off to write sketches and burlesques
for the revue, which was to be called *On with the Dance*. However, 'governed either by his subconscious will or a deliberately oppor-
tunist motive', Cochran observed, 'he contrived his sketches in such
a way that they evolved quite naturally towards a musical finish'.
When the revue was completed, it was discovered – to everyone's

embarrassment but his own – that the majority of the words and music were Noel's.

A cast was assembled: Alice Delysia; Douglas Byng, quirky comic and camp female impersonator; Ernest Thesiger, another effeminate character actor renowned for his needlework; Hermione Baddeley, chorus girl about to turn actress; and Nigel Bruce, young and good-looking and a rising star. Roger Quilter, who had written the music for *Where the Rainbow Ends*, wrote a Hogarthian sketch, 'The Rake', which, together with other scenes, was to be choreographed by Leonide Massine. Other numbers included 'Fête Galante'; a vicarage garden party, complete with scouts and choirboys; and a risqué song entitled 'Even Clergymen are Naughty Now and Then', sung by Byng (as the vicar) and Thesiger (the curate).

Coward, still appearing in *The Vortex*, handed over to his understudy, John Gielgud. The three days of final rehearsal before the revue opened in Manchester were hectic, and riven by personality clashes between author and producer. Coward discovered his name was not on the playbills, which led to a full-frontal verbal assault on Cochran in his bathroom, who was clad only in a towel. But the producer 'retained his dignity magnificently'; praising Coward's genius and complimenting him on his contribution, he hitched up the towel 'which had begun to sag around his prominent middle', and invited 'dear Noel' to take sherry with him in his sitting-room, where they amicably discussed the triumph of the revue.

They also argued over a song Cochran considered below standard. Coward fought, supported by Alice Delysia, and 'Poor Little Rich Girl' stayed, with Delysia as a French maid warning her mistress, Hermione Baddeley, of the perils of her debauched life.* It became Coward's first hit, an anthem for the world-weary 1920s:

> Cocktails and laughter
> But what comes after?
> Nobody knows.
> You're weaving love into a mad jazz pattern,
> Ruled by Pantaloon.
> Poor little rich girl, don't drop a stitch too soon.

---

* When he traitorously suggested that Gertrude Lawrence might sing it in New York, Delysia lost her temper. ' "Noel", she screamed with excellent command of . . . idiom if not of accent, "is a sheet and a boogairr." '

On with the Dance opened at the Palace Theatre on St Patrick's Day 1925. Spontaneous applause and cheering greeted various numbers, the culmination being a curtain call for Cochran, Coward and the company, and some highly satisfactory press coverage the next day, with Delysia ('Continental rages' forgiven) acclaimed as the star. The revue ran for a gratifying 229 performances in London, where the *Morning Post* acclaimed this 'decadent and brilliant' show. 'As befits Mr Coward's genius, many of the incidents are as Nature seen through a glass crookedly, and when we see some normal little typical revue duet-dance face to face, it seems positively dull – an effort to restore the company to a state of mental balance. Those arid, futile people that Mr Coward puts into plays dash about the stage, worked into a frenzy by the syncopated music.' It was an entertainment built for its time, 'bizarre, preposterous', and magnificent.

The pace of Coward's characters was reflected in the momentum of his career. *Fallen Angels* was in rehearsal, with Edna Best and Tallulah Bankhead. The mercurial Bankhead, who had been rejected by Maugham for the leading role in *Rain*,* was a last-minute replacement for Margaret Bannerman. Arriving at rehearsals, she 'tore off her hat, flipped her furs into a corner, kissed Edna, Stanley [Bell, the producer] and me and anyone else who happened to be within reach and ... embarked on the first act. In two days she knew the part perfectly.' Her subsequent performances were less convincing, however. Jeffrey Amherst claims that she was nicknamed 'Bellulah Blockhead. What a bore she was! She could have been a great star. But she could give a wonderful performance on Monday and a disgraceful performance on Tuesday. You never knew what the hell she would do. She had no discipline at all, and consequently she was totally unreliable.' After *Fallen Angels*, 'Noel said never again would she work for him. She would do the most awful things in the theatre. She'd put in her own lines, doing the splits, whatever you like!' Whatever Bankhead's misdemeanours, Coward recorded 'no sense of struggle' between the two leading ladies, as might have been expected. The struggle, as before, came from outside.

Fallen Angels concerns two young women – Julia Sterroll and Jane

---

* Basil Dean had cast Bankhead, but Maugham disliked her in the role. Tallulah went home and made a half-hearted suicide bid with a handful of aspirins, leaving a note: 'It ain't goin' to rain no mo''.' On the opening night of *Fallen Angels* she changed Coward's line 'Oh dear, rain' to 'My God, RAIN!', which the audience found hilarious.

'Captain' Henry
Gordon Veitch, RN:
Noel's maternal
grandfather

Mary Kathleen Veitch:
Noel's maternal
grandmother

Noel in
nautical mood,
aged five years:
photographed on
8 October 1904

Family album

Arthur Sabin Coward

Violet Agnes Coward

5 Waldegrave Road (now No. 131),
Teddington: Noel's birthplace

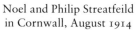

Noel sketched by
Philip Streatfeild, 1914

Noel and Philip Streatfeild
in Cornwall, August 1914

Noel at Aunt Laura's,
Charlestown, Cornwall, 1907

The Great Name: Noel, Lydia Bilbrooke, Charles Hawtrey: "He was inclined to be cheeky, and often made himself unpopular."

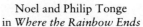

Noel and Philip Tonge in *Where the Rainbow Ends*

Noel and Lillian Gish in *Hearts of the World* (June 1917)

Centre right John Ekins, Esme Wynne and Noel

The Knight of the Burning Pestle

Rare photograph of Mrs Astley Cooper (centre), with Noel (lower right) and house party at Hambleton Hall

Noel in the Med

Coney Island, 1921: Teddie Gerrard and her 'suitors', Noel, Jeffrey Amherst and Napier Alington. The significance of the gesture remains mysterious

Davos, Christmas 1922

Benita Hume, Ivor Novello, Mabel Poulton and Frances Doble on location for *The Constant Nymph* at Achensee in the Austrian Tyrol

Douglas Fairbanks, Mary Pickford and Noel, a shipboard photocall

An exuberant Noel at Ivor Novello's Red Roofs

Coney Island, 1925: Gladys Calthrop, Noel, Bobbie Andrews and friends

Noel and Lilian Braithwaite:
the final scene from *The Vortex*

The *Sketch*

No. 1683 — Vol. CXXX.   WEDNESDAY, APRIL 29, 1925.   ONE SHILLING.

NOEL THE FORTUNATE: THE YOUNG PLAYWRIGHT, ACTOR, AND COMPOSER, MR. NOEL COWARD,
BUSY AT BREAKFAST.

'Noel the fortunate':
the front page of
the *Sketch*, 1925

Noel and Edna Best:
the final scene from
The Constant Nymph

In
conference
with
C. B. Cochran

Carqueiranne, South of France: unknown,
Gladys Henson, Noel and Ivy St Helier

Lilian Braithwaite,
Ivor Novello and Binkie Beaumont

John Gielgud   *Celebrity status*

Goldenhurst Farm: Noel's arm is on Gladys Calthrop's shoulder; Beatrice Lillie below,
G. B. Stern on far right

Violet, Noel and Aunt Vida
at Goldenhurst

Mad Dogs and Englishmen:
Far East tour, 1930

As Stanhope in *Journey's End*, Singapore:
the breakdowns of the recent past do not
seem far away; *Post-Mortem* followed

Erik Coward
on holiday in Norfolk

Home and away

Banbury – who had both been lovers of a Frenchman named Maurice Duclos; now married, they await his return nervously, and get drunk as they do. (According to some reports, the scenario was based on a real-life episode, when Noel and Gladys were both dressed up waiting for a mutual boyfriend to arrive.) Both admit to having made love with Maurice before their marriages, an outrageous admission for the time. Predictably, the censor's reaction was hostile. Refusing the play a licence, Street reported that it was 'brightly written but extremely dubious', and that the lightness with which the subject of adultery 'both about the women's obvious willingness to go wrong and about their pre-nuptial going wrong – would cause too great a scandal'. Lord Cromer disagreed, and wrote from Portofino, where he was holidaying, '. . . I take the view that the whole thing is so much unreal farcical comedy, that subject to a few modifications in the dialogue it can pass . . .'

Fallen Angels opened at the Globe Theatre on 21 April 1925. Happily, Bankhead gave a 'brilliant and completely assured perform-ance, a *tour-de-force* of vitality, magnetism and spontaneous combus-tion'. *Punch* could not remember 'a better piece of stage-craft in this type of play since Mr Maugham's *Home and Beauty*' (again Coward's work was being compared to his older rival's), but the majority of the critics found it 'vulgar, disgusting, shocking, nauseating, vile, obscene, degenerate. The *Daily Express* even went so far as to allude to these two wayward creatures as "suburban sluts".'

Good for the box office, the scandal also unleashed 'a mass of insulting letters' about the playwright, with the occasional pornographic drawing. Bishops protested, and the London Council for the Promotion of Public Morality lobbied the Lord Chamberlain to withdraw the play's licence, observing that its characters 'work themselves up into a state of hysteria in anticipation of sexual intercourse with a man with whom they have had immoral relations before marriage, and hope to do so again during the absence of respective husbands . . . The whole is a revolting sex-play and has not the redeeming feature of containing a moral lesson.' On 29 August, the last night of the run, Mrs Charles Hornibrook, a rogue public protester repudiated even by the Council for the Promotion of Public Morality, stood up during the second act: 'Ladies and Gentlemen, I wish to protest. This play should not go unchallenged.' The orchestra struck up 'I Want to Be Happy' as the hapless Mrs Hornibrook was escorted out.

Coward's public profile was higher than ever. 'Poor Little Rich Girl' was being sung or played on gramophones everywhere, and he went to 'too many parties and met too many people'. *The Vortex*, meanwhile, had transferred from the Royalty to the Comedy Theatre; Noel wrote to Basil Dean on 28 February, 'On Monday week we all rush enthusiastically into the arms of Sir Alfred Butt at the Comedy, who will fondle us lovingly until our receipts drop below £200 a week.' As they did; after that, the play moved to the Little Theatre, where it could 'jog along for ages to adequate business'.

Plans were hatched to take it to America. Coward told Dean he thought 'an English cast ... extremely valuable to the play', but the producer pointed out that this was an expensive luxury. In which case, conceded the playwright, 'I think it should be entirely American with the exception of myself.' He added, 'I've got a quite splendid idea for the new play which I shall be starting in a week or two. Will you cable me your opinion of "Still Life" [as *Hay Fever* was then known], as I have had a tentative offer for it ...' But that May, the New World assumed a more personal importance for Noel. During a performance of *The Vortex* in London a young man appeared in the front row of the stalls wearing a turned-down collar on his evening shirt (from which sartorial detail Noel deduced the man's nationality), who applauded loudly after the performance. A few days later a mutual friend introduced John C. Wilson to Noel in his dressing-room.

Coward's future lover 'walked nervously and with slightly overdone truculence, into my life'. After a drink and a chat, Wilson left, having invited Noel to lunch when he came to the States. Coward and Calthrop agreed that the man was 'amiable enough but rather uppish'. Arrogant he may have been, but John Chapman Wilson had impeccable credentials; a square-jawed Ivy Leaguer straight out of a Scott Fitzgerald novel. A few months older than Noel, he was the son of James J. Wilson and Mary Wilson, born in Trenton, New Jersey, an inauspicious beginning which Noel liked to compare to his own modest roots. However, Wilson had been educated at Andover Academy, where he had been an active member of the Drama Club, and at Yale, where, under the influence of Monty Woolley, the ebullient professor and actor, his interest in the theatre grew. He also knew the playwright Thornton Wilder there, and Stephen Vincent Benét, the poet. Besides such literary connexions, he had proved his athletic ability on the running track. After graduating in 1921, Wilson was steered by his father to Wall Street, where he had spent four reluctant years studying stocks and bonds and selling securities. His interest in the theatre was sustained by his membership of the Amateur Comedy Club, and he eventually gave up Wall Street to tour in a production of *Polly Preferred*. Returning to Broadway with high expectations, he found no theatre work, and was forced to return to finance.

Wilson subsequently worked for three months as 'assistant director' at Paramount's Astoria studio on Long Island, on little-known films such as *The Swan* and *Man Must Live*, then went to Europe to write screenplays. He spent six months in Sicily, working on some forty scenarios without much success, and was en route for New York when he met Coward. Wilson was an undeniably handsome man, reminiscent of a young, less muscled, Marlon Brando. Joyce Carey remembered his 'shiny black hair and beautiful brown eyes ... very well dressed and very charming altogether'. Wilson was typical of the sort of man to whom Coward was attracted: masculine, assertive, athletic and elegant.

Noel's sexual life had until now been characterised by speculative encounters or frustating obsessions. His friendship with Jeffrey Amherst remained apparently platonic, while dalliances with the likes of Bobbie Andrews were intermittent. Photographs of house parties at Ivor Novello's country home, Red Roofs, near Maidenhead, show a succession of elegant young men in bathing suits, the equivalent of chorus girls, attracted by the glamour of Novello and his crowd, Coward among them. He undoubtedly had a number of youthful affairs with such young men, but the romantic in him yearned for something more. In his memoirs, Coward infers that at the time the encounter with Wilson left only a lingering impression. He could not write of the attraction he felt for the American; even less could he admit that, within a few short weeks, he had fallen in love with Jack Wilson.

It is a measure of Coward's growing popularity that within the space of twelve months, *The Vortex*, *Fallen Angels* and his Cochran revue were followed by the production of *Hay Fever*. Having been rejected by Basil Dean, it was taken up by Alban Limpus and Charles Kenyon for Marie Tempest, one of the brightest stage stars of the time. Tempest professed not only to be delighted with the rewritten script but asked Coward to produce the play. She knew a rising star when she saw one.

Hay Fever is an everyday story of theatrical folk, a comedy of appalling manners. The Blisses are amoral, Bohemian and misguided: 'We none of us ever mean *anything*', says Sorel Bliss in a burst of self-enlightenment. The mother, Judith Bliss, is a great comic creation, and much of *Hay Fever*'s humour derives from the fact that an actor is writing about actors. Planning a comeback, Judith's expectations of her notices are funnier because the audience attaches them to the play they are watching: 'The satisfied grunt of the *Daily Mail*, the abandoned gurgle of the *Sunday Times*, and the shrill, enthusiastic scream of the *Daily Express*!' exclaims Judith. 'I can distinguish them all . . .'

Again Coward held up a mirror, not only to the theatre but to the society he lived in. The age sought to avoid boredom as if it were a contagious disease (to Coward, it was a fatal malady) and the Blisses of *Hay Fever* fall over themselves not to be bored. They assemble a tangle of weekend guests, whom they subsequently ignore. As Cecil Beaton observed, 'in certain circles it was considered smart to be rude. A number of wealthy debutantes became very aggressive, played practical jokes, and spoke their private language of eggy-peggy (pig Latin) in front of those . . . not . . . allowed into their exclusive circle.' Yet the cynical selfishness of these egotists is redeemed by brilliant wit, in scenes of near anarchy. It was as though Coward had come upon a 'real' (and clever) family and given them a script to perform, introducing other characters as the charade unfolds. Coward's lack of seriousness is here dramatised, his flippant, devil-may-care view of life a protest against the solemnity of his elders and betters (discredited by the mistakes of the Great War). In *Hay Fever*, the Bliss family use words to browbeat their guests and subordinate them to the family's 'feather bed of false emotions'. But what is Coward saying? That life is facile and fleeting and artificiality is all? The joy of *Hay Fever* in particular, and of Coward's work in general, is that we do not know.

Coward doubted the value of his piece, which he had written in just three days; he looked it over, and found no witty epigrams. 'I think the reason for this was that I was passing through a transition stage as a writer, my dialogue was becoming more natural and less elaborate . . .' The comedy now lay in situation and emphasis, a fact proved, forty years later, when Maggie Smith, as Myra Arundel, extracted Orton-esque humour out of the breakfast scene line, 'This haddock is disgusting.' (Likewise, in *Design for Living*, Leo ponders the ridiculousness of the word 'haddock'). In rehearsals, Tempest took Coward in hand, insisting he play scenes for her: 'You wrote it and you know, I didn't write it and don't!' Noel dutifully played Judith with the fey flourish the character required.

The Lord Chamberlain, who, for a fee of two guineas, granted *Hay Fever* a licence on 4 June 1925, had few reservations about the play. But various actor friends thought that *Hay Fever*, with its in-jokes and histrionic subtexts, was 'fundamentally too theatrical in flavour and too thin in plot ever to be a success with the public'. Edward Marsh, critic and friend of Novello's, said patronisingly, 'Not this time, Noel. Not this time.' *Hay Fever* ran for a year, 'to excellent business'.

Noel celebrated by holidaying in Spain, apparently alone. In Barcelona he saw his 'first and last bullfight. I was fortunate enough to secure a seat in the front row – and it was all too lovely. I saw fine horses gored to death and three bulls baited and finally murdered all in the course of a half an hour after which I left charmed and awed by the sportsmanship and refinement of the Spanish nation.' He moved to the Balearic Isles, and wrote to Basil Dean, 'I'm sitting on the patio of my hacienda. It is on the side of a mountain with miles of olives stretching down to the sea – and there are coloured houses dotted about like pieces of sugar in a green cake, and palm trees and bougainvilleas ... Oh dear I *do hate* being a successful dramatist – and why oh why do I write unpleasant plays. It seems so unfair that all the good sincere and honest failures ... should have to stay in London! I must think of something really lascivious to get me a longer holiday next year!' The culmination of Coward's *annus mirabilis* was to take his success across the Atlantic.

The Vortex closed in London on 16 June. G. B. Stern arrived from Italy in time for the final performance. 'I'd also like to see just *one* play which isn't by Himself (that phenomenol [sic] Mr Noel Coward)', she told Esme Wynne-Tyson. 'They say there is one at the Upper Clapham Theatre Royal ...'

It was evident that Coward was looking to the New World for future triumphs; perhaps his private life lay there too. Stern reported that 'Noel talks of going to America, to make a little home (grey – the West) for us all. He says England's played out.' She claimed that his dissatisfaction seemed to have taken an extreme if exuberant form, 'I heard a rumour that he spent a night in gaol, recently, for throwing flower-boxes about in the streets of the West End ... Our wee one must really *not* behave like an Undergraduate in Eights – whatever they may be!' This brush with the police, which may have frightened Coward (homosexuals being easy targets), made him all the more eager to get out of England. He had previously promised Violet a holiday in Paris, where he had planned to buy a flat; he now proposed she should go with him and Gladys Calthrop to New York.

They sailed in August on the SS *Majestic*, 'a gay, nervous voyage and far from peaceful'; Noel, Violet and Gladys were joined for meals by

Basil Dean, Lilian Braithwaite and Leslie Howard, the suave British actor who was 'vague and amiable and spread his own particular brand of elusive charm over every gathering'. Mercedes de Acosta and Eva Le Gallienne were also on board. Coward had met both women on his last visit to New York, when de Acosta found him 'touchingly poor, charmingly unsure of himself, refreshingly unknown and beguilingly insecure . . .' As in London (where their preponderance was supposedly due to the lack of eligible men post-war), Noel's female acquaintance in Manhattan encompassed an inordinate number of lesbians – an entire social network of their own.

De Acosta was half-Spanish, dark-haired and often dressed in a tricorne hat and highwayman's cape. Poet, playwright and later screen-writer, she espoused, and practised, free love; Greta Garbo and Marlene Dietrich were among her later conquests. She and Le Gallienne had fallen in love shortly after de Acosta's marriage to Abram Poole in 1920, and were returning from Paris, where Le Gallienne had appeared naked in de Acosta's *Sandro Botticelli*, and triumphantly in her *Jehanne d'Arc*. But their relationship was on the point of breaking up. To Noel, the two women 'alternated between intellectual gloom and feverish gaiety and wore black, indiscriminately, for both moods'. Gladys gravitated to their company and, according to Dickie Fellowes-Gordon, was openly wooed by Le Gallienne, much to Coward's amusement; by the time Dickie arrived in New York, 'Gladys Calthrop had gone off with Mercedes de Acosta's girlfriend . . . Noel shook his head and said "There'll be trouble now!"' Patrick Woodcock recalled Coward's attitude to lesbians: 'He didn't like their lack of ironic humour. Eva Le Gallienne was dancing with him on the *Majestic* . . . and she said to Noel "I think I'm taking away your Gladys" and Noel absolutely peed himself because it was so idiotic and typically humourless.'

This Bohemian boatload arrived in New York on 18 August. Noel was in high spirits, and told a reporter from the *New York Times* of his first visit to the country: 'I hadn't got a "bob", a quarter, to my name then, but I was glad that I did it because I learned a lot. I found out what "pep" meant and have tried to instil it into my London companions, but I am not sure how well I have succeeded.'

Noel, Violet and Gladys moved into the Plaza Hotel for a few days, then to an apartment ('dainty to the point of nausea') on East 54th Street, which Violet was left to organise. Rehearsals got under way for *The Vortex*, with Coward and Calthrop sweltering in the heat of high summer. An immediate obstacle was Abe Erlanger who, with Charles

Dillingham, was to present the play. He demanded that Noel rewrite
the last scene, explaining that no American could bear such a travesty
of mother-love. Memories of *The Vortex*'s rough ride to eventual
production – and acclaim – in England made this 'theatrical magnate,
soggy with commercial enterprise', very annoying indeed. Coward said
he would board the next ship home rather than rewrite his play, and
announced that the producers were barred from rehearsals. Basil Dean
and Dillingham followed Coward out of the office, pleading that, with
tact, Erlanger was quite manageable. 'I replied that I had not travelled
three thousand miles to manage Mr Erlanger, but for him to manage
me, and left them to go back to the office and be as tactful as they
liked.'

The result was that Dillingham and Erlanger gave up the production,
and Sam Harris and Irving Berlin stepped in, together with Joseph P.
Bickerton Jnr (a well-known theatrical lawyer and sometime lover of
Mercedes de Acosta). The Henry Miller Theatre was acquired and
Gladys Calthrop set off to trawl Greenwich Village street markets for
props. In the first week of rehearsals, Coward received the promised
lunch invitation from Jack Wilson. 'Flushed with pride at having even
remembered his name', Noel dictated a reply, 'and waited, in a
mounting rage, for three-quarters of an hour on the day specified . . .' It
transpired that his secretary had not posted the letter.

The Vortex opened in Washington in mid-September heat, but gener-
ated only a lukewarm response. There was a thunderstorm on the first
night, which seemed a bad omen, reinforced by a farcical scene when
Florence threw Nicky's box of cocaine out of the window and a passing
stagehand caught it and threw it back. Returning to New York having
taken just $6000, Coward and company prepared for the worst. They
opened on 16 September: 'Never before or since in all my experience
have I received such a direct personal stimulus from an audience', wrote
Coward. He felt he had delivered the best performance of his life.

The press agreed that Coward received 'the biggest ovation any
visiting player has received on Broadway in years'. The 'fine audience,
in its entirety, remained in its place until, after curtain calls we forgot
to count, the succession of responses on the stage had given place to the
single response of Noel Coward . . .' 'Brilliantly acted', wrote Alexander
Woollcott in the *New York World*; 'a good, thrilling, glib and seriously
amusing play', said Percy Hammond in the *Tribune*. The notices
confirmed what the audience had so vociferously indicated: *The Vortex*

was a hit on their side of the Atlantic too. Joseph Bickerton threw a
first-night party at the Embassy Club, where Broadway stars gathered
to 'honour young Mr Coward'. Ethel Barrymore, Michael Arlen and
the Lunts were followed by the arrival of Coward's glamorous new
friend, Lady Diana Cooper.

Although tickets were soon exchanging hands at double their face
value, the morality of Coward's work was questioned. The feared critic
Hannen Swaffer claimed that *The Vortex* would persuade America that
English society was entirely decadent, and that the producers were
'offering an insult to the British people'. Interviewed, Coward denied
the charge. 'You know perfectly well, and I presume everyone does,
that the percentage of rotters in society is very small. In London today,
despite the fact that the war left a great many people groping, shattered
mentally and morally, without any beliefs left in anything that gives
them a moral anchor to windward, fashionable society as a whole is as
sound and healthy as it ever has been.'

'I am not a propagandist', he declared, revealing a distrust of critical
interpretation which would colour his future work. 'I do not feel that it
is my mission in life to rescue these unhappy and misguided drifters. I
regard them as a poor, afflicted group who constitute a canker on the
body of society as a whole; but I am a man of the theatre ... We all
want to bring the theatre into popularity, power and prosperity. We
must have all kinds of plays to do that. Serious plays, of course; and to
have a serious play that is worth while and which will attract people
you must attack something in contemporary life.' Alexander Woollcott
also leapt to his defence, answering 'the silly people who spoke of this
as somehow an evil and corrupting play and one which would mislead
the native Americans into thinking of it as a composite portrait of
modern English life ... The sceptical can see the American prototypes
of this mother and this son in a hundred homes on our own dear Park
Avenue. So there.'

Once again New York was instrumental in changing Coward's life.
Jack Wilson came to the first matinee: 'Fortunately I remembered his
face', Coward noted disingenuously, and Wilson was invited back to
dine at the studio. 'From then on we became close friends, and a few
months later he gave up being a stockbroker in order to be my personal
manager', wrote Noel, neatly avoiding the true nature of their relationship. Wilson's interest in Coward was not entirely amorous or altruistic.
A profile written in 1937 observes that 'Wilson, in a gesture that fused
business with pleasure ... invaded the Coward dressing room and came

away with the Coward account for Barney & Co., a distinct feather in his financial cap.' It was partly Erlanger's withdrawal from *The Vortex* which installed Wilson as Coward's manager, according to the *New York Times*: 'In a stocks-and-bonds discussion with Wilson, Coward hinted that he was in dire need of a business manager . . . could Wilson recommend a desirable man? . . . With characteristic candour he named himself . . .'

Like Gladys Calthrop, deep in an affair with Eva Le Gallienne, Coward had found love in America. Metropolitan New York, in its liberal isolation from the rest of the country, was the perfect place for such liaisons. This gay group of Coward, Wilson, Calthrop and Le Gallienne, whose amorous allegiances may have seemed quite orthodox to the outsider, sashayed around town together, partying as hard as they worked. Calthrop, seduced by American glamour and Eva's charms, had decided to work for Le Gallienne's Civic Repertory Company as art director and stay on in America.

Coward was now an established figure in New York society, well known among the Four Hundred, during the day lecturing to women's groups on 'Modern Drama from the English Viewpoint', exploring the nightlife in the evening. However, there were reports that he had been refused admission to nightclubs on two or three occasions. 'But since he announces himself as Mr Coward, the shoe manufacturer – despite the fact that the shoe man has been long dead – the playwright gets ringside tables everywhere.' One particularly hedonistic night saw Coward and Michael Arlen club-crawling, having 'eluded their hordes of admirers among the socially elect'; they visited no less than nineteen establishments. The evening ended with Coward seeing Arlen on to the boat for England, announcing that he had decided that his next play would be about 'New York's contemporary life'. The result would be the scandalous *Semi-Monde*.

With *The Vortex* launched, Coward turned his attention to the American production of *Hay Fever*. The Shuberts, well-known New York impresarios, were the somewhat eccentric producers of the play, casting actors with little regard for the script. At rehearsals Noel was presented with a 'brassy blonde in a *décolleté* afternoon dress of black lace' stretched out on a bench, chewing gum: this was his Myra. Laura Hope-Crews (playing Judith Bliss) watched with amusement as Coward, with visible self-control, told the blonde that her accent wasn't quite right. The blonde merely spat out her gum and said 'Accent hell! I've got a contract.' Noel suspected the casting-couch, but without a working knowledge of the New York theatre he was unable to find suitable actors himself. *Hay Fever* opened in Brooklyn for a trial week, then came into the Maxine Elliot Theatre on Broadway for an invitation-only Sunday night show. The reaction was bad; the critics accused Laura Hope-Crews of over-acting (which was to misunderstand the nature of the play), and *Hay Fever* expired six weeks after opening.

Undaunted, Dean and Coward set to work on their third project, *Easy Virtue*, for which Jane Cowl, an actress famed for her caprice, was engaged as lead. The play concerns Larita, a woman with a past who is seen as an unsuitable wife for John Whittaker, the son of a county family. It is a situation which both typified the social concerns of the time and reflected Noel's uneasy entry into society. 'In those days,' he told Judy Garland, 'when we entertainers were considered rogues and vagabonds ... we weren't received socially – which of course saved us an enormous amount of boredom ...' Acutely aware of class and position, Coward wrote these concerns into *Easy Virtue* with a degree of irony which its title reflects.

Larita's entrance, in 'violently expensive' clothes, is a grand scene for any actress, but for the vampish Jane Cowl, with her panda-black eyes, bee-stung lips and predilection for leopardskin, it was virtual typecasting: 'How-do-you-do seems so hopelessly inadequate, doesn't it, at a moment like this? But perhaps it's good to use it as a refuge for our real feelings.' The play unfolds as a minuet of love affairs to an orchestra of disapproval, as the characters swap partners in a prefiguration of later plays such as *Private Lives*.

'If not a very good play this is at least an extremely intelligent one', noted George Street, who found nothing to censor. 'The author's frankness is chiefly in his own explanations, which have nothing to do with the stage performance.' (Lord Cromer, won over by Noel's personal visit over *The Vortex*, was positively enthusiastic: 'A very intelligent play in the most modern style. The title may arouse more criticism than is justifiable from the play itself, still it would be a mistake to insist on its alteration.') After a 'tricky' preparation, due partly to Basil Dean's passion for detail, the play opened in Newark on 7 December 1925. Coward blamed Jane Cowl for making it more melodramatic than he intended; critics accused him of facile characterisation: 'Even such an uprising youth as Noel Coward is hopelessly enmeshed in the sheer conventions of the scarlet woman', wrote Alan Dale in the *Denver Post*. 'I expected something more than a dressed-up doll, placed amid a crowd of respectable matrons, always drawing herself up to her full height and emitting banalities.'

After five months on Broadway, *The Vortex* went on tour. Coward was tired of his onerous part, and dwindling and less appreciative audiences prompted a decision that he would never again appear in a role for more than six months, 'preferably three months in New York and three months in London'. The tour was enlivened by friends, however. At Atlantic City, Fred Astaire appeared arm-in-arm with his mother, Ann, and Noel's mother, and they were snapped strolling the Boardwalk, Violet clearly in her element. A six-week engagement in Chicago promised better crowds, and checking into an expensive suite at the Lake Shore Drive Hotel, Coward took delivery of a new Rolls-Royce, and prepared to open at the Selwyn Theatre on 22 February. Unfortunately, the audience were expecting comedy, and reacted accordingly. Coward, 'trembling with rage', was restrained by Lilian Braithwaite's patriotic admonition, 'Remember you are English!' 'Never, since *Charley's Aunt* on a Saturday night in Blackpool, have I heard such uproarious mirth in a theatre', Coward maintained. 'Noel Coward died here', he wrote on his dressing-room wall, a piece of graffito which amused Clifton Webb when he played the theatre two years later.

Also in town were Diana Cooper and her mother, the Duchess of Rutland. Cooper, wife of Alfred Duff Cooper, was a great beauty and sometime actress (Griffith had filmed her for a sequence in *Hearts of the World*). She and Iris Tree* were touring in *The Miracle*, in which Diana played the statue of the Virgin Mary come to life. While Violet Coward went off for cosy shopping trips with the Duchess, Noel, Diana and Iris were invited by 'Benny' Marshall, an architect responsible for some of Chicago's grandest buildings, to his lakeside mansion in Wilmette, where he entertained such figures as the Prince of Wales. The house was full of gimmicks such as a tropical garden with a glass roof that would open for parties, a dining-room table that rose automatically from the floor, and a nautical bar with concealed hydraulic lifts which rocked the room to complete the effect. The women suspected Marshall's motives, and discovered that a new Apache Room had been decorated especially for them. The three decided that their host had intended a little impromptu orgy, so made their excuses and left.

* Iris Tree (1897–1968), art student turned actress, was the younger daughter of Sir Herbert Beerbohm Tree, actor-manager and founder of RADA. She led a wild life, and her promiscuity on tour was well known to Cooper, and, presumably, to Coward.

Noel gave Diana *Semi-Monde* to read, his most daring play to date. In a chic Parisian hotel, a series of sexual pairings take place through rendezvous, arguments, infidelities and reconciliations; sexual deviance is undisguised, and it appears to have been written for a very sophisticated audience. Promiscuity is pursued by visitors from England and the United States in this unreal world, isolated by geography and happenstance. Set in the bisexual 1920s, the play could easily be populated by characters of Coward's society: dandy aesthetes Harold Acton, Brian Howard, Cecil Beaton, Stephen Tennant; and their female counterparts, Nancy Cunard, Diana Cooper, Iris Tree and Tallulah Bankhead. None was averse to sexual experimentation, as their exploits bore witness: Vita Sackville-West's elopement to France with her girlfriend, Violet Trefusis, pursued by their respective husbands (one of whom, Harold Nicolson, was homosexual), could have inspired a sub-plot of *Semi-Monde*, amorous adventures conducted in foreign hotels to escape British censure and law, by sleek-haired men and boyish women.

The play's alternative title, *Ritz Bar*, betrayed its origins. The Ritz Hotel in New York had two bars, one a men's bar well known for its homosexual clientele. Here Beverley Nichols saw Cole Porter, looking like a 'startled leprechaun', sipping Pernod and casting his 'dark, syrupy little eyes to the white and gold ceiling', devising 'his devastating little rhymes'. The other bar was mixed; when Porter met his wife, the couple switched from the former to the latter. The Ritz Hotels in Paris and London also had bars known for their homosexual clientele; the London one was notorious enough to be closed down by the Ministry of Defence during the Second World War, deemed detrimental to service discipline.

Coward's setting allowed for women with 'excellent jewellery' and 'exquisite cigarette cases', and men in smart suits – the more waisted the cut, the more indeterminate the sex. The action takes place in the hotel lobby, over three years, 1925 to 1927. It opens with Tanis Marshall, awaiting her husband, Owen; in the corner, Inez Zuleika and Cynthia Gable, both dressed 'with rather affected simplicity', bicker in a lovers' tiff. Clearly, Coward was drawing on the liaisons of Gladys Calthrop, Eva Le Gallienne and Mercedes de Acosta, and his look at their affairs is a little dismissive. A chic woman 'somewhere between thirty and forty' meets the lesbians. 'You haven't seen a dark little American girl with a sort of wood-violet face loitering about, have you?' she asks. 'Yes, hundreds', replies Inez. Like his own lesbian friends, Coward's women seem constantly in dispute; by the end of the play, Inez is arguing with yet another girlfriend, leaving the impression that lesbian relationships are ceaselessly promiscuous and doomed to failure.

Male homosexuals are equally typecast. Beverley Ford is 'forty, extremely well dressed', chatters in an affected manner and has in tow Cyril Hardacre ('in the twenties – good-looking and slim'), apparently heterosexual. Hardacre is embarrassed by Ford's effusion, particularly in front of Jerome Kennedy and his daughter, with whom he is to travel to the Riviera. He is even more abashed when shrill-voiced Albert Hennick minces over to welcome them: 'My dear, where did you find that?' he says to Beverley, as Cyril walks ahead, 'it's divine!' When Beverley buys a copy of *Vanity Fair*, Albert urges, 'Do get *La Vie Parisienne*, it's so defiantly normal!' Coward's attitude is defined by his tone – rejecting promiscuity and effeminacy, he assumes the stance of Jerome, normal and straightfoward. Yet Jerome also wants to escape. 'The great open spaces?' asks Owen. 'Yes, where men are men.' Owen laughs, 'You mustn't let this bar dishearten you.' Jerome replies, 'Oh, these don't matter – they're not even real of their kind . . .', a telling comment from Coward, who, while presenting almost music-hall caricatures of homosexuals in the play, allows that not all are effeminate – as he was not. The heterosexuals in the play are no less sexually obsessed, and Coward's themes – decadence, moral hypocrisy, homosexual oppression – tumble over one another in near-hysteria in the partner-swapping orgy. The play ends with a bare resolution of the turmoil, the restoration of normality and the heterosexual balance – a submission to the status quo.

Semi-Monde was obviously too risqué for Britain, and Coward pursued possible production abroad for the next couple of years. In New York that autumn, he hoped Basil Dean (who had announced the play's production in *Theatre World* that August) would produce it. 'He has great ideas . . . if we can raise enough money', Noel told Violet. But in late November, his hopes had transferred to Max Reinhardt. The famous German producer was 'very anxious to do *Semi-Monde*, which will be one in the eye for everyone and place me on such an intellectual plane that I doubt if I should ever come down!' Seeing it as an exposition of his 'serious side', Coward was evidently not worried about the outrageous nature of the play; indeed, he probably relished the publicity it would attract – another *Vortex* perhaps.

But the play remained unproduced and unpublished. In 1936 Beverley Nichols tried, unsuccessfully, to persuade the Norwegian Ambassador to Paris, Baron Wedel-Jahrlsberg, to finance a production. Nichols recorded 'a very apposite remark which Noel Coward once made about sex when we were lunching together at the St James's Club. He was infuriated because the Lord Chamberlain had just censored a play of his called *Ritz Bar* . . . It was all an abomination in the eye of the Lord, and of the Lord Chamberlain. To which Noel had exploded . . . "I cannot agree that it is within the province of the Lord Chamberlain, or of anybody else, to concern himself with what I happen to do with my thighs."' (Another version of the story substitutes a different part of the body.) Perhaps as a result of writing a play which he knew would not be passed by the Lord Chamberlain's office in England, Coward spoke out against censorship publicly in America, telling the *New York Times* that the system in the United Kingdom was unfair. In passing, he remarked that American drama was 'finer' than its counterpart across the Atlantic. Coward genuinely believed, and had done since his first visit to New York, that the pace of American productions was an improvement on the slower, more conservative world of the theatre at home. Freedom of expression, especially for a homosexual writer, was important, and liberal attitudes he had encountered in America convinced him it was a better place to perform and perhaps to live. Over time, Coward's disenchantment with his homeland deepened; he despaired of its reaction to his work, and the restrictions it placed on what he could or coul not do, both onstage and off. Despite being seen as the quintessential Englishman, he would spend much of the rest of his life travelling outside Britain, and would eventually exile himself from it.

The *Vortex* tour finished in Cleveland, Ohio, to good business, and after a holiday in Palm Beach with Florence and John Magee Noel returned to New York feeling fit and well. He confirmed Jack Wilson as his business adviser, an ill-advised mixture of work and pleasure. Wilson was not unaware of the financial potential of his new friend (particularly with film rights being discussed later that year when *The Young Idea* was sold). But whatever manoeuvring may have gone into achieving his new position, Wilson appeared good at his job, investing Coward's money in American securities and drawing up a contract with options, 'so that in the event of sudden unforeseen mutual hatred, we could still continue to work together, however dourly, on a business basis'. Wilson was to return to England with Coward that spring, and Noel wondered what Lorn Loraine would make of this 'hard-headed and extremely uncompromising American'. He must also have wondered what his circle would make of a man who was so obviously his lover.

10

On with the Dance

Colin on the front page, Colin on the back page; interviews with
Colin and special articles on Colin; photographs in every conceiv-
able position; in every conceivable scene of his new play . . . Colin
Martial, London's Idol, Darling of the Gods, Our New Dramatist,
Not-Yet-Twenty-Five; seen at the Fifty-Fifty, seen at the Embassy,
seen at the Kit-Cat, at Ciro's . . .

G. B. Stern, *A Deputy Was King*

THE SS *Olympic* left New York in late March 1926, carrying
Noel, Jack and Violet, as well as Diana Cooper, Syrie Maugham
and Rebecca West. West was reported as saying that Coward
and Cooper were both 'Delightful! . . . We all came over together. But,
you know, even Diana Cooper and Noel Coward become a little trying
after a time. We all kept together – exclusively. Noel saw to that. I think
it was a publicity stunt of his: being the centre of the "smart set" on the
boat.'

Coward was followed by the Rolls-Royce he had bought, which gave
him 'many plutocratic thrills'. He drove triumphantly around town in
this emblem of his American success, a stark contrast to events at home,
where the bitter General Strike was in progress. There is no evidence of
Noel's reaction to the struggle of the workers; he was more concerned
with enjoying celebrity status, 'It felt strange after months in America
to be back again as an established star.'

Jack Wilson (nicknamed 'Dabs') was introduced to the Cowards and
to Noel's extended 'family'. He apparently acquitted himself well; in
the summer, he and Wilson drove down to see Esme Wynne-Tyson, in
a new Talbot (another acquisition, due to the frequent breakdowns of
the Rolls). They arrived at her house at Fort Brockhurst, near Portsmouth, in time for lunch; Noel sent Jack off until tea-time, leaving him

to have a long talk with his old collaborator. Wynne-Tyson was now writing novels, and had 'embraced Christian Science with tremendous ardour'; Noel compared its strictures to 'new policemen ... over-zealous in obstructing traffic'. His memoirs record little contact after her marriage and motherhood, but the truth is that she remained as Noel's conscience, a critical and intelligent voice in a world falling willingly at his feet. He continued to help Esme (in 1922 he had taken her poems to the American publishers Boni and Liveright) but her religiosity frustrated him. Her diary entry for 20 September 1927, when she visited Coward in London, records that they argued about Christian Science, 'and I saw how impossible friendship is when one is not of one mind. He does not know one more than a stranger.' Wynne-Tyson's obsession with her beliefs would mean the loss of other friends too. Ethel Mannin wrote to her in 1930, '. . . I won't come and see you, Esme, because I know I should be let in for a bout of Christian Science, which I should loathe, and I am told you are "all Christian Science now" (Noel told me that and G. B. Stern confirmed it).' Noel was so exasperated by his old friend's espousal of the 'no pain' doctrine that he took a pin and stuck it into a friend's backside to demonstrate the fallibility of Esme's belief.

In letters, he criticised her early novels, some of which dealt with facets of their life together.* He also addressed her attempts at playwriting, in comments which reflect on his own dramatic talent: '. . . you always make your characters say too much at one go – you must break up your speeches with interjections from other people – unless it's a highly strung and dramatic scene. Another thing is you dot your i's and cross your T's too much – *Dont* underrate your Audience so dreadfully – instead of letting your people *say* how and what they're feeling – let them express it more subtly – the Audience will get it all right – instead of saying "Oh how happy I am in this beautiful house" let her *be* happy in the house . . . Weigh each speech over in your mind before you write it – keep the speeches short – and dont over emphasise your points. Darling I do so want you to be *frightfully* good . . . But *do* take it seriously and dont compare it to *other* plays. That's fatal . . .' Jon Wynne-Tyson said that 'although there is more than an element of truth in his criticism of her work, there was behind it . . . a certain

---

* In *Quicksand* (1927), dedicated to Coward, Paul Myse is based on Noel; his sister, Pauline, is evidently Esme. Paul writes a revue and a much-acclaimed musical comedy, and becomes famous, in the process acquiring a 'relentless superficial humour'.

degree of satisfaction that she wasn't doing that well. In a way he was very mixed up about her.' Esme thought Noel felt betrayed by her career as a writer and because she had withdrawn her services as an actress. But she also regarded Coward's increasing fame and materialistic concerns as estranging and dehumanising. She was pleased for Noel when he introduced Jack Wilson, yet doubted the depth of the relationship; she thought Wilson 'a very nice person ... nice to talk to, a charming young man', but in the end, she said, Coward's 'genuine love was channelled into his mother'.

Jack Wilson seemed dedicated to the business of running his lover's life. A 1937 report said that after Wilson was engaged as Coward's manager, he 'served in the box-office of a theatre housing a Coward hit, and for two years he acted as company manager of transplanted Coward plays. Although Coward's personal representative at the time he insisted on this procedure that he might familiarize himself with all phases of the theatre.' His urbane good manners and transatlantic charm won easy friends, but others remained equivocal. Was he perhaps like Joanna, the interloper-seducer of *Present Laughter*, threatening the charmed circle of the playwright's 'family'? There was a degree of resentment of this American who had conquered not only Coward's affections but his professional interests too. Joyce Carey recalled that Wilson 'really was a young businessman – he enjoyed café society life more than theatre ... he was interested in it in a business way, but it wasn't his surround ...' Dickie Fellowes-Gordon thought Wilson 'nice looking, not particularly brainy. He acquired a certain amount of direction, he directed one or two things quite well.' On business matters, however, she found him 'stupid. He ought to have been a good businessman. His father was. He had a good training.' According to Charles Russell, when Wilson came to England, Lorn Loraine was moved into a back room, which she resented: 'Jack Wilson was a ... pompous American, coming in and telling everyone what to do.' It was a measure of the devotion (or perhaps control) Coward demanded of his entourage that peace was maintained, for the time being, at least.

Of all Coward's intimates, it was his mother from whom Wilson had most to fear, and it is obvious from letters that Wilson went out of his way to charm Violet. But she was unhappy about his usurpation of her role as her son's keeper. 'Having been mistress of the house for so many years,' she wrote later, in her most sarcastic tone, 'it was difficult though very stupid of me not to realise that Jack was boss.' She continued in an access of self-pity, 'How much better to have gone while you still loved me, and no crowds of grand friends and success had come between us. I shall put Bobbie Andrews in my room so you and he and Jack can cuddle up together...' (The letter seems to confirm that Bobbie Andrews was Coward's lover before Wilson.) Violet was well aware of her son's sexual proclivities, and Esme's comments about her hold over his affections were true. Violet's jealousy was almost that of a spurned lover; her ability to discomfit her devoted son was not to be underestimated.

Easy Virtue, cast and all, would be brought by Basil Dean to London when it finished in New York. Thus freed from work, Coward and Wilson set off abroad; now a rich man, Noel could afford to leave England on a whim and seek more exotic diversions. This honeymoon holiday included a visit to André Gide in Paris, the South of France, as well as Sicily and Tunis, two destinations then popular with wealthy young men of their persuasion. By the end of April he and Wilson were in Taormina. They then moved on to the luxurious Grand Hotel des Palmes in Palermo, where Jack had stayed the previous year. Even here, work was never far away. Basil Dean's proposed changes to the cast of *Easy Virtue* necessitated a cable from Coward, PERFECTLY SATISFIED JOYCE CAREYS PERFORMANCE THINK IT UNWISE TO CHANGE, and Noel embarked on a new play, 'This Was a Man'.

They sailed for Tunis on 4 May, but were back in Palermo by the eighth. From there they sought the high society of Venice: Cole and Linda Porter, and Elsa Maxwell and Dickie Fellowes-Gordon were already there. Porter had made his name with *Lady Be Good* (1924) and *Tip-Toes* (1925), and that year Gertrude Lawrence was to star in *Oh, Kay*. The Porters,* each independently wealthy, had spent the past three summers in Venice, where they threw increasingly elaborate parties – for one, they built a floating nightclub on the canal. That summer they rented the imposing Palazzo Rezzonico, where a whole series of charity shows and balls were planned, with the *jeunesse dorée* (and some not so young or golden) as guests: Tallulah Bankhead, Diana Cooper, Oliver Messel and Elsie de Wolfe (who that year, at the age of sixty, married Sir Charles Mendl).

---

* Cole Porter married the society beauty Linda Lee Thomas in 1919. Her first husband was the rich newspaper owner Edward Thomas, whom she had divorced in 1908, citing Teddie Gerrard as co-respondent. Cole Porter was later introduced to Teddie at a party. 'I don't know whether I should meet you or not,' said Teddie, 'you see, I was your wife's ex-husband's mistress.'

Here Coward experienced the liberated hedonism of Cole Porter's circle. Dickie Fellowes-Gordon recalled that the American got into trouble with the law when he tried to bed a reluctant gondolier. In addition to 'indiscriminate sexual experimentation, heavy drinking was commonplace, and hashish, opium and cocaine were tried by most members of this Lido set'. Wilson, no mean drinker, was quickly part of the scene; he, Coward and Porter were photographed in their belted swimming trunks, a tanned trio posed in diminishing size, Wilson with Coward's arm slung easily over his lover's shoulder, Porter bracing his chest to look bigger for the camera.

From Venice, Coward and Wilson moved to Paris, where there was a flurry of cables over *Easy Virtue*, confirming Joyce Carey's casting but mainly concerning the conflicting personalities of Edward Molyneux and Jane Cowl. Noel telegraphed Basil Dean, WHAT MEANING ALTERNA-TIVE MANCHESTER UTTERLY BEWILDERED STOP HAVE WIRED CANCEL-LATION MOLYNEUX FURIOUS AT JANES BEHAVIOUR SUGGEST SHE APPEAR IN COMBINATIONS. The actress had bought her own costume, much to Molyneux's fury. Noel pacified him, and told Dean that the couturier had agreed to make the dresses (for £150) and that he would meet Jane Cowl on Monday, when she doubtless received a stern reprimand. Back in London Coward showed the script of 'This Was a Man' to Dean, who thought it excellent, and announced that he would produce it after *Easy Virtue*. But as Noel's bewildered cable indicated, there had been problems, and the guardians of public morality once again challenged his work. In this case it was the Manchester Watch Committee who, as Lord Cromer had predicted, took exception to its title. After a hard-fought battle, *Easy Virtue* became *A New Play in Three Acts* for its first night in Manchester (even though, as Noel commented wryly, the cinema next door was showing *The Flames of Passion*). Jane Cowl had arrived from Paris just three days before, but gave a bravura performance and a first-night speech asking the audience for their sympathy as she was a newcomer to their country. She was 'mobbed by the gallery girls at the stage door and conveyed in triumph' to the Midland Hotel.

'London fell into Jane's lap like a ripe plum', wrote Coward. *Easy Virtue* ran at the Duke of York's for a splendid 124 performances, although its initial reception was equivocal. Esme, who had been invited by Noel, travelled to the first night in his Rolls with Arthur and Aunt Vida. She thought the play 'not so good as it should have been ...' James Agate, in the *Sunday Times*, claimed, 'Mr Noel Coward gets younger with every day, and in *Easy Virtue* has attained to that pure idealism which prompts the schoolboy who has been taken to see *La Dame aux Camélias* to believe for the next ten years that a *cocotte* is the noblest work of man if not of God.' The naivety apparent to Agate (perhaps a veiled criticism of a homosexual writing about heterosexual relationships) negated the critic's hope that this would be Coward's best play to date: 'Unfortunately, as soon as the play began to move it went to pieces.' Yet few had anything but good to say of Jane Cowl, and it was her performance (misjudged as Noel had always seen it) that carried *Easy Virtue* through.

Rather than *'This Was a Man'*, Dean decided to put Coward's 1922 piece *The Queen Was in the Parlour* into production as a follow-up to *Easy Virtue*, with Madge Titheradge, Herbert Marshall and Viola Tree in the cast. Although Noel predicted that, as a Ruritanian romance, the play would quickly date, it had a good run at the St Martin's Theatre. It opens with two young lovers living a wayward life in Paris. Coward played up contemporary excesses for sensational effect: 'Some of us dope, and some of us drink, and some of us merely go in for undiluted love in varying doses . . .' The contrast is between duty and decadence; Nadya must give up her life in Paris to be queen of Krayia. 'Your country comes first', she is told. Nadya says, 'The air is full of democracy and freedom'; to which the messenger counters, 'The air is full of the voices of cheap people crying out against the existing order of things, trying to tear down kings and queens and loyalties and establish themselves on the throne in their shirt-sleeves with their feet on the mantelpiece.'

Considering the politics of the time, and Noel's anti-intellectualism (and his opposition to, and incomprehension of, radicalism), it was apposite that the play was performed in the immediate aftermath of the General Strike. Such speeches were sops to the middle-class audiences: 'There's something so comforting about the English point of view, specially in a crisis', says Nadya. It was a statement of Coward's paradoxical embrace of the status quo.

'This Was a Man' was sent to Lord Cromer for licence in September 1926. The readers found something entirely different from the Ruritanian romance of *The Queen Was in the Parlour*. The play was set firmly in contemporary Britain, dealing with characteristic themes of love, marriage and infidelity. Lord Cromer and his men found it so lacking in morality that, of all the works submitted by the author (already

notorious for including a bedroom scene in almost all his plays), they refused to license it.

To modern eyes, *'This Was a Man'* seems no worse and no better in its presentation of 1920s mores than Coward's other works. Dedicated to John C. Wilson, the play opens in the portrait painter Edward Churt's Knightsbridge studio. Here a woman (only later do we learn she is Edward's wife, Carol) brings Harry Challoner home in the early hours of the morning. They kiss and cuddle, and Harry leaves: Carol goes to bed, unaware that her husband had been in the room.

As with *Semi-Monde*, this world of changing relationships was drawn from contemporary society. 'It's the obvious result of this "barriers down" phase through which we seem to be passing', says Edward's former lover, Zoë. 'Everyone is at close quarters with everyone else. There's no more glamour. Everything's indefinite and blurred except sex, so people are instinctively turning to that with a rather jaded vigour.' 'Oh, Zoë, I loathe this age and everything to do with it', says Edward. 'Men of my sort are the products of over-civilisation . . .' He is presented as a victim of the war: thin blood, too much intellectualisation, and lacking the Victorian spirit on which the empire was built. The play ends with his wife bedding his best friend, and Churt turning bitterly on them both.

Critically, the piece lacks dynamism, has a negligible plot, and colourless, unsympathetic characters. It becomes bogged down in verbosity, its dialogue is protracted and inconclusive, but it is redeemed by some good lines, acute social observation and nice period details.* On moral grounds – which were to be its downfall – the piece seems ambivalent, despite Coward's protests of its righteousness.

The lack of moral stricture was apparently what the censors found offensive. 'The main intention of this play is to satirise and generally score off the complacent and correct type of Englishman', George Street said in his report. 'That intention is no doubt permissible, but the means by which it is executed unfortunately involve an amount of adultery, cynically and light-heartedly treated, which makes the play more than dubious.' The Advisory Board agreed, Sir Douglas Dawson becoming almost apoplectic: 'Every character in this play, presumably ladies and gentlemen, leads an adulterous life and glories in doing so . . . I find no

---

* Coward employs the changing metropolis as a metaphor: 'London's looking so pretty with all the roads up', says Zoë. 'I'm afraid you're finding the old town sadly changed', Edward replies. 'I'm sure it's much more hygienic now', she says.

serious "purpose" in the play, unless it be misrepresentation. At a time like this [with the General Strike only just resolved] what better propaganda could the Soviet instigate and finance? ... It was apropos of just this sort of play that, during my time in Paris, *nice* French people remarked to me, "Would that we had a Censor".'

It was paradoxical that the play intended to follow *The Queen Was in the Parlour* was banned as a possible threat to national security, when *The Queen* had cried up the old values of patriotism and duty. Coward made his anger public in a series of heated comments to the press. MY VERY MORAL AND BANNED PLAY – MR COWARD THINKS CENSOR'S ACTION WAS SILLY, shrieked the headlines. '"The Lord Chamberlain has banned my really very moral play, 'This Was a Man', and so I shall content myself with its production in America and Germany, where the theatre is much more alive than it is here", said Mr Noel Coward in an interview with the *Evening Standard* to-day ... "He was very annoying over *The Vortex* ... Now he has gone one further, and actually banned a play altogether. It is really rather silly, for the play itself is quite harmless."' Coward contended that he was 'not upset ... The whole thing merely confirms my opinion of stage conditions in this country. The authorities do not encourage dramatists. Where are the Eugene O'Neills, George Kellys, and Sidney Howards here? I shall, for the future, concentrate on New York,' he threatened, 'for in America I am taken seriously, as a serious writer, whereas in England people think I am out for salacious sensation. I shall from time to time write a pleasant little trifle for London, but all my important work will be done in Germany and America' (a defiant reference to hopes of Reinhardt's production of the truly scandalous *Semi-Monde*). But this was mere sabre-rattling; Noel's immediate future was bound up inextricably with the land of his birth.

With the new stability of his relationship with Jack Wilson and the added security of professional success, Coward sought somewhere permanent for himself and his extended family to live. The Cowards left the cottage he had rented at Dockenfield, and looked for a new house in the countryside of Kent, which had appealed to Noel ever since his sojourn at St Mary's. He had decided on a redbrick house at Stone, near Rye, when he heard that a Mr Body, a neighbour at St Mary's, wanted to let Goldenhurst Farm, on the borders of the Marsh, south of Ashford.

The house was poky, with dark corridors and small rooms, and had a 'lop-sided ... Victorian air', partly the result of an extension, 'a square edifice wearing perkily a pink corrugated tin roof and looking as though it had just dropped in on the way to the races'. A barn-enclosed muddy yard, two ponds, an orchard, a line of poplars and six acres of grounds completed this shabby rural scene, but the setting claimed Coward. Behind the house the land sloped from a steep escarpment, falling away to the expanses of the Marsh and the Military Canal, with Dymchurch in the distance. The sea was a grey line on the horizon, and beyond that, on clear nights, could be seen the lights of the French coast. Coward took it at a rent of £50 a year; he now had a quiet retreat, not only for himself but for Violet, and the thought would be a comforting one when he was away.

After a short but glorious period when two Noel Coward plays were running simultaneously in the West End, *Easy Virtue* closed as Jane Cowl had to return to the States, and *The Queen Was in the Parlour* transferred to the Duke of York's. Basil Dean offered Coward a new role. Their working relationship had achieved a certain equilibrium, now that Noel could deal with the producer's occasionally fiendish outbursts, 'I don't think it ever occurred to him that actors' feelings are notoriously nearer to the surface than average people's. If they weren't they wouldn't be good actors.' Dean proposed that Coward should play Lewis Dodd in Margaret Kennedy's adaptation of her book *The Constant Nymph*, the best-selling novel of the decade. Noel had reservations, for reasons of stamina and because it meant delaying the New York production of '*This Was a Man*', but the casting of Edna Best as Tessa secured his services.

His was a demanding role, and it proved Coward a more versatile actor than he had been given credit for. Beverley Nichols described *The Constant Nymph* as having an 'unforgettable gallery of highly irritating, electric, ultra-Bohemian individuals'. Albert Sanger, a composer exiled to the Tyrol mountains, is visited by Lewis Dodd, also a composer and an admirer of Sanger's. Sanger's fourteen-year-old daughter, Tessa (Edna Best was twenty-six), falls in love with Dodd, twice her age and married; Tessa has a weak heart, and, having eloped with Lewis to a dingy Brussels hotel, dies trying to open a jammed window which her lover had been too uncouth to open for her. In the final scene a distraught Dodd carries her body to their bed.

The portrayal of 'free love' captured the public imagination, and Dodd seemed a suitable part for Coward to play. Kennedy describes Dodd as 'a lean youth' with a bony face, 'deeply furrowed . . . a thin, rather cruel mouth', and 'light, observant eyes, so intent that they rarely betrayed him'. But insiders thought Coward miscast, and Noel himself hated Dodd 'whole-heartedly'. Admitting that he gave 'a fine and convincing performance', Coward took issue with the adaptation: 'In the book his character was clearly defined and understandable; in the play he seemed to me to be a clumsy insensitive oaf with little to recommend him over and above the fact that he was supposed to be a musical genius.' With long hair, 'ill-fitting suits', spectacles and a pipe, this was not the Noel Coward the public knew. Noel found it hard work, and admitted to taking it out on Jack Wilson and Lorn Loraine.*

John Gielgud, whom Dean had originally engaged as the lead, was again Coward's understudy. Celebrating at the Ivy, Gielgud saw Coward at his customary table, just inside the restaurant door where he would miss none of the comings and goings. He called Gielgud over, 'I think I ought to tell you before Dean does, I am going to play Lewis Dodd for the first month . . . of *The Constant Nymph*.' Gielgud was bitterly disappointed, and Dean added insult to injury by offering him half salary to understudy Noel; such incidents account for Gielgud's ambivalence towards Coward. He recalled that the rehearsals for *The Constant Nymph* were not comfortable. Coward was already acquiring a reputation for being difficult. 'Noel disagreed with Dean and Margaret Kennedy on several occasions, and one morning he left the rehearsal at a standstill and retired with them to the bar, whence their voices could be heard in violent argument. Noel came in to the Ivy for lunch with a set face . . . telling me he was going to throw up the part.' Gielgud's hopes were dashed when the next morning 'the row had been patched up, and the rehearsals went on as if nothing at all had happened'.

The Constant Nymph opened in September and was 'an immediate smashing success', but Coward spent the first night in a 'dull coma of depression'. Jack Wilson came to his dressing-room after the second act to tell him of the positive audience reaction; Coward took this to be a 'well-intentioned but transparent lie' and asked his friend to leave, 'which, to my considerable irritation, he did'. The strains of the past two years were beginning to tell; and it was the pressure of what he had pursued for so long – fame and success – that threatened Coward's health. The signs were already evident in his banned play '*This Was a Man*': Zoë St Merryn comments that Edward Churt's 'vitality seems to

---

* As Dodd's reverential epithet for Sanger was 'the Master', this is a possible origin of Loraine's nickname for Coward, particularly if she was subjected to temper tantrums from her employer whilst he was playing the role.

have been snuffed out by something . . . I expect it's success. That's always frightfully undermining.' It was ironic that Coward wrote of the demands of success in a play which, when it failed in New York, would exacerbate his condition.

The initial breakdown was dramatic and public. Noel 'finally snapped' and cried throughout the performance, 'to the bewilderment, not only of the audience but of the cast'. He collapsed in his dressing-room, and a doctor was summoned to give him a strychnine injection and put him to bed, where he stayed for a week. Dr Desmond MacManus wrote to Dean from Ebury Street on 7 October, 'Mr Coward has been examined by me this morning and is suffering from severe nervous exhaustion. He has been ordered by me to remain in bed & will not be fit to act for at least a month.'

John Gielgud took over as Lewis Dodd, and according to Coward, 'played it successfully for a year, pipe and all'. But Gielgud complained that he was 'made to feel rather small. I was billed, after a few days, in the newspapers, but otherwise I was baulked of my hopes for publicity.' Coward's photographs remained outside the theatre for the whole year's run. Gielgud was accused of 'imitating' Coward's style: 'I acted as well as I could, but at first I was terribly hampered, just as I had been in *The Vortex*, by Noel's reading of the lines, which were so indelibly printed on my mind that I could not easily discover how to play the part in my own way.' The cast resented Coward's departure and that of their director, who went to America to direct his new play.

Friends also resented Noel's behaviour; like Esme, they complained of neglect. G. B. Stern, noting that his breakdown meant he would go to America earlier than expected, commented, 'But *did* he write and tell me how much he enjoyed my charming book, so courteously sent to him? No! Did he ever send me a copy of *The Queen Was in the Parlour* with dedication to G. B. Stern because she was the fifty-first? No!' Stern had remained a close friend of Coward's. Her book was *A Deputy Was King*, the second of her Rakonitz Chronicles, published that autumn, in which Coward was portrayed as Colin Martial (an antonym of Noel's surname), a playwright and actor, and herself as Toni, the heroine estranged from Giles, her husband (Geoffrey Holdsworth). Noel wrote to Violet, 'It's very good and she's done me in it! rather well at moments.'

Martial is a magnetic figure: 'Colin's outlook was so infectious: he could make trifles swell to such importance, that important things, beside them, dwindled to mere trifles . . .' His theatrical work is often the subject of discussion: 'Oh, we were talking about Colin's play. First night yesterday, you know', says Giles, noting that it would be 'pumping some new slang into the waiting world, I've no doubt'. But here was also evidence of the darker side: '. . . Colin used to solace himself over any setback, by rushing round to the studio, to plan, with a chubby relish that destroyed any sort of ghoul-like effect, how he was going to "do in" such and such an enemy; and eventually reduce the whole lot, by his staggering triumphs, to a state of abject and imploring pulp!'

Geoffrey Holdsworth had already remarked on Noel's instinct for revenge; rumours of a little black book containing the names of Coward's enemies were given some substance by Edward Holstitus, an old friend of Esme's and Noel's, who recalled 'the famous "List" of those he intended to stab in the back the moment he was in a position to do so – those who had slighted or hurt him when young. And hurt – and stab – them he most certainly did . . . until every name was wiped off. The last name on the famous List happened to be a friend of mine . . . and when Noel came into Ebury Street, in our bachelor days, to announce with glee that he had now been able to cross the name out I really felt that a great harm had been done.'*

But Stern was lenient in her portrait. Colin Martial is an affected but entertaining figure, always gossiping on the telephone, ever ready to demonstrate a new dance craze, a required ingredient for any truly exciting party. Fame suits Colin; like Noel, he flourishes in its glow. 'That's Colin Martial, isn't it?' says Queenie, a maid who, like many others, professes to be mad about the boy. 'Isn't he fascinating and attractive? I do so love his smile.'

* Holstitus added, 'It certainly struck me as odd (to say the least of it!) that Noel should carry this imaginary grievance so long and then try to do this chap a most serious hurt . . . Luckily, this actor, now dead [he was writing in March 1961], did reach the top and died fairly recently in New York.'

11

Home Chat

It's inevitable that the more successful I become, the more people will run after me. I don't believe in their friendship, and I don't take them seriously, but I enjoy them. Probably a damn sight more than they enjoy me! . . . Let them all come, they'll drop me all right when they're tired of me; but maybe I shall get tired first.

Leo, Design for Living

ON 13 October 1926 Coward ignored doctor's orders and, with Jack Wilson, left for New York. Departure from England was a wrench, not because he missed the premiere of one of his plays (*The Rat Trap*, unsuccessfully produced by Norman MacDermott at the Everyman) but because even at the age of twenty-six, Noel was mother-sick. 'I did hate leaving you so dreadfully,' he wrote from the *Olympic* at Cherbourg, 'and I cried for half an hour with Jack trying to comfort me . . . Oh dear, I really ought to have got over being a mother's boy by now, but I never shall!' Jack Wilson also wrote to Violet, thanking her for her hospitality during the past six months and adding, 'Please believe that I'll do all I can to keep Noel well and happy – he doesn't like much home life but mine is open to him and Mother would be very honoured and happy to have him with us all . . .'

Despite high seas, the crossing restored Coward's equilibrium; sleeping twelve hours a night, he became 'superior and healthy, if a trifle apprehensive!' Syrie Maugham (now separated from her husband, and opening new shops in Chicago and New York) and her daughter Liza were on board for diversion. Once in New York, he and Wilson moved into the Ritz, but soon moved out again, Coward complaining that it was too noisy and expensive. The city had expanded rapidly in the last years of the boom, 'about twenty new buildings have shot up into the air since last year, and five million more motor cars, consequently one can't move anywhere'. They found a suite at the Gladstone on East 52nd Street. 'All New York has rung me up and welcomed me so I feel very cosy', he told Violet. Soon he was out with Laurette Taylor and Gertrude Lawrence (about to open in *Oh, Kay!*). Gladys Calthrop was 'very gay', busy designing two productions for Eva Le Gallienne; Jeffrey Amherst was now a theatre critic, and invited Noel to first nights for off-the-cuff pointers. He was also taken to *Iolanthe*, which confirmed his deep dislike of Gilbert and Sullivan.*

Noel and Jack set to work on 'This Was a Man'. They opened an office within Basil Dean's office at 1674 Broadway, 'with Noel Coward Inc on the door in gold letters', he bragged. 'It's very cheap so we're going to keep it permanently – we must have somewhere to put our papers and contracts (all three!)', and having his own office made Noel feel 'extremely business-like and prosperous'. Nigel Bruce and Auriol Lee were engaged for the play, and Francine Larrimore was persuaded to play the 'unattractive' part of Carol; she was 'small and red-haired and very sexy and as far as I can gather, has already made plans about every man in the cast'. Coward considered it 'a very good cast indeed', and 'it looks like a success'.

Basil Dean was producing the play 'beautifully', but rehearsals were painstakingly slow, partly because Dean terrified Nigel Bruce. Bruce in turn drove 'everybody completely mad by being completely and abjectly stupid and trying far too hard and not listening to what he's told'. There were tears from Larrimore and tantrums with Auriol Lee, who 'snapped in and out like a jack-knife'. Noel was glad to escape for the first weekend in November, which he spent on Long Island 'in an enormous house party with all the Vanderbilts and Astors and Shufflebottoms – altogether Society's pet' – a scenario which later surfaced in his short story 'What Mad Pursuit?'.

He was besieged by old acquaintances seeking work, including Philip Tonge, who had come to America with his actor parents some years previously. Noel was enjoying himself, 'I love being here and I'm taking everything very easily and being a good boy.' Linda Porter was in town, 'and we're all having grand fun', meeting up with the Webbs, Clifton (now an actor) and his ever-present mother, Maybelle. One afternoon Jack took Noel to a Yale versus Princeton football game, 'marvellous

---

* Coward would not have been pleased with his entry in *The New Grove Dictionary*, which asserts that the pair were 'obvious influences' on his work, and judges him a 'latterday Gilbert and Sullivan'.

stuff and terribly exciting – 65,000 people all screaming their heads off!' Jack lost control in the excitement and hit Noel on the head every time his team scored. There were more sophisticated pleasures when a party was given for him, at which George Gershwin played 'and we all carried on till one o'clock'. There was even a reconciliation of sorts with Osbert Sitwell, in New York to publicise his novel *Before the Bombardment*: 'I wrote him a note saying that as we were both in a Foreign Country we ought to put an end to the Feud.' But Osbert suggested ('quite pleasantly') that Noel should apologise publicly to Edith 'in all the papers! I gave him an old-fashioned look and explained gently that he was very very silly indeed which he seemed to understand perfectly and we talked very amicably. It really was becoming a bore because he wasn't being asked anywhere poor dear owing to my popularity being the greater!'

'*This Was a Man*' eventually opened on 22 November at the Klaw Theatre. 'The first night was fashionable to a degree. Everybody who was anybody was there, that is, they were there up till the end of the second act, after which they weren't there any more.' Noel, Jack and Gladys sat with 'neatly arranged first-night faces' as their customers left; as if to show unconcern, they got 'bad giggles'. Coward thought his audience had been expecting 'something very dirty indeed' after the play was banned in England, 'and they were badly disappointed. Francine Larrimore was very good and [A. E.] Matthews too tho' he forgot most of his lines. Nigel Bruce who has never understood what it was all about from the first was all right but extremely dull and Auriol was good but also dull. For some unknown reason they played it so slowly that there was time to go round the corner and have an ice-cream soda between every line.'

Coward told Violet, 'I find on close reflection that I am as unmoved by failure as I am by success . . . a *great* comfort', but added defensively, 'I like *writing* the plays anyhow and if people don't like them thats their loss!' His confidence in the play evaporated, to be replaced by recrimination. He blamed Dean's direction, '. . . if the writing of it was slow, the production was practically stationary.' The after-show party, given by Schuyler Parsons, turned out to be more of a success than the play itself, partly because of the arrival of celebrated Queen Marie of Romania, with her son and daughter.

Coward subsequently disowned '*This Was a Man*' as 'primarily satirical and on the whole rather dull'. The play ran for a pitiful thirty-one performances. Brooks Atkinson called to mind Coward's intention to write seriously for New York or Berlin and contribute only 'pleasant little trifles' for London: 'the tone of *"This Was a Man"* is obviously serious. But the drama is trifling. Possibly Mr Coward has confused his audiences.'*

The play's failure affected Coward's already precarious health. He enjoyed New York less and less; the noise became an insistent irritation; he felt ill and lacked energy. He left the city after the opening, and spent Thanksgiving Day at Jack's parents' house in Lawrenceville, New Jersey, where the Wilsons made a fuss of him. Noel was generally 'irritable and unhappy', but the Greenbriar Hotel at White Sulphur Springs had a calming effect: 'It's a most luxurious hotel in the mountains of West Virginia', with 'mountains rushing up into the sky and wild gurgling torrents dashing along like one o'clock'. He and Jack rode along mountain trails ('The horses are very mild and sweet if a little flatulent'), and he spent the afternoon working in the out-of-season peace to finish *The Marquise*, a period comedy written with Marie Tempest in mind. 'As there are several illegitimate children in it I doubt if Lord Cromer will care very deeply for it!' He told Violet that he intended to send it to the Lord Chamberlain's office under another name, 'as they all seem so down on me in England'. On 9 December, Coward returned to New York, 'to worry about *Fallen Angels* again' (he had been trying to cast a US production), and to see the last performance of '*This Was a Man*'. He also intended to start work on a new revue, but his plans were thrown into doubt by a yet more serious threat to his health that winter.

He explained to Violet that he had been feeling 'nervy' before he had gone to White Sulphur Springs, 'just like I did in London'. When he got back to New York, the symptoms worsened, 'I began to ache in every limb and have headaches.' After sleeping for eleven hours, he woke up '*dead* tired with my legs aching as tho' I'd walked ten miles'; depression hit him 'without warning, melancholia . . . like a thick cloud, blotting out the pleasure and colour from everything'. The indication was clinical depression, with unpleasant symptoms of a 'bursting head that . . . felt as though it were packed tightly with hot cotton-wool; a vague, indefinable pain in my limbs when I lay down to rest, a metallic

---

* Coward sanctioned a German production the following year, adapted by Rudolf Kommer and produced by Max Reinhardt, at the Komödie Theater in Berlin on 25 November 1927, retitled *Die Ehe von Welt*, where it ran for seventy performances. In January 1928 it was put on in Paris, where Edward Stirling's English Players kept it in repertory for five years.

discomfort as though liquid tin had somehow got mixed up with my blood-stream, making sleep impossible and setting my teeth on edge'.

A specialist found nothing 'organically' wrong, but said that Noel was 'in a bad way as far as nerves are concerned. He said I have been living on nervous energy for years and now it has given out and that I must go away at once!' Coward was on the verge of a nervous breakdown, a reprise of the mental illness that had struck him in 1918. With the recommendation that a long sea voyage was the best way to recuperate, he planned a two-month trip, to take him farther from home than he had ever been. 'I feel I must get away from all the people I know for a while,' he explained to his mother, 'not only from the point of view of health but for my work as well. From now onwards I'm not going to work so hard anyhow – Jack will have charge of all contracts and things and I shan't think about anything.' He reassured Violet, 'I wouldn't take this drastic step unless I'd thought it out carefully . . . it really is the only thing to do . . .' Coward had to flee the claustrophobia of his self-created world; if he stayed too long (as Graham Greene observed elsewhere), he might discover how thin the ice was beneath his feet.

Coward celebrated his twenty-seventh birthday quietly in New York and, two days later, he and Wilson left for San Francisco. Jack had insisted on accompanying him that far; he was against the idea of a solo trip. They stopped off to see Syrie Maugham in Chicago, where she had opened a shop in partnership with Elizabeth Arden and a local architect, David Adler. They lunched and dined together, and Noel 'went quietly to the Theatre and *straight* back to bed and felt perfectly *awful*'. Noel and Jack travelled on in the company of the Magees, Florence and John. San Francisco was 'fresh but not cold, the streets . . . steep like Edinburgh with divine shops and Chinatown right in the middle of everything!' Diana Cooper and Iris Tree (still touring with *The Miracle*) were also at the hotel, the Fairmont, and with Max Reinhardt they had a 'grand party' on Christmas Eve, at which Paul Robeson sang. Cooper wrote, 'Noel Coward is on the edge of a nervous breakdown which he proposes to have in China.' She lacked tact, and was said to have told Coward, 'I saw your play and I didn't laugh once', to which Noel replied, 'How strange. I saw yours, and laughed right through it.' Her taste was also lacking on this occasion; she wrote of Robeson's performance, 'His voice is amazingly beautiful and soft, but niggy-wiggs have no accent or bone or grit and it doesn't stir one.'

At four o'clock on Christmas Day, Coward sailed for Hong Kong on the *President Pierce* (which Noel naturally renamed 'Peirce'). A quayside band played as Jack (wearing Noel's fur coat which he was taking back to New York) waved 'with a very forced, gay smile, then as I couldn't see any more I went below to my cabin'. He arrived in Honolulu on New Year's Eve after a bad six-day voyage which exacerbated his nervous condition. Almost hysterical and fearful for his sanity, he persuaded the ship's doctor to give him a sedative. He landed on the island with a temperature of 103 degrees, and realised he could not undertake the world tour he had planned; once again, all his arrangements had to be altered. Luckily, friends of the Magees, Walter and Louise Dillingham, had been alerted to his predicament, and had him met off the boat by their Japanese chauffeur, complete with the traditional Hawaiian *lei*.

Walter Dillingham had married Louise Acton (a cousin of Harold Acton) in 1910, at the Actons' villa, La Pietra, in Florence. On their return to Honolulu the Dillinghams built their own pastel-pink La Pietra on Diamond Head (designed by David Adler, Syrie Maugham's partner), complete with Venetian terraces and statues. The house was known to the press as 'an international celebrity centre', and Coward was comforted to discover that his hosts were 'very rich and very nice and are virtually King and Queen of Honolulu'. The energetic Louise Dillingham whisked Noel off to La Pietra, where Coward was plunged into a lunch party; dizziness sent him reeling from the table and back to the Moana Hotel. The Dillinghams arranged for a charming doctor, Paul Withington, who put Noel to bed for three days and told him it would be at least a month before he could go on with his trip. The Dillinghams sent him to their country ranch at Mokuleia, at the foot of the island's highest mountain; Withington drove him there, through banana and cane plantations. It was a tropical paradise: camellias and roses grew wild, and a coral reef guaranteed safe bathing off the beach. After supper, he and Withington stripped for a moonlight swim: in that blood-warm sea, balm to a bruised soul, virtually any trouble could be forgotten.

'The colouring of course is beyond belief, just like Robinson Crusoe', Noel enthused, captivated by the 'deep blue ocean – bright green lagoon – dazzling yellow sand – enormous cocoa palms and scarlet hibiscus everywhere'. As a young boy, he had avidly read South Sea Island romances, and acknowledged that these books 'injected into me the first insidious drops of that wanderlust which has lured me in later years to so many remote corners of the world'. That lure was the sensual freedom of tropical climes, where few clothes were needed, and the restrictions of society were even fewer.

Coward stayed there for several weeks, looked after by the French caretaker and his wife. He spent the time sea- and sunbathing, and writing a song inspired by his contentment, 'A Room with a View'. The restoration of peace brought reflections on his recent successes. Coward saw most of the world as 'greedy and predatory, and if you gave them the chance, they would steal unscrupulously the heart and soul out of you without really wanting to or even meaning to'; he also realised that ascending stars descended just as quickly. His true friends – whose loyalty did not depend on the box-office receipts of his last play – were to be valued. It was another epiphany of sorts, comparable to the moment of revelation he had had years before when touring with Esme Wynne. It left Coward more than ever aware of the instability of his calling, and the need to temper his public profile with a private assertion of self.

Still suffering exhaustion, Coward would not appear on stage at all during 1927. But when he arrived back in New York, met by Jack Wilson and Gladys Calthrop ('both looking much younger and nicer then when I had left them'), everything seemed better; even the *Olympic* (which was the sister ship to the SS *Titanic*) had been repainted. On it, Noel and Jack sailed home to England, Goldenhurst and Violet.

He discovered that *The Marquise* had opened successfully at the Criterion, with Marie Tempest, her husband W. Graham Browne and a young actor named Godfrey Winn, the 'flashy young man' who became better known as a journalist. The play was a triumphant return to form for Coward. Set among the aristocracy of eighteenth-century France (with dialogue irredeemably 1920s England), it is a high comic tale of Eloise, the middle-aged former lover of taciturn and puritanical Raoul, and Esteban, a happier man. It romps along, employing familiar Coward devices (on her arrival, Eloise says, 'The château seemed so large from the outside, but there, moonlight is very deceptive, is it not?', a line reused in *Private Lives*; and the inebriated Raoul's wild talk of debauchery compares with similar scenes in *Design for Living* and *Fallen Angels*). Raoul and Esteban fight a duel for Eloise's favours, while she delivers a running commentary, 'Really, considering your joint ages, you're doing magnificently.' She makes the two friends embrace, then confesses that they were the only men she loved: 'in this depraved age it's rather humiliating to admit it, but it's true'. Honour is restored when Raoul admits he loves her, and asks her to marry him.

It is a spirited, funny and fast-moving play, a deft crowd-pleaser. Coward arrived in London the day after it had opened, and found that it was exactly as he had imagined it, back in his White Sulphur Springs room. Marie Tempest 'brought to perfection the art of playing comedy with repressed laughter in her voice', exactly right for the part of Eloise. Although the *Morning Post* thought Coward 'still cannot write an effective love scene; his imagination is defeated when he cannot be flippant about the mating of true lovers', it found the play 'delicious and done with dexterity and delicacy'. It ran for 129 performances. 'Wasn't *The Marquise* delicious?' wrote G. B. Stern to Esme Wynne-Tyson. 'All his old sparkle and lightness back again. And I'd been getting so depressed over *Easy Virtue* and *The Queen Was in the Parlour* – the latter my godchild, damn him!'

With a playwright as popular as Coward had become, it was only a matter of time before his works were taken up by the growing movie industry and, early in 1927, his other costume drama, *The Queen Was in the Parlour*, was filmed. Coward made tentative forays into the media in the late 1920s, having sold the rights of *The Queen Was in the Parlour* and *The Vortex* to Michael Balcon's Gainsborough Films. The former was made in conjunction with the German company UFA, at their studios in Berlin, starring Paul Richter and directed by 'Jack' Graham Cutts, who had made the sensational *Cocaine* in 1921 (a title the censors insisted be changed to *While London Sleeps*).

Given the different requirements of stage and screen, and the rivalry between them, the film of *The Queen Was in the Parlour* was surprisingly well received. 'Another satisfied screen author is Mr Noel Coward,' noted a contemporary journal, 'whose "The Queen Was In The Parlour" . . . was privately shown last week. Mr Graham Cutts has made a remarkably expert film of this royal romance. Although not lacking in his characteristic faults, an over-prolonged dance-room scene, and some ice-rink diversions which have nothing to do with the story, it is by far his best film. The photography is beautiful, the settings lavish, while in Lili Damita a genuine new "star" has been found . . . Miss Damita, who is French, was discovered, quite accidentally, in a

Paris cabaret.'* The critic declared it 'a definite success', and 'a welcome change from the standardised fare which Hollywood is ... providing'.

In 1927 the British film industry was emerging from a period of depression, and was keen to find new material; writers such as Arnold Bennett and H. G. Wells were being tempted to work for the screen. Two years previously, Coward had been commissioned to write titles for productions by Michael Balcon, which probably led to Balcon's production of *The Queen Was in the Parlour*. Coward's interest in films was primarily financial; he agreed with Basil Dean (who was venturing into the business) that the medium was not yet an art – it was still referred to by some as 'the poor man's theatre'.

There were two other film adaptations of Noel's plays during the 1920s, when companies waited a year or less before filming a successful stage work. London was dotted with studios, the most advanced being that at Poole Street in Islington, started by Famous Players–Lasky (later Paramount Pictures) in 1920, and equipped with state-of-the-art facilities, housed in a former power station, on land owned by Lord Alington. It was subsequently taken over by Michael Balcon and Gainsborough Pictures, who made some of the best-known British films of the period there. To this rather dingy part of east London came the glamorous figures of Betty Balfour and Ivor Novello, the only homegrown British film stars of the period. Novello was under contract to Gainsborough, earning up to £4000 a picture. He and Isabel Jeans starred in *The Rat* ('the story of an Apache'), filmed at Islington in 1924 from a screenplay written by Novello and Constance Collier (under the pseudonym David L'Estrange). Novello was typecast for the part with his sultry good looks, dark eyes and artfully dishevelled hair; a British Valentino. Two years later, attracted by the money and quick work, Noel supplied the subtitles for a sequel, *Return of the Rat: The Count, a man of more cash than consequence, who kept his heart in his trouser pocket along with his other small change.*

The same year (1927) Gainsborough's version of *Easy Virtue* appeared, starring Isabel Jeans, produced by Balcon and directed at Islington by Alfred Hitchcock, already one of Britain's highest-paid and sought-after directors. Balcon claimed that this was Britain's retort to

---

* Actually Damita had already starred in two films by G. W. Pabst. She later married Errol Flynn (who nicknamed his wife Tiger Lil) and was said to have had an affair with Marlene Dietrich.

the criticism that its film industry aped America, failing to develop its own style, as Germany had done. 'Easy Virtue is the answer: a country-house play with country people ... the future of the cinema lies in the hands of the young writers,' he concluded portentously, 'and Mr Coward, as one of the most brilliant of them all, is a notable newcomer to British films.'

There was, however, a considerable problem in adapting Noel's dialogue to the then silent screen; its spirit was entirely lost in one-line titles. Hitchcock tried to overcome this by stressing the visual dynamic of the story, but in so doing changed the story line considerably. The film opens with Larita accused of adultery by her estranged husband; she flees to the Riviera, and there meets John Whittaker. Hitchcock's characteristic humour was evident even then: to show that the newly-weds have left France for England, a French poodle on one of their trunks is exchanged for a British bulldog. The climax comes with a second divorce trial, in which Larita's address to the press photo-graphers – 'Shoot! There is nothing left to kill' – was believed by Hitchcock to be one of the worst lines of dialogue he ever wrote.*

Coward was aware of the problem, but the box-office lure of his name on the credits encouraged directors to adapt his work. Michael Balcon later said, 'It was no doubt wrong of us to seek to bask in the reflected glory of people like Noel Coward; we followed trends and did not try to make them.' In early 1928 Adrian Brunel was commissioned to film The Vortex. Brunel had set up Minerva Films in 1920 in partnership with Leslie Howard. Having seen The Vortex, he had his reservations about filming it, not only because it was difficult to put across visually but because of its subject matter. The strict British Board of Film Censors was even less likely than their stage counterparts to take a positive view of drug-taking and sex on film.

Jeffrey Bernard, 'Wardour Street's ace salesman', was sent to argue the case with the censors, and returned triumphant. 'It's OK, except that the mother mustn't have a lover, and, of course, her son mustn't take drugs.' A new script was written. 'When Noel read the script he was speechless for a moment,' Brunel recalled, 'and then let out a torrent of criticism that even the telephone couldn't stop.' The script was changed, but was still unrecognisable, 'We took the risk of letting the mother have a platonic boy-friend and the son very nearly take to

---

* Yet Lindsay Anderson commented that Hitchcock's Easy Virtue was 'almost as prodigious an accomplishment' as Ernst Lubitsch's adaptation of Lady Windermere's Fan in 1925.

drugs!' Coward screen-tested to reprise his stage role on screen, but eventually Ivor Novello was cast as Nicky; Willette Kershaw, a fey American actress who seemed to subsist on vegetable extract pellets, was engaged as Florence. Brunel was in the Austrian Tyrol shooting *The Constant Nymph* with Novello and Frances Doble when an executive demanded *The Vortex*, and it was edited in his absence. This, and some hastily written 'peppy' subtitles, resulted in an unsatisfactory product.

The film was released in March 1928 to equivocal notices, and the failure of this new attempt at bringing Coward to the screen underlined the inherent problems: as film historian Rachel Low observed, 'epigrams depending on a throwaway delivery looked merely facetious in the portentous pause of a title'. Unlike Hitchcock's attempt, Brunel's film had not made a successful leap from one medium to another. 'At all events the loss of dialogue and the absence of action were fatal to the film', Low wrote.

It was not until the advent of the talkies that a convincing film could be made from a Noel Coward play. (Talking pictures had arrived with *The Jazz Singer* in 1927, but two years later, Coward remained doubtful: 'I'm not interested in them at present', he told an American reporter. 'So many of them sound as if the speaker's palate had been cut.') As Balcon learned to his cost, sound was vital to Coward's work on screen; in 1928 he commissioned Noel to write *Concerto*, a costume romance for Novello. The script 'cried out for music', and despite having agreed to pay Noel £1200 (in monthly instalments of £100), Balcon suggested calling the film off. Coward agreed, and returned the money. This honourable gesture brought good fortune; Noel reused the *Concerto* plot profitably for his most successful musical, *Bitter Sweet*.

In the wake of his recent illness and his absence from the stage, Coward sought home comforts, and decided to buy Goldenhurst outright, 'at a ridiculously small price'. The house became his country retreat, and the venue for weekend parties for the great and good of London theatre and society.

All 'family horrors of sentimental value' were banished to Violet's and Vida's bedrooms, and Syrie Maugham was summoned to provide an appropriate interior. Local antique shops were searched for suitable fixtures; a trip to an auction at nearby Herstmonceaux resulted in the pillaging of a seventeenth-century Cornish tin 'Winged Time' allegory, and a large Grinling Gibbons wood carving, intricately baroque, which were hung on Goldenhurst's walls, now rendered fashionably pale. 'Syrie's' supplied a sofa long enough to accommodate five or six posteriors, and the curtains and coverings were in pale green and beige. Another whimsical touch was Coward's songsheets pasted along a connecting corridor, at the end of which was the Big Room, with two grand pianos back-to-back. With bare white plaster, exposed beams, and open fireplaces, Noel now had a stylish set for his impromptu performances, or home movies of his travels and the Mickey Mouse cartoons he loved. He even stage-managed the approach to his new home; as his later neighbour, Patricia Frere, noted: 'The house [was] ... practically on the road, with a farm gate entrance. Noel bought the wood behind [so] you went in by another entrance ... this nice drive through the woods to the house. It was a better arrival point.'

This island of West End sophistication amid the rural idyll of the Romney Marshes might have caused local concern, but Mrs Frere and other neighbours 'took him for granted. No loud parties – nobody would've heard if there had been. He was awfully good to people. He gave the farmer, whom he scarcely knew, quite a big tract of land, which he would've bought, but he gave it to him.' By such good neighbourliness Coward eased himself into country life; not that he seemed to take much notice of the environment; as one visitor, Katharine Hepburn, recalled, 'It was nice, but it was Noel in the country, you know. He wasn't interested in the country. It was just like the city, only the temperature was different.'

Old cine films bring Goldenhurst summers to life in flickering black and white, the stars at their ease in casual wear and shorts, cavorting on the Kentish lawn, showing off for the camera. Noel, in pale linen and narrow espadrilles, larks about boyishly, revelling in the freedom of his home and the confidence of the host. But guests could sometimes prove difficult. Elsa Maxwell and Dickie Fellowes-Gordon came over from Paris, Dickie bearing 'a big jar of French coffee, because I knew English coffee was so *bad*. When we arrived and I gave it to Noel, he said, "Oh dear, I do hope Dickie isn't going to be *difficult* this weekend!"' Thus did Dickie earn her nickname, 'the Black Bitch'.

In summer 1927 Coward and Wilson toured Europe: Vienna ('fearfully grand'); Budapest ('huge and flat and hot and stupid'); and Achensee, in the Austrian Tyrol, 'far far too crowded with pot-bellied Germans in mustard-coloured plush hats with Alpenstocks tramping about everywhere'. They left the next day, ending up at Lac d'Annecy above Aix-les-Bains, with a 'sweet little terrace and balconies outside our rooms looking across at the most lovely mountains'. 'I've never felt so well in my life,' he wrote home, 'travelling agrees with me. We've been everywhere second class and thoroughly enjoyed ourselves – not being grand is somehow a tremendous comfort for a change ... It's quite the most beautiful place I've ever seen. We have our own little boat and bathe from it all day. We're very sunburnt and I feel marvellous.'

From Aix they went south, to Edward Molyneux's luxurious villa, La Capponcina, on Cap d'Ail. It was another outpost of the international set, who worshipped the sun and descended on one another's summer residences in a succession of house parties. Molyneux had opened a salon in Monte Carlo to capitalise on this lucrative new market of the Côte d'Azur. Coward turned 'ebony' on a balcony with views of mountains to the left, Monaco ahead, and 'deep blue sea' to the right, intermittently working on his new revue. Syrie Maugham was down too, and came to lunch at La Capponcina, responding with an invitation to weekend at her own villa nearby.

But the weekend was fraught with tension, partly because of Syrie's strained relationship with her husband, now spending most of his time with Gerald Haxton. Also there were Beverley Nichols, then writing plays and music; Frankie Leverson, a dancer who had taught the Prince of Wales; and Doris Delavigne (later Castlerosse), another sexual adventurer, former flatmate of Gertrude Lawrence and supposed model for *Private Lives*' Amanda. As the guests assembled for dinner, Gerald Haxton tried to shock Syrie by telling her how he had seduced a twelve-year-old girl in Siam for a tin of condensed milk. Afterwards they all went to the casino, and Haxton got very drunk. Back at the villa, Nichols, investigating gurgling noises from Haxton's room, found him naked on his bedroom floor, covered in thousand-franc notes and his own vomit.

According to Nichols, it was not only Haxton whose behaviour was reprehensible. Perhaps encouraged by the dissoluteness of his fellow countryman, Jack Wilson sneaked into Nichols's bedroom in the early hours of the morning, and tried to make love to him. Coward burst in, looking like 'the wrath of a thousand Chinese gods'; coldly, he ordered Wilson to leave, and accused Nichols of having invited him in. In a letter to Cole Lesley in 1976, Nichols wrote, '"Did Noel ever tell you the true story of what happened between Jack and myself chez Syrie, ... or rather, what did not happen? It is a very strange story and I have an uncanny feeling that it clouded my relations with Noel for the rest of our lives ... he never forgot it, nor did I – though my conscience is as clean as a newly polished whistle. Jack behaved like every variety of bitch." '*

Although his involvement with Jack was, like most of Noel's romances, understood to be an 'open affair', the manner of Wilson's attempted seduction of Nichols, who was a rival of Coward's in other respects, was hurtful and coloured their future relations. Tellingly, Wilson was not included in plans to go to Biarritz with Edward Molyneux, and returned to London, where he busied himself with less dangerous affairs.

On 13 September, Coward returned to England, to find Gladys Calthrop back from America, 'with a hard black hat and mumps', caught from Eva Le Gallienne with whom she had just fallen out. Noel had lamented the temporary loss of his designer, and had work for her to do. He had written a new play called *Home Chat* (after a women's magazine of the same name), inevitably set in Mayfair society. Janet Ebony is discovered in a train crash to have been sharing a *wagon-lit* with Peter Chelsworth, much to her husband's and her family's dismay; they refuse to believe the couple's innocence, so she determines to play the vamp, allowing herself to be discovered in Peter's flat, supposedly making love. The play ends as Janet really does go off with a lover – but the assembled and chastened company are now so convinced of her original innocence that they do not believe this either.

In *Home Chat*, comedy disguises deeper themes; Coward's couples strain to communicate: 'We none of us ever say what we really mean', Sorel complains in *Hay Fever*. Nor did Noel. Whatever meaning there might be in his dramas is hidden because he could never write directly about his own experiences. Conventional morality is replaced by Cowardian morality: a self-constructed code of conduct based on traditional values of duty, discipline and loyalty, yet compromised by a homosexual lifestyle and sensibility (hence his anger at Wilson's betrayal). It is not surprising that his dramatic worlds were upside-down, considering the inverted emotional acrobatics required to create them. In *Home Chat*, flippancy rules, everything is false, hypocrisy and suspicion are rife; it is a play almost cynically concerned with the futile chase of sex.

He seems to have been concerned as to how the play would be

---

* Nichols used the incident in his published indictment of Maugham's behaviour towards his wife, *A Case of Human Bondage*, but substituted Haxton for Wilson and Maugham for Coward.

received. It was sent to the censor (under its original title *To Err Is Human*): 'This reads like a Noel Coward play', wrote George Street, indicating that it had been submitted under another name, as Noel had told Violet he might do with *The Marquise* in an attempt to avoid prejudice. 'It is an amusing light comedy and the main part of it, though risky in a way, might well pass, but a characteristic immoral twist is given at the end ... The main idea, an innocent woman pretending to be guilty, is not pretty but is certainly not a fatal objection.' Lord Cromer passed the play on 27 July.

The production went ahead, under Basil Dean's aegis, with Madge Titheradge as Janet (Coward had written the part with her in mind). Perhaps because of similarities to '*This Was a Man*', he claimed a presentiment of *Home Chat*'s failure. Rehearsals proceeded with 'sinister smoothness', and on the opening night his suspicions grew as the audience seemed restless. He writhed in his chair, 'sniffing disaster and seeing no way of averting it'. As the curtain came down, there was booing from the 'cheaper parts', although one witness disputed this: 'The curtain rose several times because of the mild applause, and then Noel was ill-advised enough to take a call ... there was no dissent until he came on stage.' Coward went out to support his cast, since Basil Dean was nowhere to be seen. He bounded on to the stage 'with my usual misguided valour', booing began, and someone shouted 'Rotten!' 'We expected better', called someone else, to which Coward replied, 'So did I', and left the stage. The notices were not as bad as Coward maintained, but many took the line of the *Westminster Gazette*, that '... the gallery was right. We expected better.'

Coward later maintained that *Home Chat* was his least favourite work, 'a thin little play ... I wrote it without taking enough trouble. When you have a failure, it's always your fault, nobody else's fault. But actors do a certain amount of damage.' He tended to apportion blame, and in this case he was probably right to do so; the play was 'very slowly directed by Basil Dean' and hampered by an elderly actress (probably Nina Boucicault) who forgot her lines. 'It was a little better than bad but not quite good enough, and that was that.'

Coward escaped to Europe for two weeks to avoid the reverberations of the flop. He sensed an anti-Coward feeling in the air and he was not wrong. James Agate came to his defence in a broadcast on the BBC, stating his belief in the young playwright's work. But such support could not stem the incoming tide.

*

Given the failure of *Home Chat*, which ran for just thirty-eight performances, the precipitate production of *Sirocco* can be seen, in hindsight, as rash, and indicative of the arrogance Coward readily acknowledged. The play had been written in 1921, and revised for production; it was nearer 1924's *The Vortex* than 1927's *Home Chat* in content, substance and style. Dedicated to Mrs Astley Cooper, its title derives from the sirocco wind of the Alassio region, said to drive the unwary insane – which should have warned audiences that this was no comedy.

The play relied on notions of foreign passion; its portrayal of the British in 1920s Italy evokes an atmosphere similar to that of E. M. Forster's *A Room with a View* (1908),* in that it introduces the closeted, buttoned-up sensibilities of the English to the sensual, free-living Italians; a clash of cultures which, in *Sirocco*, produces conflict.

Sirio Marson, half-English, half-Italian but with Latin looks and temperament, seduces Lucy, a young English wife left temporarily in Italy by her husband. When he arrives to reclaim her, he accuses Lucy of 'glorying in your – your – degradation'. She retorts that he wants her back for the sake of his good name, not for love, shouting, 'We have no tie of any sort but the memory of a short service in Church . . . We've been bored, bored, bored' – the *cri de coeur* of her generation. But she now realises that 'free love' is 'hateful and sordid and cheap'. Sirio is effete, unserious, immature; a contrast to the post-war woman, who wants to be liberated. As Sirio leaves, she exults, 'I'm free – free for the first time in my life', then, burying her face in her arms, cries, 'God help me!'

The play thus ends in a desolate cry of despair; or at least that was Coward's intention. But his desire to shock seems to have overcome his better judgement, and the play predictably aroused the censor's attention; the original copy sent to Lord Cromer's office is thick with blue pencil. Lines such as an Italian exchange – 'Sirio: Guardo dove vai bastardo incretinito. Giuseppa: Un bastardo sei te, figlio, d'una cagna' – had the censors reaching for their dictionary.† But while Street noted

---

* It is perhaps no coincidence that Noel used Forster's title for one of his songs; a knifing scene in the play also recalls Forster's novel. It is tempting to see a comparison between Forster and Coward as middle-class mother's boys, homosexual, dealing with contemporary cultural issues of class, sex and society.

† George Street noted the 'long string of abuse. I do not understand it, but the Lord Chamberlain no doubt will. Of course few people in the audience will.' However, Lord Cromer's holidays on the Italian Riviera had not resulted in a grasp of the language. Sir George Crichton had to write to Sir Hubert Montgomery, 'Dear Hubert, Could you possibly

the violent love scenes and bad language, he thought it 'hardly an immoral play, as the sinful ménage comes to grief'. As did the play itself.

Sirocco ought to have been a Josef von Sternberg film, with artfully directed carnival scenes and the seductive Marlene Dietrich to enliven matters; but it was anchored to the London stage, and Ivor Novello was cast as Sirio. Novello had not been impressed when Coward had shown him the script two years previously, but was talked into the part by the playwright and Basil Dean. He seemed to enjoy rehearsals, 'behaving on the whole gaily, as though he were at a party'. His co-star, Frances Doble, was however 'frankly terrified from beginning to end. She looked lovely, but, like Ivor, lacked technique.'

On the evening of 24 November 1927 Noel set off with Violet, Gladys and Jack Wilson, 'elaborately dressed and twittering with nerves', for what would be his most humiliating night in the theatre. Coward's first impression was of restlessness in the house, then during Novello's love scene with Doble, the gallery burst out laughing, compounding uproar with sucking sounds whenever the couple kissed. What Coward had written to shock came over as farce. The *Evening Standard* commented, 'It was understandable that the gallery should have laughed a good deal . . . a love scene that consists of few words and many kisses is almost more than the silliest parts of the house can stand.' Matters worsened; catcalls 'and various other animal noises' punctuated every other line, reaching to a crescendo in the final act. As the curtain fell, even Violet's deafness had been penetrated. 'Is it a failure?' she asked her son wistfully.

Against Dean's advice, Noel went onstage. He shook Ivor's hand, and kissed Frances Doble's; as he left, the booing increased in volume. Prickling, Coward returned centre stage, bowing and smiling at the wolf-whistles and catcalls which he weathered for seven minutes. Frances Doble, called for by the crowd, received the first friendly applause of the night. 'Ladies and gentlemen, this is the happiest moment of my life', she said, somewhat bizarrely. Noel heard Ivor 'gurgle', and broke into laughter himself. The booing started all over again, and the curtain came down for the final time. Raymond Massey claimed that he saw at least three fist fights between Coward baiters and supporters. Even getting out of the theatre was hazardous. Coward was warned not to leave by

get one of your knowledgeable people in the Foreign Office to give us a translation of the Italian [in] the enclosed play. It would be very kind if you would do this for us as no one here knows a word of Italian.'

the stage door where a hostile crowd awaited him. This fixed his resolve, and he marched out, to be spat at. 'The next day I had to send my evening coat to the cleaners', he said, with a wryness worthy of Wilde, with whose varying fortunes Coward may have felt some sympathy. Noel sought to rise above it all; he ascended in the tiny lift to Ivor's Aldwych eyrie, where the critic Edward Marsh joined him and Novello for supper. Marsh was impressed 'by the dispassionate courage, free from all trace of self-pity, with which the two routed aspirants, neither of whom would have been surprised to be told that he was irreparably done for, discussed the failure and its causes'.

The press was also up in arms. The notices, said Noel, had not one good word for the play, with only two exceptions: a defensive piece by Edgar Wallace, and a review by the *Observer*'s St John Ervine. Ervine acknowledged Coward's display of courage at the first night as 'wholly admirable'; he saw the play as a 'tract' against 'cinema romance', and insisted it was not pornographic; he added that Novello had given 'the best performance that I have yet seen him give in any play'. The *Sketch* disproved Coward's contention of uniformly bad reviews, 'Just as the third act was the making of *The Vortex*, so it was the salvation of *Sirocco* ... The scene in which the lovers part ... is magnificent.' But the impression was of a monumental flop; the next day, half the pre-sold tickets for the next three performances were returned.

Coward dramatised the event as 'the most abysmal failure I have ever had'. He had been proud that the play 'was completely different ... from anything I had done hitherto'; but afterwards realised it was 'only passably written and poorly constructed'. He considered it 'badly directed by Basil Dean and inadequately acted by Frances Doble and Ivor Novello'. This was ungracious, and blaming Dean meant an acrimonious end to their relationship. Coward held aloof. 'My first instinct was to leave England immediately', but this would be an admission of defeat. He decided to be in evidence for a week, and then to go to America, trusting that a year's absence would make British hearts grow fonder. He appeared at his usual table in the sheltering stained-glass emporium of the Ivy, then, after a few days of toughing it out, escaped with Jack Wilson to Europe, rather than to America. They stayed at Neuilly with Edward Molyneux in the designer's 'quiet, lovely little house'; rural peace was a relief after the trauma of recent days. He told Violet that their lives were 'very simple ... sleeping 12 hours a night'. But he remained depressed and 'exceedingly upset' by press coverage of his failures.

It seemed that there was no halfway point for Coward with the media. He came to realise that they sought to polarise opinion; in their simplistic world, things were all good, or all bad – this is what sells papers. As a playwright, he knew that drama required conflict; stars were built up, then demolished, and were seldom realistic figures. This was the nature and the price of fame. But it did not alleviate the frustration, nor did it stop Coward coming to the decision, made when in Paris, that he would never give another interview. Yet the quandary remained: his image and his career were dependent on the publicity.

He and Jack spent Christmas at St Moritz, where they celebrated Noel's twenty-eighth birthday. They went tobogganing and skating all day, and Noel felt 'marvellous'. At the end of December, he returned to what still seemed a hostile territory, but the new year would bring his greatest success yet.

12

Bitter Sweet

I believe in doing what I can
In crying when I must,
In laughing when I choose
Heigho, if love were all
I should be lonely.

'If Love Were All', *Bitter Sweet*

IN late summer 1927 the Lunts had arrived from the United States, where they had finished their run in *The Second Man*, a comedy by a new American writer, S. N. Behrman. Keen to involve Coward in a British production of the play, they gave an impromptu runthrough of the piece in his drawing-room. Noel promptly acquired the rights, seeing himself as 'Clark Storey', a novelist torn between two women, described as a 'cynical, intelligent dilettante'. To those who did not know him, perfect typecasting for Noel Coward.

Coward had learned his lines for the play in St Moritz, cabling Dean from Paris, where he was delayed: CROSSING SUNDAY IF POSSIBLE WORD PERFECT ANYHOW FIRST TWO ACTS. In London, he rehearsed with co-stars Zena Dare, Ursula Jeans and Raymond Massey. Dare recalled that it was 'a very sophisticated, *chic* play – rather *avant-garde* for 1927'. She had not been on stage since her marriage in 1910 and found it difficult to readjust, 'constantly breaking into tears during rehearsals'. Coward took her aside and told her it could not continue, 'After all, if you were working for the Post Office you couldn't behave like this, could you?' She was invited to Ebury Street, where they worked together. 'His patience and forbearance were terrific,' Dare said, 'and of course I did get better.'

Behrman arrived from New York, and met the company at the Playhouse Theatre. 'Noel was in great form', he wrote; 'he'd been, the night before, to the Pantomime and he did an imitation of Miss Florrie Ford, the principal "boy". He described her: beyond middle age, corpulent, with a garish voice and a garish smile. He became Miss Ford ... he sang Miss Ford's song, "If your fyce wants to smile well LET IT." Miss Ford's smile was cosmic. Noel "let it" amply before all of us.' Behrman was amazed at Coward's technique at rehearsals, running through the words so fast that it was like listening to a play in a foreign language. 'Noel must have felt this because he called out to me, "We're probably going too fast for you but don't worry about the tempo – our audience will understand us." The third act began with Noel reading some pages he had just written, crushing them up and throwing them in the waste-basket while he stigmatised them, "Trash, trash, trash". When he'd read this, he confided to us, "Don't be surprised if there's a little burst of applause when I say that"' – a reference to recent events. There were rumours that Coward was the real author, anonymous because of the *Sirocco* débâcle; with its elegant use of language and simple plot, involving just four characters, *The Second Man* seemed to bear his imprint; but he admitted he had not contributed one word to the production.

The play opened on 24 January. Behrman noted the difference between the cultural and social position of the theatre in New York and London. 'The actors' dressing rooms were, after each performance, lively and entertaining social centers where you could meet the most brilliant figures in London society.' Even the players were socially elevated: Zena Dare was the daughter-in-law of Viscount Esher; Raymond Massey the younger brother of the governor general of Canada. Coward was astounded when Behrman asked, 'Who is that man? He seems to be well connected.' 'Well connected!' cried Noel. 'It's Prince Arthur of Connaught! Queen Victoria was his grandmother.'

Notices for the play were good, and between performances, rehearsals began for Coward's new revue for C. B. Cochran. Noel had offered to release Cochran from their contract, but the latter reasoned that after two failures Coward would be motivated to make the revue a success. Soon Cochran was announcing to the press, 'What I have seen of this revue "book" is some of the most brilliantly witty work Coward has ever done.' Lorn Loraine contributed the title – *This Year of Grace!*; all Noel had to do was to write the music. One of the first songs to be put down on paper, with Elsie April's help, was 'Dance, Little Lady'. As sung by Sonnie Hale and Lauri Devine, it was a reprise, in both tempo and sentiment, of 'Poor Little Rich Girl', and like that song, it was a critique of the archetypal flapper:

> Dance, dance, dance little lady,
> Youth is fleeting – to the rhythm beating
> In your mind.
> Dance, dance, dance little lady,
> So obsessed with second best
> No rest you'll ever find.

In a dance-mad era, incessant movement took the place of intelligent thought, and Coward's admonishing voice was apposite:

> But I know it's vain,
> Trying to explain
> While there's this insane
> Music in your brain.

The song even had a 'patter' section, which showed the influence of black music heard when Noel was in the States:

> When the saxophone
> Gives a wicked moan,
> Charleston hey hey,
> Rhythms fall and rise,
> Start dancing to the tune,
> The band's crooning –

Full of internal rhymes, the sequence is virtually an early rap.

Its 78-rpm pirouette seemed innovative, but Beverley Nichols – himself a composer – claimed that 'the first eight bars revealed themselves as identical with a charming Edwardian ballad'. Coward admitted the plagiarism, 'but I didn't realise this when it came into my head, and now it's too late to do anything about it'. Anyway, this was no wistful period piece, but a harsh attack on modern life:

> And when the lights are starting to gutter
> Dawn through the shutter
> Shows you're living in a world of lies.

Perhaps influenced by his visits to Berlin cabarets and their contemporary satire, Coward had uniquely injected the social criticism of his plays into an English revue song.

The show also featured another potential hit song, for which Noel would always be remembered, 'A Room with a View', written in

Hawaii, now sung by Jessie Matthews, Sonnie Hale and Adrienne Brune. As both dramatist and composer, Coward's success in revues lay in his ability to create vivid scenes to accompany his songs. At rehearsals he was at pains to realise them, applying strict theatre discipline even to these flimsy sketches. Sheilagh Graham, then a Cochran 'Young Lady', recalled a rehearsal in Soho. 'No, no. That's not the way to do it! Let me show you', Coward told her. 'He took me in his arms. "Now, look at me as though you were disdainful of me . . ."' Unsure what disdainful meant, she 'promptly turned my most dazzling smile on him'. 'Oh, my God', said Noel. 'Let's go on to the next scene.'

The mixture of contemporary reality and glamorous fantasy in *This Year of Grace!* gave the revue formula a Coward twist. The opening number was set in a tube station, with disgruntled passengers vexed by a street urchin whistling an insinuating dance tune, the equivalent of today's overloud personal stereo; but so infectious is the rhythm that the passengers soon join the dance. There were pertinent jokes: a booking-clerk and newspaper vendor chat: 'What we want in England is more and better birth control', says Harry, when Charles, 'a very exquisite young man', enters. 'All right – you've won,' says Fred, 'I'm all for birth control.' Charles buys a ticket for Queen's Gate, and Fred remarks, ''Arry, that's wot the Russian Ballet's done for England.' In the Lido scene, the Venetian playground of the rich was contrasted with the mundane English version (the world of Noel's childhood holidays): 'There's sand in the porridge and sand in the bed/ And if this is pleasure, we'd rather be dead.' The style of the show was underlined by the chic decor of Gladys Calthrop, Doris Zinkeisen and Oliver Messel. Messel's designs for 'Dance, Little Lady' included bizarre *papier-mâché* masks, pop-eyed and open-mouthed, worn by dancers in shiny suits surrounding an intimidated Tilly Losch. Set to a saw-edged soundtrack, it was one of the great *mises-en-scène* of 1920s musical theatre.

The revue ran for 316 performances, earning Coward the immense sum of £1000 a week in royalties, and further income from sales in their thousands of the hit songs in sheet music and gramophone records. Noel was restored to grace, and his audience delighted in the self-referential jab of the number 'Any Noel Coward Play', in which an actress declared, 'Ladies and gentlemen, this is the happiest moment of my life' to boos and catcalls. However, acclaim was not universal. Writing in the *London Mercury* A. G. MacDonnell, author of *England, Their England*, noted, '*This Year of Grace* is, without exception, the dullest revue it has ever been my misfortune to see. There was hardly a single scene, situation, line, or gesture that was amusing. Of the far-famed "Coward wit" there was not an iota, or, if there was, it ought not to be far-famed ... As for the lyrics, they were innocuously neat and harmless except for one tiresome mannerism. Mr Coward has apparently just discovered the internal rhyme and uses it *ad nauseam*.'

MacDonnell was representative of elder critics frustrated by what they saw as a talent wasted on frivolity: 'If he turns his mind and his energy and his industry a little more to thought and study ... he may yet live down his colossal success', MacDonnell wrote later. Yet, bound up in his Englishness, he could not but acknowledge the extraordinary nature of the phenomenon, in a comment predicated on notions of class and the outsider: 'In the last hundred years only Disraeli and Wilde and Shaw have started from nothing and conquered England as Mr Coward has conquered. It is curious that he is the first Englishman [sic] to do so.'

Characteristically, Coward would confound the expectations and exhortations of the critics. His next musical left Jazz Age stridency behind, and adopted an altogether more whimsical genre, signalled by a number in *This Year of Grace!*, 'Teach Me to Dance Like Grandma':

> I'm getting tired of jazz tunes
> Monotonous,
> They've gotten us
> Crazy now . . .
> Teach me to dance like Grandma used to dance
> Sixty summers ago!

The idea of an operetta occurred to Coward in the early summer of 1928, when he and Gladys Calthrop were staying with her solicitor, Ronald Peake, in Surrey. Mrs Peake put on a record of *Die Fledermaus*, which sparked romantic associations in Noel's imagination. Inspired by *The Merry Widow* and other Edwardian musicals, he thought sentiment might make a welcome (and profitable) return to the London stage after the brittle subjects of recent years. Once again he tapped into the spirit of the times: Viennese romantic songs and books, a return of the waltz, even the longer dresses being worn by women in the late 1920s all heralded this revival. But for the moment, Coward put his imagination on hold: he had learned to allow for the fermentation of his ideas.

When *The Second Man* finished its run, Cochran and Archie Selwyn (the producer-manager) tried to persuade Coward to go to Broadway that autumn with *This Year of Grace!*, with Beatrice Lillie taking Sonnie Hale's place. Noel liked the idea, and he and Cochran set off on the *Mauretania* for a reconnaissance expedition. 'I can never stay away from New York long', Coward told reporters, lounging in his Ritz-Carlton suite wearing pyjamas 'that included two vivid blending colors'. 'It's a fact that I feel at home when I reach these shores.' Did he prefer American audiences? 'Oh, decidedly. Your New York audiences are marvellous, simply marvellous. They are so "welcoming". They want you to be good instead of bad. They are waiting for you to be good.'

He renewed old acquaintances and, through Constance Collier, met Jed Harris, 'the new phenomenon of Broadway ... an extraordinary creature with an authentic flair for the theatre' – and therefore of great interest to Coward. He thought Harris 'one of the most interesting self-devouring egos' he had ever encountered, and reminded Noel of a praying mantis.

Harris had produced *Broadway* in 1927, 'a melodramatic production depicting gangster violence in a Broadway night club', and *The Royal Family*, which Coward later directed, as *Theatre Royal*, in London. Harris went on to produce *The Green Bay Tree* (1933); starring Laurence Olivier, it was the first major Broadway play to deal with homosexuality. He was 'a man of considerable reputation with the ladies despite his rather sinister looks', Katharine Hepburn recalled; 'Laurence Olivier said he used Jed as his model for Richard III – a terrifying creature.' Harris's friends included Ben Hecht and Charles MacArthur, hard-drinking and fast-living Manhattan men, far removed from the genteel world of the West End theatre. The relationship between Harris and Coward was not lacking a certain rivalry. Harris's son recalled a later meeting, when his father 'was looking for an actor in London for *The Green Bay Tree* ... He had been going around the theatre, he'd seen Shakespearean productions and said he was very tired of seeing English kings played by English queens. Anyway, they were talking together about affairs, and my father asked if he had ever slept with a woman. There was a pause, and Noel said to him ... "It would be like going to bed with a porpoise."' S. N. Behrman later noted a divide between the two men: had they quarrelled? 'Not at all,' said Coward, 'we just don't speak to each other. The truth is, you know, I am harder and more sophisticated than Jed.'

On Broadway, Coward saw Harris's production of *Coquette*, in which Helen Hayes 'tore our emotions to shreds'. Manhattan provided one of the 'richest two weeks', from a theatrical point of view, he had ever spent; and all on an expense account. However, he and Cochran failed to find suitable performers for *This Year of Grace!*, so they took the boat home. The *Berengaria* was crowded, and they had to share a cabin: 'Although we both viewed this prospect with slight apprehension,' noted Coward, 'it turned out to be extremely cosy.' The enforced intimacy gave them ample opportunity for chats after lights-out, and Noel, who was working on the first act of *Bitter Sweet*, read it to Cochran, whetting the showman's appetite to stage the operetta.

Back in London, family arrangements changed again. With their son a wealthy man, there was now no need for the Cowards to run a boarding-house; indeed, it was embarrassing that they did. Noel retained his rooms in Ebury Street as his London *pied-à-terre*, and Arthur went to Goldenhurst to look after the gardening, a duty uncomfortably shared with Aunt Vida. Meanwhile, Violet drove her new car into the window of a grocer's shop in Ashford. Coward wrote about these happenings as a comic interlude, but matters soon took a more serious turn.

Erik, Noel's seldom-seen brother, was now twenty-three, and had drifted from job to job. 'His assets were little above average', wrote Coward coolly, admitting that his shadow 'lay heavily' on his sibling. In truth, Erik annoyed Noel and knew it; his visits to Goldenhurst were timed not to coincide with his brother's. Yet he was similar to Noel in many ways, and one shared aspect was their sexuality. Erik's intense friendship with his cousin Leslie Makeham is obvious from photographs of the two with their arms around each other (Erik a less handsome version of his brother, Leslie decidedly better looking). They spent all their time together; playing golf, visiting Norfolk, affecting Noel's style in dressing gowns and tanning themselves in the sun. Both worked in the City, often side by side; but Erik, like his brother, yearned to travel.

His prospects were discussed 'at length' by the family, and it was agreed that he should go to Ceylon in autumn 1928 as a tea planter – the empire still called its sons and daughters to far-flung colonies. On 1 July Erik wrote to Violet from Bognor Regis, where Arthur had arrived with a letter and 'news of the general fracas which once more seems to have arisen through no fault of mine . . . Noel is apparently prepared to provide £350 providing he hears nothing further on the subject . . . It's kind of Noel to be so liberal', Erik conceded, '. . . but his hardness so gets the better of him that he trusts nobody and nothing that is not a stone cold certainty. I know he has a pretty poor opinion of me . . . But he will receive a pleasant surprise one of these days . . .' Erik arrived in Ceylon in late August. There, high in the mountains above Kandy, where even the weather seemed English, he made friends with Eric Halsey and his wife, and stayed at their bungalow in Matale; photographs show him sitting on a verandah, looking the part in pith helmet and shorts. He spent three years working there until illness, already manifesting itself that October with bad stomach pains and fever, forced him to return home.

Back at Goldenhurst, further domestic friction exploded when Jack Wilson planned to rebuild the abutting barn as family accommodation, leaving the house to him and Noel, out of range of the bickering Cowards. The family objected, hinting that Noel was embarrassed for them to be seen in front of his 'new-found "grand" friends'. 'As my new-found "grand" friends that year consisted solely of Bobbie Andrews, who had come down for a couple of weekends,' maintained Noel, 'this argument seemed unjust.' The result was that Coward and Wilson had the barn converted for their use. The finished building was then coveted by the family, who promptly used it to entertain their own 'new-found "grand" friends' when Noel was away.

It is strange to think of the Cowards sharing a house with their son's lover; Noel's friends certainly found it odd. Dorothy Dickson, another of Cochran's 'Young Ladies', recalled visiting Goldenhurst one weekend: 'There were two houses and the father and auntie lived in the house next door. They were – excusez-moi – rather common . . . I saw the father the first time I went down there. I never saw him again. I thought, "Well either he's too old to speak, or he just doesn't know enough about the theatre" – we were all talking and so on. I just got the impression that he was really very ordinary and not at all [likely to have produced] a genius such as Noel Coward.'

But same-sex couples were no novelty in that part of the country. Following in Coward's footsteps, Gladys Calthrop had moved into a converted mill in Aldington, the nearest village to Goldenhurst. The stream still ran under the drawing-room, and prompted the name 'Wuthering Depths' from Coward. She was later joined there by her new girlfriend, Patience Erskine.* With Calthrop and other figures

---

* Gladys had recently conducted an affair with Mercedes de Acosta, much to Eva Le Gallienne's dismay. Patience Lina Erskine was a scion of the Earls of Buchan; an amateur mathematician, she was devoutly uninterested in the theatre world.

such as the actress Jeanne de Casalis and the publisher Erica Marx* in the area, Coward had 'a little circle of friends' to hand, according to Patricia Frere, who had met Noel when her father, Edgar Wallace, wrote his positive review of *Sirocco*; her husband Alexander was a director of Heinemann, Coward's publishers.

The Freres came to live in the area a few years later, and Patricia remembered Goldenhurst as a 'beautiful old house, really very old . . . he built on to it, but with very good taste, building at an angle. His father and mother lived in the old part, and he lived in the new bit. They were pretty separate. Anything could go on in Noel's part of the house. It was divided by a big "playroom" as the Americans call it . . . with a table always ready for chess, and another for backgammon, and jigsaw puzzles.' One evening she and her husband had been invited to dine with Coward; after drinks in the new part of the house, Noel announced, 'It's quite a long way to the dining-room. I intend to take a box lunch with me.'

'His mother we loved,' Patricia Frere said, 'a killing old girl. Perfectly outspoken . . . Say anything in front of anyone. His father – well, Noel was very good to him, [but] he was a stupid old boy . . . I don't even remember what Arthur Coward looked like . . . I only met him about twice in my life. He was tucked away.' As were Aunts Vida and Ida; 'You knew they were there, but they didn't appear.' Some perceived a degree of embarrassment for Coward about this encumbrance of relations; John Gielgud found Noel's parents 'very tiresome. His mother was pretty stupid, and his aunts were impossible. He was sort of ashamed of them.'

But Coward had more painful problems: he was suffering from haemorrhoids, and needed an operation. Visitors to the nursing home where he was operated on hedged uneasily around his 'complaint', much to his amusement. The news was important enough to warrant an item in the *New York Times*: 'Noel Coward Operated On; Dramatist Stricken in London – "This Year of Grace" Postponed.' Coward recuperated in the South of France, near Cap d'Antibes, where he was photographed sunbathing with Beatrice Lillie, about to star in the American production; she with Eton crop, in pyjamas and embroidered waistcoat; he in dressing gown, bathing cap and espadrilles, looking frail. But Noel returned to work on the show with vigour, taking a six-

---

* Erica Marx ran the Hand and Flower Press, which published Robert Greacen's *The Art of Noel Coward*.

week dancing course to limber up, combined with rehearsals in the gloomy Poland Rooms. He also wrote new numbers for the show, among them the song 'World Weary', the result of his enervating post-operative interlude. The song showed a certain frustration with the theatrical world, a mood which perhaps led Coward in a new direction that year, when he made a tentative foray into the realms of Blooms-bury. Or did they come to him?

Coward first met Virginia Woolf in January 1928 at Sibyl Colefax's house in the King's Road. A month later Woolf confessed to her lover, Vita Sackville-West, that she had fallen 'in love with Noel Coward, and he's coming to tea. You cant have all the love in Chelsea . . .', she insisted, 'Noel Coward must have some.' Having seen *This Year of Grace!*, she wrote telling him that some songs 'struck me on the forehead like a bullet. And what's more I remember them and see them enveloped in atmosphere – works of art in short . . .' Woolf apparently encouraged Coward in his desire to write fiction: 'I think you ought to bring off something that will put these cautious, creeping novels that one has to read silently in an arm chair deep, deep in the shade.' This was praise indeed from so stern a critic. She elaborated enthusiastically to her sister, Vanessa Bell, 'He is in search of culture, and thinks Bloomsbury a kind of place of pilgrimage. Will you come and meet him? He is a miracle, a prodigy. He can sing, dance, write plays, act, compose, and I daresay paint – He rescued his whole family who kept boarding houses in Surbiton, and they are now affluent, but on the verge of bankruptcy, because he spends so much on cocktails. If he could only become like Bloomsbury he thinks he might be saved.'

Bloomsbury gathered quite uncharacteristically around Coward's flame. Harold Nicolson and Vita Sackville-West also met him at Lady Colefax's salon, and he subsequently invited them to dinner. 'Noel very simple and nice', Nicolson recorded in his diary. 'He talks of the days when his mother kept lodgings in Ebury Street and he himself had a top back room. Gradually he began to make money and took the top floor for himself, finally descending to the first floor and ejecting the lodgers. "As I rose in the world I went down in the house." Completely unspoilt by success. A nice eager man.'

Noel's eagerness to stress his humble origins seems to have been designed as a play to the egalitarian Bloomsberries. His relationship with Woolf continued erratically throughout 1928, with a certain amount of soul-baring from Coward. 'I have been lunching with Sibyl to meet Noel Coward; and I enjoyed it', Woolf told Roger Fry. 'He says the English theatre is so degraded that he will not produce any serious work here in future. He says the middle classes make his life a burden. Old women in Gloucester write and abuse him for immorality. Lord Cromer can force him to leave out any sentence, or ban the whole play. He says they are infinitely more civilised in America and Berlin. So he is off to produce his plays in New York. There he makes £1000 a week, and he can say what he likes . . .'

Woolf was not surprised to receive a letter from Coward later that year, an unashamed panegyric upon her latest book, *Orlando*, a tale of a sex-changing hero/heroine based on Vita Sackville-West. 'I am still hot and glowing with it', Noel wrote fervidly from Manhattan. 'At the risk of sounding insincere', he was 'completely at your feet over it . . . Oh I do so congratulate you and thank you for the lovely "unbuttoned" feeling you've given me and I hope to God it will last. . . . If ever I could write one page to equal in beauty your "Frozen Thames" description . . . I should feel that I really was a writer. Please when I come back to England let's meet and talk a good deal . . .'

This surprising relationship had sufficient novelty to continue for some time; Coward's reservations about intellectuals were put aside for the favours of the famously so. His courting of Woolf was unabashed but it is also evidence of Coward's aspiration to become a more serious writer than his public perceived him to be.

Towards the end of October Coward returned to New York, where Cochran was already setting up the production of *This Year of Grace!* During the try-out week in Baltimore, a combination of Noel's pre-show nerves and Beatrice Lillie's 'devilish' behaviour created a crisis. Lillie was 'uppish, temperamental, tiresome, disagreeable, inconsiderate, [and] insufferable', complained about the quality of her material and refused to speak to Cochran. Coward, unable to stand any more, took a day off and the final rehearsal had to be managed by Cochran – not entirely the professional behaviour expected of the author.

The revue opened at the Selwyn Theatre on Broadway on 7 November, relaunching Coward in New York. He and Lillie appeared socially inseparable at charity balls and fashionable nightclubs, providing the American papers with ample fuel for romantic speculation. The pair were endlessly asked to sing 'Lilac Time', and a midnight benefit performance arranged by Archie Selwyn was a highlight of the season. To Cecil Beaton, also in the city, Coward was enjoying 'the triumph of his

New York career'. He met Noel at a lunch party given by the publisher of the *New York Evening Post*, Mrs Schiff, where he found his rival 'very charming and gracious' towards him, 'which was touching and I liked him for it, but although he talked hard . . . the entire time he didn't succeed in saying anything amusing or clever. He was extremely badly dressed in trousers too short and his face was sweating at every pore.'

Beaton's comments on Coward's sartorial sense were ironic, considering their subsequent meeting on the boat back to England the following April. Severely seasick, Cecil emerged on deck after two days of 'semi-coma' to find Noel and Venetia Montagu. 'At once they attacked me. "Why do you write such malicious articles? Why do you say such nasty things about Mr Coward?"' (Beaton had continued scathing about Coward's career, saying in 1925 after seeing *Fallen Angels*, 'I do think the play will help to ruin old Coward. It is quite definite that he won't live long. People will get so tired of him.')

Coward 'showed more aplomb, investigating me out of a detached curiosity'. But as the pair mimicked the photographer – 'Oh, it's too, too luvleigh!', accusing him of flamboyant gestures, an 'undulating' walk and 'conspicuously exaggerated' clothes – Beaton felt 'speechless with inferiority'. Yet Coward agreed to sit for a sketch by Beaton, for which he went to Noel's cabin. 'We've been absolutely beastly to you,' admitted Coward, '. . . let's hope you've learnt a lesson. It is important not to let the public have a loophole to lampoon you.' Noel explained how 'he studied his own "façade"' carefully, 'his voice . . . was definite, harsh, rugged. He moved firmly and solidly, dressed quietly . . . "You should appraise yourself", he advised. "Your sleeves are too tight, your voice is too high and too precise. You mustn't do it. It closes so many doors . . . It's hard, I know. One would like to indulge one's own taste. I myself dearly love a good match, yet I know it is overdoing it to wear tie, socks and handkerchief of the same colour. I take ruthless stock of myself in the mirror before going out. A polo jumper or unfortunate tie exposes one to danger." He cocked an eye at me in mockery.'*

Coward had learned what was acceptable; his advice, part of the self-defence mechanism of a homosexual man, was not to *look* queer. Crucial in Beaton's account is the final mocking gesture; with that raised

---

* When Beaton published his diaries, Coward made a belated apology: '. . . I, who usually pride myself on my psychological judgement, cannot believe I was such an ill mannered clot to you so many many years ago. Happily it *was* many many years ago and Time and a great many Tides have obliterated it, but oh dear! It's a sharp lesson . . .'

eyebrow, Coward betrayed the fact that he had overcome (or outwitted) prejudice, and that Beaton had not. The security of his place in the meritocracy allowed Coward to assert his rebellious character and he never lost his childlike propensity for anarchic wit. When a chorus girl from *This Year of Grace!* fell ill after drinking hooch in a speakeasy, Cochran announced pompously, 'Every one of us is an ambassador for Britain. We have a duty to uphold our country's reputation . . .'; Coward replied in a stage-whisper, 'Rule Britannia!' During one performance, Alexander Woollcott, sitting with Harpo Marx, ostentatiously opened a newspaper as Coward began to sing 'A Room with a View'. Noel responded by giggling, 'then rallied and cooed the rest of it in baby-talk which sent an exasperated Woollcott storming out of his box'. Coward's maturity often seemed tenuous, from his use of baby talk (especially with the intimate 'family'), to petulant tantrums when crossed. Kenneth Tynan wrote of him, 'I submit . . . that infantilism may be the essential cocoon within which certain kinds of talent need to flourish. It is a virtue, not a fault, in Coward that he never discarded – and was never embarrassed by – his childhood . . . Whether by genetic luck or environmental good judgement, Noel Coward never suffered the imprisonment of maturity.'

This Year of Grace! continued to play to packed houses; so good was business that Coward was persuaded to remain in the production after his usual three-month maximum. New York was fun, with Woollcott's Sunday breakfast parties at his apartment, at the secluded 'dead end' of the East Fifties, overlooking the East River. These parties were attended by the Round Table stalwarts, with the portly Woollcott sitting 'in grandeur in a comfortable armchair, unshaved, in his bright green pyjamas with all the fly buttons undone, marshalling the guests as a ringmaster'. Coward stayed in the city throughout January and February, fielding press enquiries about his marital status: '"I'm afraid I'd make a frightfully inadequate husband. You see, I like being alone so much. Besides, I'm too much the egotist."' He worked on songs for *Bitter Sweet*, one of which famously came to him on a taxi ride, the insistent melody of 'I'll See You Again' triumphing over the beeping horns of the gridlocked New York traffic. Coward had intended to ask Gertrude Lawrence to play Sari, but her voice was not strong enough; Evelyn Laye, his second choice, was not available (she blamed Cochran for the fact that her husband, Sonnie Hale, had fallen in love with Jessie Matthews, his co-star in *This Year of Grace!* Laye told Coward, 'I'd rather scrub floors than work for *him* again').

Soon afterwards, Coward ran into Peggy Wood* in the lobby of the Algonquin. He had known her since his first visit to the States – she was a friend of Teddie Gerrard, Cecile Sartoris and Lester Donahue – but had not heard her sing. They repaired to his studio at the Hotel des Artistes; Noel was impressed by her voice and her 'lack of "star" manner', and promptly offered her the part. Wood was engaged by Cochran 'on the assurance from Mr Coward that I had not grown fat in the ten years since he had last seen me play on Broadway'.

The author and producer returned to England in the spring to search for a male lead. They followed various tips in Germany and Austria, and a young man was discovered whose name was Hans Unterfucker. Despite Coward's mischievous desire to see it writ large on West End billboards, they returned to London, and found George Metaxa 'who had been available all the time'. Metaxa had appeared in Cochran's last revue, *Wake Up and Dream*; thirty years old, he had been *chef de cabinet* in the Romanian Ministry of Agriculture, and now specialised in playing exotic foreign noblemen. The part of La Crevette posed no problem: Coward had written it for Ivy St Helier, his mentor from *Wild Heather* days. A diminutive and idiosyncratic character actress and singer, her tragi-comic mien was the perfect foil for the romance at the heart of Coward's piece. Noel read and sang the completed work to Cochran, who announced to his general manager, Hal Lewis, that *Bitter Sweet* would provide his old-age pension. Rehearsals began at the end of May, with a huge cast assembled for the ballroom scenes. Using a microphone, Coward directed operations from the dress circle, as though he were back with his toy theatre in Clapham; productions such as *Bitter Sweet* and the revues were realisations of his childhood fantasies, adult versions of the peg-dolls and cardboard scenery. The artifice excited Noel, the super-reality of the theatre, epitomised by the ideal love of the romantic musical.

Bitter Sweet opens in the gay clatter of modern high society; Dolly Chamberlain, a well-bred English girl, leaves her lover to elope with a musician, just as Lady Shayne had eloped, fifty-four years previously. The scene change from 1929 to 1875 is practically a cinematic dissolve to the production's great hit number, 'I'll See You Again', sung by Peggy Wood and George Metaxa. Reprised at the end, the song summed up the nostalgic tone: the simple sentiment of love represented by the

* Having begun her career as an opera singer, Wood later appeared in the 1965 film of *The Sound of Music* as the Mother Abbess, singing 'Climb Every Mountain'.

haunting tune is the theme of the play, and its set-pieces and period scenes assert fantasy, rooted in a dim memory of an unlived past. Although modern tastes would find the love and despair too artificial ('Oh God!' says Dolly, 'I'm so utterly, utterly miserable'), contemporary audiences, who expected formality, saw them as effective emotional scenes. The show's heart-tugging sentimentality was underlined by what Alan Jenkins called a 'terrific risk' on Coward's part: the killing-off of his hero in a duel on stage. 'Even though the tragic mood is softened by the jazzy up-to-date last scene, the lump in the throat does not quite depart.'

'People are tired of speedier and speedier shows', Coward said on the production's American opening. 'After all, a chorus girl can only wave her arms and legs about so much.' The antithesis of the mid-1920s cynicism of previous Coward shows, *Bitter Sweet*, with its swirling waltzes, lavish costumes and luxurious sets, was a panacea to the woes of world depression. Theatre audiences had not seen its like for years – a spectacle of melody and colour which swept all before it.

Yet within the songs of Coward's musical were sentiments as bitter sweet as its title. Most autobiographical of all was the sublime 'If Love Were All':

> I believe the more you love a man,
> The more you give your trust,
> The more you're bound to lose.
> Although when shadows fall
> I think if only –
> Somebody splendid really needed me,
> Someone affectionate and dear,
> Care would be ended if I knew that he
> Wanted to have me near.
> But I believe that since my life began
> The most I've had is just
> A talent to amuse.
> Heigho, if love were all!

Bitter Sweet was licensed by the Lord Chamberlain's office on 28 June 1929, with George Street commenting drily, 'there is very little to quarrel with. Noel Coward is in a sentimental, not a salacious mood.'

The first night – in Manchester, as was customary with Cochran's shows – was 'riotous'. The reviews were 'almost incoherent' with praise, and the three-week run was immediately sold out. The London first night was something of an anticlimax – the audience was fashionably cool, although they thawed by the finale. Coward refused a curtain speech, saying he made these only when his audience booed. The notices evinced 'rather grudging patronage', as if regretting their effusiveness over *This Year of Grace!* and embarrassed that Coward had followed one hit with another. The *Evening Standard* talked of 'the common-placeness of popular musical comedy . . . steps away from the rarer and more delicate form of light opera'. 'It would be too bad', Coward observed acidly, 'if I were encouraged to believe that there was anything remarkable in writing, composing and producing a complete operetta.' Coward had written it 'tongue in cheek', alleged some critics. 'This was not "real Coward"', wrote W. J. Turner. 'Inept as the incidents of old-fashioned musical comedy were, it would not be possible to find in the annals of Daly's Theatre anything more preposterously unreal than this.' It had 'finally smashed' his 'hopes of Mr Coward, for a more inane and witless composition never left the pen of a distinguished author'.

Coward's suspicion of the press (and particularly of the Beaverbrook papers, which he considered had waged a vendetta against him ever since *Sirocco*) was illustrated by an annoying incident on the first night. During the duel scene, Hannen Swaffer, Gordon Beckles and Ewatt Hodgson, dramatic critics of the Express group, performed a mock fight with their umbrellas. Cochran complained to Beaverbrook, but Noel knew that would do no good. However, James Agate saluted Coward's achievement as 'a thundering good job . . . a thoroughly good light entertainment'. The theatre-going public agreed, embracing it with enthusiasm. Despite the rise of the cinema, the theatre was still a major source of entertainment; many homes had pianos and, as with Coward's previous musical efforts, sales of sheet music, gramophone recordings and the published work brought a sizeable income; they also promoted Coward as a household name outside the audience catchment area of the West End, and spread his fame and the popularity of the show throughout the country.

It was difficult to ignore the production, appearing as it did in every medium. Cochran commissioned Max Beerbohm to do a series of *Bitter Sweet* caricatures. 'Max took a great liking to Noel Coward himself and was enchanted with the play', wrote David Cecil. 'Its nostalgic evocation of the Victorian and Edwardian epochs chimed deliciously with his own backward-looking daydreams.' Beerbohm would also have appreciated the wit of 'Green Carnation', which poked fun at the very group of 'greenery-yallery' aesthetes the venerable dandy personified:

> Faded boys, jaded boys, womankind's
> Gift to a bulldog nation
> In order to distinguish us from less enlightened minds,
> We all wear a green carnation.

It was Noel's comment on the Uranian decadents, purveyors of a camp sensibility he eschewed. The homosexual overtone was an 'open secret'; the audience privately understood, but pretended otherwise. The blatant descriptions ('Our figures sleek and willowy,/ Our lips incarnadine,/ May worry the majority a bit') puzzled the Lord Chamberlain's office. Street's report muttered that 'the "green carnation" young men in Act III might be offensively bi-sexual but that is not indicated', and Lord Cromer thought 'the "Green Carnation" young men may be very objectionable', but it was allowed to pass. Perhaps its concluding refrain reassured the censors,

> We feel we're rather Grecian,
> As our manners indicate,
> Our sense of moral values isn't strong.
> For ultimate completion,
> We shall really have to wait
> Until the Day of Judgement comes along

which signalled disdain for the more obvious members of the homosexual fraternity. The song also contained the line, 'We are the reason for the "Nineties" being gay'. (In 'Mad About the Boy', the idol has 'a gay appeal/ That makes me feel/ There's maybe something sad about the boy'.) Although modern usage of 'gay' is seen as a recent development, it was certainly employed in theatrical circles in the 1940s (Kenneth Williams uses it in his wartime diaries); and in 1936, Stephen Tennant quotes from *Far from the Madding Crowd*, 'What kind of person is he?' 'Oh Miss – I blush to name it – a gay man', regarding his former lover, Siegfried Sassoon. As the 1920s had its own code words for homosexuality (two of the most common being 'musical' or 'so'), the usage of 'gay' may well be older than is assumed.

As great a success as *Bitter Sweet* was, not everyone was convinced. Ethel Mannin thought its music 'the essence of all the musical-comedy staleness and all the *Blue Danube* sentimentality ever orchestrated'. But such views Coward saw as killjoy; let the country wallow a little – bad times are just around the corner.

Given the success of the British *Bitter Sweet* (it ran for a remarkable

697 performances, outdone only by *Blithe Spirit*'s tenacious wartime stretch), it was obvious that Cochran would ask Coward to agree to an American production. This became a *fait accompli* when Evelyn Laye proved available (he had his reservations about Peggy Wood's performance); Laye would surely guarantee Broadway success. She had realised how 'small-minded and foolish' she had been to turn down the role, and anyway was broke, having lost £10,000 on the stock market. Elsie April put her case to Coward and Cochran, and she was immediately engaged. As the British show would continue, an entirely new cast was required for New York, and so Coward, Cochran and Calthrop set off for the South of France to find a new Carl, but neither the Riviera nor Paris yielded a suitable lead. However, Princess Jane di San Faustino – one of Noel's 'new-found "grand" friends' – came up with a Roman; rather short in the leg but with nice long eyelashes. He'd do, said Noel, and was booked. Cochran and Calthrop returned to London, and Coward went off to Avignon to stay with the Bolithos.

Noel had met William Bolitho at one of Alexander Woollcott's parties on his last New York trip. South African-born, Bolitho had fought in the war, which 'tortured and all but broke him'; he was the only one to escape from a trench cave-in on the Somme in 1916, saved by a passing English soldier, who pulled him out by the feet. He had become a journalist and when Coward met him had just published an acclaimed psychological study of five mass murderers (such as Burke and Hare), *Murder for Profit*, which Noel had read with fascination. Bolitho was tall, blond and blue-eyed, with a strong Afrikaans accent, and Coward took an immediate liking to him. They dined together in New York at the Plaza, and Bolitho described the encounter in his column for the *New York World*.

He felt he was 'watching the embryo of an authentic great man; in fact, the tadpole of a genius'. 'On the one hand, negatively, he is unprepossessing, which will save him from the mantrap of romanticizing himself. He has a low forehead – so he will never be tempted to aim for the Nobel Prize, nor feel the fatal duty of making the world a better place. He has good, easy-fitting manners, which shows he has escaped the social distemper fatal to so many Englishmen who have worked their way up, the malady, for example, from which the promising genius of Wells, Kipling, Hardy, Wilde, never properly recovered. Coward has an intact core of hard-bitten, unashamed, touring actor on which all his graces can build securely. Most of all, my suspicion, or confidence, is attached to the look of his eyes . . . a certain quality, a glint rather than a gleam . . . like the refraction of light from a polished steel cutting surface . . .'

When not in New York, Bolitho lived at La Préfete, near Avignon, with his Viennese wife Sybil, tending their 'English garden oasis'. Coward spent much of his stay in the swimming-pool, while Bolitho finished what was to be his last book, *Twelve Against the Gods*. He appeared only at mealtimes, conversing 'with fire and grace and beauty . . . Of all the minds I had ever encountered,' Noel wrote, 'his, I think, was the richest and most loving.' It was intellectual stimulus to rival that of Bloomsbury. In New York, Coward had told Bolitho of a 'rather neurotic' novel he intended to write, about a young man who commits suicide out of boredom. The writer told Coward, 'almost sharply, "Be careful about Death, it's a serious business, big and important. You can't go sauntering towards Death with a cigarette hanging from your mouth!"' Coward heeded the reproof when he wrote his play *Post Mortem*, dedicated to his friend; the advice was also prescient – Bolitho died two years later of peritonitis.

Coward said he was 'turned . . . inside out' by Bolitho. He 'stimulated the best of my ambitions, readjusted several of my uneasy virtues, and banished many meretricious ones'. Bolitho's piece on *Bitter Sweet* was 'one of the very few journalistic excursions relating to myself that I have ever wished, proudly, to keep'. Bolitho wrote of the quality the play had: 'You find it faintly when you look over old letters the rats have nibbled at . . . there is a little of it, impure and odious, in the very sound of barrel-organs, in quiet squares in the evenings, puffing out in gusts that intoxicate your heart. It is all right for beasts to have no memories; but we poor humans have to be compensated.' Noel returned to London 'strongly elated and bursting with gratitude' to his philosophical mentor, 'for the strange new pride I found in myself'.

The encounter made the rehashing of the *Bitter Sweet* material for America seem tedious; the only consolation was working with Evelyn Laye. Peggy Wood and Ivy St Helier crept into rehearsals to see how their counterparts were doing. 'We saw just part of it', but they agreed that 'apart from Evelyn . . . Noel had to take . . . all those he'd rejected for the London production'. The result was, according to Wood, a second-rate version; she asked Coward why he didn't wait and let the London cast do it. He explained that he was afraid New York would have copied his show by then; he had to get in first.

Cochran was unable to go to New York, and Coward was left in charge, helped by Jack Wilson. There was a two-week try-out in Boston, with a full Sunday evening rehearsal at which the awful truth dawned: the Roman tenor's English was unintelligible and his acting was hopeless. Why this had not been discovered during the weeks of English rehearsals is unclear, though it may have been a result of Coward's professed boredom with the proceedings. Dickie Fellowes Gordon had a different version of the story, claiming that it was she and Elsa Maxwell who were responsible for the tenor's discovery: 'We found him a marvellous leading man who was Italian, from a small orchestra in Venice. He was good-looking, his English wasn't too bad, no worse that Metaxa . . . but they [Coward and Jack Wilson] took a dislike to him, because he was too masculine. He wanted a woman and that annoyed them. So they dragged a very unattractive man out of the chorus and got rid of him.' Coward claimed to feel 'desperately sorry' for the unwanted Roman, his dismissal now inevitable. Gerald Nodin, who had understudied the part in London, was chosen, the wrong type for the part, but ambitious enough 'to make the utmost of himself' (a subtextual joke of Coward's; as Hugues Cuenod, who sang in the production, notes: Nodin was 'a very good-looking chap who went through the company like a pack of salts').

The Boston show was a hit and when the production opened on Broadway on 5 November, police had to be called to cordon off Sixth Avenue. It was a brilliant affair – literally – as floodlights illuminated arriving celebrities and flash bulbs popped ceaselessly. It was Evelyn Laye's American debut. 'Noel – who I knew was secretly as nervous as I was – came in with a little ornamental box which, when he pressed a spring, released a mechanical bird. "There you are, ducks," he said. "I wanted to be the first to give it to you!" . . . "the bird" is the symbol of the audience's loud disapproval.' But, Coward told his mother, Laye was 'the most triumphant success I've ever seen. When she made her entrance in the *last* act in the white dress they clapped and cheered for two *solid* minutes and when I came on at the end they went raving mad. Reporting that Laye was 'weeing down her leg with excitement', Coward complimented his mother, 'How right you were about Evelyn – she certainly does knock spots off the wretched Peggy!'*

What Noel called 'probably the most distinguished first night ever seen in New York' reverberated beyond its auditorium. The following

---

* Laye replaced Wood in the English production in November 1930, when the *Tatler* noted that Miss Wood had been 'ordered a rest'.

night he took Elsie April and Cissie Sewell (Cochran's dance instructor) to see *Whoopee* as a reward for their 'having worked like dogs'. During the performance its star Eddie Cantor stepped forward and announced, 'the greatest theatrical genius alive to-day', and the spotlight fell on Coward. 'I had to stand up and bow to me great American Public!' he exulted. 'All this . . . in the middle of somebody else's show!'

The *New York Times* noted that Coward had, 'in bland defiance of the New York custom, not only appeared for a curtain call . . . but . . . responded with a few words. Mr Coward . . . [is] to embark on a trip around the world . . . in a week or so, linger a few days in Hollywood, and then sail for the East. He will be joined in Tokyo by Jeffrey Holmesdale [Amherst], who used to write pieces about the theatre for the *New York World*, and together they will venture deep in Japan and China. Mr Coward may be gone for a long time.'

With *Bitter Sweet*'s American launch secured (it ran for 159 performances), Coward could look forward to his Far Eastern tour. He privately thought that the American *Bitter Sweet* did not match up to the London original; still, his name was in lights on Broadway, his photograph was in the *New York Times*, and the success of the show remained untarnished by more important news – the crash of the New York stock market. 'Everybody is losing millions, poor old Syrie [Maugham] has lost practically all she had, but it really serves them right for gambling', he purred. He thanked God that Jack had invested only in gilt-edged securites 'and never speculated so I'm perfectly safe, but it really is horrible, people hurling themselves off buildings like confetti!' The atmosphere in New York encouraged Coward's travel plans. His escape had been planned 'under a general sense of futility' after his encounter with William Bolitho; it was time to recharge his batteries. On the Saturday before he left for California, Gertrude Lawrence threw a leaving party, and presented him with a tiny gold notebook from Cartier's – a reminder that he was to write a play for them both.

Coward left New York on 17 November 'in a blaze of glory', taking the train via Chicago to Hollywood, where more parties in his honour were promised by Charlie Chaplin, Ronald Colman and Marion Davies; movie moguls had put their cars at his disposal, hoping to lure him to their studios. 'God forbid, but I shall use the cars and probably wee wee in them', he told his mother in another infantile reversion. He spent ten hectic days under what Scott Fitzgerald called Hollywood's 'anxious sunlight'. The glare seemed to induce a paranoid state; his impression was that he had been 'whirled through all the side-shows of some gigantic Pleasure Park at breakneck speed'. Post-Bolitho, the values of the place affected and even threatened him. Hollywood was an immovable force to be resisted, its attractions too obvious and fleeting. A chaotic series of parties engulfed Coward in an all-consuming culture which claimed any celebrity for its own; he went driving down Sunset Boulevard with Gloria Swanson discussing dentristry, and played tennis at two in the morning with Charles MacArthur, under 'artificial moonlight', after which they dived fully clothed into a floodlit pool. Laura Hope-Crews appeared spectrally from behind a fountain, whispering, 'Don't be frightened dear – this – THIS – is Hollywood!' And that was enough to induce a permanent aversion to the place.

Coward sailed from San Francisco on the *President Garfield* on 29 November, on his most extensive travels to date, and certainly his most expensive (costing more than $7500). But it was also a long-awaited escape from everyone and everything – even from Jack, whom he had left in Chicago. That Noel was to meet Jeffrey in Tokyo may well have been irritating to Wilson, who realised that Coward still had an emotional attachment to Amherst.

Coward considered his future: he had achieved fame and success, but how long would they last? He was only as good as his next show – the perpetual dilemma of the successful artist. Until now, his youth and nervous energy had provided the impetus; now that he had got it all, what next? Watched by the media of two continents, Coward (who would be thirty in two weeks) needed to consolidate his position. The situation was as brittle as one of his comedies; it might all fall apart like a house of cards if he lost the delicate balance. His experience of Hollywood sharpened his sense of doubt, but he saw this feeling of dissatisfaction as a good sign. 'Perhaps my uneasiness was the true indication of my worth,' he wrote later, 'the inevitable shadow thrown by thin facility; a deeper mind might suffer more . . . There seemed no criterion by which I could judge my quality, or rather so many criteria that they nullified each other.' Until now, 'there had been no necessity to look either to the right or the left . . . success was the goal – "Noel Coward" in electric lights. Now I found the electric lights so dazzling I couldn't see beyond them . . .'

Coward accepted that 'nobody . . . could find my own truths for me', and concluded that the voyage, in cutting him off from that world, might answer a few questions. 'It would be enjoyable to return to my startled friends with, in addition to the usual traveller's souvenirs, a Strindbergian soul.' But like his dalliance with Bloomsbury, that was a pose: a man of artifice become a man of intellect. In trying to find himself, Coward found only other masks to wear.

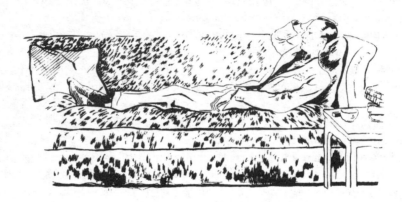

13

Private Lives

The swift, hard, rattling farcical-comedy, at which he aimed so many shots, is brought to glittering perfection in *Private Lives*. It is technically a masterpiece – not of the art of writing plays, but of the art of writing Mr Coward's plays. For, as I think we have discovered by now, Mr Coward's plot is the contrast between brilliant cosmopolitanism and stodgy Anglo-Saxondom, his standby is Infidelity and his device of stage-craft is the Bicker ...

A. G. MacDonnell.

THREE years after his first, unhealthy arrival in Honolulu, Coward returned to Hawaii 'on a calm opalescent sea', at dawn. Once again he was offered the Dillinghams' hospitality, and spent four days at La Pietra, then sailed on the slightly down-at-heel *Tenyo Maru* for Yokohama. He worked throughout the voyage on the novel he had described to William Bolitho (*Julian Kane*), but, discouraged by its 'obvious dullness' and the effort involved, gave it up and applied himself to the lesser requirements of drama.

He arrived in Yokohama in a snowstorm, and went by taxi to Tokyo, where he discovered that Amherst, delayed on his freight boat, would be three days late. The night before he was due, Noel went to bed early, 'but the moment I switched out the lights, Gertie appeared in a white Molyneux dress and refused to go again until four a.m., by which time *Private Lives*, a title and all, had constructed itself'. Wary of this facility, Coward did not write it down there and then. He pushed the play to the back of his mind, and waited until it needed to reappear.

Amherst, who had been mixing in risqué company in New York (he had befriended a young boxer named Gerry McCarthy who was later shot dead in a Jersey City brawl), had decided he was becoming 'egg-bound, mentally', and had travelled to the Pacific with another friend, Whitney Warren. They parted in Pago Pago, and Jeffrey sailed on to join Noel in Japan. They found Tokyo a 'sad scrap heap of a city', sacrificed to Western aspirations, and when an earthquake hit they were glad to leave. From Nagasaki they embarked on a rough crossing for Korea, then took a train to Mukden. The British consul (brother of Frank Tours, musical director of *Bitter Sweet*) took them to a New Year's Eve fancy-dress party, 'strange ... and, beneath its gaiety, exceedingly touching'. Amid the amateur pierrots, now dusty images of the last decade, Coward discerned his countrymen's isolation, 'condemned to stay in that grim, remote place perhaps for years'.

They travelled on to Peking by train (with twenty-seven pieces of luggage and a gramophone), lying 'in a heap wrapped in fur coats', drinking brandy and fending off intruders by playing Sophie Tucker's 'Some of These Days' at full volume. In the Cathay Hotel in Shanghai, Noel was laid up with flu, which turned out to be a fortuitous indisposition: armed with an Eversharp pencil and a pad of paper, he wrote *Private Lives* in four days.

As he recovered, the weather improved, and he enjoyed Shanghai, 'a cross between Brussels and Huddersfield'. They got to know three naval officers from HMS *Suffolk*, moored on the Yangtze. Soon they were dining riotously on board the ship, and having a 'fairly rowdy' time. Noel persuaded the navy to let them travel 'Grey Funnel' on the ship from Shanghai to Hong Kong. It was an environment in which he may have felt at home: his grandfather Henry Gordon Veitch had after all spent twenty years in the navy, and a great-uncle had been an admiral. Indeed in his encounters with the navy from now on can be seen Coward's preparation for his wartime role as Captain Kinross in *In Which We Serve*. Naval hospitality provided them with a cabin each, and use of the captain's bathroom; the captain even allowed Noel to film with his movie camera, which was strictly against the rules. 'I think we behaved adequately well on the whole', Noel said, learning naval etiquette and jargon which he later used to advantage.

Their week in Hong Kong followed a routine: Amherst took the ferry across the harbour to the city, leaving Coward 'propped up in bed in a dark blue flannel dressing-gown, with note books scattered about and a portable typewriter, busy getting *Private Lives* down on to paper'. He sent copies to Jack Wilton and Gertrude Lawrence, and waited for their replies. From Shanghai they took passage on a battered tramp steamer for Haiphong, sharing a cabin with a multitude of bedbugs and cockroaches, and were driven in a hired car along the coast to Saigon. The drive took a week, and 'while jungles and rivers and mountains and rice fields were unrolling by the window of the car', Coward wrestled in his mind with a complicated new song, 'Mad Dogs and Englishmen':

> In tropical climes there are certain times of day
> When all the citizens retire
> To tear their clothes off and perspire.
> It's one of those rules that the greatest fools obey,
> Because the sun is far too sultry
> And one must avoid its ultry violet ray.

The achievement was all the more impressive because Coward had no pen and paper; he sang it 'triumphantly' to Jeffrey, accompanied by a chorus of tree frogs.

In Singapore, chronic dysentery struck Amherst for the second time, and he was admitted to hospital for six weeks, leaving Coward with time on his hands. He made friends with an English touring company, the Quaints, among whom was a young John Mills, who was to become a protégé of Noel's. Coward was persuaded to play Stanhope in their production of *Journey's End*. R. C. Sherriff's play was one of the first to deal with the still traumatic memory of the war, and William Bolitho's influence encouraged Noel in the role, which was 'long and demanding' and perhaps out of his range. 'I gave a sort of lachrymose, sobbing performance,' he recalled, '. . . entirely the wrong performance for the play.' The critics tendered 'polite notices', although one was 'smart enough' to see that his performance was over-emotional.

Certain sections of Singapore society were also displeased. After Amherst was released from hospital, he and Coward attended a lunch at Government House. The governor's wife, Lady Clementi, was a puritan who had demanded that all copies of Somerset Maugham's works be removed from local bookshops on the grounds of immorality. Over lunch she alleged that Sherriff's play was a 'vile libel' on the British army, and attacked Coward personally for playing Stanhope. 'None of our soldiers ever drank in the 1914 war', she insisted, claiming personal knowledge from her father, who had been a general. Coward turned to Amherst, who had served in the trenches, and asked if he could confirm this particular statement. 'Never drew a sober breath', Amherst answered. Lady Clementi visibly bristled, and lunch ended quickly. Coward composed a song in honour of their erstwhile hostess:

Oh, Lady Clementi, you've read a lot of G. A. Henty
You've not read Bertrand Russell and you've not read Dr Freud,
Which perhaps is the reason you look so unenjoyed.
You're anti-sex in any form, or so I've heard it said,
You're just the sort who would prefer a cup of tea instead
You must have been a riot in the matrimonial bed
Whoops – Lady Clementi.

'Noel sang this at various parties. All the grander and rather more elderly ladies would exclaim, "Oh disgraceful, disgraceful. Sing it again, Mr Coward, please sing it AGAIN."'

From Singapore, they took a night train to Kuala Lumpur, and had their only argument of the whole trip, occasioned by Amherst wanting the window open, and Coward wanting it closed. 'Or vice versa. We didn't speak for quite ten minutes', said Amherst. A Prairie Line freighter, with a canvas swimming-pool, took them to Ceylon, where they were met by Erik Coward. Noel had been due to meet Violet there; she had gone to Ceylon because of reports of Erik's ill-health, but had to leave before Noel arrived, possibly because of illness. 'It's so beastly for you to have had such a dreadful time poor darling', Coward wrote. Erik gave Noel and Jeffrey a comprehensive tour of the plantation at Naralia, but Noel found the stay a strain, partly because of lack of empathy between the brothers but also because he knew Erik had been ill. He was relieved when they went back to Colombo to the Galle Face Hotel, where Cole and Linda Porter appeared, also having been on a Far Eastern tour. Despite the comparative luxury of the hotel, with its jazz orchestra and swimming-pool, Linda Porter 'couldn't wait to get back to Paris to have her hair properly washed and set'.

They were also subjected to Cole Porter's home movies, which sent Jeffrey to sleep. Coward had also been filming his trip, but remarked to his mother, 'Jack says I shall *never* need a projector, as none of my films ever come out.' He and Jeffrey bought uncut emeralds for which the island was famous, but discovered they were cheap because they were clawed. Nonetheless, they had them made into cufflinks: 'the "Coward emeralds"', Noel quipped to Chips Channon. Colombo also provided contact with London, and Coward and Gertrude Lawrence managed to bicker across thousands of miles via the telegraph when Miss Lawrence said that there was nothing wrong with *Private Lives* that couldn't be fixed. Coward retorted that the only thing that would be fixed was her performance. It was typical of Lawrence to play hard-to-get when she had badgered Coward for so long to write the play; her cables announced obstacles in the shape of Charlot contracts and 'Moral Obligations', to Noel's increasing annoyance. Wearied by the effort and expense of this telegraphic skirmish, he lost his temper, and dictated a final cable announcing that he would find someone else to play it.

Coward and Amherst sailed from Ceylon to Marseilles on a boat of the P&O Line, a marked change from their recent unconventional trips. 'Life on board was strictly *de rigueur*', Amherst recalled. They were asked to judge a fancy-dress competition, and when they awarded the prizes to 'two Eurasian ladies, pretty and young with much the best costumes', they annoyed the planters' wives whose caste consciousness forbade fraternisation. When he discovered that there wasn't a mother among them whose daughter didn't dance and sing, Noel took his revenge with the second song of comic genius his trip produced. It began with *politesse*,

> Regarding yours, dear Mrs Worthington,
> Of Wednesday the 23rd,
> Although your baby,
> Maybe,
> Keen on a stage career,
> How can I make it clear,
> This is not a good idea

and built to the rage of the seldom sung last verse,

> One look at her bandy legs should prove
> She hasn't got a chance,
> In addition to which
> The son of a bitch
> Can neither sing nor dance
> She's a *vile* girl and uglier than mortal sin,
> One look at her has put me in
> A tearing bloody rage,
> That sufficed,
> Mrs Worthington,
> Christ!
> Mrs Worthington,
> Don't put your daughter on the stage.

The voyage also resulted in further creativity, of more serious intent. Reverting to the pessimistic theme of his abandoned novel, *Julian Kane*, Coward wrote *Post-Mortem*, a tirade against the errors of the Great

War, very much in the wake of William Bolitho's influence and his performance in *Journey's End*. An idealistic young officer, John Cavan, is mortally wounded in the trenches; thirteen years later his ghost returns to his loved ones to discover what lessons have been learned. Gradually disillusioned by what he sees of 1930s society, Cavan's previous optimism about the fighting spirit of his peers turns sour.

Under 'the flare of a Verey light', a visual metaphor, an officer reads the *Daily Mercury*. 'It's absolutely beastly about the Germans', he laughs, presaging Noel's later song. The poet-soldier Perry Lomas protests, 'Oh, Christ! . . . That muck makes me sick!' The strong anti-press feel of the play is an attack on Lord Beaverbrook, Coward's sworn enemy. Lomas foresees that 'one day someone will go too far and say something that's really true and be flung into prison for blasphemy, immorality, lese majesty, unnatural vice, contempt of court, and atheism, then there'll be a glorious religious revival and we'll all be rushed across the Atlantic to conquer America, comfortably upheld by Jesus and the Right!' After his 'death', Cavan confronts his still grieving mother; she has lost faith in God, the 'flimsy mysticism of their threadbare Christian legend'. It was the attitude of the playwright; that year, Coward told Laurette Taylor, mourning the death of her husband, 'Christians astonish me. The more they believe in a beatific future the more they weep when a loved one goes to it. A pagan and his pagan relatives are the happiest people. They die easily . . . because they have no regrets for the past and don't believe in the future.'

Lomas is next on the visitation list of Cavan's ghost. The relationship between the two men is evidently emotional: Perry sees John's visit as 'a farewell salute to things that have lain unsaid between us'. Cavan is embarrassed, 'Oh, Perry! Don't be such an ass.' 'It's true!' says Lomas, 'nothing to be ashamed of.' It is the kind of attachment bred by confinement in the trenches, facing imminent death together, and is underlined by the love of another young soldier, Babe, for the officer, Armitage.

In *Journey's End*, Raleigh likewise worships his officer, Stanhope; J. R. Ackerley's play *The Prisoners of War* also explores the love of Jim Conrad for a younger, heterosexual officer, Allan Grayle. At the time of the play's publication and performance (1925), it was 'talked about in London clubs as "the new homosexual play"'. Coward was certain to have seen the production, if not read the published work.

Coward's wartime contact with men who served on the Western Front also informed the play; especially men such as Scott Moncrieff whose Uranian sensibilities eulogised the young boy-soldiers about to die. And Perry Lomas appears to be based on Siegfried Sassoon, in his vituperative anti-Establishment tirades, the central didactic of the play. 'Bunk! Bunk! Bunk!' Lomas exclaims hysterically. In a shocking twist, Cavan hands Lomas the revolver so he can shoot himself. 'What's a little death among friends?' says Perry. 'Better than life among enemies', John replies. It is perhaps the blackest moment in Coward's work.

The play splutters to an end like a badly made firework, with bursts of sharp emotion. The final short scenes show Cavan's trench comrades, now aged, at dinner, suspended in time; they say that in another war they would readily send their sons to fight, ignorant of the reason why. It is this ignorance that Coward addresses in *Post-Mortem*. Back in the trenches, Cavan is carried on a stretcher, and exclaims, 'You were right, Perry – a poor joke!' It is the closing note of the play.

Post-Mortem was intended as a retort to those critics who thought Coward able to deal only with flappers perched on sofas drinking cocktails. But crucially, Coward never pursued its production, appearing to lack confidence in it; partly because he expected unfavourable comparison with Sherriff, and partly, perhaps, because he felt unsure of his motives. Had he written the play because anti-war dramas were then fashionable? Somerset Maugham would publish his own, *For Services Rendered*, in 1932, and much anti-war literature had emerged, by poets Graves and Sassoon, and prose by writers such as Erich Maria Remarque (whose *All Quiet on the Western Front* was filmed in 1930, to critical acclaim). The cynical considered that Coward was unwilling to risk a production of a piece so unlike the rest of his work: 'Mr Coward is afraid to put *Post-Mortem* (in which appears his most fearless hatred) on the stage because, rest you merry, it would be unsuccessful in making money', accused Sean O'Casey. O'Casey was perhaps waspish because his own anti-war play, *The Silver Tassie*, had been turned down by the Abbey Theatre. He added that 'its queries, its chastisement and its fearlessness' would effectively be 'cancelled by the gorgeous recantation of *Cavalcade*'. The play would also have been heavily censored in England, considering its language and anti-religious statements.

Coward wrote, 'I tore my emotions to shreds' over the writing of the play. 'The result was similar to my performance as Stanhope: confused, under-rehearsed and hysterical ... however, it had some very fine moments. The truths I snarled out in that hot, uncomfortable little cabin were all too true and mostly too shallow. Through lack of detachment and lack of real experience of my subject, I muddled the issues of the play.' *Post-Mortem* had purged his system 'of certain accumulated acids'.

The experience of travel, the influence of William Bolitho, the writing of *Post-Mortem* (and the ghosts it conjured from his past) had combined to produce a more considered, serious mood, but one which left him with conclusions about his limitations. At thirty, Coward did not feel himself capable of being 'a serious playwright'.

That May, Noel returned to a serious family feud. Violet, enraged by Arthur's idleness and flirtatious ways with local women, wrote to her husband, 'I have never been so miserable in my life as since I came from Ceylon, and who are you to dare to make my life so unhappy. What have you ever done for me or for either of your two fine boys to help them on in life.' She accused Arthur of making no effort to earn a living, though perfectly healthy 'and will no doubt live to be 100, a burden on Noel, not to speak of putting your wife on him too'. She had decided, she told him, to ask Noel to find a house, 'with a little less grandeur than you have here [Goldenhurst] which will do you good. Her anger was exacerbated by anxieties over Erik's health, and their elder son was piggy in the middle. Noel's relationship with his father had the appearance of toleration; Arthur's attitude to his son's career was, according to Noel, 'always one of faint bewilderment'. But for Arthur and Violet, the rest of their lives together would be lived in an 'uneasy truce' in which Noel would often have to play the mediator.

Arrangements for the production of *Private Lives* soon overtook such domestic considerations. Gertrude Lawrence had been placated, and was holidaying with Edward Molyneux in the South of France, where Coward joined her to discuss the play. Writing in retrospect, Coward claimed an intimate knowledge of Gertrude Lawrence possessed by few others. While not sexual, it was a love-hate relationship similar to that he had with Esme Wynne (though less intellectual); fraught with quarrelsome reunions – a potent force which, harnessed by Noel's script, became raw and exciting. Yet the now legendary nature of their partnership is belied by the facts: they performed together in just four plays, *Hannele*, *Private Lives*, *Tonight at 8.30*, and its revival.

Coward wrote of Lawrence that she had 'an astounding sense of the complete reality of the moment ... quick humour, insane generosity and a loving heart'. She was as wayward a woman as he had known, changeable and extreme. Her features, set and determined, were evidence of this: not beautiful, but attractive; like her voice, not good, but charming. Her appearance was of a knowing woman of the world – blood-red nails, bias-cut Molyneux gowns, arched eyebrows indicating a certain arrogance. But she was ultimately elusive. 'To disentangle Gertie herself from this mutability is baffling, rather like delving for your grandmother's gold locket at the bottom of an overflowing jewel-case.' As an actress, said Coward, she lacked discrimination; as a woman, she often lacked sense, spending her money recklessly, flirting aimlessly, and engaging emotions with little regard for the long-term effect of her dalliance. (Because Lawrence had paid no American taxes, she had been warned by her lawyer, Fanny Holtzmann, that financial ruin loomed. A clever and persistent woman, Holtzmann negotiated with Cochran to give Lawrence a percentage of the management profits on *Private Lives*, which became a CCL (Cochran–Coward–Lawrence) production, each putting up £1000 for the play.)

The relationship was unequal. Coward's talent and intelligence exceeded Lawrence's, but actors do not require intellect to be successful, and he may well have had her in mind when he gave his opinion of the performers of his art: 'What fascinates me about acting is when a beautiful talented actress can come on the stage and give a performance that makes your blood curdle with excitement and pleasure, yet she can make such a cracking pig of herself over where her dressing-room is or some such triviality, for which you hate her. Intelligent actors never do that, but then they're seldom as good as the unintelligent ones. Acting is an instinct. A gift that is often given to people who are very silly as people. But as they come on to the stage, up goes the temperature.'

To actress Elspeth March, as to countless other fans, Lawrence had a unique ability to influence the theatrical thermometer, but the idea of anything other than a professional relationship between Gertrude and Noel was 'absolutely ridiculous. The only person Noel really loved? Ridiculous. They had *blazing* rows. But she was his sort of woman. The figure, the face, the background, everything. Gertie was a real man's woman.' John Gielgud, who 'didn't quite aspire to [Coward's] social circle', found Lawrence 'so mercurial. I never quite understood his friendship with her – it was rather shadowy, I think. He was very fond of his women friends, he liked to take them out to dinner, and dancing, and all that.' The potency of their public relationship seemed to depend on their temperamental natures and their svelte and streamlined symbolism of an era; it was this unique relationship which Coward sought to exploit in *Private Lives*.

If *Post-Mortem* was Coward's attempt at serious drama, *Private Lives* was his attempt at serious comedy. It is based on misdirected love, misplaced marriage and an inability to communicate. We enjoy the predicament faced by Elyot Chase and Amanda Prynne – lovers separated, remarried to others, and now unwillingly reunited, honeymooning with their new spouses in the same hotel. The situation is close to farce, and yet more subtle, as they seek to conceal their past from Sybil and Victor. But the play is not just the 'lightest of light comedies', as the author dubbed it, it is an exposition of his preoccupations, a situation comedy where the situation – two people in love and unable to live together – is tragic.

The director Alan Strachan wrote that contemporary critics 'missed the underlying sadness of these glib and over-articulate people who twist their lives into distorted shapes because they cannot help themselves'. Certainly the worst judge of a production is often its creator, 'Authors usually write shockingly badly about their own work,' Terence Rattigan said in 1956, 'and the author of *Private Lives* is no exception.' In deprecating the play ('psychologically unstable'; 'as a complete play it leaves a lot to be desired'), Coward sought to ward off intellectual dissection. Yet Rattigan saw in the play's 'equation of love and hatred' an 'objective truth that endows it with that touching quality ... so often the concomitant of great comedy'.

Private Lives epitomises Coward's apparently effortless ability to structure a 'well-made play', using a classic comic formula of two pairs of characters: its three acts set the scene, further the action, and resolve the situation. This satisfying dynamic provides the framework for his bickering one-liners and ripostes. The audience does not expect reality from a Noel Coward play; they saw aspects of real life in his characters but accepted the situation as a vehicle for wit. The 'what if' – what if *their* private lives were thus threatened? – is a fantasy they can look at from the comfort of their marital stability; the frisson of anarchy is enjoyed at one remove. Yet perhaps they had something to fear from Noel Coward's world: the ordinary and commonplace should beware the omniscient author, the homosexual outsider wielding an axe ground on a disregard for convention.

Women are well treated in Coward's plays only if they are deemed to be 'heroines'. Otherwise they are featherheaded or scheming creatures, trying to dominate men, as does Sybil, whom Elyot accuses of subconscious 'age-old instincts ... mincing up little bits of experience for future use, watching me carefully like a little sharp-eyed, blonde kitten'. Elyot's over-feminine wife is matched by Amanda's over-masculine husband. Their spouses lack chic or finesse, and are representative of stultifying English parochialism (neither consider sunburn attractive, while both Coward and Lawrence were avid followers – if not setters – of the new fashion for sunbathing, their perpetually glowing skins radiating the decidedly un-British glamour of the Mediterranean). The audience suspects that natural levels of suitability will be restored by the end of the play, when the couple prepare an 'all-change', but Coward's sublime twist – and another example of rebellion – is to turn Victor and Sybil into a bickering couple like Amanda and Elyot. They are sucked into the playwright's world, rather than the other way around.

Throughout the play, Coward toys with convention. To Victor's statement, 'I'm glad I'm normal', Amanda replies, 'What an odd thing to be glad about. Why?' 'Well, aren't you?' he says. 'I'm not so sure I'm normal', she answers. The explicit sexual rebellion, and implied sexual inversion, of Amanda and Elyot means they operate as amalgams of their creator's personality. In Amanda's words, it is the prevailing theme of the play, 'I think very few people are completely normal really, deep down in their private lives.' With its niggling dialogue, the play is childishness at a sophisticated extreme. Coward remained essentially childish throughout his life, and in *Private Lives* he presents Elyot and Amanda reverting to childhood; symbols of escapism in an age obsessed with escape.

That summer, Coward and Jack Wilson set off for the South of France, where Gertrude Lawrence had rented Molyneux's villa to learn her part. En route, they stopped off in Paris to meet the playwright Sacha Guitry, with whom Noel's work was often compared.* 'Nobody else could possibly have worn so superbly frivolous a dressing-gown with such dignity', said Beverley Nichols when he met Guitry in the Twenties. '"I once wrote a play," he told me, "called *Je t'aime*. There were five acts in it, and nothing whatever happened in those five acts, *nothing . . . On parle, on aime, on cause, on sort, on revient – voilà tout*. That play was one of my greatest successes."' The *New York Times* had written in 1926, 'Not seldom Mr Coward shares Monsieur Sacha Guitry's knack of saying nothing – amusingly.' Coward and Guitry had much in common; and there was a suggestion that *Private Lives* be translated

---

* As early as July 1920 when, in a review for *Time and Tide*, Rebecca West likened Coward's *I'll Leave It to You* to Guitry's work. Guitry had first appeared in London in 1920, in *Nono*, with his second wife of five, Yvonne Printemps.

for Guitry's Théâtre de la Madeleine; he also offered to write a play for Noel, although neither suggestion came to fruition.

Gertrudge Lawrence was installed at Cap d'Ail with her daughter Pamela; G. B. Stern and William Powell were also there. Coward and Lawrence rehearsed *Private Lives*, often reaching fever-pitch, to the bemusement of their friends; Lawrence recalled that her other guests 'wandered in and out, amused themselves as they wished, and looked on Noel and me as two quite pleasant but quite mad creatures'. At the end of July they returned to London to begin full rehearsals with the rest of the cast. Coward had chosen Laurence Olivier to play Victor but, to Noel's surprise, Olivier announced that he would prefer the lead. Coward patiently explained that only a good actor could play a bore without himself being boring, and pointed out that the part would be a wise career move, considering Olivier's recent desertion of *Journey's End* for a part in *Beau Geste*, which had failed ostentatiously.

Coward was charmed by Olivier, as was Olivier by the older man. Cole Lesley wrote, 'Noel adored Larry, there is no other word for it, and Larry adored Noel.' In Olivier's memoirs, a reference to a 'nearly passionate involvement with "one male" has been interpreted as meaning Noel. Later, when Olivier was discussing Coward with his son Tarquin (Noel's godchild) he was told that Noel had questioned the boy about the possibility of homosexual feelings. 'Are you sure you said no?' Olivier asked his son, 'he can be very persuasive.' 'Did he persuade you?' Tarquin asked. 'Christ no, but he tried, when I was much younger. I've never been queer.'

Whatever the relationship, it flowered during the rehearsals of *Private Lives*. Coward, eight years Olivier's senior, became avuncular, recommending that he read the Brontës, Maugham and Arnold Bennett. Olivier acknowledged Coward's influence, 'He was a great mind-opener and very inspiring ... I think Noel probably was the first man who took hold of me and made me think, he made me use my silly little brain. He taxed me with his sharpness and shrewdness and brilliance and he pointed out when I was talking nonsense, which nobody else had ever done before. He gave me a sense of right and wrong.'

One notable visitor to the *Private Lives* rehearsals was T. E. Lawrence, whom Coward had met lunching with Sir Philip Sassoon, his Kentish neighbour. The Arabian hero's visit to the theatre thrilled the cast; afterwards they all went to eat at an obscure restaurant where Lawrence could be sure of anonymity – Adrianne Allen* noticed that

---

* Adrianne Allen (1907–93) played Sybil; she later married Raymond Massey.

he hardly took his eyes off Coward. The two struck up a correspondence: Lawrence, obsessive about his 'ordinary' role in the ranks of the RAF, signed his letter with his serial number; Noel replied, 'Dear 3381721 (May I call you 338?) . . .' When he saw the play proper, Lawrence wrote to Coward that the 'finished product' looked good. 'Yet I'm not sure that the bare works you showed me that afternoon [in rehearsal] were not better. For one thing, I could not tell always when you were acting and when talking to one another . . . Gertrude Lawrence is amazing. She acts nearly as well as yourself. I was sorry for the other two. They were out of it.' Lawrence acquired an edition of *Private Lives*, 'The play reads astonishingly well. It gets thicker, in print, and has bones and muscles . . . For fun I took some pages and tried to strike redundant words out of your phrases. Only there were none. That's what I felt when I told you it was superb prose.'

Pre-production drama came in the now customary battle with the censor; this time the lines were drawn over Elyot's and Amanda's love scene. George Street was of the opinion that the 'amorous business' of Act Two went 'very far and seems to need a caution . . .' Lord Cromer wrote urging 'caution in production' in Act Two, and concluded that it was 'an immoral play written in this author's amusing style' which, after amendments to passages offensive to Catholics and the flippant use of 'Gods', could 'reluctantly' be allowed a licence.*

Private Lives received its premiere on 18 August at the King's Theatre in Edinburgh, and embarked on a countrywide tour to Liverpool, Birmingham, Manchester and Southsea. 'Assurance of success seemed to be emblazoned on the play from the first,' Coward wrote, 'we had few qualms, played to capacity business and enjoyed ourselves thoroughly. We felt, I think rightly, that there was a shine on us.'

The stars of the show carried on their rows offstage. During one shouting match, Everley Grigg, who was playing the maid, found Noel and Gertie engaged in a 'full-scale fist-fight'. 'Stop it, stop it,' she cried, attemping to pull the protagonists apart, 'I love you both.' They stopped

---

* These recommendations were not enough for the London Council for the Promotion of Public Morality – those 'futile moralists' – who accused *Private Lives* of being 'weak and pointless', 'its morality . . . on a par with that of street dogs'. But the Bishop of London, President of the Council, told the Lord Chamberlain, '. . . I have just had two girls to dinner, whom I know very well, and they . . . tell me that the account of "Private Lives" was exaggerated . . . no further steps should be taken.'

dead, and Coward turned on Grigg: 'Well, you're fired for a start! How dare you interfere when I'm talking to my friend!' Well into the London run, Coward and Lawrence continued to argue; Lawrence insisted on changing the way she played Amanda, choosing unsuitable accessories, adopting different positions and gestures. This outraged her co-star, who threatened to stop speaking to her. She continued; he stopped speaking – for two weeks. Only after arbitration was communication restored.

The London venue for *Private Lives* was Sidney Bernstein's brand-new state-of-the-art theatre, the Phoenix, partly designed by Giles Gilbert Scott and set at the edge of theatreland on Charing Cross Road. Bernstein, heir to a chain of music halls which he had transformed into cinemas, was now venturing into theatre. The Phoenix had a plush interior, decorated with murals reproducing Italian Renaissance master-pieces. At first Coward had refused to open there (considering a new theatre bad luck), but after Bernstein had shown him the special noiseless fans, the magenta upholstery of the auditorium, and the cloakrook with its 1200 hatracks (one for every seat), Noel decided that the Phoenix was ready to receive the audience of a Coward first night.

This was the usual glittering affair, and the newness of the venue meant considerable publicity. The critics allowed that the play was the work of one 'who knew the business of the actor from the inside'. *The Times* thought that the dialogue, 'which might seem in print a trickle of inanities', became onstage 'a perfectly timed and directed interplay of nonsense'; the *Observer* found the play superficial to a sophisticated degree, the effect 'as light and shiny as can be . . . Their style is mainly in their clothes; as conversationalists they are mere back-chatterers', but allowed Coward 'the courage of his cunning', conceding nothing 'to the old rules of playmaking, of characters, of constructions. He trusts to his wits and wins.'

Whatever the reservations of the critics, the play was a box-office hit, cleverly assisted by its musical number, 'I'll See You Again', and by Coward's recent success with *Bitter Sweet* on both sides of the Atlantic. The three-month run of *Private Lives* was sold out within a week of the opening, and quickly repaid the trio's investment, taking £3200 each week. It was highly profitable for Coward who, apart from his actor's salary, received his royalty as dramatist (from the gross receipts), as well as his one-third of the profits.

He was once more spread across the nation's newspapers and magazines. In one, an account of Coward at work was provided by the operatic bass and part-time caricaturist Fernando Autori: 'Punctually at the minute, Mr Noel Coward shakes my hand in his dressing room. He wears a rich make-up costume of vest and pant . . . He is not at all embarrassed by his slight costume, knowing I wish to sketch him all around the compass. His face in talking changes a thousand expressions, and I regret my pencil is not a movie pencil to depict all of them. The telephone rings and rings, and Signor Coward has for each occasion the lovely phrase with darling in it. Then it is time for him to go to the stage; I follow him to the wings . . . while someone put on his coat and someone stick a cigarette in a cigarette holder in his mouth. On the stage, he is as lively as in the dressing room – plays piano, quarrels with his Signorina Gertrude Lawrence, has his head knocked with a Master's Voice, and many other troubles. Back in the dressing room he offers me cigarettes, whisky sodas, everything – presents me to all the artists, talking, talking all the time. His desire is to meet Mussolini, know what I think of the show, is there sentiment sufficient in the singing, would an Italian audience find him simpatico . . . To all I say "Yes," because I think so, and because he leaves me no time for to say more.'

As if to reflect the durability of his latest achievement, a bronze life mask was taken of Noel's face by Paul Harmann in 1930. Now in the National Portrait Gallery, it gives a glimpse of the playwright at the height of his powers. The hair is scraped back from a rounded, definably intelligent forehead; the nose is long and blunt, faintly Roman, with a large raised lump on the right-hand side (photographs usually featured his left-hand profile). His eyes, almond-shaped, taper to slits, the upper lip a bare line. The skin seems tight and taut, tensely drawn across the bones; at thirty, it was smooth but hatched by a crosswork of faint lines, giving an appearance of having lived perhaps too hard. (Writing in the *Observer* seven years later, St John Ervine reflected that 'neurosis and incipient TB have helped to give him that curious old look he has'.)

Now, with the play which assured his theatrical immortality, Coward took a clever (to some outrageous) step. Although it was clear the play could run and run, Coward closed it in London after three months, despite being informed by Sir Cedric Hardwicke that it was 'unprofessional' to close a hit. Others said darkly that he would regret this decision. But it was to his career as a writer that he looked first; if he played on, there would be no time to write the successes in the first place. 'It is, of course, more than possible that I might write and appear in a play that wouldn't run three weeks', he wrote in 1937. 'In that bleak moment, age permitting, I shall turn gratefully to a revival of *Private Lives*.'

*

Coward and Wilson spent Christmas at Goldenhurst, now a bona fide country estate where Noel could take long walks without leaving his property. He was also able to establish his own Christmas traditions, as Patricia Frere observed. 'Noel used to give lovely Christmas parties . . . He got on beautifully with children, really "on terms". There was a Christmas tree, of course, and much too expensive presents to every-body on Christmas Eve . . .' She recalled one party, when her young son enjoyed Uncle Noel's hospitality, 'In one of the rooms was a hooded fireplace with a sofa straight in front of it . . . Harry [her son] was three or four, and Nanny had come down to collect him. He was found on the sofa . . . Coley one side and Noel the other, with a good supply of mince tarts. Noel was looking at him rather quizzically. What he was doing was licking the mincemeat out, eating it, and handing the empty, filthy, sticky, empty tart to Noel . . .' Coward's dry forbearance with children was legendary. David Niven once watched, helpless, as his young son crept up behind Coward and bashed him over the head with a silver plate. Coward remained quite still, and remarked that he would give the boy a chocolate-covered hand grenade for Christmas.

In the New Year, Coward turned his attention to his next project – the most adventurous production he would attempt. He had begun thinking about what would become *Cavalcade* during the London run of *Private Lives*; emboldened by success, he now wanted to test his 'producing powers' on a grand scale. He imagined epic scenes at the London Coliseum which even D. W. Griffith might have been hard put to replicate: the storming of the Bastille, the massacre of the Huguenots; even the decline and fall of the Roman Empire seemed a suitable subject for his dramatic blockbuster. But whatever he did, it would require a story: Coward's search for material took him to Foyle's on the Charing Cross Road, where he found old copies of the *Illustrated London News* and *Black and White*. Their yellowing but evocative scenes of the Boer War recalled distant memories of childhood, of the troops' songs of the times – 'Dolly Gray' and 'Soldiers of the Queen'.

Back at Ebury Street, he played them on the piano, where he was discovered by G. B. Stern in a state of 'high excitement'. He asked her if she knew anything about the Boer War and, being ten years older, Stern told Coward 'about newsboys down the street, about the siege of Mafeking, about Bugler Dunne. I recited "The Absent-Minded Beggar". I am afraid I sang "Dolly Gray" and "Bluebell" and "A Little Boy called Taps". "Remember that: newsboys down the street," said Noel crisply to Gladys Calthrop . . .' Stern also remembered the children of her family being taken by an elderly cousin, 'Kruger' Rakonitz, on to his balcony at Oxford Terrace to watch Queen Victoria's funeral procession. 'We found the title that same evening. I kept on saying, "You want something like 'Pageant' or 'Procession'"" and then Noel shouted, 'Cavalcade!"'

Cavalcade was born in a remembrance of popular culture from late Victorian days, and the result was something between musical, drama and tableau; Coward had originally planned to follow a group of 'bright young people of the nineties' through the lives of their children, but decided on a greater theme; thirty years of English life seen from both sides of the social divide; the families of the well-to-do, and those who served them.

For the moment, however, all this had to be put to one side, as Coward went to New York to deal with the production of *Private Lives* on Broadway. It opened in Times Square Theatre on 27 January 1931. Walter Winchell wrote that it was 'something to go silly over'; Robert Littell called it 'an admirable piece of fluff'; and Brooks Atkinson remarked that the playwright 'has nothing to say, and manages to say it with competent agility for three acts'. Other critics were percipient about the childish quality, and the nature of the relationship with Lawrence, regarding the actors and the characters they played as one and the same. 'They are only adults under the skin', noted the *New York Review*. 'They are really sulky adolescents on long legs and the humour they distil is infectious and superb.'

The success of *Private Lives* in the United States enabled Coward to sell the film rights profitably to MGM, together with those of *Bitter Sweet*. But Noel resisted the lure of Hollywood, even though Laurence Olivier and his wife Jill Esmond (who played Adrianne Allen's part in the US *Private Lives*) had secured lucrative film contracts there. The movie business was no magnet, 'For one thing, I don't think they'll give me enough money to make it worth while, as I demand more than they would pay their biggest stars!' he told Violet, and he'd 'rather have a nice cup of cocoa really'.

Working in a penthouse flat on West 18th Street, with a view of the Empire State Building and the noise of the traffic below, Coward consulted old magazines and his memory for *Cavalcade*. But until he began writing there was a sense of trepidation, and he was eager to get home, despite the fact that *Private Lives* continued to play to capacity crowds throughout its Broadway run. When Gertrude Lawrence fell ill, Noel had to play five performances with an understudy. They then decided to close the theatre for two weeks; to make up the twelve-week run, the last night was put forward to 9 May. As the closure coincided with Holy Week ('when business is always bad') this was a blessing in disguise. It meant Coward and Jack Wilson could take a fortnight's holiday in Bermuda.

It was Coward's first visit to the Caribbean. They stayed in Havana, which Noel described as 'very very beautiful and filled with lovely old buildings, but also very gay and smart'. He and Jack drove through sugar and banana plantations surrounded by 'masses of every conceivable flower', and dined alfresco 'outside the town, with trees hung with lights and Spanish orchestras playing very softly'. In Nassau, they met the Oliviers, and spent their time fishing and visiting the islands in a motor-boat, filming all the while with cine cameras. 'It's the best sort of holiday for me,' Noel commented, 'nothing but sun and sea.'

Coward, Wilson and the Oliviers shared a garden and swimming-pool, and Noel, ever the sunlover, decided that they should spend most of their time nude. After initial objections, they all agreed it was rather liberating. One lunchtime Jill Esmond went to Noel, holding a salad bowl as he served himself. 'Darling Jilli,' he said, 'have you any idea how lovely you are, just like that?' Then Noel decided Larry was too hairy and, as his wife lay asleep, he and Jack grabbed hold of Olivier and began to snip away at his pubic hair. Jill woke to see Noel at work. 'There,' he said, 'that's much better, don't you think?' 'Yes,' said Esmond, 'much.' But she saw it as evidence of Coward's homosexual feelings towards Larry, with which she later confronted Noel, 'and shooed him off', according to her son.

Back in New York, with Gertrude Lawrence recovered, the play ran out its final days. Noel's longing to get home was mitigated by the approbation of New York and beyond; that year he was declared the world's highest-paid writer, with an estimated annual income, since 1929, of £50,000.

14

Cavalcade

Have you considered acquiring all the rights to Noel Coward? . . .
He writes English like Congreve, and when G.B.S. goes will be the
main force in the English theatre. I should nobble him, if nobble-
able, on both sides of the Atlantic . . .

T. E. Lawrence to F. N. Doubleday

BACK at Goldenhurst, Coward turned his attention to the proposed venue for his spectacular; the Coliseum was unavailable,
so Cochran had secured the Drury Lane Theatre. Noel had
detailed his requirements for *Cavalcade* in a three-hundred-word telegram from New York: a pivot stage to contain the Mile End Road,
Edwardian reception rooms, a seaside resort and Trafalgar Square on
Armistice Night, with precise requirements for lighting effects, a full
orchestra, fog effects and a company of Guards. There was an additional
enjoinder that 'no detail of this should reach private or particularly
Press ears'. These were specifications equivalent to those of a modern
stadium concert, and Coward's script required no more than thirty
seconds' interval between each of the play's twenty-three scenes. The
stage was divided into six hydraulic lifts, timed to rise or fall on light
cues, and automatic lighting was employed; all of which would necessi-
tate complex and painstaking rehearsal.

Coward and Calthrop now had to produce their script and designs.
Calthrop moved into Goldenhurst, and the pair worked industriously;
Coward wrote facing the window and the view of Romney Marsh,
which appalled Maugham, who told him that good writers looked at
blank walls when they wrote. The final speech at the end of the play
proved most difficult to write, but Coward told Tarquin Olivier that he
went to bed, and 'awoke at 7.30 in the morning and without a second's
hesitation wrote out the speech. He went down for breakfast. When he

returned he found no need to alter a word, not a comma. His mind had worked on it all night.'

Having cast his main characters, Coward found recruiting the crowd scenes a 'depressing business'. With unemployment high, more than a thousand people applied for four hundred jobs, and although it was possible to engage this vast number only by restricting salaries to thirty shillings a week, they still kept coming; the endless lines of actors queuing for bit parts reminded Coward of his own beginnings. Cochran's attitude to the 'lower ranks' displeased his author; Cochran offered vast sums to individual artists, and indeed, to Coward himself (the production costs alone were £30,000, raised almost single-handedly by Cochran), but he was less than generous with those scrabbling for bit parts. Coward also discovered that Cochran had engaged three society girls for walk-on roles, and suspected they had not been hired for their talent; Noel told the girls they were not suitable, but Cochran persisted. Coward retorted that for each girl he would engage two extras who needed the work.

His relationship with Cochran began to crack under the strain of the production of *Cavalcade*. This was partly due to Cochran's personality; the showman had become something of a pastiche of himself. His biographer, James Harding, paints an unappealing portrait of him, then in his fifties, his 'fair hair ... thinning and whitening, his girth ... fattening and his face becoming more rubicund, yet his desire for women remained insatiable ... Cochran was better placed than most in that, ageing though he looked, girls slept with him for the sake of his patronage and influence.' Rows broke out between the two men. The technical difficulties of the final 'Chaos' scene made Noel want to cut it; Cochran said that this was only temporary weariness and frustration, and insisted on rehearsing it; Coward gave way. But Cochran's control was compromised by frequent absences due to illness, and Coward was increasingly dismissive of the impresario's opinion.

Some involved in the production were disappointed that Coward had written so few new numbers, but Coward, backed by Cochran, considered that the emotional effect of the familiar music would 'electrify the assembled company' – the potency of cheap music, as one of his characters would observe. In retrospect, *Cavalcade* appears highly commercial, but politics and history played their part and, ironically, out of the financial misery of the time, Coward's fortune was made.

Three years into the Great Depression, Britain had come off the gold standard, and *Cavalcade* opened during this financial crisis; as a direct result of the threat to national prosperity, the jingoistic play became an enormous success. By the time it was published by Heinemann in early 1932, *Cavalcade* was as popular in print as it was on stage. With its smart jazz Thirties cover, and dedicated to G. B. Stern, the frontispiece sets the keynote, quoting from the final speech, 'Let's drink to the hope that one day this country of ours, which we love so much, will find dignity and greatness and peace again.' Although Coward denied any knowledge of politics (or that an election was imminent in the autumn 1931, when *Cavalcade* might influence for the better the fortunes of the Tory party), his patriotic tone was prescient. Once again he had tapped into the national mood.

Opening on New Year's Eve 1899 (the year of its author's birth), the play alternates between above- and below-stairs. The usual Coward mechanicals – the servants, Ellen and Bridges – are elevated to more important roles; from their mouths come the playwright's basic (perceived) beliefs, as in Bridges' dictum, 'We've got to 'ave wars every now and then to prove we're top-dog . . .' Servants withdraw 'covered with respectful embarrassment', and their mistress says, 'Small things are so infinitely touching, aren't they?' *Cavalcade* unashamedly reaffirms stereotypes: the characters seem almost Dickensian as Coward mixes comedy and tragedy. Bridges appears drunk in front of Lady Marryot, only to die dramatically, as a result of his drunkenness, run over by a coach. History was reduced to affecting vignettes: two lovers chat on a ship; when the girl takes her coat from the rails, the name *Titanic* is revealed. The great crowd scenes such as the Armistice celebrations focus on personal tragedy, as Jane Marryot faces the death of her son, while Ellen mouths, 'Things aren't what they used to be, you know – it's all changing.'

The play closes where it began, on New Year's Eve, with the aged Jane and Robert Marryot drinking to 1930. Jane's patriotic speech affirms that after the desolation of the war, her faith in England has been restored: 'to the spirit of gallantry and courage that made a strange Heaven out of unbelievable Hell . . .' Yet Coward throws in a final scene of near-anarchy – a raucous nightclub, with Fanny singing the cynical 'Twentieth-Century Blues' ('What is there to strive for/ Love or keep alive for?'). The chaotic ending, six war 'incurables' juxtaposed with jazz-age decadents to a soundtrack of cacophony and the National Anthem, is a cross between a Busby Berkeley musical and *The Three-penny Opera*. But the overwhelming impression of the production was of nostalgic national introspection and sentimentality, somewhat redeemed by Coward's handling of his material, technical skill and sense of spectacle. The result was a triumph of style over content.

On 22 October 1931, King George, Queen Mary, the Prince of Wales and other members of the royal family firmly sealed the play's success with their presence. The *New York Times* reported that the family were 'known to have been stirred deeply by Mr Coward's patriotic panorama of British history. If Mr Coward receives a knighthood in an early honours list it will set a record for so young a theatrical personage.' 'I was told on all sides', Coward wrote, 'that I had done a "big thing" and that a peerage was the least I could expect from a grateful monarch.' Age may have been one reason why his name was not in the New Year's Honours List of 1932; other rumours as to why he was not officially recognised would become ever more bizarre over the years.

Cavalcade was embraced by Fleet Street, who decided that if the British people needed flag-waving, they would lead the parade. The *Daily Mail* serialised the play, and the *Telegraph* wrote that it encompassed 'All the pent-up emotion of a sorely-tried nation – joy and relief that a crisis had been faced and passed . . .' But Coward's intentions were far from clear, and the evolutionary and emotional links between *Cavalcade* and his last work, *Post-Mortem*, are less surprising than they might seem. Jane Marryot has her direct parallel in Lady Cavan, both bereaved mothers who fulminate against the mistakes of war made by politicians. But whereas in *Post-Mortem* the attack is vehement and unalloyed, in *Cavalcade* 'ideas are quickly defused by sentiment'. In private, or in a published but unperformed work, Coward was willing to risk his hand, questioning authority and the Establishment; but in the public glare of the limelight, he refused to take himself seriously. Although Jane Marryot questions the idea of *pro patria mori*, no serious credence is allotted to her opinions as it is to long speeches by Perry Lomas or John Cavan in *Post-Mortem*. 'In *Post-Mortem*,' John Lahr writes, 'words failed Coward to convey his disgust at chauvinism and at the waste of life. In *Cavalcade*, he abandoned words and conveyed the irony brilliantly with sound and image.'

Coward's own comments indicate equivocation about the hijacking of *Cavalcade* for political ends: 'God seemed to be, politically at least, firmly ensconced in his Conservative heaven and all was right with the world', he wrote in his third volume of memoirs, *Past Conditional*. 'There was a feeling of hope in the air and a sort of rebirth of honest, homely patriotism . . . I had been assured on all sides that I had done a great service for England by writing it and producing it at such a timely moment. I suppose I believed all this? It is difficult to believe that I did. But perhaps the laurels rested comfortably enough on my head and I accepted the tributes without irony ... I know that it made many people cry and gave to some of them a feeling of hope for England's future, so perhaps I did do them a service after all, for it is better to hope than to despair. In any event either emotion may turn out to be illusory and a waste of time.'

When Coward gave Esme Wynne-Tyson a copy of the play, he inscribed it, tongue-in-cheek, 'From a National Hero'. His own family were not above questioning his motives; that summer, Erik wrote to Violet, 'Noel is getting a Cadillac, is he? For all his supposed patriotism, he seems to prefer most American things. I can't think why . . .'

Sean O'Casey found little to admire in *Cavalcade*, or in its author, and later launched a virulent attack on Noel in his trilogy of essays, 'Coward Codology'. 'In spite of the hysterical scene of a woman kicking her little children's toy soldiers to pieces (a very foolish thing to do), the central theme, it seems to me, was the marching of a million of men to battle, murder, and to sudden death ... Is this play, or pageant, or spectacle, a representation of England during the last thirty-five years? No, be God, it isn't, for England has something more to show for herself than war and sex. *Cavalcade* is but the march-past of the hinder parts of England, her backside draped with a Union Jack, the middle parts of England paraded with drum, trumpet and colours.' Defenders of *Cavalcade* argued that it was an all-round 'good thing'; it employed many actors at a time of high unemployment, and 'kept the film wolf from the door of our nearest approach to a National Theatre'. But O'Casey took issue with the very notion of *Cavalcade* as a popular play, pointing out that it did not succeed 'in even filling Drury Lane nine times a week for a year'. He condemned Coward's flippancy, and concluded that *Cavalcade* was 'a tawdry piece of work . . . Noel Coward hasn't yet even put his nose in the front rank of second-class dramatists let alone into the front rank of first-class dramatists.'

While some criticised Coward for the obviousness of his play, others berated him for its 'classism' when mass unemployment and poverty affected millions of Britons. Ethel Mannin lambasted Noel under the heading, A PLAY WHICH MAKES ME RAGE. Her objection was to the portrayal of classes, and she cited Mrs Bridges' change in attitude to Lady Marryot after the war, no longer calling the 'fat Mamma "your ladyship" or "Ma'am" ... we are meant to deplore the passing of servility in servants ... All round me were fat, white, bejewelled and befurred women whom one felt sure were thanking Mr Coward for showing ... that servants are no longer what they were ... If only one could have felt that Coward was making this point as a challenge to class distinctions, if only he had ... used the opportunity to put *the upper classes* in their place for once ... But Noel Coward is now a very successful young man, and sometimes success makes people forget, so that they instinctively ally themselves on the side of money and power.'

Beverley Nichols, at that time a fervent pacifist, was also disgusted by *Cavalcade* and its sentiments. He maintained that Coward 'ought to be a white-hot pacifist' (without explaining why), 'but somebody waved a Union Jack in front of him, and he tripped up, and he wrote *Cavalcade*. That play is about the finest essay in betrayal since Judas Iscariot ...' Nichols argued that Coward had pandered to the middle classes and their unthinking patriotism for the sake of publicity and career. Certainly, in the light of *Post-Mortem*, Coward's patriotism seems cynically crowd-pleasing, and his equivocation cannot convince us otherwise. Yet to him, the question of patriotism was beyond politics; it was an instinct for self-preservation, a territorial defence. Years later, having given up British citizenship, he claimed a desire to celebrate 'a most remarkable race', of whose shortcomings he was only too well aware, 'because I have suffered from them personally. I despise our national docility, the silliness of some of our laws, our meek acquiescence ...' However, much as he loathed these things, 'what I love about my country is really quite simple. I love its basic integrity, an integrity formed over hundreds of years by indigenous humour, courage and common-sense.'

Cavalcade became an almost unwanted measure of Coward's success: perhaps more than the other hits of the Twenties and Thirties it was the barometric high point of his popularity. It also confirmed the onset of reaction in his ideas. With the advent of a dour decade, he declined to try to become a serious writer or to join in the polemics of his intellectual and privileged peers. Noel, who'd had to fight his way up, had the typical respect of his class for his country's past, as opposed to the younger generation's rage at its destruction. However much he lampooned the stately homes of England and their scions out in the midday sun, he remained a spokesman for this threatened empire.

The new-found National Hero had now acquired a new London residence. He had outgrown his rooms at Ebury Street, and in 1930 had sought a smarter address, in Belgravia – the whitened sepulchure of the upper classes and the upwardly mobile. Noel's stake was less grand than the tall stucco terraces of Eaton Square, but chic for all that. 17 Gerald Road, a converted eighteenth-century coach-house, was previously Chester Studios, workplace of the Victorian artist Henrietta Mary Ward, and subsequently the home of the dancer Frankie Leverson, who had refurbished the interior in Spanish style. It is likely that Noel had been a guest there before he bought the lease. Studio flats were fashionable among young professionals of the period; light and space made them ideal for working and entertaining. Gladys Calthrop had taken just such a property, a 'lofty studio apartment with huge windows on the top floor in Spenser Street [close to Gerald Road] ... Her bedroom had been fashioned out of some sort of greenhouse.'

Gerald Road also had the great advantage of seclusion and quiet: Coward was especially sensitive to noise, and raged if his 'bubbers' (his sacred afternoon nap) was disturbed. The front entrance was through a high gate into a short dark tunnel, formed by the house above, lit at night by a Spanish iron lantern. Inside was one enormous room, 33 feet by 25, and 25 feet high, vaulted with triangular oak cross beams; under a huge east-facing window, a raised dais was in effect a miniature stage, and there was even a gallery, with a theatrical box above the front door. Upstairs were bedrooms, and a sun terrace. Attached to the rear, in Burton Mews, Coward also bought the lease of a house for use as Lorn Loraine's office.

Once again, Syrie Maugham was called upon; she installed deep, light-coloured sofas, limed Louis Quinze-style chairs and fashionable brown and white zebra-print cushions. A romanesque chair provided a thronelike perch for the prince of the West End, and a dash of chrome and frosted Lalique glass and geometric rugs gave a modernist touch. The bathroom featured a large fitted mirror over the bathtub. 'Each time when I'm shaving in the morning,' he told a disapproving Lord Maugham (the writer's dour brother), 'I say to myself, "Pretty picture! Pretty picture!"'

It was an impressive place in which to entertain; John Gielgud recalled one party there 'when there were at least fifty people up on his balcony'. A guest invited to the studio for cocktails asked Noel who would be there. '"Just ourselves", he replied; which turned out to mean a throng including Joan Crawford, Douglas Fairbanks Jnr, and Laurence Olivier.' Fairbanks described it as 'a page out of *Vanity Fair* or a Michael Arlen short story. The theatrical stars of the day mingled with Mayfair's playboys and girls, and the aristocracy with the plutocracy and politicians. Even a member of the Royal Family, the young, elegant, and very handsome Prince George [whom Fairbanks said was addressed by Noel as 'P.G.' and whose photograph featured prominently on a Gerald Road sideboard], came with the Countess of Dalkeith.' It was, commented *Vogue*, 'a party in the enlightened tradition, all very white and witty'.

Here, Coward revelled in the success of *Cavalcade* (changing his telegraphic address from PLAYBRIT (a patriotic if egotistical statement) to CAVALCADE, KNIGHTS, LONDON). He was flying high, and the 'yellow press' delighted in discussing his massive earnings, placing him above George Bernard Shaw and A. A. Milne. The *New York Times* assessed his income at $6000 a week, with *Cavalcade* earning over half that sum, and provincial tours of *Bitter Sweet* and *Private Lives* contributing to the coffers. Coward was undeniably at the peak of his international career.

Characteristically, Noel stayed around for just two weeks of adulation. One reason for his departure was his health – he was afraid of the delayed effect of recent stress – but he was also concerned by his name and work being appropriated for political ends by the media. There is also the suspicion that Coward was becoming exasperated by Jack Wilson's behaviour. Wilson was spending a lot of time (and a fair amount of his friend's money) in New York, settling business matters. But he had also become involved with David Herbert, second son of the Earl of Pembroke, then working as an interior decorator, and the two men shared an apartment on East End Avenue.

The liaison was no secret to their circle; together with other affairs of that group of young men, Wilson and Herbert were satirised in the eccentric Lord Berners' privately published spoof novel, *The Girls of Radcliff Hall*. Hugo Vickers remarks that it was easy for insiders to recognise Cecil Beaton as 'Cecily Seymour', hopelessly in love with the unfaithful 'Lizzie Johnson' (Peter Watson); 'Oliver Mason' (Oliver Messel) as an incorrigible gossip; and 'Daisy Montgomery' (David Herbert), who conceives a passion for 'Helena de Troy' (Jack Wilson). De Troy 'became immediately a great favourite with the whole school', wrote the author, 'and Daisy Montgomery, in particular, was simply crazy about her'. Daisy cuts off a piece from de Troy's rubber mackintosh to sleep with it under her pillow; it is subsequently stolen by Lizzie Johnson, although Berners afterwards informs readers that Daisy 'had set up an antique shop with Miss Helena de Troy in Bath'. (Berners was implying that Wilson/de Troy also had an affair with Peter

Watson, Beaton's inamorata, which could not have ameliorated Cecil's spikiness towards Noel.)

Given the state of his relationship with Wilson, Coward was glad to arrange another adventure with his old friend Jeffrey Amherst. Noel knew no better traveller than Earl Amherst, as he had now become (his father, the 4th earl, had died in 1927). After their Far Eastern tour, Amherst had trained as a commercial pilot at Hamble in England, and was awaiting his licence to begin work at Heston Aerodrome. He often took Coward flying, as did Gladys Calthrop, who 'flew very well, when she remembered where she was going'. Amherst once flew with Calthrop to Germany, where they met Hitler at the chancellery in Berlin. 'The double doors opened and in flounced Hitler, dressed in a short black coat and striped trousers, for all the world as if he had come to measure one for a new suit. But when he harangue[d] us in his hysterical German . . . he came ten foot high. It was very frightening.'

However, it was not by air but by sea that Amherst's and Coward's new adventure began. They left England on 29 October, en route for Rio de Janeiro. It was supposed to be an educational holiday: they learned Spanish from a Linguaphone course for the Argentine leg of their trip, and Noel read some history; there was also an odd encounter with a flamboyant Spanish woman who appeared to be involved in socialist espionage, and tried to persuade Noel to take a packet ashore for her at Rio. When he refused, she spat at him, 'turned on her high shiny black heels and scuttled off'. Their three weeks in Rio were filled with social activities, as everyone in town sought to meet Coward. They stayed in an hotel on Copacabana, where they were one day accosted 'by a good-looking lady who was accompanied by a very tall, handsome young man with a formidably good figure, both in their bathing suits'. She introduced herself as Marjorie Large, and her companion was Daan Hubrecht, twenty-one-year-old cavalry officer son of the Dutch ambassador. Large was the English wife of a Brazilian, and she and Daan were involved in a holiday romance; when Coward and Amherst, taken by the Dutch boy's charms, insisted Daan accompany them on their trip, Hubrecht's parents were visibly relieved.

As guests of a large maté tea company, they set off for the Brazilian interior. Two days out from São Paulo, they reached Porto Epitacio, as far as the train would go, and were ferried on a flotilla taking maté downstream. They sailed along the muddy river, home of piranha and crocodiles, for two days and nights. Coward found the hundreds of miles of dense virgin forest either side of the river 'quite terrifying – you can't walk more than a few yards and it's filled with snakes and orchids and parrots'. They disembarked close to the Iguaçú Falls, donning mackintoshes to brave the spray and film, then sailed on, changing boats frequently, until the final stretch to Buenos Aires on a regular passenger ship, whose captain objected to their short-sleeved shirts at dinner, saying they were an affront to the women passengers. They refused to change, so were in effect confined below deck for two days, where they threw their own cocktail party for the stewards. On reaching Buenos Aires, they stepped off the boat '*exquisitely* dressed', cut the captain, shook hands with the stewards, and climbed into the luxurious limousine awaiting them.

Hubrecht left to rejoin his family in Rio, and Coward and Amherst took a slow train across the pampas to stay on a cattle ranch on the edge of the lake at Nahuel Huapi, surrounded by snow-capped mountains. This was real wilderness: the nearest town was 470 miles away. The ranch belonged to the Basualdos, one of the richest families in the Argentine, five brothers who shared the property with their wives, one being the former New York dancer Leonora Hughes, whom Noel knew. The ranch was the last word in luxury, every bedroom with a marble bath, enormous open fireplaces and 'perfect food'. The Prince of Wales and Prince George had stayed there the previous year, and Coward was proud that they (and General Pershing) were the only other people to have followed this adventurous itinerary.

Crossing the lower Andes, partly by mule, to Chile, they encountered some Royal Navy officers at the hotel bar and were soon invited to 'a couple of fairly libidinous "guest nights"', details of which Coward kept to himself. From Santiago they climbed to La Paz, 15,000 feet above sea level and practically airless. Inca and Mayan ruins were impressive, although Coward noted 'it really *isn't* very central'. At Arequipa they stayed a week at an establishment run by an old American lady, Tia Bates, and met Sidney Bernstein, now losing money after the first flush of success with *Private Lives*.* Bernstein was glad to have company, and made their party up to three once more. By now the high altitudes and cold weather were getting to Noel, and although Lima was warmer he would be glad to get back.

At Panama, the trio separated. Amherst sailed home to London;

---

* Bernstein sold the theatre soon after, apparently without any animosity towards Coward, whose insistence on taking the play off after three months adversely affected the Phoenix's future.

Bernstein to New York, via Cuba; while Coward was bound for San Francisco on a Norwegian freighter, in the owner's suite. The hot, slow ten-day journey was spent mostly naked, donning shorts only in the evening to dine with the captain and indulge in a 'piss-up' with the crew. 'Those raucous evenings', he recalled, 'were sufficiently charged with maritime romanticism to remain for ever in my memory. One of the crew members, a strapping bearded young Viking clad in the briefest pair of shorts I have ever seen, not only played a guitar but actually wore a single gold earring.' He was never happier than when sunning himself, and the gentle movement of the ship soon had his imagination working. From the first night out, he worked on *Design for Living*, which took only eight days to complete, with two days in hand before his arrival in California.

Met from the ship by Jack Wilson, Coward revisited Hollywood in a round of parties and films. MGM's version of *Private Lives* missed the point, but Noel approved it and the performances of Robert Montgomery and Norma Shearer. As the film was about to start, Montgomery pressed an expensive wristwatch, engraved 'N.C.', into Coward's hands, 'This is to prevent you from saying what you really think of my performance!' The film had done well at the box office, which encouraged MGM to invest in the rights for *Hay Fever* (never filmed) and *The Queen Was in the Parlour*, re-shot by Paramount as *Tonight Is Ours* in 1932, with Frederic March and Claudette Colbert. The rights to *Cavalcade* had proved difficult to sell until a Mrs Tinker saw it in London, and cabled her husband, a Fox Films executive, recommending they buy.

Coward attended the first technical conference about *Cavalcade*. A scriptwriter rose to say, 'The opening of the picture as I see it should be as follows', and gave a winsome description of wintry birds in their nests suddenly waking to spring. Appalled by this 'treacly symbolism', Noel 'remembered' a previous appointment, and fled mid-meeting. Fox redeemed themselves by hiring a British director, Frank Lloyd, and left him to get on with it (out of apparent lack of interest, much to its author's satisfaction). A crew was sent to London to film the stage production, which became the basis for the movie version. An English cast – Diana Wynyard, Irene Browne, Frank Lawton and Ursula Jeans – played it straightforwardly, and the result was a great success. 'As far as I can remember *Cavalcade* opened more or less simultaneously in Hollywood and New York and was acclaimed on all sides as one of the greatest pictures ever made, which, at that time, I honestly think it was.'

In addition to being faithful to Coward's play, the film had the added advantage of expanding scenes which even Cochran's lavish production could only hint at; however, Hollywood gloss threatened to overwhelm the theatrical nuances. The result was more like silent cinema than modern talkie (Louella Parsons called it 'greater even than *Birth of a Nation*). Yet even in America, there was opposition to *Cavalcade* and its celebration of patriotism at a time of deep depression, and some American reviews of the film were scathing about its morality. The *New York Herald Tribune* said, 'Mr Coward has turned into a sort of moral Fascist ... Like all other Fascists, political, religious or intellectual, he couches his new beliefs in terms far too simple to ... carry even a modest burden of truth ... Whatever the sins of "The Vortex" ... it had none of this new quality of smugness.'

California furnished another diversion, in the shape of a Warner Brothers star, James Cagney. Originally a dancer, Cagney was now famous for his psychotic gangster roles, such as *The Public Enemy* (1931), in which he pushes half a grapefruit in Mae Clarke's face. The young Cagney was apparently engaging enough to inspire a song; when the composer Ned Rorem met Coward later, he 'had heard that he and James Cagney were [lovers] ... from many different sources. That the song "Mad About the Boy" was written for Cagney. I thought it was so incongruous, that's why it stuck with me.' Coward's American agent, Charles Russell, said Noel told him 'he had a rough and tumble with James Cagney, a wrestling match on the floor'.

But whatever its attractions, Coward's low opinion of Hollywood was confirmed. They all 'work too deuced hard. They get up at 6.30 ... stand around all day under the red-hot lights ... eat hurriedly at mid-day, and because they are too tired to sit up late at night have their supper served on trays. That's no way to live, and certainly no way to work.' Writers got the worst deal of all: 'How they accomplish anything in the rabbit hutches to which they are assigned is beyond me. They even punch time clocks', Noel added, an authentic note of disgust in his voice.

15

Design for Living

Let's make the most of the whole business, shall we? Let's be
photographed and interviewed and pointed at in restaurants! Let's
play the game for what it's worth, secretaries, fur coats, and de luxe
suites in Transatlantic liners at minimum rates! Don't let one shabby
perquisite slip through our fingers! It's what we dreamed many
years ago and now it's within our reach.

Leo, *Design for Living*

*D*ESIGN *for Living* had arrived in New York before Coward,
and the Lunts were already being besieged by theatre managements keen to snap up this starry three-hander. A great
quantity of flowers and champagne were sent as inducements, but the
independent producer Max Gordon was the successful applicant – he
hadn't sent so much as a Hershey bar. Gordon had endeared himself to
Coward with his intelligent comments on *Private Lives*; Coward was
not to know that Gordon had no capital at all, and had to raise it on
the back of the promise of *Design for Living*.*

Coward returned to England in the spring of 1932, to be greeted at
Goldenhurst by an ever-growing menagerie: two dachshunds called 'the
Coconuts', a Sealyham, two cocker spaniels, a mongrel and his cat,
'Proust', all cared for in his absence by a special doggy domestic. He
settled down to work on his new revue for Cochran. At one of the early
auditions he was surprised by the assurance of a fourteen-year-old
South African boy, thrust on to the stage by his mother to sing 'Nearer
My God to Thee' in a pure treble while executing a brisk tap dance.

---

* Max Gordon maintained that Coward had contacted him, rather than the other way
around, offering him the play on hard terms: 10 per cent of the gross for the three leading
actors, and 10 per cent for Coward as author. Noel and the Lunts would put up $20,000, but
Gordon would have to raise the further $30,000 required.

'My mother said Mr Coward might not give me enough time so I should do the tap dance while I sang', says Graham Payn. 'Noel was so astonished that he said, "Better give the boy a job!"' This stage mother, Sybil Payn, was a more professional and driven version of Violet; the boy, Graham Philip Payn, a handsome edition of Noel at that age. Payn was engaged as a pageboy and urchin street-singer, to perform in 'The Midnight Matinee' and 'Mad About the Boy' respectively. Sybil Payn's insistent promotion of her son forced his retention in Coward's memory, but not for quite the right reasons. Joe Mitchenson, Coward archivist and friend, tells that Payn went backstage on the first night 'and said, "My mother doesn't think I've got enough in this show," and Noel said, "Oh, I think we'd better cut your second number – it's not all that strong." He wasn't having a youngster telling him he hadn't enough to do in the show.'

Coward could now call the shots with Cochran, and decided he would drop the over-choreographed and over-designed traditions of a Cochran revue. Noel fixed the running order of the scenes and sketches, and announced his title, *Words and Music*. The production, direction and casting were to be as he ordered; Gladys Calthrop had designed *Cavalcade* single-handed, and could surely cope with this revue. Cochran was annoyed by the lack of co-operative spirit in his old collaborator, but success had given Coward the upper hand, and he remained adamant. Cochran, who had been instrumental in that success, assumed the unsatisfying role of theatre manager. He thought *Words and Music* 'a jaded, sulky piece of writing with overtones of bitterness ... It may have been an interesting Coward revue, but it was not a Cochran revue.'

Cochran's opinion was vindicated by the relatively short run of *Words and Music*, which opened in Manchester on 25 August and in London on 16 September, where it played for just 164 performances – far short of the two years Coward had anticipated. And yet it was an excellent showcase of Coward's talents: from the sophisticated opening of 'Debutantes': 'Shall we escape the strange "ennui"/ Of civilised futility?', to 'Children of the Ritz', the revue dazzles with irony. These are the Bright Young Things, post-Depression:

> In the lovely gay
> Years before the Crash
> Mr Cartier
> Never asked for cash
> Now shops we patronised are serving us with writs
> What's going to happen to the Children of the Ritz?

followed by 'Mad Dogs and Englishmen', sung by Romney Brent, wearing a leopardskin solar topee and clerical collar.

The great hit of the show, 'Mad About the Boy', opened outside a cinema at night, with traffic and music blending Gershwin-style. The audience saw women – housewife, schoolgirl, typist, servant-girl, street-walker – all gazing at stills of a matinee idol. The reality is revealed; the star himself, 'in an elaborate dressing-gown and having his nails manicured. His feet are in a mustard bath and he obviously has a bad chill. He also wears pince-nez, as, off the screen, his eyes are weak. His secretary stands beside this shadow of an idol with a pile of "Fan Mail". He tosses the letters casually aside merely saying gloomily, "Send a photograph, send a photograph".' There is a hint of femininity about the boy, perhaps apt considering the homosexual interpretation inevitably put on the song.* Besides the Cagney story, another rumour was that Coward had written it as a serenade to Douglas Fairbanks Jnr, who is mentioned in it. 'Although Noel loved the young Fairbanks,' an American paper said years later, 'Doug definitely didn't love him back, although the two men became good friends.' The song could also have been a comment on matinee idols who appeared heterosexual – not just Ivor Novello, but stars such as Valentino, Astaire, Robert Taylor, Cary Grant and Errol Flynn.

Of the other numbers, a *Journey's End* burlesque – a musical version of Sherriff's play – was not perhaps in the best of taste (the Lord Chamberlain's office thought that 'this sort of "gala" edition of a fight in the late War might offend public opinion'). With former Quaint John Mills as 'Harry Happy' to underline the skit, it was virtually a parody of *Post-Mortem*. The note of self-reference and satire continued to the revue's finale, when street cleaners were heard to remark, 'You'd never think there was a Crisis, that's wot I say – you'd never think it, not for a moment you wouldn't', another ironic comment from the creator of *Cavalcade*.

The critics appreciated Coward's tougher approach; the *Sketch* thought that *Words and Music* had single-handedly 'rehabilitated' the revue. *The Times* said, 'in this revue his satirical pieces have ... the active fierceness which is the distinction between genuine satire and empty sneering'. Once again, it seemed, Coward had delivered the

---

* For the 1938 New York revue *Set to Music*, another verse was added, to be sung by a businessman in his office: 'Mad about the boy,/ I know it's silly,/ But I'm mad about the boy,/ And even Doctor Freud cannot explain/ Those vexing dreams/ I've had about the boy ...' The verse was cut by the management, who considered it too daring.

goods, but the ticket-buying public did not agree – a reminder that critical acclaim by no means ensures popular success.

Behind the scenes of his public life, Coward was experiencing family problems. Reports from Ceylon indicated that Erik's illness had worsened, and the doctors insisted he return to England. Although he had suffered bad stomach pains for nearly four years, Erik thought that all he needed was 'a sea voyage and good food and rest'. He left Columbo for home on 13 July. Coward was shocked when he saw his younger brother. 'He seemed to have shrunk to half his normal size, his face was gaunt and drawn and it was obvious he was very seriously ill.' Noel arranged for him to be admitted to a private nursing home in Portland Place, run by Almina, Lady Carnarvon, and sought the best medical advice. The president of the Royal College of Surgeons, Lord Moynihan, examined Erik, and diagnosed testicular cancer, so far advanced that there was no hope of survival beyond six months.

Noel had the responsibility of breaking the news not only to his parents but to Erik himself. Knowing that Erik was waiting to hear, Coward conspired with Almina Carnarvon to tell his brother that he was suffering from hyperplasia of the abdominal glands, which could explain the symptoms; Erik was ambivalent, but accepted the verdict. Noel suggested he recuperate at Goldenhurst. 'I also, in a moment of inspiration, told him that he could repay me by making an accurate and detailed index of all my gramophone records.' As Dickie Fellowes-Gordon recalls, not all the family were so sensitive to the young man's condition, 'Auntie [Vida] used to hint to this poor soul that he'd "better make the most of this" before they could stop her.'

One effect of this tragedy was to exacerbate Noel's antipathy to religion, particularly on his mother's behalf. 'Everything is so tragic and cruel for you, and my heart aches dreadfully for you but that's no good either except that it proves even to me (who didn't need much proof) how very much I love you. The next letter I write to you won't be like this at all, it will be crammed with gay description. This sort of letter only makes us both cry and that's sillier than anything. I'm saying several acid prayers to a fat contented God, that Father in a dirty nightgown who hates you and me and every living creature in the world.'

On 28 September the Court Circular of *The Times* announced, 'Mr Noel Coward has gone abroad for several weeks. He intends to have a complete holiday and no letters will be forwarded.' He was off with the navy again, having recently renewed his friendship with the Mountbattens. Lord Louis Mountbatten was now stationed in Malta, and invited Noel to join him in Greece on the HMS *Queen Elizabeth*.

Coward left London for Paris, where he spent a few days with the Mendls and Lord Lloyd at the Villa Trianon. It was a peaceful stay, and Noel realised how physically exhausted he had been by recent events. His mind was still full of home, and he wrote Violet pained letters of sympathy, 'I'm trying to take your advice about not thinking of you but it's very difficult and I find I think about you all the time.' He then embarked on the Orient Express, but it was a far from luxurious journey; he had to sleep standing for two nights, 'jogging along' through a hot and dusty Serbia. At Salonika he was met by 'several angry Greeks', and the after-effects of severe earthquakes. Finally, he was ferried to Lemnos, to meet the *Queen Elizabeth*.

Coward was always a welcome guest of the Mountbattens, even when he said he was 'disgusted at the size [Mountbatten's] tummy had got to', as the naval commander wrote. Noel put him on a diet, 'No potatoes, no bread or pastry (only Ryvita), no butter, no sugar, chocolates or sweets etc. In a fortnight it reduced my tummy girth by an inch and in a month I expect to be lovely and slim.' Mountbatten was an easy-going friend, and the two enjoyed each other's company. The *Queen Elizabeth* sailed to Egypt and, after a few days, back to Genoa. Coward returned to England, but his few days at home were unhappy, as he knew that he was probably leaving his brother for the last time; Violet's grief was transparent. On 23 November he left for New York on the *Empress of Britain*. His transatlantic trips were now deluxe affairs; on this occasion he occupied a suite furnished in waxed maple, pink brocade furniture and apple-green shaded lamps, with a miniature bar, cheval glasses and a twenty-foot private deck. When he disembarked in New York, reporters noted Mr Coward's procession towards the gangway, 'scattering largesse among a posse of stewards, waiters and boot boys who lined his path'.

He moved into an apartment at 2 Beekman Place, overlooking the snowy East River, with Katharine Cornell and her husband, Guthrie McClintic,* among his new neighbours. Work began on *Design for Living* almost immediately; 'bliss', Coward told his mother, because the

---

* Guthrie McClintic, 1893–1961, actor, producer and director, was born in Seattle and married to Katharine Cornell, 1898–1974, the glamorous German-born actress and lesbian.

Lunts were 'so utterly sure and concentrated on what they're doing there's no work for me at all except to try to be good in my own part!' The rest of the cast were capable, including Philip Tonge, making a brief appearance as a reporter in Act Two. 'He's very good in it', Noel reported, adding: 'It does seem funny when I look back and remember how much in awe of him I was, life certainly plays very strange tricks on people.'

Gratifyingly, New York reassured Coward of his fame. 'The Press fall over themselves to say nice things about me and I'm altogether New York's white-headed boy.' Parties abounded, and theatre visits, 'some of them very good, particularly a musical by Jerome Kern called *Music in the Air* which is divine'. His heart was heavy, however. 'I couldn't be so silly as to wish you a Happy Christmas,' he wrote to his mother, enclosing money for her present, 'but please buy yourself something completely unnecessary and think of me when you're doing it.'

The cast left for Cleveland on 30 December, where their first week was already sold out. 'Somehow, by a sort of underground telegraph,' reported the local paper, 'word had filtered through that it would be very, very naughty.' Noel reported, in an encouraging and rare letter to Erik, that 'the play is a wow here and we have to have extra chairs in the aisles at every performance. We're all very good I think, I so wish you could see it.' Coward told him that the film of *Cavalcade* had opened in New York, and was a great success; the first night was a 'super riot! The notices are quite incredible, I've never seen so many superlatives. They've kept it completely English and just like the play and Jack who was there said it was the most moving thing he had ever seen when the enormous Broadway First Night audience rose to its feet and cheered at God Save the King! They're sending me a special print of it to Pittsburgh where I shall have a private showing . . . All my love to you and hand out some to everybody else and get well soon. Your heroic National-Minded Patriotic Bro.'

Design for Living was Coward's 1930s update on the morals he had examined in *The Vortex*. In its way, it is more shocking than the drugs and boy-love of the earlier play; barely below the surface are hints of bisexuality and free love that go unchallenged within the Bohemian lifestyles of the protagonists. But the gloss of sophistication served, as it so often did, to divert attention from darker themes.

The world of the play is the international *beau monde*, a transatlantic high society dressed by Molyneux and furnished by Syrie Maugham;

the title was redolent of Le Corbusier and Bauhaus chrome, as precise a period reference as *The Vortex* was for the early Twenties, and modernism – in the guise of scientific, medical and psychological theory – underpins the facetious wit of the piece. In an artist's garret in Paris, Gilda, a thirty-year-old woman of definable chic, banters with the art dealer Ernest Friedman; we are soon aware that the play is concerned almost entirely with sex. 'All the hormones in my blood are working overtime', Gilda tells Ernest. 'They're rushing madly in and out of my organs like messenger boys.' Gilda ought to marry Leo, the writer, but is equally attracted to Otto, the painter. The symmetry of the various couplings that follow – Gilda and Otto, Gilda and Leo, Leo and Otto, Gilda, Leo and Otto – is an elegant dance of sexual confusion, more than farce yet not serious drama. From Paris to London, from London to New York, the characters pursue each other across the Western world, blithely unaware of a real world beyond their modern interiors, tailormade and flash-fire epigrams.

Coward's ironic design for living revisits the atmosphere of the Ritz bar, a flexible *ménage à trois* in which the superficial rules and flippancy is all. Love is a dirty word, morality is absent. Who cares what Mrs Hodges, the token representation of the lower classes, thinks, confronted with behaviour which she cannot approve or understand? The author's stance – shocking for the time (it was not surprising that Coward evaded the Lord Chamberlain by producing it on Broadway) – leaves the audience up in the air at the play's conclusion, as the three participants embark on a shared sexual life.

A pivotal scene – as far as self-revelation by the author is concerned – is when Otto and Leo, temporarily spurned by Gilda, get drunk together and fall into each other's arms:

> Leo (*haltingly*): The – feeling I had for you – something very deep, I imagined it was, but it couldn't have been, could it? – now that it has died so easily.
> Otto: Thank God for each other, anyhow!
> Leo: That's true. We'll get along, somehow – (*his voice breaks*) – together –
> Otto (*struggling with his tears*): Together –

Teasing and blatantly flirtatious, in the light of Coward's homosexuality and Alfred Lunt's bisexuality, this loaded charade had implications for any spectator aware of Noel's sexuality; the overall tone of *Design for Living* was unmistakably homosexual. Even Gilda, with her mannish good looks, could be an effeminate man. John Lahr, in his percipient critique of the play, writes, 'Coward's comic revenge at the finale is the victory of the disguised gay world over the straight one.'

Hand in hand with the overt sexuality is the dominant theme of celebrity, and how to deal with it. We are among a professional meritocracy led by a playwright (Leo), a portraitist (Otto) and a society decorator (Gilda), each in successive scenes attaining their goals (just as the Lunts and Coward had promised themselves all those years before). However, their race for fame and fortune is at the root of their essential dissatisfaction, distancing them from their original enjoyment together in poverty. Leo/Noel embraces fame, yet realises the artifice of it all; he comments 'grandiloquently', 'It's all a question of masks, really; brittle, painted masks. We all wear them as a form of protection; modern life forces us to. We must have some means of shielding our timid, shrinking souls from the glare of civilization.' Leo and Gilda read the reviews of his first night. 'It's a knockout! It's magnificent! It'll run a year', exclaims the author. '*Change and Decay* is gripping throughout', he reads from the *Daily Mirror*, '"But" – here we go, dear! – "But the play, on the whole, is decidedly thin."' 'My God!' says Gilda, 'they've noticed it.' It sums up *Design for Living*'s reflection of *its* author: plays within plays, a disregard for convention or serious opinion, the inversion of principles; a rebellion of its own.

The early days of *Design for Living*'s American tour were not entirely happy.* Jeffrey Amherst, Gladys Calthrop and Daan Hubrecht had sailed across on the *Bremen* for the opening. 'The house [was] full, great excitement. But with the fall of the curtain after Act One, Noel stormed off the stage in a blind rage. It was a serious comedy. The oafs had laughed all through the first act, he'd be damned if he would go on with the play. Alfred Lunt was near to hysterics, Lynn Fontanne was in tears.' Calthrop shook her finger at Coward, 'reminding him that . . . it was the public who paid his salary, and . . . if he insisted on writing funny lines he must expect the audience to laugh'.

The run was also affected by depressing news from home. Noel wrote from Pittsburgh, 'Oh Darling, a very sad letter from you to-day. I do wish I could do something but I *know* there's nothing to be done. Christmas must have been awful, and New Year's Eve! It really is amazing how much human beings have to bear sometimes. How wonderful if he could die quietly in his sleep. I am so glad the nurses are

---

* This was also the case offstage: the emotional tangles of the play were reflected in real life, as, staying with a family in Cleveland, Noel fell hopelessly in love with the young son of the household.

nice and that he doesn't suspect anything. Bear up my darling, perhaps in the long run he will turn out to be lucky after all! Anyhow he could never go through what you're going through. Snoopie.' Two days before *Design for Living* was to open in New York, Coward received a telegram telling him that Erik had indeed died in his sleep. Coward's reaction was to send for his mother (and Aunt Vida) immediately; they arrived in New York ten days later.

Design for Living was well received, the American critics perhaps impressed by the rumour that Lunt, Fontanne and Coward were receiving the highest salaries ever paid to a trio of leading actors in a Broadway play.* Brooks Atkinson in the *New York Times* thought Coward ought to have 'cut the cackle and come to the main business, which is his brand of satire and comedy', but when he did it was with 'remarkable dexterity'; in an 'impish mood', Noel was 'enormously funny'.

Coward decided to break his rule and play in *Design for Living* for another two months. He rented a cottage at Sneden's Landing, on the banks of the Hudson River, again with Katharine Cornell and Guthrie McClintic as neighbours. The cottage was fairly primitive, but only thirty-five minutes from Broadway. Violet and Vida stayed with him, delighted at being among his smart friends.

Coward's high profile could cause problems, however. Celebrity kidnapping threats were fashionable after the abduction and murder of the Lindbergh baby, and Coward was advised to employ a 'delightful' private detective named Tommy Webber, 'bulging with armaments'. This was perhaps justified; that year, a twenty-six-year-old English actor named Frederick Manthrop was arrested in New York after demanding $2000 'under threat of death' from Coward and a Mrs John Sloane. And Elsa Maxwell recounted how she and Noel had been followed by 'four shabby men in an enclosed delivery van' from West 47th Street to the Empire State Building, where they 'made enquiries about Mr Coward and drove away only after three building guards drew pistols to escort Mr Coward and Miss Maxwell to their car'. 'They weren't kidnappers but celebrity hunters', said a spokesman for Mr Coward. 'They were a bunch of kids from Jersey over to see the stars. They had been following Tallulah Bankhead, too. Really, it's rather embarrassing

* Tickets for the first night of *Design for Living* were $11, $9 more than the average. Coward's weekly salary was reported to be $5000, while the Lunts each received $7000. The discrepancy was because Noel was also getting a 10 per cent author's royalty.

to Mr Coward.' Like a modern-day pop star, Noel was often pursued by obsessive fans, and would satirise the type in *Present Laughter*, in the character of Roland Maule.

After three months of Violet and Vida (quite long enough) Coward saw his mother and aunt off for England. *Design for Living* ended, and after the closing-night party at the Waldorf-Astoria and a playful poke in the ribs from Tommy Webber's pistol, Noel left for Bermuda, to cruise on HMS *Dragon*. His host was Captain Philip Vian, a contemporary of the Prince of Wales at Osborne and later an admiral of the Fleet: tall, 'with piercing blue eyes and extremely aggressive eyebrows', Vian exploded on first introduction, 'What the hell are you doing on board this ship?' Coward replied, with some degree of embarrassment, that he was 'exhausted, over-worked and on the verge of a nervous breakdown and had joined the ship in order to be nursed back to health and strength and waited on hand and foot'. Vian responded by inviting him to drink gin in his cabin. 'At the risk of infuriating him by my theatrical sentimentality,' wrote Coward, 'I must flatly admit that I am very fond of him indeed.'

He ended up in Trinidad, and began to work on a new musical play. Told of a romantic island off the coast, he arrived at Point Balaine's one hotel, run by a former sailor and his wife, to whom Noel took an immediate liking. A two-floor wooden building, with outlying bungalows, its atmosphere was pure Somerset Maugham, with whirring ceiling fans, lush tropicality and the only contact with the outside world a motor launch. Coward exploited the setting in his next play, *Point Valaine* (announced as *Point Balaine* in the US press), also written with the Lunts in mind. His other effort, *Conversation Piece* – a Regency fantasy inspired by *The Regent and His Daughter* by Dormer Creston – was for Yvonne Printemps, wife of Sacha Guitry and star of the Parisian stage, although, by the Thirties, somewhat past her peak.

Back at Goldenhurst he worked on the score for *Conversation Piece*, asking Cochran to keep it secret, but soon the newspapers discovered the next project of Britain's brightest playwright. A hit song was needed, and he obliged with 'I'll Follow My Secret Heart', one of his most indicative lyrics:

> I'll follow my secret heart
> My whole life through,
> I'll keep all my dreams apart
> Till one comes true.

> No matter what price is paid,
> What stars may fade
> Above,
> I'll follow my secret heart
> Till I find love.

For Coward, whose love was necessarily secret, it was a statement of intent.

He finished the score in November, and spent the pre-Christmas period travelling to and from Paris, trying to persuade a reluctant Printemps to take the role. She agreed, then changed her mind, in true *prima donna* style. By January she was rehearsing, in her charming fractured English, and played with aplomb through attendant crises, such as the death of one of her dogs in Paris, whose final gasp she heard on a rare trans-Channel telephone call in her dressing-room.

A 'polite, but faintly raffish play', *Conversation Piece* was basically a vehicle for Coward and Yvonne Printemps, its songs, glamorous costumes and mime scenes an attempt to replicate the success of *Bitter Sweet*. The 'Regency Vogue' fashion of the times gave it a chic reference point, and Coward's sugary fantasy had a satirical edge to sharpen it for modern audiences. When it opened at His Majesty's Theatre on 16 February 1934, James Agate thought it 'confused', but admitted that the wit, 'when we are allowed any', was 'at once unexpected, mordant, and bitter-sweet'. Beverley Nichols wrote in his diary, 'I have given up facile criticisms ... of his work and gratefully accept his charm, his sturdy avoidance of anything "shymaking" and his supremely brilliant direction. His performance was remarkable but left me with a sense of strain.'

The production saw the final breakdown of the relationship between Coward and C. B. Cochran. There had been disagreements over the casting: Cochran had approved of Printemps – indeed, he maintained it had been his idea to use her, not Coward's; but when Noel took the lead, Cochran considered it a mistake: he felt it would take his attention from the direction of the play, that his French accent would sound too English against Printemps', and that Coward 'lacked the romantic quality the part needed'. With the success of the piece, all seemed forgiven. On the first night, Cochran gave Coward a present, as he usually did: a Georgian snuff box, large enough to serve as a cigarette case, inscribed, 'In memory of a not altogether unsuccessful association'. It was the epitaph to their friendship.

Two weeks later Cochran received a letter from Coward, 'I have decided . . . to present my own and other people's plays in the future in partnership with Jack . . . This is . . . the result of our increasing activities in New York . . . where we have bought interests in several productions of other managements and, as you know, have controlled and virtually presented several of them.' Coward flattered, 'Without your encouragement and faith in me and my work it is unlikely that I should have ever reached the position I now hold in the theatre . . .' Cochran's reply was constrained, 'As you say, the development you refer to was inevitable, and I wish you and your associates the best of good fortune. Meanwhile, believe me, Yours as ever, CBC.'

Coward was hurt by the formality of CBC's reply; for his part, Cochran was bitter about Coward's curtailment of their relationship. His biographer James Harding claimed that a more vindictive man might have 'taken a malicious pleasure in the fact that none of Coward's later musical shows ever succeeded as well as those . . . in the grand days of their partnership . . . Without Cochran's flair and intuition an essential ingredient was missing.' Harding maintained that Coward 'always believed . . . that Cochran had cheated him'.

Life was again presenting Coward with a set of choices and another period of change; even beyond the unstable environment of the theatre, a state of ambivalence prevailed in his relationships.

Coward had kept up his friendship with Virginia Woolf by post, and now wrote another fan letter, 'This is just to tell you how very much I loved "Flush". It is quite exquisite and the most marvellous picture of an age. I do, with all my heart, congratulate you on a very difficult job most tenderly and beautifully done.' Sibyl Colefax's relentless hospitality brought the two together again, 'on a cold foggy night' in January 1934. Woolf had written to her nephew, Quentin Bell, '. . . I have to dine with Colefax tonight to meet Noel Coward whose works I despise but they say hes very good to his old mother. And Sybil [sic] wont take no, even in the fog . . .' Woolf reported back on the evening, saying that Coward 'called me Darling, and gave me his glass to drink out of. These are dramatic manners. I find them rather congenial . . . Then he played his new opera on Sybils grand piano and sang like a tipsy crow – quite without self consciousness. It is about Brighton in the time of the Regency – you can imagine. I am to go and see him in his retreat. He makes about twenty thousand a year, but has several decayed uncles and aunts to keep; and they will dine with him, he says, coming out of

Surbiton, and harking back to his poverty stricken days. So he has to combine them with the half naked nymphs who sing his parts, which is difficult.'

Woolf felt she was on display, and that Coward was party to Colefax's manoeuvres. '. . . Colefax writes that she is furious. Cant believe that its not a personal insult that I wont roast myself and fry myself talking to her and Noel Coward. Lord – what dusty souls these women get!' Colefax reproved Woolf for 'insinuating that her dinner was merely a snob dinner to bring celebrities together. The truth was Noel [Coward] adores me; & I could save him from being as clever as a bag of ferrets & trivial as a perch of canaries.' Post-*Cavalcade*, it seemed that Woolf no longer thought Coward capable of salvation; his ubiquitousness as a celebrity turned her against him. Later in the year, she dined with Clive Bell, Aldous Huxley and the Kenneth Clarks. 'Talk at dinner about . . . Noel Coward . . . at Monte Carlo, laying his hand on A[ldous]'s arm: this is divine – a Jazz like the rest. The variety of his gifts: but all out of the 6d box at Woolworth's. Beating & beating & beating – an omelette without eggs, said A. Nothing there: but the heroic beating . . .'

E. M. Forster also met Coward at Colefax's in 1935; Stephen Tennant recorded Forster's account of 'a lunch party with Sibyl and Noel Coward talking awful drivel – he said the stupidity of the whole party was indescribable – he imitates Noel C. The sometimes patronising reaction of the intelligentsia gave Coward good reason to despise its more egregious offenders. Jeffrey Amherst tried unsuccessfully to introduce Noel to Roger Senhouse, and maintained that 'in those days Noel was inclined to fight shy of anything he thought highbrow and he looked askance at Bloomsbury. He took against those rather esoteric productions in little theatres by obscure authors. Slightly petulantly one day he announced he would write a Russian play for the Pitoeffs and their Compagnie des Quinze (who were really only thirteen). "It will be played entirely in the dark and will be titled *Seven Pass while the Lentils Boil*."'

Coward was acutely aware of the social and intellectual distance between him and the mandarins of Bloomsbury. Many years later, he read Michael Holroyd's biography of Lytton Strachey. 'It's a fascinating picture of the Bloomsbury lot', he admitted. 'If Mother had been able to afford to send me to private school, Eton and Oxford or Cambridge, it would have probably set me back years. I have always distrusted too much education and intellectualism; it seems to me that they are always dead wrong about things that really matter, however right they may be in their literary and artistic assessments ... My good fortune was to have a bright, acquisitive, but not, *not* an intellectual mind, and to have been impelled by circumstances to get out and earn my living and help with the instalments on the house.'

Strachey himself was equivocal about Coward, and unimpressed by his work in the early Twenties. They had a chance meeting later. 'I met you a few years ago', Noel reminded Bloomsbury's high priest. 'Rather a nice interval, don't you think?' Strachey replied.

16

Tonight at 8.30

Free from love's illusion, my heart is my own; I travel alone.

Noel Coward, 'I Travel Alone'

IN March 1934, Noel Coward, Jack Wilson, Alfred Lunt and Lynn
Fontanne formed a partnership as Transatlantic Presentations Inc.,
initially to produce S. N. Behrman's *Biography*. It was a 'friendly
agreement which provided that thereafter all were eligible for partner-
ships in any stage venture in which any one of them was involved'.
Funds were paid into production accounts in London and New York
for the purpose; 'the extent of the participation of any of the four in
any one play is elastic, depending upon the relative enthusiasms of
individual partners for the play in question'.

Coward was not enthusiastic about appearing in Behrman's comedy
of American manners, but its similarity to his own work (it concerned a
much-courted portrait painter) suggested that he should direct it. He
cast Ina Claire and Laurence Olivier in the leads, and although business
was initally good, largely due to the draw of Coward's name, its
disappointing run boded ill for one half of Transatlantic Presentations,
the new Noel Coward–John C. Wilson company, set up to replace
Noel's arrangement with Cochran. Hugh 'Binkie' Beaumont, the rising
young theatrical impresario in charge of the production, pronounced it
a '"*dis-ah-ster*" . . . he lengthened the vowel into a moan of despair'.

Financing his own productions proved a mixed benefit for Coward:
the increased control was welcome, but all depended on persuading
others to invest, no easy task. Dramatists had an advantage over
producer-managers: they could write a number of plays and absorb the
failure rate without having risked their own money. But Coward was
now reinvesting in himself, a gamble which might lead to greater profits
or might plunge him into debt. Profits made on one production could

be wiped out by the failure of another, but Coward was to some extent insured against such loss; even if his plays took only a few hundred pounds a week, he was entitled to his stipulated percentage of the gross receipts; as he pointed out when he was congratulated on some newly acquired property, 'Yes, it was bought entirely out of my failures.'

Coward was intending to appear on Broadway that year in another playwright's work, that of Keith Winter, with whom he was romantically involved. Winter, six years Coward's junior, had been a schoolmaster before his play, *The Rats of Norway*, set in a Northumbrian preparatory school, achieved success in 1933. Directed by Raymond Massey, it starred Gladys Cooper and Laurence Olivier in what the American reviewers would call 'a turgid affair concerning repressed and misdirected sex impulses in an English school'.

Fair-haired, fresh-faced and earnest-looking, Winter had planned to become an 'acrobatic dancer' until a rugby injury 'dispelled my dreams'. Oxford-educated, Winter, who was a friend of G. B. Stern's, was not a typical companion for Coward, but their affair was intense and apparently tempestuous. After the success of Winter's *The Shining Hour* in 1934 – again with Gladys Cooper, a tale of jealousy set in a Yorkshire farmhouse – Coward agreed to appear in his third play, *The Ringmaster*. But illness would prevent Coward from fulfilling his promise and it was not produced until the following year, with Laurence Olivier as the bitter and sardonic wheelchair-bound protagonist, not a part with which Noel would have been happy. It was perhaps a lucky escape for him, as the play closed within a week. Considering the speed with which Noel plunged into his next romantic intrigue, it seems that the affair with Winter ended abruptly and unhappily; there is no further mention of him in Coward's extant diaries or letters, nor does he allude to their relationship. (Winter later became a film scriptwriter, working on Powell–Pressburger's *The Red Shoes* in 1948, and in Hollywood as a contract writer. He died in New Jersey in 1985.)

Coward had other commitments in 1934; that April he accepted the presidency of the Actors' Orphanage charity, and decided to play a more active role than had his predecessor, Gerald du Maurier. The orphanage, Langley Hall, was home to some who were not really orphans but illegitimate children of members of the theatrical profession, often with living parents who could not afford to look after them or did not want to. A distinct stigma attached to the place; Roy

Williams, who was there from 1929 to 1940, has only recently been able to admit it. He tells a fascinating tale of Noel rescuing a modern-day Dotheboys Hall. 'When I went in 1929 [aged five] it was a pretty awful place, really Dickensian and badly-run...' A teacher named Austin ruled with the cane, and just before Coward's first visit had given some young offenders an unprecedented twenty-four strokes; the school had risen in protest, the children going 'on strike'. Noel was 'horrified to discover that former presidents had ... just let it run under this awful character, Mr Austin'. He took direct action, and in 1938 the school moved to Silverlands in Chertsey, Surrey, with a new headmaster, and 'the place became much kinder. We also became co-educational. Before, if a boy was seen looking at a girl, that was cause for him to be punished ... it was very daring for that time – not many orphanages, or private schools even, became co-ed.' Coward also introduced school uniforms, and trips to see the Lord Mayor. 'Then there was the Theatrical Garden Party [which raised funds for the orphanage], to which the Duke and Duchess of Kent were always dragged along.' Coward would travel down with Lorn Loraine, often bringing other committee members, such as Evelyn Laye; he even prevailed upon Douglas Fairbanks and Mary Pickford, who donated a home movie camera to the school.

Uncharitable tongues had it that Coward's attentions were not entirely altruistic; Roy Williams thought it possible that 'he did it in the hope that this would be his contribution to charity and society and that there might be some reward for that ... and when he realised there wasn't going to be any, his interest dropped'. As with any high-profile celebrity, there were many approaches to Coward from charities and individuals. His employee Bert Lister said that Lorn Loraine 'saved him a lot of money. She used to forward the begging letters he got – at least ten a week – to the charity offices on Queen Anne's Gate. And they were grateful because they wanted customers. It saved Noel thousands.'

Nor was his vigorous approach entirely popular at the orphanage: 'I think Noel hurt some committee members' feelings, like C. Aubrey Smith. He wanted to be a working president...' There were other problems too; although Williams recalls no sexual indiscretions by the staff, Cole Lesley noted that one master appeared rather too interested in the girls' evening baths. When he began comparing them to 'pretty little pink seals', he was urged to take another post.

*

The film of *Design for Living* also appeared that year, directed by Ernst Lubitsch and scripted by Ben Hecht. Starring Gary Cooper (in Coward's role), Miriam Hopkins and Frederic March, it ignored the subtleties of the play in favour of a straightforward romantic triangle. The characters were Americanised, and their names changed – Gilda became Gilda (pronounced 'Jilda') Farrell; Leo, George Curtiss; and Otto, Thomas Chambers. Cooper's slow-speaking masculine manner, even when clad in well-cut suits, could not convey the sophistication of Leo; nor did Lubitsch intend him to. The result was innocent and 'larky', with no relevance to Coward's original themes. There had been, wrote one critic, 'a partial cleansing for the screen of a stage story notorious for its wealth and variety of moral code infractions'. So little remained of Noel's original script that Hecht joked, 'There's only one line of Coward's left in the picture – see if you can find it.' *Variety* judged it 'an improvement on the original' – impudence made bearable for the author by the £10,000 fee.

In the meantime, Coward was back in Malta with the Mountbattens. Edwina Mountbatten was still recovering from the bad publicity of her libel action against the *People*, which claimed she'd had an affair with Paul Robeson. She denied even having met Robeson, a lie which hurt the black actor and singer. Society gossip about the two was rife, and was made worse by the high-profile court case (forced on the Mountbattens by Buckingham Palace). Coward sympathised with Edwina because, bizarrely, Essie Robeson, Paul's wife, had believed herself to be in love with Coward himself. The Robesons first met Coward in 1926, probably introduced by their mutual friend Rebecca West. 'The play was trash,' wrote Essie when she saw *The Vortex*, 'but he emanated a sweetness and personality right over the footlights.' According to Essie's diary, she saw a lot of Coward during the winter of 1930–1, when he was the recipient of her woes about her marital difficulties with Robeson. His attentions are evident from a letter Robeson wrote to Essie in January 1931: 'I had a talk with NC. We talked frankly as he said he knew all the facts ... He was noncommittal, and rightly so. After all, his business with you is your concern, not mine ...' Robeson's biographer, Martin Duberman, found 'no evidence of a sexual affair ... Nonetheless, the oblique reference in Paul Robeson's letter leaves the matter in doubt.'

Essie and Noel 'stopped traffic' when they arrived together at the NAACP (National Association for the Advancement of Coloured

People)* annual ball at the Savoy. 'Noel danced with me often. He was conspicuously attentive ... to the confoundment of all those present.' The young black woman was flattered by the attentions of the most eligible young playwright-about-town, and there was reflected glamour in the dalliance for him too. But their relationship, although intimate, was probably platonic, and Coward may well have become embarrassed by her attentions, although not as embarrassed as Edwina Mountbatten by stories of association with Essie's husband. It was said she had come out to Malta to evade the continuing rumours, but even there the officers' wives knew of the affair and there was a distinct coolness towards her.

Coward left *Conversation Piece* on 23 April, and joined the Mountbattens at the Villa Medina in Malta, with King Alfonso of Spain and a thirteen-year-old Prince Philip, future Duke of Edinburgh. The lavish lifestyle of the Mountbattens suited Noel. He enjoyed the sun and the warm, clear water, zooming about on the *Lizard*, Mountbatten's green motor boat, attempting to water-ski and picnicking on the rocks at Gozo. He wore little but brief shorts and a hat he had bought in China. Coward's thank-you letter epitomised the flirtatious relationship he maintained with Mountbatten:

> Dear dainty Darling,
>
> I *couldn't* have enjoyed my holiday more ... Please ask Peter [Murphy, Mountbatten's great friend] not to foul the guest cabin in any beastly way because I do so want to use it again ... Please be careful of your zippers, Dickie dear, and don't let me hear of any ugly happenings at Flotilla dances, Love and kisses, Bosun Coward
> (I know Bosun should be spelt 'Boatswain' but I *don't* care!)

Coward had promised Cochran he would return to *Conversation Piece* to rally a flagging box office in the latter part of the run, and he reluctantly went back to London. But after just twelve performances Noel collapsed mid-performance and was operated on the next day for acute appendicitis. With no pressing work until the autumn, and in need of further convalescence, Coward decided on another holiday, the summer being closed season in the theatre. Chartering a yacht, the *Mara*, and a crew, Coward set sail for Cannes. Aboard was a new friend, a handsome young actor named Louis Hayward.

---

* Coward and Beatrice Lillie were among the first of their profession to volunteer for a benefit show for the Negro Actors' Guild on 11 December 1938, helping to raise $25,000 for 'the ill and needy of the profession'.

They had met two years previously when Hayward was appearing in *Another Language* at the Lyric Theatre. In late 1933 Coward had cast him as Simon Bliss in a revival of *Hay Fever* at the Shaftesbury Theatre, and subsequently as the Marquis of Sheere in *Conversation Piece*, where the young actor made a definite impression in tight white breeches and kiss-curl coiffure. Ten years younger than Coward, Hayward (whose real name was Seafield Grant, but whom Noel called 'Sugar') had been born in Johannesburg. He had appeared frequently in the West End in parts suited to attractive young men and had also begun a successful film career in Britain. Coward found him irresistible; a sequence of photographs in Noel's album show Hayward riding and leaping fences, romantic in shirtsleeves and breeches.

But what ought to have been a romantic cruise ended in disaster. Having sailed along the Italian coast, they anchored off Corsica at L'île Rousse, where a violent storm blew up while they were ashore, breaking the yacht against the rocks; Noel and the crew had to walk twenty miles to find help. In his memoirs, Coward dramatises the scene with a 'fainting French Captain', and himself taking the boat's wheel, 'upheld by gin and my ex-appendicitis truss'. In fact, Hayward and he merely waded out to the wreckage the following day to retrieve what they could. Noel had lost his typewriter, passport, money, clothes and, more importantly, the manuscript of his autobiography.

Much was made of the incident in the press on both sides of the Atlantic; it was always good to maintain one's public profile, especially if the story could be elaborated. Newspapers reminded their readers that the world's most renowned contemporary playwright had only recently recovered from an operation during which he was 'in a critical condition for several days'. Friends had visions of a *distrait* Noel returning shoeless, but he was snapped in Paris looking suave in a spotted cravat, with not a lock of hair out of place. Of the fact that Louis Hayward had been on board (a scenario straight out of *Home Chat*), no mention was made.

The usual debonair Mr Coward arrived back in London to produce *Theatre Royal*. George Kaufman's and Edna Ferber's comedy, like *Hay Fever*, portrayed a histrionic family, this time the Barrymores, a veritable stage dynasty. Marie Tempest, Madge Titheradge and Brian Aherne*

---

* Brian Aherne (1902–86), British actor who had been in the 1913 production of *Where the Rainbow Ends*, and who later became a close friend of Coward's, as well as a lover of both Dietrich and Garbo.

were cast, but Aherne was contracted in Hollywood. Until he could be released – in time for the London opening – Laurence Olivier would take the part on tour. Despite receiving £100 a week, Olivier was not pleased, but did it as a favour for Coward. However, he was so successful that Coward persuaded him to take the play into the West End. It looked set for capital city success, provided the strange Indian character who came onstage in Edinburgh, muttering mock Hindi, didn't cause the entire cast to break down in giggles when they realised their director had made an unscripted entrance.

On 2 November Coward and Edwina Mountbatten were photographed at Southampton Docks, she in leopardskin coat and hat, he in smart suit with a cigarette in his fist. Coward had been invited by the Governor-General of Canada, Lord Bessborough, to stay with him at Government House in Ottawa; Lady Louis was still feeling the backlash of her libel suit, and vanished from society for the next few months. They were joined by Bessborough's wife and young son, who had been on holiday in England, and were good friends of the Mountbattens.

From Canada, Coward went to the Lunts' farm in Wisconsin, to discuss the new project, *Point Valaine*; the three of them arrived in New York on 19 November. Jack Wilson had negotiated for Noel the purchase of a house at Saco Hill, Fairfield, Connecticut, which he had seen while its former tenant, Edna Ferber, was still living there, and from this new base, Coward began work on rehearsals for *Point Valaine*, the fourth production he directed that year. New York had not been starved of Coward during his absence. *Home Chat* had opened in Brooklyn (with Philip Tonge among the cast), and *Conversation Piece* opened at the 44th Street Theater with Yvonne Printemps, where it played for six months to packed houses, despite Brooks Atkinson's calling it 'passing dull'. And on 27 October, Noel was heard for the first time over the American airwaves (so the *New York Post* maintained) when WABC transmitted a Coward entertainment from London.

Of *Point Valaine*, Coward wrote that he was 'honestly attempting to break . . . new ground by creating a group of characters and establishing an atmosphere as far removed as possible from anything I have done before'. The play was certainly a new departure for him, evoking Maugham in its heady tropical atmosphere, with the thwarted passions of a female hotel owner, her Slav lover and various other guests. As if to stress the difference between this and earlier, more innocuous offerings, Coward sprinkled his play with bad language – 'bastard' and 'bloody' – this was an American production, and not subject to Lord Cromer's blue pencil. There is also a sexually ambiguous male couple, and a visiting writer, Mortimer Quinn, perhaps an evocation of the play's spiritual father, Somerset Maugham, a man whom Coward would see as increasingly bitter even as he plundered the world for material. '... I always affect to despise human nature. My role in life is so clearly marked: cynical, detached, unscrupulous, an ironic observer and recorder of other's people's passions. It is a nice façade to sit behind, but a trifle bleak ...' He also avers, 'What discourages me most is confusion. The dreary capacity of the human race for putting the right labels on the wrong boxes.'

The play is an unsatisfactory piece which fails to explore the questions it raises. It was to be a vehicle for the Coward–Lunt–Fontanne talents, but the Lunts were reluctant to appear in it, and Lynn predicted it would run no longer than six weeks. 'Nonsense! Absolute nonsense!' said Coward. Yet his leading lady's premonition was confirmed on the first night by a 'soggy and comatose if not actually hostile' audience. The Lunts were received coolly when they came on; Coward, Wilson and Calthrop sat at the back 'and watched the play march with unfaltering tread down the drain'. Dickie Fellowes-Gordon was there with Elsa Maxwell: 'the public didn't like it. They didn't like the Lunts not being perfect, and neither of their characters were very nice ... There was a big party afterwards and he said "Oh darlings, what a flop!"' It was the only failure of the Lunts' joint career.

Coward admitted that the play was written 'out of the innocent desire to create two whopping good parts for the Lunts, which I did, and failed to write a good enough story to show off these parts. The result was half-hearted, neither comedy nor tragedy ...' George Jean Nathan thought it 'the kind of thing ... Maugham might ironically write to order for Hollywood, provided that Hollywood paid him $100,000 in advance, plus agent's commission, and provided, in addition, that he was recovering from a prolonged jag and had a slight touch of the 'flu ... It is impossible to believe that Mr Coward, a fellow of some humour, could have written such zymotic bilge with a straight face ...' The only actor to get good reviews was Louis Hayward, whom Coward had imported to play Martin, a handsome young aviator. When the play opened on Broadway on 16 January 1935, he was singled out for praise, a personal success which helped launch Hayward in Hollywood.

Coward, too, was beginning to find the silver screen an interesting prospect. He needed the money, as a letter written by Lorn Loraine to Violet Coward indicates: 'We have got to go very, very easy on money and economise rigidly wherever it is possible', she warned. 'Mind you, I am pretty sure the shortage is only temporary and would never have arisen if it were not for the fact that all Noel's personal earnings have to go into a special tax account as soon as they are received ... Both the bank accounts have overdrafts and there is very little coming in just now – a good deal less than has to go out.'

The Scoundrel (originally entitled *Miracle on 49th Street*), which Coward agreed to film in the early weeks of 1935 for a fee of $5000 (less than he would have earned in Hollywood, but he was promised a share of the profits), was written by Charles MacArthur and Ben Hecht, a team already celebrated for *The Front Page*, successfully filmed in 1930. Hecht was also responsible for the *Design for Living* script, for which Coward presumably forgave him. In 1935 Hecht and MacArthur took over the Astoria studio in Long Island City:* one of the few East Coast studios remaining, it was close to New York, and therefore 'a holiday from Hollywood'. The two writers committed themselves to produce, write and direct four films, but the 'Astoria Experiment' became an excuse for 'a two year party that kept going seven days a week'. Hecht and MacArthur stuck up life-size female nude photos in their offices, hired prostitutes as secretaries, and had large lunches sent from plush Manhattan restaurants. In this schoolboy atmosphere, Coward made his first serious appearance on film. The result won Hecht and MacArthur an Academy award, and is the one movie of any interest made during the Astoria experiment.

Noel's decision to infiltrate a medium he had previously scorned may have been prompted by the financial rewards, but he maintained otherwise for the benefit of the press. 'What really induced me to try them', he said when asked why he had suddenly decided to make films, 'was because I wanted the experience ... I might be terrible. I've taken some screen tests and I don't think I'm quite at ease yet in front of the cameras...' This pleading evaporated as soon as the Coward confidence was asserted; his performance for *The Scoundrel* remains a unique record of the charisma he possessed, then at its devastating height. Part of the reason for the impression he made may have been the control he had over the film's production; Hecht and MacArthur's

---

* Jack Wilson had worked at the studios as an assistant director before he met Coward, and was probably instrumental in the casting of his friend and client in the film.

delight at having secured Coward made them accord him consultancy rights on each scene before it was shot. He did not add or alter dialogue; he was eager only to see the 'rushes' at the end of each day to judge his performance. The literary flavour of the screenplay had attracted him, and cameos by Alexander Woollcott and Edna Ferber introduced a Round Table atmosphere, stressed by Manhattan location shots (such as a scene filmed in the Hapsburg House restaurant). The film also derived visual strength from the camerawork of Lee Garmes, who had shot *Morocco*, *Dishonoured* and *Shanghai Express* for von Sternberg.

Shooting began on 23 January. Coward's first scene, as an egotistical publisher, Anthony Mallare, has him emerging from the shower, making his screen debut proper naked (though half-hidden), his wiry body wet and his dark hair hanging over his face in an angular fringe. As he slicks his hair into its appointed place, and dresses in a sharp double-breasted suit and bow-tie, the image is focused: Noel Coward appears, theatre idol, would-be screen god. As a 'literary Don Juan', Mallare seduces a young poet, Cora Moore (played by Julie Haydon): 'Before telling a woman I love her, I rattle my tail six times . . .', he says. '. . . I regard heaven as unfit for all women under forty', he quips, laughing languidly to himself. For the first time an audience had a chance to see his facial mannerisms close up, his barely extant upper lip drawn into a supercilious grimace. It contributes greatly to the air of urbanity Coward exudes in *The Scoundrel*; a svelte panther in Brooks Brothers and a carnation.

Cora's boyfriend, Decker, tries to shoot Mallare, but the bullet bounces off his cigarette case. Yet Mallare gets his just deserts when his plane crashes; in stormy seas, his drowned body floats, and Coward's voice intones that his spirit will not rest until he finds one person to cry for him. A phantom in a black leather coat, he searches the bleak streets of the soulless city, and finds Cora looking after the desperately ill Decker, who shoots Mallare and then himself. This time the bullets pass right through Mallare, and Decker falls down dead. Mallare appeals to God, 'I want no mercy for myself, none, but I do ask for them. Give them back what I took . . .' Decker comes to life; Cora turns to Mallare, tears in her eyes, thanking him; Mallare looks to heaven – he is saved.

The Scoundrel is high drama, an odd mixture of German expressionism and Hollywood glamour, but Coward succeeds in transcending fantasy with a convincing, if camp, performance. It established him as an unlikely hearthrob: American newspapers anticipated that 'Noel Coward's feminine following . . . will soon be nationwide. For he's in the movies now!'* (The newly formed Legion of Decency did not think so, condemning the film. Even in America, Noel discovered, there was no escaping the righteous.)

Coward was equivocal about the experience, and was frustrated by the filming process. 'The picture was made quickly and fairly efficiently; most of its speed and efficiency being due to Lee Garmes, the cameraman', he wrote. 'The direction of Charlie MacArthur and Ben Hecht was erratic, and I, who had never made a picture before, was confused and irritated from the beginning to the end . . . I made a success in it and so did everyone concerned, but I still wish that it and they and I had been better.' Some critics thought the film too full of 'unpleasant characters . . . a pretentious straining for bizarre effects'; but others judged it 'a singularly adult picture, a most devastating study of New York literary celebrities', which 'builds to an end as emotional, as mystic, and as forceful as any motion pictures have yet offered us'.

The Scoundrel received a muted response in America, although its idiosyncratic character guaranteed continued showings in 'art house' cinemas. Modern critics have called the film 'Coward's finest screen performance', claiming that 'he is perfectly cast, and brings to the part an icy composure and malevolent charm'; it remains a resonant evocation of the actor's charisma, despite his reservations. 'I thought I was very good,' said Coward years later, 'in the parts I was dead.'

Coward set off by train for Hollywood, where he made friends with Ruth Chatterton and Joan Crawford, and found a floodtide of film offers. He was to make a second film for Hecht and MacArthur (*Down to Their Last Yacht*, into which he had ploughed his share of the profits on *The Scoundrel*), and was being considered for the part of the Trappist monk in David Selznick's *The Garden of Allah*, co-starring Marlene Dietrich. Dietrich saw *The Scoundrel* in California and noted the good work of 'her' cameraman, Lee Garmes. She later rang Coward in England to congratulate him on his performance ('I act with an incredible swiftness once my feelings are involved'), but when she gave her name, Coward hung up. Dietrich called back and quickly 'said a few words about his film', quoting part of the dialogue. Noel explained that he 'was afraid of . . . a certain kind of practical joker and had

---

* 'In my private fantasy, I *am* Noel Coward: brilliant, witty, adored by women', wrote Alan Jenkins of his youthful self in 1930. 'I do not yet know that he is homosexual: when I find out, the shock lasts for two days.'

believed that someone using my name wanted to play a dirty trick on him. We talked for a long time and were friends from then on', Dietrich wrote.

Dietrich had a magnetic attraction for Coward, as for many of her homosexual fans: they were 'kinder, nicer than "normal men"', she said. 'Our relationship repeatedly astonished me, because my interests were completely different from his. I was neither brilliant nor especially witty, so I didn't like invitations to soirées. I didn't belong to his milieu. I had other habits, shunned the limelight, and didn't view the world as he did. Despite all that, we were inseparable.'

Their friendship grew: Dietrich became Coward's glamorous cab service, picking him up or dropping him off on his visits to Hollywood or New York, and they shared each other's intrigues and romances. Marlene was sought for her opinion of a dress rehearsal, 'Marlenah! I must not appear effeminate in any way. Do be a dear – watch out for anything that could be considered less than "butch", if you see me being at all "queer", tell me immediately.' But their relationship remained demarcated by each other's star quality. Dietrich's daughter, Maria Riva, commented, 'For Dietrich, it was his style, brilliant success, and the "Noel Coward", as he lived his own creation of himself, that was her "chum". The sensitive, vulnerable, serious man, so easily lonely, hidden so well beneath the throwaway charm – him, she never took the time to find . . . If she had . . . it would have confused her.'

Through Dietrich and other film stars, Coward gained an insight into the film industry which confirmed its dubious attractions. In 1935 he nearly succumbed to a lucrative few years in the movies, when the monolithic giants of the Californian dream industry tried to ensnare him. But Edna Ferber advised, 'What is there in it for you? You are a writer. Go away and write.' Without even staying to see the result of the screen test he had done for Irving Thalberg, and abandoning the proposed Hecht–MacArthur film, Noel sailed for Honolulu on the *Tatsuta Maru*. He restarted his autobiography, and after joining up with the Dillinghams in Honolulu, sailed on to China, and thence to Japan and Bali.

Coward was due to deliver *Present Indicative* to the New York publisher Nelson Doubleday that autumn; he was also working on a series of one-act plays, nine altogether, to run in varying order on three consecutive nights at the theatre. It was a bold idea, risky and innovative, to be called *Tonight at 8.30*. By late summer he was back at

Goldenhurst, describing to Gertrude Lawrence the elaborate new vehicle he had created for their talents. The playlets not only had wonderful roles for both of them but their variety would avoid the dreaded boredom. He had finished writing all nine by the end of August, and rehearsed them with Lawrence in Goldenhurst's Big Room. Then followed full cast rehearsals in London, to open in Manchester and with a nine-week provincial tour before opening in London.

Coward's serious work of recent years invested *Tonight at 8.30* with maturity. The most successful piece was 'Still Life', a tale of suburban extra-marital love which gained classic status as the 1945 film *Brief Encounter*. In 'Still Life', the roles of the buffet manageress and the stationmaster are more prominent as a happier, working-class counterpoint to the doomed affair between the doctor and the housewife who meet by chance on a railway platform; that Laura's and Alec's love is seen as superior to the working-class affair perhaps illustrates Coward's endemic snobbery. 'The Astonished Heart' also involved extra-marital relations, with an acclaimed psychologist reluctantly drawn into an affair, leaving his wife distraught; the play ends with his suicide. But it lacks 'Still Life's' empathy, and the Cowardian dialogue which elsewhere delighted in its formality here seems stilted.

A third playlet, 'Fumed Oak', is 'an unpleasant comedy', in which a browbeaten husband asserts himself in a devastating speech and slaps his wife. Only occasionally witty, its characters are 'nothing more than a music-hall joke', again at the expense of the working classes, as well as being evidence of Coward's stereotyping of women as harridans who oppress men. (The silliness of the conventional women in Coward's work crosses class barriers: Doris in 'Fumed Oak' has her upper-class equivalents – Mrs Whittaker in *Easy Virtue* and Sybil in *Private Lives*. Bound by their (heterosexual) prejudices, they are inferior to the mannish Amanda and Larita, and are the bane of men's lives.) 'Ways and Means' is another 'light comedy' – a pair of unlucky casino gamblers, Toby and Stella, conspire with a burglar to restore their fortunes; while 'Shadow Play' concerned more Mayfair marriage crises, with three good Coward songs and a decidedly experimental fantasy scene ('Small talk, small talk, with other thoughts going on behind'*).

Of the comedies, 'Hands Across the Sea' is one of the most successful, an unmistakable caricature of the Mountbattens; Noel was using his

---

* Citing this, Kenneth Tynan later claimed that Harold Pinter derived his 'elliptical patter' from Coward.

society friends as fodder for his imagination. Lady Maureen Gilpin is 'a smart, attractive woman ... nicknamed Piggie by her intimates' who insists that her reluctant husband – Commander Peter Gilpin ('tall and sunburned and reeks of the Navy') – help entertain unexpected visitors. The forgotten guests recall the bad-mannered Bliss household of *Hay Fever*. 'Everyone's making such a noise', says Piggie to the telephone. 'The room's filled with the most dreadful people.' It is one of Coward's funniest pieces and in the opinion of Terence Rattigan was 'the best short comedy ever written'.

'Red Peppers' is a pure music-hall joke, an excuse for Coward and Lawrence to send up the theatre of their youth with basic humour (the Lord Chamberlain objected to 'farting' and 'raspberries'), and was the outright populist piece of the collection. 'Family Album', 'a sly satire on Victorian hypocrisy, adorned with an unobtrusive but agreeable musical score', was spiked when George V died; its black jokes about death necessitated replacement with 'We Were Dancing'. This tropical love tangle set on the fictitious South Sea island of Samolo, is 'little more than a curtain-raiser'. The orphan of the suite, 'Star Chamber', reverted to the theatre for its setting, with various actors at a meeting of the Garrick Haven Fund (mirroring some of the excesses of the administration of the Actor's Orphanage). It did not appeal, and was performed just once, for a Saturday matinee.

Tonight at 8.30 ('We Were Dancing', 'The Astonished Heart' and 'Red Peppers') opened in Manchester on 15 October 1935. In his programme notes, Noel suggested that the 'short play, having a great advantage over a long one in that it can sustain a mood without technical creaking or overpadding', deserved resurrection. 'From our point of view behind the footlights ... the monotony of repetition will be reduced considerably, and it is to be hoped that the stimulus ... the company ... will derive from playing several roles instead of only one will communicate itself to the audience.' His ploy worked. The production took £26,000 in nine weeks in the provinces before it opened in the West End.

The tour was suspended for Christmas, which Coward and Jeffrey Amherst spent in Scandinavia. Back in her home country was Greta Garbo, the reclusive superstar, and (to the tabloid public) putative lover of Noel Coward. The pair had probably met through George Cukor, and by January 1936 the *New York Times* was printing rumours of an affair. Such publicity was not unwelcome as it diverted attention from their individual predilections. Noel saw Garbo's reclusiveness as a silly pose; it was not an attitude he would tolerate. About to enter a Christmas party, Garbo balked, 'Believe me, Noel, I really and truly cannot go in, I cannot face it.' 'Yes you bloody well *are* going in', said Noel, ringing the bell and pushing the actress into the house. As with Marlene Dietrich, he flattered her artfully, and appeared eligible without being too eligible. 'My little bridegroom', the inconstant, teasing star jokingly called Coward, saying she 'wished the newspapers were right'.

Tonight at 8.30 opened in London at Bernstein's Phoenix Theatre, which Noel now regarded as 'his own'. 'The Astonished Heart' was sandwiched between the period whimsy of 'Family Album', and the theatrical pastiche of 'Red Peppers'. What would the critics say to this new form of entertainment? The *Observer* (in the voice of Ivor Brown) thought the 'variety of the programme . . . a tribute to Mr Coward's interest in experiment. The presentation of it is a real piece of work.' *The Times* did not think much of 'Family Album' or 'The Astonished Heart', but acclaimed 'Red Peppers' as the 'theatrical success of the evening . . . a robust end to an otherwise slim or perilous entertainment'. The *Daily Mail* called it 'second-rate entertainment'.

Once again, the critics and the public diverged in their opinions, as box-office business continued to be good. If the press had found *Tonight at 8.30* an untidy mix, they were wrong, Noel declared. 'I love criticism,' he said, only half in jest, 'just so long as it's unqualified praise.'

On 20 January, George V was on his death-bed, the wireless silent save for a ticking clock. That evening, *Tonight at 8.30* carried on regardless, but at the end, as the audience was about to leave, Coward came out front in his dressing gown and announced the king's death. The photographer Barbara Ker-Seymer was there: 'He signalled for the orchestra to strike up and the entire audience stood to attention (including my friend who was a dedicated communist) and led by Noel Coward sang the National Anthem. I couldn't help thinking at the time that [he] must have been in his element . . .'

Tonight at 8.30 continued its run, with the usual arguments between Coward and Lawrence. When it was agreed that Jack Wilson would present the show in the States, Coward cabled: EVERYTHING LOVELY STOP CRACKING ROW WITH GERTIE OVER 'HANDS ACROSS THE SEA' LASTING SEVEN MINUTES STOP HER PERFORMANCE EXQUISITE EVER SINCE. Lily Taylor, then wardrobe mistress for H. M. Tennent, said, '"Oh, they *hated* each other! Noel *hated* her!" She said Gertie couldn't care less about anything, and she spent all her money and had a very jolly time. She was a lovely woman, and everybody adored her. But of course, Coward was beastly to her . . . he did scream at people . . .'

As others close to the Master testified. Leonard Cole went to work for Coward in 1936. Then aged twenty-seven, he worked as a shop assistant in Kent. Slight but presentable, Lesley Cole, as he now called himself, was living in a bedsit in Chester Row in London when a series of coincidences led to his being told that Noel Coward was looking for someone to work for him. The following Monday Lorn Loraine interviewed Cole at Burton Mews, and called Coward for his approval; Cole was engaged as a cook-cum-dogsbody for a probation period, and Noel took little notice of his new employee, save to remark on his rather mincing walk. But soon Cole distinguished himself by providing good feed-lines. 'What would you say to a little fish?' he asked one lunchtime. 'I should say Good Morning, little fish', replied Coward.

Noel's trust in 'Coley', as he became, grew, and Cole's absolute loyalty to the point of subservience made him the perfect factotum. The inversion of Leslie Cole's name came about partly as a result of his wish to be seen as something more than a 'cook-valet'. By reversing Christian and surname, 'Cole', which Coward called him, became a more acceptable appellation.*

His ability to deal with the often erratic behaviour of his master soon made Cole an indispensable member of the team, but his first experience of those darker moods must have been terrifying. Coward's temper had always been thin, and he had not grown out of his childish tantrums; he was quite capable of throwing himself face down on a sofa or bed and beating the cushions with his fist when people or plans thwarted him. Cole records cries of 'I wish I were dead' and 'What *am* I to do?' as Coward lay supine – often naked – wallowing in self-pity. His status and celebrity allowed him to get away with it, but that did not make the behaviour acceptable to those who witnessed his irrational fits of pique. Cole Lesley admitted to his master's selfishness: 'It was total, but if he only thought of himself and getting what he wanted when he wanted it, this was because he very genuinely believed other people did, or should do, the same and were fools if they didn't.'

His selfishness would approach megalomania, born of early success and an artifical life within the theatre. 'He was . . . a vain man', Rebecca

---

* Vivian Matalon said, 'I remember reading one of his books, and he referred to Coley as "my personal servant". I thought, "What an awful thing to write about anybody" . . . I later asked Coley, and I said, "Did that hurt you?" He said, "More than I can tell you" . . . I think he [Coward] thought that's what he was . . .'

West said. 'He talked constantly about himself, thought about himself, catalogued his achievements, evaluated them, presented to listeners such conclusions as were favourable, and expected, and waited for applause.' (Though she added, 'His sensitivity knew this and was shocked, and he regularly rough-housed his own vanity by considering himself in a ridiculous light. This he did for the good of his soul.') That Coward could not countenance opposition is well-attested, and a vicious instinct for revenge was apparent in his black list and its victims. Age did not assuage this ill-temper, and as the Twenties and Thirties gave way to a less certain future, these characteristics assumed greater importance.

Tonight at 8.30 ran for 157 performances, and once more Coward was a social lion. Harold Nicolson recorded an evening at Sibyl Colefax's. 'After dinner, Rubinstein plays some Chopin ... After Rubinstein has played three times, the King crosses the room towards him and says "We enjoyed that very much, Mr Rubinstein." I am delighted at this, since I was afraid that Rubinstein was about to play a fourth time. It is by this time 12.30 and the King starts saying good-bye. This takes so long that at our end of the room we imagine that he has departed, and get Noel Coward to sing us one of his latest songs. The King immediately returns on hearing this, and remains for another hour, which is not very flattering to Rubinstein.'

In June Coward took off again, for Venice and the Lido. Admiral of the Fleet Sir Dudley Pound brought his boat in (photographed on deck in shorts, Coward's arm resting chummily on the admiral's shoulder), and Noel and friends – Doris Castlerosse, Ivor Novello, Douglas Fairbanks and Lady Ashley – went aboard for parties. Lady Castlerosse and Coward were given an open guest list by Sir Dudley and Lady Pound for one party. Castlerosse confided, 'Noel, I have a dreadful feeling we've asked too many queer people.' Coward reassured her, 'If we take care of the pansies, the Pounds will take care of themselves.'

At Goldenhurst, weekends were 'gilded' that summer. The air show at nearby Lympne was celebrated with a party to which Godfrey Winn brought a new actress, dark-haired, ravishing and sharp-eyed, whom Coward took to at once – Vivien Leigh, who had recently become Laurence Olivier's lover. One minor actor visiting assumed a major role: Alan Webb, the new focus of Coward's romantic attentions. The affair with Louis Hayward had ended bitterly; Noel later wrote that it was 'emphatically not one of the happier episodes of my life'. Hayward's capacity to make Coward jealous had been well demonstrated when he had a shipboard romance with Natasha Paley, Jack Wilson's wife-to-be. Hayward subsequently married Ida Lupino, the British film actress and director. Many years later, when Coward was filming at Television City in Hollywood in 1956, Hayward was making a TV series of *The Saint* on a stage next door; the bitterness had evidently endured, 'Noel wouldn't even walk over and talk to him', recalls Charles Russell.

As with Hayward, Coward provided his new boyfriend with work, in supporting roles in the *Tonight at 8.30* plays. Alan Webb was thirty, son of Major Albertoni Webb, and had trained at the Royal Naval Colleges at Osborne and Dartmouth (doubtless part of his appeal to Coward) but took up acting instead. John Gielgud remembers Noel's relationship with Webb, 'Alan Webb was his best critic, in my opinion . . . Webb was a very caustic and brilliant actor, much under-rated. He was one of the few who dared to oppose Noel.' 'Short, masculine, a little rough but definitely camp', Webb was another of the dark and handsome types Coward fell for. Theirs was a passionate affair which lasted for much of the rest of the decade.

On 15 September 1936 Coward's production (for Transatlantic Presentations) of Jacques Deval's *Mademoiselle* opened at Wyndham's Theatre, with Isabel Jeans, Cecil Parker, Madge Titheradge and Greer Garson. The play did well and with this success behind him Noel sailed to New York, where he and Gertrude Lawrence were to star in *Tonight at 8.30*. For Lawrence, the departure was near-permanent; she would only once work in Britain again.

Coward had bought Woollcott's Riverside apartment in the Campanile co-op at 450 East 52nd Street as his new Manhattan *pied-à-terre*, and there he prepared to take his nine-play show on the road. They opened in Boston, and at the National Theatre on Broadway on 24 November. Critics thought the production a hit-and-miss affair, not least because of pot-luck of the scheduling; Brooks Atkinson advised his readers to 'consult your . . . favourite astrologist' before they visited the box office. Coward had stressed to reporters that it would be a limited season; more limited than he knew – he was stricken with laryngitis. At first he missed only a couple of nights, but soon broke down again. His doctor advised that he was suffering from 'overwork and nervous exhaustion', and told him the show could not go on.

He had in fact suffered another nervous breakdown, necessitating his return to England. It is noteworthy that Noel never wrote about this period of his life: *Present Indicative* ends in 1931, *Future Indefinite* begins in 1939, and there is only a fragment of a third volume, *Past Conditional*, covering 1932 to 1933. It was a time of personal instability. Jack Wilson's infidelities had introduced a note of distrust; Coward had his extended family, but love eluded him. His affair with Louis Hayward had ended painfully and now Alan Webb proved difficult to deal with, taunting Coward by bragging of other liaisons.

Such were the pressures that led to this fresh failure of nerve; Coward's façade of bravery, the glittering exterior he presented to the world, crumbled. This fragile sensitivity was a trait of his fictional characters: Nicky Lancaster; Amanda and Elyot; Gilda, Otto and Leo, and the entertaining quarrelsome dialogue was in real life the evidence of emotional instability. Creativity goes hand in hand with such hypertension; it can tip over into mental instability, as it did with Coward. His breakdowns were escape routes from stress, as were the bouts of foreign travel; the depressive who travels to avoid ennui. That remained the prescription. After returning to England in time for the coronation of George VI (Edward VIII having abdicated, to Coward's satisfaction), Noel took Alan Webb for a holiday in Nassau, where he had been so happy with Jack in 1931. The arrival of Joyce Carey, and the restorative light and sun, helped to disperse the recent gloom.

The rest of the summer was divided between Goldenhurst and Gerald Road, gathering his latest reviews. *Present Indicative* had been published in March, and reprinted twice within the year. These memoirs, written with style and panache, had the effect of consolidating Coward's personal myth, which is what certain friends alleged it to be. Esme Wynne-Tyson accused Noel of exaggerating and falsifying parts of his early life; his account of her receiving stolen goods vexed her, and she considered that he wrote merely for effect, with little regard for the truth.

It was as though Coward were conforming to the convention of the first novel as memoir, blurring fact and fiction. Events were jumbled, chronologies ignored, and certain key people misrepresented or omitted. He had not set out to write truth; he was an entertainer and there was no room for pedantry or facts if they slowed the action. Like the Hollywood scriptwriters he professed to despise, Noel edited his life story and presented the highlights: tragedy and drama were there, overlaid with British phlegm. Oddly enough, the one fact which could have been most damning – his homosexuality – was not disguised. Anyone with any knowledge of the theatre world or its rumours could have read between the lines of *Present Indicative* and made the connections. Nothing is overtly stated – that would have risked legal recourse and, perhaps worse, social estrangement – but there is no mention of an emotional relationship with a woman, save for the closest and most enduring emotional tie in his life, between himself and his mother. His readers did not expect a warts-and-all memoir; biographies of the time (and particularly autobiographies) were cloying and vapid. Coward presented a memoir mercifully free of these faults.

The distinguished novelist and playwright St John Ervine, writing in the *Observer*, was fascinated. He approved Coward's courage, integrity, fortune and fame, yet could not envy him, '. . . I doubt if he has had a tenth of the happiness he must seem to the majority of people to possess.' *Present Indicative* was a revelation to the critics; Coward was not the man they had thought or hoped. 'I am amazed and disturbed at the slenderness of his intellectual resources,' wrote Ervine, wondering if Coward had 'ever read a great book, seen a fine picture or a notable play, listened to music of worth, observed a piece of sculpture, or taken any interest in even the commonplaces of a cultured man's life'.*

The two men were friends. Years earlier, Coward had written to Ervine thanking him for a letter of praise, 'I can't tell you how very much I appreciated your letter and I'm awfully glad to have proved to you that my real ambition is to write good stuff and not fritter away my talents on flippant nonsense.' Aware of the critic's stern demands, he had also said in a letter appreciative of Ervine's *The Wayward Man*, 'When I read a novel like yours it makes me despair of ever writing myself because my imagination doesn't feel strong enough to reach things which have not actually happened to me – and constant repetitions of Parisian coquettes having cocktails in the Ritz bar are apt to become a bore.'

Ervine and Coward had continued to correspond, Ervine often publishing positive notices of Coward's plays. But the playwright had not lived up to Ervine's expectations, and he saw Coward's facile smartness as a direct result of the war, in the aftermath of which 'glibness was all'. His proposed antidote was that Coward 'should become an industrial life insurance agent in Huddersfield, living exclusively on his commission from premiums, and refusing vigorously to

---

* T. S. Eliot remarked, 'I doubt if Mr Coward has spent one hour in contemplation of the study of ethics'; to which Noel replied, 'I do not think that would have helped me; but I think it would have done Mr Eliot a lot of good to spend some time in the theatre.'

speak to anyone with an income of more than ten pounds a week. I think he'd grow if he did that. He *must* grow. We need a developed Coward.'

Ervine's optimism was not matched by other critics of *Present Indicative*. Despite its wide appeal (the book sold 33,000 copies in its first year of publication in America), critical opinion generally despaired of there being anything deeper in the Coward psyche, and Cyril Connolly's review was perhaps the most incisive, and damning. For Connolly, the book was 'almost always shallow and often dull', leaving a picture 'carefully incomplete, of a success ... a person of infinite charm and adaptability whose very adaptability, however, makes him inferior to a more compact and worldly competitor in his own sphere, like Cole Porter'. The ironic self-deprecation of Coward's memoirs did not deflect Connolly's attack; he found 'an essentially unhappy man, a man who gives one the impression of having seldom really thought or really lived and is intelligent enough to know it. But what can he do about it? He is not religious, politics bore him, art means facility or else brickbats, love, wild excitement and the nervous breakdown. There is only success, more and more of it, till from his pinnacle he can look down to where Ivor Novello and Beverley Nichols gather samphire on a ledge, and to where, a pinpoint on the sands below, Mr Godfrey Winn is counting pebbles. But success is all there is, and that even is temporary. For one can't read any of Noel Coward's plays now ... they are written in the most topical and perishable way imaginable, the cream in them turns sour overnight – they are even dead before they are turned into talkies, however engaging they may seem at the time. This book reveals a terrible predicament, that of a young man with the Midas touch, with a gift that does not creep and branch and flower, but which turns everything it touches into immediate gold. And the gold melts, too.'

Coward found Connolly's piece 'venomous and ... inaccurate to the point of silliness'; upsetting and incomprehensible. Its tone of condescension marked the end of Noel's flirtation with the English literati. Recently, Osbert Sitwell had announced in the *Sunday Referee* that 'Mr Coward, with his frisky tea-shop dialogues, has gained among nitwits a certain reputation for wit', and Brian Howard declared, 'I've always felt that Mr Coward's works could have been written by some tremendously shrewd bird, especially the music.' Coward nurtured his distrust of the bluestockings and beauty-lovers; the names of Mr Connolly and others were entered in his little black book.

Despite the personal nature of Connolly's attack (particularly the reference to Noel's nervous breakdowns as due to 'love', which seemed to derive from private knowledge) and the questionable judgements about his plays, there is truth in his assessment of Coward's life as being predicated on success. There was always the proud boast that he was the man who wrote *Cavalcade*/*Bitter-Sweet*/*Private Lives*, a self-affirming mantra. By such boasts, Coward confirmed what Connolly had written: he was defined by his fame. It was, after all, what Noel Coward had been invented for.

17

To Step Aside

There is a brief reference to fetishism on page 7 ... Coward is a
funny fellow, he never seems to grow up. He worked the same idea
some years ago, with old boots!

Lord Chamberlain's report on *Operette*, 14 May 1938

AFTER a Mediterranean cruise with Admiral Vian, Coward
returned to Goldenhurst to work on a new musical. He also
agreed to resume his work as director of *George and Margaret*,
partly on Jack Wilson's initiative, but also at the urging of Binkie
Beaumont. Beaumont, young hope of the old H. M. Tennent company,
was one of the most influential theatre men in London, and effectively
replaced Cochran as Coward's producer.

Coward had met Beaumont at the Fifty–Fifty Club just before
Christmas 1924. Born in Wales (his nickname was Cardiff slang for
Negro), Beaumont was dark and feminine-looking, with a moon face
and feline manners, given to such phrases as 'Very *bijou*, my dear',
cribbed from Ned Lathom and Tallulah Bankhead. He once gave a
party for Bankhead and Lathom in his flat, ordering every kind of
delicacy from Fortnum & Mason, including an ice-cream cake shaped
like the Sphinx. 'Just a few bijou items, simple peasant food, my
dear...', he told Bobbie Andrews. Beaumont's companion was John
Perry, sometime playwright and actor in the Gielgud mould, who had
lived with Gielgud in St Martin's Lane (Bert Lister, later Coward's
dresser and stage manager, also shared the flat) and his house near
Henley before becoming Beaumont's lover. The outspoken Lister
recalled, 'Binkie Beaumont could charm the hind legs off a donkey. He
was very clever with money. You'd go up to see him at the Globe – in
that tiny lift only one person – or two if they were fond of each
other – could fit. He wouldn't discuss money. It was only when you

got outside that his secretary told you the bad news.'

In his encounters with Coward – at the Ivy, the Embassy, or any number of parties – Beaumont had made various efforts to work with the playwright, who promised to consider any suggestions. When Coward's association with Cochran ended, Beaumont approached him with a new proposal. *George and Margaret*, a farcical comedy by Gerald Savory, had been running successfully in the West End (saving H. M. Tennent from bankruptcy). It was said that Coward, via the Duke of Kent, had been influential in the visit of the new king and queen to the play, a royal endorsement which made for good business. As a return favour, Beaumont suggested that Coward should direct it on Broadway. Coward, who thought the play excellent, agreed.

Lister also remembers Coward's reticence with Beaumont. 'I always had to go up and see Binkie because Noel wouldn't speak to him. They weren't friends at first – except on first nights, when they'd shake hands and wish one another luck and all that bullshit. It was dominance. What Noel said was the last word, there was no arguing. But Binkie did.' John Osborne later observed that Beaumont 'took great satisfaction in tearing the wings from writers, especially the rich and famous. Rattigan and Coward ... both suffered humiliation from his lizard tongue.' This Osborne partly ascribed to the 'sexual politics' of their profession.

Before beginning work on *George and Margaret*, Coward was invited by Eleonora von Mendelssohn, grandchild of the composer and god-daughter of Eleanora Duse, to stay at Schloss Kammer am Attersee, a 'sinister, possibly haunted' castle near Salzburg, where this intense beauty was pursuing her infatuation with Toscanini. Von Mendelssohn and her co-host, Alice von Hofmannsthal, constantly entertained large groups of friends, including Max Reinhardt, Mercedes de Acosta, Diana Cooper; Nicolas Nabokov (composer brother of the novelist); Cecil Beaton and Peter Watson; George Hoyningen-Huene and his boyfriend, Horst P. Horst; and David Herbert. There were odd and vaguely riotous goings-on, and in one case, a guest had to be asked to leave, and did so 'exhibiting rudely her behind'.

There was also the singer Fritzi Massary, toast of Berlin nightclubs and musical comedies, whom Coward had first seen in 1922. Although Massary professed never to have heard of Coward ('I never went to the theatre'), they became friends, and he began to think of roles for her to play. Being Jewish, and recently widowed, she was keen to leave

Germany. Coward told her, 'If you learn English, I'll write a play for you.' Massary said, '"I can't", but then he sent me a teacher from London. So he persuaded me, and I went to London . . .'

The vehicle Coward constructed for Massary's talents was *Operette*. The taste for romantic European fantasy had grown in proportion to the worsening political news; following in the swirling dance-steps of Lehar's *The Merry Widow* and Novello's Viennese productions, senti-mental and winsome songs abounded. Dickie Fellowes-Gordon and Coward parodied one particularly sugary number which Richard Tauber had sung in the eponymous film *I Kiss Your Hand, Madame*:

> I will not kiss your hand madame,
> You're such a bloody bore
> For years and years I've planned madame
> To sock you in the jaw
> If you're feeling blue madame
> And don't know what to do madame
> Or to make the moments pass madame
> Then take my hob-nailed boot madame
> And shove it up your arse.

Such jokes notwithstanding, Coward resolved to write something in this Mittel Europe mode for Massary.

George and Margaret rehearsals began in Manchester. Coward had decided to change the play for an American audience, replacing senti-ment with wit, but his style clashed with the author's, and the play suffered. There were other problems, too: the removal of Richard Bird caused bad feeling (a friend of Novello's whose sacking was engineered by Coward and Beaumont), and Noel's temper was short. Alan Webb was playing a lead role, and Coward shouted at his lover, 'Alan, you're no bloody good, you must either be a juvenile or a midshipman with piles.'

Coward sailed for New York on 1 September on the *Queen Mary*, in company with Gertrude Lawrence and Evelyn Laye, arriving in time to attend the marriage of Jack Wilson to the heiress Natasha Paley.* Paley was the morganatic granddaughter of Tsar Alexander II, and had

---

* She had appeared with Katharine Hepburn, Cary Grant and Brian Aherne in Cukor's *Sylvia Scarlett* (1935), based on Compton Mackenzie's book about a girl masquerading as a boy to escape France ('She's a boy! It's Mr Hepburn to you!' wrote one reviewer). The film was later condemned by the Legion of Decency for its coded homosexuality.

been married to the Parisian couturier Lucien Lelong. She was a celebrated social figure: Beaton found 'her quality of beauty so rare and alluring', and posed her against upturned bedsprings, her blonde hair scraped back into a black hat and a bunch of freesias at her neck.

That Coward's and Wilson's passion was a thing of the past was widely known to New York café society. But Wilson's subsequent affair with David Herbert had been superseded by his latest attachment, and legal problems experienced by Herbert had come at a convenient time, as Beaton had recorded on a visit to New York in 1935: 'Telephone conversations with Natalie [Paley], Nicholas [Nabokov] . . . went down to Jack's room to hear the scrape David had got into – and to hear of his departure. I hated Jack's rather supercilious tone, as much as to say "Well the boy must deserve what he gets if he will know inelegant people." Poor David's very sad at being banished from the country as a result of a frame-up . . . it suits Jack Wilson beautifully to have David out of the way just as his love Natasha returns from Hollywood.'

Wilson's mercenary attitude to his romantic liaisons resulted in the rumour that Noel and he had arranged the marriage to draw attention from their relationship. (Despite its supposed secrecy, the wedding was widely publicised on both sides of the Atlantic, complete with photographs, which seemed to support the theory.) It was ironic that on his arrival in New York, Coward was quizzed by reporters about rumours that he too was to marry. '"Who? Me!" gasped the startled playwright. "For heaven's sake, who is it now? It can't be Gladys Calthrop. That thing's been bobbing up for years. No, it can't be Ruth Chatterton, either. People just can't bear to see me being a happy and unmolested bachelor."' Jack Wilson's marriage also raised questions about his partnership with Coward. Was it true they were about to split? asked Ward Morehouse, compiler of the 'Broadway After Dark' column. The notion was absurd, said Noel, 'I think he has the best critical faculty of anybody I've ever met in the theatre. He's merciless in his criticisms and he's generally right. His judgements are superb . . . He has been far and away the most important person in my life . . . Anything I do, now and for ever, will be in association with John C. Wilson.' It was a statement Coward came to regret.

To friends, the marriage seemed odd. 'Jack took to drink in a big way after he got married, strangely enough', Dickie Fellowes-Gordon said. 'She took to drink too, of course. Funny marriage, that was. I can't imagine why they got married . . . but they seemed to get on all right.'

Wilson's increasing consumption of alcohol severed the relationship with Coward, who could not countenance indiscipline. Katharine Hepburn remarks that Wilson 'wasn't of Noel's calibre ... I didn't think all that much of him ... [Noel] was a hard-worker. He had no patience with weakness. He just thought it was stupid.'

Meanwhile Coward was receiving reports of new upheavals at home; Goldenhurst's housekeeper had left in high dudgeon when hit in the eye by a pat of butter, and Vida and Arthur had clashed over garden management. Noel tried to placate from afar, to which Violet replied, 'I shall keep your twaddly letter to show you one day. To think that *you* could write such tosh!' Arthur was carrying on with a local floozie called Miss de Pomeroy, said Violet, and such was the antipathy between his parents that Noel had his father moved to rooms above the garage. But Violet did not have to put up with much more from her spouse; Arthur Coward gave up his unremarkable life that autumn. He died on 12 September, aged seventy, leaving £545 6s 1d to his wife. As Arthur's life made little impression on his son, so his death occasioned only a brief comment, 'Father died at Goldenhurst ... Went to Gennesee to stay with Lynne and Alfred. *George and Margaret* opened in New York to faint praise.'

Both press and box office for *George and Margaret* were lukewarm, and Jack Wilson, who had put up most of the money for the American production, lost heavily. It also suffered from comparison with the work of a younger English playwright: Terence Rattigan's *French Without Tears* had critics talking of him as the new Coward, perhaps even more talented. Rattigan was younger, better educated, and more intellectually rigorous; but he was also hesitant, cynical and less driven than Noel and would prove no match for Coward's determination to stay in the spotlight.

Noel returned to England, and Goldenhurst, where he worked on *Operette*. Cole Lesley was the first to hear 'The Stately Homes of England' and 'Where Are the Songs We Sung?', the quality of which seemed to disprove the critics' claim that Coward's talent was fading. The musical's plot was slight and familiar: an Edwardian musical comedy actress (Fritzi Massary) nobly refuses to marry the heir to a peerage, who will have to resign his commission if she does. There is also a musical-within-a-musical, 'The Model Maid', in which Massary was Countess Mitzi. With a prologue of pre-war ladies and gentlemen and much genteel elegance, the general impression was of another attempt to repeat the success of *Bitter Sweet*.

Gladys Calthrop provided magnificent sets and costumes, and rehearsals went well. For Massary, it was an introduction to Coward's foibles: 'he came always very late ... and always looked in the mirror. His secretary told me that he was very vain. So I said to the cast, "He's really very pretty." One day he came very, very late, and we were waiting; and so I said, "Now at last the pretty king is coming." And from that moment on the whole cast called him "the pretty king".' Linda Gray, who had a supporting role, recalled that Coward's demands were exacting: 'Noel was a perfectionist, and when he conducted *Operette* on several occasions it was quite electrifying. He disliked noise in the theatre when rehearsing and very often begged the cleaners to "silence those angry Hoovers".'

Operette opened in Manchester on 17 February, a first night attended by a plethora of celebrities, including the Kents, the Gloucesters and the Princess Royal. Despite a month's worth of full houses, Coward and Beaumont considered the production too long, and the burden on Massary (then fifty-five) too great. Coward rewrote, cut and rearranged it, but these interior tensions made for an unsatisfactory whole. Alfred Lunt thought that '*Operette* was not one of Mr Coward's best productions. It had charm, of course ... but the music was not his most memorable', and Massary was 'disappointed in the music. I liked Noel and admired him, but *Operette* I didn't.' The improved version opened at His Majesty's Theatre, after an invitation-only dress rehearsal which Coward later confessed was 'a great mistake'; *Operette* was the 'least successful musical play I have ever done', and when it failed he concluded that it was the book of the piece which let it down. What he did not see was that musicals were changing, and he was not. Binkie Beaumont concluded that Coward's talent had temporarily deserted him.

The critics seemed to agree. James Agate doubted 'whether Mr Coward's tunes are as good as they used to be', while Ivor Brown alleged that Coward had become too much a part of the Establishment he had previously satirised, an example of which was Noel's membership of the Athenaeum, previously thought to be the exclusive domain of 'the eminents of College, Church, and State'. (His application to the more suitable Garrick Club, theatreland's watering-hole, was supposedly 'blackballed' on account of homosexuality, but the inclusion of the club in his 1922 number 'Down with the Whole Damned Lot' is a more likely reason. Coward did become a member later.) Although he poked fun at the aristocracy in 'The Stately Homes of England', he was, by association, a supporter of its traditions and values, an essential part, in his opinion, of what it meant to be British. To be on intimate terms with lords and ladies was no creative stimulus (there was a limit to how many satirical songs an earl could inspire) and perhaps it was true that Coward's exalted status had blunted his talent. But the threatening war would undermine the society in which Noel had so much faith, and would set the scene for the next few turbulent years and, paradoxically, his next great period of success.

In April 1938 Coward took another cruise with Admiral Vian, visiting Egypt and Palestine. His previous trip had been curtailed at Gibraltar because of the Spanish Civil War; this time the ship became an indiscriminate target for pot-shots by warring Arabs, Cypriots and Albanians. Europe was becoming a dangerous place. He made a visit to Rome, and attended one of Mussolini's Fascist rallies, where his previous interest in Il Duce succumbed to reality. The dictator looked 'like an over-ripe plum squeezed into a white uniform', and Noel laughed loudly.

There followed a bizarre occasion at the Villa Mauresque on Cap Ferrat, when Somerset Maugham warned his guests that Noel was 'on his uppers', all his money gone on recent flops and bad investments; Maugham determined to give Coward a 'square meal'. Noel arrived looking affluent and not particularly hungry, and greeted Maugham, 'Willie, *cher maître!*' with an embrace. Generous cocktails were poured, and quantities of stodgy food produced. '*Servez bien Monsieur Coward,*' said Maugham, '*il a l'air d'avoir faim.*' Noel struggled through, too polite to refuse, until he was shown by Robin Maugham to his car. 'Wonderful old boy,' said Coward, 'but a trifle over-hospitable, don't you think?' Meanwhile Maugham drew his guests' attention to the supposed speed with which Noel drank his cocktails and ate his steak-and-kidney pudding, '*and* the chocolate souffle? He probably hadn't had a square meal for weeks.'

At Goldenhurst, the larder was not quite bare. Here guests – who had included Maugham just a few months before – reported odder events. Lilia Ralli, the Greek-born friend of the Duchess of Kent, had a restless night in the French Room, a new guest room built off the long passage. Coward came to the conclusion, based on the evidence of other disturbed nights, that local tales of a suicide walking the path over which the room had been built were true and that it was haunted by a lovelorn Kentish lad. Unlike his fictional counterpart, Charles

Condomine, however, he did not call in psychic assistance to deal with the uninvited visitor.*

Visitors to Goldenhurst often met Alan Webb, who stirred political arguments to fever-pitch; his hotheadedness did not endear him to some of Coward's older friends, but he was given free rein. Some found Coward's vehement political ideas (of which he did not always have a firm grasp, tending to polarities) to be a bore. By mixing with politicians, he acquired a fleeting comprehension of world affairs which, like his amateur medical knowledge, he enthusiastically employed. Ivor Novello received a hard punch from Coward for his 'cowardice' when he cried during Chamberlain's 'I have in my hand a piece of paper' speech. But to Bob Boothby, who lived nearby, Noel's ideals seemed genuine: 'He cared about the political policies we pursued in the Thirties more passionately than anything else. Not unnaturally this bored the theatrical world. But he used to come over to The French House quite often and talk with me, alone, into the deep watches of the night.'

In November Coward arrived in New York to begin rehearsals for his new revue, *Set to Music*, in which Beatrice Lillie was to star. Since her role in the American production of *This Year of Grace!*, Lillie had worked in revue on both sides of the Atlantic, and had pursued a flamboyant private life, conducting an affair with Charles MacArthur while remaining married to Sir Robert Peel. Her professional association with Coward had continued; she was the first to sing 'Mad Dogs and Englishmen', for *The Third Little Show* revue on Broadway in 1931; and in 1935 sang duets with Noel at the Rainbow Rooms. She was also inclined to take liberties – Coward had been surprised that his permission had not been sought for her performance of 'Lilac Time' on American radio.

Their love-hate relationship was typical of Coward's relations with his leading women. She matched his wit effortlessly, once having Harrods send him an alligator with the message, 'So what else is new?' However, her cavalier attitude to performance tested Coward's patience sorely, and at one point during *Set to Music* rehearsals, Noel was driven to scream at the cast, 'This is the most disgraceful thing I have ever witnessed! How dare you, every one of you, behave in this outrageous

---

* Subsequent tenants of the house describe a feeling of being watched when playing the piano, which they ascribe to Coward's continuing presence. His ghost has also been reported in more unlikely venues: the bar manager of the Little Theatre in Wells claimed to have seen his spectral form, clad in a smoking-jacket during an amateur production of *Cowardy Custard*.

manner!' He swore at Lillie, who told him to get out. 'Never to return, dear girl', he retorted. But they made up that night at a party and, on opening in Boston on Boxing Day, she acquitted herself well. The show went to New York and to critical acclaim.

Coward's failure in his home country and success in the United States exacerbated his frustration with Britain and its critics. Brooks Atkinson lauded *Set To Music* in the *New York Times* as being Coward and his co-star Lillie 'at their best ... With his familiar prodigality of talents, Mr Coward has written it and staged it, sketches and songs alike, some of it having been retrieved from a revue he wrote for London last season ['The Stately Homes of England', 'Mad About the Boy' and 'Children of the Ritz']. On the spur of the moment it seems like the best show he has written ... For light amusement, written and acted with impeccable taste, this London revue is off the top of the pack.'

This situation was indicative of the times: London was preoccupied by the threat of war, and not in the mood for Coward's nostalgic meanderings; on Broadway the lights shone as they always had, and America turned its back on the European squabble. Paradoxically, the revue was very English, not only because of the presence of adoptive aristocrats such as Beatrice Lillie, and the real thing in Penelope Dudley-Ward, but because of its themes. Musical numbers included the needling wit of 'I Went to a Marvellous Party': 'Quite for no reason/ I'm here for the Season/ And high as a kite,/ Living in error/ With Maud at Cap Ferrat/ Which couldn't be right ...', referring to a world not far from *Semi-Monde* and earlier Coward plays, 'Poor Lulu got fried on Chianti/ And talked about esprit de corps/ Maurice made a couple of passes at Gus/ And Freddie, who hated any kind of a fuss,/ Did half the Big Apple and twisted his truss,/ I couldn't have liked it more.'

Soon American sophistication began to pall, however, and Coward set off for Honolulu. Eschewing the exhausting company of Louise Dillingham, he rented a shack on the beach at Mokolaeia, where he began writing the collection of short stories published as *To Step Aside*, a prose version of *Tonight at 8.30*. Using the time release on his camera, he snapped himself on his verandah, clad in Hawaiian shirt, suntanned and slicked-down hair, looking pensively out to sea, the picture of a romantic exile. Introspection encouraged his writing, which emerged in the form of short stories. Pleased with his efforts he returned to New York in March, sailing back to England briefly, before going to Switzerland to finish his stories at the Beau Rivage Hotel at Lausanne.

Perhaps even more than later efforts at fiction, Coward's first collection of short stories contained much that was autobiographical, as well as being strongly influenced by the two masters of the genre, Saki and Maugham. The protagonist of 'The Wooden Madonna' is a 'second Noel Coward', who decides to write an espionage novel (after Maugham's *Ashenden*) on the shores of a Swiss lake; Aubrey Dakers's suede shoes establish his sexuality for the *cognoscenti*, confirmed when we learn he had been an antique dealer.* He is subsequently fooled by a real agent, in a neat comic denouement. 'Traveller's Joy' is set in down-at-heel suburbia (where the houses are like 'respectable women who are beginning to take a drink'); Hubert Darrell, an ageing actor, makes love to Miss Bramble, a hunchback. Its details convince: the landlady's open window, the cord of its blind banging against the pane, and Coward's habitual use of brand names – Icilma vanishing cream and Houbigant face powder – root his stories in some reality.

In 'Aunt Tittie' the influence of Maugham is obvious; it tells of the orphaned boy Julian and his life with his theatrical and wayward dancer aunt, Titania. She introduces him to her world of tarts (both male and female) and warns him against older men. The tale ends mournfully with Aunt Tittie's death from a burst appendix. Coward writes affectingly because of his almost naive ability to access his past; Anita Brookner observes that he 'still retained unromanticised memories of his theatrical childhood . . . a certain true pathos underlines the false pathos which springs so neatly off the page'. Edith Sitwell later declared 'Aunt Tittie' 'a real masterpiece . . . it brings tears to my eyes every time I read it . . . The end of the story is almost unbearable.'

The most lively story is 'What Mad Pursuit?', about a celebrated writer, Evan Lorrimer, a pale reflection of his creator. 'Evan, like so many people who have attained fame and fortune by their own unaided efforts, was a firm self-disciplinarian. He apportioned his time with meticulous care: so many hours for writing, so many for reading. He ate and drank in moderation and indulged in only enough exercise to keep himself fit. He contrived, although naturally of a highly strung, nervous temperament, to maintain an agreeable poise both physically and mentally and to derive a great deal of enjoyment from life, admittedly without often scaling the heights of rapture, but also without plumbing the depths of despair.' Invited to Long Island for what he thinks will be a peaceful few days, he discovers his hostess is intent on

---

* Homosexual antique dealers also appear in *Pomp and Circumstance*, and his pastiche of Cole Porter's 'Let's Do It' notes that 'even nice young men who sell antiques/ Do it'.

showing him off in an interminable series of parties. These boast a good sprinkling of homosexuals: the lesbians Leonine and Shirley, who predictably end up bickering, both boyishly dressed; and the 'Russian fairy' Suki. Considering the prescriptive climate in which it was written, the overtness of such references in Coward's prose is extraordinary. Evan fancies the movie star Don Lucas, 'He was even handsomer in real life than he was on the screen. His young finely modelled face healthily tanned by the sun; his wide shoulders and long curling lashes; his lazy, irresistible charm . . . "It was exactly," thought Evan, "as tho' some clear-eyed, vital young God from the wider spaces of Olympus had suddenly walked into a nightclub."' (The same movie star – perhaps modelled on Louis Hayward – reappears in Coward's 1951 play *Relative Values*, in which the homosexual aristocrat Peter Ingleton flirts with Lucas.)

'What Mad Pursuit?' portrays a society and a time reminiscent of early Evelyn Waugh or later Nancy Mitford. Coward's setting allows for a stream of eccentric characters, such as the aged, and hilarious, Mrs Grouper Wendelmann, to whom Lorrimer is introduced. '"That book of yours", she said portentously, and cast a furtive look over her shoulder as though she were about to impart some scurrilous secret, "is great literature – No, it's no use saying it isn't because I know – Henry James used to be an intimate friend of mine and I knew poor Edith Wharton too, and believe me," her voice sank to a hoarse whisper, "I *know*."' The scenario was too good to be tucked away in the playwright's prose; Coward recycled the plot in his play *Long Island Sound*, written in 1947 but not produced. Indeed, many of his stories seem to be sketches for dramas; Anita Brookner has commented on the 'peculiar neatness with which Coward always finished his sentences and which was so tightly drawn that it skidded off into epigram . . . evident in the ground plan of these stories, a ground plan which corresponds to the well-made play'. As well as being able to deal with themes and events which the theatre censor would not allow, they succeed because the scene-setting and characters are so well observed. The plots are less substantial; the effect is all.

Yet beneath this glib showiness could be found vital clues to the writer's personality. 'Cheap Excursion' concerns the conspiratorial love affair between Jimmy, the assistant stage manager, and Diana Reed, the star: 'nearly forty and desperate', she is making a fool of herself over Jimmy (a dilemma Noel had faced in his affair with Louis Hayward, among others). Coward addressed the dichotomy of private and public:

Diana Reed finds a magazine picture of herself, 'the reminder of herself as others saw her . . . how shocked they'd be if they could see her now'; brought low by love, she is driven into the streets to look for Jimmy. Lust belies the public image: 'Diana Reed, that smooth gracious creature whose stage loves and joys and sorrows they had so often enjoyed, furtively loitering about in the middle of the night in the hope of spending a few minutes with a comparatively insignificant young man whom she liked going to bed with.' For Coward, there were always the tensions of his sexuality (and the problems of pursuing an active homosexual sex life), and at the same time not being what he was supposed to be. As an actor, he liked to appear to be what he was not. When Cole Lesley wrote his memoir of his master, great play was made of the 'revelation' that Noel Coward did not spend his evenings lounging decadently in his dressing gown drinking champagne, but preferred, like a character from one of his later musicals, to retire early to bed with 'a little "eggy" something on a tray' (another infantile reversion).

Just as his earlier dalliance with Bloomsbury or his attempt to write serious plays seemed to be efforts to escape his public image, so his ventures into prose-writing sought to prove he could do something more. Despite the claims to domestic banality, the stories were a reaction against ordinariness. As the homosexual outsider who feels challenged by normality, Coward almost always expresses the opinion of otherness in his work, nowhere more vivid than in his tales of the middle class. 'The Kindness of Mrs Radclyffe' is a parable of the priggish, snobbish, interfering Mrs Radclyffe who vexes and upsets (intentionally or otherwise) practically everyone she meets in her day, from husband to servants to daughter and best friend. Yet even here are touches of Coward: 'a disciplined mind in a disciplined body', she has 'a poor opinion of those . . . who allowed themselves to be swayed this way and that by emotions and circumstances over which they had little or no control'.

Of all the stories in *To Step Aside*, 'Nature Study' is probably the most acute. It is told in flashback to the Twenties. Jennifer Hyde marries Ellsworth Ponsonby, then visiting Taormina. He 'has quite a lot of complexes really', says Jennifer. 'The Catholic Church, Italian Gothic, Walt Whitman and not overtipping. He's a beauty lover, I'm afraid.'*

---

* 'Beauty lover' seems to refer to the Uranians of his youth. In 1949 Coward read Oscar Wilde's *De Profundis*, 'Poor Oscar Wilde, what a silly, conceited, inadequate creature he was and what a dreadful self-deceiver. It is odd that such brilliant wit should be allied to no humour at all . . . The trouble with him was that he was a "beauty-lover".'

Ponsonby seems drawn from Maugham; he has married for security, but is unable to have sex with his wife and instead becomes 'a hundred percent rip-snorting beauty lover'. His wife is the victim (as Coward saw Syrie Maugham), but she copes with the blackmail he is threatened with in New York (evidently a threat of sexual exposure). Yet more appositely, the story recalls other recent events: Jack Wilson's relationship with David Herbert in New York, and Herbert's flight from the city to escape legal proceedings. In the light of Coward's disintegrating relationship with Wilson, 'Nature Study' (the ironic title refers to the sexuality dissected) is a veiled but bitter comment on Jack's marriage to Natasha Paley.

18

Present Laughter

Joanna: You never get tired of fixing people's lives, of being the
    Boss, or everybody adoring you and obeying you?
Garry: Never. I revel in it.

Noel Coward, Present Laughter

THE London production of *Design for Living* had been running at the Theatre Royal, Haymarket, since 25 January 1939, directed by Harold French and produced by Binkie Beaumont. It was Coward's farewell to the Thirties, his last pre-war production. Beaumont, frustrated in his attempts to get Noel and the Lunts to recreate their New York roles in the West End, had agreed to a new cast; Diana Wynyard, Anton Walbrook and Rex Harrison were the *ménage à trois*, with Alan Webb as Ernest.

Both Coward and Beaumont had been worried about the chances of a licence from the new Lord Chamberlain, the Earl of Clarendon, but, when the play was submitted in September 1938, the reader said 'the play is pure Coward and despite the immorality of its theme, the Public would not, in my opinion, be justified ... in raising any serious objections to what is, after all, only an artificial Comedy of Manners.'* The play was passed, although the implacable Public Morality Council lobbied the Lord Chamberlain throughout the run of the play, saying it had 'an injurious influence' and was 'a very nasty play' with no 'useful moral lesson'. The long-suffering correspondent at St James's appended a testy note, 'The Theatre is *not* a pulpit.'

The play ran for most of 1939, but critics were disappointed; what

---

* Only one reference was blue-pencilled: Gilda's reply to Leo's remark that *The Times* is the 'organ of the nation': 'That sounds vaguely pornographic to me'; another line which Coward would reuse, this time in *A Song at Twilight*.

Brooks Atkinson had found merely wordy positively annoyed his British counterparts. Perversely, Sean O'Casey criticised *Design for Living* for being too ordinary; the characters 'barge at each other in the most conventional way possible, without one curious twist of word or turn of phrase'. The prospect of three men fighting over Gilda 'as if life would end because Gilda slept with Leo instead of Otto' was ridiculous; altogether, they were 'poor wincing worms in a winecup'. 'It remains, in the aggregate of its parts, good entertainment,' *The Times* said, 'though with a bitter taste and sometimes with a callow "daring"; Miss Wynyard and Mr Anton Walbrook are not perfectly cast.' Others agreed that Walbrook and Wynyard were too elegant and serious; only Rex Harrison rose to the occasion.

Coward spent the last summer of peace at Goldenhurst, on one occasion going over to Glyndebourne, where Mozart failed to engage him – the composer's work was 'like piddling on flannel'. He preferred Verdi and Puccini, and found Wagner particularly dilatory: 'I wish he'd get on with it.' There was an impatience in Coward's assessment of the finer arts, as if he had no time for their more subtle points. But he did not have the modern ubiquitous access to music, and the pop songs of the period sounded much better on gramophones than did the Ring Cycle. At Goldenhurst, he applied himself to his own creative talents; war might threaten, but his muse remained vigorous and defiant. Rising every morning at 6.30, he worked on two new plays: *Present Laughter* (originally called *Sweet Sorrow*); and *This Happy Breed*, which he completed at the end of June. It would be four years before either was to see the boards of a stage.

Present Laughter has always been seen as a piece of autobiography, in which the convoluted private life of playwright Garry Essendine is subject to the demands of casual sexual partners and those of his extended family of friends. But it also concerns a menopausal play-wright coming to terms with his middle age and inherent instability. The household is run by Monica, Essendine's secretary, 'a pleasant, rather austere woman' in her forties; she is unmistakably Lorn Loraine, a model of efficiency and acerbity, adept at keeping her own counsel. Like Lorn, she is intimate (carrying out her secretarial duties with Garry as he takes his bath) and unflappable, dealing calmly with his overnight conquest, Daphne. The other organisers of Essendine's life – Henry and Morris, his manager and producer – also perform their often thankless tasks in the face of their friend's irascibility (it is not difficult to see the figures of Binkie Beaumont and Jack Wilson in this pair), and Essendine's estranged wife Liz draws on Joyce Carey, a characterisation underlined when Carey took the part in the 1942 production. (One Essendine retort to Liz recalls Carey's forays into dramatic writing: 'And you! One of the most depressing, melancholy actresses on the English Stage. Where would you be if I hadn't forced you to give up acting and start writing.' Carey had written the successful play *Sweet Aloes*, of which it was said that Coward was jealous, and discouraged her from further, potentially usurping efforts.) In *Present Laughter*, the Family – 'five people ... woven together by affection and work and intimate knowledge of each other' – are allowed their say, subject to constant remonstration from their master: 'Never mind me, I'm only the breadwinner', Essendine whinges.

The play includes some of Coward's best dramatic writing; maturity anchors his wit and the dialogue is adroit. A sense of past achievements and assumed fame creates the atmosphere; like *Hay Fever*, *Present Laughter* toys with the thespian at home. It is telling that Coward's best works deal with celebrity, success and fame, and *Present Laughter* exemplifies the essence of his self-reflection: the actor playing an actor in a play about a playwright. 'Don't love me too much, Daphne!' Garry implores melodramatically, in virtual pastiche. 'I am not free like other men to take happiness when it comes to me – I belong to the public and to my work ... The work, the drudgery, the nerve strain? That is my job, the one thing to which I must be faithful.' His is a deeply theatrical narcissism, his oxygen:

> Monica: You could never get rid of Miss Erikson, she worships you.
> Garry: Everybody worships me, it's nauseating.
> Monica: There's hell to pay if they don't.

The premise of *Present Laughter* is Essendine's promiscuity; the notion that his charm is infallible. But he is now nearing forty, and it is time to settle down; Coward too was nearing forty, and for him too it meant a re-examination of his life, most particularly his emotions. There are discernible allusions to Garry's bisexuality; he admires an admiral's son with 'vast strapping shoulders and tiny tiny hips like a wasp', and later, the butler announces with an undeniable innuendo, 'The gentleman's in the office and the lady's in the spare room if you want either of them.' But Coward's opinion of sex is vouchsafed by Essendine to his emotionally confused inner circle, 'To me the whole business is vastly over-rated. I enjoy it for what it's worth and fully intend to go on doing so for as long as anybody's interested and when the time comes that they're not I shall be perfectly content to settle down with an apple and a good book!'

Present Laughter is crucially about control, and 'Coward was always in control', as Anna Massey agreed. 'You never felt he lost control. And he was always surrounded by loving guard dogs. He never went anywhere alone. To that extent, he was rather like royalty. I don't think you'd ever see Noel Coward go to Boots and buy some Kleenex on his own.' Garry Essendine presides over his clique, dispensing the 'daddy-knows-best' wisdom for which he was famous. Threats come from outside: Roland Maule, a would-be playwright from Uckfield (a typically Cowardian *double-entendre*), is a precursor of the Angry Young Men of the Fifties, and an offshoot of the leftist intelligentsia of the Thirties (Coward may have drawn on Keith Winter as his model). Maule accuses Essendine, 'Every play you appear in is exactly the same, superficial, frivolous and without the slightest intellectual significance ... All you do with your talent is to wear dressing gowns and make witty remarks when you might be really helping people, making them think! Making them feel!'

But the ultimate threat to Essendine's equilibrium and his family circle comes in the 'exquisitely gowned' shape of Joanna, wife of Henry, lover of Morris, and now seducer of Garry; although she is modelled on Natasha Paley, the stranger in the Family's midst, she also represents Coward's own love affairs. Anarchy threatens as this highly charged circle is about to fall apart; it is entirely fitting that Coward's most autobiographical play should end in an argument. Joanna storms off, Henry and Morris are sent away by Liz, who announces she is coming back to Garry. Morality is restored. They tiptoe out, leaving Maule and Daphne in spare room and office, and his promiscuous bachelor days behind.

To the uninitiated, the portrait of the author as Essendine was exaggerated, unreal; they objected, as they had done to *Hay Fever*, that the play was too histrionic. The truth was that it was nearer Coward's character than he might have liked to admit. The self-portrait was certainly evident to the scrutinisers of St James's Palace, but they saw it, too, as a surprisingly moral play. Geoffrey Dearmer's reader's report* for the Lord Chamberlain was submitted on 18 July 1939, when the

---

* Geoffrey Dearmer, a poet, novelist and playwright who had served in the war, was examiner of plays for the Lord Chamberlain from 1936 until 1958. He then produced 'Children's Hour' for BBC Radio.

play was still entitled *Sweet Sorrow*: 'The title is ironic, since the "sweet sorrow" of parting with his admirers is the one thing which that all too popular actor Garry Essendine cannot achieve . . . The play is practically all talk. Garry rants for pages and never bores (Coward will obviously play the part himself) . . . The Joanna–Garry one occasion intrigue is the only "affair" in the play. Its boomerang consequences should be a warning. In fact the comedy is a highly moral one, or it would be if it were not so artificial. Coward's limitation is that his characters are too clever to be real. But their artificiality accounts in a large measure for their inoffensiveness. Recommended for licence.'

Present Laughter's subject was Noel Coward as celebrity. Fame requires constant renewal, ever brighter, ever more spectacular effects. Coward produced them, time after time, but at a cost: such demands had led to nervous breakdowns in the past. Did he drive too hard, too soon, depleting his talents too early? In the next few years, he produced the highly successful trio of *Present Laughter*, *This Happy Breed* and *Blithe Spirit*, but to some this triumphant cluster resembled nothing so much as the last flowering of his genius.

Having finished *Present Laughter* and *This Happy Breed*, Coward decided to undertake a tour of Northern Europe 'to see what was going on'. He claimed he wanted to discover the situation for himself, but the secrecy of his later war duties gives some credence to the theory that he was acting as an informal, freelance intelligence-gatherer. His close contacts with government sources and romantic notions of espionage combined to give a mysterious air to his mission, little of which he dispelled in his memoirs. (In *Future Indefinite* he simply says that he discussed his plan with Robert Vansittart at the Foreign Office.) New evidence suggests that he had been associated with the 'Z' organisation, a partly private agency run by a Colonel Claude Dansey (who was probably homosexual and claimed to have been seduced at school by Robbie Ross). Dansey was financed by the rich South African brothers, Solly and Jack Joel, and enlisted the likes of Alexander Korda in gathering information on Nazi Germany. It is said that in the late 1930s Coward went to Paris for Z, possibily to make contact with an agent. His European tour seems to have been part of these duties.

The itinerary included Warsaw, Danzig, Moscow, Leningrad, Helsinki, Stockholm, Oslo and Copenhagen – an altogether chilly tour. In Warsaw, he conducted an informal survey, speaking to 'musicians, artists, critics, actors, soldiers, airmen and politicians', in all of whom

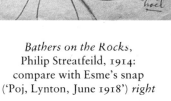

Easter greetings
to Violet

Bathers on the Rocks,
Philip Streatfeild, 1914:
compare with Esme's snap
('Poj, Lynton, June 1918') *right*

'Hair as shiny as wet coal':
Graham Payn

Noel in the pool

An island exile

Lorn Loraine

The view from Firefly Hill, watercolour by Beaton

Firefly

Sculpting on the
veranda of the Old
Lookout, Firefly Hill

Dust jacket for
Pomp and Circumstance

Noel, unidentified
artist, Cole Lesley,
Gladys Calthrop,
Blanche Blackwell
and Clemence Dane
at Blue Harbour

Two Nuns,
Noel Coward

Noel, Graham Payn,
Charles Russell
and Cole Lesley,
Firefly, 1955

Lorn Loraine, Noel and Joyce Carey arrive in California, 1958

Noel on the set of
Nude with Violin, New York, 1957

Bill Traylor

Cole Lesley at Les Avants

Joyce Carey and Alan Webb

Being photographed by Richard Avedon,
New York, March 1961

At Goldenhurst in
favourite Nehru jacket

Blue Harbour, 1993

Noel Coward's grave, Firefly Hill, 1993

Poster for *Brief Encounter*, 1945

Programme for
Sail Away, 1961

Album covers,
1955

he detected 'the same fatalistic conviction that war was not only inevitable but imminent'. He delivered a private letter to the High Commissioner of Danzig, Professor Carl Buckhardt, a mission accomplished with a certain amount of derring-do, crossing frontiers and evading possible Nazi interception. His journey on the Moscow express was accompanied by enough vodka to banish the sense of doom that had descended upon him; far from being the land of *Anna Karenina*, with Greta Garbo about to throw herself under a train, the Soviet Union was grey and depressed, and (had Coward but known it) its dictator was depleting the population far more effectively. Wandering around Moscow, he realised he was under surveillance, and amused himself by trying to lose his follower, 'an innocuous little man with a green velour hat'. Finally, he walked up to him, shook his hand and said he hadn't seen him for ages and how were Anna and the children?

Coward took a midnight train for Leningrad, glad to leave Moscow, and was met by a woman wearing boots, black coat and scraped-back hair, 'who seemed to have stepped directly out of the film *Mädchen in Uniform*'.* She drove him to the Astoria Hotel, where his attempts to engage the waiter in conversation were distracted when he saw the telephone was off the hook – another ear listening. This is unlikely to have been paranoia; he was, after all, a well-known figure, and his presence in Russia seemed odd. Noel picked up the receiver and said, 'That will be all for the moment. Thank you so much', and hung up.

In Helsinki he had a bemused meeting with Sibelius (he confused the Finnish composer with Delius); in Stockholm, he again felt a 'leaden wariness' in the air. The British minister asked him to take the diplomatic bag with him to Oslo, which he did, but on the way to Copenhagen, Coward was seized with a need for the sun of the Côte d'Azur.

He flew to Paris and south to Cannes, and was soon ensconced in the Carlton Hotel for a week of sunbathing before he had to report for the rehearsals of *This Happy Breed* and *Present Laughter*. A last pre-war party assembled: Joyce Carey, Alan Webb and Marlene Dietrich, and Coward visited Maugham at the Villa Mauresque, and Maxine Elliott at the Château de l'Horizon, both sequestered in their secluded Riviera retreats. The atmosphere of the times was summed up in the frail figure

---

* A 1931 German film dealing with lesbianism in a boarding school, and starring Romy Schneider and Lili Palmer.

of Elliott, once a king's mistress, now fatally ill, waving goodbye from the beach.

Binkie Beaumont had not been keen on the idea of a double bill, preferring to do only *Present Laughter*, but Coward felt that *This Happy Breed* was a necessary balance to the comedy, especially given the political situation. He told Beaumont it was all or nothing; the producer settled for all, and booked a six-month tour. He hoped to follow *Design for Living* with the two plays, although the news made that increasingly unlikely. After the first week of rehearsals, Coward, Carey and the Wilsons were spending the weekend at Goldenhurst when a Sir Campbell Stuart rang Noel, requesting a midnight meeting in London; Stuart was managing director of *The Times*, and had worked on propaganda in the First World War. Bob Boothby, who was driving up to town that afternoon via Chartwell, records that Coward asked him to take him to see Churchill (rather than the other way around, as Noel wrote), to seek his advice: 'There we found a small party, and Churchill not in a very good mood.'

After dinner, and a performance of 'some of my lighter songs', an impatient Coward was eventually taken aside by Churchill, to be told, 'You'd be no good in the intelligence service . . . Get into a warship and see some action! Go and sing to them when the guns are firing – that's your job!' Coward was irate; he wanted to be more than a mere entertainer of troops. If Churchill thought that someone singing 'Mad Dogs and Englishmen' above the noise of a twenty-pound gun would be a vital contribution, the war effort was in pretty bad shape. 'He was very depressed on the way home, but . . . Churchill was right', said Boothby. 'He never really liked or appreciated Coward . . . But he knew that Coward's particular genius could only fulfil itself in his own world.' Noel was not convinced; he saw his talent to amuse as a handicap to being taken seriously, and he knew that if he 'bungled this moment, and by so doing betrayed my own code of morals', he would not be able to live with himself. But Coward did betray himself, in his comment, 'whether books or plays I lived to write in the future would be inevitably and irrevocably tainted by the fact that I had allowed to slip through my fingers the opportunity to prove my own integrity to myself'. This smacked of one eye on immortality, the other on the box office. Certainly the glamour of a secret assignment was attractive, but he also had to exorcise the ghost of his shadowy performance in the previous war. He was determined that his role should be a noble one.

The midnight interview with Stuart provided reassurance. Coward had been cast, and the part had been written for him. Jean Giraudoux, the French minister of information, would 'take it as a personal compliment' if Noel were to go to Paris to set up a Bureau of Propaganda, liaising with the French Commissariat d'Information. Coward was flattered; good use would be made of his skills as a writer, and 'it would at last give me an opportunity to use my mind and imagination'. That night, he dreamed he was a clown in the Cirque Medrano, 'and that Winston Churchill was in a box applauding vociferously'.

Over the next two weeks, Coward interspersed rehearsals for the theatre with rehearsals for war, in briefings with Stuart or Colonel Dallas Brooks, his second-in-command, a 'large and good-looking and impeccably dressed' Royal Marine, typical of his regiment – 'which means that he was efficient, sentimental and had perfect manners'. Brooks supplied a secret code, which appeared simplistic to Coward's devious mind, consisting as it did of calling people by different names. There were dress rehearsals of *This Happy Breed* and *Present Laughter* on 30 and 31 August, which went surprisingly smoothly. But the next day Germany invaded Poland, and the denizens of the Phoenix Theatre knew war was inevitable. Noel took Joyce, Gladys and Jack to lunch at the Ivy, as usual, where they were 'very bright and jocular and made little jokes to tide us over'.

On the day that war was declared, Coward and his chief-of-staff, David Strathallan (son of the Earl of Perth), were due at Campbell Stuart's secret headquarters; they had got as far as St John's Wood when the air-raid sirens went off, so they took cover in a nearby block of flats. The possibility of being bombed out with babies wailing in their ears sent both men back outside, defying ARP wardens. They made it to the HQ, which, as the locals gave them directions, did not appear to be very secret. The 'mock Tudor villa' was in fact Bletchley Park, the Buckinghamshire country house taken over by the SIS (forerunners of MI6) for the duration. Here Coward had a terse meeting with Admiral Sir Hugh Sinclair, head of SIS and the owner of Bletchley. It was decided that Coward should go into D section, the 'dirty tricks' department; already there was Guy Burgess, and Kim Philby was about to join.

Although Coward's approach to the war seemed flippant, he was convinced of its rightness. Since the early 1930s he had been aware of the German military build-up, his travels enabling him to observe the effect the National Socialist government was having on the Continent.

'With a few individual exceptions the German people have always been antipathetic to me', he wrote unrepentantly in the mid-Sixties. 'There is something about the Teutonic mentality that grates on my nerves ... No nation with a grain of genuine humour could have accepted seriously the grotesque ranting and roaring of Adolf Hitler. His physical appearance alone should have been sufficient for a belly laugh.' Coward's reductivist theories betray his lack of understanding of politics, and, indeed, of the nature of fascism. It was a consequence of the life he led: within his world, stereotyping was not only acceptable, it was necessary; to dramatise life was to exemplify characters and aspects, to reduce them to theatrical types. Although Noel possessed genuinely humane qualities which abhorred racism and anti-Semitism, his belief in the values of the British way of life remained unshaken – at least for dramatic purposes, as his latest play showed.

This Happy Breed has been seen as a patronising portrayal of the class from which Coward himself came. It is true that his '*Cavalcade* for suburbia' reflected his background, but only to a superficial degree; it is the lower middle class in Coward's imagination, rather than the reality. The play opens in 1919, at 17 Sycamore Road, Clapham Common. The Gibbons family have just moved from Battersea, and the mother-in-law Mrs Flint and Aunt Sylvia constantly argue, like Violet and Vida. This is 'Fumed Oak' territory, full of carping women who don't know their places; and crucially *This Happy Breed* is about the importance of knowing one's place.

The ex-soldier Frank Gibbons is a sceptic; when Ethel tells him they ought to be grateful he survived the war, he asks, 'Who to? I don't 'old with a God who just singles out a few to be nice to, and lets all the others rot.' She is upset when, like the 'heroes' of *Post-Mortem*, Frank says he would go to war again (war and defence of the realm being the subtext of this late Thirties play – it is no coincidence that the title came from Shakespeare's *Henry V*). During the General Strike, Ethel speaks of reports of 'riots and people being arrested and houses being bust down and soldiers charging the crowds and all sorts of horrors'. Coward is not quite as reactionary as he seems, and in the feminine concerns of Ethel, as with Jane Marryot in *Cavalcade*, there is a genuine note of dissent.

Edward VIII's abdication speech is another threat to the country's stability.* Two years later, the Munich settlement is announced ('I've

* The Lord Chamberlain objected to the intention to broadcast the speech on stage. Dearmer

often thought Mr Chamberlain must be a Christian Scientist at heart',
says Sylvia, a backhanded gibe at Esme Wynne's religion), and Frank
calls it 'betrayal'. The play ends in June 1938 with a two-page speech
delivered to Frank's grandson in his pram: 'The trouble with the world
is, Frankie, that there are too many ideals and too little horse sense . . .
Human beings don't like peace and good will and everybody loving
everybody else . . . they're not made like that. Human beings like eating
and drinking and loving and hating. They also like showing off,
grabbing all they can, fighting for their rights and bossing anybody
who'll give 'em half a chance. You belong to a race that's been bossy
for years and the reason it's held on as long as it has it that nine times
out of ten it's behaved decently and treated people right . . .' He blames
the politicians for 'letting down the people who trusted us and allowing
noisy little men to bully us with a lot of guns and bombs and
aeroplanes'; but 'we know what we belong to, where we come from,
and where we're going. We may not know it with our brains, but we
know it with our roots . . .'

This atavistic sense of belonging was Coward's notion of Englishness,
a continuance of the imperial values prevailing at his birth. He could
gloss over the misery of the Depression; now insulated by his income,
his experience of poverty as a child was remote. Whether or not the
family in *This Happy Breed* was a caricature, or an accurate representation of the great British public, Coward was equivocal. Five years
later, his 'Burchells of Battersea Rise' sang, 'We resent and detest and
despise/ Being talked of as "This Happy Breed" in the Press,/ If the
author we meet/ We'd be happy to greet/ Him with two lovely black
eyes/ From the Burchells of Battersea Rise.' The play is a natural child
of *Cavalcade*: no change was recommended; unremitting and reassuring
status quo was the order of the day, and the play is a controversial
exposition of Coward's assertion of middle-class values: 'from above to
above, pretending by mimetic means, to come from below', as Douglas

---

recommended that this 'should surely be cut . . . It would be embarrassing for everybody and
quite intolerable for any member of the Royal Family who might see the play.' Coward
insisted that the reference was crucial, but the king was consulted and permission was declined.
Three years later, when the play was actually performed, Coward applied again. Sir Alexander
Hardinge replied, '. . . I always feel that the British people look upon the Abdication as a
discreditable episode which they would like to forget altogether. I believe that it will be
distasteful to them to rake it up again, and definitely repugnant to the Royal Family.' Even in
1950 the Lord Chamberlain refused to allow a recording of the abdication speech to be used
in a charity performance of *This Happy Breed*.

Dunn wrote. In an era of stereotypes, when Cockneys were condemned to be chirpy and Belgravians to be sophisticated, the barriers were insurmountable. Although Coward had managed that remarkable leap, he was not about to encourage further social acrobatics.

Before leaving for his Paris appointment, Coward drove down to Goldenhurst with Joyce Carey to see his mother and Jack and Natasha Wilson. Jack had conscientiously blacked out the windows and replaced ordinary light bulbs with blue ones. 'A lot of nonsense,' Violet complained, 'I can't see my hand before my face, I nearly fell downstairs, and the whole thing's idiotic!' They dined gloomily, and Coward said a sentimental goodbye to his house and friends.

He crossed the Channel in a Vega Gull aeroplane, surreally attired in bowler hat, dark suit, gas mask, parachute and lifebelt. He found Paris hot, dusty and deserted, and only the Ritz and Maxim's appeared obstinately open for business. Together with the naval attaché, Captain Holland and David Strathallan, he dined at the Ritz on caviar, filet mignon and pink champagne. Confusion reigned. Coward had difficulty finding anyone who knew what was going on, or what he should be doing, and he began to wonder if his mission was about to fall apart. Eventually he met with Giraudoux and dined with him *en famille*, urbanely discussing theatre but not propaganda. It was the same with André Maurois, who, when drunk, sounded distinctly unconfident about the venture. Noel was even more discouraged.

Meanwhile the RAF dropped leaflets politely exhorting the enemy to drop their guns, like good chaps. But, amateurish as the war seemed, Coward's own attitude was less than serious; his account of his Parisian duties is reminiscent of an Ealing comedy, with redundant officers in bed drinking bismuth, presiding over chaos and farce. Noel's attempt to call British HQ in code, with his irascible interlocutor bellowing, 'What the bloody hell are you talking about?', is a scene straight out of *Our Man in Havana*. He wrote his report and marked it *Secret, Confidential, and Dull*, and a proposed mathematical code was hampered by the playwright's gross innumeracy. Although these self-deprecating anecdotes may have been a cover for Coward's work for the SIS, his aptitude for that work was doubted, more especially as D section's projects were achieving mixed results. 'It wasn't Coward's cup of tea', wrote journalist John Simpson.

Noel decided to fly home and explain in person the difficulties he was facing. He was greeted by Lorn Loraine at Gerald Road as a returning warrior, and after seeing the Wilsons (who were about to leave for America) he reported to Stuart, who promised to follow Coward back to Paris to assess the situation. Stuart and Brooks duly arrived, and Coward was installed in a well-appointed office at 18 Place de la Madeleine, with Strathallan and a Scottish secretary, Miss Cameron; Cole Lesley arrived to perform his usual duties. Coward was to concentrate on black propaganda (answering to the Political Warfare Executive), and acquired a full complement of staff: a 'bogus' Squadron Leader, Bill Wilson; a French-speaking radio expert; Paul Willert, whose duty it was to liaise between any useful refugee contacts; and Peter Milward, a friend of Edward Molyneux's, who volunteered to find useful material in the French media.

Life was a good deal more comfortable with staff around him, and more so when he found a flat on the Place Vendôme, with Chanel and Schiaparelli as close neighbours. The *beau monde* of Paris had resurfaced by November, with Elsie Mendl's salon at the Villa Trianon at Versailles and the Windsors' dinners at the boulevard Suchet. The one concession to the war seemed to be that it was considered chic not to wear evening dress, except in the presence of the Duke of Windsor, who had announced 'in no uncertain terms' that *le smoking* was *de rigueur* at boulevard Suchet. Coward noted that 'an unpleasant rash of functions and entertainments' provided 'a form of occupational therapy for those ... whose nerves had been cruelly jolted by the events of the last eighteen months'. He participated, if only because there was little else to do. Boothby recalled Coward's work for 'a ridiculous organisation in Paris which was supposed to be some kind of Information Service, but consisted chiefly of endless and purposeless lunch, dinner and drink parties. On the two occasions when I saw him there, I told him it was a farce; and he agreed with me.'

So Coward partied with Lady Mendl and dined with Edward Molyneux, and began keeping a diary for the first time, a new discipline to his life. Work at the office followed a set routine: by 9.30 a.m., Coward was installed at his desk, ready for the day's business. Miss Cameron would be bashing away at the typewriter next door (proof merely of her extensive social circle, noted her boss), while Coward waded through dull missives redundantly marked 'secret', most of the good stuff having already appeared in the European edition of the *Daily Mail*. 'On the whole, I think I give a good performance', he told the press. 'Occasionally I don't come to until the middle of the first act, but there I am, nonetheless, going through the business.' His intermittent tardiness may have been due to his idiosyncratic emergency precautions; during air raids, incipient claustrophobia drove him to eschew the Métro for the stone staircase of his house. When the warning sounded, he gathered up some pillows, a pack of cards and a bottle of gin, and tucked himself under the stairs, playing solitaire until the all-clear came. Two or three times a week a diplomatic bag arrived from London, mostly containing private mail: gossip from Violet, Joyce, Lorn and Gladys, with the occasional verse from Clemence Dane. He flew home once a month, often spending his first night at Clemence Dane's Covent Garden house, catching up on all the news.

Coward had known Dane (she had taken her name from a London church; her real name was Winifred Ashton) since the Twenties, and admired her gusto and naivety in equal measure. She was striking in appearance, tall, with an aquiline profile, and large in girth, and had trained as an artist and as an actor. Her successful novels (among them *Regiment of Women* (1917)) often dealt with theatrical subjects, and her first play, *A Bill of Divorcement*, was an immense success when it opened at St Martin's Theatre in March 1921. (On Broadway it helped establish Katharine Cornell as a star, and was filmed by George Cukor, with Katharine Hepburn playing her first film role as Sydney Fairfield.)

Dane lived above a greengrocer's shop at 26 Tavistock Street, Covent Garden, with her secretary, Olwen Bowen, herself a writer of children's books, but who now devoted herself to the care of her companion. 'One climbed up a rickety staircase and there was Winifred, surrounded by her paintings, sculptures, a piano and goodness knows how many books, where she would give many after-the-theatre parties . . .' Coward relished tales of her eccentricities, which were legion; Jeffrey Amherst wrote that when fire broke out in one of the warehouses opposite No. 26, Dane 'dashed out in her dressing-gown, her hair flying, to persuade the firemen to keep the fire going long enough for her to get it down in paint on canvas'. As a sculptor and painter, she was talented, and was famous for her unintentionally hilarious vocabulary, fond of telling friends the secret of sculpting was to 'dip your tool in hot white wax'. For Coward it was fun to arrive at Dane's chaotic literary and artistic salon, to hear the latest gossip, and meet his old intimates. They played The Game, a sophisticated form of charades at which Coward and Joyce Carey excelled. 'Winifred used to go mad to try and guess the Game', Judy Campbell recalled. 'She was a large lady, with raven locks pushed up on top of her head with tortoiseshell combs, and I have this vision of her, hair around her shoulders and combs on her lap, desperately trying to get the clues.'

It was only a matter of time before Coward used his colourful friend in one of his dramas, and sure enough she provided the inspiration for *Blithe Spirit*'s Madame Arcati, the unworldly psychic riding her bicycle, described as 'a striking woman, dressed not too extravagantly but with a decided bias towards the barbaric' (Coward's lesbians are often dressed 'barbarically'). 'I had my first trance when I was four years old and my first ectoplasmic manifestation when I was five a and half', exults Arcati. 'What an exciting day that was! I shall never forget it. Of course the manifestation itself was quite small and of very short duration, but, for a child of my tender years, it was most gratifying.'

19

Could You Please Oblige Us with a Bren Gun?

Could you please oblige us with a Bren gun?
The lack of one is wounding to our pride.
Last night we found the cutest
Little German parachutist
Who looked at our kit
And giggled a bit
Then laughed until he cried.

Noel Coward, 'Could You Please Oblige Us with a Bren Gun?'

LIFE had become oddly routine in this 'crisis'. Coward's major achievement in Paris was to have a commercial radio station, which could have provided enemy bombers with cross-bearings, shut down, but the complications involved convinced him that 'men of apparent integrity, occupying positions of considerable responsibility, can, when financial interests are involved, behave with shoddy evasiveness'. If Coward had been naive in believing otherwise, it was to his credit.

He may also have been naive in believing that his work in Paris would counter critics at home. Emmanuel Shinwell had already tried to raise a question in Parliament about Coward's relationship with the Royal Navy – why was this man being carried about on personal cruises by ships of His Majesty's Fleet? Now the press questioned the usefulness of his posting in France. Coward claimed that he was being 'victimised, even more than usual, by my own publicity value'. He blamed Stuart for issuing a press statement about his activities, leaving the field open for tabloid speculation; one story claimed Coward had been seen in the Ritz bar 'hissing unutterable secrets into the ear of a female Polish spy'. Coward was particularly incensed by a photograph in the *Telegraph*, showing him 'sauntering along the Rue Royale in naval uniform';

followed by a *Sunday Pictorial* demand to know why he was wearing a uniform he was not entitled to. Even though Mountbatten had offered him the honorary rank of Lieutenant-Commander RNVR for his work for the Royal Naval Film Corporation, Noel had yet to don the uniform of the Senior Service. What the newspaper picture showed was his taste for sharp navy-blue blazers, which imparted a nautical air; but on a weekend in London, he was still questioned by Churchill as to the veracity of the rumours. Added to that, there was more salacious gossip spread about him and his staff, with Peter Milward implicated in sexual indiscretions. These Coward diffused, telling David Strathallan (of whose Catholicism he was suspicious) that it really didn't matter if Milward did it with Chinese mice, as long as he didn't bring them into the office.

Endless intrigue and argument made Coward restless, and he felt he was achieving little in Paris. Early in 1940 it had been suggested to the Ministry of Information that prominent writers such as H. G. Wells, Maugham and Coward be used to explain the British position to the Americans: 'Carefully selected Britishers of outstanding ability and reputation could form a British mission under the leadership of the British Ambassador.' Coward persuaded Sir Campbell Stuart that a tour of the United States could provide important information in assessing American reaction to the war, and the likelihood of their involvement; it was also, Coward later admitted, a plea to get away from an increasingly bleak Europe. The German invasion of Norway and Denmark had made the crisis in Paris more tangible, and Coward turned this to his advantage, telling his boss that the six week tour he proposed was even more important now.

At the end of April he left Paris for Genoa, to sail for New York. It was the wartime route to travel the Atlantic and, together with fleeing Scandinavian consuls, he had a rough crossing on the SS *Washington*. The trip allowed for a little ad hoc intelligence-gathering: Coward met a suspicious-looking European, and having chatted to him and obtained his name, returned to his cabin to look him up in his list of suspects. The man's name was at the head of the list. Noel asked the purser for his dossier, and concluded that the suspect was an agent either for the Soviets or the Germans, probably the latter.

On his arrival in Manhattan, the *New York Times* accepted Coward's proffered reason for his trip, that he was 'to arrange with his agent . . . to put on a play in New York in the Fall'. Coward said he would leave his two new plays – *Sweet Sorrow* and *This Happy Breed* – with Jack Wilson: 'Both were written by me for me, and must wait until after the

307

war. No matter how long the war lasts it won't affect my suitability for either role, since I could play both wearing a long white beard.' Coward had announced he would not write any plays for the duration, a sacrifice which had the added bonus of taking the pressure off his creative duties. This may have been convenient at a time when ideas for new dramas were not forthcoming (although he professed to be annoyed by American friends who were trying to persuade him to return to the theatre). In fact, he did work fitfully that summer on *Time Remembered*, set at a Connecticut house-party in September 1940, where an Englishwoman arrives with her children to escape the London Blitz. Appalled by her friends' blindness to the situation in Europe, she returns home to be with her husband. The play was never published or produced, perhaps because of its anti-American tone, which was superseded by America's entry into the war.

It was a relief to be back in New York, where wartime restrictions did not apply, and Coward dined, partied and gave interviews, then went to stay with Jack and Natasha Wilson in Fairfield, on the edge of Long Island Sound. The Lunts joined the house-party on Sunday, and it all seemed like old times again. But duty called, and Noel flew to Washington DC, with a letter of introduction to Mrs Roosevelt from their mutual friend, Paul Willert. That night he was to dine with her, after an interview with her husband.

The President struck Coward as an admirable man, for all the stories he had heard of Roosevelt's 'political treacheries'. From an elaborate array of cocktail equipment, he made Noel a perfect martini, despite a rule prohibiting hard liquor in the White House, and confided his equivocal attitude to the European war, a policy determined by heavy opposition to any involvement. Public figures such as Charles Lindbergh campaigned against US action, and it was Coward's mission to counter-act such publicity. Back in New York, his socialising was overshadowed by the news that Germany had invaded Holland, which sparked off 'general hysteria'. It seemed 'the beginning of the end' for Europe, but the Allied Relief Ball at the Hotel Astor went ahead that evening: Coward decided 'the only thing to do was to put on bright faces and endure it as best we could'. He sent cables to his boss, saying he wanted to return as soon as possible, but Stuart told him to go on with his tour, which he did, visiting Salt Lake City, Omaha, Cincinnati and Cleveland.

In Los Angeles, he stayed with Cary Grant, who shared a house in Santa Monica with Randolph Scott, but was in the throes of a public love affair with Barbara Hutton (which disgusted Coward). Being back in Hollywood was like walking into a Technicolor film after the grainy black and white of war-torn Europe. Coward enjoyed this dose of moviedom, and the attention. He visited the set of *The Philadelphia Story*, starring Cary Grant, Katharine Hepburn and James Stewart, and Coward helped the director, George Cukor, by giving Stewart 'a big hug of praise' when the actor was having trouble with a speech. (In August, Cukor would return the favour by producing 'The Astonished Heart', starring Gladys Cooper, at El Capitan in Hollywood, as a benefit for British war relief.) But as the Hollywood parties continued, news from Europe worsened: the British Expeditionary Force was trapped, and Dunkirk was only a week away. Like the heroine of *Time Remembered*, Coward could not bear being so far from the action, and decided to return to Britain, but could not get a plane reservation until 8 June.

In the meantime, he was summoned back to Washington, and the White House; this time his interview with the President was conducted with Coca-Cola and without jokes. Dunkirk had been evacuated, and Roosevelt spoke admiringly of the British ability to make a defeat seem like a victory. Asked if he thought Germany could successfully invade Britain, Noel said, 'beyond all logic and reason', that it could not. 'If that isn't blind faith', said Roosevelt, 'I should like to know what is.' Coward reflected the determination of his fellow countrymen, unable to countenance the possibility: but they were facing the threat; he was three thousand miles away.

The *New York Times* reported Coward's departure on the Clipper on 9 June, noting that he had been on a 'six-week furlough from secret British Government duties'. Just before the plane landed in Lisbon, they discovered that Italy had entered the war. The British Ambassador in Portugal summoned Coward to tell him that he could not return to Paris, as the German advance was threatening the capital. Had Noel taken the train, he would have arrived in Paris one day ahead of Hitler. With his name firmly on the Nazi liquidation list (as he later discovered), it would have been one of his less propitious entrances.

Coward soon felt his usual homecoming depression; his mother country was frustrating and life was difficult. He began to organise the evacuation of the Actors' Orphanage to America, and Violet and Aunt Vida to North Devon. It seemed that his war was going to be decidedly dull, had if not been for further forays into the secret world of wartime espionage.

In *Future Indefinite*, Coward refers to an anonymous 'Little Bill' who would offer him a job 'which, in his opinion and in mine, would be of real value to the war effort, and would utilise not only my celebrity value but my intelligence as well'. 'Little Bill' was Sir William Stephenson, head of British Security Co-ordination in the States. A short, slight Canadian millionaire, he was already employing Alexander and Zoltan Korda, Ian Fleming and Leslie Howard as his 'boys' in romantically dangerous exploits, recreated by Fleming in the James Bond stories. Coward's new task would involve espionage of a sophisticated nature; he looked forward to the sort of duties for his country that Somerset Maugham had performed in the previous war. Coward's account of the events is clouded, both by the secrecy which still bound him in later years and by the haphazard nature of his recollections; only at the end of his life did he discuss the events openly, recalling that he had been summoned to St Ermin's Hotel in Caxton Street. 'I had to meet a contact in the foyer. I waited in this squalid place and eventually a man said "Follow me" . . . he wheeled me round and into an elevator. It was only labelled to go up three floors. To my absolute astonishment it went to the fourth instead.

'Well this was the – ah, the Special Operations Executive. What we called later the Baker Street Irregulars.* Some chap was saying President Roosevelt wanted us to do his fighting. And Little Bill was there, very calm, with those sort of hooded eyes watching everything.' Coward's new mission was to join Stephenson (codenamed 'Intrepid') at Intelligence headquarters in New York, where he would receive further briefings. With the United States still not actively involved in the war, the operation of British agents remained illegal; Stephenson used 'informal' means to train and maintain agents, and encourage US participation in the war.

Coward had a 'confusing talk with Winston Churchill' before he left. 'He knew I'd done something in France for intelligence but couldn't get it into his head that what I wanted was to *use* my intelligence . . . he kept saying, "No use, you'd be no good – too well known." I said, "That's the whole point . . . nobody will think I'm doing anything special" . . . Eventually I got it through to him – I was fluent in Spanish and could do the whole of Latin America, where the Germans were very active . . .'

* The amateurs who helped Sherlock Holmes; the SOE headquarters moved to 64 Baker Street.

Intriciate plans were laid for Coward's trip to South America. He was to undertake an extensive lecture tour under the auspices of the British Council, a cover for the anti-Nazi work which he would really be pursuing. He decided his mother must be evacuated to America, fearing that were the Germans to invade England she would be tortured to get back at him; he consulted on the matter with Joe Kennedy, the American ambassador, who agreed. But just days before he was due to leave, Colonel Dansey rang him to say the entire project was called off. Coward was furious and blamed self-seeking politicians; even his friend George Lloyd seemed to have betrayed him by not providing the necessary British Council cover. The affair deepened his distrust of British politics, and coloured his view of the country as a whole; it was a sense of futility and frustration which would resurface in his post-war diatribe, '*Peace in Our Time*'. Duff Cooper saved the day, however, and arranged for Coward to sail to the States, armed with a personal letter to Lord Lothian, the British ambassador.

Coward returned to New York, where an official from the British Information Service instructed him to tell the press that he was there on theatrical business. Noel had already run the gamut of the media mob at Ellis Island, and said he had been 'the soul of discretion'. But this was not quite the case: the *New York Times* reported that Coward was 'on a mission for Lord Alfred Duff Cooper, British Minister of Information', and that he 'would go to Washington tomorrow to report to the British Ambassador'. 'The situation in Great Britain is serious', said Noel, 'but it is simply marvellous the way everyone is behaving.' Coward's condescension may well have annoyed the Americans; but he did explain that he hoped to evacuate the 68 children of the Actors' Orphanage 'in his personal charge' to the States for the duration: 'Mr Coward said he already had arranged with English members of the Hollywood film colony to give them shelter.'

Coward charged Fanny Holtzmann – Gertrude Lawrence's voluble lawyer – with arrangements for the orphanage. Roy Williams describes its wartime fate, 'I left the school in July 1940, and later that year Noel Coward was the prime mover in arranging for the school to be moved over to America for the war. The ship they went on was in the convoy that the *City of Benares* was in, which was sunk. Luckily their ship had developed engine trouble and had to turn back to port, and they went over on their own. They were housed in the Gould Foundation . . . just outside New York, and . . . went to the local school. That was really the end of the school as a school. Noel criticised it for spoiling the children, with the best accommodation, always being visited by actors and actresses, getting lots of publicity.'

After checking in with Stephenson at his New York office in the St Regis Hotel, Noel visited 'Camp X', British Security Coordination's base on the north shore of Lake Ontario, 300 miles north-west of Manhattan, where agents were trained, sabotage devices tested and espionage techniques taught. But Noel's major weapon was his 'celebrity value': 'My disguise was my own reputation as a bit of an idiot . . . whole lot of tiny things are the stuff of intelligence. Smallest details fit into a big picture, and sometimes you repeat things and wonder if it's worth it. I travelled wherever I could do – Asia and what was left of Europe. And I ridiculed the whole business of intelligence, because that's the best way to get on with it – ridicule and belittle ourselves, and say what an awful lot of duffers we are, can't get the facts straight, all that sort of thing.'

He despaired of the Americans understanding his approach to the business, but he 'learned a lot from their technical people, became expert, could have made a career in espionage, except that my life's been full enough of intrigue as it is. All that technical expertise isn't worth a damn if you don't get the best out of people, though.' Coward's overt task – to 'talk up' support for the Allies – entailed his bright and breezy presence at endless interviews, engagements and parties, making patriotic speeches, singing songs, and generally trying 'to make myself look as attractive as possible' – essential to his more secret duties. It all cost money (about £11,000) which was drawn from Noel's private New York bank account, as the government did not pay him expenses. Part of the reason may have been because they preferred the arrangement to remain casual, but the American Neutrality Bill made it impossible for foreign agents to be paid to conduct propaganda in the US, and those who went had to support themselves financially. Coward naturally thought that there would be some sort of reimbursement eventually; if not financial, then perhaps some other reward; perhaps a knighthood. But the feeling about Mr Coward in Britain did not involve such honours, as he discovered from the *New York Times* of 7 August: 'Commons Questions Coward's Visit Here'. The House of Commons took time out from urgent questions of national finance today to discuss why Gracie Fields and Noel Coward were allowed to go to the United States . . .'

Harold Nicolson, parliamentary secretary to Duff Cooper, replied that 'Mr Noel Coward has gone to the United States on a short visit with the knowledge and approval of my Right Honourable Friend . . . Mr Coward is not acting in the function of an ambassador. His qualifications are that he possesses a contact with certain sections of opinion which are very difficult to reach through ordinary sources.' An MP asked, 'Is the Parliamentary Secretary aware that a feeling is rising in this country that if a man has a certain publicity value and money, he can get out of this country quite easily, often on short visits, and probably not returning, during a time when this country is going through great stress and anxiety?' Nicolson blustered: 'I think that is grossly unfair.'

There was perhaps a subtext to the protests, echoed in Joyce Grenfell's comments to her mother: 'What do you think about Noel Coward going to America? . . . I think it is a great mistake. Everyone knows his past history and altho' these things don't matter in one if merely writing stuff for the theatre, it is definitely a pity . . . that the man who represents this country at a time like this should be famous as a "queer".'

In New York, Coward made a statement to the press. He patiently explained (so far as he could) the nature of his mission, and said, 'It seems unfortunate that they [the House of Commons] have so much time to waste at the moment. I was sent here to take a message to the Ambassador in Washington and to discuss with him certain possibilities for the future. It is a pity for them to talk before they make sure of their facts.' This was true enough, but had Coward been more circumspect, the outcome might have been different. He was in fact intensely annoyed by the incident, and concerned that it would jeopardise his work, dissuading Stephenson from using him. Stephenson reassured him, saying he had telegraphed London to reaffirm his confidence in Coward, and Noel continued with his mission. It was decided that he should work for British War Relief, which would give him a good excuse for travelling around the country.

The US press, sharply divided over whether America should enter the war, remarked on Coward's appearance at the World's Fair at Flushing Meadow. Among the bullet-holed Spitfires and Hurricanes and a specimen air-raid shelter at the British Pavilion, Noel spoke to bolster support for the war effort. 'The actor was bronzed and well-fed', noted one unfavourable journalist, Sylvia Taylor, 'but oldish, heavy, and lined. He walked in with his characteristic easy stride, neat in his Bond Street suit of dark cloth, and . . . came forward to the podium. And I recalled his autobiography . . . and how he had boasted of escaping service in the last war, and here he was escaping service in this war.' Coward's masculinity was impugned: '. . . I also recalled how he was worshipped by so many weak young men, who thought of him as their belle ideal [sic] of playwright, society darling and paragon of virtue. And also of the remark made by an MP that Coward should be called home to England, for he was a poor representative of British democracy . . .'

As Coward spoke, the writer 'noticed little Lord Lothian . . . who happens to be listed as a member of the Anglo-German Union, and as a fascist. Well, now . . . Coward – and Lord Lothian.' Coward's relationship with Lothian was not as warm as he indicates in *Future Indefinite*; not surprising, considering Lothian's pro-Munich stance in 1938. But America was facing its own crisis of isolation, and criticism of the playwright did not abate; further press coverage noted that Coward, 'who is fast becoming Noel-fussbudget, is not making himself too popular with his New York British colleagues . . . complaining about certain young Englishmen who are still in mufti. Noel is a little too quick to call some of his countrymen by his last name – a great deal of what he is saying in the theatrical district would sound better if he were in uniform – over there and not in the well defined safety zone of New York.' Having tried to persuade the Oliviers to return to London (and professing himself disappointed at their refusal), Noel announced that all English actors of military age should go home, a remark which caused Gladys Cooper to publicly cut him in Hollywood.

A happier aspect of his visit was a reunion with Gertrude Lawrence, who had married Richard Stoddard Aldrich, the manager of a theatre in Cape Cod. Coward had sent her a message after her fourth of July wedding, 'Dear Mrs A. Hooray Hooray/ At last you are deflowered/ On this as every other day/ I love you, Noel Coward'. Moss Hart was negotiating a contract with Lawrence for *Lady in the Dark* and sought Coward's assistance in persuading her. She eventually signed, and on the first night of the show Coward sent another telegram: 'Hope you get a warm hand on your opening'.

But Coward's position in America remained difficult, and his sense of uselessness sometimes reduced him to tears. In desperation, he turned to Richard Casey, the Australian minister to the States, who suggested that he travel to Australia to entertain the troops as a guest of the Government. Not only could it be seen as a patriotic duty (away from the carping American press), it was another chance for travel, always exciting to him, even if he would be paying for it himself. Lord Lothian was consulted, and thought it an excellent idea, saying the situation in America would have changed by the time he returned (he was probably relieved to be rid of this amateur ambassador). Duff Cooper agreed too, on the proviso that Coward was back by March 1941, when there would be 'something of great importance' to be discussed.

After a summer of sweaty diplomacy and part-time espionage, Coward organised an apartment in New York for his mother and Aunt Vida for the duration, then left for California and the Pacific. A surprise detour in the three-week voyage to Australia was via Japan and the China Sea, which delighted Coward, who had fond memories of the area. But at Yokohama passengers were forbidden by the Japanese to disembark; Coward persuaded his table steward to get him a crew pass, and disguised as a 'tough American seaman' he set off with 'the boys' on a bar and brothel crawl. Noel found this disappointingly dull, but he was surprised at the number of Germans they met, information which he duly noted for 'Little Bill's' benefit.

His reception in Sydney gave Coward an attack of nerves; microphones were thrust at him and flashbulbs popped incessantly. Unable, for once, to produce his 'Mayfair witticisms', Noel choked out, 'Hello, Australia – I am very happy to be here', before being whisked off to his hotel.

His seven-week tour was taxing, and sometimes hazardous. At a military concert at Ingleburn Camp outside Melbourne, some 'diggers' tried to shout Coward down before he had even begun. He merely announced that he was going to sing for three-quarters of an hour, whether they liked it or not; and at the end of his performance was applauded enough to know that they had. His reception by the 1700 soldiers was enthusiastic, and the press ran photographs of Noel at the piano, surrounded by husky Australian troops, a row of them sitting on top of the instrument, their bare legs hanging over the keys as he played.

His government-appointed entourage included an ADC, a secretary and 'a fair, tough young man', Jim Wilcox, who acted as his press representative and saw him through the exhausting coast-to-coast itinerary. He attended the Australian premiere of *Design for Living* at the Minerva Theatre in Sydney, where police had to restrain enthusiastic crowds; he was mobbed by 900 'business girls' at a Red Cross lunch. Melbourne, Adelaide, Perth, Fremantle and Canberra passed in a flash. At Brisbane exhaustion overcome him, and Cairns, Townsville and

Darwin had to be cancelled as he recuperated by sunbathing and surfing, before returning to the fray.

His visit to New Zealand was less fraught. The country had a more leisurely pace, and his engagements were fewer and farther between. However, the crowds were appreciative, and welcomed Noel loudly; he rubbed noses with Maoris, played to several thousand men at a troop concert outside Dunedin, and evaded (just) censorship of his lyrics in Wellington, where the mayoress informed him that 'The Stately Homes of England' was an insult to the Mother Country. Noel demurred, and the lady replied, 'You see – he can't take criticism!'

On 3 February 1941 Coward flew from New Zealand on a Clipper whose captain, Crowther Beardsell, had flown him from Batavia to Singapore in 1936. On Canton Island, Coward stayed in a luxurious American-style hotel, and visited the official British Residents, the Flemings, who raised and lowered the Union Jack every day, and saluted the king; Coward used the endearing pair as the basis of his short story 'Mr and Mrs Edgehill'. Canton Island was a theatrical setting, where 'local conflicts and dramas and comedies swell to terrific proportions', all theatrically enclosed by the reef, *Point Valaine* style. Additional drama was provided by a cyclone, which meant Noel had to stay sixteen days, by the end of which he felt he had been living on the island for months.

He returned to Britain via Los Angeles, Bermuda, the Azores and Lisbon, full of anticipation about the job 'Little Bill' was to offer him. 'I had had some intensive briefing in New York and Washington and was now in a state of, alas, premature exaltation.' But even before he reached Bermuda, the whole operation was called off. 'A greater power than we could contradict has thwarted our interests', Stephenson informed his would-be secret agent. Stephenson had received a telegram, sent in code from London:

APRIL 2ND FOR NOEL COWARD (A) REGRETTABLE PUBLICITY GIVEN TO YOUR VISIT LONDON BY ENTIRE BRITISH PRESS WHICH WOULD INCREASE ON YOUR ARRIVAL UNFORTUNATELY MAKES ENTIRE SCHEME IMPRACTI-CABLE (B) COMPLETE SECRECY IS FOUNDATION OF OUR WORK AND IT WOULD NOW BE IMPOSSIBLE FOR ANY OF OUR PEOPLE TO CONTACT YOU IN ENGLAND WITHOUT INCURRING PUBLICITY (C) WE ARE ALL VERY DISAPPOINTED AS WE HAD LOOKED FORWARD TO WORKING WITH YOU BUT THERE ARE NO FURTHER STEPS TO BE TAKEN . . .

'God, what enemies I must have', Coward wrote in his diary, suspecting Churchill and Beaverbrook (then Minister of Supply). The tabloid press reported his American and Australian travels as though they had been holidays; touring the tropics and singing a few songs sounded like an easy life to blitzed Londoners.

Coward's homecoming was perforce not happy. Press interviews were held at Gerald Road, principally to answer the questions raised in Coward's absence. Where had he been, what was he doing, whose money was he spending? Noel reprimanded the gentlemen of Fleet Street for their less than fair treatment of him; sensational reports of his exploits had no basis in truth, he told them. They nodded amiably; the next day none of it was reported correctly or accurately. Having broken his no-interview rule, Coward felt betrayed once again; such incidents did not endear him to a country whose ways he came increasingly to deplore. This opinion was reinforced when Anthony Eden (whom Coward had considered a friend) 'virtually cut' him in the Carlton Grill because of the publicity surrounding Coward's foreign travels. ('A foolish mistake on his part', Noel wrote, 'although perfectly consistent with his career.')

He resumed his place in London life, now under the threat of invasion. One evening at Gerald Road Noel and his friends discussed what they would do if the Nazis did come; the debate began seriously, but ended with Noel donning one of Gladys Calthrop's turbans and a pair of high-heeled shoes, mincing up and down the street soliciting the Gestapo. But the destructiveness of the war was made vivid on 16 April, when Noel came home to find the skylights blown in, and Dallas Brooks, who had been staying there, hit by the bedroom chandelier. As Coward helped his friend, another bomb fell; this time Burton Mews was hit, and the office badly damaged. Noel ran into the street with a pocketful of morphine capsules to administer first aid, but was told that the injured had been taken to hospital. Just then, two well-dressed girls passed by, 'You know, dear, the trouble with all this is you could rick your ankle.' Noel burst out laughing; the warden suspected hysteria and recommended he go inside at once.

The full extent of the damage to the studio was evident the next day: shattered windows and fallen ceilings, and a 'hopeless, beastly smell in the air. I suddenly felt miserable and most profoundly angry.' Unlike the Eastenders who had recourse only to the Underground, Coward could move into the Savoy for the duration. Considered 'safe' because of its iron and concrete construction, the hotel on the Embankment had already become a home from home for Margot Asquith, who brazened out the blitz in her eyrie there. With the Thames a known flight path for German bombers, it was not unusual for the Savoy to shake with the nearby explosions, flushing out the hotel's odder occupants. During one midnight raid, Coward saw a vision descending the hotel staircase, in a dressing gown more lavish than any he owned, 'every hair pinned on end'. It was Stephen Tennant, the flamboyant aesthete.

The move to an hotel had made Coward a tourist in his own town, and he felt two unusual emotions: relief at being back, and surprise at the 'charm and quality' of London, re-evaluated in its threatened state. This was a cue for a sentimental song, and he promptly wrote it. 'London Pride' struck the right chord with his public (whose allegiance he had been in danger of losing). Created from the cry of a lavender seller, the song was a paean of pride, and no less effective for that.

Three days later, Coward, Calthrop and a friend from the RAF named Bill Taylor were dancing in the crowded Savoy Grill. Two bombs dropped on the Embankment, the second blowing in the doors of the restaurant. 'With gallantry, tinged, I suspect, with a strong desire to show off', Noel took to the platform where Carroll Gibbons was playing the piano 'and sang several songs before anyone could stop me'. He was joined by Judy Campbell, singing the song she made famous, 'A Nightingale Sang in Berkeley Square'. Two days later, the Savoy offered him a river suite for the rate of his single room. He was now without a home. One weekend he travelled down to Kent to visit Gladys Calthrop and Patience Erskine, and went over to Goldenhurst. Emptied of its furniture and commandeered as an army headquarters, it seemed it would never be his again.

20

Play Parade

It is positively frightening to think what may happen if he outlives his success – at the moment he is on the highest wave of his career so far . . . But his hand twitches nervously for more triumphs – and the applause of the matinee audience does not satisfy him – he is waiting already for the evening audience to arrive.

Cecil Beaton on Noel Coward, war diary

BY 1941, Coward's finances were under pressure, partly because none of his plays was being performed. At the beginning of the war, the government had closed down all non-essential media: BBC radio was reduced to non-stop news and organ music, and its television transmissions had been suspended for the duration. Theatres and places of entertainment were closed, putting the entire profession out of work; Bernard Shaw called it a 'masterstroke of unimaginative stupidity', depriving the people of something which might boost their morale. Two weeks later, the authorities gave in to the entertainment industry and the ban was lifted, but only for performances during daylight.

Wartime required a particular sort of entertainment, and Coward knew he had to come up with a good commercial proposition. In his diary for 22 April he wrote, 'Spent morning with Lorn discussing financial troubles which are considerable. Also discussed play as possible solution. Title *Blithe Spirit*. Very gay, superficial comedy about a ghost. Feel it may be good.' The scenario had evolved from the idea of a large French house (perhaps Elsie Mendl's Villa Trianon) visited by the ghosts of its past. Coward and Joyce Carey (also writing a play) set off for the Italianate folly of Portmeirion – Clough Williams-Ellis's fantasy village in Wales – and the plot for his new play emerged. Just seven days after his arrival, *Blithe Spirit* was all but complete.

'Disdaining archness and false modesty', Coward knew it would be a hit. 'My gift for comedy had obviously profited from its period of inactivity.' Such was the precision of his script that only two lines needed to be cut in production: for a man with a notoriously low threshold of boredom, it was a necessarily rapid talent. Coward was justified in being sanguine about *Blithe Spirit*: it is one of his most durable, best-constructed plays, with an adept plot and brilliant comic structure. He gave the formula of marriage and infidelity a twist with the introduction of the paranormal: a man whose dead wife returns to haunt him and his second wife. *Blithe Spirit* is set in an idyllic never-never land, itself an escape from the drastically changing 1940s. Madame Arcati became the scene-stealer; originally an unimportant role, Coward described to Cecil Beaton that 'a character takes hold . . . and writes itself', and Arcati 'had refused to leave the stage'. Clemence Dane declined the part created for her, and it was Margaret Rutherford who perfected the dotty eccentricity of the character, a foil for the sophistication of her sceptical hosts.

The story is akin to a supernatural *Private Lives*, with the barriers to communication being the abyss of the afterlife. But there is also a vague misogynism – the female as encumbrance to men. Vivian Matalon, who directed Coward in his last plays, thought '*Blithe Spirit* . . . the only play in which he is unpleasant about women. Condomine's mother nagged him, Elvira laid someone else on their honeymoon, Ruth is a shrew, Madame Arcati is a fool, even the maid has a perpetual cold.' Nonetheless, *Blithe Spirit* shines, a clever comedy brimming with style and elegance. It broke box-office records and confirmed that Noel Coward was worthy of his legend.

The play was put into rehearsal almost before Coward's fingers had left the typewriter keys. A John C. Wilson/H. M. Tennent production, under Beaumont's aegis, the cast was quickly settled: Ruth would be played by Fay Compton, Charles by Cecil Parker, and Elvira (the name came from Beaumont's housekeeper) by Kay Hammond. The casting of Margaret Rutherford as Madame Arcati was not so easy; when Coward sent the script to her, she returned it with a polite refusal. Beaumont decided to take Miss Rutherford out to lunch, to discover why she had turned the part down.

Rutherford was a character actress of distinction who had been a success as Miss Prism in revivals of *The Importance of Being Earnest*. She had had an extraordinary childhood: her father had murdered her grandfather, and was sent to Broadmoor; on his release the family went to India, where her mother hanged herself. Margaret was brought up by her aunt and, when she discovered her family history, became mentally unstable. Her condition improved when she was acting, but a doctor was often waiting in the wings with a sedative injection so she could continue. Little of this history was known to her fellow actors, although John Gielgud knew of her mental problems, and both Coward and Beaumont would have been aware of them.* Rutherford explained to Beaumont that she believed in spiritualism, and did not want to be party to its mockery. Beaumont pointed out that the play poked fun at *fake* mediums, not genuine ones, and that, as she was a fraud, mockery of Arcati was justified. Rutherford retorted, 'Will you explain how she raises *two* ghosts if she is a fake?' 'By chance, Margaret dear. Even fake mediums can have a stroke of luck and this doesn't stop them from being fakes, does it now?' The next day Rutherford rang to say she would do the play, on condition that it was played straight. 'I regard this as a very serious play, almost a tragedy. I don't see it as a comedy at all.' Beaumont declared, 'Of course, she always wanted to do it. She's far too sensible not to realise what a terribly good part it is. But she needed a face-saving way of saying "yes", and that's exactly what I gave her.'

The problem of creating a ghost (or two) on stage occupied Coward and Calthrop. They considered the Victorian trick of reflecting an actor in the wings on onstage glass, and even consulted members of the Magic Circle about spectral effects, but in the end Calthrop designed an all-white ensemble for Elvira, grey-white dress, face and hair to match.

Blithe Spirit opened in Manchester on 16 June, and in London on 2 July. Its first night in the West End did not augur well: 'The audience, socially impeccable from the journalistic point of view and mostly in uniform, had to walk across planks laid over the rubble caused by a recent air raid to see a light comedy about death.' Noel had hoped that the black humour of *Blithe Spirit* would coincide with the (less than blithe) spirit of the times, but it was met with catcalls of 'Rubbish' and 'Why should he get away with it!' and Graham Greene called the play 'a weary exhibition of bad taste'. John Gielgud did not think much of it either: 'I thought it was terribly over-written. It was a good joke, but he spun it out too much.'

---

* Around this time, Stephen Tennant proposed to Rutherford, but refused her admittance when she arrived for the weekend at his home, Wilsford Manor. She was later found by the butler in the coal cellar, eating coal.

Opposition also came from the clergy. In the *Star*, a Reverend James Colville contributed a piece entitled 'Should We Laugh at the Dead?' in which he opined that 'death and the hereafter' were not 'suitable subjects for farcical treatment'. Although his play made fun of the subject, Coward's interest in the supernatural was real, if sceptical. In the 1960s he went to a séance with Nancy Spain and Philip Astley, Gertrude Lawrence's former lover. The medium announced the departed Gertie's presence, calling for Noel; she was wearing her white Molyneux gown from *Private Lives*, reported the medium. 'Christ! It must be tatty by now', said Coward.

Despite the initially negative reaction to *Blithe Spirit*, it would run for an unprecedented 1997 performances. It remains one of Coward's most satisfying plays, its constant revival a testament to its enduring appeal.

Rehearsals for the play had been overshadowed by the sinking of Mountbatten's ship, HMS *Kelly*, off Crete on 23 May, with Mountbatten clinging to the bridge. When he surfaced he was machine-gunned by Junkers dive-bombers. Noel was relieved to hear that Dickie was safe, having acquitted himself bravely: the story was to provide Coward with an opportunity to show his own usefulness in the war effort.

Soon after *Blithe Spirit* opened, Coward was approached by the film producer Anthony Havelock-Allan, whom he had met in the early 1920s. Havelock-Allan was now working with Two Cities, a production company run by Filippo del Giudice, a colourful character addicted to fat cigars and dark glasses, who had made his name producing the film of Rattigan's *French Without Tears* in 1939. 'He got the idea that he wanted to make a big propaganda film', Havelock-Allan recalls. 'He thought it would do his reputation good, which was perfectly legitimate, and that it would also do the company some good.' Del Giudice wanted someone well known to write the piece, and suggested Coward, who said he would be glad to do it, so long as the subject was the Royal Navy, and he had complete control. Privately, his immediate reaction was negative; he respected neither the medium nor its methods. However, when he was dining with the Mountbattens, the tale of the loss of the *Kelly* provided the inspiration he needed. Here was the scenario for *In Which We Serve*: adventure, a patriotic tribute and a panegyric to his favourite service rolled into one.

The story made perfect drama, from Mountbatten's initial address to his crew – 'In my experience, I have always found that you cannot have an efficient ship unless you have a happy ship, and you cannot have a happy ship unless you have an efficient ship' (which Noel used almost word for word in his screenplay) – to the cowardice of a stoker who deserted his post, 'out of the 240 men on board this ship, 239 behaved as they ought . . . and as I expected them to'. For reasons of security and perhaps awareness of some antipathy towards his vaulting ambitions, Mountbatten did not want the film too closely based on his story, but his support made the project possible. (In fact, Mountbatten's story was one of recklessness: the *Kelly* spent only 57 days out of dry dock during more than eighteen months of service.) 'About three weeks later,' says Havelock-Allan, 'we got a telephone call, Noel saying "I have an idea".' But Coward realised that he did not know how films were made. He asked Ronald Neame, whose work he had seen and liked, to be the lighting-cameraman, and expressed a further need for someone to 'hold my hand . . . to be my righthand man'. Thus began Coward's fruitful relationship with David Lean.

Lean was a celebrated film editor and putative director, who had been turning down offers to direct 'quota-quickies', made cheaply in England by American companies to meet a requirement that a certain percentage of films shown should be British in origin. He was suggested to Coward as an excellent technician and editor, and Noel realised that Lean's knowledge and ability would make the film technically possible while allowing him to retain authority and his artistic reputation. An attractive character, thirty-three, handsome and always elegantly dressed, Lean's contribution was vital to Coward's work in the 1940s.

Having set up the machinery for production, Coward went off to Plymouth to do the necessary research. The naval base held other attractions too: Michael Redgrave, with whom Coward was now romantically involved, was stationed there. Redgrave, nine years his junior and with the good looks of a matinee idol, had been a socialist and aesthete at Cambridge, and took up a stage career in 1934, following the method acting theories of Stanislavsky. Professionally and politically, he could not have been further from Noel, but emotionally there was mutual appeal. Redgrave had met Coward through the Actors' Orphanage committee, of which Redgrave was a member, and Noel invited him to the second night of *Blithe Spirit*. Redgrave joined the navy as an Ordinary Seaman in July 1941, and the friendship grew with the bond of matters maritime. 'Noel is an expert on slang', Redgrave said. 'He knew more naval slang than me in spite of the time I spent in the Navy.' That summer Redgrave asked Coward for some new songs to sing in a ship's concert. He was sent 'three or four . . . including one . . . "Could you please oblige us with a Bren Gun?"' Redgrave had just learnt it (in the lavatory after lights-out) when he received a cable about the lines, 'Colonel McNamara who/ Was in Calcutta in ninety-two,/ Emerged from his retirement for the war'. Noel cabled, PLEASE CHANGE MCNAMARA TO MONTMORENCY STOP THERE IS A REAL AND VERY ANGRY MCNAMARA IN THE WAR OFFICE.

The intensity of his relationship with Redgrave was obvious to contemporaries. Redgrave was often at the cottage in Buckinghamshire which Coward took over during the filming of *In Which We Serve*. Bert Lister, then his valet, remembered his employer's excitement on finishing a week's shooting on the film and about to leave for Plymouth for a rendezvous with Redgrave; Rachel Kempson, later Redgrave's wife, told Coward how upset she had been when her husband chose to spend his last night before leaving on active service with Noel instead of her.

In mid-August, Coward visited the Home Fleet at Scapa Flow for research purposes; a cruise on the *Nigeria* helped his imaginative efforts, as did frequent trips to Portsmouth (familiar to Noel from his childhood sojourns in the area), where he stayed with the Packers at their house, Fareham Croft. 'Bertie' Packer was captain of the naval school, HMS *Excellent*, and his wife recalled that 'much of Noel's material was gathered there'. She was taken aback to discover, on viewing the completed film, that she too had inadvertently provided material for the project: 'I was astonished . . . to hear the Captain's wife . . . quote word for word what I had said at dinner at Fareham Croft. Noel had drawn me out and right after dinner dashed upstairs and I guess he wrote it down. It was to the effect that a naval wife knew and accepted her husband's ship as his "grey mistress" – a rival she could never conqueror but one she came to love.'

Official encouragement for the project also came from Sidney Bernstein, now Films Adviser to the Ministry of Information. The Minister, Brendan Bracken, had argued that the project would monopolise the scarce resources of the film industry, and asked Bernstein to dissuade Coward from making the film. Bernstein asked Noel if he really thought he could play Mountbatten: 'Of course I could', said Coward. 'Aren't I an actor?' With heavyweights such as Bernstein and Mountbatten behind him, Coward felt reassured that the film would receive its proper treatment.

Three months after their initial discussions, the production team were invited to hear Noel read a rough draft. 'There was a slight silence at the end,' says Havelock-Allan, 'and with one voice we said "I'm afraid Mr Coward, that story would take some eight or nine hours on the screen." It started before the war, with scenes in the Café de Paris, scenes in the China station, then ... in the West India station.' Coward bowed to their superior knowledge. 'So we went away, and we wrote something completely different ... we decided we'd start with the laying of the keel of a destroyer in 1939, and make it the story of the ship, from the time it was thought of to the time it sank off Crete. Coward approved, and we were ready to start casting.'

The most contentious casting was Coward's own. The company were concerned that the 'dressing-gown and cigarette-holder' image would not align with a 'tough naval captain', and there was open criticism in the press. Further advance criticism came from the censors, who thought that showing one of His Majesty's ships actually sinking was a threat to morale; intense lobbying was required to retain the all-important scene. Noel, meanwhile, readied himself to don uniform as Captain Kinross.

In January 1942 Coward and Gladys Calthrop (Art Supervisor on the film) leased neighbouring cottages close to Denham Studios. John Sutro, the film producer, and his wife Gillian were also living nearby, and one freezing snowy night, invited Coward to dinner, together with Cecil Beaton. 'Noel and I have never got on well', Beaton admitted to his diary. 'We have said bad things about one another's works ... However, here we were, face to face.'

Beaton's acidulous account is a vivid glimpse of the forty-two-year-old playwright at war. The Sutros sat in relative silence while the two men talked. 'Gin, burgundy and a lot of apricot brandy loosened any remaining restrictions', Beaton wrote. 'Noel never stopped the pace for two hours. He got very squiffy – his eyes closed up and his face became drawn and haggard but he spoke with lucidity and brilliance.' Artfully employing his accustomed charm, Coward told Beaton he admired his war work, 'I've been hiccuping off at the outbreak of the war – thinking I'd done a wonderful thing to give up those two plays [*Present Laughter* and *This Happy Breed*] and do a job that anyone could have done. You've done so much better. You used to stand for everything I dislike – I've been beastly about your being Elsa Maxwell's darling and Elsie Mendl's puss – but I've been wrong. Let's be friends ...' Later they went to Coward's cottage 'to drink a huge container of cocktail'. Beaton's acute eye took in the decor: photographs of the Kents and Mountbattens, Toscanini and Rachmaninov on display, and a mixture of 'comfort and "art"' which Cecil thought revealed 'something lacking in him'.

It was impossible for Beaton to disguise his envy: 'He talks of himself as having had such tremendous success [and] glamour during the last fifteen years that he wouldn't think it terrible if a bomb killed him today. *Private Lives* . . . will go down to History as a play by Congreve or Wilde! He talks of *Blithe Spirit* as being a "bloody good play". He will not talk about the birthpangs of the creation for the reason that there are none, or if so they are not interesting to him. "If I type easily then I know the stuff is good!"' Late into the night, Coward spoke emotionally of his childhood and the theatre, and it was one o'clock before the two embraced and went separately to bed.

The shooting of *In Which We Serve* began on 5 February. Coward graciously deferred to the production team's knowledge. 'I'm much too old to . . . start learning that kind of technique,' he told Havelock-Allan, 'so will put myself entirely in your hands.' Havelock-Allan still defends Coward's decision to play Captain Kinross: it was 'a measure of his skill as an actor, he was able to play lots of parts for which he was totally unsuited . . . his performance was always interesting, if not quite convincing. He was enormously limited, physically. He moved very peculiarly, one of the most extraordinary walkers I knew. His hands down to his sides – his fingers always together. He would walk very quickly, in short steps. He had very hunched shoulders, and he said he always looked like a Chinaman . . . Yet he played so-called good-looking young men . . . convincingly. His knowledge of acting, and his timing, were absolutely impeccable.'

Coward's presence on set seemed to elevate the business of film-making to a higher level. The tall figure picking his way elegantly over the cables, assuming his character of Captain Kinross with unselfconscious ease: here was someone more than a movie star, distinguished by the fluidity of his movement, the subtlety of his gestures, the details of his appearance. The fact that Coward was not classically handsome did not matter: the effect was of someone undeniably attractive, and important. It was an effect carefully studied and assiduously maintained.

His performance in the film is an approximation of a naval captain, a Cowardian impression. Dedicated to the Royal Navy, the film opens – to the strains of a score composed by Noel – with the words, 'This is the story of a ship' (the HMS *Torrin*) and scenes of its construction; soon the ship is in action off Crete. Neame's atmospheric camerawork creates the semi-documentary tone of the film, cut with Lean's flash-backs and Coward's mannered dialogue. In a scene on the ship's bridge, which might as well be the *Private Lives* balcony, an officer remarks of the sunset, 'Someone sent me a calendar like that last Christmas, sir.' 'Did it have a squadron of Dorniers in the upper right-hand corner?' enquires Kinross. 'No, sir.' 'That's where Art parts company with Reality', says the captain. 'I believe you're right, sir. Cigarette?'

Such episodes are contrasted by violent action sequences: the battle raging over Crete, followed by the captain's order to abandon ship. As the ship sinks, the camera closes in on Coward floundering underwater, an out-take from *The Scoundrel*. His life unreels before him; he is driving home to his wife Alix (Celia Johnson) and children Bobbie (played by nine-year-old Daniel Massey) and Lavinia (Ann Stephens), a perfect middle-class family: it is odd to see Coward play the conventional father. The dialogue seems archaic and hilarious to modern audiences. 'Is there going to be a war?' asks Alix. 'Yes, I think there is', answers Kinross. 'Does the chintz look all right?' ask his wife. 'Absolutely first-class', he replies.

Reality returns with the shipwreck, as survivors swim for a dinghy; Noel's stroke is far from Olympic standard as he saves crew members. Again the film follows the lives and loves of the various men clinging to the life-raft: Bernard Miles and Joyce Carey in lower-middle-class scenes reminiscent of 'Fumed Oak'; John Mills at Christmas dinner with his family, *This Happy Breed* revisited. The early years of the war, the Battle of Britain and Dunkirk, are seen through 'ordinary' eyes, and there is a downbeat ending: Miles's wife and mother-in-law are killed in the Blitz; Richard Attenborough deserts his post, and many of the *Torrin*'s crew are lost.

One film historian, Gerald Pratley, wrote, 'it is important to remember . . . that it is a motion picture about war made in wartime, during a period of history when no one spoke about "anti"-war films. It reflected quite accurately the sentiments of the three classes which made up British society, working, middle and upper class, in the simplified way in which all people then looked at war.' Coward's performance is an English caricature, more theatre than film, a personal interpretation of Englishness, patriotism and the 'Britain-can-take-it' mentality in which Noel was steeped. His speeches as Kinross are in the mood of *This Happy Breed*, exhortative and belligerent; they contrast sharply with a scene in the opening sequences when a copy of the *Daily Express* floats by with the headline NO WAR THIS YEAR. Beaverbrook was enraged by this slur on his paper. Coward was already a target; now Beaverbrook made 'Laard Mountbatten' the subject of a personal vendetta in his newspapers.

Much of the film's impact came from its cast, which included up-and-coming actors who would become household names: John Mills, Richard Attenborough and Celia Johnson.* Johnson would define the Coward heroine for the public in the 1940s; quintessentially English and irredeemably middle class, a domesticated Amanda perhaps, with a voice so well-bred that it ought to have had a pedigree of its own. She landed this, her first major film role, by uncharacteristic means. Usually shy, she saw Coward at a party late in 1941 and, knowing that he was casting the film, asked for the part. He invited her for a screen test, where they 'talked for hours ... until we'd exhausted every topic of conversation. Then suddenly Noel began to spout bits of "The Walrus and the Carpenter" at me. What was the sun doing? he said. Shining on the sea, I told him exuberantly, shining with all its might. If seven maids with seven mops swept it for half a year, he said, considering the situation gravely, do you suppose (and he dropped his voice because he wanted a very sad bit for the camera) that they could get it clear? I doubt it, I told him with an absolutely miserable face, and shed a bitter tear ... It looked quite crazy in the rushes. But Noel seemed to like it and I got the part.' Coward admired her professionalism, and the fact that before an important take, she could be sitting 'doing the *Times* crossword, lay down the paper and pencil, go on and do the scene, tears in the eyes, come back and finish "Nine Down"'.

The long and protracted business of filming bored Coward with its endless set-ups, early calls and long periods of apparent idleness. 'After six weeks,' recalls Havelock-Allan, 'he was so confident of what was happening that he only came to the studio when there were scenes in which he was involved.' He found the British film industry 'extravagant to the point of lunacy and, on the whole, fairly inefficient'. But he gave full credit to David Lean, and the fact that Lean was able to stamp his personal style upon a production overshadowed by Coward's looming (and egotistical) presence says much for his ability.

Coward felt sufficiently proud of his work on *In Which We Serve* to invite the royal family to visit the set. This was good publicity, of

---

* Celia Johnson began acting in the 1920s. G. B. Stern's *Debonair* brought her to critical attention, and she was successful in Keith Winter's *Old Music* in 1937. She married Peter Fleming, brother of Ian, in 1935.

course, duly shown on newsreels across the country as a taster for the film itself, as well as underlining Noel's connexion with royalty. It was intensely important to him that the film should succeed, not only because it was his first film effort or because it was his tribute to the Royal Navy, but because it was his contribution to the war effort, and had to be seen as such. Its success was confirmed in 1943, when Coward was awarded a special Academy Award for 'outstanding production achievement', his first and only Oscar.*

The Second World War came at a good time for Noel Coward. After the madcap Twenties and the bleak Thirties, the war redefined British-ness and served as an antidote to the disillusion and decadence of the inter-war period. Its revival of the values of empire and Britain's greatness was congenial to Coward: the quality of fortitude required (and mythologised) by the war neatly coincided with the fortitude displayed by Noel (an ironic turnaround of his performance in the First War). Whether assumed or not, it made little difference: the values he espoused dovetailed with the Dunkirk/Blitz/'Britain-can-take-it' spirit, and he was able to exploit them fully. *Cavalcade* had announced his patriotism; the films, plays and concert tours of the early 1940s helped cement his image in the hearts and minds of the British public.

But he was only reaping the rewards of hard work. Like any superstar, Coward had sought to stay one step ahead of his public; tantalising them, changing with them and for them, manipulating the limelight. His celebrity status between the wars led naturally to a role as unofficial ambassador during it. In his wartime travels to Europe, America, and the Middle and Far East, he represented the apparently undamaged sway of the imperial power clad in Savile Row armour. Churchill's exhortation, to go and sing while the guns were firing, might have vexed Coward, but it was good casting, for his best contribution was his image, his representation of Englishness.

Yet some found Coward's ubiquity too much for them. The diplomat Charles Ritchie recorded a party given by Lady Victor Paget for Beatrice Lillie; among 'a gathering of pansies and theatrical blondes', he saw Coward, who sang 'London Pride' 'in a manner which I found all the more revolting for being sincere'. Ritchie saw with some acuity the changing world of wartime London; with other guests 'Lord S. and

---

* The film was released in the United States in December 1942, when it was used in conjunction with a wartime campaign to conserve rubber.

latest girlfriend and Hore-Belisha – an obscene spectacle', and David Herbert 'looking more *racé* than he knew', Ritchie described the evening as 'a réchauffé of a gay twenties party with everyone looking that much older and trying to get back something which is not there any more'.

'London Pride' was a soundtrack for Coward's simplified war: banal but touching; an evocation of emotion, an emblem of resistance. Ironic then that its composer was now accused of going on one foreign trip too many, and was punished by the law for so doing. In the autumn of 1941, Coward was summoned to appear in court, accused of having flouted British currency regulations by taking more than the permitted limit of pounds to the United States with him on his last visit.

To Noel the whole affair was a case of 'celebrity-baiting'. He was outraged at his treatment, the result (as he saw it) of a concerted campaign by the press and Parliament. (After the war, Coward was told by Fanny Holtzmann that the prosecution had been initiated by 'a lot of the Hollywood and New York British renegades, livid with jealousy about me and resentful that I should ask them to subscribe to the Orphans [Actors' Orphanage Fund] and not subscribe myself'.)

To be thus rewarded was indeed galling for a man whose patriotism was so publicly displayed. Represented by the larger-than-life figure of Dingwall Bateson, Coward went to trial on 30 October. The prosecution tried to establish that his US trip had not been on official business at all. They also alleged that Coward had sold shares 'without the Treasury's consent' (one hundred shares of American Can, receiving $11,420; one hundred Chrysler Corporation shares for $8599; and one hundred General Foods Corporation shares for $4798). Bateson contested that his client was 'morally innocent', and that, being a man who was 'bored with business', he was ignorant of the regulations.* Noel maintained that he 'always left most of his financial affairs to his American representative, John C. Wilson, who had bought and sold stocks without his specific knowledge'. It was added that Mr Coward could not pay a 'large fine' (a punitive sum of £43,062 was being

---

* Coward provided an itemised list of his expenses from October 1939 to May 1941, an intriguing insight into his finances at the time. Rent of hotel suite and country house, £3270; travel, £770; wages, £970; shares bought and contributions to theatrical ventures, £4908; storage and repayment of loans, £460; sent to Paris, £2660; amusements, restaurants, etc, £200; apartment, expenses, £590; cash, £190; theatrical charities, £13; war charities, £2; income tax, £280; medical odds and ends, £90. To counter any criticism of the figures for charitable donations, 'Mr Coward testified that the charities listed were by no means the limit of his contributions, but only those included within the charge.'

quoted; George Arliss had recently been fined £4500 for a similar offence).

The presiding judge accepted defence evidence that Coward could not be expected to live in America without expenses, and commented on Noel's financial vagueness. The outcome was a guilty verdict, with a nominal fine of £200 plus costs, but the ordeal was not yet over. He was brought before the Mansion House to answer questions on his American securities, and here Jack Wilson's mismanagement resulted in a fine of £1600.

War news worsened during the autumn of 1942: Singapore fell, and the Japanese invaded Sumatra and Burma. The navy losses hit Coward particularly hard, as they were men and ships he knew; Gladys Calthrop's son, Hugo, a naval captain, had been killed in Burma. The defiance of *In Which We Serve* seemed all the more necessary. The premiere was held on 17 September in aid of naval charities. 'The preponderance of naval uniforms and gold lace gave considerable *cachet* to the occasion', Noel noted with satisfaction. Its success countered the bad publicity of the court case, and his next career move capitalised on this new public profile. After discussions with Beaumont, he agreed to direct a twenty-eight-week provincial tour of *Present Laughter*, *This Happy Breed* and *Blithe Spirit*, to be dubbed *Play Parade*. Noel assembled a cast headed by himself, and including Joyce Carey, Dennis Price and Beryl Measor. There were new faces, one of which was James Donald, a good-looking and sensitive young Scottish actor who had appeared in *In Which We Serve*, and twenty-six-year-old actress-singer, the elegant and beautiful Judy Campbell. Another member of the entourage was Charles Russell, who had also played a small part in *In Which We Serve*. He recalled 'escaping being one of [Noel's] boys' when he declined an invitation from Coward to go out for a drink, but was subsequently invited to stage-manage and understudy on the *Play Parade* tour.

From the tedious sound stages of Denham, Coward had returned to the more comfortable territory of the theatre, appearing for two weeks as stand-in for Cecil Parker in the London production of *Blithe Spirit*, his first stage appearance since *Tonight at 8.30* in New York in 1937. During this stint, news came of the Duke of Kent's fatal air crash. Coward felt close to tears at that night's performance, and did indeed cry at the funeral at Windsor, in memory of a nineteen-year friendship. He had often seen the Kents during the filming of *In Which We Serve*, as their house, Coppins, was close by. Judy Campbell was told by

Gladys Calthrop that 'Noel was finding it very hard to cope with'. She assumed there was more to the relationship than just friendship: 'I know he was in love with Alan Webb, and Keith Winter . . . He seemed to be unlucky in love.' Others were less sympathetic; after Kent's funeral, his cousin the Marquess of Carisbrooke (himself homosexual) told Coward, 'You know of course, Noel, that you can never be Dowager Duke of Kent.'

The adventurous project of *Play Parade* went well. There were none of the customary squabbles or behind-the-scenes fights that usually accompanied such tours, although the privations of wartime Britain made it a very different experience from pre-war excursions. Luxury hotels and cars were now replaced by the blackout, food rationing and air raids. Nonetheless, conditions were better than most Britons were having to face, and Coward admitted, 'I was engaged on a pleasant and profitable acting job which contributed nothing actively to the war effort.' Foreseeing a bad press for his apparent evasion of 'real' war work, Coward gave four to six concerts a week in munitions factories and hospitals in the tour towns. His accompanist was Robb Stewart, a rather fey Mancunian habitually garbed in dirty mac and shabby, much-darned evening dress. Stewart took over Elsie April's function as Coward's amanuesis, although with some trepidation; April apparently warned him against Coward's predilection for plagiarism: 'Don't show him any of your music.'

'Robb was beautiful,' Bert Lister recalled, 'he'd stand by Noel and say something like "the second violin is too low" and Noel would shout it out as if he'd thought of it.' Coward seemed to put up with his accompanist's eccentricities for the sake of his talent. Lister's wife added, 'Robb used to say . . . in his camp Manchester accent, when he was late for a show, "I'm terribly sorry Noelie, I had a blackout." He was the only one allowed to call him "Noelie".'

The contrast between the two people with Coward on his canteen concerts could not have been greater; the tramplike Stewart and the glamorous Judy Campbell. Campbell found the *Play Parade* tour 'great fun – Noel took great care of me'. Driving to the concerts, he would give her tips, as Hawtrey had done for him: ' "Never gesture below the waist, always above it. Always make the audience believe they are your honoured guests, take your time, don't hurry. Never appear to be nervous . . ." And although Noel didn't believe in drinking before a theatrical performance, it didn't matter so much with the concerts, so we'd have a nip of gin from a hip flask before going on.

'We visited the navy hospitals in Portsmouth, and one of them had a ward for mentally-disturbed sailors . . . Noel and I would work our way round the wards, he starting at one end, and I at another. That way I discovered how truly the men loved him, because I "did" the beds he'd just done. They called him "Captain Coward", because a lot of them had been in *In Which We Serve*, and they were surprised that Noel remembered their names. It was a trick he had, he told me, "like royalty – it's something I've picked up".' Life imitated art imitating life: Kinross and Mountbatten likewise made a point of recalling their crew's surnames. 'Afterwards we were having drinks, and were just about to leave – Noel was very good at leavetaking – when they asked him to go and see someone who was about to have "deep sleep" treatment. When some mental cases are so disturbed, they put them to sleep for a day and a night. Anyway, this poor sailor had been shipwrecked in the North Sea three times, and had been stranded in freezing water for hours, and had fishbite – the fish actually bite your legs . . . Noel . . . stayed there for well over half an hour, talking to the boy in the dark, telling him it would be all right. Later we got a letter from the hospital saying that Noel had done more for that boy than all their treatment could.'

Coward was less of a hit with ordinary factory workers. Few seemed interested, at best listening politely, at worst considering the perform-ance a patronising gesture. Often, no sooner had they set up than a buzzer sounded and the employees trooped off back to work. Noel decided his own songs were not appropriate, and reverted to standards like 'If You Were the Only Girl in the World' and 'There'll Always Be an England', to little effect. 'They really wanted to hear Vera Lynn, or Workers' Playtime', says Campbell. Coward concluded that he would rather perform for a group of 'hostile aborigines' than to 'over-tired, and obviously ravenous, factory girls' and a soundtrack of metal trays clattering with lunchtime crockery. By the end of the year, the idea was jettisoned.

Cecil Beaton joined the company in Bristol to take photographs of the productions. He judged *This Happy Breed* 'a first rate play – a real play – of tremendous reality and humorous understanding of human nature. It's baffling to me how anyone of Noel's standing can have written it. For sheer egomania I have never known anything like him. It is positively frightening to think what may happen if he outlives his success – at the moment he is on the highest wave of his career so far.

He is surrounded by a court of admirers and goes from one victory to another. But his hand twitches nervously for more triumphs – and the applause of the matinee audience does not satisfy him – he is waiting already for the evening audience to arrive. Off the stage he must continuously tell of his excellent tributes: "Really this hotel – they call me urgently . . . to sign a football for the boy servants" – "Bring those press cuttings back to the hotel for me to read" – "Doesn't matter about me, I only wrote the play" – "Don't bother about me I only wrote *In Which We Serve*." It is always Noel that gets up from the table and walks out through the restaurant followed by Joyce Carey and the others of his loyal band.'

The entourage processed to the Midlands and the north-east. In December Joyce Grenfell saw *Present Laughter* and *This Happy Breed* in Edinburgh. *Present Laughter* was 'a perfect piece of escapist froth, quite beautifully played and with such speed and polish . . . It's wildly funny and witty and sometimes wise and always a delight to the eye for Gladys is good at that sort of thing.' The following evening Grenfell went to Noel's hotel with Richard Addinsell (celebrated for his 'Warsaw Concerto', he also scored the film of *Blithe Spirit*). She watched aghast as Coward made 'a sharp and beastly attack' on Addinsell for writing film music. 'Noel hates movies and radio but even so it was unkind and unnecessary and I did so mind for D[ick]. He took it well though and tossed it off; but he was hurt, all the same.' Grenfell compared Coward to her aunt, Nancy Astor, 'in that he can't resist hurting where he knows it will make the most sting. It's a form of bullying and power . . . it was cruel of Noel and what's more he knew it. You could see him doing it deliberately. I wonder if he has a heart? C. A. Lejeune in the O[bserver] said she thought it had at last caught up with him when she saw *In Which We Serve*. He has and he hasn't. What he has got is colossal and complete ego.'

Down south, conditions were better, at least for the stars of the show. Campbell was put up in the same hotels as Coward and Carey, leaving the rest of the cast to fend for themselves. Campbell confesses, 'I was absolutely in love with Noel. I wasn't half as sophisticated as I looked, and lived in hopes . . . One night in Scotland, *shivering* our way through the love scene in *Present Laughter*, he folded me in his arms then slid his hand under my dress and over my naked breast, and I thought, "Ah, at last!" But afterwards he just said, "Thank you Judy dear, that's the first time my hands have been warm all evening."'

'Noel hated method acting. He thought it was pretentious . . . When we were doing *This Happy Breed* ... he had a little ginger moustache and a ginger wig and an open collar – but he reeked of Chanel No. 5! Dear little Robb Stewart thought he could make scent and imitate Chanel No. 5 and we all bought it off him to encourage him but really it was nothing like.' The fact that Coward had come onstage wearing perfume seemed 'a gesture against that thing of having to become your role'. Coward was fond of scent, and would liberally use 'Vertible' by Guerlain, which the painter Christian Bérard commended for its aphrodisiac qualities. Even as the tour wound its way round wartime Britain, Coward kept up the appearance of a sybarite. In February, Harold Nicolson entered his sitting-room in the Grand Hotel, Leicester, 'as he was having his bath. A valet was opening countless scent bottles and folding his clothes. There was a large apparatus in the corner, in front of which Noel, clad only in a triangulo, seated himself with an expression of intense desire and submitted himself to five minutes of infra-red, talking gaily all the while.'

Attempts to keep the weather at bay were frustrated in the West Country, where Coward star came down with a cold, followed by a serious case of jaundice. This laid him up in the Imperial Hotel in Torquay for several weeks. 'I have had a bloody awful time,' he told Cecil Beaton, 'and have been very ill, very yellow and very cross.' His dresser-cum-valet, Bert Lister, took charge, nursing him 'with a fervour that Florence Nightingale would have envied'. Lister had been introduced to Coward by John Perry, who told him that Noel wanted a 'secretary-cum-dogsbody to go with him on tour'. Recently invalided out of the Royal Marines (where he had been ADC to Evelyn Waugh), and with Cole Lesley having been drafted into the army, Lister became a loyal Coward employee. He possessed sharp humour and no subservience: '[Coward] called me "Nanny" because when we were on tour in Torquay and he was ill he shouted at me for coming to him with my hair all messed up' (clad only in a towel). '"A nice fright for me to open my eyes and see that!" The next day I hired a nurse's outfit and took him his breakfast wearing it.'

Coward sought the recuperative peace of Tintagel in north Cornwall, storing up energy for the next leg of the tour. He had agreed to stage *This Happy Breed* and *Present Laughter* in London for eight weeks, plus an extra week in Plymouth to compensate for the cancelled week due to his illness. After that, he was in theory free. He refused to go into ENSA, disliking organised entertainment for the troops (and the possible subsuming of his celebrity), and decided instead to travel the war zones of the Middle East, 'where I considered I would be most needed'. Back in London, Violet, now sharing a flat in Eaton Mansions with Aunt Vida, celebrated her eightieth birthday, a reminder of his own advancing years. Balding, his face craggier, his figure now subject to middle-aged portliness, he yet retained his elegant profile and remained a potent draw for London box offices.

In April, *Present Laughter* and *This Happy Breed* opened on alternate nights at the Haymarket, giving the metropolitan press a chance to comment. Of *Present Laughter*, *The Times* wrote, 'the second act sees the wittily impudent and extremely well-invented French farce in full swing, and Mr Coward and a most amenable Miss Judy Campbell together bring it to a brilliant climax with a mocking variation on the seduction scene'. *This Happy Breed* also had a good reception: 'Mr Coward keeps firm control of his narrative and in his own part occasionally permits himself to speak for an England which, though tired, is still possessed of an invincible stamina.' They played to capacity, partly because a theatre-starved London was eager to see any new play: 'It was very glamorous and everyone came', recalled Charles Russell. 'They were great plays – but then, they had been written before the war.'

After the success of *In Which We Serve*, the Lean/Havelock-Allan/Neame team, now working as Cineguild, proposed that they continue the successful and profitable working relationship with Coward. 'Noel Coward was very generous', Lean said. 'He didn't really enjoy film direction. He liked writing and acting best, and by the time *In Which We Serve* was finished he said, "Well dear boy, you can take anything I write and make a film of it."' It was decided to film *Blithe Spirit* and *This Happy Breed*, which was in production by spring 1943.

Lejeune, doyenne of British film critics, wrote, 'In the strictest sense, this is a Coward project rather than a Coward film. The master wrote the original play, has supervised the shooting script, cast the parts, and keeps a tight hand on every detail of the production, but he will neither direct the film nor appear in it.' During the initial stages of the film's development, the production team 'worked on a few pages of the script at a time. Then they would dash off to wherever the Coward company was playing that week, and the author himself indulged in slashing cuts in dialogue.' He had certain stipulations: 'Coward has a horror of what he calls "film mania"', said Lejeune. 'Film people, he says, have a morbid passion for being lavish. Since the essence of "This Happy Breed" is the relation of the family to the house, his cameras will be allowed the freedom of No. 17, but no more, except to take a peek across the fence at John Mills, the boy next door ... We even hear rumours of an opening shot, pure Orson Welles in its dash and functionalism, that features the dirty rim left in the bathtub by No. 17's previous tenants.' (An idea which was not incorporated in the final edit.)

'It was pleasant to be concerned with the picture but not trapped by it', Coward wrote. He was pleased with the end result, particularly the muted Technicolor, which gave the film a pale, nostalgic colour wash. There were only four Technicolor cameras in England at the time, and British film-makers such as Michael Powell used them with a delicacy their American counterparts lacked; so subtle was their use in *This Happy Breed* that audiences hardly noticed it was a colour film.

Contemporary critics have seen the film of *This Happy Breed* as 'detached and patronising. [Coward's] view of history is exasperation; he plays to the new enjoyment of British audiences, the pleasure of recognition of themselves. He wants to compliment them, but he almost caricatures them.' Such critiques focus on Coward's archaic ideals and sociological shortcomings to the detriment of the film's artistic and emotional effect. It remains an affecting tribute to a mythical England; a Cockney neo-romantic townscape, a snapshot of a city and a people that existed only in Noel Coward's head.

21

Don't Let's Be Beastly

Don't let's be beastly to dear Noel
For you can't deprive an actor of his role;
Though he steals the scenes from Winnie, from Monty and from Gort,
He's as loath as Rudyard Kipling to sell the empire short . . .

US newspaper, undated cutting

O N the bridge of HMS *Charybdis*, on the first leg of his Middle East tour, Coward 'fell automatically' into his Captain Kinross stance, 'and it was only with a great effort that I restrained myself from pushing Captain Voelcker out of the way and shouting orders down the voice pipes'. During the voyage, he became 'godfather' to the ship and an honorary member of the wardroom; as they docked at Gibraltar, the ship's band played the waltz from *Bitter Sweet*. For Coward, the navy and sentimentality went hand-in-hand: Plymouth ratings, Portsmouth invalids and Pinewood film extras alike, they seemed to show uncomplicated affection for him. It was his personal challenge, and triumph, to place himself firmly in the hearts of the public. 'The critics might not have liked him', commented a wartime resident of Plymouth, 'but we certainly did – Noel was loved by the public.'

At the Rock Hotel, Binkie Beaumont was in charge of a 'concert party' of Beatrice Lillie, Dorothy Dickson, Vivien Leigh and Leslie Henson, 'all deeply sunburned and bubbling with their experiences in North Africa'. Coward visited the military hospital, where it seemed that most of the casualties had been caused by 'bits of Gibraltar falling on them'. He flew to Algiers for three days, to give troop concerts, and while there his attention was drawn to a 'virulent attack' in the *Daily Herald* by Spike Hughes (a music critic previously considered a friend) on the lyrics of Noel's newest comic song, 'Don't Let's Be Beastly to the Germans':

> Let's be sweet to them,
> And day by day repeat to them
> That sterilization simply isn't done.
> Let's help the dirty swine again
> To occupy the Rhine again
> But don't let's be beastly to the Hun.

The song had friends in high places; at Chequers, it had pleased Churchill so much 'that Noel was almost hoarse by dinnertime'. It was broadcast the night before Coward left England, when he became the first person to use the word 'bloody' over the airwaves, necessitating a hurried disclaimer from the BBC.*

Hughes accused Noel of 'appalling taste and mischievous disregard for public feeling' after its broadcast. Coward professed himself amazed at this reaction, 'the satire . . . was surely not all that subtle'. But the 'misunderstanding' was rooted in something deeper; the press continued to take shots at Coward's 'playboy' war work. Three months later, newspapers were still receiving letters of complaint. 'We are bitterly disgusted and ashamed at Noel Coward's song', wrote a WAAF. 'Do you think the British people will tolerate this?' Others objected to the reactionary political sentiments. American newspapers looked on with bemusement: 'It is cynical, sarcastic and controversial,' wrote the *New York Times*, 'therefore, it is perfect Coward. And since it is perfect Coward, a lot of people are offended . . . left-wingers and rightists, service men and women and civilians, writers and ordinary radio listeners have given the debonair playwright–composer–singer such a tongue-lashing that he may be . . . pleased he's in the Middle East under the auspices of the British Ministry of Information.'

Coward sailed back to Malta on HMS *Haydon*, when a nearby ship was hit and sunk by a torpedo. As danger threatened, Coward put on his Gieves waistcoat and 'most meticulously' filled his cigarette case, 'reflecting that a cigarette is at least an aid to outward nonchalance'. Such examples of British phlegm were recorded in *Middle East Diary*, Coward's hastily published account of a trip during which he was constantly filmed and photographed; some saw the book as a name-dropping piece of self-promotion. Even to Cole Lesley, it was 'undeniably a mistake. It was difficult for the war-weary British to feel sympathy

---

* 'Let's soften their defeat again/ And build their bloody fleet again.' Noel's lapse occasioned more humorous comments, such as Tommy Handley's 'If I were Noel Coward, I would be able to say what I think of you.'

for his exhaustion, alleviated the next day by lying in the sun by a swimming-pool with a drink.'

There were other pleasures too. On HMS *Haydon*, Noel noted a rating 'six foot, youngish and dressed in an abbreviated pair of faded blue shorts ... a body that would make Gary Cooper envious'. In Malta, he encountered a blue-eyed, blond fighter pilot named Billy Drake whom he had met at a 'successful, if slightly libidinous party' in Paris in 1940. In such sexual allusions, Coward conflated heroism and desire in a manner redolent of First World War trench poetry, 'We must remember these young men, not personally, because we happened to love certain individuals among them, but as a whole Nation which has escaped devastation and possible extinction because of them.' In the heat of Sicily, he saw 'convoys of lorries returning festooned with half-naked, dusty, healthy-looking troops'. Such scenes recall nothing so much as Philip Streatfeild's paintings: 'the surprising sight of the troops bathing on the beaches completely nude'; 'sailors everywhere, the whole world seemed to be composed of sailors; muscular, sunburned and cheerfully expectant'.

In Cairo he stayed in Shepheard's Hotel, where intrigue was masked by the chatter of cocktail parties and purring Rolls-Royces. Still gathering intelligence, Coward enjoyed the colonial atmosphere, joined by his old travelling companion, Jeffrey Amherst, now a wing commander and stationed in Egypt. Noel found him looking 'far from well', and blamed the attack of amoebic dysentery he had suffered on their Far East tour, 'I don't believe that his inside has ever been quite right since ...' He met King Farouk in a nightclub, and was annoyed when the king paid his bill 'as I had only had a beer and two packets of Gold Flake'. There were more concerts in Alexandria, and a meeting with Lawrence Durrell, whose *Alexandria Quartet* described a city 'bathed in glamorous corruption'. In August he arrived in Beirut, a mixture of the South of France and Beverly Hills, its nightclubs geared to sophisticated society. Robert Flemyng remembers Coward's performance at a military hospital there, 'run by some colonel who was frightfully unpopular ... There was something wrong with the microphone ... this colonel got up on the stage, and he was obviously directing things. Suddenly it snapped on [for the audience] to hear Noel saying to himself "You're very very fat and very very silly, get off this fucking stage."'

He spent a week touring the canal zone, giving concerts and making hospital visits, deeply impressed by the medical staff's ability. Sholto

Douglas invited him to a party to meet King Farouk; at 1.30 a.m., he was told by the king to 'come and sing for your supper'. Douglas noted Coward's reaction to being treated as an entertainer, 'If looks could have killed, the one shot at Farouk by Coward . . . would have resulted in his losing his throne far quicker than he did.'

While Coward was staying with the Caseys at Mena, a South African general, Frank Theron, persuaded him to plan a tour of South Africa. The idea had been mooted during the filming of *In Which We Serve*, but Noel had been too busy to consider it seriously, although accounts of the country from William Bolitho and Louis Hayward had fired his imagination. Now the trip seemed more feasible, and the number of Allied wounded in hospitals there made it a positive duty. Coward discussed the project with Norman Hackforth, who was touring the Middle East with ENSA, and who had worked intermittently as an accompanist to Coward since 1941, performing tasks similar to those of Elsie April and Robb Stewart and helping to write such songs as 'London Pride' and 'Won't You Please Oblige Us with a Bren Gun'. The new engagement Coward offered was attractive, and Hackforth agreed to the South African visit at the end of Coward's current tour.

There was a further trip to Tripoli, where hospitals were crowded with casualties from Salerno. Peter Daubeny, who was with the Eigth Army, recorded Coward's performance. 'I thought, what an ordeal! What guts he must have!' The curtains parted 'to grudging applause . . . He was dressed as a Desert Rat, but somehow had managed to give his disguise a Cartier finish', and the audience was 'swiftly bludgeoned into submission by his sheer vitality and determination . . . [They] roared, stamped and shouted for encores, using every flattering artifice to keep him with them, like children being kissed good night. His triumph was complete.'

Coward later said that 'performing for the troops can be awful. Contrary to general opinion, they're not very bright.' Such arbitrary judgements would get him into trouble. Coward visited a hospital for South African casualties, and was impressed (he told a Rotary lunch in Johannesburg) that 'among those broken and suffering men he had found only one whose morale was low, and he had had his toenails out'. But there were also about a hundred American soldiers, casualties of Salerno: 'I talked to some tough men from Texas and Arizona, they were magnificent specimens and in great heart but I was less impressed by some of the mournful little Brooklyn boys lying there in tears amidst the alien corn with nothing worse than a bullet wound in the leg or a fractured arm' – a throwaway line he came to regret.

Algiers was cold and put Coward in a bad temper. His working tour was over, and he took off in a storm-battered DC3 and enjoyed the flight over a calm Mediterranean to Gibraltar. He relaxed in Government House for a few days, and watched HMS *Charybdis*, his 'godship', steam out of harbour. On his return to England, he was told it had been sunk off France on 23 October, with just nineteen survivors.

In December, Coward went to New York, telling the press that he was going to catch up on Broadway shows and see friends, and denying that he was there 'to confer with the Internal Revenue Department regarding settlement of his American play royalties'. Brendan Bracken had sanctioned the trip, during which Coward was to make propaganda broadcasts. Moving into Jack Wilson's flat on East 55th Street, he found that two years of war had made little difference to the Americans, or to the high life of New York. This he resented. The city seemed 'almost intolerably shiny, secure and well-dressed, as though it was continually going to gay parties while London had to stay at home and do the housework'. His irritability stemmed from a bout of flu, which he overcame to lunch with the Roosevelts in Washington. He sang 'Don't Let's Be Beastly to the Germans' for them, and was asked to include it in a government broadcast; in New York, he made two more broadcasts, one on Christmas Day for the benefit of the Free French, transmitted direct to occupied Paris. Coward spent Christmas with 'Little Bill' Stephenson and his wife, May, who lectured him on his health, and insisted he must take a holiday in the Caribbean, where they had a villa. After a farewell party given by Neysa McMein, Coward flew south, via Miami, to Kingston, Jamaica. .

He was met by a naval officer who drove him up tortuous hairpinbend roads and into the Blue Mountains, where the well-to-do had villas in the cooler heights. The Stephensons' house, Bellevue, was 1300 feet above sea level, with a stupendous view of Kingston and the Port Royal peninsula below. Jamaica soothed Coward out of his illness. Its heat was modified by rainstorms which cleared the air and left the luxuriant vegetation greener than ever; the exotic flora and fauna, the paradisial landscape and a colonial society redolent of the days of Empire all combined to enchant him. He decided that this might be a place to live, 'The spell was cast and held, and I knew I should come back.' He was soon caught up in island life. There was a press reception at Kingston (wherever Noel went there was a press reception), and lunch at King's House. The Jamaican-raised theatre director Vivian Matalon, then a young boy, caught a glimpse of this celebrated visitor to the island: 'I wanted to see what a famous person looked like, and there was Coward with a mass of reporters, and I just watched him, because I'd never seen a famous person before and I thought they would look different, and he didn't.' But there was evidence of the playwright's 'otherness': 'There was a young American soldier, who had been detailed to look after him and see him around, and hindsight tells me that that was something else, probably, but I remember going up to him and saying, "How do you know him?" ... I clearly saw that I embarrassed him.'

The island would provide limitless inspiration for Coward. Just as his Far Eastern tour had resulted in 'Mad Dogs and Englishmen', so colonial Jamaica sparked off the witty account of the would-be missionary, 'Uncle Harry', whose attempts to preach to the islanders come comically undone:

> The natives greeted them kindly and invited them to dine
> On yams and clams and human hams and vintage coconut wine,
> The taste of which was filthy but the after-effects divine.

This first stay was all too short, and in late January he began the adventurous journey by air to Africa, via Brazil, Ascension Island, and thence to the Gold Coast. From Accra he flew to Khartoum, where Bert Lister had arrived two weeks previously with Noel's heavier baggage; Lister was 'in a suicidal rage', stricken with tonsillitis and unable to travel. He could not leave Bert, so he postponed the flight to Pretoria. Lister recovered by the end of January, and they flew low over the savannah, elephants and hippos cavorting on cue, to Bulawayo in Rhodesia, where Coward telephoned his South African host, Myles Bourke, who assured him everyone was still eagerly awaiting his arrival. Bad weather delayed them further, and three days later they finally made it to Pretoria. Coward's precise demands for concert arrangements were met by a long-suffering, ever-patient Bourke, who had to fire an Air Force dance band who were supposed to open for Noel; Coward thought they would steal his thunder. He also stipulated that General Smuts and his cabinet should attend his first performance: Myles muttered, 'True, O King.'

Although cities such as Pretoria, with its monumental brick and stone government buildings, echoed Old World stability, South Africa was not a happy place. Coward found a 'ferment of racial problems and political unrest', an 'underlying, perilous discontent' apparent even to the most casual visitor. The land, he thought, seemed about to lose patience with its 'fractious tenants' and tip them into the Indian Ocean. As a guest of the government, Coward knew he had to guard his tongue, aware that his 'strong contempt for any sort of racial discrimination might if expressed . . . imperil the success of my tour'. He was on war work, and bound by certain rules. But he managed to let slip in a farewell broadcast that he thought 'Cape coloureds' ought to be allowed to form their own repertory company, a 'heresy' deleted from the script by a censorious official of the South African Consolidated Theatres. This organisation was responsible for mobilising Coward's shows; by donating the use of their theatres countrywide, funds raised were maximised. Richard Harmell, the organisation's president, was 'the greatest entrepreneur I've ever met in my life', says Bert Lister. He and Coward lobbied Harmell with their complaints, mainly about money. They had economised on their entourage, and 'Coward was paying for us all the time we were in Africa. So I thought "Fuck this" and I got a bill from the hotel and went to see Dick Harmell and said "I can't get any money out of him" [Coward] – which was true, but not really true 'cos we had plenty! Dick said "Leave it to me. Any bills you get, Bert, bring round to me." He deducted it from the takings [which were for charity] . . . He arranged all the travel and everything. Sometimes we'd be an hour late . . . but the people were still there to welcome us, thousands and thousands . . . I asked Dick about it and he said, "Yes, I had machine-guns keeping them in position."'

After initial publicity in Johannesburg, including a radio broadcast on the SABC, Noel set off by train, in a private coach supplied by the government, on a spectacular journey across the semi-desert Karoo, tipping down into the sweep of Table Bay and Cape Town under its cloud-topped plateau. Despite arriving two hours late, Coward found more than 30,000 Capetonians crowding the streets to welcome him. From a balcony on Adderley Street he was introduced to the crowd as 'best known to you, perhaps, as Captain Kinross in that immortal film, *In Which We Serve*', and after a brief speech he was whisked to the Mount Nelson hotel, noting as he left that 'the crowds melted away with almost disconcerting swiftness'.

The next day Coward lunched with General Smuts, the South African premier and anglophile, in the House of Assembly. He had met Smuts briefly in London, and was now introduced to his wife, a homely woman known as Ouma. 'She was wearing a dress that looked like a duster and a pair of army boots!' Lister says. 'I wouldn't've let my wife use that dress as a duster. Mind you, she was a sweet old thing. Noel got on very well with them.'

The first night of his tour proved daunting. The concert opened with the Cape Town Municipal Orchestra playing Wagner and Rossini, requested by Coward, according to Norman Hackforth, so as to 'bore the bejesus out of the audience ... [after that] they'll be only to delighted to see us'. After a ten-minute interval, 'he went on and made a right cock-up of it. A lot of people had paid a lot of money – it was packed – Smuts was in. When he came off ... I clouted him across the chops. I said "You cunt! Behaving like that in front of those people! You're not fit to lick their boots!" We had three-quarters of an hour. He went back and did his two best comedy songs, and it was a riot.' Although shocked by the violence of Lister's attack, Coward said, 'I have never been so nervous again.'

Noel's musical menu had been chosen with particular care. All the crowd-pleasing hits were there: 'Mrs Worthington', 'A Room with a View', 'London Pride' and 'Don't Let's Be Beastly to the Germans', together with recitations of his poem 'Lie in the Dark and Listen' and Clemence Dane's 'Trafalgar Day, 1940'. Material from other composers included his witty reworking of Cole Porter's 'Let's Do It', and 'Mad Dogs and Englishmen' had them cheering. The finale came from *In Which We Serve*, 'There Will Always Be Ships'. The result was success, with three shows at the Alhambra, and no less than thirty-five camp and hospital shows in the arena, constantly changing the programme for the sake of variety. At several of the troop shows Coward noticed a civilian, 'a nice-looking man in a navy-blue suit'. He sent Lister to invite the stranger for a drink. After whisky had 'mellowed' the man, 'and he had begun to suspect that I was not quite the clipped, ultra-sophisticated, affected type that he expected me to be', the visitor admitted his true status – he was a London reporter sent to see Coward 'booed off stage'.

Soon afterwards, the British press reported questions in the South African parliament, asked by Dr P. J. van Nierop, why a 'music hall crooner' should be receiving such preferential treatment, including private cars and trains. Smuts explained that Noel was a guest of the Government, and giving his services in aid of the Comforts Fund. South Africa seemed rife with pranksters, or perhaps saboteurs: before he arrived in Pretoria, someone telephoned prominent people in Johannesburg in the middle of the night, asking them to meet Coward at the airport. In another incident police were sent by a hoaxer to the home of one of his hosts. The *Argus* regretted that their visitor 'must have formed a queer impression of the mentality of some people in South Africa'.

There were other hazards too, in the shape of the demands of society hostesses; Noel had not allowed for South African hospitality, the unwritten rule being that no visitor shall go hungry, unaccompanied or unentertained. In the suburbs of affluent Cape Town, fervent hands wrote out endless invitations; Coward's refusal of these blandishments looked set to start a social civil war; eventually he had to succumb to one weekend social round redolent of 'What Mad Pursuit?' Coward resorted to subterfuge and slipped away to call Bert at the hotel; Lister arrived in a car 'with some garbled talk about an important telephone call from London', allowing Coward to make good his escape.

A quieter weekend was spent with Lord Harlech, the high commissioner, and evenings with the Cameron McClures, to whom he had been introduced by Gwen ffrangcon-Davies and her friend, Marda Vanne.* On hearing of Noel's interest in Cape Dutch architecture, Cameron McClure took him on a tour of the historic buildings of the city. According to Lister, McClure and Coward became good friends; McClure was a radio announcer, and Lister rather cynically thought that his subsequent promotion was a result of the friendship.

South Africa brought other liaisons. Coward was said to have had a relationship with an erstwhile Capetonian, Sonny Heseltine, described by his friend Emlyn Williams as 'tall, slim . . . with fair hair, blue eyes and a vague hospitable smile, the handsomest captain in any public school'; and Roy Moseley alleges a Coward conquest in Rhodesia a month or so later, with Bill Milton, an RAF officer. Milton 'found himself . . . at a party for Noel, at Meckle's Hotel in Salisbury, after Coward had given a performance . . . Bill was good-looking . . . six foot, well built, handsome.' The guests began to leave, 'until he found himself alone with the Master. He said, "Well, I knew what that meant . . ."'

Coward left for Durban, urged by Smuts to take the Garden Route through the south-eastern Cape. The very end of Africa, it was a

---

* Dame Gwen ffrangcon-Davies (1891–1991), English Shakespearean actress since 1911. In 1942 she had gone to South Africa with Vanne, a Johannesburg-born actress, touring the country in a series of plays which included *Blithe Spirit*.

spectacular seascape and the journey took four days and five nights. From Port Elizabeth they turned north, through Zulu territory to the Indian Ocean coast, and Durban. Coward relished the heat, staying at Umdoni Park, fifty miles out of the city on the north coast, in a rest-house for officers, with a tidal pool cut out of the rocks where he could swim in surging shark-free waters. At the King Edward Hotel on Durban's promenade his reception was again ecstatic, crowds gathering under the palm trees to cheer their visitor. His demeanour was princely – opening bazaars, attending receptions and on one occasion inspecting a women's lavatory in a Victoria League hostel 'before anyone could stop me'.

From Durban they processed inland again, to Pietermaritzburg, Bloemfontein, Kimberley and back to Pretoria. Coward took time out to write his comic tribute to 'Nina', the Argentine lady who would not dance, nor 'sacrifice her principles for sex', to an insistent samba beat in his head:

> She said that frankly she was blinded
> To all their over-advertised romantic charms
> And then she got more bloody-minded
> And told them where to put their tropic palms

followed by the sublime refrain, sung at tongue-twisting speed:

> She said I hate to be pedantic
> But it drives me nearly frantic
> When I see that unromantic
> Sychophantic
> Lot of sluts
> For ever wriggling their guts
> It drives me absolutely nuts!

Such was the complexity of the verse that when Coward first presented it at the Pretoria Country Club, his mind went blank after the first verse and he was forced to start it over again.

The last stop was Johannesburg, the teeming gold-rush metropolis with sprawling leafy suburbs and black ghettos sharing uneasily a plateau over five thousand feet above sea level. The rarefied air did not diminish Coward's energy; he played more concerts in those two weeks than ever before. There were three days of visits to the gigantic Baragwanath Hospital (in what is now Soweto), where he performed on canteen table tops and delighted the audiences. The two farewell public concerts at the Empire Theatre, netted £6000 for the Comforts Fund (the entire toured earned £22,000 from twelve public appearances: Coward's figure; the *Johannesburg Star* put it at £18,000). Coward judged these two his best performances of about 100 he had made; it was an excellent note on which to leave.

Coward and Lister took a much-needed break visiting the Victoria Falls, before beginning their Rhodesian tour: nine shows in eleven days. The programme from the Palace Theatre in Bulawayo gives a flavour of the entertainment: the Bulawayo Municipal Orchestra presided over the first half, with selections from *The Barber of Seville* and *Sleeping Beauty*, with Una M. Etheridge at the piano; after an interval, 'Noel Coward – In Selections from his Repertoire; at the Piano: Norman Hackforth'. The audience was advised that 'the total proceeds of this performance will be donated to the National War Fund', and included was 'a message from the Prime Minister of South Africa, the Right Honourable Field-Marshal J. C. Smuts', expressing 'a deep debt of gratitude to Mr Noel Coward for . . . his self-sacrificing and noble work'.

Coward's wartime duties were not to end in Africa; he received a telegram from Mountbatten, now Supreme Allied Commander in Southeast Asia, asking him to perform in Assam and Burma. 'I knew he would not have asked me to go unless he considered it really important', and with Lister and Hackforth, Coward decided that it must be done. On 16 May, he sailed on the destroyer HMS *Rapid* for Ceylon, leaving Lister and Hackforth to fly to Cairo. (Where Lister spent his time 'living the life of Riley . . . That boyfriend of Coward's, Lord Amherst, had a house by the river [in Egypt]. I went to lunch with him twice. He was a charmer. So was Lord Mountbatten.') Lister is sceptical about stories of Coward's relationship with Mountbatten, 'I don't think he was a boyfriend of Noel's. Everybody he spoke to was meant to be a boyfriend of his.'

On the voyage, he wrote his short story 'Mr and Mrs Edgehill', and was met at Colombo by Michael Umfreville, ADC to Mountbatten, who drove him to Kandy. Mountbatten briefed Coward and warned him conditions would be tough, especially as it was the monsoon season. The mission assumed proportions not concomitant with singing comic and sentimental songs to indifferent and captive audiences, but it was part of Coward's talent that he created, out of such a situation, a successful event which reflected both his own patriotic motives and his theatrical ones.

Calcutta was 'an authentic foretaste of hell and damnation'. Norman Hackforth arrived from Cairo (leaving Bert in Alexandria suffering from malaria), and they acquired an upright piano and a travelling microphone, driving in a jeep through the monsoon rain, followed by the piano on a lorry. At Imphal, with the Japanese just beyond the mountains, Noel spent ten hellish days, a punishing round of ad hoc concerts and hospital visits made worse by the nearness of war. Noel was appalled and fascinated by the wounded, and by the smell of a clearing nearby in which were stacked hundreds of rotting Japanese bodies. His reception was mixed, and he was booed off stage by 'two thousand coloured troops', GIs who had never heard of him. Metropolitan India required a more polished entertainment, as an old adversary noted. On 1 July Cecil Beaton wrote in his diary that he dreaded Coward's arrival in Calcutta, sharing Emerald Cunard's view of the playwright, 'He's too slick. He's the Artful Dodger of society.' The pair had dogged each other's footsteps; Beaton too had toured the Middle East, seeing the same people in Egypt and elsewhere. In India he was intimate with the group of ADCs who surrounded General Wavell and Dick Casey – 'the Pansies' Parlour', as they were known, and it was not surprising then that Beaton resented possible eclipse by Coward.

Watching Coward in concert, Beaton was fascinated to observe his technique, 'the more I see it the more technical I realise it is. Nothing is left to chance'; it was a brilliant effect, created by 'tremendous wit and polish'. But Beaton found his presence inimical; he portrayed an egomaniac exhibitionist, with vestiges of an uninformed intolerance: 'Noel shouted and said he had become more and more imperialistic and would like to beat the black and yellow buggers down the street. Only way to comply [sic] with them. Why do a lot of intellectuals talk balls and give them self government. Not fit to look after themselves.' Yet irresistibly drawn by this lodestone of envy, Cecil visited Noel's room, finding him 'at a dressing table covered with bottles'; they talked theatre, Noel talking 'heartlessly' about Ivor Novello's recent brush with the authorities (he had been convicted of misusing petrol coupons, and had been jailed for a month). 'He's been fighting like a steer to keep going as before the war and hasn't done a thing for the general effort', Coward commented with apparent vindictiveness, then seemed to dismiss the subject.

Beaton's portrait seems almost grotesque – Coward's outrage when his Red Cross speech was interrupted for the news 'amused' Beaton and, far from privations and danger, Coward's tour of the Far East seemed little different from a theatrical tour in Britain, his 'progress from one port of call to another . . . done with the greatest comfort and luxury – no strain – with dozens of people to help him in every way. Today he rather reminded me of Stephen Tennant – so unselfconscious and spoilt was he – in a "mood" . . . demanding that people should come to see him rather than that he speak to them on the telephone . . .'

The comparison was apposite. The unworldly Tennant, relic of the 1920s, had become an eccentric and wilful manipulator. For Cecil to see the strains of social engineering in these two larger-than-life characters was flattering for neither: Stephen Tennant, living in 'decorative reclusion' in his Wiltshire retreat, could ignore the war by virtue of aristocratic privilege and wealth; Noel Coward could breeze through it with the aplomb of one utterly sure of his talent, popularity and essential Britishness, a status which made travelling only slightly more uncomfortable than when he toured with Jeffrey Amherst and twenty-seven pieces of baggage. Like Tennant, Coward operated best with an audience. At another lunch, Beaton watched as Noel flattered General Wavell over his anthology of verse, *Other Men's Flowers*. 'He never misses a trick . . . The multitude . . . are so beguiled by a world celebrity that their critical judgement disappears entirely, and a group of hearties laughed convulsively when, at the end of the cocktail party, he said "Now I must go and change for dinner. I shall come down in five minutes' time looking ravishing."'

Coward continued his tour in Delhi, Bombay and Madras, then returned to Ceylon. After a performance in Mountbatten's honour at Kandy, and yet more camp shows, 'what I had been dreading for a long time finally happened'. Coward suffered a complete collapse. He weighed only nine stone, two under his usual weight. He sought sanctuary at the Galle Face Hotel in Colombo, there to recuperate by the swimming-pool, facing the calming Indian Ocean. A homeward-bound plane was found, and Noel was on his way to England.

The film of *This Happy Breed* had been a hit since its opening in June. James Lees-Milne recorded his visit to the charity premiere with Loelia Westminster and Ann and Esmond Rothermere, 'It was in colour, and quite horribly and insidiously sentimental, so that I had constant lumps in my throat and wanted to cry, realising all the time that my lowest emotions were being played upon.' Coward's new-found success in films would solve the pressing problem of his bank balance; just as the cash crisis of 1941 had inspired *Blithe Spirit*, so this present dilemma had a solution. Noel persuaded Cineguild, who had just finished filming *Blithe Spirit*, that his playlet 'Still Life' could be realised on screen. But immediate funds were required, and war travels had taken their toll on the Coward coffers. He agreed with alacrity to two theatrical revivals in late 1944. The first was the British production of *Point Valaine* at the Old Vic (in Liverpool for the duration of the war) with Mary Ellis (who had made her name in Novello's *Glamorous Nights* and *The Dancing Years*) and Frederick Valk. Ellis disputes Coward's account of the production as a failure, 'We all thought it was a wonderful play ... and were wondering "Is he going to take it to London?"' But the fact that it had been a flop in New York apparently sealed its fate. The second revival did better business; but then, *Private Lives* always did. Produced by and starring John Clements and Kay Hammond, it toured for fourteen weeks before being presented at the Apollo for 716 performances, providing welcome funds for Noel Coward Ltd.

Meanwhile Coward fulfilled a promise made to General Slim in Assam by broadcasting on behalf of the 14th Army (which the general had lamented as the Forgotten Army), a gesture which earned him a 'full page of unqualified abuse' from John Gordon in the *Sunday Express*. Gordon later asserted that Coward seemed 'oblivious to the fact that the newspapers were unable to perform their duty because of official restrictions'. But this press storm was nothing compared to the furore that *Middle East Diary* caused when it was published in New York. The *New York Times* reviewed it on 5 November; within ten days, the New York City council was being asked to halt its production, and the mayor, the diminutive Fiorella la Guardia, assailed Coward's reputation. There were even calls to 'kick this bum out the country' next time he set foot in the city.

The uproar resulted from Coward's perceived insult to the fighting boys of America; referring to 'mournful little Brooklyn boys lying there in tears amidst the alien corn' was unlikely to improve Anglo-American relations already strained by disputes over how the war was being fought. If Noel's satirical 'Don't Let's Be Beastly to the Germans' aroused British ire, this new *faux pas* started a bush fire in the States, where some were all too willing to torch Coward's reputation. The *Brooklyn Daily Eagle* reminded its readers of Coward's financial misdemeanours in 1941, and added that his Middle East tour consisted of 'a quick drink before almost every assignment', followed by an afternoon swim. 'Private Marion Bilash of 78 S. 1st Street said there were no quick drinks for the GIs at the battlefront . . . The husky young private suggested Coward might become more enthusiastic about Brooklyn boys' gallantry if he fought side by side with them at the front. "On second thought," he mused, "I'd like to see him with a toothache."'

The *Eagle*'s campaign was relentless. Two days later it printed a piece calling Coward 'a quite useless member of society, a relic, a Dresden china ornament left over from another day, cracked and stuck together with mucilage'. The city council's representative told reporters, 'If he tries to come back here, I'll see that he spends all of his time on Ellis Island until a boat comes to take him back.' There were public hearings, and the welfare committee urged New York producers and publishers to stop production of Coward's work; a W. R. Hary quoted from *Present Indicative* to show that the author had tried to evade military service during the First World War.

Having initially denied the imputations, Coward's defence was to lie low, but his refusal to accept responsibility for what was deemed an insult only exacerbated the rage in Harlem, Queens and Manhattan; in Brooklyn there were those who feared for Noel's safety next time he visited the city. The council resolved to condemn Coward 'for the libel published by his reflecting upon the valour and courage of Brooklyn's fighting forces . . . [and] affirms Mr Coward's appraisal of himself . . . in his book, "Present Indicative", in which he characterizes himself as "a poor weakling, a spineless creature of no integrity, unable to cope with anything more formidable than a row of footlights and a Saturday-night audience".'

Elsa Maxwell came to her friend's aid in her *New York Post* column: 'I happened to recall John Keats' [one of Coward's favourite poets] "Ode to a Nightingale", and sure enough, in stanza six occurs these lines: "Through the sad heart of Ruth, when sick for home,/ She stood in tears amid the alien corn". So perhaps the poetic reference in Mr Coward's diary, from one of England's most lyrical and beautiful poets, might not have been meant as an insult.' The facility of Maxwell's poetic memory elicits suspicion: had Coward alerted her to the provenance of his inflammatory comment, to publicise in her column?

He must have been glad that there were three thousand miles of ocean between him and his verbal assailants. He was now in Europe, taking part in a series of ENSA concerts, 'a tiresome experience and almost entirely uninteresting'. Liberated Paris had a feeling of 'malaise ... compounded of recrimination, shame and bitterness'. The shadow of suspected collaboration hung over Cocteau and Picasso, Colette and Sacha Guitry, and Coco Chanel, all part of the *beau monde* with whom Noel had been friendly before the war. Maurice Chevalier insisted to Coward that he only once appeared in Germany, thereby securing the release of ten prisoners, and that he had sung on radio as the Gestapo had a hold over him. 'I believe him,' Noel wrote in his diary, 'and at all events it is not for me to judge.'

It was a time of uncertainty about the future, although Coward's pragmatism stood four-square against vicissitudes. As the Allies advanced, the Germans unleashed their final weapons, V1 and V2 rocket bombs, but social life continued, as James Lees-Milne found, taken by John Sutro to a 'film drinking party. It was hellish; thick smoke, stifling heat and everyone talking at cross purposes at top speed. Noel Coward was there, red in the face, assertive, middle-aged and middle-class. I left at 11.' Lees-Milne revealed certain social opposition to Coward which would soon reach open hostility: 'Emerald [Cunard] recounted her row with Noel Coward ... He greeted her with, "Emerald darling!" She replied, "Why do you call me 'darling'. I don't know you very well." Then she said, "I have never liked you." And again later, "You are a very common man." Tony Gandarills [sic] practically had to separate them.'

In February Noel returned to Tintagel for a week of solitude, planning a revue for that summer which would be called *Sigh No More* and feature his new romantic interest. The following month he returned to Paris to perform for the Stage Door Canteen with Marlene Dietrich and Maurice Chevalier; Lister recalled 'terrible rows – he only wanted me to star Graham Payn in the show!' The jealous Lister was not at all convinced of the talents of Noel's new friend, and expressed his feelings with customary vehemence, 'I wouldn't have anything to do with it. I had to move out of the Ritz into another hotel because we wouldn't speak.'

David Lean's *Blithe Spirit* opened in April 1945. The lavish stylishness of the Technicolor film (as Rank's first attempt to break into the American market, it had a generous budget) did not meet with Coward's approval. Before he left for his Far Eastern tour, Coward had wagged a finger at Lean, 'Just photograph it, dear boy.' Lean showed the finished work to Noel. 'After the film the lights went on. There was a ghastly silence and I said, "Well, what do you think?" He said, "My dear, you've just fucked up the best thing I ever wrote." '

History proved Coward wrong: *Blithe Spirit* is a successful film, with a good cast (although Constance Cummings, with an idiosyncratic catch in her voice and mannered diction, was thought by some to be not quite right; the crew expressed their disbelief at Charles Condomine/Rex Harrison being interested in her 'when he's got that much better looking bit upstairs'). Harrison was a perfect purveyor of Coward dialogue, his brusque, no-nonsense manner toughening the edges of the witty lines. All tweeds and English hauteur, Harrison was a natural inhabitant of Coward's upper-middle-class world, representative of a rational, stable 'reality' which the interloping spirits stirred into an elegant, anarchic cocktail. With its servants and smart cars and the 6.45 from London (clearly the setting is Goldenhurst, or its symbolic equivalent; a signpost announces 'Ashford 8 miles', and the telephone has an Ashford number), that world was but a short step from a territory where even the reality of death is an excuse for wit.

David Lean saw that 'the time was right for a comedy. People had endured the darkness of war; we had done two films which, while not without humour, were about the trials and tribulations of wartime and daily life. Noel, who taught me a great deal of what I know, had said earlier, "always come out of another hole", by which he meant if you do a story like *Cavalcade* follow it with something completely different . . .' The critic Gerald Pratley remarked that Lean was 'as much at ease with Coward's pre-war cynical manner and frivolous, heartless people as he had been with the "commonplace" lives of the "ordinary" people'. The result was 'an immensely tasteful and brilliantly funny picture'.

The war was drawing to its close. On 3 May, as German surrender approached, Coward dined with Juliet Duff in Belgrave Square. 'There were only four of us: Juliet, Venetia Montagu, Winston Churchill and myself. Emotion submerged us and without exchanging a word, as simultaneously as though we had carefully rehearsed it, the three of us rose to our feet and drank Mr Churchill's health.' It was a scene no less moving for its theatricality; Coward could never overlook dramatic potential, even if it meant drinking with the enemy. 'There he was, gossiping away with us, the man who had carried England through the black years . . . so ineffably charming, that I forgave him all his trepasses and melted into hero-worship.'

VE Day was celebrated at Clemence Dane's, afterwards convening, with thousands of other Londoners, outside Buckingham Palace. But the pessimist in Coward wrote, 'as in all celebrations of victory, an inevitable undertow of sadness … there was still the future to be fought'.

22

Peace in Our Time

A new world, serious, and rather frightened, took its place, a world that looked on Mr Coward's flippancy with suspicion. But Mr Coward was not dismayed. The first world fell at Mr Coward's feet: the second he has had deliberately to conquer.

Sunday Times, 14 September 1952

THE post-war years were as turbulent as those they succeeded. The election of a Labour government exemplified the changing nature of British life, and notions of class were challenged as 'the era of the working man' dawned, the death knell for the world between the wars which Coward represented. This was a period of stress for him; it seemed that early success had trapped him under the sediment of his youthful triumphs, from which it was hard to emerge. Inspiration was not as forthcoming as it had been for the *enfant terrible*, now a middle-aged stalwart of the status quo. A playwright's fortunes are all too visible, and the ensuing years challenged Coward's conception of himself, as his audience began to move away from the values his plays represented. Perhaps it is true, as some said, that Coward had done his best work by the time he wrote *Blithe Spirit* in 1941, the rest of his career being one long 'conjuring trick'. To those who watched from the wings, the illusion (seemingly done by mirrors and sleight-of-hand) was painfully achieved.

Coward often said that when he was happy professionally, his private life was sure to suffer; and vice versa. If this was true – and the failure of *Sigh No More* indicated a downturn in his theatrical fortunes – the Fates augured well for his new relationship.

Graham Philip Payn was born on 25 April 1918, at Pietermaritzburg in Natal, South Africa. His father, Philip Francis Payn, known as Frank, and his mother, Ellen Fleming Graham, known professionally as Sybil

Graham, had met as children in South Africa. They married, only to divorce in 1926; Frank Payn, an electrical engineer, continued to support the family, but Graham saw little of him. His mother went to Germany to have her voice trained, and subsequently went into partnership with a tenor, Joel Myerson, to tour Australia. But the tour was cancelled and Myerson abandoned Sybil, who had to work as a barmaid to get back to South Africa. Meanwhile Graham was brought up by various relatives in Pietermaritzburg. It was not a happy childhood, as Payn recalls, 'I was always with aunts and uncles who didn't really want me. I was only with my mother briefly, and then she was more like a manager than someone giving me mother-love.' But when he moved to Johannesburg, he discovered a certain aptitude for singing, and on his mother's return in 1930 they agreed to go to England to try their luck. They found lodgings in Kilburn, where the local school authorities were remarkably understanding when his mother took him off on auditions, one of which was for *Words and Music* in 1932, when he first met Noel.

Payn had already made his London stage debut as Curly in *Peter Pan* in December 1931 and, having worked with Noel Coward, he began to get other work. He trained at the Italia Conti School and soon found parts which suited his talents; in August 1939 he was in *Sitting Pretty* at the Prince's Theatre; in the spring of 1940 and of 1941, he scored a modest but notable success in *Up and Doing* at the Saville Theatre. Soon the *British Theatre Yearbook* would be calling him 'our leading *jeune premier*', who 'sang and danced delightfully'. Payn could also boast of being an early television performer, appearing in BBC variety shows televised from Alexandra Palace. When war broke out, he enlisted, but was invalided out of the army with a hernia. He fell back on his theatrical talents to entertain the troops in revues; it was not an easy occupation; as he says, 'Soldiers would immediately suspect me, and blow me kisses – but I hit 'em with "Alexander's Ragtime Band".'

Coward had kept track of Payn's career since *Words and Music*, seeing such revues as *Up and Doing*, which featured 'London Pride', and had gone round to Graham's dressing-room to compliment him on his performance. In April 1944 Payn was appearing in *The Lilac Domino*, and invited Coward and Lorn Loraine to the first night. They appeared during the second interval. 'What has happened between then and now?' demanded Noel, referring to the previous revue. 'How could you have learned such awful habits? You were terrible!' 'I thought, "Fuck him",' recalls Payn, 'and got on with the show. But he was right.

I was doing all this "cheerful chappie" stuff, grinning stupidly with a glass of champagne and a girl on each arm.'

Prior to meeting Coward, Payn had not had a homosexual relationship. He had been engaged to a girl in Wimbledon, and affairs with chorus girls had proved unsatisfactory. 'After the third abortion – and they cost £75 in those days – I decided I'd had enough.' His mother encouraged the friendship with Coward: 'She didn't mind about the homosexual stuff at all', partly because of her theatre background, partly (one suspects) because she saw it as a route to the top for her son. But for Graham, it was real affection: 'I hadn't had that love from my parents, so when Noel gave me it I appreciated it more.' Coward was avuncular – Noel called himself 'Daddy', and Payn, 'Little Lad'. He saw in Graham a version of his youthful self, and sought to encourage his new friend's theatrical ambition.

At first, the homosexual world in which Coward moved seemed strange. There were jealousies and old scores to settle; Noel's ex-boyfriends disliked Payn, partly because he was not a 'proper' homosexual, and was suspected of gold-digging; they spread rumours about his being married. In truth, Coward and Payn had an open relationship from the start, which contributed to their deeper loyalty as friends and the longevity of their partnership. 'Noel and I played around – he had his swingabouts, and I had mine', Payn observes, though all subsequent relationships were with men. What was different was that Graham refused to recognise jealousy, so that the old tortures Coward had experienced with Jack Wilson and others fell away. 'All his other chums had made him jealous, they knew how to make him jealous – Jack Wilson, Louis Hayward, that awful character actor, Alan Webb.'

It is easy to see Payn's appeal: a handsome face with a firm jaw and high cheekbones; a fresh appearance, with dark curly hair and a good figure, slim without being slight; a soft voice and an acquiescent manner. He had little of the obvious femininity paraded by Noel's more flamboyant homosexual friends, and was a presentable companion with a particular glamour. William Marchant noticed this when he met the two lovers backstage at *South Pacific*: 'With hair as shiny as wet coal, a winning smile and ruddy complexion, he brought something of the outdoors into the overheated dressing room. He kissed [Mary] Martin as if it were the fadeout of a particularly romantic film.'

Yet some doubted whether the affair would last. 'Nobody ever lasted more than three months with him', says Lister. 'Lornie and I used to dread when the last week or two was coming because it would all die down, and there'd be a space before somebody else would come along. It went on and on like that, year after year. Until Graham Payn . . .' Pat Frere saw it as a '*coup de foudre* . . . Everyone [was] rather surprised . . . he didn't seem quite Noel's genre. But . . . it worked wonderfully – Graham and Coley and Noel, a happy triangle – absolutely extraordinary.' Dickie Fellowes-Gordon maintained that 'the great grand passion didn't last too long. After that they just became two slaves, Graham and Coley. Wherever Noel went, they went too, as kind of attendants. But in the beginning he was absolutely [stricken] – I've never seen anything like it. The Jack Wilson thing was nothing compared to that.'

Unlike Wilson, when Payn was introduced to Coward's intimate friends, he was accepted easily; Cole Lesley, who had spent most of the war stationed near Oxford, accepted the newcomer with apparent equanimity. 'He was quick and intelligent,' Lesley wrote, 'although his IQ as such was not spectacularly high.' There was no braggadocio about Noel's new love, and there was true love between them. Coward told Vivian Matalon 'that he wrote "Matelot" [from *Sigh No More*] for Graham Payn, and he played [it] to him . . . He finished playing the song, and Graham burst into tears and said "I love you" and Noel said "And that was the point where I fell in love with Graham."'

The new spirit of romance in Coward's life was reflected in his latest project. If *In Which We Serve* was his tribute to the the war efforts of the armed services, *Brief Encounter* (based on 'Still Life' from *Tonight at 8.30*) was his homage to the phlegmatic qualities of the British which Noel perceived the war to have defended. It was a middle-class version of the world he had examined in *This Happy Breed*, and a rearguard action against encroaching change.

Brief Encounter dealt with a near-scandalous theme for its time; indeed, Cineguild were apprehensive about the film being passed by the British Board of Film Censors. The story reflected problems faced by couples often separated for long periods during wartime, and *Brief Encounter* was 'the first film which dealt with middle-aged love outside the confines of marriage', wrote the film historian James Robertson. 'Duties and responsibilities to others ultimately triumph over sexual desire and emotion, but had the ending been otherwise, the BBFC might not have been so tolerant . . .' As with earlier Coward works, the film escaped censorship because of its moral resolution; it was passed uncut in September 1945.

To be able to make the film at all required some convoluted deals.

MGM had acquired all the rights to *Tonight at 8.30* in 1938, which they stockpiled. The producer Sydney Box persuaded MGM to sell him the rights, and thereafter sold them, singly, to the Rank Organisation, obliging Cineguild to pay Rank £60,000 for the right to perform a piece which their screenwriter had already written. The film would cost £270,000 (of which £1000 went to Celia Johnson, and £500 to her co-star, Trevor Howard) – no mean budget at the time.

The scenario was written by Havelock-Allan, Neame and Lean, who claimed the film's success was due to 'luck, but you won't have any luck if you haven't got a good script. Luckily, Noel proved to be very good at adapting his plays to the screen. We all worked with him, of course, [but] the dialogue was always his.' Havelock-Allan recalls that 'by the time we got to shooting, Noel was in India . . . so we would cable him, to say "Look, we've decided to send them rowing. We need a little more dialogue . . ." He cabled back saying "I'm sending you a minute and forty seconds. If you really mean a minute, take out the following words . . ." We mapped out what [the couple] should do, and occasionally said to him, "Should they do this?" Curiously enough, he wanted them to go to a cinema so that they could say when they came out, "It was a terribly bad film. It nearly always is."'*

Brief Encounter is unimaginable without Celia Johnson as Laura. Her 'ordinary' features – huge eyes and sculptured bone structure – and essential Englishness represent the romantic spirit of the film; apparent serenity, sentiment without mawkishness. Similarly, Trevor Howard's plain good looks and diffident manner give an edge of realism to Alec. The Cineguild team had seen Howard in Rattigan's *French Without Tears*; the rushes for *The Way to the Stars* (made in the same studios) convinced them that Howard was perfect for the part. But it is not only the lead roles which make the film work. Joyce Carey, as Myrtle, manager of the station buffet, is described as 'reasonably jaunty except on those occasions when a strong sense of refinement gets the better of her'. One of the crew watched Carey pour tea daintily into the buffet cups. 'Not like that', he told her, showing her the professional 'caff' method, swooshing the beverage across the cups without stopping. Carey's extraordinary Cockney-cum-genteel accent is a comic joy of the film. 'I don't know to what breed you refer', she says to her fiancé on

---

* The film was *Flames of Passion*, which was playing next to the Manchester theatre where *Easy Virtue* opened in 1926; a neat if belated revenge on the local council which had demanded that Coward's play be retitled.

the subject of dogs; and famously cries, 'There go me Banburys', as her cakes are knocked to the buffet floor.

The symmetry of *Brief Encounter*'s plot, beginning and ending at the station,* reflects the orderliness of its setting (in which anarchy threatens). We are ostensibly in the Midlands, but the accents, surroundings and characters are indisputably Home Counties. All the details of suburban England are present: the Boots lending library, the Kardomah Café, the cinema matinees – Betjeman country, overlaid with Coward's fantasy romance and demanding mores: duty and discipline, the pull of emotion and one's place in the scheme of things. Laura's brief encounter is an escape from suburbia, just as Coward's escape from his suburban origins was a considerable dynamic in his life and work. He was equivocal about his origins. To acknowledge their humbleness indicated how far he had come, but he found the values they represented claustrophobic and hypocritical. In *Brief Encounter*, he subtly blames British inhibitions for the doomed affair. 'Do you know, I believe we should all behave quite differently if we lived in a warm, sunny climate all the time', says Laura. 'We shouldn't be so withdrawn and shy and difficult.'

The film is suffused with restrained emotion, an atmosphere underlined by the soundtrack, from the implied grand passion of Rachmaninov's second symphony to a plaintive barrel organ plantively playing 'Let the Great Big World Keep Turning', evoking once again Coward's dictum from *Private Lives*, 'Strange how potent cheap music can be.' Even when uttered for the first time, the phrase must have sounded familiar. Laura's narration – her confession to her husband – is wistful and disembodied. 'The thing I like best about *Brief Encounter*', Noel commented later, 'is that the love scene is played *against* the words . . . He's a doctor and talks about preventative medicine and the different diseases one gets, and all the time he's looking at her. And then she says, "you suddenly look much younger" – which cuts right through and forces them back to ordinary dialogue.'

Initially, public reaction to the film was worrying. David Lean showed it in Rochester (while making *Great Expectations* on location), where a rough crowd laughed at the love scenes, and groaned 'Isn't 'e ever goin' to 'ave it orf with 'er?' But it received excellent notices when it opened at the New Gallery on 26 November 1945. Trevor Howard was

---

* Probably based on Ashford, Kent, where visitors arrived en route for Goldenhurst. In the film, the Lake District station of Carnforth was used.

unaccountably not invited, and had to go as his agent's guest; Noel failed to recognise his leading man, and had to be introduced to him by Celia Johnson. However, Howard was made into an instant star by the film, and *Brief Encounter* went on to win the *Prix Internationale de Critique* at Cannes in 1946, as well as an Oscar nomination.* Fifty years later, it is seldom off cinema or television screens.

As peace settled uneasily over the country, Coward surveyed the war and its effect on his life. When Novello (whose spirit was supposedly broken by his imprisonment for flouting petrol restrictions) told Coward 'how he evaded fire-watching and flew to the shelter whenever danger threatened', the incident sparked off deep-seated feelings in Coward. Novello and Bobbie Andrews 'and their selfish, pathetic triviality' revived his emotional witness to war, his hospital visits, his 'service' with the navy. 'I must hang on to those moments or I shall not have survived the war.'

It was difficult to be optimistic. Goldenhurst was empty and neglected and Britain seemed to feel the same way, with Churchill having resigned and the Labour Party (whom Noel called 'a shoddy lot of careerists') in power. All his efforts during the war seemed as nothing, although he was amused to hear his name had been found in the 'Black Book' issued in Germany in readiness for invasion in 1940. Rebecca West was listed, as were Churchill and the high and mighty of British politics and society. 'My dear,' wrote West, 'the people we should have been seen dead with!' The feeling of futility prompted Coward to debate remaining in Britain; but for the moment, he lost himself in work on *Sigh No More*. Rehearsals went bumpily, brightened by the occasional flash of inspiration; Coward took to his bed early 'with a new idea for a song for Graham . . . called "Matelot"'. Hinting at a return to pre-war form, the revue had some good Coward numbers, particularly 'I Wonder What Happened to Him?', a skit on colonial rule in India with near-to-the-knuckle lyrics:

> D'you remember young Phipps
> Who had *very* large hips
> And whose waist was excessively slim?

* Howard played Alec again in Otto Preminger's colour TV version of *Tonight at 8.30* in New York in 1954, with Ginger Rogers as Laura. Preminger said, 'Forget about the picture you made. Here we have something different – we have Ginger Rogers. You must pick her up with you, take her to the counter for coffee and pinch her ass.'

> Well, it seems that some doctor in Grosvenor Square
> Gave him hormone injections for growing his hair
> And he grew something here, and he grew something there.
> I wonder what happened to her – him?

Sigh No More opened in Manchester on 11 July. Seeing the show three weeks later, Coward was depressed; Cyril Ritchard and Madge Elliott were spoiling it with 'raucous vulgarity'. They were duly told off, and hasty improvements made for the London opening on 22 August, when Carey and Payn were hits, and the notices were 'good for box-office but patronising for me', Noel noted. The critical reaction was indicative of Coward's profile in the new, post-war period. *The Times* was disconcerted by its lack of a definite style, and in the *British Theatre Yearbook*, Peter Noble wrote that the revue 'lacked wit, contained not one clever sketch, was wholly pre-war and quite unreal, had at least one scene which was in questionable taste, lacked cohesion and was over-long'. Noble asked, 'has the playwright reached a turning point?' He acknowledged Coward as an institution, but attacked his work of recent years, particularly on political grounds. *This Happy Breed* lacked 'any perception as to the real lives of the common people . . . Mr Coward does not understand the working class and . . . in any case, he dislikes them intensely.' Noble referred to *Sigh No More*'s 'The Burchells of Battersea Rise':

> We may find if we swallow the Socialist bait
> That a simple head cold is controlled by the State,
> Though we know Winston Churchill is wise
> And we'd love him to win the election again,
> If he's forced to say 'Yes'
> To the Beaverbrook press
> There'll be loud animal cries
> From the Burchells of Battersea Rise.

Coward stood 'for all the things which the war has brought to an end. What will he do in the new world which we are now trying to build from the ruins of the old?'

Sigh No More's fate made Noble's point. It began to lose money, and Beaumont told Coward that unless he took a cut in his royalties the show would have to come off. Noel agreed, and the show ran for 213 performances. This was common practice, especially by a businessman of Beaumont's shrewdness, but it looked remarkably like blackmail.

*

Coward's relationship with Graham Payn was not without its initial upsets. Hermione Baddeley, who had been appearing with Payn at the Saville Theatre before *Sigh No More*, met him in Shaftesbury Avenue; he was in tears; Coward had 'thrown him out', and he was sure the romance was over. It was not, and when *Sigh No More* opened, Payn gave Coward a tardy first-night present of a gold cigarette-holder over lunch at the Bon Viveur. Soon Payn moved into Gerald Road and to Coward's new seaside house, to establish a post-war domesticity which defined Noel's 'family life' from then on.

Coward had leased White Cliffs at St Margaret's Bay on the south-easternmost coast of Kent, close to Dover. It was set on a sea ledge below overhanging chalk cliffs and faced the Channel, a welcome breath of sea air after the rationed stuffiness of London. The building was unremarkable, but Noel, assisted by Gladys Calthrop (who had bought a house nearby), turned it into a Coward ménage, immediately recognisable by the tin Wings of Time affixed to the outside wall. There was also a pair of terraced cottages abutting White Cliffs, into which Noel persuaded his mother and Aunt Vida to move (although Vida disliked the place, Violet loved it).

Graham Payn arrived with a bottle of champagne to toast the new residence. 'An evening of enchantment,' Coward wrote, 'I know this is going to be a happy house.' The early autumn was warm, and they sunbathed and walked on the downlands above the house; the sky – no longer a conduit for 'doodle-bugs' and death – was clear. Ships slipped by, strung at night with coloured lights, although the calm could be rudely stirred by sudden storms and high seas almost breaking over the house. Coward, Payn and Lesley spent peaceful days at White Cliffs that autumn, doing up the house, driving into Dover for provisions, and walking the cliffs. Coward began to write verse again, and thought up the plot for a new operetta.

Samolo, retitled *Pacific 1860*, was a lavish piece of escapism which Coward hoped would score a hit with a war-weary public. He had created the fictional island of Samolo for 'We Were Dancing' in *Tonight at 8.30*, and with Lesley's assistance, planned out in precise detail its history and geography, a virtual Baedeker's Guide to be printed in the programme notes. Its star was to be Yvonne Printemps, but Printemps was unavailable, and Coward sought the services of Mary Martin, the Texan singer famous for her rendition of Cole Porter's 'My Heart Belongs to Daddy'. An American star was a suitable choice, for *Pacific 1860* sought to capitalise on American musicals of the period, experiencing a golden age since *Oklahoma!* in 1943. It was agreed, by Noel Coward Ltd and H. M. Tennent, that the show would reopen the bombed Drury Lane Theatre, but rebuilding permits were no great priority when thousands of houses were needed,* and Drury Lane would not be ready until the late autumn. The closing of two Coward shows within a month – *Sigh No More* on 23 February (a run of less than eight months), and *Blithe Spirit* (a more impressive four and a half years) on 9 March – did nothing to cheer him. Events appeared to be conspiring against him, so four days later he went to France.

Paris was an escape for those who could afford it, with unrationed food and drink and the liberated atmosphere of a city which knew how to enjoy its victory. Duff and Diana Cooper were now installed in the British Embassy, presiding over a social renaissance. For reasons of hedonism, fashion and legality, this resurgence had a strong homosexual flavour; Nancy Mitford recorded one evening that of the twelve people she had 'in before dinner . . . I was the only normal one . . . It is rather strange one must admit. Nature's form of birth control in an over-crowded world, I daresay.' Paris had become 'quite giddy, people doing all sorts of things they will regret later'. The atmosphere was a reprise of *Semi-Monde*: the painter Edward Burra told William Chappell of 'a cute party with Noel C. Cocteau & Berard. no mention of Bobbie [Helpmann] who was dipping *ces longs cils & plongeant ses regards clair et surpris* in a *gin vermut au Ritz Bar* I've no doubt . . .'

Coward met Marlene Dietrich and her *amour*, Jean Gabin, and saw Boris Kochno's ballet, during which Dietrich 'talked about herself a good deal'. He and Graham took off for the south, with its pre-war memories. They visited Maxine Elliott's Château de l'Horizon, recently occupied by the American army, and dined with the Windsors; Coward could seldom resist royalty, even the deposed variety. Back in England, there was an encounter with reigning monarchy at a revival of *This Happy Breed* at Windsor: 'The Queen thanked me for the play and . . . said how sweet it was to see me again.'

In these accounts of royal encounters – high tea with the Duchess of Kent at Coppins, intimate chats with the Queen – there is no hint of the disappointment Coward is supposed to have felt at the lack of official recognition of his war work. Theories still circulated about the reasons for the oversight: his court case, his homosexuality, Churchill's disap-

* As Coward was well aware: on 20 January the *Sunday Express* announced that a question would be asked in Parliament about repairs done to White Cliffs.

proval. According to Jon Wynne-Tyson, an old friend of his mother's and Coward's, who worked at Whitehall vetting those considered for honours, reported that Coward was not considered because of his involvement with Prince George. 'They don't forgive lightly ... the currency thing, and leaving the country, gave them a marvellous excuse, filling in the appropriate document in Whitehall: "No to Noel Coward".'*

There had been a brief flurry of expectation during the *Play Parade* tour, when Mountbatten had intimated that 'his cousin' would like to award Coward a knighthood in the New Year's honours list of 1943. But the idea was squashed, leaving Coward to wonder 'if Winston Churchill has been obstructive'. Mountbatten 'explained that he considered sabotage had been at work, so that's that and I shall not reconsider the matter'. Lister recalled that his employer waited nervously until one a.m. for the call from Mountbatten. When it came, 'Noel broke down and cried.' Others blamed the press. When Coward had made his speech about the press neglecting the efforts of General Slim's 14th Army, John Gordon pointed out that restrictions prevented such reports, and went on to quote from *Present Indicative* on Noel's First World War record. The day after his piece was published, he lunched with Lord Beaverbrook, his boss, who reported, 'We've just had a Cabinet meeting and your article about Coward came up. Churchill told us he had put Coward down for a knighthood in the Honours list about to be issued. The Cabinet put its feet down in view of what you had written and insisted on Coward's name being taken off the list. Churchill had to agree.'

Whatever the cause, Coward had good reason to feel bitter. His contribution to the war effort since *In Which We Serve* had been exemplary, and surely his work for 'Little Bill' merited some recognition? Rumours became yet more convoluted, including one that Coward's currency trial had been a 'blind' for espionage work and that he expected to be cleared later; things went wrong, and he was left out in the cold. Coward's own comments do not make matters any clearer. Years later, he said, 'I was told that the King would like to honour me, and I replied that while I would, of course, do anything he wished, I would rather he didn't offer me a knighthood. After that I heard no

---

* Maugham's lack of an honour was also claimed to be due to his sexuality. His biographer wrote, 'there can be little doubt that he had been systematically excluded from the Honours List for nearly forty years'.

more . . . I had to think of the billing you know,' he joked, 'the name on the marquee. Noel Coward has a certain ring to it. Sir Noel Coward is not quite the same.'

No such honour would come for another thirty years. Whatever Coward felt about it, he had become disenchanted with Britain. He felt hounded by the press, unappreciated by the public, unrecognised by the establishment. Society had grown tired of the erstwhile witty young man about town. To survive the bleak years ahead, he would have to repeat what he had done twenty years before: invent another Noel Coward altogether.

In May 1946 Coward was back in Paris, working on the French version of *Blithe Spirit*, and appearing at a gala concert with Payn ('nervous . . . did his numbers well but was not relaxed enough') and Dietrich. Noel had to make a second appearance when Grace Moore, the opera singer, left the stage with a sore throat. 'I flew from my dressing-room . . . and sang "Mad Dogs" and "Germans", neither of which I had rehearsed. This really tore the place up, which was jolly gratifying and I felt was deserved, as I had behaved well all day and not lost my temper.'

Finances had improved, with income from *Blithe Spirit* and revivals. His consumption continued to be lavish, and he had begun an art collection as well as adding to his stable of fast cars. On Molyneux's advice Noel bought a Vlaminck oil for £1000 and later one for £450; in June he acquired an MG18 hp drophead coupé for £1350: such were a bachelor superstar's symbols of prestige. His real-estate problems had been solved by Lorn Loraine's idea of charging the upkeep of Golden-hurst to Patience Erskine, Calthrop's girlfriend. This was mutually satisfactory; it gave Erskine a home and set Coward's mind at rest about the house, which had been courting ruin.

At White Cliffs, Coward made use of his isolation to work on the large portfolio of musical numbers his new operetta demanded. A budget of £40,000 was agreed with Prince Littler, director of Drury Lane, and by July auditions had begun and the final title, *Pacific 1860*, had been established. After a happy summer holiday in France, making friends of Ginette Spanier (directrice of Balmain) and her husband Paul-Emile Seidmann (whom he nicknamed 'Marie-Antoinette'), Coward returned to England to meet his star-to-be Mary Martin, her manager-husband, Richard Halliday, and their five-year-old daughter, Heller, at Southampton. The following night he threw a party at Gerald Road, at which 'everybody fell in love with Mary on sight'. To Charles Russell,

Martin had no '"star grandeur" . . . she was a genuine kind of girl'. His partner, Lance Hamilton, noted that Halliday was 'a wonderful husband and never leaves her side. He even washes her hair and I think often designs her clothes.' But Martin brought unwelcome news; Jack Wilson had done his best to prevent the pair from coming. Wilson's disloyalty was accepted phlegmatically, 'He has obviously changed. I don't think he really cares any more for England or for us, which is very sad.'

Coward's wartime prosecution had called Wilson's managerial abilities into question, and the other qualities which had drawn Noel to him were being eroded by his increasing dependency on alcohol – a lack of discipline which Coward found intolerable. That February, Coward had heard from Beaumont, recently returned from the States, 'unhappy stories of Jack's attitude'. The relationship, begun so passionately, would end in recrimination but, even then, Noel could not sever links entirely. It was a weakness which continued to cause him pain. A month later, Coward read slaying notices of the Broadway production of *Present Laughter*. 'I see clearly that I shall have to have a showdown with Jack', he wrote. 'I cannot afford to have my valuable properties bitched up.' But Wilson wrote back, explaining that the first-night audience had been 'social steel', and business was good. Noel was not convinced.

After a request for intervention to Aneurin Bevan, the Minister for Health, Drury Lane got its building permit, and the opening of *Pacific 1860* was set for mid-December, with rehearsals to begin on 4 November. Continual delays were embarrassing for Coward, with his American star having nothing to do, so when a trip to Paris to see the French version of *Blithe Spirit* (*Jeux d'Esprit*) was deemed necessary, he decided to take Martin and Halliday with him. They were well rewarded: there was a spectacular Molyneux party, and Cocteau's new film, *La Belle et la Bête*. Less happy was *Jeux d'Esprit*: 'flat-footed, obvious and badly-directed', and the company didn't know their words, a cardinal sin for a Coward cast. The director was exhorted to do better, but the play was not a success.*

Back at White Cliffs, Aunt Vida died on 8 November. She had fallen and broken her hip, and had been bedridden since, in the cottage she

---

* Other Coward plays had done well in France since the translation of *Hay Fever* as *Weekend* had been produced in Paris in 1928. This was followed by *Le Printemps de Saint-Martin* (*Fallen Angels*, 1928), *Au Temps des Valses* (*Bitter Sweet*, 1930), *Les Amants Terribles* (*Private Lives*, 1933), and *Sérénade à Trois* (*Design for Living*, 1935).

shared with Violet. 'She looked very pathetic and little' to Coward when he went over to say goodbye. A constant in his life, her loss was felt by her nephew; for Violet, it was the end of a love-hate relationship. 'Doesn't she look pretty, like a little snowdrop', she said when she saw Vida in her coffin. 'It's a pity she looked so disagreeable when she was alive.'

Pacific 1860 resembled nothing so much as *Bitter Sweet* in a tropical setting. Graham Payn played Kerry Stirling ('slim and dark and [with] more romantic imagination than is altogether comfortable for him'); Mary Martin, the outrageous Elena Salvador, a world-famous opera singer who wears men's riding breeches and falls in love with Kerry. Like Larita in *Easy Virtue*, her morals are questioned and yet she is essentially better than her detractors; another reflection of Coward the outsider. Her friends counsel Elena to forget her 'fantastic folly', her love for this young man. 'Your career has been unparalleled and your success unqualified', says Felix. 'And now . . . because of the sudden flare up of a romantic emotion, you are prepared to sacrifice everything that all those hard years have brought you.' Writing a painful farewell note to her beloved, she leaves the island, but returns a year later, and the two lovers are reunited – a happy ending which appeared to reflect the joy Coward had found in his love for Payn.

The preparations for the production were less joyous, and its star was '*at last* showing signs of being tiresome'. Martin refused to wear either hats or wigs as Calthrop's designs dictated. Payn thought that Martin's husband was behind much of the fuss, 'either that, or Mary used him as an excuse . . . Of course, Gladys *was* wicked. Mary said she was allergic to bows, and the dress came back with hundreds of tiny bows on it.' Charles Russell had another explanation, 'Gladys rather took a fancy to Mary – and I think Mary was a bit that way inclined too. But she wasn't interested in Gladys, so Gladys started getting bitchy about Mary's appearance . . .'

Rehearsals were uncomfortable in an unheated theatre. Coward had to sit on a sugar box, wearing two sweaters, a fur coat and an eiderdown over his knees, watching his shivering company turn a pale shade of mauve. The whole exercise was fraught, but the first night on 19 December was 'really triumphant. Mary wonderful; Sylvia Cecil stopped the show; Graham magnificent.' Afterwards Coward's intimates convened at Clemence Dane's, but his old friend was not very forthcoming: 'Winnie never said one word of praise to me . . . Dick Addinsell never

said one word about the music. They were both vile . . .' This sour note
was a foretaste of the press the next day, 'The blackest and beastliest
day of the year', wrote Noel. Not only were the notices uniformly
dreadful, but his dog, Matelot, which Graham had bought him, had
died; both he and Payn were 'horribly upset'.

The reasons for Clemence Dane's *froideur* were made clear when
Coward telephoned her the next day. She delivered an extended
character analysis. 'She told me that for the last three years I had been
. . . so unbearably arrogant that it's grotesque; that everyone is laughing
at me; that I am surrounded by yes-men; that the reason *Pacific 1860* is
so bad is that I have no longer any touch or contact with people and
events on account of my overweening conceit; that I have ruined
Graham . . . that I have encased Mary Martin in a straitjacket . . .
crushing her personality; that I am disloyal and behaved badly over *Sigh
No More* (cutting Dick [Addinsell]'s music).' Dane's diatribe recalled
the accusations against Garry Essendine in *Present Laughter*; it seemed
that the flaws in Coward's character had been made more visible by the
war. Others saw them too. Charles Russell, then acting stage manager
for Coward, outlined the odds, 'It was just after the war, and the theatre
was cold and unoccupied and they had a terrible time setting it up. It
cost a fortune. Coward didn't care about money – when it was other
people's. He fell out with Mary Martin, and gave her Graham Payn as
a leading man. It was laughable.' Clemence Dane's telephone call
ended peacefully enough, with Coward promising to be less arrogant.
But privately he thought her judgement, and that of his other
friends, wrong. Not only that, her writing was deteriorating, and her
conceit was close to mania; he thus turned the arrow to point at its
firer.

Noel toyed with the idea that *Pacific 1860* might be reworked, but
rejected such kow-towing. Dane's criticisms seemed even more apposite
as Coward decided 'if the critics and the public don't like the show,
that's their affair but I won't muck about with it and alter something
that I consider charming and accurate'. He was taking no account of
other people's opinions (unless sycophantic), a dangerous tactic in a
medium which demanded compromise between author, producer and
performer. To outsiders, it was par for the course; John Gielgud
maintained that Noel 'bossed his friends about – people like Gladys
Calthrop and Jeffrey Amherst – he over-rode them. He would listen to
them, but not take any notice.'

*

At the end of March 1947, Prince Littler indicated he was putting two weeks' notice up on *Pacific 1860*. Coward was relieved. The four-month run had been dreary, and hard on Payn, 'whose big chance it should have been. However, that is the theatre.' To rectify matters, Coward decided to revive *Present Laughter* and alternate it with a new play, *Might Have Been*, if it could be ready in time. Rehearsals of *Present Laughter* began, with Joyce Carey in her old role as Liz, and a newcomer, the South African actress Moira Lister, as Joanna. Coward was once again Garry Essendine. It opened at the Royal Court Theatre in Liverpool on 7 April, transferring to the Haymarket on 16 April. The production received excellent notices, broke box-office records in its first week, and ran for two years and 528 performances.

Moira Lister recalls the apprehension she felt at appearing on stage with the Master. As Joanna she had to deliver a slap to Garry's face, and out of nervousness she gave him 'the most almighty slosh across his face'. Coward winced, but said nothing until the final curtain. 'Then, even before we could get off stage he turned on me like a viper and said that if I ever did that again, he would hit me right back in front of the audience.' The following night, nerves a-jangle, she hit him even harder, and ran off at the curtain call before he could catch her.

Encouraged by this new success, Coward resumed work on *Might Have Been*, for which Lorn Loraine provided a better but more contentious title, '*Peace in Our Time*'. Taking its cue from Saki's 1914 invasion fantasy, *When William Came*, the play was to hypothesise English life under the Nazis. Coward had seen at first hand the effects of the occupation in Paris, and the stigmatising of collaborators such as Colette, Chevalier and Chanel; he wondered if England would have suffered the same 'atmosphere of subtle disintegration, lassitude, and, above all, suspicion'. He set his sombre fantasy in The Shy Gazelle pub, between Knightsbridge and Sloane Square (giving his local garage a namecheck along the way), and filled it with character types: Cockney stalwarts, tarty women, intellectual homosexuals, all supposed denizens of the public house – despite their air of having just checked out of the Savoy. Only the circumstances are drastically different; Churchill has been executed, the royal family are prisoners at Windsor, and the Isle of Wight is a concentration camp. The phlegmatic patriots of the pub are a stalwart lot, full of *This Happy Breed*-style speeches, with the added spice of sensationalism: an escaping prisoner of war is branded on his forehead; the publican's daughter is tortured to death. Polemical and politicised, '*Peace in Our Time*' ends with hand-to-hand fighting in

Sloane Street as the reinvasion of Britain is triumphant. One wonders whether Coward would have liked a reinvasion of his own, in the new socialist Britain.

Crucially, for a man of exquisite timing, he had misjudged his moment. The British public did not want to be reminded of years of deprivation and war; the depressing picture of a defeated people undergoing shortages and domination was all too close to the truth, since Britain was still suffering from austerity and rationing. His audiences expected the escapism of his late war films, *Brief Encounter* and *Blithe Spirit*. That he had not delivered the goods underlined Clemence Dane's criticisms.

The play was put into production, with Coward seeking a new, young cast. He wanted Kenneth More to play the young resistance fighter, and More recalled being terrifed when invited, alone, to Gerald Road. When Noel walked towards him with what seemed predatory intent, More burst out, 'Oh Mr Coward, sir! I could *never* have an affair with you, because – because – *you remind me of my father!*' Coward laughed and said, 'Hello son'. Another young actor he had wanted for the play was Dirk Bogarde. He too was invited to Gerald Road where Coward pre-empted his nerves by announcing, 'I shan't jump on you. I'm not the type, and Gerald Road Police Station is immediately opposite. Would you care for a whistle or will you merely shout?'

'Peace in Our Time' opened in Brighton on 14 July, in terrific summer heat, and a 'fairly silly holiday audience' gave it an ovation, encouraging Coward to think he had a success on his hands. 'In spite of all the press have said about me, I seem to be loved by the public. It is a lovely feeling and I am grateful.' Elspeth March, who played one of the leads, thought that the 'jingoistic' nature of the play was responsible, 'the applause was like a cannon – you reeled back, it was so enormous . . . Noel came on and made a marvellous speech, telling the audience he was so proud of us, that the acting was of the highest traditions in the British theatre. It reduced us all to tears.' In London, the reception seemed positive, and Noel celebrated by buying another Vlaminck to add to the 'Coward collection'.

At the end of July Coward and Payn left for New York. Noel enjoyed showing off his new friend; they saw the Wilsons at Fairfield, dined at the chic Oyster Bay home of Horst P. Horst – now living with Valentine Lawford – with Greta Garbo, Margaret Case and Christopher Isher-wood. In Chicago they saw Tallulah Bankhead in a surprisingly good production of *Private Lives*. It would tour every American state bar three, grossing more than $1.5 million, of which ten per cent would go to Noel Coward Inc.; at least in this piece of business, Noel had cause to be grateful for Jack's participation. Taken aback by the offer of an Augustus John picture as a present, Coward noted that Tallulah was 'a curious character; wildly generous, a very big heart and can be both boring and amusing'. But Tallulah darling was by now becoming a parody of herself, her taste for alcohol and narcotics turning her seductive features into those of a raddled addict. They saw Carmen Miranda in cabaret, and after the show, the singer joined Noel, Graham and Tallulah at their table. 'Tallulah was nicely thank you and proceeded to be noisy and vulgar from then on. Carmen Miranda wisely disappeared. Tallulah screamed and roared and banged the table etc., and I wished the floor would open.' They drove to a Chicago dive, where 'callow youths became hypnotised' by a bebop band, 'and began to wriggle and sway and scream exactly like a revival meeting'. This display of modern club culture pained Noel, assailed by 'the heat, the violent noise and Tallulah still shrieking'. At another club, he was seated under a trumpet-player, 'whereupon I walked out and came home. I am forty-seven and sane.'

In New York, Coward's approval was sought for new projects. Lillian Gish, who was playing in *The Marquise* in Bucks County, wanted to bring it into New York; the author did not. He was also opposed to a revival of *Tonight at 8.30*, proposed by Gertrude Lawrence and Fanny Holtzmann, her energetic lawyer. It seemed that if Britain was not keen on Coward, America might take him over. He was offered a handsome contract by Paramount; if he would commit himself to three films as actor, author or director, they would pay him $500 a week for twenty-three years. But this was another form of enslavement, and Coward told the agents that he valued his freedom. 'They went on about England being finished, etc., and I suddenly saw the headlines: "Noel Coward signs up to American Film Company. Another rat leaving the sinking ship." All my instincts told me violently to refuse. So I did and they were astounded.'

Coward was inclined to reconsider the Gertrude Lawrence *Tonight at 8.30* revival. Jack Wilson and Graham Payn thought it a good idea, and it could be a means of reviving Payn's career. News from England encouraged some sort of action; Beaumont had cabled to say he was unhappy with '*Peace in Our Time*', the usual prelude to drastic measures. Coward was annoyed at the prospect of its failure: 'Really, if that play turns out to be a flop I shall be forced to the reluctant and pompous conclusion that England does not deserve my work. That is a good play, written with care and heart and guts and it is beautifully acted and directed . . .'

Coward's only religion had been his patriotism; for him, as for his peers, it was a shared experience of love of one's country, a feeling that you were working for it, not in spite of it. Thus the apostasy came that much harder: 'I have sick feeling about England anyhow', he wrote, echoing the sentiments of *'Peace in Our Time'* and its idea that the country would have been less complacent and lazy had the Battle of Britain been lost. 'We are so idiotic and apathetic and it is nothing to do with "after the war" because we were the same at Munich and before that.' He was seriously considering his options.

Autumn 1947 also marked a nadir in Coward's relationship with Jack Wilson, still ostensibly his partner and producer in the US, despite his many failures. On 28 September Noel finished his new play, based on his short story 'What Mad Pursuit?', his tale of a misspent weekend on Long Island. *Long Island Sound* was ceremoniously read to the Wilsons and Neysa McMein, but they were not impressed: 'Jack prophesies that the press will crucify me for it.' A couple of days later, Wilson interrupted Coward at dinner to tell him that Payn would not be able to rehearse *Tonight at 8.30* without a permit (which Coward had already arranged with Fanny Holtzmann). Coward realised that Wilson was no longer to be trusted.

Matters worsened at rehearsals for *Tonight at 8.30*. Wilson had been making remarks about Payn's place in the show, saying, 'I am the biggest baby-sitter in New York', and referring to him as 'Payn-in-the-ass'. The only way to avoid theatrical suicide would be for Coward to stay with the production until it opened in Baltimore, to prevent Wilson from causing trouble. At the same time, Coward learned that his royalties had been 8 per cent of the gross on a recent tour of *Blithe Spirit*, but Wilson had got 5 per cent 'for his kindness in letting them do it', plus 5 per cent of the profits. On the train to Baltimore with Fanny Holtzmann for the opening of *Tonight at 8.30*, he heard further accusations; she told him that under Wilson's management he had been overpaying tax and that his financial affairs had been mishandled for the past twenty years. Such allegations were hardly unbiased: pursuing Coward as a lucrative possible client, Holtzmann was not above trashing the opposition, and the outcome was that she and her brother David were hired.

Of the opening night, Coward wrote, 'Graham better than ever.

Lighting bad as ever. Electrician sacked.' In Boston weekly receipts were $4000 down on Baltimore. On the first night on Broadway, Coward defied New York custom by going onstage to extol the production. He then led Graham Payn to the front, presenting him to the audience. For those who knew of their relationship – as many of the first nighters did – this was an additionally unacceptable act. To friends it seemed Coward was risking his reputation. Frith Banbury thought that Noel had 'allowed his heart to overcome his head . . . But no one said nay, and Graham . . . hadn't the nous to say "Come on, my dear, this isn't . . . a good idea." It really destroyed Graham's career, in a way.' The New York press slaughtered the show, and singled out Payn for special contempt. The second cycle of *Tonight at 8.30* seemed to go well the following evening, but by 24 February Noel knew he had a flop on his hands. It was time to leave Western civilisation behind.

23

Island Fling

I am beginning to believe that my news value is higher than that of anyone in the world, with the possible exception of Stalin and James Mason.

Noel Coward's diary, 26 January 1946

LOELIA Westminster had told Coward about Ian Fleming's house in Jamaica, which he hoped to rent for his forthcoming holiday, returning to the island which had made such a strong impression during his brief visit there in 1943.

In the late 1940s, Jamaica was still a peaceful British colony, the product of centuries of rule by the plantocracy, aristocratic owners of the sugar-cane and banana plantations, and supplemented by expatriate escapees from Europe and America. Morris Cargill, a broadcaster and columnist on the island's newspaper, the *Daily Gleaner*, for more than forty years, portrays the island as 'a great place where English families sent their black sheep ... and gave them an allowance. They were remittance men ... [who] sipped a rum punch before lunch, and then slept after lunch ... crawled out for another rum punch before dinner, and ... crawled back to bed. Jamaica was a real outpost of Empire. There was a lot of colour prejudice. You had to be awfully careful with anyone who was coloured – you couldn't take them to your friends' house. The manager of the Myrtle Bank Hotel gave me a season ticket, "That's how we keep the niggers out", he said.'

A change in Jamaican social life was presaged in January 1947, when Carmen Pringle opened the Sunset Lodge Club in Montego Bay. 'For a brief spell, which ended in 1960, certain very rich and certain rather poor upper-class English people drank, idled and committed adultery in the sunshine, creating an atmosphere reminiscent of that of Happy Valley in Kenya.' Tropical passions upturned conventional morality:

Cargill says that he must be one of the few men to have lost his girlfriend to his father's mistress.

The fashionable north coast of the island, from Montego Bay to Falmouth, Ocho Rios, Port Maria and Port Antonio, contained a notable homosexual community, led by Coward, Edward Molyneux and Ivor Novello. Ann Fleming complained, 'We are the only heterosexual household for 50 square miles ... Gielgud is on our left, Noel on our right and beyond two newcomers who have called their house "Moot Point"!' Here, on the lush lower slopes of the Blue Mountains, the expats built country estates sealed off from the poverty of their surroundings. Life was idyllic. Under Jamaica's bleaching sun, tempered by sudden rainstorms, palm, rubber, guava, paw-paw and banana trees rose out of rampant undergrowth; wild ginger and hibiscus bloomed surreally. Blue-green lizards splashed with red, electric-blue butterflies and beelike hummingbirds ornamented the scene, with ominous black John Crow vultures wheeling above. Days were spent lounging by the pools, and at night 'neighbours' were visited in villas strung along the coast. Eating alfresco, they were served by black waiters in immaculate white coats. Only the tree frogs in the darkness beyond reminded them that they were on a tropical island rather than in a Park Lane hotel. The drive home, along dangerously unmade roads strewn with tethered goats or crawling land crabs, was seldom accomplished in a sober state.

Coward was not the first celebrity to discover the island's charms. Errol Flynn established his own colony at Port Antonio; Clara Bow, Claudette Colbert and Bette Davis all had Jamaican retreats. In 1947 Fleming had built his house, Goldeneye, on thirty acres of limestone promontory close to the shanty village of Oracabessa, and west of the nearest large settlement on the north coast, Port Maria. The house was designed by local architects Scovell and Barber, who would be employed by Coward; Goldeneye's horizontal slit window which framed its tropical views was replicated in Noel's own dwellings. Yet during his three-month stay (for which he was charged £50 a week rent by Fleming) Coward professed to find the place uncomfortable, and dubbed it Golden Eye Nose and Throat because it reminded him of a hospital.

But one could forgive cold showers, hard beds and inadequate cuisine when stepping out of the door and into paradise. For Noel, the island presented the perfect retreat after the stress of the *Tonight at 8.30* débâcle; brilliant white sand, Kodak blue skies and warm seas were balm to a bruised soul. 'So far, it all seems far too good to be true', he observed. Jamaica had bewitched him again with alarming speed and by March he was considering investing in property; by mid-April he was viewing land. He found the site for his Jamaican home five miles along the coast east of Oracabessa and Goldeneye, on the brow of the hill before it made its descent to Port Maria. It was sufficiently hidden to be secluded, but open to the sea, with a coral reef for protection. Here he and Graham watched the sunset 'gilding the mountains and the sea'; as if on cue, a double rainbow appeared in the sky.

After a week in New York, it was back to Britain, no longer entirely friendly territory. He was met at Southampton by the press: what did he have to say to a story that he was sick of England? 'Charming!' he said, 'I am getting sick of this press persecution.' He was diverted by a lunch with Tennessee Williams and Gore Vidal, although 'both gave out a sort of "end of the world feeling"; they were good company but doomed'. Vidal recalls Coward 'did a two-hour "audition" (Tenn's disgusted word) of his career, leaping up every now and then to caress the ivories of the adjacent grand. Coley served us kidneys, which we both detested.'

One of the Coward 'family' was experiencing crisis: Gladys Calthrop had suffered a nervous breakdown and been 'clapped into a nursing home at Swiss Cottage'. This was blamed partly on her menopause and her grief for her dead son, although Coward might have felt guilty about the vicious reprimands he had delivered during *Pacific 1860*, when he had blamed bad relations with Mary Martin on Calthrop's 'arrogance' with the costumes. Now he found Calthrop 'infinitely pathetic and lonely'. It upset Coward greatly, 'It is terrible to see someone you love in any sort of mental state.'

Calthrop had spent the war working in the Women's Voluntary Service, in which she was 'a sort of glossy figurehead', says her doctor and friend, Patrick Woodcock. Her relationship with Patience Erskine was uneven; she told Woodcock that Erskine was 'in love with her', implying that the emotion was not requited. Erskine was not a glamorous figure, described as 'a middle-aged lady, slightly on the stoutish side, with a very hoarse voice, a gin-throat', and the relationship would eventually end in 'a lesbian row'. (In July 1966, Coward noted a dinner with the two in Kent, at which 'Gladys was snarling at Patience and vice versa'.)

Coward had had to balance the affections of his designer and other members of his coterie; as Woodcock recalls, 'Joyce Carey and she didn't get on . . . she was very competitive.' The fact that Carey arrived later gave Calthrop a precedence she was loath to concede. Calthrop was 'a very severe depressive', and her mental illness required electric shock therapy, which could diminish the personality. It was no coincidence, perhaps, that her role in Noel's life declined in the post-war years.

Rising above the misfortunes of his friend, Coward cast a French production of *Present Laughter* (*Joyeux Chagrins*) which he had decided to direct and appear in – a hefty role in a foreign tongue. The tour began in Brussels on 29 October and went well, but in Paris Noel's voice, never very strong, vanished completely, and despite electrical treatment he was admitted into hospital. He had recovered by the following week, and the play opened to 'the most chic, smart, glamorous and truly awful audience' he could remember. It included his mother, who was photographed with her son backstage. Now aged and bent, she wore heavy jewellery and stood weakly in his embrace, her crooked hand on the sleeve of his dressing gown; Coward's cheek pressed to hers said much of the age-old connection.

'Apparently it was a great success', Coward wrote, but he felt the play was not understood; despite good notices, he remained unconvinced of its success. He approached his forty-ninth birthday sensing a career crisis, 'I suppose this succession of failures is good for my soul, but I rather doubt it.' The feeling was intensified by excellent notices of Lawrence's performance in Daphne du Maurier's play *September Tide*. He professed a 'deep pleasure' on his friend's behalf, but her success must have made the failure of *Tonight at 8.30* all the more galling. He was further unnerved when he was approached after a performance by a young Austrian man who wanted to show his appreciation by kissing him. Noel evaded him, but the Austrian planted a firm kiss on his 'idol' as a photographer's flash went off. The photographer was from *Samedi Soir*, a Parisian tabloid; the incident had been engineered to provide a homosexual scene.

Joyeux Chagrins finished on Boxing Day with an audible sigh of relief from Coward, who returned to the arms of his family. There was some serious financial talk with Loraine, but money problems were to be partly solved by the £10,000 (and ten per cent of the profits) which Coward would receive for extra dialogue for the film of *The Astonished Heart* which Sydney Box was to produce. A further collection of *Tonight at 8.30* stories – 'Fumed Oak', 'Family Album' and

'Red Peppers' – was planned; perhaps 1949 would be a good year after all.

Coward began the year at White Cliffs, working on his screenplay for *The Astonished Heart*. Financial affairs were still uppermost; Dingwall Bateson advised him not to buy White Cliffs, but to raise a mortgage on Goldenhurst to pay for its repairs; Bateson also thought Coward should keep Fanny Holtzmann on, provided 'she does not go too far'.

In mid-January Coward met Graham Greene. Greene had in the past been caustic about the playwright, attacking him in two scathing articles in the *Spectator* in 1941. Coward's riposte was to write 'The Ballad of Graham Greene': 'Was ever a mind so mean/ That could have vented – so shrilly vented/ Such qualities of spleen . . .' However, when Alexander Frere, director of William Heinemann and publisher to both, introduced them at his Albany flat, the two writers discovered they liked each other; the friendship led to Coward's elegantly comic appearance in Carol Reed's film of *Our Man in Havana*.

In February Coward returned to Jamaica and his newly built house, Blue Harbour. His plans had not been carried out exactly, and his ideas for the house to be on different levels, clinging to the cliffside, had apparently been discarded by Scovell in favour of a monolithic block. 'Good God! it's the Flat Iron Building!' Noel exclaimed as he and Graham Payn drove round the corner. Yet despite its external tendency to modernistic brutalism, and within to English suburbanism (the interior, ordered by Coward's agent Reggie Aquart, was painted pink and so redolent of Surbiton that Noel rechristened the place 'Kozy Kot'), the house was 'entrancing. I can't believe it is mine.' He called on Ian Fleming, with whom Ann Rothermere* was staying, then returned to his own verandah, 'and almost burst into tears of sheer pleasure'. Here he could find happiness.

Blue Harbour eventually expanded into three 'cottages': the main house contained a sitting-room, dining-room and bedroom; Noel's house was fifty feet to its left and a smaller guest house sixty feet to its right. As future guests were to complain, the interiors left much to be desired. Lance Hamilton observed that the guest-house lavatory and shower were divided from the bedroom by a wall which did not reach to the ceiling. 'This meant that all those "bathroom" noises could not be concealed

---

* Ann Charteris had married Lord Rothermere (brother of Lord Northcliffe, fellow press baron and rival of Beaverbrook's) in 1945, and became the lover of Ian Fleming soon after.

from whoever you happened to share the house with. As this was the principal guest house . . . [later] to be occupied by Lynn Fontanne and Alfred Lunt, Vivien Leigh and Laurence Olivier, I can only suppose that they finished on terms of great intimacy with each other's bowels . . .'

Wedged into the side of the limestone cliff, Blue Harbour was unpretty but functioned well, with its open-air terraces and rooms with unglazed windows; facing the north-east, it caught the early morning sun, perfect for a writer addicted to rising at dawn. The drawback was the loss of spectacular sunsets as the sun slipped behind the Blue Mountains to the west; night fell at Blue Harbour like a safety curtain. The house felt secure, solid enough to withstand the frequent hurricanes, and the rocks below formed protective coves for private bathing. Coward also built a salt-water swimming-pool, so near the sea that it was hard to tell where one ended and the other began. This provided a cooling refuge when even the pebbles on the beach were too hot to walk on. Not that Coward eschewed the charms of the Caribbean; like Fleming, he was addicted to snorkelling along the coral reefs, face-to-face with the vibrant-coloured fish, listening to the crackle of the denizens of the reef eating the smaller fry.

But there was one major obstacle to complete happiness. Cole Lesley – by now as essential to Coward's professional and private well-being as a ready supply of cigarettes – had refused point blank to come to Jamaica. Lesley felt exhausted, and perhaps undervalued, by the constant demands of his employer. 'He didn't have a life of his own', Lister says, 'but he had far more brains than Coward. He translated Coward's plays in French, and taught Noel how to speak French . . .' Diana Cooper once referred to him as Coward's *alter ego*, and Rebecca West noted that Noel said of him, 'Coley paints better than I do and is as funny as I am, and often funnier, and he works hard to prevent me noticing it. How I wish I could thank him, but it would spoil it all.' Lesley was now living in a flat in Burton Mews, with his friend Claude; it was his first long-term relationship, and he was keen to maintain it. The demands of the four months in Paris, where he had to run Coward's life virtually single-handedly, had taken their toll, and his health had suffered. He had been frightened when he witnessed Gladys Calthrop 'give way completely (with every reason on that particular day, I must add)', and worried that he might go the same way. Now he rebelled. Friends were shocked at his denial of his master's wishes, but Coward had to accept; Lesley was of the opinion that the break did them both good (he later relented and went out to Jamaica). The insurrection served to remind

Noel that he could not always rely on absolute devotion. It was a lesson which the author of *Present Laughter* would do well to remember.

In Jamaica, Coward lunched with Lord Beaverbrook at his house at Montego Bay; they had met on the *Queen Elizabeth*, and called a mid-Atlantic truce. It seemed hypocritical to some friends, and Mountbatten, who was still a target for Beaverbrook's papers, expressed reservations. In this Coward sensed 'self-justification ... as though I were being subtly briefed for any future talks I might have with Max ... I do so resent having my intelligence underrated.' At Montego Bay Beaverbrook took Coward to see Ivor Novello's house, 'quite quite horrid ... exactly like a suburban villa'. (A subsequent visitor to Jamaica asked Coward if one could see the sea from Novello's house. He replied certainly – if one stood on the dining-room table).

Just as the Riviera had been a gathering place for international society before the war, so now Anglo-American stage, screen and political celebrities were beginning to arrive in Jamaica in droves. But despite social interruptions from Novello's house guests and others, Coward worked well, writing a new musical, provisionally entitled *Over the Garden Wall*, about which he felt 'the authentic thrill'.

Coward returned to London to find the rushes of *The Astonished Heart* ready to view. What he saw did not entirely please him. Michael Redgrave's portrayal of the psychologist who has an extra-marital affair and eventually commits suicide was unconvincing. After emergency meetings with Anthony Darnborough and Sydney Box (the co-directors) and Redgrave, Coward decided to play the part himself; he told Redgrave the news, and thought he took it remarkably well. Redgrave's account is somewhat different; he felt he had been edged out.

The result was very much a Coward production; not only did he star in it and write the screenplay, he composed the music too. 'Everybody is so *decent*', Coward told C. A. Lejeune when interviewed on the subject. 'We've been having a bit of trouble with the Johnston Office.' Breen [Joseph J. Breen, administrator of the Production Code] didn't approve of my going away with the Other Woman, in order to get the thing out of my system. He said the film must have a moral message ... I suggested we leave the moral message to the cook. Now she quotes the wrath of God from Deuteronomy* in triumph, and it's very

---

* The threat levelled at those who do not obey the Commandments: 'The Lord shall smite thee with madness, and blindness, and astonishment of the heart.' Deuteronomy, 28.28.

naughty, but highly effective.' The film was not successful, however; the performances are wooden and too stagey. Graham Payn looks handsome without bringing his role to life; Celia Johnson shines, but has little room for manoeuvre. Coward's performance is bad; his clipped, stiff manner seems to yearn for release from its costiveness. Unlike *Brief Encounter*, the story suffered from filmic enlargement. 'We're all trying so hard to be wise and well-behaved,' says Leonora, 'it's a dreadful strain.' The viewer probably agreed.

Havelock-Allan found Coward's performance 'totally stilted . . . He hated doing it, he didn't want to do it at all, but it was the only way to save the production.' And Coward was nervous without David Lean's guiding hand. But he made a great deal of money from *The Astonished Heart*; a £25,000 appearance fee plus a percentage of the net profit (although Rank had suggested that Noel should appear in it without a fee 'as a gesture to the British Film Industry'). Rank also gave Payn a year's contract, and a part in *Boys in Brown*, with Dirk Bogarde and Richard Attenborough (another of Coward's protégés) as rather elderly Borstal boys. That was not successful either, and did little for Payn's putative film career.

That November Charles Russell's revival of *Fallen Angels* opened. 'I have never yet in my long experience seen a more vulgar, silly, unfunny, disgraceful performance', wrote Coward. Since the *Play Parade* tour, Charles Russell and his partner Lance Hamilton had worked as stage managers to both Coward and the Lunts, and had also opened a theatrical costumier's on Soho's Greek Street, providing costumes for *Sigh No More*, among other productions. In September 1948 they proposed starting a management company, and decided to produce *Fallen Angels*. After touring, they suggested to Coward that they should bring it in to the West End, with Hermione Gingold and Hermione Baddeley. Baddeley agreed, but Gingold was more difficult to engage. Since her adolescent encounter with Coward, she had grown into a mischievous comedienne, with a penchant for wicked innuendo and younger lovers. Now in her early fifties and hardly beautiful (she was described as looking like a man in drag), Gingold was an excellent foil to her softer, younger (forty-four) and more amenable rival, Baddeley, with whom she fought a long-standing war of assertion; Gingold would sometimes introduce the other Hermione as her mother.

In their burlesque of *Fallen Angels*, the Hermiones fought cattishly over the laughs, often trampling on each other's lines to get the upper hand; at one point Gingold, jealous of the success Baddeley was having with one joke, circumvented it by stuffing her shoe in the champagne ice bucket and ruining her rival's pay-off. Noel hated the production when he saw it in Plymouth, and 'flew' at Peter Daubeny (co-producing with Russell and Hamilton), demanding he cancel the London opening. 'It would have cost £9000 to get out of the contract', says Russell. 'I said, legally, you can't stop it . . .' The play went to the Ambassadors Theatre, where it ran for nine months – longer than the original production. Back in Jamaica, Coward wrote in his diary, '*Fallen Angels* a terrific success. Livid.'

Coward's new musical was now named *Hoi Polloi*. Prince Littler had told him that the script needed extensive changes before it could be staged, which vexed Noel. 'I am getting sick of other people's silly unimaginative minds trailing all over my work.' But after a discussion with Beaumont, he decided to rewrite the second act. Robb Stewart's friend Neville Phillips recalls it had 'started off as another musical altogether . . . about a sailor coming home after the War, and it was all set in suburbia . . . Prince Littler hated the book . . . and no one would touch it. So what [Noel] did was to keep the numbers . . . and set it in a nightclub . . .' Coward recognised that the beauty of this idea lay in the economy of scenery; he had also discovered the perfect title: *Ace of Clubs*. By January 1950 it was finished: 'it really does feel very good indeed'. But it was turned down by theatre manager Val Parnell, and Coward suspected Littler of being behind the rejection.

He had already asked Pat Kirkwood to star in the show as 'Pinkie', the nightclub singer. Kirkwood, whose voice, looks and long legs had earned her many admirers, was warned against the role by her agent (such was the word about town of Coward's fading career), but she told Noel that 'she would rather be in a flop by me than in a success with Littler or Parnell'. Heartened, Coward performed his songs for Tom Arnold, producer of many of Novello's successes, who agreed to do the show. However, Arnold and his assistant, Clem Butson, had second thoughts. Could Coward reconstruct it? This was galling for a man who, for twenty successful years in theatre, was used to making demands rather than receiving them; it cut deep into Coward's pride to be told his work was not good enough. He discussed the situation with Lorn Loraine and Gladys Calthrop, and they decided to produce the show themselves, on a tight budget, with Pat Kirkwood and Graham Payn paid on percentages. 'It will mean using our imagination and ingenuity like mad . . . but I think it is the right way. I would like to

prove that talent and material count more than sequins and tits.'
Coward guaranteed two-thirds of the money, and would take no
royalties until the production had paid for itself.

Ace of Clubs, with its Soho jewel heists and chorus girls, was a
strangely artificial creation, more like a British film comedy than an
attempt at an American musical. Woven with a thin plot of intrigue and
blackmail are numbers such as 'Three Juvenile Delinquents', a post-war
phenomenon: 'We thrill the Sunday readers,/ But the silly bleeders/
Haven't got a clue.' The best, however, was the sublime 'Sail Away',
sung by Graham Payn as Harry the sailor: 'When the storm clouds are
rushing through a winter's sky/ Sail away – sail away/ When the love-
light is fading in your sweetheart's eye/ Sail away – sail away.' Yearning,
romantic, escapist, it is perhaps the story of its writer's life. Of his
musical, Coward later wrote, 'At least it anticipated the present rash of
Soho-Gangster British musicals by some years, so I can always comfort
myself with the reflection that it was "Before its Time".'

'Quite obviously a smash success', Coward wrote of the first night in
Manchester. 'Graham nearly stopped the show twice, with "Sailor" and
"America". He became, before the first act was half over, a star.'
Coward's optimism was misplaced. On 7 July *Ace of Clubs* opened in
London, to a starry first-night audience that included Frank Sinatra,
and all seemed to go well until Noel came onstage at the end, when the
audience began to boo. Moira Lister recalled, 'The jeers and catcalls
were redoubled when a spotlight suddenly picked out the playwright
... For several minutes, Coward stood there and took it all. Then ...
with one hand ostentatiously to his mouth he let out one vast, long
yawn. To a man the booing stopped, as if switched off by current.
"Thank you, ladies and gentlemen", Coward said pleasantly. "And now
perhaps you will allow me to thank my cast?"'

The notices were sufficiently downbeat to dampen the celebrity-
studded party thrown for Coward by Charles Russell and Lance
Hamilton, and by the end of the month he had retreated to Jamaica,
where he heard that box-office takings were falling rapidly. 'Oh Christ!
It seems as though it is a flop after all. I really am very, very angry.' He
blamed a fickle public, and claimed he felt worse because of the impact
it would have on Payn's career. Some blamed Coward for substandard
work. Bert Lister alleges that 'after Elsie April died – and Little Lad
[Graham Payn] arrived on the scene – he couldn't cope ... Elsie April
put him on the map with his music, and Robb [Stewart] continued ...'
Stewart felt he had been used, according to Neville Phillips. 'He was

very badly paid ... and when Coward went away he was expected to go and work in a club or a bar to make a living, until he got back, and then drop everything and work for the Master again. After *The Ace of Clubs*, they really came to blows.' Coward resented Stewart working on his own music, and found his eccentricity increasingly infuriating. The relationship rapidly deteriorated. To Stewart, it seemed that the Family closed ranks, and he maintained he was put on Coward's 'black list ... whenever somebody was writing a book ... [Coward] refused to let them see Robb'. Stewart was left with little to show for nine years of service to 'Noelie' save for a first-night present from *Pacific 1860*, 'a hideous painting of a steamer leaving Dover, all grey'. He died of cancer in 1988, and is not mentioned in either Sheridan Morley's or Cole Lesley's books about Coward.

At the beginning of September, Coward visited the Wilsons in Fairfield, Connecticut, at their house on the flatlands close by Long Island Sound. Jack was now a confirmed alcoholic and would never recover from his addiction. He was also becoming increasingly treacherous, telling Anita Loos, 'Dear Noel, so blessed, he never had any looks to lose.' In 1951, he produced Coward's play *Home and Colonial*, retitled *Island Fling*, with Claudette Colbert in the lead, and Noel cabled that he would be over to see it. Wilson asked him not to come, and Coward realised that he had 'bitched the play ... and doesn't want me to see for myself'. In August of that year Noel wrote to him, confirming the end of their association. 'This is a relief as I think very little of him as a theatre man', Coward wrote coolly, the passions of the past all spent.

Yet, in 1950, Wilson had still had enough influence to persuade Coward to consider a proposal which might have altered the course of events. Rodgers and Hammerstein wanted Noel for a musical which Gertrude Lawrence had asked them to create out of the play *Anna and the King of Siam*. Wilson thought it would be an excellent career move, and Noel had to agree that two per cent of gross profits (up to $1000 a week if it was a hit) would be welcome. But he had his own work to consider, and a long run was anathema to him; anyway, a substantial percentage of the money would be syphoned off by increasingly punitive British taxes. Rodgers pleaded with Coward to reconsider. 'Obviously I could get practically anything I want, within reason', observed Noel, but the deciding word came from Edna Ferber, who told Coward there could be no 'food' in it for him. He suggested Yul Brynner for the role, and *The King and I* was a runaway success. It was not the only such opportunity Coward missed in the early Fifties. Two years later, in July 1952, Wilson brought another proposal: the Theatre Guild wanted Coward to write a musical version of *Pygmalion*, to co-star Mary Martin. Noel thought the idea dubious and again turned it down. Four years later, Lerner and Loewe produced *My Fair Lady*.

Returning to London, Coward ordered a major reorganisation of his affairs. Lorn Loraine was to be his 'representative', and Leonard Cole's name was officially changed to Cole Lesley, and his job description from 'servant' to 'secretary'. During an intimate talk with Gladys Calthrop, Coward suggested that unless she was really excited about any new project with him, she was not to get involved. Jeffrey Amherst wrote, 'having worked ... in those spacious days before the Second World War when only the best was tolerated, she found it dispiriting to have to meet the post-war shortages and restrictions...' Calthrop's lack of professionalism was a weakness Coward could no longer tolerate in the new, streamlined business he envisaged. Thus ended thirty years of collaboration, without an audible whimper.

The New Year of 1951 saw the publication of Coward's second collection of short stories, *Star Quality*. Fiction was a therapeutic antidote to the compromising business of the theatre. 'You sit there, on your balcony or wherever you are, and write a short story ... you don't then have to go through all the misery of casting, rehearsing and ultimately being panned by the critics ... It's so lovely to be able to write it ... correct the proofs, take out all those extra adjectives and ... there's an end to the whole thing.'

This new clutch of tales showed an improved grasp of the genre. While it again bore the influence of Saki and Maugham, *Star Quality* indicated a style of Coward's own, cross-pollinated by his dramatic writing. Adept description, narrative and character portrayal enhance these simply told stories. The details delight: the air stewardess who smiles as she asks people to fasten their safety belts 'hoping to rob the sinister command of any urgent implication'; Lisbon from the air 'like a map flung down onto a rumpled green carpet' (in *Future Indefinite*, Canton Island from the air is 'a small cluster of winking lights looking like a Cartier bracelet flung down on to black velvet'). Inevitably, social sophistication seeps in, with knowing references; a dust-jacket photo of writer Elwyn Brace Courtland, 'a strange face, with wide-apart eyes and high cheekbones; his hair, which was cut in a fringe, made him look artificial, like a Dutch doll', was a clear reference to Truman Capote's controversial first novel, *Other Voices, Other Rooms*, with its languid photo-portrait (which Coward later described as more of a 'pre-face').

His subjects recall the recent and distant past. In 'Ashes of Roses', an actress is reunited with her first lover with one thing on his mind, 'sex. Sex in any reasonable form whatsoever. This may or may not have been something to do with his t.b. tendencies . . .' 'This Time Tomorrow', about the pre-flight nerves of Louise, is riven with nostalgia for the old social status: the glamour of pre-war travel was now more accessible. As the masses for whom Coward represented high living began to sample its reality for themselves, his version paled into parody. In the title story, Coward restated his own standards: 'star quality' as exemplified by the actress Lorraine Barrie, who possesses all the characteristics of a Tallulah Bankhead or a Gertrude Lawrence, 'the least intelligent, most conceited and most tiresome bitch that I have ever encountered in all my long experience of the theatre . . . To meet, she can be alluring, charming, very grand, utterly simple, kind, cruel, a good sort or a fiend – it all depends on what performance she is putting on for herself at the moment. What really goes on, what is really happening deep down inside, no one will ever know – least of all herself.' Aptly, at a pre-publication party in New York, both Gertrude Lawrence and Tallulah Bankhead were present, the former looking 'lovely and . . . at her best'; the latter 'awful and . . . at her worst'.

He and Graham Payn returned to Blue Harbour at the end of the month, entertaining Ian Fleming, Ann Rothermere and Cecil Beaton to lunch; 'an orgy of photography' depicted host and guests in a typical Beaton composition. Such a volatile group was bound to give way to occasional squabbles or fully-fledged drama. To Peter Quennell, it seemed that Coward played up to Ian Fleming, 'who was himself resolutely, even at times aggressively heterosexual'. Noel treated him 'as if he were a distinguished member of the opposite sex, almost a *prima donna*; and Ian, oddly enough, responded and dropped some of his masculine defences. He enjoyed being admired and teased, and having a bouquet or two thrown at his feet.' Fleming's lover, Ann Rothermere, was a different prospect. A striking-looking woman with angular features, her social connexions made her one of London's most popular hostesses, and she gathered around herself a devoted group of intellectual and political admirers. Coward's relationship with her was bound to be equivocal; the threat of intellect and attraction of social charm in one woman was a difficult mix for even Noel's practised talents.

In Jamaica, Coward immersed himself in work. In October 1950 he thought of the idea for *Nude with Violin*: 'it really could be a wonderful satire on the dear old art lovers; it will have to be kept at a high artificial pitch throughout', but the play refused to come easily. Almost as recompense, a new comedy, *Moxie*, was conceived, the initial idea probably due to Lorn Loraine. The play was re-titled *Relative Values*, and was completed in April; 'Oh, the bliss of writing dialogue after prose'. Not since wartime had Noel's muse transported him along the highways marked by the high-speed successes of *Private Lives* or *Blithe Spirit*. Reading it aloud to Joyce Carey and Cole Lesley, he was convinced of its 'entertainment value'.

In May Coward went to stay with the Lunts in Wisconsin, where they were treated to a reading of *Relative Values*; like Wilson and Beaumont, they thought it excellent. In New York, Coward saw Gertrude Lawrence and Yul Brynner in *The King and I*, and enviously noted that the production must have cost at least $300,000, money which in recent years seemed beyond his reach; though compared to the sums required to mount *Cavalcade* it was, in relative terms, no immense figure. But *Cavalcade* had been written by a younger man, and Coward was now feeling his age. After a bout of neuritis in his arm, alcohol was proscribed, fruit and vegetable juice taking its place. Noel affected not to mind, but the diet had a windy effect hardly commensurate with a playboy image, and staying dry in New York was then no easy matter.

By June he was in London for discussions with Beaumont, who thought that *Relative Values* ought to run to three acts, not two. Graham Payn's appearance in *The Lyric Revue* augured well, as did the business; the revue played 313 performances and included 'Don't Make Fun of the Festival', Coward's satirical look at the Festival of Britain (from whose committee he had resigned in disgust). The festival had been organised by the Labour government to celebrate the new Britain; Coward's ironic contribution to the festivities was *Relative Values*.

He knew that he had to write a certain hit if he was to disperse the memory of recent failure, so he mined familiar territory. The theme of the play is class, family and breeding – hence the punning title. After Lady Hayling's haughty opening remarks, 'I am perfectly aware that nowadays all social barriers are being swept away and that ... any suggestion of class distinction is laughed at', Coward sets out to show that this is not the case. The Earl of Marshwood's imminent marriage to a movie actress is the focus for this question of social station, set against the faded aristocratic patina of Marshwood House, East Kent, in the early summer of 1951. *Relative Values* represents the two worlds between which Coward was caught: English tradition and American glamour, a case of Hollywood meets Hambleton Hall.

The snobbishness is obvious but highly enjoyable as the comic plot twists towards the re-establishment of 'natural' social balance. The starlet is unmasked as the long-lost sister of the ladies' maid. The butler's final speech echoes the restoration of privilege: 'I drink to the final inglorious disintegration of the most unlikely dream that ever troubled the foolish heart of man – Social Equality!' But is this speech (virtually a parody of his *Cavalcade* toast) Coward's real opinion? In the game of bluff and counter-bluff in which he revels, we do not know. We are left with the only discernible stance of the playwright: an amused, wry smile at his creation.

Gladys Cooper was to play the Countess of Marshwood. She too had experienced a bad patch and '*Relative Values* was ... most important. More so, perhaps, for the dramatist than for the actress, since the actress ... had come to take herself less seriously.' The inevitable contretemps came when Cooper said she was used to learning her lines at rehearsal. Coward told Sewell Stokes, 'I did not expect word perfection at the first rehearsal, but had rather hoped for it by the first night!' Cooper's difficulty with her lines led Noel to nickname her 'the Hag', and Judy Campbell, playing the starlet, recalls Coward being 'very bad-tempered ... with Gladys Cooper ... Noel was describing to us when she first refused to learn her words ... and there came a merry whistle from the wings and she said, "Careful what you say, ducks, I'm still here!"' But when the play opened in Newcastle on 15 October, Cooper acquitted herself well. After a six-week tour, it came into the Savoy Theatre. 'Beaumont knew that it might get roasted, but he knew there was a public for it', says Frith Banbury. 'He vetted every single person who got into that first night, so that they would be ... a sort of ordinary audience, and they loved it, and ... it was a success. But it had to be very carefully handled.' In making a comedy out of class, Coward was treading on dangerous ground. 'Happily, his latest play [is] the best he has written for several years', said Harold Hobson, the esteemed critic of the *Sunday Times*. 'He is about to enter 1952 as much as a rebel as he was in 1925. Though not, of course, against the same things ... In *Relative Values*, democracy and social equality have a very bad time, and the audience a very good one.'

'Well, well, what a surprise!' Noel wrote. 'Rave notices. Quite a lot of them irritating and ill-written but all, with the exception of the dear little *Daily Mirror*, enthusiastic and wonderful box office.' The play was a hit; at last, it seemed, his patience and determination had been rewarded.

24

A Bouquet of Violets

Noel Coward . . . handed London's West End a gift at half an hour
after midnight today – a bouquet of violets dipped in vitriol.

Popper photo caption, 17 June 1952

COWARD had meanwhile discovered an entirely different kind
of success. In June rain had once again dampened the Theatrical
Garden Party in aid of the Actors' Orphanage, and, sitting in a
tent with Norman Hackforth at the piano, Coward gave twenty-minute
recitals of his best-known numbers. Outside a sign declared, 'Noel
Coward At Home: Admission Three Shillings'. The popularity of the
stunt gave Noel the idea for a cabaret season at the Café de Paris, where
Beatrice Lillie had been successfully appearing. He and Norman Hackforth decided to try a month-long engagement, to test public reaction.

He opened at the Café de Paris on 29 October. This red and gilt
cavern, with its symmetrical twin staircases sweeping down to a tiny
stage, was the perfect arena for his art. The hesitant timbre of his voice
projected into the darkness; the occasional flamboyant gesture punctuated comic numbers; the solemnity of his now lined face as he sang
more serious songs – a spotlit figure in evening dress, pinpointed by
diamond-glitter eyes. It was the essence of Noel Coward. To some, it
was all a glorious confidence trick: 'his personality almost persuaded his
audiences that he could sing'. 'I can't sing,' Coward was to admit, 'but
I know how to, which is quite different.'

Kenneth Tynan was in the audience, watching as Coward 'came
thudding down the stairs . . . balanced before the microphone on black
suede-clad feet . . . upraising both hands in a gesture of benediction . . .
Baring his teeth as if unveiling some grotesque monument and cooing
like a baritone, he gave us I'll See You Again and the other bat's-wing
melodies of his youth. Nothing he does on these occasions sounds

strained or arid; his tanned leathery face is still an enthusiast's ...
Amused by his own frolicsomeness, he sways from side to side, waggling
a finger if your attention looks like wandering. If it is possible to romp
fastidiously, that is what Coward does.'

The evening was a 'triumphant success'. His celebrity audience
watched from their elegant supper tables: Princess Margaret, in an ivory
satin gown and huge white fur jacket (with her dancing partner, Lucian
Freud), and the Duchess of Kent (the *Evening Standard* noted that both
women smoked cigarettes through long holders all evening); Beatrice
Lillie led the applause. It was glamour *par excellence*, and Coward
revelled in it. He gave twenty-four performances, for a weekly wage of
£1000. It was a visible success, and 1952 began with a repeat appearance, this time with Mary Martin, in aid of the Actors' Orphanage.

Contrary to appearances, however, the finances of Noel Coward Ltd
remained unstable. Coward turned his attention to a revival of *The Vortex*,
in which Dirk Bogarde was cast as Nicky Lancaster. Bogarde thought
that Noel was 'alarmed. Never said so, just went off to Jamaica and
sent me a telegram on the first night: DON'T WORRY DEAR BOY IT ALL
DEPENDS ON YOU.' Coward's enthusiasm for Bogarde had not waned,
although he was not above sending up the suave British star. Walking
across Leicester Square with a friend, Coward saw advertised Bogarde's
new film (in which he co-starred with Michael Redgrave): *The Sea Shall
Not Have Them*. 'I don't see why not,' said Noel, 'everyone else has.'

In New York at the end of January, Coward read his new play
Quadrille to Alfred Lunt and Lynn Fontanne, for whom he had written
it, and who were duly 'ecstatic'. The day after he arrived, he heard of
the death of George VI, 'a horrible shock'. He sent off cables to all the
royal family, perhaps less a gesture of sympathy than of faith. He left
for Jamaica, where Ian Fleming and Ann Rothermere were about to
marry. Rothermere observed, 'he continues to pose as intimate friend of
the royal family ... "My dears, I have dispatched my letters to the
Queen ... the formalities one must observe obscure the feelings, but
between the conventional beginnings and ends I was able to put in my
whole heart"!'

Ann Rothermere's aristocratic disdain for Coward was an indication
of how he was sometimes treated by the upper classes among whom he
liked to be seen as a peer (and whose mores he appeared to defend in
Relative Values). Nonetheless, Coward and Lesley were witnesses at Ian
Fleming's marriage to Ann at the parochial hall in Port Maria. It was
'an entirely hysterical affair'. The bride was 'very nervous. She had on

an eau-de-nil dress, and she shook so much that it fluttered. I can't think why she should have been so terrified, but she was. The principal official of the ceremony spoke very close to them, which I don't think they cared for, so they had to turn their faces away when they said, "I do. I do." After the ceremony Coley and I were so unnerved by the whole experience that I tied a shoe to my own car and drove home.'

In April Laurence Olivier and Vivien Leigh arrived in Jamaica. Leigh was having a 'suppressed nervous breakdown', and the Oliviers' relationship was tense, due to her ill health and Olivier's philandering. They stayed a week, and Noel left soon after they did, returning to New York, where the producers of *The King and I* were worried about Gertrude Lawrence's voice. She had been increasingly ill, and audiences had begun to boo her. Coward tried to convince Lawrence to leave the production and do a straight play, but she refused. He returned to England, unaware that he would not see her again. Another old friendship resurfaced in London. Coward lunched with Esme Wynne-Tyson, now 'fattish with white hair ... very cheerful and somehow touching because she talked more absolute nonsense than I have ever heard in my life'. He found the change 'from a bouncing, sexy, determined girl into this arid, muddled, moralising, elderly crank' extraordinary. 'It is her complete compensation for being a failure as an actress, as a writer and as a wife. It is also a supreme compensation to her for my career of nasty, enviable, materialistic success.' Esme found Noel changed too; she was critical of his lifestyle and sexual adventures, and would later remind him of his youthful wish 'to have the world at your feet, theatrically speaking. How surely that wish came true!' In turn, an acerbic portrait of the mature Esme emerged as Carlotta in his play *A Song at Twilight*: 'a very remarkable character, a mixture of adventuress and evangelist. Her strongly developed sense of moral rectitude has impelled her to ... confront me with my past misdemeanours and upbraid me for my lack of conscience.' Podge and Stodge were figures in a misty past, a boy and girl whose relationship had been submerged by a sea of experience and worldly knowledge. Coward indeed achieved success; but, Esme asked, at what price?

Throughout June, Coward reprised his Café de Paris turn, driving down to Goldenhurst in the early hours.* In July *The Globe Revue*, which

---

* His reckless driving earned him a £1 fine that summer. His case came before Greenwich Court on 27 August, when he was found guilty of speeding in his cream-coloured Jaguar.

featured not only a Noel Coward number but his protégé, opened to good notices. Graham Payn sang 'Bad Times Are Just Around the Corner', was praised in the notices and for his sartorial sense in the *Tatler*, where he featured as 'one of the singing and dancing stars of *The Globe Revue*, photographed in an unusual tartan jacket for leisure hours at home. The buttons are cloth covered.'

Rehearsals had begun for *Quadrille*, with the Lunts as co-producers. Cecil Beaton was to design the set and costumes; although they had known each other for more than twenty-five years, it was the first time playwright and photographer had worked together. Beaton wrote to Coward, 'I am utterly enchanted by the play . . . nothing on earth that I know of would prevent me from doing the job.' *Quadrille*'s evocation of the past provided Beaton with an excuse to wallow in the decor and fashions of the previous century. 'A Romantic Comedy' (Coward always subtitled his plays, lest anyone should mistake their intent) set in mid-Victorian England, Boulogne and the South of France, the play is another tale of partner-swapping, a variation on *Private Lives*, with older protagonists. It opened in Manchester, to excellent notices, his third batch of adulatory press cuttings in a year.

Before *Quadrille* opened in London, Coward took a holiday on the Riviera, gambling at the casino and witnessing a performance by Mistinguett, the aged French star, relic of the Folies Bergère and 'a truly terrifying sight' (even twenty years earlier Stephen Tennant had described the performer as 'looking exactly like an old Baboon dressed like Jessie Matthews'). In Rome he visited Tennessee Williams 'in an apartment of desperate squalor', and together they went driving on the Appian Way in Williams's Jaguar, over which he appeared to have little control, admitting cheerfully that he could only see with one eye.

Coward was pleased to return to England; as he said, work was more fun than fun. But the fun was cut short abruptly on the weekend of 6 September. He was at the Folkestone races when a friend, Anne Attree, said, 'Did you hear the one o'clock news? Gertie Lawrence has died.' Coward returned to Goldenhurst, stunned. The next day was helped by the presence of Graham and their friend Simon Lack, with whom Noel played croquet 'in between phone calls'. Fanny Holtzmann rang from New York, and told him Gertie had known she was dying, and had spoken of Noel; this was indeed upsetting. *The Times* asked for an obituary, and he broke down in tears while writing it: 'We first worked together as child actors in the Playhouse Theatre, Liverpool; since then, whether we have been acting together or not, we have been integrally part of each other's lives . . . I wish so very deeply that I could have seen her just once more, acting in a play of mine . . . Her quality was, to me, unique and her magic imperishable.'

Noel took calls of sympathy from Douglas Fairbanks, Clemence Dane and Joyce Carey, 'but no words from the Lunts. It would have been nice if they had rung me up.' In fact, they were irritated by what they saw as Coward's over-played grief, and by his radio obituary in which he had said, 'No one I have ever known, however brilliant and however gifted, has contributed quite what she contributed to my work.' They deemed this a personal insult.

Coward's relationship with Lawrence had begun to cool after her marriage to Richard Aldrich, whom Noel did not like; he also thought she had evaded her patriotic duties during the war. But his tributes remained effusive and theatrical. Peter Quennell told an anecdote about Coward's behaviour when Lawrence died. 'That same day, two of his friends were motoring across Kent and . . . decided they would visit him. Earlier, they had read reports of the great comedienne's death, but the news had slipped their minds and they . . . were preparing to ring the bell when the door was flung open . . . There stood Noel . . . "You *darlings*," he cried, "I *knew* you'd come . . ." Not until several minutes had passed – minutes of speechless embarrassment – did they understand his tragic welcome and begin to fall into the dignified consolatory parts he had intended they should play. His own part – heart-broken but still hospitable – he enacted to perfection. With a few sighs and some faint autumnal smiles, he produced a tray and glasses; and, standing, they drank a silent toast in beloved Gertie's honour.' Sentiment as artifice: for Coward, it was a mechanism to deal with the difficult dispensation of social sympathy. Quennell points out, 'I do not suggest that his sorrow was insincere, but that sincerity and insincerity are relative terms as applied to any well-known actor, whose life is made up of the real and the unreal, the natural and the artificial, in extremely puzzling proportions . . . Off stage, when did Noel act, and when was his private behaviour truly spontaneous?'

Quadrille opened on 12 September at the Phoenix Theatre, the site of Coward and Lawrence's triumphant *Private Lives* in 1930, and *Tonight at 8.30* in 1936. On this occasion, however, the London reviews were appalling. Not that Noel cared; the production was sold out until Christmas.

He was now firmly in his fifties, and the years were taking their toll.

In November he decided to have all his upper teeth taken out, which provided a witty quip later that month when, at a Czechoslovakian spy trial, he was accused of being a British spy. Noel wanted to tell the press that, 'owing to a recent dental operation, my lips were sealed, but refrained on account of undue flippancy'. André Simone, a Jewish editor and 'veteran propagandist', alleged that 'Coward told him in Paris in 1939 that he knew that he worked for the French intelligence and he was therefore inviting him to work for the British intelligence service as well'. On 28 November a statement prepared by Noel was read on the BBC's Hebrew service which described as 'a complete fabrication' the allegations 'that he had held an important post in the British intelligence service. He said he had never been connected with the British intelligence service.' Coward could not reveal at the time that he had met Simone in Paris in 1940, when he was working in his French office; he was not about to blow his own cover. Simone was hanged after conviction as a British intelligence officer.

Christmas Day was spent quietly in Kent. The day after Boxing Day, he gave a dinner party for the Flemings, Loelia Westminster, the Connollys and Peter Quennell. Barbara Connolly was told to 'wear your oldest clothes', but when she arrived at Goldenhurst she found both Ann Fleming and Loelia Westminster in satin gowns and diamonds. 'Noel Coward and his friend were both dressed in very new-looking Tyrolean clothes. The house was like an oven, so that soon people's eyes began to puff and close. We ate a cold supper of dry chicken, tomato salad tasting of fertilisers, peas like pellets and lettuce with brown edges. Afterwards we played games. Peter and I groaned when we learnt our fate.' Others complained of the fare *chez* Coward, particularly in Jamaica. 'The food was awful, always covered in pickled walnuts', says John Pringle. 'The desserts looked like they'd been made in toilet seat moulds.'

The rest of the winter was spent in Jamaica, where Coward's new retreat was being built on Firefly Hill. Noel and Graham Payn had discovered the site in 1949, when they were staying at Goldeneye. At the end of a hilly lane pitted with enough rocks and potholes to wreck their car's suspension, they found a wide green field, with a long, low, roofless stone building at its eastern end. This, they subsequently discovered, was a look-out built by the seventeenth-century pirate Captain Morgan. The building, with thick stone walls and ancient flagged floors, was not spectacular, but the view was. The Blue Mountains fell down to lush lower slopes, separated from the sea by a thin strip of silver sand; the effect was breathtaking. (Later, when Noel brought up flasks of potent martinis for his guests, he told them that the dizziness wasn't due to the drinks at all but to the altitude.) The land, which had cost him £150, was now worth about £5000, so the construction of his retreat seemed all the more viable. Noel hoped to sell Blue Harbour (retaining a section of its beach) to give him further financial latitude with his new house, but when it was put on the market in September 1952 it failed to attract offers to match the £25,000 it had reputedly cost, and was withdrawn.

Jamaica spurred Coward to work early every morning before the sun grew fierce; the afternoon was spent floating in the cool of his seaside pool, or painting. He had always painted and drawn: in childhood, bold depictions of Nell Gwynne and theatrical scenes; as a teenager his letters to Esme Wynne were embellished with comic sketches. In the Twenties, he took up the hobby seriously, but career pressures left little time for it. He began painting again in the Thirties 'in watercolours, usually seascapes with ships in sepia or low-toned keys', Cole Lesley wrote; 'rather naive but, as in everything he attempted, with a style of his own'. G. B. Stern remembered, 'Both at the same time, we had been seized with a passion for doing what was not our job . . . Noel sold me the painting he did that morning for £1 18s 6d. The sum shows clearly enough that bargaining took place, and that his original valuation was £2 . . . It really might be a good deal worse: a rather solid yet Whistlerish effect of dark blue archways across the Seine at night. He called it "Where the Bee Sucks".' Later, on a visit to Churchill at Chartwell one Sunday, Noel was converted to oils. He set up studios at Goldenhurst and White Cliffs, and he and Cole Lesley trawled junk shops for Victorian pictures to paint over, blithely ignoring the possible value of the canvases. But it was in Jamaica that Coward pursued painting most seriously; indeed, Churchill turned up in Jamaica that month, with more artistic advice and his wife Clementine and their daughters, Sarah and Mary.

Another amateur artist to arrive was Katharine Hepburn, together with Irene Selznick, driving around the island in a zippy open-top sports car (not usual for Jamaica, being assumed to cause sunstroke, but after Hepburn's stylish arrival Coward followed her lead and used convertibles). They stayed for several days, and enjoyed each other's company and artistic endeavours; Hepburn sketched a figure on the bark of a tree, which Coward later cut out and framed. She remembers Blue Harbour as a 'pretty good house. A lot of people – too many. I don't like a lot of people . . . we stayed in his guest house, which was next to his house. We used to eat at his house – but not with Noel. He didn't really like to do the things I liked to do. I loved to play tennis, and he wasn't too much on sports . . . I don't think he was a great swimmer. He liked to lie in the sun, he liked to talk. That whole group of people . . . just liked to talk '

Hepburn could not persuade her host to participate in anything resembling exercise, except for a dip in his salt-water swimming-pool, usually naked. Nudity was the norm at Blue Harbour; Miguel Fraser, the butler-manservant, recalled that no one was allowed to wear swimming costumes in the pool. When John Pringle was invited with his wife, Liz, to meet the Oliviers, he arrived to find them 'naked on Noel's terrace, Vivien draped over Larry's cock. It was some introduction!' Jamaican life was uninhibited, and relations with the local community were apparently unaffected by such behaviour. Maurice Cargill observes that 'the working classes were always delighted if you were spending a lot of money, and they could keep a lot of his groceries. He was very popular from that point of view. He was very good to his staff.' Coward's donation of some of his land to the town as a playing field certainly helped.

His homosexuality was an open secret, noted Cargill. 'I never discussed the matter with him. The only time he ever talked about it was very funny. He used to ask me . . . to keep an eye on his property, and he complained bitterly that his staff were robbing him. And they were. He had a fellow called Fred up at Firefly, and Fred was feeding the neighbourhood with Noel's groceries. I told him, "You've got to fire the fellow you know." But he wouldn't do it. Anyway, Noel came back . . . he was complaining again about his staff. I said, "Noel, it's your own bloody fault. I told you over and over again that Fred is robbing you, and you won't fire him." I got quite cross about it. He looked me straight in the face and said, "You think I'm fucking Fred, don't you?" It was exactly what I was thinking . . .' Certainly the masculine charms of native Jamaicans did not elude Coward, as his paintings indicate. Many feature well-developed Afro-Caribbeans, diving naked off jetties or lying about in the sun. Some closer studies were made, such as 'Purple Interior': a tall black nude on a bed, the man's clothes strewn about the room, the window open to a Jamaican seaview. The languid pose of the man, stretched lazily and at full length, and the detailed manner in which his musculature has been painted render unequivocal the picture's sexual tone.

However, Cargill noted that Coward kept away from the local gay cliques, finding their sometimes outrageous behaviour not to his taste. 'Noel didn't really get involved,' says Cargill, 'he kept himself very aloof. We promised him in the press that we would give him peace and quiet . . . He could come here and the newspapers wouldn't bother him, no reporters and that sort of thing . . . I always saw to it that the *Gleaner* kept off him . . .'

Late in 1952, Beaumont had suggested that Coward ought to mark the coronation of Elizabeth II by appearing in Shaw's political parody, *The Apple Cart*. Noel read it, and agreed that King Magnus was a good part for him. It would be his first appearance in another playwright's work since his stint in *Journey's End* in 1930. Shaw's play was a witty and subtle allegory, not typical Coward territory; Noel found its long sentences required a different sense of timing from his own spitfire bursts of dialogue. 'There is a twelve-minute speech in the first act that is quite frightening', he observed. But when the play opened in Brighton he was surprisingly calm. 'I never intend to indulge myself in first-night nerves again. It is a waste of time and unnecessary. This is big talk but I am determined to strain every un-nervous nerve to carry it through.'

Picture Post sent a journalist and photographer to Brighton to mark Coward's appearance there. Noel disliked the reporter, Robert Mullins, but liked the photographer, Dan Farson. 'Revealing no star temperament whatever,' wrote Farson, 'he posed uncomplainingly on the Sussex Downs, playing a pinball machine on the Pier, lying on top of Margaret Leighton on stage at a dress rehearsal, receiving his guests, Graham Greene and Laurence Harvey, in his dressing-room after the first night . . .' Backstage Farson watched Coward fussing with the back of his wig. 'His dresser tut-tutted, "It doesn't *matter*. It's only the behind." "I'll have you know," Coward retorted crisply, "that in its day my behind has been much admired and *much* sought after."'

Coward returned to London ready to open at the Haymarket, but bedevilled by lumbago could only get through the opening night on codeine, aided by 'belladonna plasters'. Reviewers greeted his performance equivocally; while Noel spoke his lines clearly enough, he lacked projection, more noticeable because of the Shakespearean and classical training of the other players. Charles Russell was dispatched to move around the auditorium, to check how well Coward could be heard. 'I told him people were on the edge of their seats trying to hear what he said. He said that's exactly what they should be doing!'

The run depleted his stamina, but towards the end of May he perked up, looking forward to his new series of appearances at the Café de Paris. Coronation fever was upon London, with 'swarms of people and a perpetual misery of traffic congestion'. Coward opened at the Café on 26 May to 'roars and cheers', much like Coronation Day two weeks later, which Noel watched mostly on television. This, according to legend, was the occasion for one of his best-known quips; as the procession of foreign dignitaries rolled past, a carriage came into view containing the very large Queen Salote of Tonga and a small man beside her. 'Who's that man sitting next to her?' someone asked. 'Her lunch', Coward replied. 'Oh Noel, that was so funny', Dickie Fellowes-Gordon said when next she saw him, but he denied responsibility, 'I didn't say it. I wish I had. It was a member of White's . . .'

Pomp and circumstance agreed with Coward; it was a reminder and remnant of his Empire-tinged youth. It even put him in a good enough mood to wax generous about John Gielgud's knighthood (despite the actor's recent conviction for indecency) in the Coronation Honours list, 'I am really glad because he has deserved it for years.' But, commented his friends, so had Noel.

As the 1950s got into their swing, Coward was determined not to be left behind. He took Gladys Calthrop to see Johnny Ray, the semi-deaf heartthrob, one of the first of a new breed of singing stars, at the London Palladium. 'He was really remarkable', wrote Noel, 'and had the whole place in uproar.' Coward visited Ray in New York when he was ill – a friend was surprised to see him pat the handsome singer's leg *under* the bedsheets.

The Apple Cart continued to play to capacity crowds, with coronation London full of ticket-buying visitors eager to see Coward. When the run finished on 1 August, Noel and Graham Payn set off for a motoring tour of Italy. The country was 'enchanting', but, in the travel boom of the Fifties, full of tourists. Venice was threatened by 'Germans, Swiss, Americans in vast hordes'. The global pervasiveness of America was too much for Coward. In his song 'Why Do the Wrong People Travel?', he lampoons the citizens of Omaha and Houston, with their cameras, loud voices and louder shirts. Yet in his post-war career, these were the voices whose calls for encores he needed to hear.

While in Jamaica for the winter, he began writing *Nude with Violin*. In this satire on modern art, Coward's prejudices are mouthed by the elegant, all-knowing butler, Sebastien, who speaks of his deceased master, the artist Sorodin, and his disaffection with his work: 'I don't think that anyone knows about painting any more. Art, like human nature, has got out of hand.' As one of Coward's servants, Sebastien represents the playwright's refinement of this useful breed, from the one-dimensional factotums of the early plays (mere mechanicals in *The Vortex* and *Easy Virtue*) to the protagonists of *Relative Values* and *Nude with Violin*. It was his nod towards egalitarianism, but *Nude with Violin* is as much a fable as was *Relative Values*: its comic characters are two-dimensional cyphers; even the names are baroque whimsies, such as Marie-Celeste, the maid. The young journalist, Clinton Preminger Jnr, represents New World values and modern gullibility, running in with a cable from his editor about 'Rude with Violin'; NY dealers are 'crazy with excitement', and *Life* wants it for their cover. But Sebastien reveals that his master's paintings were all done by others, and 'Nude with Violin' was painted by Sorodin's young son. Threatened with exposure by an art dealer, Sebastien points out, 'If the news leaks out that the great Sorodin's masterpieces were painted by a Russian tart, an ex-Jackson Girl, a Negro Eleventh Hour Immersionist and a boy of fourteen, the rot will spread like wildfire. Modern sculpture, music, drama and poetry will all shrivel in the holocaust.'

It was too easy a parody, and Coward was siding with the reactionaries rather than the modernists. It was a further example of his entrenchment in the past; in *Nude with Violin*, he was a world away from the rebellion of *The Vortex*. Opinions, faith, beliefs often change drastically within a lifespan: what Coward believed in 1924 was not what he believed thirty years later. But perhaps he had never really rebelled; had he not been homosexual, he might have been a conservative, run-of-the-mill playwright. Being a sexual outsider gave his work its edge.

Nude with Violin was a comment on those who try to intellectualise their reactions to art; and Coward's anti-intellectualism underlies *Nude with Violin* like a primer. In reaction, there had always been positive creation: the energised younger Coward had been able to turn his scepticism to witty effect. But as he aged into occasional irascibility, the effect seemed more laboured, underlain by a sour quality. With *Nude with Violin*, the critics would again allege he had lost the touch, but he was to prove that what seemed a depleted seam was not yet exhausted. 'My dear,' he had told David Lean, 'always come out of another hole.' And so he did, redefining his art for the second half of the century.

It was an art Coward continued to practise with apparent ease. He finished *Nude with Violin* in just over three weeks, and left Jamaica for Miami, and then New York, where society sank its claws into its favourite adoptive son once again. Elsa Maxwell proclaimed it 'Noel Coward Week in New York', and documented her old friend's trawl of the cocktail parties. Ina Claire threw one in her Sherry-Netherlands apartment, at which a bronzed Cole Porter, just back from St Moritz, chatted with Artur Rubinstein, the Gilbert Millers, George and Valentina Schlee (he was Garbo's mysterious 'walker'; she the renowned fashion designer), Jack and Natasha Wilson, and Truman Capote, the latter working on his musical, *House of Flowers*, with Harold Arlen. Valentine Lawford noted that 'Noel sang some of his songs in his new [musical] play [*After the Ball*] – but it was all, once again, about the British Empire. Can one go on laughing indefinitely about how sure the British were in 1900 that Britannia rules the waves? ... as much as I like Noel, his songs were slightly old-hat, though he sings with endless charm. His tunes also were unoriginal and un-virile, in contrast to the Jewish-American-negro, hard talent of Arlen's amazingly pretty songs...'

Back in England Coward had a chance to see his first copy of *Future Indefinite*, published by Heinemann on 29 March. A companion to *Present Indicative*, *Future Indefinite* took his life story from 1939 to 1945; while acknowledging that it was not a proper sequel, Coward declined to explain his decision to begin in 1939. The war years were covered by his recent diaries, but the gap between gave rise to theories that he had something to hide. The book garnered 'mixed reviews'. Ian Fleming was full of praise, 'On every page there are passages of brilliant observation, wit and humanity', but noted 'a rather querulous note of self-justification'. Other critics were less kind: 'Autobiography written on the instalment plan is a delicate art of which few men are masters, and Mr Noel Coward is not one of them', wrote the *Telegraph*. There was 'a jarring, glossy magazine note' about his accounts of intimate suppers with the great and the good. In the *Daily Express*, W. A. Darlington wrote that 'the reason for the book's dullness is simple. The enthralling part of the life story of a celebrity is his rise to fame. Once he is famous, his doings among the other VIPs lose narrative tension and are a mere matter of "happily ever after".' Gerard Fay wrote of a 'light-weight championship' between Coward, Beverley Nichols, Godfrey Winn and Ivor Novello, which Noel sidestepped by choosing to document his war rather than publish a second volume of autobiography. There was a 'touch of dejection in Coward's later writing ... in some of which it is difficult to see exactly where the borderline between fact and imagination lies'.

It was not a propitious homecoming. *After the Ball* was on a twelve-week tour, and Coward saw it for the first time in Bristol. He was disappointed. The direction lacked style, and the speeches and songs were inaudible. 'Mary Ellis acted well but sang so badly that I could hardly bear it. The orchestra was appalling, the orchestrations beneath contempt, and poor Norman [Hackforth] conducted like a stick of wet asparagus.'

After the Ball was a collaboration between Coward and Cole Lesley, an ambitious attempt to turn Oscar Wilde's stage play *Lady Windermere's Fan* (now out of copyright) into a musical. Charles Hawtrey had parodied the play, and Coward had decried its author as a 'beauty-lover'; perhaps the auguries were not good for the meeting of dandy wits, rivals in spite of the generation that separated them. To Mary Ellis, Coward's 'timing and wit didn't match Wilde's story'; the balance of Wilde's play was upset and overturned by intrusive (although some good) songs. Part of the reason for its failure was that it was a co-operative effort; Lesley's investment in the production was clear from a letter to Stephen Tennant, who visited the cast in Southsea. 'In the drawing of the rose you have, for me, somehow crystallised all the charm and all the nostalgia of "After the Ball" so that it becomes a pledge for the play's success', said Lesley, a success which 'means a very great deal to me'.

Unfortunately, Tennant's gift was not an effective talisman. Eric Keown wrote in *Punch* that 'the basic melodrama of the original' had caused Coward to create 'operatic ding-dong' to illustrate 'moments of crisis'; this over-the-top quality detracted from what could be 'enjoyed simply as musical comedy'. Coward had failed to enliven the piece. 'If one is going to convince an audience of hard bitten, tough moderns that it is terrible for a young married woman to visit a bachelor in his rooms', observed an American reviewer, '. . . you will not do it the way selected here.'

After seeing *After the Ball*, Coward re-orchestrated the score and rehearsed the cast as the production progressed. 'Everybody was unhappy, miserable', says Ellis. 'He could do cruel things, always for the right reason, but it might have been better if he'd done them less cruelly . . . there was nobody who could satisfy him . . . except himself. One day at rehearsals he got up, and said "I see it this way", and practically played the whole first scene of Mrs Erlynne . . . I said "I can never play it as well as that" ... He was furious.' Ellis thought Graham Payn's performance uninspiring, 'He played the juvenile something-or-other, and had a dance and a song and that was it...' Coward had written the part of Mr Pepper for him, which added to the lack of balance. Coward professed himself pleased with the revamped version, which opened at the Globe Theatre on 10 June. 'An obvious success', said Noel. 'Mary was bloody good and at least sang quietly.' The press was not bad, but Coward felt that the cuts he had made would reduce the chances of its long-term success. 'It is now, subtly, a bit lopsided', he admitted. 'Personally I would give it about six to eight months, which is definitely better than nothing.' In the event, *After the Ball* ran for 188 performances.

On 16 June, Marlene Dietrich came to see the play; her arrival caused a traffic jam in Soho, and delayed the start of the show. A few days later, Dietrich threatened to upstage Coward with her own cabaret at the Café de Paris, in a sequinned reprise of her Berlin days, enhanced by the lighting of Joe Davis, whom Noel had introduced to her.

He also introduced Dietrich from the tiny nightclub stage, before she swept down the curving stairway. His preface mythologised the evening's star in delicious internal rhyme: 'Though we all might enjoy/ Seeing Helen of Troy/ As a gay cabaret entertainer,/ I doubt that she could/ Be one quarter as good/ As our lovely, legendary Marlene.' Noel had brought the Oliviers along to enjoy the show, as this 'Venus in furs', as Tynan called her, held sway. The evening was recorded and released – complete with Coward's introduction – as a lavish album, the first one thousand copies drenched in the scent Arpège. Its success influenced Noel's own recordings, which were to establish his fame among a new and younger audience, as would a new venture. When Dietrich had been asked to perform in Las Vegas in December 1953, Noel had advised her against the idea, saying it would be no more than 'saloon singing', but her runaway success there made him reconsider his judgement.

The vicarious pleasure of Dietrich's triumph was followed by a personal one when, as president of the Actors' Orphanage, he presided over the *Night of a Hundred Stars* organised by Charles Russell and Lance Hamilton. The pair had revitalised the Theatrical Garden Parties, previously dogged by pitiful attendances, frequent rainstorms and small proceeds, sometimes as little as £500. Russell had suggested that 'the stars belong under a roof. You can't put them in Regent's Park and hope it doesn't rain. So that's how "Night of a Hundred Stars" at the

Palladium came about.' Coward signed letters composed by Lance Hamilton, inviting stars to appear, and they made £10,000. Noel received an ovation and sang a duet with Dietrich, and news of his 'cosy personal triumph spread round theatrical London like *feu sauvage*'.

Yet amid all this hectic business was deep sadness. For some time now Coward had been watching helplessly as his mother's health declined. She became more deaf and crippled, yet still strained to keep up a bright appearance for her son. By 28 June, it was clear she was dying; she died two days later, aged ninety-one. 'I went round at eleven o'clock and she recognised me for a fleeting moment and said "dear old darling". Then she went into a coma. I sat by her bed and held her hand until she gave a pathetic little final gasp and died.' It was a mercifully brief exit. Noel was lucky to have had it so, as he was lucky to have had her throughout his life. She was always there at his first nights, though not at the parties afterwards, as the papers noted: 'A frail, white-haired figure who, later, would listen to the applause, smile contentedly, and then go straight home.' One reported that in the film of *The Astonished Heart*, she 'could not bear to see her son die even a film death'.

'Fifty-four years of love and tenderness and crossness and devotion and unswerving loyalty', her son recalled. 'Without her I could only have achieved a quarter of what I have achieved, not only in terms of success and career, but in terms of personal happiness . . . she has never stood between me and my life, never tried to hold me too tightly, always let me go free.' She was the one constant in his life; now she was gone. After the funeral at St Albans, Teddington, he flew to Paris. 'This week has been fairly idiotic. I have drunk a lot . . . seen heaps of people, gone through each day and night . . . dully . . . Mum, with her usual tact, has been content to sit quietly in my subconscious and not bother me. The only bad pang I have had was . . . from the impulse to send her a postcard.' Coward told Oliver Messel that he felt 'desolate and suddenly rootless . . . She was an old, old lady and it was "high time" and all that, but it didn't mitigate the sense of loss and the feeling that the most important link of all had gone.'

He flew south to stay at the Villa Mauresque for 'an escapist holiday'. Maugham was surprisingly good company, 'merry as a grig and very mellow and sweet'. But Coward underestimated the depth of his grief, and suffered 'a sort of minor nervous breakdown . . . a feeling of nullity'. He arrived back in London unable to face resting for a year as he had planned. Circumstances abruptly underlined the decision: Noel was £19,000 overdrawn. He returned to the Café de Paris, but the cold weather of autumn did not agree with his larynx. 'It is always dangerous for me to sing at this beastly time of the year', although the audiences didn't seem to care 'so long as I can get the comedy numbers over'. A Royal Command Performance at the London Palladium followed, during which Charles Russell and Cole Lesley arrived in his dressing-room to tell him 'to be prepared for a fate worse than death'. This only stirred him to greater heights, and the next day's papers 'announced, with unexpected generosity, that I was the hit of the show'. It did, however, convince him that the offer of a Palladium season (to repeat the recent success of Danny Kaye) was not a good idea; an intimate audience in the Café de Paris was one thing; the auditorium of the Palladium quite another.

But there was a new audience to whom Coward could play, one whose glittering jewels and tightly packed wallets had a different provenance from the accoutrements of the royal, aristocratic and theatrical celebrities who applauded him from their supper tables at the Café de Paris. Noel was about to be rediscovered by America and what he dubbed 'Nescafé Society'. The bright lights and big money of Las Vegas beckoned.

25

Live in Las Vegas

Las Vegas, Flipping, Shouts 'More!' as Noel Coward Wows 'Em in Café Turn.

Variety, 15 June 1955

COWARD spent Christmas 1954 in Jamaica with John Gielgud as a house guest, 'amusing, talkative and most considerate'. Noel 'used to read to us in the evening the work he'd been writing during the day, which rather amused me', says Gielgud. 'He would take our comments and go back and revise it ... He used to come down from his little house and make a great entrance on the swimming-pool for cocktails, then, like a royal routine, return for dinner.'

Coward often took his guests to visit Morris Cargill, who lived up the hill on his farm, Charlottenburgh. Cargill remembered Gielgud's visit, 'What a vain man ... when you'd go down to Blue Harbour, he wouldn't bother to talk to anybody. He'd sit by a window showing his profile ...' Cargill's favourite visitor was Laurence Oliver, 'Larry used to demand ganja, and he always used to maintain that Charlottenburgh ganja was the best in the world. Noel didn't approve of anybody smoking ganja – he was very stuffy about that. When Larry Olivier and one or two other people came up to Charlottenburgh and smoked my ganja out there Noel would sort of tolerate it but was very sniffy about it ...'

Visitors remained an equivocal pleasure. Natasha Wilson represented 'the most perfect house guest, as she never spoke to anyone before luncheon', although, as Lance Hamilton pointed out, 'as no one ever saw Noel before luncheon, I never understood how he knew'. When Charles Laughton and his manager Paul announced they were coming for lunch, 'Noel found it very tiresome', John Gielgud said. 'Laughton arrived, in a very sulky mood, with Paul, and of course they did stay for five hours.' As a character in Coward's unpublished play *Volcano* observes, 'The most beautiful thing about having people to stay is when they leave.' Keen not to commit a similar sin, Gielgud departed on New Year's Day, leaving Noel to consider 1955 and the rest of his sabbatical. 'I have at least a few months in hand before I resume singing and acting and showing off and being a fascinating public legend.'

Coward began work on a prose project, a short story, of which he had written 19,000 words by mid-January. It was obvious that it intended to be somewhat grander, so he decided to start again. The result became his Samolan-set novel, *Pomp and Circumstance*. Like *South Sea Bubble* (the revamped *Home and Colonial* play he was also working on), the book drew directly on local politics. That month, Coward stayed with Sir Hugh Foot, governor-general of Jamaica, at King's House in Kingston. Foot (brother of Michael Foot) was left-wing; his fictitious counterpart, Sir George Shotter (who appears in both *Pomp and Circumstance* and *South Sea Bubble*), is a 'rabid socialist'. Foot was pleased with the election as chief minister of Norman Manley, head of the left-wing People's National Party. The Foots were regular guests of Noel's, and vice versa. He later immortalised one gathering, at Blanche Blackwell's house, Bolt, on the hill above Blue Harbour:

> I will now propose a toast
> To the land we love the most
> Though the land we love the most may be kaputt, putt, putt
> But to get a social jolt
> We are lunching at the Bolt
> With the Governor and Lady Foot, Foot, Foot.
> I should like to drink a Stein
> For the sake of Auld Lang Syne
> Though the thought of Auld Lang Syne is far from sweet, sweet, sweet,
> So to get a social thrill
> We are trudging up the hill
> To have luncheon with dear Blanchie and the Feet, Feet, Feet.

In both book and play Coward sought to capture the sometimes farcical nature of island life, where issues were blown out of proportion. 'Jamaica 300', the tercentenary of British occupation, was celebrated in 1955, and the preparations for this and Princess Margaret's visit provided ample source material. An edict was issued saying Her Royal

Highness would not dance with black Jamaicans; Coward thought this stupid, 'Jamaica is a coloured island and if members of our Royal Family visit it they should be told to overcome prejudice.' Like her fictitious counterpart, Sylvia Foot insisted on welcoming black Jamaicans to Government House, much to the horror of the plantocracy.

In March, Russell and Hamilton arrived with a proposal from Bill Paley, head of CBS, who had asked if they could interest Coward in appearing on American television. 'At that time they couldn't get film stars to appear on TV. The studios kept them under contract and wouldn't allow them to do it.' Paley suggested that Coward could repeat the show he had done with Mary Martin at the Café de Paris (which Russell and Hamilton had produced). Coward agreed to Paley's proposal for three television shows: a one-hour special with Martin, and productions of *Present Laughter* and *'Peace in Our Time'*. Although the pair brought more lucrative sponsorship offers from General Motors and Chrysler, he decided to go with CBS and Ford's $450,000 because of their greater TV experience and better organisation. Russell and Hamilton, now appointed Noel's US agents, would receive $125,000 to produce the shows, plus 10 per cent of Coward's fee.

Back in London, Coward gave a party at Gerald Road to publicise that year's *Night of a Hundred Stars*. Two hundred people crammed into the studio, including Margaret Leighton, Baroness Ravensdale and Nancy Spain. Douglas Fairbanks Jnr stubbed out a cigarette on his host's rug, much to Coward's annoyance, and by the end of the party the library was full of empties and the floor covered in bottle tops. Coward found his homeland 'a bit dull and complacent. Perhaps Mum not being here any more has loosened my "roots" grip.' He was glad to return to New York on 15 May, where he settled a problem with the help of Marlene Dietrich. Norman Hackforth had been refused a work permit to accompany Coward in Las Vegas, and Dietrich suggested he use 'her' pianist and arranger, Peter Matz. Matz revamped the Coward tunes for an American market, establishing new and more modern configurations for old favourites. His work was a major contribution to Noel's success as a cabaret entertainer in America.

The prime motive for Coward's decision to play cabaret in Las Vegas was money. The shock of being overdrawn had made the finances of Noel Coward Ltd a pressing matter, so when a New York theatrical agent, Joe Glaser ('a brisk little Jewish go-getter', who acted for Louis Armstrong and Billie Holliday), proposed a three-week season in the

Nevada desert, Coward agreed. He was promised $15,000 a week, with another $60,000 from the Desert Inn (where he would appear) for options in the company formed to deal with his television ventures.

Las Vegas was 'a fabulous, extraordinary madhouse', a mass of neon and concrete that rose like Babylon from the plain, surrounded by towering pastel-coloured mountains. Coward found this temple to Mammon 'almost stimulating', seemingly run by gangsters with good manners. 'Their morals are bizarre in the extreme. They are generous, mother-worshippers, sentimental and capable of much kindness. They are also ruthless, cruel, violent and devoid of scruples ... curious products of a most curious adolescent country.'

He and Cole Lesley arrived on 5 June, sweltering in the hundred-degree heat, which Coward loved. The movie cameras were present to capture the arrival of this English alien: Noel striding from the plane, elegant in dark suit and bow tie, carrying (with a perceptible swing) a bucket bag. It was a royal arrival, with only the cheering crowds missing. They were in place for the first night: Frank Sinatra chartered a train from Los Angeles, bringing Judy Garland, Humphrey Bogart, Lauren Bacall, David Niven, 'Swifty' Lazar (Coward's literary agent in the States), Joan Fontaine, Zsa Zsa Gabor, Laurence Harvey *et al.*

Noel knew from his first few bars that he had the starry crowd in thrall. Performing in front of a backdrop painted to represent the Houses of Parliament, he was onstage for little more than half an hour but this concentrated airburst of charm was precision targeted for maximum Stateside effect. 'Coward's opening at the Desert Inn produced a notable crush, even for Las Vegas', the *New York Times* magazine reported. 'He appeared in a knowledgeably tight, double-breasted midnight-blue dinner jacket with a red carnation in his lapel. His hair is thinning, his shoulders are slightly hunched, his voice is a little nasal, his ears are large and his walk toed-out. He offered himself serenely, almost sedately and with an air of absolute authority. All he did was to sing his own songs and a parody of Cole Porter's "Let's Do It", the lyrics of which may be described as naughty. He sang "I'll See you Again", "Someday I'll Find You", "I'll Follow My Secret Heart", "Poor Uncle Harry", "A Bar on the Piccola Marina", "World Weary", "Nina" and "Mad Dogs and Englishmen" and several others. The room was drenched with nostalgia, both real and assumed ... "Thank you for giving me such a wonderful welcome. I'm terribly touched by the way you received me." He concealed his *touchment* artfully. Later, in his dressing room, which was banked with flowers and which reverberated with cries, both tender and hoarse, of "Noel" and "Darling", Coward received several planeloads of Hollywood celebrities, to say nothing of a middle-aged lady with odd red hair in a black gown of Spanish influence who was puffing agitatedly on a small cigar. "Noel," she said, "you brought class to Las Vegas. Now, you must bring class to Hollywood." "Darling", murmured Coward with eyes closed.'

The exuberant artificiality of this scene – the entertainer armed for public exposure – captures the spirit of the performer, as strong as ever in his mid-fifties, pinched and prettified for the stage; the almost nervous gestures to the face – as if to wave away criticism or to punctuate a devastating line – were conducted by a symbolic cigarette; a ramrod poise was achieved by tightly gripped cuffs. Due adulation was accepted from the lesser mortals of Las Vegas, allowed a glimpse of a rarefied level of human sophistication.

'I have made one of the most sensational successes of my career,' he recorded a week later, 'and to pretend that I am not absolutely delighted would be idiotic.' Modesty was thrown to the wind in the face of 'screaming rave notices . . . I am told continually, verbally and in print, that I am the greatest attraction that Las Vegas has ever had and that I am the greatest performer in the world.' It was a satisfying riposte to the 'mean, envious little sods' who said he had 'massacred' his own songs at the Café de Paris. 'I really feel that I don't want to appear at home much more.' The Master was slowly turning his back on his *alma mater*, 'pull the ladder up, Joe, for I'm all right!'

This self-celebration was abruptly curtailed by a sudden and violent fever. Sheer adrenalin could not carry him through this time, and his doctor insisted he cancel the show for one day. But Noel was back up there the following evening, and 'the triumph continues'. By now audiences were delivering 'a screaming ovation', and now he knew how Johnny Ray felt. Hollywood kept on coming, eager to see Noel Coward reborn as the ultimate cabaret star. But what really pleased him was that Mr and Mrs Midwest came too, and loved it. It proved he still had the common touch: 'How much I owe to those hellish troop audiences in the war.'

Peter Matz, Coward's new accompanist, marvelled at his ability to size up an audience: 'A certain joke might be too obscure for the second show . . . because the first six tables look as though they're sleepy, or eating or drinking too much. So he would just give them a break of an extra raised eyebrow . . . to say that the joke was coming, and of course an audience loves that.' The lessons of Charles Hawtrey were well remembered. The performance was recorded, and released as the *Noel Coward at Las Vegas* album. For its cover, he stood in the desert (at a temperature of 118 degrees) immaculate in evening clothes and black tie, delicately holding a cup of tea; a pillar of European culture in the arid vistas of the New World.

After visits from Cole Porter and Tallulah Bankhead, the engagement came to an end. Coward flew to Hollywood, virtually on the wings of his own triumph, where he was offered film parts and engagements galore. 'Paramount want me to do a picture with Danny Kaye and *The Sleeping Prince* and/or anything I bloody well like on my own terms. MGM want me to play the Prince in *The Swan*. Twentieth Century-Fox are sitting with their fingers crossed.'* The glory was increased by memory of the recent past, when Noel was in the wilderness, with not even a mirage of the Desert Inn on the horizon.

Hollywood loved success, as he knew from experience, and its doors were thrown open. Porter, Bogart and Sinatra all held parties in his honour, and at Sinatra's, the director Charles 'King' Vidor was prompted to pull off his amethyst and gold buttons and cufflinks as an impromptu present; Coward 'protested mildly and pocketed them'. The 'violent week' took its toll, and on 11 July Coward flew to Chicago, where he checked into the Passevant Hospital for an intensive three-day check-up supervised by Dr Ed Bigg. Every aspect of the Coward physique was examined, from blood checks to 'tickling my balls'. Nurses bustled in and out. 'How ya comin'?' asked one. Noel replied that in his present state he 'saw little hope of such a contingency arising'. The prognosis was optimistic, but the doctors found a curvature of the spine (Coward was now noticeably round-shouldered, a legacy from his father), which could be arrested by better posture; and an inclination to a 'nervous stomach'. Dr Bigg recommended less alcohol, but also less roughage – 'bad for my colon, which apparently is over-sensitive, like so many of my friends ... In fact he advised moderation in everything. We then got into a long discussion of morals and sex taboos and homosexuality, which convinced me he is one of the wisest and most

---

* *The Prince and the Showgirl*, based on Rattigan's play *The Sleeping Prince*, was to star Marilyn Monroe, but Coward did not like the idea of appearing with her – 'sometimes stars do not very much care for other stars', observed Lance Hamilton – and would consider the part only if Judy Halliday played the chorus girl. He had also been asked to play the phlegmatic British commanding officer in David Lean's *The Bridge on the River Kwai*, but turned it down on the grounds that he had spent most of his film career in or under water.

thoroughly sensible men I have ever met. I shall go to see him once a year.'

Returning to New York in a heatwave, he met Mike Todd, the flamboyant Broadway producer, and agreed to guest star in his first (and only) film, *Around the World in Eighty Days*. At a party given by Todd to announce his appearance, Noel told reporters, 'It's what they laughingly call a cameo part. When Mike Todd first offered me this part I said "No" very firmly. Ten minutes later I said "Yes" equally firmly.' He would not be paid for his two days' work; instead he would receive a Bonnard painting valued at £4500; as a tax-free scheme, it appealed to both parties. Noel's presence in the film was a magnet which helped Todd to attract other big names. (The film featured forty-four famous actors, including former Coward players such as Beatrice Lillie, John Mills, Robert Newton, Trevor Howard and Hermione Gingold.) Such was Coward's pulling power that shrewd New York businessmen couldn't believe he had not asked for a percentage in the movie. But as Noel's life insurance policy was about to mature, swelling his deposit account by £20,000, and with the Las Vegas fees added to his Jamaican reserves, his financial future at last looked secure.

He filmed his scenes for *Around the World in Eighty Days* at Elstree Studios on 30 August. The compressed screen time encouraged Coward to turn in a caricatured, flamboyant performance. Laurence Olivier had been due to play with him, but turned down the part, and Gielgud was enlisted, 'charming to work with. He was, as usual, a little false in his performance but very effective.' Coward was head of a domestic employment agency, and dealt with Gielgud as Phineas Fogg's frustrated butler, driven to leave by his master's demands. 'How *do* you take the temperature of toast?' mused Coward, in slicked-back toupée and frock coat.

He returned to Jamaica to write songs for his TV show with Mary Martin, with Peter Matz's help. Martin and Richard Halliday also came out for informal rehearsals, but idyllic press shots of Noel and Mary by the pool or at the piano at 'Coward's luxurious winter estate' belied the true atmosphere. The Americans were exceptionally noisy, and Halliday's drinking and 'bad character' convinced Coward he wanted nothing to do with him. One evening Halliday turned on him 'with snarling, whining hatred', accusing him of 'cheese-paring'. Coward informed Martin that he would not work with her husband: he could not risk losing his temper, or the bad publicity that would ensue.

The couple left Coward in peace on 25 September. He and Matz continued to work, under the threat of an approaching hurricane, which meant they had to keep the radio on all day to heed the storm warning. In the sweltering sessions of song-writing, only fifteen-minute bursts were possible before they had to cool off in the pool. Matz watched in amazement as Coward wrote out whole songs, such as 'What's Going to Happen to the Tots?', almost without pausing (a satire on modern morals, it updated a 1927 version, which might account for the speed of transcription). Meanwhile the threatened hurricane shook the house, but was less disturbing than the Hallidays' shrill voices.

At the beginning of October Coward flew back to New York to rehearse his TV shows. Charles Russell had found an apartment for him in the same block as his own, 404 East 54th Street. When Coward moved in, Russell told him of the young actor who lived upstairs, a good-looking American called Alan Helms. 'Well, we must take what God sends us, mustn't we?' Coward quipped. Rehearsals for *Together with Music* took place on a 'closed set'; CBS barred all extraneous personnel for security reasons. They went well, but Richard Halliday's presence soon began to grate, and he and Noel had full-scale shouting matches on set. His wife, although 'a great performer', was 'painfully naive and has no clue about playing comedy and never will have', and the comic scenes which Coward tried to work out with Martin were killed by Martin's '"Rebecca of Sunnybrook Farm" quality'. The result, Coward feared (if only for the balance of the piece), would be that 'I shall play rings round her.' There were to be three live performances before an invited audience at Studio 72 (an old Broadway theatre), only the last of which would be televised – the first live 'spectacular' transmitted in colour.

There were, however, last-minute problems with the sponsors. CBS had sold the airtime to the Ford Foundation, and their advertising people came up with pastiches of *Private Lives*: lovers on a balcony watching Ford models pass by, with a commentary that led from 'very flat, Norfolk' to 'and so is the Thunderbird Hardtop, with the interchangeable hoods and seat belts and push button drive and automatic window washer and the plastic seat covers extra'. Russell and Hamilton thought it best not to show these to Coward. Nonetheless, Ford had to be advertised, and the studio was filled with the new models, making the performing space a tight squeeze. During the ninety-minute programme there would be several commercials, when the live show would have to stop dead. Worse was to come. Ford were determined that such 'offensive' lines as 'Nina's' 'Sycophantic lot of sluts/ For ever wriggling their guts' be excised. 'One of the directors ... told Coward that he thought the Bible Belt wasn't ready for such language yet, and that it was vulgar. "Vulgar?" said Coward. "I'll tell what you what vulgar is. That" – pointing to a row of coloured Ford cars – "*that* is vulgar."' Only hours away from airtime, Coward informed the would-be arbiters that for thirty-five years he had been concerned with 'productions of impeccable taste', that he considered their interference 'impertinent', and that since he was employed to entertain the majority, he had 'no intention of being dictated to by a minority'.

The show went on – on Coward's terms. *Together with Music* was a *tour-de-force* of his performing style. Preserved on videotape (the only extant film of Coward in cabaret mode), his television manner convinces completely; for all his denunciations, he used the medium in that same effortless, controlled manner that defined his theatrical ability. 'Nina' is sung with hip-swivelling and finger-wagging camp and punctuated by a final flamenco-style flourish of the hand; 'Mad Dogs and Englishmen' is taken at dizzying pace, the 'papalaka' asides ('pay no attention, that's native talk') thrown aside for an audience left trailing behind. By the time they catch up, Noel has taken his bow and is acknowledging the applause before it arrives. The effect is startlingly modern; not for nothing did Tynan claim that Coward had 'invented the concept of cool'.

A lavish post-production party was thrown by Bill Paley for the cast, crew and guests, and the first reviews appeared even before it had finished. Reaction to the programme – viewed by millions across the United States – was excellent, but it didn't get the viewing figures CBS had hoped for (although the press claimed thirty million, the figure given by the Trendex ratings was seventeen). Bill Paley said how pleased he had been with the show, and was sorry that the ratings were not better, 'but Noel didn't have to worry. The ratings ... would improve ... by the third show there would be a great difference.'

Viewers may have been disconcerted by Coward's sly digs at American culture. Out of the deluxe context of Las Vegas, and beamed by interstate television into the heart of the Midwest, his camp cowboy swagger to 'Deep in the Heart of Texas' might have been offensive. But the newspapers liked it; they considered Coward had devised a new form of entertainment. 'There has certainly been no more informal show since the beginnings of television. These two could very well set a trend that a lot of other entertainers might imitate.' Some thought

Coward hadn't gone far enough. Regretting the fact that he had toned down the 'sexy innuendo' of his 'Let's Do It' parody for America ('Even Liberace, we assume/ Does it'), one writer said that 'most Americans who have followed Noel's career are aware that he's a bit queer. But they would consider it in poor taste for him to flaunt his peculiarities in public. And he's too smart for that . . . if Coward had sung his parody in Las Vegas the way he did in London, some of those tough cowboys out there might have run him out of town.'

Even now, Coward's sexuality could be held against him. He read in *The Times* that a magistrate's court in London had voted against altering the laws on homosexuality. Noel's attitude was equivocal, 'Any sexual activities when over-advertised are tasteless, and for as long as these barbarous laws exist it should be remembered that homosexuality *is* a penal offence and should be considered as such socially, although not morally. This places on the natural homo a burden of responsibility to himself, his friends and society which he is too prone to forget . . .' For Coward, taste and discretion were all: while he railed against the blackmail such laws encouraged, he felt that 'abnormal sex' ought to be kept entirely private. It was an Edwardian attitude: sex happened, but ought not to be flaunted; to do so laid one open to the censure of the scandal-hungry press – as it did in America, later that month. A magazine called *Rave* published a piece in which Coward read that he was 'the highest-paid British "tulip" (better than "pansy", I thought) who had ever been imported into America, that during the war I sang "Mad About the Boy" to an RAF officer at Biggin Hill and was ducked in a pond by his incensed comrades; that I had set up a young man in Jamaica in a travel agency. All this was printed clearly and with a refreshing lack of innuendo.' None of it was true, and to sue would invite further publicity. But he had to protest. 'I *never* sing "Mad About the Boy"' – the pitch was much too high for him.

A new dilemma faced Coward that autumn. With all the time he was spending out of England, it was ridiculous to be paying up to £20,000 a year in income tax. He was subject to a high rate of up to 50 per cent, with surtax on top. 'It was a great incentive for people to get out', says his adviser, Leslie Smith. Coward's finances were still suffering from Jack Wilson's mismanagement, which had left Noel Coward Ltd a less viable concern than it should have been (considering the enormous sums earned by Coward in the past). He had made no money by selling film rights to any of his post-war works, and such sales had their tax complications anyway; Noel had been particularly annoyed, when the rights for *Blithe Spirit* were sold, at having to pay American as well as British tax, with the result that he received just 7 per cent of the fee, while the agent got 10 per cent.

Coward was officially employed, 'on a modest salary', by Noel Coward Ltd, which was the holding house for all the income – play royalties, film fees, and any other earnings. The expenses submitted to the Inland Revenue by the company were enormous – £100,000 a year – comprising the running of the houses, salaries, parties and so on; there were 'very generous allowances', observes Smith: 'Gerald Road, Burton Mews, Mrs Loraine's salary, Goldenhurst, Blue Harbour and Firefly'. John Basden, a specialist in theatrical accountancy, was Coward's accountant in Britain, adept at obtaining good deals from the tax inspector, and Fanny and David Holtzmann worked on his American finances. In the mid-Fifties, Coward discovered that Basden had 'used the proceeds of an endowment policy – which Noel had ear-marked in his mind as a nest-egg – for the purposes of paying some of Noel's tax. Noel nearly went up the wall.'

The result was a drastic decision to sell up and move out, no easy matter then, when currency restrictions meant money had to taken out gradually, over nine years. His tax counsel told Coward he must 'destroy all his connections with the UK, and resign from all his clubs . . . and dispose of all his homes and property here, move all his belongings abroad or sell them'.

In Jamaica, Morris Cargill was party to the financial dealings of his friend. 'Noel was busy going broke. He owed a lot of money to the income tax people in England . . . I happen to be a lawyer [and] my speciality was company income tax law. [Sir Dingwall Bateson] came out . . . and we had a long conference about Noel's affairs. We set up a structure. But one of the things was that he had to ration Noel, he had to put him on an allowance. He hated it! He came out one day, storming up to Charlottenburgh. "You little shit!" he said, "you're starving me to death, that's what you're doing!" Just like a spoilt child, you know. I let him go on, till he calmed down. We got him sorted out very nicely.'

Noel wrote to Joyce Carey of his impending exile. 'I could not obviously have done this while Mum was alive but even then, and all my life, I have got out of England as quickly as I could as often as I could. I think on the whole that I have not done badly by England and I also think that England has not done very well by me. The general public love me and are, I feel, proud of me but this does not apply to the press, the politicians and even the present darling Royal Family – or, if they are, they haven't made it apparent . . .'

Coward was lucky in that his work did not tie him to England; anyway, recent events had indicated that America was a more fruitful market for his talents. It was sad for him to cut the umbilical cord, but that connection had already been severed with the death of his mother. The proposition quickly became a *fait accompli*. Escaping the whirl of figures, Noel left for Havana, Mexico and Hollywood. 'The joke will certainly be on me if one of the planes . . . plunge[s] me into eternity, but if it does my first gesture in the afterlife will be to form a limited company, establish residence and set about avoiding (not evading) any celestial income tax . . .'

Christmas 1955 found Coward back in Hollywood, to rehearse *Blithe Spirit* for CBS. New York was rapidly losing its position as a centre for television; not only was land cheaper in Hollywood, but most of the stars lived there.

Lauren Bacall had been chosen to play Elvira, and Claudette Colbert, Ruth. Neither woman was easy to work with; Colbert was '*extremely tiresome*', and Bacall was 'no comedienne'. Colbert recalled that Coward was 'unremittingly difficult'. When she apologised for fluffing her lines – 'I knew them backwards last night' – Noel retorted, 'Yes, and that's the way you're saying them this morning.' Colbert had always regretted the fact that the distance between her nape and shoulders was short: 'The thing Noel said that hurt me most – but funny it was – he said, "If she had a neck, I'd wring it."'

Russell and Hamilton were dismayed that Coward wanted Graham Payn in *Blithe Spirit*. 'We thought Graham was safely in London . . . but Coward said, "Oh, Graham's here, he can play Dr Bradman."' Russell reminded him that 'three years before he'd had Graham on Broadway, and brought him to the front instead of Gertie Lawrence . . . Hedda Hopper had attacked him in the press for it . . . With Hopper and Louella Parsons watching a live TV show, it would be disastrous . . . We just said no.'

Preparations followed the usual precise requirements: Coward demanded a month of rehearsals on a fully furnished set (in the poltergeist scenes of the play, even the furniture had to be rehearsed), and all but essential personnel were barred ('That's so the men spending their money won't bother their ulcers', Noel told a journalist). He also requested a studio audience for an early rehearsal, to judge reactions.

These were unprecedented demands for a medium used to casual drama production methods. But just as camera rehearsals began, an abscess was discovered on Coward's sciatic nerve in his right leg. A doctor was sent for, 'and injected the damn thing eight times with the thickest needle I have ever seen'. Numbed with novocaine, he continued, although he seemed bad-tempered for much of the rehearsals. But the ninety-minute show was 'played without nerves and *on* nerves ... the result was that the performance went like a bomb'. The invited audience were described as 'very hep' by the *New York Herald-Tribune*, who likened it to 'a smart Broadway opening with a terribly fashionable cast in front of an upper-drawer audience'.

Critics judged the show 'light as thistledown and merry as an epigram tossed off in a glittering drawing room'. One paper remarked on the dialogue, 'just about the most emancipated we've heard in a television comedy ... uproarious boudoir innuendo; several well-placed hells and damns; and one of the funniest rebukes of all time ... Noel Coward tells his purring, ectoplasmic wife, "Don't call me 'lover boy'. It's vulgar and inaccurate."'

With this new TV triumph behind him, Coward left for Bermuda to do some house-hunting. His financial advisers recommended residence in the British dependency because it was still in the sterling district as well as being a tax haven, and dollars were accepted there. 'Yes, it is a wrench all right,' wrote Noel, 'but I *know* I cannot maintain Golden-hurst *and* Jamaica, and it will be better to say goodbye now, when I can at least profit by it, than wait for a few years and be forced to part with it at a loss of thousands.' Yet when it came to be sold, Goldenhurst could not even reach the asking price.

Coward found a house called Spithead Lodge in Warwick Parish, Hamilton, on the steep shore edge, which he hoped to buy, half on mortgage, for £18,000; not cheap, but 'it will surely be worth it', he thought. Dingwall Bateson informed his client that both Goldenhurst and Gerald Road should be sold before 6 April, the beginning of the financial year, and that he would not be allowed to visit England between then and April 1957; after that, he could return for only three months a year.

The London operations of Noel Coward Ltd were again revamped. Graham Payn would share a flat in London with Cole Lesley, and Lorn Loraine would move the office to her house at 32 Milner Street. Coward had to resign as president of the Actors' Orphanage, 'which frankly is a great relief, it has cost me a lot of time, energy and money for twenty years'. With *South Sea Bubble* about to open, Noel had to accept that he might never see the play; the drawbacks of exile were beginning to appear. *Nude with Violin* had been postponed until the summer while John Gielgud paid his surtax bill by appearing in a film remake of *The Barretts of Wimpole Street*.

In February Coward repaired to Jamaica, where the house on Firefly Hill was finished. He had commissioned Pat Marr-Johnson, a Jamaican neighbour and architect, to build it; the result was another 'ugly house' like Blue Harbour, recalls Morris Cargill. 'I thought it was dreadful, but funnily enough, Noel . . . didn't seem to have much in the way of taste either in his furniture or in his houses . . . He shared this with Ian Fleming. Neither of them had any good taste at all. They couldn't choose a curtain.' Originally stone-faced in a crazy-paving style (Coward later had it rendered and whitewashed to look less gloomy), the impression was part modernist 1930s bungalow, part military fort. Its slit windows – more redolent of a machine-gun emplacement than of a cosy retreat – underlined the defensive atmosphere of this icing-sugar pillbox, a fey modern counterpoint to Captain Morgan's fiercely hewn look-out. The resemblance to the Watchhouse (the Portmeirion villa in which Coward wrote *Blithe Spirit*) may not have been coincidental; it was as though Coward sought to recreate the atmosphere of that creative retreat.

The house had few rooms: a studio, a modest music-room, and a sitting-room, with its open, unglazed window framing a grandiose widescreen view, reminiscent of one of the Edwardian 'Panoramas' Coward had seen as a child. Below was Port Maria, the successive bays beyond, and the Blue Mountains in the distance. (When Coward showed Lynn Fontanne the view, the staggered ranges of valleys and hills stretching into the distance, he said, 'Isn't it marvellous?' 'No,' replied the actress, 'it reminds me of too many empty seats.') Below, too, were his neighbours, Blanche Blackwell at Bolt House, the Flemings at Goldeneye, and his own guests at Blue Harbour. From this theatrical vantage point he could look down on their goings-on, and affairs which he would soon be documenting anew.

The view was enough to distract any writer from his work. But work here Coward did, at a large, plain wooden desk. The simple interior did not feel like the abode of a wealthy man, more the monastic retreat of one who thrived in a hot climate. Its *raison d'être* was its setting. Noel would spend more and more time there, secluded from the hubbub below and from the incessant sound of the sea, which he now found disturbing. Sometimes he would descend only to Blue Harbour to swim, or for dinner; when he had a swimming-pool built, at great expense (Graham Payn recalls that it required 'seventeen lorryloads of water' to fill), his visits to his original island home virtually ceased, and invitations to Firefly became a rare ticket.

Despite his new isolation at Firefly, life was no quieter for him in Jamaica. Ian Fleming wrote to his wife with reports of Truman Capote's visit, 'hustling and twittering along with his tiny face crushed under a Russian commissars' uniform hat . . . Just taking him off to Noel for drinks and dinner . . .'

'The Noel evening was typical', he reported. 'His firefly house is a near-disaster and anyway the rain pours into it from every angle and even through the stone walls so that the rooms are running with damp. He is by way of living alone up there and Coley has to spend half the day running up and down in the car with ice and hot dishes of quiche Lorraine! A crazy set-up. N. is going to sell Goldenhurst and Gerald Street and become a Bermuda citizen! So as to save up money for his old age. I can see the point but expect the papers will say some harsh things . . .'

Blanche Blackwell was a new arrival on the island. Sister of Robert Lindo, who had sold Coward the land for his Jamaican houses. She had come to live in the family home situated strategically between Golden-eye, Blue Harbour and Firefly. It was a symbolic position, for Blanche was to find herself caught between two friends. Coward appreciated this young, good-looking girl; 'feisty' might be the word a midwesterner would apply. Ian Fleming appreciated her charms too; as she recalls, 'He treated women badly, but I was not the sort of woman to just take it. I think what he liked in me was my willingness to defy him.' Soon the talk was that Blanche and Ian were lovers. This not being the case (yet), Blanche became vexed at the gossip Noel was spreading. 'One night I got on my horse and rode over to his house. I said "Noel, I know what you think, and it isn't true."' But during 1956 he worked on a new play, *Volcano*, inspired by Blackwell's affair with Fleming, which did indeed blossom. The 'volcano' of Noel's play might well have been the wrath of Ann, when she discovered what was happening.

Coward relished the affairs of the Flemings: Ian conducted romances with Loelia Westminster and Rosamond Lehmann, while Ann was involved with Hugh Gaitskell. Loelia Westminster once looked on in amusement as Coward bartered for Fleming's Polaroid camera in return for taking in Lehmann when her presence at Goldeneye grew too disruptive. Peter Quennell – who recalled that Fleming's method of dismissing Lehmann was to throw an octopus at her – also remembered Noel's comment to Ian: 'You're just an old cunt-teaser, aren't you?' In *Volcano*, inspired by these island flings, Coward dealt with themes of jealousy and envy, passion and principle. Set on Samola, to a soundtrack of native drums and the ominous rumble of the neighbouring volcano, the play is riven with inter-couple bickering. Adela, a widow in her forties, and Guy Littleton, thirty-five, are unconsummated lovers. Guy's wife Melissa arrives on the island; for anyone who knew her, it would be hard to ignore the aspects of Ann Fleming invested in this society beauty: 'I'm afraid I've never found it easy to be on really friendly terms with other women. I suppose it is because I find men so much more interesting.' Guy is seen as a heartbreaker; Keith, a school friend, admits to his wife, 'I *was* in love before I met you. So much in love that it twisted up my whole life . . .' She asks, 'Who was it you loved so much? Who twisted up your whole life?' At which the butler announces, 'Mr Guy Littleton'.

This revelation confirms Guy's ability to wreck other people's lives with his promiscuity. The final scene of the play returns to Adela's verandah, ten days later. Guy comes in bearing seashells from a scuba-dive (as Ian Fleming did for Blanche), and attempts an amorous reconciliation. Adela dismisses him, 'You wreak too much havoc, swaggering through people's lives touting your illusion that physical love is "the one irreplaceable ecstasy". Shakespeare described your creed more accurately, "An expense of spirit in a waste of shame". I'm tired of the noise you make with your shrill, boastful trumpeting. Please go away and leave me alone.' Adela 'slowly dashes each of the seashells, one by one, to the ground'.

Volcano could be taken as an implicit criticism of heterosexual lust, as personified by Guy Littleton; it is certainly an indictment of mindless passion, as Noel saw it. It came at a period when Coward was entering late middle age, and eschewing the sexuality of his youth, when he had been as promiscuous as these characters. It seemed he had put those days behind him.

Volcano never saw the limelight. Binkie Beaumont, when given the play to read, turned it down, telling Coward it was not a viable proposition. Charles Russell thinks that the piece went unproduced because 'it wasn't good enough'. But Coward refused to let it lie, and asked Russell to deliver a manuscript of the play to Katharine Hepburn in New York, at her house on East 49th Street, in the hope that she would consider the part of Adela. 'Someone answered the door with a mop and a headscarf', Russell recalls. 'I didn't recognise Katharine Hepburn for a moment. She lifted her arm up and asked me to put the script under there!'

Back in England, the break-up of the Coward empire continued. On her return to London Lorn Loraine had been charged with selling off Noel's 'principal pictures'. Leslie Smith thought 'it was a case of them wanting the money – they didn't have to sell them'. The auction was at Sotheby's on 19 April. Also there were Richard Attenborough, who bid for a Boudin; Gladys Calthrop (who got bored and went out halfway through to do some shopping in Bond Street); and Nancy Spain, who told the readers of the *Daily Express* that the occasion 'felt more and more like a funeral' as she spotted members of 'the Old Brigade of Coward Faithfuls'. The auctioneer, Peter Wilson, 'had a very grand manner', Smith recalls. 'When he was conducting the auction, you couldn't tell if he was taking real bids or not.' Smith watched as one painting was knocked down, 'It hadn't been sold, he was buying it in for Noel ... instead of announcing it hadn't reached its reserve ... it was done very discreetly.'

Fourteen pictures in total were sold, two Vlamincks, a Bonnard and a Boudin accounting for £11,000. Four Christopher Woods and a John Nash helped to bring the total to £12,990. Lorn Loraine also sold Coward's Jaguar, and oversaw the sale of Gerald Road and Goldenhurst. Gerald Road went for £11,000, not a bad price; it was a desirable town house, after all. Goldenhurst was a different proposition. The six-bedroom, five-bathroom property, plus tenanted farm with 149 acres of land, was originally offered at £17,000. But it failed to sell, so the farm was sold off separately, and the house, with thirty-two acres, went to auction on 31 July 1956. 'There wasn't a bid in the room', recalls Smith. The auctioneer neglected to mention the house's most famous tenant, content to refer to its possible Roman origins. The bidding crept up to £6600, short of the reserve price (£7500), and the property was withdrawn. Goldenhurst was eventually sold in September of that year, to a retired colonial civil servant recently returned from Kenya, for an undisclosed sum. 'From Mr Coward's point of view the price is disappointing', admitted the estate agents.

That Coward was literally selling out was public knowledge, and the British press reaction was mixed. The *Daily Express*, notably Conservative in outlook, wrote 'more in sorrow than in anger' of the loss of a great British playwright, driven out by a Labour government. Noel thought the article well-judged, but knew his friends would indulge in 'a certain amount of head-shaking and disapproval'.

Coward's next project was his third television special. He reread *Present Laughter* and cut it to an hour and twenty minutes, 'without, I think, impairing its essential quality', but removing the more blatant sexual references for the benefit of 'millions of Bible-thumping, puritanical, asinine televiewers'. 'They didn't like the idea of Gary Essendine being chased by both boys and girls', says Charles Russell. Rumours circulated that the project had been cancelled, but Hamilton told the press on his return, 'It can't be off, actually. It's a commitment. We have a contract as big as the Magna Carta.'

However, the Ford Motor Company announced that the show would not go ahead because the ratings for the previous two had not been good enough. To Coward, this had been done deliberately to 'humiliate me as publicly as possible', because of his comments about their products and lack of taste. ('People who object to the profanity in "Blithe Spirit" are crackpots,' Coward had told a reporter, 'and Mr Ford should be happy if even one of them doesn't buy his car. They would be a menace on the highway.') The press were commenting on the feud: 'Insiders feel that no one, other than possibly Mr Coward, would be too unhappy if the spectacular were eased out because his appeal is considered too sophisticated for most viewers and, as important, he has proven difficult to work with in the past.' Coward's imperiousness had annoyed Ford and CBS, maintained Russell. 'People didn't like him because he'd led Mary Martin a song and dance, playing Lord and Master, he was an Englishman, and queer to boot.'

Coward decided to fly immediately to New York, in a whirl of indignation ('Like darling Mum, I fairly blossom in a crisis'). Bill Paley was 'twitching with apprehension', and an agreement was reached: a press release announcing that Noel's show had been postponed until October, when the new CBS series, *Playhouse 90*, would be launched with *This Happy Breed* (an acceptable alternative for the Midwest). But as the publicity worsened, realising they had nothing to fill the gap, Ford returned to the original arrangement, allowing Coward to do the show on 5 May, as his contract had stipulated.

While in New York, Coward saw Rex Harrison and Julie Andrews in *My Fair Lady*, 'really quite enchanting from every point of view'.

Ironically (considering that Coward had been offered the role of Henry Higgins), Harrison had protested to lyricist Alan Lerner that 'Why Can't the English' made him sound too much like Noel, and he asked Lerner 'to find some less Cowardly words'. Noel was concentrating on the narration of Ogden Nash's verse which he was to read to the accompaniment of Saint-Saëns's *Carnival of the Animals* at Carnegie Hall. 'Coward spoke the rhymes, alternately standing beside a mike and sitting informally in an armchair, with fitting tongue-in-cheek', but the performance was not particularly successful; Coward blamed the presentation and an unprepared audience. The following night he did a version for *The Ed Sullivan Show*; with fifty-two million viewers, it was the largest audience he would ever play to. He followed this with another TV appearance, on Ed Murrow's *Person to Person*, filmed in Russell's and Hamilton's apartment at East 54th Street, because it was larger than his. Coward's performance was urbanity itself. 'Tell me,' asked Murrow, 'have you found anything special to ease the tensions after a hard day's work?' 'Certainly,' Coward replied, 'but I've no intention of discussing it in front of several million people.' Murrow asked about his painting. 'I just happen to have one here', Noel replied cheekily, taking a Jamaican street market scene to the camera. 'How would you describe the style?' asked Murrow. 'Erratic', replied Noel. 'Actually, it's known by my friends as Touch and Gauguin.'

For *This Happy Breed*, Coward much preferred working in the television studios in New York to those of Hollywood. There was less clutter and fuss ('those prehistoric monsters lunging at you', as he called the cameras), and the scale seemed more human. The technicians even presented him with a bunch of chrysanthemums after a dress rehearsal, and after rehearsals he could go home and cook himself an omelette. 'You could never cook your own omelette in Hollywood, old sport', he told a reporter. 'That's one of the things that's wrong with the place.'

This Happy Breed was transmitted live at 9.30 p.m. on 5 May. Coward paid tribute to Edna Best's performance as Ethel; Best had recently suffered mental illness, but that evening 'the rapport between us was so strong that it gave the play a little personal magic that it has never had before either on the stage or the screen'. Critics found the show 'frequently touching and always understanding', with 'genuinely warm scenes', although Coward's portrayal of the young Frank Gibbons failed to convince; at fifty-six years of age, perhaps that was too much to expect even of a stage magician. Despite generally good reviews, the ratings were lower than for previous shows, which explains why

Coward was not issued with a speedy return invitation to US network television.

In mid-May he returned to Europe on the SS *Liberté*, a slow boat to soothe his spirits. With £60,000 in his Bermudan bank account (which had swollen to £111,000 by the beginning of June), and six successful American engagements in ten months, he felt justified in taking things easy. But on his arrival in France, Coward was faced with hostile press reaction about 'renouncing my native land where I earned all my riches. This view seems to arise from the belief that the great British public made me. In fact I have made most of my money in the United States.' Coward sought to prove his honesty regarding his financial dealings. He pointed out that in 1949 he could have bought his Paris apartment in the Place Vendôme for £8000 had he not observed currency restrictions. 'Of course, I was an unspeakable fool. I could have got an American to buy the flat for me and I would have paid him back in New York.'

Coward found the media intrusion 'sickeningly vulgar', a symptom of the post-war world. Paris was another reminder of the passage of time, meeting old bright young things at Chantilly: Diana Cooper, Olga Lynn and Iris Tree. But Diana was at last beginning to look old, and at Chantilly 'the past lay over the house heavily, like a curse, instead of something lovely to be remembered'. Marlene Dietrich too was showing 'signs of wear and tear', intensely preoccupied with 'her love affairs . . . How foolish to think that one can ever slam the door in the face of age. Much wiser to be polite and gracious and ask him to lunch in advance.' At Biot, he saw Edward Molyneux, and lunched with Winston Churchill, who was staying nearby. Churchill was pathetically enamoured of a young woman, Wendy Russell, and pointed to a Toulouse-Lautrec nude, saying 'in a voice dripping with senile prurience, "Very appetizing!"' That a man of Churchill's stature should be reduced to an impotent fantasy sex life was 'pitiable'. Noel's worldliness (especially in amatory matters) allowed a charitable view, and he 'forgave the old man his resolute enmity of years, then and there. He, the most triumphant man alive, after all has lived much less than I.' He also saw the Windsors; the duke, now deaf, was 'completely idiotic', and Noel reflected wryly that he had been 'sucking up to two men who had been steadfastly against me since I was in my twenties'. It seemed a pity that Max Beaverbrook was not there to complete the trio.

He was glad to return to Bermuda at the end of June. 'What I have been doing is what is laughingly known as "settling in"', he told Nancy

Mitford. 'The house is enchanting and my own little private cottage a veritable *rêve* because it goes straight down into the limpidest sea . . .' 'The island itself is much, much nicer than I thought it would be', although Coward had to build a stone wall to deflect prying eyes, and passing cruisers would announce through loudspeakers that Spithead Lodge was formerly the home of Eugene O'Neill, and was now the residence of Noel Coward. Out practising his breast-stroke when the first announcement drifted across, he found himself the subject of 'about twenty nuns peering at me through binoculars'. 'The other morning I was caught, practically naked, covered in dust and sweat and carrying a frying-pan in one hand and a slop-pail in the other', he told Nancy. 'I paused graciously while they took their bloody snapshots, and pressed on with my tasks and occupations. Noel Coward is *so* sophisticated.'

Coward was in his cooking phase, eagerly trying out often disastrous recipes on his house guests; he signed off his letter to Nancy Mitford, 'I must stop now and go back to my tasks and occupations, one of which is to frost a rather rubbery angel cake which I made yesterday.' Due to the heat, he often wore just an apron while cooking. Once he answered the door to a cleric, calling to welcome him to the island. 'Just a minute', said Noel, remembering he had something in the oven and, turning to attend to it, presented his naked rear to the shocked clergyman.

The social demands of British colonial life soon buried the play-wright's hopes for peace under a pile of invitations. 'I would like to be able to tell you proudly that I have written thousands of witty words since I saw you,' he told Nancy, 'and that my novel is finished and a new play started. Unfortunately it would NOT BE TRUE. What is true is that I haven't written a bloody word except a short note in the third person saying that Mr Noel Coward would be delighted to attend the Admiralty Fête and draw tickets for the Raffle.'

26

Pomp and Circumstance

Mr Noel Coward, at over fifty, still retains that power to surprise, scandalise, and amuse which made him the adored, as well as the abused, *enfant terrible* of the 1920s. You never know whether he will be stormy petrel, petard, pianist, Puritan or, even, very occasionally, puerile; though you can be certain he will never be peasant, poet, pedant, or Pecksniff.

Harold Hobson, *Sunday Times,* 29 April 1956

COWARD'S exile did not mean that his name was forgotten in Britain; in April 1956 his professional life continued with the opening of *South Sea Bubble* at the Lyric Theatre. Like many of his post-war works, its history was erratic. It began life under the title *Home and Colonial* in 1949, when Coward first took up residence in Jamaica, and was inspired by a mixture of Evelyn Waugh's *Decline and Fall* and colonial eccentricity. Intended for Gertrude Lawrence, the heroine of the piece was Lady Alexandra, or Sandra, a Diana Cooper–Edwina Mountbatten figure also to appear in *Pomp and Circumstance.* Coward drew on the chic, charming, yet flighty aspects of these two society beauties for his portrait of the governor's wife, threatened with seduction by Hali, a Samolan nobleman. The comedy included the goings-on at Government House and 'scandal with local Busta' (Busta-mente, the Jamaican prime minister, caricatured in the play as the blackmailing politician father of Hali). Coward saw it as a 'heaven-sent opportunity to get in a lot of Jamaican stuff'.

Lawrence had been unable to play Sandra, and in June 1950 Coward and Beaumont asked Vivien Leigh to take the part in London. But the Oliviers had 'violently disliked' the play, which was 'a surprising and salutary jolt' for Coward, but 'I have a strange feeling they are right'. It was 'curiously overwritten', he admitted, 'I seem, in later years, to have lost my gift for economy.' It was not until March 1955 that he resurrected the play, rewriting it almost entirely and renaming it *South Sea Bubble*. Vivien Leigh was now 'madly enthusiastic' to do the play (a description which Beaumont thought a little too apt), and rehearsals began in February 1956, under the direction of William Chappell.* On its opening in Manchester Coward was told of 'a roaring success', and 'a comedy triumph' for Leigh. It owed much to Leigh's portrayal of the charming Sandra, whose breathless entrances seemed typecast for the heroine of *Gone with the Wind*. When the play was published, it was dedicated to her. But Leigh had the support of a cast of experienced Coward actors – Alan Webb, Joyce Carey and Arthur Macrae† – who could handle dialogue demanding meticulous timing for comic effect. Harold Hobson wrote that it was 'an almost perfect example of co-operation between author, company, and director'.

The political satire depends on the old clash of imperial and socialist values, with Sandra, like the real governor's wife (Sylvia Foot), representing modernity. When reprimanded for using the word 'appetisers', she says, 'I know a lot of others too. They're all part of the progressive modern trend. I can say "Lounge" and "Phone" and "Let's have a small one before we buzz".' It was no coincidence that Nancy Mitford's teasing essay on 'U and Non-U' had been published that year.

The play shows how self-referential Coward's work had become. 'I really must apologise for this barbarous idea of George's of having communal breakfast', says Sandra. 'He saw a country-house comedy once in which everyone was frightfully witty all through the last act and kept on helping themselves to kedgeree.' 'My God,' she exclaims, 'there really *is* kedgeree.' As its title suggests, *South Sea Bubble* is a gossamer-thin construction; reactionary perhaps, but beneath the crowd-pleasing conservative values is acute observation, and Cowardian wit to carry it. Chappell's style of direction was quite the opposite of his manner of speech, and Harold Hobson noted that he 'caused his players to take [the first] act at what must be the fastest speed ever heard on the West End stage; it is almost incredible that the players, speaking as rapidly as

---

* Chappell had designed and produced *The Lyric Revue* and *The Globe Revue*, which featured Coward songs (and Graham Payn), and had designed the revival of *The Vortex*. An elegant, diminutive figure, friend of Helpmann, Ashton and Edward Burra, Chappell was notoriously late for rehearsals. 'The excuse was always the same. "Grannie fell on the fah" – he was too lazy even to pronounce the word "fire".'

† Arthur Macrae had played Sholto in a 1931 revival of *The Young Idea*, and Edward Marryot in *Cavalcade*. He was one of Carey's closest friends, and was also homosexual.

they do, should remain both human and audible.' In his opinion, it was 'the best play Mr Coward has written for a long time', and Leigh's performance 'shines like the stars, and is as troubling as the inconstant moon'. In that remark was an intimation of the instability of Leigh's personal life, complicated by a sudden announcement: 'Vivien Leigh has decided, rather erratically I think, to have a dear little baby,' Noel told Nancy Mitford, 'which means that she will leave my play at the height of its success. This is all being, 'ow you say, most strange if not downright curioso.' He was annoyed that the Oliviers had left it until now to tell him their news. The couple had reasoned that to announce Vivien's pregnancy earlier would have been to jeopardise the bookings for the play. Anyway, with Leigh's medical history – she had already had one miscarriage – they wanted to be doubly certain. A month later, Leigh left the cast on a Saturday, and miscarried the following day, 'as inevitable as anything could be', wrote Noel. Leigh was said to have become pregnant to upstage Marilyn Monroe, then about to appear with Olivier in *The Prince and the Showgirl*. Her emotional balance was severely disturbed; according to Vivian Matalon, Coward wrote his later *Suite in Three Keys* trilogy for Leigh, 'but then he said he couldn't work with her . . . that she was madly in love with him'.

The problems with Leigh set the tone for the next troubled months of Coward's life. On 2 September he flew to New York after two busy months in Bermuda, where a certain 'irritation and tetchiness and a feeling of unease and dissatisfaction with everything' had begun to pervade his domestic life. He ascribed this to having lost weight. Although he had regained his youthful figure, his face looked drawn. John Dempsey, his former masseur, had set up a health club in Bermuda, and was shocked when Coward called in. 'Christ you look old!' was Dempsey's less than tactful greeting. Noel was visibly displeased. He had been short-tempered with Graham and Cole, 'neither of whom could have sweeter dispositions'. Coward saw the writing on the wall 'which said, in so many words, "Don't be a cunt!" . . . to be slim and svelte is important only up to a point. At the age of fifty-six youth is no longer essential or even becoming.' He promptly put on six pounds and felt better.

On 20 September he sailed back to Europe on the *Queen Mary*, to see *Nude with Violin* open in Dublin on the 24th. Landing at Cherbourg, he was ambushed by the press, after comments on 'tax avoidance'. They followed him to Paris, where he went underground at Ginette Spanier's. A siege mentality predominated; Marlene Dietrich stayed over, sleeping on the couch so that Noel could have the spare room. Dietrich was 'in a tremendously *hausfrau* mood and washed everything in sight, including my hairbrush (which was quite clean), and gave me a wonderful new sleeping-pill suppository [Supponeryl], which I rammed up my bottom and slept like a top'.

Gielgud was better in *Nude with Violin* than Coward had anticipated, but had introduced 'fussy inessentials', due, Noel thought, to the director's 'over-anxiety'. Gielgud now regrets his involvement. '*Nude with Violin* was a very silly play and I was very stupid to do it.' The part had been intended for Rex Harrison; when Harrison turned it down, Coward planned to change Sebastien into a woman, and have Yvonne Arnaud play it. She too refused, leaving Gielgud, who was eager to do something light, to agree to the original version. 'It's very broad and a bit vulgar,' he wrote, 'but full of surefire situations and brilliant curtains ... I should have to be rather clever at creating a character out of a "type" which does not really exist in life.' It was also a type – the knowing or conspiratorial butler – which provided Gielgud with a few choice roles during the latter part of his career.

When Coward arrived he found that Gielgud had 'neglected his own performance for the sake of the rest of the production'; a common fault with him. Noel 'helped him build it up, adding lines in two of the scenes, 'but ... he did not do nearly as much rewriting as John had been hoping for'. Noel was irritable, partly because of the continuing clash with the British media. He was bombarded with questions about his self-imposed exile: was it true the Queen had 'firmly scratched' his name from the next honours list because of it? How much money did he owe the British government? Coward found this interrogation impertinent; worse still, it had nothing to do with the play he was trying to promote. The *Evening Standard* came up with 'Criticisms? I haven't read them yet, says Noel Coward', and cartoons appeared of Noel surrounded by retitled plays, 'This Unhappy Greed', 'In Which We Serve (and don't pay tax)' and 'Brief Encounter (Catch me!)'.

The fuss roused Noel to an unprecedented act: he wrote to *The Times*,

Sir, [2 October 1956]
   Amid the hail of inaccurate and frequently malicious publicity that has been beating down on me of late I wish to say 'Thank you' to your Correspondent, who not only interviewed me in Dublin and quoted me correctly but who also had the intelligence to consult an official of the

Inland Revenue and extract from him a clear explanation of my position regarding income tax as a non-resident in the United Kingdom.

As you probably suspect, all this Press hullabaloo regarding my private affairs has distressed me considerably, as I – not unnaturally – resent any implications regarding my personal integrity. I made up my mind to give up my English domicile after mature consideration and on the most expert legal advice.

In my own circumstances I consider this action as entirely justifiable and requiring neither defence nor vindication. Nevertheless, I am grateful, but not surprised, that *The Times* should have taken the trouble to place the facts clearly before the public on September 26 unadorned by either prejudice or misinformation.

Yours faithfully,
Noel Coward,
Shelbourne Hotel, Dublin.

There was an undeniable antipathy towards Coward around the time of *Nude with Violin*. Not only did the national press review the play before it opened in London, thus flouting theatre convention, but its views were prejudiced. 'Poor John [Gielgud] was completely bewildered,' wrote the author; 'he had never had the dubious pleasure of opening a Noel Coward play before.' Coward behaved as if nothing was untoward. Vivien Leigh came over to visit, and he attended a charity ball at which he spoke in aid of disabled children, avoiding the 'rock'n'roll session' afterwards. He also dined with the British ambassador, Sir Alexander Clutterbuck, in Dublin, where (the *Daily Mail* could not resist noting) he was officially on British territory.

While in Dublin, Coward was cheered by the arrival of Terence Rattigan's preface to the *Theatrical Companion to Coward*, due to be published in 1957. Noel was surprised to find it 'wittily and charmingly written, in no way effusive yet managing to say the nicest possible things about my work', among them, that the book's subject was 'simply a phenomenon, and one that is unlikely to occur ever again in theatre history'.

Joe Mitchenson and his partner, Raymond Mander, had published similar works on Shaw and Maugham, and decided Coward should be next. They were given full access to Coward's files, and the finished product – cast lists, synopses and critiques for all his work to date – was indeed flattering. 'He couldn't have been more full of praise', observed Mitchenson, who saw that the book came at a crucial time for

Noel, 'he was in a very bad state. He was very down, very low . . .'
Coward's diary entry when the book was published bore this out: 'The
only thing that has happened that is nice is *Theatrical Companion to
Coward*. [They] have done a wonderful and, to me, highly flattering
job. Thank God for a tiny ray of pleasantness.'

The reception of *Nude with Violin* in Liverpool was good, and
business was better. Coward left for a rather wet Bermuda, then New
York, where he recorded his *Noel Coward in New York* album,
capitalising on the success of the Las Vegas disc. Here, too, he read the
notices of the London opening of *Nude with Violin*, 'full of praise for
the acting and blame for the play'. In his introduction to the published
version, Coward noted that it was 'a satirical light comedy which
received almost unanimous abuse from the critics and ran to capacity
for eighteen months'.

This was a characteristic Coward comment; as Rattigan noted in his
foreword, Noel suffered from a 'persecution mania' where critics were
concerned. Rattigan's argument was that Coward's plays had not dated;
and that he had developed, his comedy being 'more carefully constructed, gracefully composed and stylishly expressed'. That *Nude with
Violin* was not one of Coward's better plays did not mean much to the
theatregoing public. Advance bookings were good, and as Noel wrote,
'it will sit next door but one [on Shaftesbury Avenue] to dear *South Sea
Bubble*, which is packing them in and shows no signs of weakening.
This really is my most effective answer to the critics after all.'

The world was changing around Coward. The first night of John
Osborne's *Look Back in Anger* on 8 May 1956 threatened to render all
other plays obsolete, just as *The Vortex* had done thirty years earlier.
The old aristocracy of the theatre had reigned too long, and the kitchen-
sink dramatists represented drastic change.

Luckily for Coward, there was an escape route from the increasingly
egalitarian homeland. Jamaica was welcoming; its heat could seep into
Noel's bones and dispel the damp of Bermuda and the rigours of
modern life. As Osborne and his fellow angry young men were shocking
the West End, Coward was writing poetry. He read the results to
Gladys Calthrop and Clemence Dane, whose praise encouraged him. 'I
am trying to discipline myself away from too much discipline, by which
I mean that my experience and training in lyric writing has made me
inclined to stick too closely to a rigid form. It is strange that technical
accuracy should occasionally banish magic, but it does.'

He had written verse ever since his discovery of grammar. Early efforts had included 'Vegetable Verse' ('The Sinful AspaRAGus/ To Iniquity Will Drag Us'), and the more perfervid outpourings he and Esme Wynne wrote in competition. His ability was thereafter channelled into his lyrics, usually written after the music, and with the aid of a rhyming dictionary, but now he sought to expand into blank verse. The results would be the long, Betjemanesque compositions of 'Not Yet the Dodo'. He hoped the new-found freedom would inform his other work; in January 1957, he noted, 'This writing of free verse . . . is opening up . . . some new windows. My sense of words, a natural gift, is becoming more trained and selective and I suspect, when I next sit down to write a play, things may happen that have never happened before. All this gives me a curious cerebral excitement. I'm feeling happy and creative and non-bothered. I need this peace badly and have needed it for years.'

Another new outlet was sculpture, which Noel and Cole went at with their usual enthusiasm. Coward, never abashed by inexperience, produced a 'Negro head' and two full-length figures, which he and the house guests then admired 'from every angle'. Clemence Dane enlivened proceedings by exorting the modellers to 'Stick it right *up* dear, ram it, ram it, and wiggle-waggle it out again.' The results of this hobby remain at Firefly, a collection of lumpy busts and indeterminate figures, not without charm, gracing the bookshelves of Coward's bedroom.

Charles Russell and Lance Hamilton arrived on 23 December, in time for a 'nasty' Christmas – unpleasant because there were no plans for its culinary celebration. On Boxing Day the butler-chauffeur, Alton, got very drunk and almost ran over a boy on a mule. His disgrace made 'the atmosphere . . . wretched' for two days. There was also a certain coolness between Coward and Russell's partner. He had developed a dislike for Lance Hamilton, mostly minor irritations: his loud and annoying laugh and his 'sort of monkey face'. To Elspeth March, it seemed that 'Noel looked down on them both. When I arrived in New York the *on dit* around town was they called Lance and Charles "the kitchen maids", and that must have come from Noel . . .'

Russell and Hamilton discussed financial matters with Coward. He had cut his working relationship with the Holtzmanns, and decided that Charles Russell would be his agent and representative in New York (not the Hamilton-Russell Corporation: 'there had been some trouble in New York and the appointment decided on was for Charles only'). With no American dollars to pay Russell a salary, it was decided that he should receive a commission 'on the collection of fees and royalties on the earlier, English-owned properties plus an ordinary agent's commission of 10 per cent on all future activities'. This agreement was drawn up by Dingwall Bateson in Dublin in September.

Coward's general financial status now displeased him. He decided that 'nothing that was originally promised me has really come true, except that I am a bit better off than I was'. This was ungrateful, considering the work Russell and Hamilton had put in to achieve the successes he had enjoyed in America. His chief complaint was that he had been forced out of his home country by press persecution, yet was still paying tax there, in America and even in Jamaica. 'The whole business sickens and bores me', he wrote. Yet time and again he dwells on money, partly because he had no idea of the financial workings of the business his talent engendered. (Later, when relations with Russell soured, Lorn Loraine had to remind Coward of the details of their agreement, 'I did not realise that you had forgotten this agreement with Charles.') This ignorance often gave the impression that he was suspicious of those who dealt with his finances, particularly after the perfidies of Jack Wilson.

Contrary to the impression he now conveyed to Russell and Hamilton, Coward had 'more actual money in the bank than I have ever possessed in my whole career', and his assets were at least £100,000. Considering he had been £19,000 overdrawn two years previously, this was a notable reversal of fortune. But his sense of financial instability stemmed from his life as a freelance entertainer, and could be traced back to his early years, when his mother made great sacrifices to further his career, and when Noel himself was the family provider. The fallow post-war years had scared Coward, but it was only after Violet's death that he felt free to leave England permanently. He had questioned his own talent – was it failing him, was it no longer good enough to earn him a living? When he said that nothing he had been promised had come true, he voiced doubts about the resurgence of his popularity, particularly in the States; the celebrity-led success of Las Vegas had to be weighed against the less enthusiastic ratings for his TV shows. Add to these misgivings the negative press reaction at home (if it was still 'home'), and these were fraught times indeed.

Terence Rattigan, 'light, sweet, ready to giggle, incredibly silly over his emotional life, weak and stubborn at the same time', arrived at Blue Harbour. Rattigan was drinking too much and getting fat, his host decided: 'on this I lectured him mildly. I think he must be careful now that he is in the forties: he has so much to contribute and it mustn't be frittered away.' It was the voice of experience. Binkie Beaumont and his boyfriend John Perry also came; to Ann Fleming, this was an amorphous mass of 'pansies': 'Noel Coward appeared last night with a party of persons called "Perry", "Terry", "Binkie" and "Coalie"[sic] . . .' According to Charles Russell, Coward assailed his captive audience with ideas for new productions in which Graham could star. 'They were subjected to . . . finger-wagging . . . about how they should give Graham work . . . They couldn't go outside and hop on a bus! After that experience, they said they'd never go back.'

Soon Noel was left in happy seclusion at Firefly, where he had now moved to enjoy his solitude and poetry-writing. But there were still too many distractions: meetings about the Designs for Living craft business he was sponsoring in Port Maria;* more visitors, island society and its demands. Noel wished he could find a 'little shack' as he had in Honolulu, where the only distractions would be the roar of the waves and the wind in the palms. Instead, it was canasta with the Flemings and Phyllis Calvert to dinner. 'One can't say NO, NO, NO, go away from Jamaica, go and live in Palm Beach or the South of France! But, oh dear, I wish they would.'

Having had seven quiet months from a professional point of view, Coward was now 'sniffing the sawdust again'. He decided he would play in *Nude with Violin* himself, on Broadway, and concentrate on the American theatre scene, which he hoped to exploit in favour of a new idea just beginning to germinate in his mind. '. . . I shall have to wait until I get to my Steinways in Bermuda to see whether or not I can still hook on to the 'fluence.' There in mid-May, he began to work on what was to become *Sail Away*, a musical with a more chequered history than any of his previous efforts.

Returning to England on the *Queen Elizabeth*, Coward sailed into unfriendly waters. Photographs of the Master in his cabin showed him snappily dressed: a checked tweed sports jacket, check bow-tie, trousers belted with an 'NC' monogram in gold, gold cuff-links matched by slip-on shoes buckled with large chains. It was a decidedly ostentatious outfit, and caused the *Daily Mirror* to print a half-length photograph,

---

* Charles Marsh, an American millionaire, had given Coward $1000 for use in helping the local community. Coward set up a textile-weaving concern, which expanded into selling other locally made goods, including plates he had designed. There was a break-in at the premises, during which only Coward-designed items were taken; Noel commented that the burglar must have had impeccable taste.

complete with a key to Coward's accessories. 'Is the bow-tie too loud?' it pondered. 'More like Texas than Tooting? Is he showing too much of a rather crumpled silk handkerchief? Are the cuff-links too large, and does a successful playwright *really* wear a leather belt? Is the jacket too long and too colourful, with its silver thread and check-and-dot pattern?' – an ironic criticism considering Coward's sartorial advice to Cecil Beaton on a sea-crossing, thirty years previously.

Lorn Loraine, Cole Lesley and Charles Russell rescued him at Southampton, and drove him to London, where he was installed in the Oliver Messel suite at the Dorchester. London seemed to have acquired 'a curious "welfare state" squalor', which reminded Coward of Moscow; he was stranded, in luxury, high above the city that had once been his own. 'It is a curious sensation being home again and in an hotel, as though I were here and not here at the same time.' He gave a party in his suite, which Messel attended as well as Mike Todd and his new wife, Elizabeth Taylor. He also saw Eddie Fisher* at the Palladium, who 'made a speech and announced very sweetly, my presence, whereupon there was a terrific hullabaloo, very heart-warming'. Noel went backstage to offer advice; Fisher ought to maintain the distance between himself and his audience. He 'respectfully disagreed', and commented, 'I suspect that Coward had an interest in me beyond professional advice . . .' Fisher had been on the *Queen Elizabeth* with Coward on the way over from New York, and together they had won £400 on the 'ship's auction' (money gambled on how far the ship had travelled that day). 'We met in the steam room one day', Fisher recalled. 'I was flat on my stomach getting a massage and he said, "Let me just pat you, dear boy, let me just touch it." He was referring to my bottom and I broke up with laughter.'

Old notions of celebrity were being replaced by a new cast list. When Coward saw the Mountbattens, he found them lacking in humour, now full of 'an overweening pomposity'. Whatever the attitude of surrogate royalty, there was warmth from the real thing. At the Theatre Royal in Windsor to see his godson Daniel Massey, Coward was summoned into the presence of the Queen, Princess Margaret and the Queen Mother. 'How lovely to see you again,' said the Queen Mother, 'we have been most angry on your behalf. For the press to attack your integrity after all you have done for England both in the country and out of it is

---

* Then highly successful, Fisher was appearing in an American TV show called *Coke Time*, an apposite title in view of the singer's later drug habits.

outrageous, but don't let it upset you, and remember that we too have had our troubles with the press!' Coward maintained that he would rather be favoured in this personal way 'than be knighted to a standstill', but this conversation could only have increased his suspicions that official honours were being withheld elsewhere – more especially when Cecil Beaton received a CBE in the New Year's Honours List.

He rehearsed Michael Wilding (Gielgud's replacement in *Nude with Violin*), but was horrified by his disastrous performance. Wilding 'made an absolute shambles of the play and a fucking fool of himself'; Coward accused him of 'hypochondria, hysteria and acute lack of talent', and Wilding burst into tears. Coward and Beaumont considered replacing him, but he then turned in a good performance, which showed the tirade had some effect.

There were other dramas offstage. When Graham Payn came to say goodbye on Noel's departure, Coward suddenly saw 'how deeply unhappy' his friend was. 'I realised how good he has been under all rebuffs and how lonely inside.' Payn's attempts to find work were met with increasingly solid stone walls, and his career was affected by the bad publicity surrounding Coward in England. It was a dilemma addressed in theatrical circles, and the gossip was audible. Kenneth Williams records in his diary for January 1958 a dinner with the now elderly Isabel Jeans and Stanley Hall, theatrical wig-maker, when 'they all said Graham Payn would be better off as an agent and I became angry and said what right had they to make such judgements'.

Payn felt that the roles Coward created for him 'just weren't strong enough. He could only write for women, or for himself. None of the parts he wrote for me were good enough, really.' But there was no doubting Coward's sincerity in his concern: 'I long for him to get a good job and make a success and I believe that eventually he will', he wrote, halfway to New York on the SS *United States*. 'But, oh Lord, the waiting about is ghastly ... my heart aches for him.' A month later Payn was 'happy as a clam' in *Tonight at 8.30* at the Theatre Royal in Windsor, where it was playing for two weeks. Lorn Loraine reported, 'quite a lot of first-hand accounts of Little Lad and all good. I do so hope it will be an "open sesame".'

From New York, Coward flew to California, to be met at the airport by his usual glamorous taxi-service in the shape of Marlene Dietrich. He and Clifton Webb holidayed in 'Rocky Mountain country', where the only noise was a squirrel on the roof, a Western idyll exchanged for the intense activity of the auditions for *Nude with Violin*, due to open on Broadway on 14 November. Back in Bermuda, Noel dined at Government House with the governor, and 'wickedly' discussed the Wolfenden Report on Homosexuality, which was before Parliament. This may have been a risky social ploy, as Coward's homosexual reputation had created certain problems for him in Bermuda. 'He was ... upsetting some young coloured men', said the masseur John Dempsey. 'You didn't ask coloured people to come into your house then . . .' But whatever problems his sexuality presented to life in a British colony, they were as nothing compared to an emotional crisis on the horizon – an offstage drama to rival any of Coward's onstage scenes of passion.

Rehearsals for *Nude with Violin* began in New York in early October. It seemed set for an easy passage; the cast were word-perfect before they started, and despite several having contracted Asian flu, they were ready to open with a week in hand 'for polishing'. But *Nude with Violin* was also to propel Coward into emotional turmoil. On 26 October he wrote, 'My secret news is that I fear that Old Black Magic has reared itself up again. This is stimulating, disturbing, enjoyable, depressing, gay, tormenting, delightful, silly and sensible. Perhaps I was getting a little smug and too sure of my immunity. It may also be that now that I'm slim as a rail again I'm more attractive not only to myself but to others. I can already see all the old hoops being prepared for me to go through. Ah me!'

His reluctance to accept emotional attachment was rooted in the bitter disappointments of the past, and in notions of self-discipline, self-denial and the work ethic: 'If I were one who ever had the capacity or the inclination, for falling hopelessly in love, to the point of catastrophe, it would have taken too much of my time', he told a journalist that year. 'I wouldn't have been able to do all the work I have done.' Kenneth Tynan observed of Coward that 'the successful homosexual is answerable to nobody . . . no wife whose tastes he has to consult, nor are there children about whose schooling he needs to worry . . . [Coward] conserved his energy for his art: none of it was sacrificed on the altar of domesticity' – what Cyril Connolly defined as the pram-in-the-hall 'enemy of promise'. 'Work was primary, and not to be dislodged by human allegiances from its central place in his life.' Coward might well 'travel alone', but he could not always escape his emotions.

His relationship with Graham Payn was now that of intimate friendship; both had their 'extra-marital' affairs, and made no secret of them. The new object of desire was an actor whom Coward had cast as Clinton Preminger Jnr in *Nude with Violin*. Russell recalls his debut on the scene, and the deeply disturbing effect this late-flowering love affair was to have upon Coward. When casting began, 'there were six actors auditioning for a part. Coward choose the worst one. We couldn't understand why, until we realised that Coward intended to have a romance with the boy. His name was Bill Traylor.'

William Traylor came from the remote Midwestern state of Montana. He had a master's degree in drama, and had played in stock productions and small roles on televison. Aged twenty-seven, six foot two, dark and plainly attractive, his first break on Broadway was the role of the inquisitive reporter in *Nude with Violin*. Coward rewrote Traylor's part 'so that he became a main character. He had him as the journalist chasing him – Coward – around the furniture . . .' It seemed that the chase was successful. 'Bill had to go back to Noel's flat after the performance [where] they would . . . have sex. Bill hated it. He was a Catholic boy, and not really queer. He would make any excuse not to go . . .'

It is an odd image: Coward, in the extraordinary stage make-up for *Nude with Violin*, consisting of 'severely taped eyelids and a slightly silvered crew-cut' that made him look like a fey Oriental skinhead ('I'm made up like Theda Bara'), a near-grotesque caricature of the youth he was pursuing, metaphorically and actually. To illustrate Sebastien's increasing wealth, he also used subtle props: a ruby ring in the first act, which became emerald in the second, and diamond in the third. The pose was also struck beyond the confines of the stage, in a large, full-page newspaper advertisement for Rheingold beer, showing Noel as the butler, bearing a tray of the beer, raising a glass in his right hand as product endorsement: 'My beer is Rheingold – the *Dry* beer!' says Noel Coward, with a healthy plug for the play in the accompanying copy.*

Previews of *Nude with Violin* were 'grim', and although anticipation of Coward's return to Broadway was great (the management had taken out full pages in the newspapers, 'Welcome Back, Noel!', endorsed by Helen Hayes, Rex Harrison, Peggy Wood, Katharine Cornell, the Lunts and Edna Best), the influential critics Brooks Atkinson and Walter Kerr

---

* Coward's initial appearance in advertisements had been in 1931, when 'this remarkable young man, the brilliant author of *Cavalcade*' had recommended Phosferine (a mild stimulant) to newspaper readers; he later lent his name to Gillette razor blades and the Jamaican Tourist Board.

were 'contemptuous'. 'It is delightful to have Mr Noel Coward back in the theater', wrote Kerr. 'It would be even more delightful to have him back in a play.' 'The old assurance has gone', Brooks Atkinson said baldly. These opinions amounted to the kiss of death. Coward raged against the shock of the new from an entrenched position as an Old World reactionary; the New World critics decided he just wasn't fashionable, no matter how he might redecorate his themes.

The play's apparent failure left Coward to seek consolation in love, but here matters were no happier. According to Charles Russell, Noel had discovered one night that Traylor had a date with one of the actresses, Sally Cooper (daughter of Gladys Cooper), after the show: 'This sent him into a rage, and he told us we had to fire Sally ... we made up some excuse about the part not being good enough for her. And Coward carried on with Traylor ... One night in Philadelphia, Cole Lesley, Lance and I knew Coward was giving Bill a finger-wagging lecture in the room next door. So we knelt down to the gap below the door to listen – all three of us! Noel was telling Bill to be faithful to him, and if he *wasn't* faithful, then not to let him know!'

'I'm no good at love,' Coward had once sung. He now wrote in his diary, 'All the gallant lyrics of all the songs I have ever written rise up and mock me while I lie in the dark and listen. It has little to do with the person involved, little to do with anyone but myself. To me, passionate love has always been like a tight shoe rubbing blisters on my Achilles heel ... I resent it and love it and wallow and recover ... and I wish to God I could handle it, but I never have and I know I never will.'

Coward played out his last Broadway season to half-empty houses in the dreary slush of winter. During the tour of *Nude with Violin*, there was one engagement where 'the takings were so low that we were only filling a strip of the centre stalls. Noel hated that. One morning ... he told us he'd lost his voice.' Russell rehearsed the understudy ready to take his place. 'When I told Noel this, he shouted "What!" and leapt out of bed. Such was his fury that he ran, absolutely naked, into his drawing-room, and threw himself face down on the sofa, arse in the air, beating the sofa with his fists in rage.' His behaviour was partly the result of emotional frustration; the affair with Traylor took a sharply tragic turn just before the play was due to close. 'The phone rang in the middle of the night', says Russell. 'It was Bill's flatmate, telling us Bill had tried to commit suicide ...' Coward was distraught. 'He said "How could it happen? We were out last night, drinking stingers, he seemed fine" ... I asked him if Bill had been drunk, and he said no ... Noel went to visit Bill in hospital – Bill was in a straitjacket, frothing at the mouth . . .'

Considering the seriousness of the incident, it is surprising that Coward's involvement was not made public. 'We hushed it up, and the gutter press didn't get hold of the story . . .' However, the *New York Post* reported that Traylor was in the Roosevelt Hospital recovering from an overdose of ten sleeping pills. He had been discovered by Hugh MacMullan, who was staying with Traylor at his apartment at 16 East 63rd Street. MacMullan 'told police the actor was apparently intoxicated when he came home early today. He said Traylor spoke with him, went into the bathroom and staggered out, to fall unconscious. Mac-Mullan said he found the empty pill bottle when he went into the bathroom to get cold water to revive the actor. He called police, who sent an ambulance.' The report – SLEEPING PILLS FELL ACTOR IN COWARD SHOW – could not have done either Noel or the show any good.*

Later, Coward recalled 'the months of November and December and the ecstasy and the nightmare. I know I couldn't bear to live it all over again but I wouldn't be without it . . . My only valid excuse is that, at moments, the pain was unendurable and when the heart is in pain it is liable to strike out.' Coward blamed Traylor's weakness: the composer Ned Rorem later recalled Coward telling him 'he had just had a boyfriend – within the past year or two – who he was very [in love with] . . . Noel said "I simply had to get rid of him. He was drunk all the time and there was no dealing with the situation."'

Cole Lesley wrote, 'Sometimes we lived those months over again in reminiscence, Noel praying such an experience would never occur again, and it did not.' Less concerned about Traylor, Coward felt he had 'let the side down' – an example of his retentive attitude to physical emotion. Such indiscretion was embarrassing; his attachment to Traylor was widely known throughout the cast, and Traylor's gesture of despair was a shaming episode. Once again, Noel's attempt to establish a serious emotional relationship had failed. Some years later he was to write, in one of his final short stories, 'Bon Voyage', of a (female) writer

---

* Bill Traylor never worked with Coward again. His subsequent career seemed to move as far away from this unhappy affair as possible: he joined Lee Strasberg's Actors' Studio, and married an American actress, Peggy Feury, with whom he had two daughters, and appeared in stage, film and television productions, including *Dynasty* and *The Rockford Files*. In 1973 he founded the Loft Studio, where his students included Sean Penn, Lily Tomlin, Nicholas Cage and Anjelica Huston. He died in 1990.

who unexpectedly falls in love on a cruise ship. 'She had been in love, really in love, three times in her life, and not one of those strained, overecstatic overcoloured episodes could be said to have been really successful . . . She was no good at love, or rather at "being in love". She was too concentrated, too inherently suspicious, perhaps too egocentric ever to be able to sustain an intimate relationship with any other human being.'

Certainly, with the Traylor episode over, he was glad to leave New York, its snows and depression, for the warmer climate of California, and then Jamaica.

Emotionally and physically exhausted by recent events, Coward was homesick for Europe: 'I'm tired of the unbrave New World', he wrote. America had been good to him, and Bermuda was financially beneficial, but the commercialism he had witnessed closely over the previous six months had 'sickened' him. It was symptomatic of what he felt about the second half of the twentieth century as a whole: despite 'all this brilliant scientific knowledge of atom splitting and nuclear physics, etc., we are *still* worshipping at different shrines, imprisoning homosexuals, imposing unnecessary and completely irrelevant restrictions on each other . . . People are still genuflecting before crucifixes and Virgin Marys, still persecuting other people for being coloured or Jewish or in some way different from what they apparently should be. There are wars . . . in Indonesia, Algeria, the Middle East, Cyprus, etc. The Pope still makes pronouncements against birth control. The Ku Klux Klan is still . . . ready to dash out and do some light lynching. God, for millions of people, is still secure in his heaven, and *My Fair Lady* opened in London last night.'

He was back in New York a week later, to dine at Sardi's and visit Cole Porter – emblems of the old appeal. Porter's leg had been amputated after years of extreme pain caused by a riding accident. It had been a 'cruel decision', involving 'much sex vanity and many fears of being repellent'. He saw Marlene Dietrich, Montgomery Clift and Roddy McDowall, and also visited the Actors' Studio, Traylor's refuge, where method acting was preached in an old church. 'Lee Strasberg (God) sits with a henchman on either side of him and a tape recorder at his feet so that no pearl that drops from his lips should be lost. We saw . . . a young man, very grubby, crawling about on the floor making guttural noises and . . . trying to stab a gramophone which was playing one of his mother's records. His mother was apparently Maria Callas

... Then Mr Strasberg went off into a long dissertation on the art of acting, most of which was pretentious balls.'

William Marchant, attending the studio as an observer, took Noel to the Theatre Bar on West 45th Street, the method actors' hangout. Here Coward was interrogated by two young friends of Marchant's. The idea that acting could be a search for identity, using emotions from the actor's life, was to Coward 'a total misunderstanding' of how to prepare a scene. 'You don't like American acting at all, Mr Coward?' asked his interlocutors. Noel replied, 'I regard many American actors as being in many respects superior to our own in England. Marlon Brando, for one, despite his having told me that I wrote plays as if I didn't know that there were people in this world who are starving to death. I'm told he's a millionaire now. I wish I were.'

27

Prisoner of a Legend

Much faith is needed to believe in the Immaculate Conception and I find that even more is required for me to believe in my own sixtieth birthday. I still think of myself as irrepressibly precocious, and capable of anything.

Noel Coward, *Plays and Players*, December 1959

I N May 1958, Coward set off to satisfy a longing he had felt for France. A week later, he was installed at Edward Molyneux's house, La Vieille Ferme, in Biot, visiting the casino at Cannes, and winning £500. It seemed a good omen for a future life in Europe. 'I dream nostalgically of Switzerland in snow . . .,' he wrote, 'my heart is definitely leaning to the older world.'

The ageing superstars of international society still paraded across the continent in a sometimes desperate attempt to keep up appearances. In Paris the previous year, Coward had found the Woolworth heiress Barbara Hutton 'not very drunk but weaving' in her Ritz suite. Coward had not approved of Cary Grant's short-lived marriage to Hutton. Now he listened to the world's richest woman read her poems of loneliness, despair and unrequited love. 'She is a tragic epitome of "Poor Little Rich Girl"', capable of 'great kindnesses but her money is always between her and happiness.'

Others had taken drastic steps to address the problems of growing old. Coward went to stay at the Villa Mauresque, where Somerset Maugham – now eighty-three, his face a cracked and desiccated old plum – lived in isolated splendour with Alan Searle, who had replaced the reprobate Gerald Haxton. Maugham was still able to dive off the board into his pool, and to gossip endlessly; age would not alter that propensity. But the old man's bitterness seemed remote in the Mediterranean sun: when he had seen Maugham the previous summer, Coward had been 'deeply impressed by the charm of old age when it is allied to health and intelligence'. In fact, Maugham had been injected with animal protein by a Swiss doctor, Professor Niehans,* and professed to be revitalised by the treatment. Robin Maugham recalled his uncle announcing, ' "Ner-now, Noel Coward is coming to stay . . . and I der-don't want him to know I've had a goat" . . . That night Noel leaned forward to me. "I must tell you that your uncle really is a remarkable man," he said. "This afternoon he took me for a walk up the mountainside, and there he was hopping and skipping from boulder to boulder like a mountain goat." There was an awkward silence.'

Coward and Maugham attended the Frank Sinatra Gala at Monte Carlo, organised by Grace Kelly, at which Noel introduced Sinatra in French. The event was 'ghastly but successful', and Noel was not feeling goatlike; he refused to dance at the gala 'because I even hate walking', he explained to another guest. 'I resent having to put one foot in front of the other.'

He discussed his future movements with Cole Lesley. He now found Bermuda dreary and suburban, and thought Jamaica 'on the turn'; he would begin serious house-hunting in Europe. 'The life here appeals to me and the climate is temperate. I would not like to live here all the year round, but then I have never liked living anywhere all the year round.' His dissatisfaction with his current situation came as no news to others. John Gielgud thought 'he was never the same after leaving England, though he wouldn't have admitted it. I think that tax business, and the way people reacted to it, shocked him . . . He wasn't much good as a tax exile. He didn't do a lot with his money. His houses were commonplace, the food dreadful, the decoration pretty amateurish.'

On Coward's return to New York, the *Herald-Tribune* rang for a progress report. 'It's my musical year', he claimed, talking of plans for his ballet for the Festival Ballet company. He also planned an adaptation of another dramatist's work; perhaps an unwise venture, in the light of *After the Ball*'s fate. Again in conjunction with Cole Lesley, Coward translated Feydeau's *Occupe-toi d'Amélie*, renaming it *Look After Lulu*. A *belle époque* boulevard farce, it had been successfully filmed in 1949 by Claude Autant-Lara; for his production, Noel appointed Cyril Ritchard, *Sigh No More*'s star, as director; Cecil Beaton, fresh from his

---

* Professor Paul Niehans used a derivative of goat or sheep placenta as a rejuvenating therapy, and the Duke and Duchess of Windsor and Pope Pius XII were among those who received the injections. It was not an entirely new technique; in *Private Lives*, Amanda and Elyot discuss cow and monkey gland injections.

success with *My Fair Lady*, as designer. His first choice for Lulu, Shirley MacLaine, was not available, and Carol Channing refused to play a 'prostitute'; instead Roddy McDowall and Cyril Ritchard recommended a new starlet, Tammy Grimes. Described by Brooks Atkinson as possessing 'pointed features' and a 'squeaky voice', Grimes recalls that Coward came to see her cabaret act, and asked her to play Lulu. 'I said, "I'll do it." He said, "Don't you think you'd better read the script first?", and I said "It's not necessary. It's better than this!"' Meanwhile, Coward was riding around New York on the back of Roddy McDowall's Lambretta. 'He was a wonderful insulter', recalls McDowall, who was accused of having 'very common hair' and of using Noel's fame. '"Stop trying to climb to success on my shoulders", he used to say.'

Before *Look After Lulu* rehearsals, Coward returned to England, celebrating his fifty-ninth birthday by a visit to the theatre with Vivien Leigh. Leigh was drinking heavily, and attacked Noel 'violently' for not casting her in *Look After Lulu*, but the day ended happily with a party thrown by Gladys Calthrop at the house in Cadogan Place which she shared with Jeffrey Amherst. Beatrice Lillie, Joyce Grenfell, Peggy Ashcroft, Rex Harrison, Kay Kendall and Gladys Cooper toasted their friend's health, a somewhat premature gesture; days later, Coward was struck down with pneumonia. His doctor forbade visitors and telephone calls, and he spent Christmas largely on a diet of beef broth. Having recovered, he flew with Cole Lesley to Geneva. It was now only a matter of time before he would be back in Europe on a semi-permanent basis. He registered as a 'subsidiary resident' (subsidiary to Bermuda, where he remained domiciled), which enabled Coward to open a bank account at Crédit Suisse, and thereby to operate more easily in Europe, earning money tax-free. Loel Guinness advised him to buy a substantial property to convince the Swiss authorities that he intended to live there.

Coward liked Geneva, 'I don't really mind settling there ... It's very near everywhere else ... attractive in its own right and has much to recommend it.' The reasons for living in Switzerland – its nearness to everywhere, the tax advantages, and so on – were hardly better than those for buying Spithead Lodge (which he was now determined to be rid of). Despite his professed love of travel, he had come to regret the lack of a stable home. For that, he had only himself to blame.

Coward had decided to accept a part in Carol Reed's film of *Our Man in Havana*. Playing a British agent, he would receive £1000 a day plus

Noel and Lorn Loraine at Gerald Road:
a stage set for *Present Laughter*

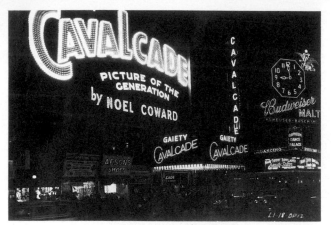

Noel and Laurence Olivier
on board ship, 1931

The film of *Cavalcade* opens
on Broadway, January 1932

With Gertrude
Lawrence in
Private Lives,
1930

Noel, Harpo Marx, Tallulah Bankhead and Jack Wilson, at Paramount Studios, 1932:
note Miss Bankhead's corsage

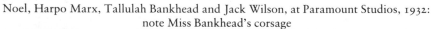

Natasha Paley and
Jack Wilson at Goldenhurst

Noel at the wheel,
leaving David Herbert at Wilton

Noel and Alan Webb
in Nassau, March 1937

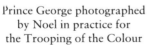

Prince George photographed
by Noel in practice for
the Trooping of the Colour

Touring South America:
with Jeffrey Amherst at the
British Embassy in Santiago,
January 1932

The romantic exile: Noel's shack
at Mokolaeia, Honolulu, January 1939

With the Lunts in *Design for Living*, New York, 1933: the final scene

With Louis Hayward
and Yvonne Printemps in
Conversation Piece, 1934

Back from the dead
in a black leather coat:
Noel and Julie Haydon
in *The Scoundrel*, 1935

'Captain Kinross'

Wartime visit to Australia, winter 1940

David Lean, Noel and Ronald Neame share a joke on the set of *In Which We Serve*; Gladys Calthrop displays her profile

Play Parade, 1942:
Noel as Frank Gibbons
in *This Happy Breed*

White Cliffs, St Margaret's Bay: Noel's house on the far right; Violet and Vida's terraces to the left.

A stage set for *Volcano*: Ann Rothermere, Graham Payn, Cecil Beaton, Noel, Natasha Wilson and Ian Fleming snapped by Beaton's time release, Blue Harbour, January 1951

The age-old connection: Noel and Violet on the first night of the French production of *Present Laughter*, 1948

With Marlene Dietrich at the Globe Theatre, June 1954

Live at the
Desert Inn, Las Vegas,
June 1955

On location for
Bunny Lake is Missing
with Olivier, September 1965:
'I play an elderly,
drunk, queer masochist'

Elegantly comic:
our man in Havana,
April 1959

The Midnight Matinee,
Phoenix Theatre, early on the morning
of Noel's seventieth birthday

Exit from Buckingham Palace,
a knight: Gladys Calthrop, Sir Noel
and Joyce Carey, 13 April 1970

Final bow

expenses; the engagement was for thirteen days. 'Knowing Carol's reputation for working over schedule I think I ought to get at least £20,000 out of it.'

There was also time to see Graham Payn in his new part in *Brouhaha*, 'a great success. God knows, he had earned it. This, I am sure, is the turning point.' No sooner was one problem resolved than another arose, in the shape of Vivien Leigh. She was in despair after Olivier had left her, escaping from her unstable behaviour. John Osborne thought Coward 'possibly more helpful than anyone. His cold eye saw quite correctly that Vivien must reconcile herself to the divorce Olivier was set upon ... Unlike most of the spectators to the whole miserable indignity of their situation ... he appeared not to stoop to the silliness of "taking sides".'

Coward brought the same 'cold eye' to bear on other heterosexual relationships, including Osborne's amatory intrigues. The same objectivity had made him a dramatist, although increasingly this facility seemed not to be employed; it had last surfaced in his unproduced *Volcano*, perhaps his most intense examination of marital relationships since *Private Lives*. Coward's ability to create such works had noticeably declined; he preferred to concentrate on lighter subjects. In New York for the opening of *Look After Lulu* in New Haven, he was spotted with Ritchard, discussing the production over lunch. 'Both men were dressed in opulent dark suits with snow-white handkerchiefs peeping from their breast pockets, white shirts and dark ties ... "It's r-r-really the most innocent play," said Mr Ritchard, "but it's got the façade of utter and complete naughtiness ..."' 'Everyone was convinced that with Cyril directing a play of mine there would be the most ghastly rows', Coward told the reporter, but maintained, 'Everybody is as happy as a bird dog.' Privately, Coward had his reservations about Ritchard's direction. The first week went well, taking $29,000 in six performances, but when it opened in New York the notices were bad.

Once again, Coward had to face failure. As with Wilde, the comic styles clashed; the plot of *Look After Lulu* was situation comedy, enough to stifle any subtlety of Coward's. Roddy McDowall felt 'at odds about *Lulu* ... Feydeau was a playwright of action, of total farce, and Noel is high comedy, not farce ... the two of us were having dinner in New York, and I asked him how he managed to survive well over a decade of rejection, from the critics, from every quarter ... "It's very simple," he said, "they're wrong." That attitude was ... wonderful, but the pain must have been enormous.' A 'supreme theatrical redundancy, a burlesque of a burlesque', wrote Kenneth Tynan. 'Either Mr Coward has fallen among sycophants too affectionate to gainsay him,' observed Tynan all too accurately, 'or he has at his fingertips an open-and-shut imposture case.'

After six weeks of declining business, *Look After Lulu* closed. 'The general consensus of opinion is that Cyril over-directed it, that Tammy didn't quite come up to expectations and that Roddy, although an excellent actor, is not intrinsically a comedian', decided Noel. Ignoring the fact that his cast had pleaded with him to cut the text, he blamed the usual factors: the destructive influence of New York critics, and the stultifying effect of theatre coach parties. Oh, and 'it was a bit common and lacked coherent style'.

Retreating to Jamaica to lick his wounds, prior to the shooting of *Our Man in Havana*, he was joined by Alec and Merula Guinness. 'Naturally he chose the dates for our visit,' Guinness wrote, 'so I found it a little odd to come across a reference to us in his published diaries (a book I suggested to my favourite bookshop would be more suitable on the fiction tables than the non-fiction) saying, just before our arrival, that he hoped we wouldn't stay too long.'

To Guinness, Coward's existence seemed predicated on the unreal. When Guinness's watch, shaving gear and fountain pen were stolen from their bedroom, Cole Lesley 'nearly had a fit – not about our very minor losses but for fear we might tell Noel. "The master mustn't know! Promise you'll never tell him!" ... any attempt at recovery would cause trouble in the village and there was Noel's reputation as a kindly and tolerant employer to be considered.' Later, on the bumpy drive up to Firefly, Noel ran over a goat. 'He burst into tears, handed over the driving to someone else, and remained greatly dejected for the next few hours. Ten shillings was sent down to the goat's owner. "Give them ten shillings for a goat," one of the guests said, "and they'll stand in the road throwing their children under the wheel of the car." "I shall never, never drive again!" Noel said, which brought an audible sigh of relief all round.'

Lance Hamilton reinforces Guinness's impressions. 'Blue Harbour was beautifully run, mostly by Cole ... whatever disturbances occurred, and quite a number ... did, were kept well below the surface ...' Coward expected 'everything to be absolutely one hundred per cent ... if the tiniest thing goes astray, there is a crisis. The moment he wakes up he expects a smiling attendant to appear with breakfast ... if the attendant does not appear on the instant, that is a crisis. If guests are late in arriving, or for meals, that is a crisis. Or if guests are late in leaving, that is a double crisis.'

Coward and the Guinnesses flew to Havana, where they were accommodated 'in a very gilded hotel and given vast over-decorated suites: Noel's suitably furnished as a Mandarin's palace'. This was shortly after Castro had taken over from the dictator Batista, 'and the city was full of excitement and chaos. Rich American businessmen were withdrawing rapidly and there were no tourists . . . Men in the streets would often stop us, pull up a trouser leg to show scars from electric shock torture inflicted by Batista's police, and then laugh, saying, "Viva Fidel!"'

Coward found Carol Reed a 'charming, courteous and meticulous director', whose instructions to Noel to play down his expressions and mannerisms would have been useful during *The Astonished Heart*. Shooting went well; they met Ernest Hemingway with Graham Greene, and were invited to dinner at his house. After eating, Hemingway beckoned to Guinness. '"Come in here," he growled, "away from the others." He led the way into his study. "I can't bear another minute of Noel's inane chatter. Who's interested in a bunch of old English actresses he's picked up from the gutter? Not me. If he wags that silly finger once more I may hit him."'

'I have just finished a new play which is all about old English actresses and will have little or no American appeal', Coward told Nancy Mitford, chiding his 'darling pen pal' for her 'wicked subversive Americaphobia . . . without America we should have no Coca-Cola, no Marilyn Monroe, and hardly any really good literature about sex'. He had been busy with his own literature: 'I think I shall dedicate [*Pomp and Circumstance*] to you . . . [it] is two-thirds done so be prepared.' In New York, he read his new play, *Waiting in the Wings*, to Katharine Cornell, Guthrie McClintic and the actress Nancy Hamilton; these Americans, at least, were suitably enthusiastic.

Back in England, he saw Vivien Leigh twice, and *A Taste of Honey* once, 'a squalid little piece about squalid and unattractive people. It has been written by an angry young lady of nineteen [Shelagh Delaney] and is a great success.' Noel professed to find the exponents of the kitchen-sink style dull at best, whereas John Osborne was positively offensive. *The World of Paul Slickey*, his musical about a gossip columnist, was 'appalling from every point of view'. Osborne observed that at the curtain-call, 'John Gielgud was booing, not waving. So was Coward.'

*

451

That summer Coward and Lesley went to Geneva to view properties. Most were highly priced because of the favourable tax position, but Leslie Smith had spotted a chalet advertised in the *Telegraph*. Coward found the house 'roomy but fairly hideous', with wonderful views: below, Lac Léman, with Montreux, Vevey and Lausanne to the west, and on the far side of the lake, Evian and the French Alps. The vista was partly obscured by tall trees which Coward subsequently felled; Ian Fleming commented that only Noel could buy a house in Switzerland without a view, to which he replied, 'On the contrary – it overlooks a wonderful tax advantage.' The owners were about to retire to Hindhead, and had been offered £12,000; could Noel match it? He could, and did.

His Chevrolet arrived, shipped over from Jamaica, and he and Cole set off for Monaco, where he won FFr 600,000 at the casino. Such a windfall would prove useful in Switzerland, where the decoration of Les Avants had begun. 'We have made ourselves dizzy and quite hysterical trying to choose chintzes, carpets, wallpapers.' Cole Lesley told Leslie Smith 'that the Master was going mad, spending far too much, and he'd had to cut down on the expenses without Noel knowing'. Lesley substituted haircord carpet for Coward's choice, 'Noel wasn't to know that it was cheaper – he liked it just as well.'

The house – later immodestly dubbed Chalet Coward (or even, in sillier moments, Shilly Chalet) – was filled with the trademarks of a Coward interior: two baby grand pianos, his X-frame chair, and the tin Wings of Time, fixed above the drawing-room mantelpiece where they would provide a visual prop for subsequent photo sessions. The theme was theatrical; a screen was covered in old photographs of Edwardian actresses, and the lavatory was papered with songsheets of Noel's hits. Upstairs were two floors of bedrooms: Graham's immediately above the sitting room, and Noel's above that. His bedroom had the air of a hidden retreat in the eaves (a reminder of Coward's childhood attics); a clever panel of mirrored doors concealed a study with views across the valley, to the lake and Alps beyond. Even the bathroom had a theatrical effect with blue and white striped pelmets, and a vivid blue shower of ultra-modern design, with jets playing from the sides. But as with Firefly, the views dominated the interior: the sitting-room's french windows opened on to a sunny balcony, and the lambent alpine light, unfiltered by smog, shone into this newest Coward residence. At sixty, Noel had found a house that would be home.

It seemed odd that he should end up in this most genteel of communities. The Swiss efficiency and the chocolate-box landscape made it an almost artificial setting; it may have been this which most appealed. Les Avants, teetering above Montreux, was also somewhat inaccessible, and the mountains provided a defence, physical and symbolic, against the uncertain modern world. It was no coincidence that the lower slopes of the Alps bore a resemblance to the Blue Mountains of Jamaica, for mountains meant remoteness, seclusion and a physical isolation from the clamorous hordes.

Coward returned to London in June, to see Graham Payn and tell him about the new house. Payn had not been happy in Jamaica, preferring city society to island isolation. It sometimes seemed that there was little to keep them together, as they pursued different lives and lovers; yet, whenever he was in England, it was Payn whom he saw first. Coward recorded that they had taken 'a great shine to the East End and we drive down and go to different pubs', where Noel was impressed by 'the exquisite manners of true Cockneys'. According to one close friend, Noel's East End expeditions were for liaisons of a basic earthiness; he was feasting with panthers, as Wilde had done. He even liked the fact that many of these men did not know who he was. A companion on one such trip recalls that when they introduced themselves to the two men they had picked up, one said that the only Noel he knew was Noel Coward. Coward admitted his identity, but the man refused to believe him, even after he had produced his driving licence.

Noel's part in *Our Man in Havana* was completed on set at Pinewood, and the film was released early the following year. Coward was the perfect incarnation of a British secret agent, impeccably (if surreally) dressed, exchanging secrets in a lavatory with the taps running; 'as inconspicuous as a hippopotamus in a tank of goldfish', wrote C. A. Lejeune, but she dismissed the idea that Noel 'stole the show': 'Coward, a practised showman, plays him with all his skills precisely as required. It is as stupid to say that he steals the film as to claim that the man with the loudest laugh is the life and soul of the party.' When the *Daily Mail* praised him at the expense of Guinness and Carol Reed, Coward conceded, 'I *am* very good, the picture *is* very slow in parts and Alec *is* dull at moments.' His excellent reviews heralded a renaissance of his film career, and raised the fees he could charge – an easy way to earn large sums, and a significant source of income for Coward in later life.

After rehearsals in Barcelona (where Noel enjoyed the wild parties that the cast and its entourage threw) and Lausanne, the *London Morning* ballet was produced at the Festival Hall on 14 July. Noel's excursion into 'serious culture' was unsuccessful; Peter Williams, the designer then working with Anton Dolin, said it looked more like a Cochran revue than a ballet. *The Times* described it as 'a succession of varied characters passing outside Buckingham Palace – schoolgirls, teddy-boys, ladies of easy virtue, nuns, a spiv and his family, an old man in his bathchair, and others. The atmosphere is frankly artificial and it is out of date too – so is the music, much of it penned in the reign of our previous queen.' The visual impact was its greatest asset, resembling one of Coward's crowd scene paintings, and unfortunately, just as two-dimensional.

On 20 July *Look After Lulu* opened in Nottingham, produced by Binkie Beaumont, starring Vivien Leigh and directed by Tony Richardson,* who rang John Osborne. 'He pleaded, "I *mean*, you've got to come up. Noel's *determined* to be WITTY. All the time." I did go, and saw what he meant immediately, but didn't fail to be somewhat transfixed.' Osborne saw Coward from the creative distance between *Look Back in Anger* and *The Vortex*. Coward represented the old world, as did Beaumont. But Coward was an artist, and to Osborne, Beaumont was the enemy, lashing out at dramatists, 'especially the rich and famous', with his 'lizard tongue'. At the after-show supper, Beaumont said, 'with a gleam of satisfaction, "Of course, Noel's *quite* uneducated"'. To Osborne, sitting next but one to Coward, it seemed 'a clumsy piece of treachery, a fair example of the reverence for academic skill and a classic misapprehension of its link with creative imagination'.

A week later the production opened at the Royal Court Theatre. It was brought in as a 'sure-fire' hit (an attempt to keep the otherwise radical Royal Court in business†) but as the critic Irving Wardle wrote, 'it failed to do the trick and became a byword among experimental companies on the folly of selling out for fairy gold'. Harold Hobson killed with kindness: 'The trouble is that Mr Noel Coward is too witty and Miss Vivien Leigh too beautiful: for the kind of play that *Look*

---

* Richardson (1928–91), stage and film director, was part of the 1950s–1960s British scene, with films such as *Look Back in Anger*, *A Taste of Honey* and *Tom Jones*. He married Vanessa Redgrave, daughter of Michael.

† Osborne, visiting the theatre, saw Vivien Leigh, Anthony Quayle and Max Adrian rehearsing and assumed that by some freakish nightmare he had been 'suddenly transported from Sloane Square to the heart of Shaftesbury Avenue'.

After Lulu is, beauty and wit are as unnecessary as peach melba at the North Pole.'

In deference to the modern age, Coward turned to television and tried his hand as an interviewer. He was engaged for a projected series of conversations with the 'great figures' of the twentieth century. Noel was not quite sure that the first subject, Darryl Zanuck, the American producer, deserved such promotion, but the pilot film was successful. However, the prospect of a whole series alarmed him and even £120,000 in fees could not sway his decision. 'To do something I wasn't really enthusiastic about would be idiocy, and I should . . . do myself a great deal of harm.' His wisdom was rewarded by a new film role, in Columbia's *Surprise Package*, for which he would receive £35,000 plus expenses. Stanley Donen (dancer-turned-director of *Singin' in the Rain*) was directing this story of an American gangster (played by Yul Brynner) who tries to steal an exiled monarch's crown from a Mediterranean island. Mitzi Gaynor was his girlfriend; Noel (predictably, after his *Apple Cart* role) was the king. Coward enjoyed filming with Donen, who was less of a taskmaster than Carol Reed. Brynner banned journalists from the set, allowing only Robert Muller to interview Coward, and the result was run in the *Daily Mail* ahead of Noel's sixtieth birthday. 'He denies that his creative energy is finally beginning to flag', wrote Muller. "I am as anxious to be good as ever", said Coward. "Time's winged chariot is goosing me."'

Coward finished the film on 9 December, two days ahead of schedule, and went to Paris to conserve the days he was allowed to spend in England. Here the seemingly ageless Marlene Dietrich was appearing in a one-woman show at the Olympia (now pinning her skin up under her wig to ease the crow's-feet around her eyes, validating Coward's Café de Paris quip that 'nowadays sex is a matter of lighting'). 'She has developed a hard, brassy assurance and she belts out every song harshly and without finesse. All her aloof, almost lazy glamour has been overlaid by a noisy "take-this-and-like-it" method which, to me, is disastrous.' Star quality depended on mystique as well as performance; 'they would have loved her more if she had been more remote and not worked so blatantly hard'.

At the end of December, Noel moved into Les Avants, and staff were engaged. A Parisian cook called Marcel arrived with his *soi-disant* wife, with whom Noel foresaw problems; less so with a charming Italian butler named Piero. Over Christmas Coward dined with the Queen of

Spain (sister of the flamboyant Marquess of Carisbrooke), now living in exile in Lausanne. She requested Noel sit on her left, which flattered him; Broderick Haldane, the photographer, found it extraordinary that this most famous man of theatre should be so impressed by the mere fact of a defunct royal title. Then Vivien Leigh arrived for Christmas, and spent most of it sobbing on Cole Lesley's shoulder. Coward had to deal with three door-stepping journalists, whom he 'utterly cowed ... with excessive good manners' and a pre-lunch drink. In the New Year, he travelled to England for Lady Pamela Mountbatten's marriage to David Hicks, at Broadlands, where the coach taking guests from the house to Romsey station was trapped in snow, resulting in the spectacle of Noel Coward and titled friends getting out to push. Such exertion could not be blamed when, on his return to Switzerland, phlebitis struck his right leg. The British press delighted in reporting the gruesome details, speculating that the blood clot 'may break up and portions be swept away by the circulation to lodge in other vessels'.

Under threat of a stroke, he was given strict instructions to rest – no visitors, no telephone calls. Unable to walk, Coward was carried about by Piero the butler, even on and off the lavatory. Enforced indolence encouraged Coward to finish his novel, *Pomp and Circumstance*, and by mid-February he was able to walk unaided. But his phlebitis returned, together with a congested lung; it seemed as though his body was beginning to fail him. This was the longest period of illness he had yet experienced, and it gave him a 'curiously detached feeling ... I find the idea of going about again, travelling to different places, going to theatres, seeing people, etc., quite extraordinary, as though it were something I didn't know anything about.' Increasingly, Coward came to accept ill health as part of his life; his unwillingness to take exercise, stop smoking or eat better seemed a gesture of defiance in the face of old age.

'Noel Coward – the prisoner of a legend', announced the *Guardian*'s W. J. Weatherby in yet another commemorative article; while his name continued to attract audiences, his reputation was unable to change with the times. Coward was well aware of the problem and was seriously considering the future. He expressed his thoughts in a confidential letter to Charles Russell, who wanted him to appear in a new television spectacular, this time with Ethel Merman. Coward demurred, for a number of reasons; one was his phlebitis, which remained a serious threat. He had been told 'that it was time for me to withdraw a little from the public side of my life and devote my energies to writing and composing and avoiding quite so much physical exertion'. He also felt he had 'done' television. 'I have always prided myself on my capacity for being just one jump ahead of what everybody expects of me, which is the principal reason that I have never paid a return visit to Las Vegas, any more than now I would pay a return visit to the Café de Paris . . .

'It has always been a problem in my life to choose what to do next. . . . I have watched my contemporaries continuing, almost desperately, to do the same thing, and . . . although I am sure I would do the Spectacular with Merman professionally and possibly brilliantly . . . many, many of the people looking at me would be saying "Isn't he wonderful . . . to be doing that at his age."' He announced his intention to 'write one more good musical, several more good plays and a few more good books. By doing this my whole legend will be properly consolidated, and everything that takes me away from this, whatever the money involved, I think at this stage would be a mistake . . . If a *really* wonderful part in a film comes along I will accept it; apart from this I wish to stay quiet for quite a while and make as few public appearances as possible.' It is clear that Coward still felt sufficiently in control of his career to manipulate matters to that all-important end: the proper consolidation of his 'whole legend'.

In March 1960, still feeling 'a little wobbly', he flew to London, then to Paris to see Dietrich ('tired and staggeringly beautiful'). A third stop was Tangier, with its beach scenes reminiscent of the film he had just seen, *Suddenly Last Summer*. Dietrich noted that although, like Somerset Maugham, Noel liked picking up boys on Moroccan beaches, 'at least he does it politely, *sotto voce*'. But Coward disliked the seamy side of the city. David Herbert, expatriate social leader of what Cecil Beaton called 'the oriental Cheltenham', showed him around, and Rupert Croft-Cooke entertained him with local gossip. Yet Tangier's delights were '*not* for me. There are too many cliques and feuds and, of course, too many people.'

Travelling allowed him time to reconstruct *Waiting in the Wings*, due to open in Dublin on 8 August. Before leaving England, he had discussed the play with Sybil Thorndike, and hoped her enthusiasm would translate into acting in it. His choice for director was Frith Banbury. 'He asked me to direct *Waiting in the Wings*, the most *ghastly* sentimentalising of old age, which I loathed, really, when I read it . . . We all know how hideous old age can be, and to pretend it's like that – no.' Banbury turned the play down. Coward's romanticism was far removed from the trends of contemporary theatre but when, that May, he saw *The Care-*

taker, he suddenly realised, 'I'm on to Pinter's wavelength. He is at least a genuine original . . . *The Caretaker*, on the face of it, is everything I hate most in the theatre – squalor, repetition, lack of actions, etc. – but somehow it seizes hold of you . . . *Nothing* happens except that somehow it does. The writing is at moments brilliant and quite unlike anyone else's.' So impressed was he that in 1963 he agreed to put up £1000 to help finance the film of *The Caretaker*. He described Pinter as 'a sort of Cockney Ivy Compton-Burnett'; when they met, they discovered a surprising amount in common.

'What he liked was a kind of objectivity of the stage', said Pinter, who saw a shared desire not 'in expressing ourselves, but in expressing objectively and as lucidly as possible what was actually taking place in any given context'. Their dramatic humour was not as far apart as it may have seemed; odd-sounding names and disembodied lines uttered in an idiosyncratic British manner – Tynan compared Pinter's 'elliptical patter' to Coward's stylised dialogue. Both dramatists relied on emblematic figures – polar opposites socially, but representative and evocative. Pinter said that Coward's 'class of people who never seem to need to earn any money . . . wasn't intended to be an accurate representation of a given class . . . [it] was an abstraction, a world which became his own, the world of Noel Coward, and can therefore be seen only as a fiction . . . that's a marvellous achievement, to have created your own world . . .' Maggie Smith later observed that Coward's characters 'whirled around in his head all the time'; like Buss's painting of Dickens and his creations, the casts of Noel's plays awaited their fate in their creator's world.

Their realisation required co-operation and sometimes compromise. Coward had trusted few people as he did Binkie Beaumont, but by 1960 relations with his producer had soured. Ever since Beaumont had behaved 'badly and greedily' over the US production of *Nude with Violin* (he wanted 2 per cent of the gross takings, and a share of subsidiary rights, quite unheard of), Coward had felt Beaumont was taking advantage of him. Now there was disagreement over changes to *Waiting in the Wings*; Beaumont asked Noel for a complete rewrite, which the author refused. His reaction was to turn to Michael Redgrave's theatrical (and amatory) partnership with the American producer Fred Sadoff. The swarthily handsome Sadoff had been a founder member of the Actors' Studio, but regarded himself as a jack-of-all-trades. Added to this, Redgrave's inexperience in production made for technical and administrative delays calculated to infuriate Coward, who was soon regretting Beaumont's absence. But then he learned of a new example of Beaumont's perfidy.

Gladys Cooper asked Coward why he had written a play about retired actresses without a part for her. 'I explained that I had written it *for* her but that Binkie had told me she had turned it down without comment.' Coward was shocked, and was left wondering if the report that Edith Evans had '*loathed*' the play could be a lie, too: 'It's not very nice, is it?' The reasons for Beaumont's behaviour are lost in the tangle of jealousies and envy rife in the enclosed world of the theatre, but he told a mutual friend that Noel's relentless promotion of Graham Payn (who was to star in *Waiting in the Wings*) made him decide he could no longer work with Coward. If this is so, there were better ways of ending the relationship than in mistrust and deceit.

In June Coward recorded the theme tune he had written for Stanley Donen's film *The Grass Is Greener*, while allowing the use of 'Mad About the Boy', 'I'll Follow My Secret Heart' and 'The Stately Homes of England' as background music. He was rewarded with a fee of $15,000, 'not to be sneezed at'. Unfortunately, the production was disappointing: the *Hollywood Reporter* said, 'It's too bad Coward couldn't have written the wisecracks too.'

Work on *Waiting in the Wings* with its director, Peggy Webster, and its producers (and investors) Sadoff and Redgrave, was held up, Noel thought, by Redgrave's inefficiency. There was a 'real blazing row in the course of which Peggy and I roared at him, banged the table and generally frightened the fuck out of him'. Sadoff proved a more amenable impresario, and able to help cool some of the on- and offstage battles. 'Sybil gives a really great performance', wrote Coward, 'and so, to my joy and relief, does Graham. I've never seen him so relaxed and charming.' The play opened in Dublin on 6 August, with a cast of veteran actors and actresses – Sybil Thorndyke, Lewis Casson, Marie Lohr – and a clutch of lesser names resurrected to populate his comedy about the sort of nursing home for which they were all too often destined.

Waiting in the Wings is the perfect set-up for Coward's comic 'types', and for theatrical in-jokes. But 'beneath the froth of some of its lighter moments, the basic truth [was] that old age needn't be nearly so dreary and sad as it is supposed to be, provided you greet it with humour and live it with courage'. Once again, details anchor the piece in Coward's autobiography, the author rewriting history as if to root himself in its reality. The inefficient theatrical charity committee that runs The Wings is obviously based on the Actors' Orphanage; and the modern world is chastised for its presumption in parries at contemporary theatre: 'An honest bit of blood and thunder's a lot more healthy and entertaining than all this creeping about in the pitch dark and complaining.' As ever, the tabloid press is attacked; a journalist, Zelda, seems 'quite a well educated young woman, it's curious that she should write so abominably'. Her boss is Lord Chakely, 'a barking old tyrant', at whose 'social conscience' Coward also takes a poke. Such comments did not encourage good reviews.

Coward considered the play contained 'two of the best scenes I have ever written'; and its critical battering may have contributed to its being one of the last stage plays he wrote. For him, it was a 'serious play on a theme which . . . remained an intrinsically sad one'; John Lahr saw it as 'a resonant metaphor for his own fears of ageing and of being put artistically out to pasture', Coward's 'most powerful and passionate post-war play'. By addressing his own late middle-age preoccupations, Coward was looking to his own mortality. Lahr notes, 'Death is what's really waiting in the wings.'

Some found Coward's attitude cynical. Charles Heriot wrote in his reader's report for the Lord Chamberlain's office, 'There is a heartless sentimentality about this piece that I find very distasteful. Mr Coward is the last person in the world to write a whimsical, hint-of-tears comedy about a home for aged and indigent actresses . . . There is an emetic hint of patronage about the whole thing as if he were saying "Poor, funny old cows! I might make something out of their quaint little ways . . ."'

Waiting in the Wings opened in London on 7 September. 'I have never read such abuse in my life . . . I was accused of tastelessness, vulgarity, sentimentality, etc. To read them was like being repeatedly slashed in the face.' Not even the performances were praised, which, considering the reputation of some of the cast, was additionally galling. 'There is a lot of old shop talked and a lot of old songs sung, and it gets more nauseating . . . as the evening wears on', wrote T. C. Worsley. A lone defender, Harold Hobson, thought it would 'give a great deal of quiet and legitimate pleasure to many theatregoers', and, claiming special knowledge, said that far from being the cynical man he was held to be, Coward had devoted 'his time, his talent, and his money to helping those of his colleagues less fortunate than himself'. Business was healthy, but Noel was sorry for his elderly company. 'This ghastly cold douche . . . cannot but have laid them low inside.' But he found some personal consolation in the acidity of the attacks, 'I suppose it is foolish to wonder why they hate me so. I have been too successful too long.'

Back in Les Avants, heavy demands were made on his reserves of sympathy. Margaret Leighton came to stay, in the throes of divorcing Laurence Harvey, and Noel despaired of 'these silly ladies' who 'muck up their lives', regretting the time when women 'just stayed put and, as a general rule, got their own way and held their gentlemen much longer. It really isn't surprising that homosexuality is becoming as normal as blueberry pie.' Then Clifton Webb's mother, Maybelle, died. Webb had been inordinately attached to her; but Noel thought 'the late sixties is rather late to be orphaned'. When Webb rang in floods of inconsolable tears, Coward threatened him, 'Clifton, if you don't stop crying, I shall reverse the charges.'

Another visitor was Lionel Bart, the composer and lyricist whose *Oliver* Noel had admired. 'He is a curious creature, not actually very prepossessing looking but rich with talent and a certain Jewish-looking charm.' Bart recalled that Coward 'called me out of the blue and invited me to his home'. Bart thought it was one of his friends playing a joke, and said, 'Noel who?' 'Coward, you Cockney cunt', came the reply. Bart 'spent a weekend listening to some very good advice and the very first rendition of his work on *Sail Away*, which he played . . . at the piano. Noel lent him a large sum, and remained a close friend, dispensing advice on his love life. Bart represented new blood, the sort of contemporary success which Coward hoped for in his forthcoming production.

In November 1960, *Pomp and Circumstance* was published; it had been a long time in the writing. 'Rattling around loosely in the novel form was enjoyable – and quite a change', Coward told the *Saturday Review*. 'I don't think I was too verbose . . . I wrote the book in bursts, and for a while I was a little discouraged with the progress. But God came along and gave me . . . phlebitis, which kept me in bed, and I could do nothing but write.'

The novel was clearly influenced by Nancy Mitford, to whom it was dedicated; like her later novels, it was a weave of fact and fiction, a *roman-à-clef* of high society. It is set in Samola, a territory by now so convincing that Coward could have exploited it as E. F. Benson did his town of Tilling. Here are stock Cowardian characters, archetypes transported from Weybridge to the Caribbean, with a smattering of sexual inverts (like the local lesbian pair, Daphne 'one of the boys' Gilpin and Lydia French). Such references were seen by reviewers as an attempt to modernise his work; they did not know that there were such models even in Coward's earliest writing.

Coward had been reading Proust, whose influence can be detected in his prose: 'a sort of gentle nostalgia made up of homesickness and remembrance of things past . . .' The book is concerned with the changing modern world, as the use of Elgar's title suggests, but it refuses to be serious. As Coward told reporters during its gestation, the book was 'not in the least significant and it has absolutely no message'. Given the seriousness and introspection of current literature, this was a minor rebellion in itself.

In November Coward returned to Les Avants, and was visited by Vivien Leigh and Jack Merivale, her new lover; he called on the Nivens, who had recently moved to Glion, a train-ride away up the mountain. At the end of the month, he met Binkie Beaumont in New York. 'He was amiable and gossipy and I didn't really care for him any more.' Noel suddenly saw 'all the pallid little wheels whizzing round: the fear of me, the lack of moral courage, the preoccupation with money, etc., and there it was, clearly and unmistakably the end of a long friendship'.

After a launch party for *Pomp and Circumstance*, he flew to Jamaica to celebrate his sixty-first birthday with a party arranged by Blanche Blackwell and Morris Cargill. Cargill had staged a firework display, and a misdirected rocket let off by 'some Jamaican cretin' avoided blinding the Master by inches only. He was not amused. Blackwell remembers Coward being 'touchy about certain things'. 'He hated to be made fun of. I remember Mrs Cargill was to bake him a birthday cake, and she told me she'd iced an upside-down baking tin instead. I knew Noel wouldn't like this . . . but she went ahead and did it anyway. As soon as Noel went to cut it, he just left the party . . . He was very annoyed.' His thin temper had not improved with the years.

He was 'now definitely beyond middle age', as the mirror confirmed. His hair had receded to the back of his head (although he would never have recourse to a wig. 'I shall never wear a toupee, Monica, however bald I get', says Garry Essendine, '. . . I intend to grow old with distinction'). His face had deepened rather than aged; the *maquette* for the Chinese sage of his later years was there even in his youthful visage. That the sleek head was increasingly bald hardly mattered; the emollient smoothness was merely enhanced. The effect was that of an elderly Jamaican lizard sunning itself on a shoreside rock. The diamond confidence and animal grace seemed untarnished by his stoop and the tendency to a paunch, but the eyes betrayed a flicker of insecurity. In the bluster of activity with which he surrounded himself was a sense of evasion from the final certainty of loneliness, acknowledged in lyrics such as 'I Travel Alone'. Even in his sixth decade, rest or retirement were as far away as ever; there was still the desire for the smash hit, the refusal to accept limitations. To have come this far, and still have so far to go, must have been unsettling. It explains the irrationality of some of his actions, in the recent past and in the near future.

28

Sail Away

When you feel your song is orchestrated wrong
Why should you prolong
Your stay?
When the wind and the weather blow your dreams
  sky high
Sail away – sail away – sail away!

Noel Coward, 'Sail Away'

HAVING had the all-clear from Dr Bigg, Coward entered his sixty-second year 'with a well-ordered liver and high hopes'. He was looking forward to working on *Later than Spring*, and on Boxing Day the singer Marti Stevens (Marlene Dietrich's friend, known to Noel as 'The Blonde Beast') arrived in Jamaica; she was being considered for a part in the new production. 'I am bashing away at the musical,' he told Lance Hamilton, 'and it is coming along fine. I'm changing the title from *Later than Spring* to *Sail Away*. It's more appropriate to the story, gayer, and I can use the number!' ('Sail Away' had been one of the successes of *Ace of Clubs*.)

The piece had started out as an idea for a film, a 'brittle, stylised, sophisticated, insignificant comedy', with a 'fascinating *femme du monde*' (Dietrich) and 'an equally fascinating but prettier *homme du monde*' (himself), with an 'articulate pair of companion secretaries' (Graham Payn and Marti Stevens). The plot would be entirely obvious, but with dialogue and lyrics brilliant enough to 'redeem its apparent banality'. The specific genesis for *Sail Away* was a song Coward had written for Beatrice Lillie: 'A Bar on the Piccolo Marina' tells of the newly widowed Mrs Wentworth-Brewster's discovery of the delights of Italian lovers, an abandonment expressed in its naughty refrain, 'funicula-funiculi-funic-yourself'. On the Marina Piccola on Capri was a restaurant patronised by Beatrice Lillie, Gracie Fields and Coward on his visit to the island in September 1954. Gloria Magnus, the owner, had been married twice, latterly to Manfred Magnus, whose manly endowment was, in her words, 'like a pimple on the dome of St Paul's'. When they visited Capri, Gloria left him for a local boatman named Pietro Cerotta, with whom she set up her restaurant. Vivacious, attractive and habitually dressed in tailored trousers and a turban, she talked a mixture of Cockney and inaccurate Italian, and liked to entertain foreign sailors:

> When both her daughters and her son said, 'Please come home, Mama,'
> She murmured rather bibulously,
> 'Who d'you think you are?'
> Nobody can afford to be so lahdy-bloody-da
> In a bar on the Piccola Marina

Mrs Magnus was too good a character to lose, and her fictional counterpart became one of the main characters in the musical, which returned to a familiar post-war Coward theme: exasperation with tourists. 'Why Do the Wrong People Travel?' suggests that 'The Taj Mahal/ And the Grand Canal/ And the sunny French Riviera/ Would be less oppressed/ If the Middle West/ Would settle for somewhere rather nearer'. 'Useless Useful Phrases' required a vocal dexterity similar to 'Mad Dogs' in its litany of surreal phrasebook responses: 'My mother is married/ These boots are too small,/ My aunt has a cold,/ Shall we go to the opera?/ This meat is disgusting,/ Is this the town hall?' Coward's intention was to emulate the success of American musicals, still in their 'golden age'. 'If I can really pull it off, it will mean financial security for life', he wrote.

In England, *Pomp and Circumstance* was on the bestseller lists (in the US it had sold 28,000 copies), and was praised by P. G. Wodehouse. Reviews had not been good – the *Sunday Dispatch* called it 'a preposterous piece of work . . . [a] stale and stuffy book'. But in early 1961 Coward undertook an altogether more provocative literary excursion. He had recently read *Waiting for Godot*, which he thought ridiculous; he noted the failure of John Arden's *The Happy Haven* (like *Waiting in the Wings*, set in an old people's home, but performed in masks and 'apparently disastrous'); and 'a turkey' from Shelagh Delaney (*The Lion in Love*). Even Kenneth Tynan was 'now enquiring rather dismally *where* all the "destructiveness" is leading us'. Coward decided to put his views in three essays, intended ultimately for a book on the theatre, but now to be published in successive issues of the *Sunday Times*.

In his first article, he set out his case, maintaining that 'my age and experience entitle me to offer a little gentle advice to the young revolutionaries of today and also to those of our dramatic critics who have hailed their efforts with such hyperboles of praise'. His advice consisted of one catch-all maxim: 'Consider the Public'; the new playwrights were in danger of alienating 'the goose that lays your golden eggs'. The 'salt-of-the-earth' types so enamoured of the 'New Movement' did not have exclusive rights to human emotion, nor had vulgarity a place on the stage. He cited as offensive Delaney's *A Taste of Honey*, where 'the heroine parodies the labour pains of her imminent childbirth'; and Beckett's *Endgame*, where 'one of the characters urinates in his trousers'. Only Pinter's *The Caretaker* had earned his approval.

His second instalment, on the 'Scratch-and-Mumble School', maintained that it always had been and always would be easier 'to play realistic drama than artificial comedy. That this is not generally accepted by our modern pseudo-intellectual groups merely proves that they don't know nearly so much about the theatre as they think they do.' This seemed to deny the validity of serious drama, and was a tirade against intellect. 'The Method' made him yawn; it indicated a lack of respect for the disciplines and traditions of the theatre as he knew it. But the theatre had changed, and this was the graceless complaint of a usurped monarch. His last piece attacked the critics, 'seldom loved or envied. The awareness of this must, in course of time, lower his morale and corrode his spirit . . .' In portraying them as less than moral, Coward was merely broadcasting his martyrdom.

The essays say more about Coward and the state of his personal art than about the theatre generally. He betrays a lack of confidence in contemporary theatre, and general dissatisfaction with the world. Robert Bolt, the playwright assigned by the *Sunday Times* to defend his peers, wrote of his generation's concerns, which were certainly not those of Coward's. Discussing theatre as a 'human activity', Bolt wrote that modern playwrights lived under the shadow of the atom bomb, and that alone was enough to make them consider tragedy rather than comedy, which 'simply isn't suitable for what we want to say'. Bolt expressed what others felt; Coward was not only old-fashioned, he was beyond redemption.

'The bridge of a sinking ship, one feels, is scarcely the ideal place . . . to deliver a lecture on the technique of keeping afloat', said Kenneth Tynan, drama critic for the rival *Observer*. Was it really 'unpardonably right wing' for actors to wear anything but tight jeans and T-shirts nowadays? 'Nothing of my invention could rival the following authentic excerpt . . . "The first allegiance of a young playwright should be not to his political convictions, nor to his moral or social convictions, but to his talent." This wins my medal for the false antithesis of the month; for what if the author's "talent" is inseparable from his conscience and convictions, as in the best writers it is?'

The closure of *Waiting in the Wings* gave Coward's critics ammunition, and a correspondent reprimanded the *Sunday Times* for allowing 'the silly old man to make such a spectacle of himself'. But one young playwright defied the backlash. 'Mr Coward, like Miss Dietrich, is his own invention and contribution to this century', John Osborne wrote. 'Anyone who cannot see that should keep well away from the theatre.'

In Jamaica Ian Fleming (nicknamed Thunderbird) had come down with bronchitis, giving Coward an opportunity to employ his medical skills; as Ann Fleming described to Evelyn Waugh, 'happily Noel Coward . . . proved himself a Florence Nightingale, changing Thunderbird's sopping pyjamas, turning the mattress, and fetching him iced drinks. Noel has always found T-B fearfully attractive and jumped at the opportunity to handle him . . . T-B's language was something horrible, he blamed me for exposing him to homosexual approaches . . .' Waugh replied, 'I always thought Thunderbird was keen on Coward. I am glad the passion is reciprocated.'

In New York Coward read a draft of *Sail Away* to its putative producers. 'Everybody raved about the score but [they] were dubious about the book.' Their reservations were well-founded; Coward had found it hard to write, caught as it was between the disciplines of drama and musical. Auditions were held without much success, until Coward dined with an effervescent singer-actress called Elaine Stritch whom he had admired in Walter Kerr's 1958 musical, *Goldilocks*. Stritch was 'wildly enthusiastic and very funny . . . but I foresee leetle clouds in the azure sky. She is an ardent Catholic, and has been "in analysis" for five years! Oh dear.' His month in New York concluded with a reluctant private performance of the *Sail Away* score to eight women organisers of theatre parties; Noel's tolerance was rewarded by a request from one of them which could represent a quarter of a million dollars at the box office. A further fillip came in the shape of Joe Layton, 'the most sought after ... young choreographer on the scene', to whom he took a great liking.

Financing the production proved a problem, until Coward's New York lawyer, Donald R. Seawell, announced that Helen Bonfils, a wealthy patron living in Denver, had agreed to contribute the whole $400,000 'without batting an eyelid! She is apparently the third richest woman in America.' Bonfils had told Seawell that he could have committed her without even telephoning, 'I know Mr Coward's work. That is enough for me.' 'To have had that pledge of belief ... from a stranger affected me for days', said Coward. Bonfils would produce the show with her partner Haila Stoddard, and Seawell, as Bonard Productions, in association with Charles Russell. Coward returned to Jamaica in March, in order to finish the book of *Sail Away*. By 2 April it was done. 'I don't remember ever having worked with such dogged determination', Noel wrote. He had purposely restricted the book, 'in the belief that the public would be relieved at not having to sit through acres of dialogue between numbers. In fact I have used a revue formula with a mere thread of story running through.'

Oliver Smith, acclaimed designer of *My Fair Lady* and *West Side Story*, came out to work on the designs, with an efficiency Coward wished he'd had on other post-war musicals. Noel contributed his own graphics in the form of a colourful poster design (and later album cover), depicting a high-kicking male dancer (a tribute to Joe Layton), and a balloon-bearing, chihuahua-holding Stritch figure, together with a Coward study on the reverse of the programme of Layton rehearsing the dancers, all muscular thighs and tight short-sleeved shirts.

'Everything is proceeding fairly well. Our only serious worry is Charles [Russell], who has taken to having hysterical scenes ... I think he has developed a sort of *folie de grandeur* and sees himself as a great impresario ... he *has* been alone and rather frustrated for a longish time, but these violent outbursts augur ill for the future, and I certainly do not intend to tolerate them when I am in rehearsal.' Russell felt resentful at what he saw as ill-treatment by his employer; Coward begrudged him his percentage, and told him, 'You look ill. You look like you've got cancer.' 'Well, he said this so many times, for about a week, I started to take it seriously, in spite of myself, and I paid $35 for a check-up in the hospital. No sign of it. So I told Coward this. Then he began saying that I was going deaf ... and accused me of needing my ears de-waxed. "What, you've never had your ears cleaned out?" he said. So I went to the doctor, who told me the truth ... There was this great build-up against me.'

Coward arrived in Paris, primarily to see the dancer Grover Dale in *West Side Story*, with a view to casting him in *Sail Away*. But there were other diversions too, among them an evening with Ned Rorem, an 'avant-garde American composer, amiable but a trifle too "advanced" for me'. 'I knew all about him and he knew nothing about me', says Rorem, then thirty-seven years old and a talented composer who had escaped his American Puritan upbringing to become a darling of Bohemian society in Paris. Blond and handsome, Rorem's charms were obvious. 'In Paris there was an American ... who ran a travel agency – he was also an intellectual – and every Sunday afternoon he would have gang-bangs at his house. He would invite people and drink tea or something and if you wanted to you could go into [a] sideroom ... which was dark. One day he said, "Oh, Noel Coward was just here ..."'

The following evening Rorem was at the Club Elysée with Philippe Erlanger when Coward sat down at the next table. Rorem, wearing dark glasses, removed them when cigarette smoke got underneath, and heard Noel whistle 'Smoke Gets in Your Eyes'. 'After all this ridiculous batting of eyelashes, I said to him ... "I was where you were yesterday ... just after you left."' The two men went back to Rorem's apartment. 'We talked there until six in the morning, about Edith Wharton, about love, about alcoholism, about music, about me ... he was a very good listener. Then he said, "Why don't we go over to that bed." I had feared that, and said, "Yes, but what if it doesn't work?" And he made the perfect remark: "From what I now know and feel about you, anything that happens on that bed will be the right thing."'

Rorem discovered that Coward's was an acquiescent desire. 'Later, I mentioned it to the American ... he said, "Yes, he likes to be held. I think he likes to be childlike, and pushed around a little bit." I know exactly what he meant, that Coward wanted to be protected, in a way ... it's not wild sex, it's juvenile sex, and I appreciate that, and I like it, but if you get two of them together, nothing much happens – nothing explodes. There's no such thing as a sophisticated sexual person – no matter who they think they are – when it comes to sex, especially when a person is as old as he was, they know they can have everything they want, except someone who will lust for them. Therefore, even though they're very spoilt people, they take it pretty easy when they're going to make a pass at somebody ... On the other hand, he wasn't used to being rejected. I'm not very good at going to bed with well-known people, I suppose because it has to do with a conflict of one's ego. In the case of Noel, of course I was flattered . . . People think that famous people all go to bed with each other, but they don't. They send out for call boys . . . Noel could have done that [but] . . . he was more attracted to the so-called common man, not rough trade, as Cole Porter was.' Noel left the apartment on the Quai Voltaire at dawn and, going down the stairs, stage-whispered to Rorem, 'Brief Encounter!'

Less intimate meetings in Paris included dinner with Katharine Hepburn and Spencer Tracy at the Escargot, and lunch with Nancy Mitford. Back in England, he went to Dirk Bogarde's party for Judy Garland at his house in Beaconsfield. Coward sang with Garland; Bogarde recalls a 'blinding, glorious, heart-stopping performance'. However, according to Sylvia Sims who was also there, Garland was less impressed when Noel played the score of *Sail Away* for the guests; she fell asleep. Coward's relationship with Garland was empathetic, evidenced by a later magazine piece which published a taped conversation between the pair: they swapped stories, anecdotes and theatrical techniques, each immersed in the tradition since childhood. Later they booked adjoining suites at the Savoy in London, where Garland's daughter, Liza Minnelli, delighted in Uncle Noel's company. Joe Mitchenson recalled that 'Garland was the only person who could hold a room and talk with Noel not talking . . . At the first night of *Waiting in the Wings* she was up in Graham's dressing-room . . . and there was a circle of people around her . . . Noel was not interrupting at all, which was unusual.'

Later in June there was another memorable encounter, this time with Princess Margaret and her new husband, an uproarious occasion which ended with throwing empty Cointreau bottles from the window of Snowdon's riverside studio. 'Not an intellectual occupation,' Coward noted drily, 'but enjoyable.' There followed the wedding of the Duke of Kent to Katharine Worsley in York, with Noel staying at Richard Sykes's Yorkshire pile, Sledmere. Sledmere's butler, the irascible Irishman Michael Kenneally, was impressed by Coward's sophisticated appearance, although the effect was somewhat diminished during the service when Noel 'nearly knocked Her Gracious Majesty for a burton', and some mothballs escaped from his trouser pocket.

In New York, *Sail Away* appeared to be on course. Theatre party advances guaranteed business for months ahead, even before rehearsals had begun; it 'had one of the biggest advance sales in Broadway history', reaching nearly one million dollars. Morton Gottlieb, general manager for the production, sought to maximise income through commercial sponsorship, persuading American Express and Cunard to pay about $100,000 (a quarter of the costs) in return for what is now known as product placement. 'I got Coward to have the crew's uniforms say Cunard,* and on one of the songs it mentioned a competitor of American Express ... he changed the lyrics to include American Express.' Far from finding this gross (as he had Ford's sponsorship of his television shows), Coward 'loved the idea of ... saving a hundred thousand dollars on the show'.

'Everything is going so well that it is almost frightening.' Jean Fenn arrived to take up her part; she was a talented singer with the Metropolitan Opera, and had flown from San Francisco to audition for Coward. Expecting some opera heavyweight, he was delighted when 'in walked this tall, gorgeous creature with heavenly long legs' and a glorious voice. Elaine Stritch was presenting problems, going absent without leave, but after the first proper week of rehearsals, she 'saw the light'. Noel professed himself happier with the company than he had been with any since *Bitter Sweet*.

Sail Away opened in Boston where it was a sell-out, assisted by Jacqueline Kennedy's visit to the show. The Kennedys subsequently invited Coward to their Cape Cod house, flying him there in their private jet. But there was still work to be done on *Sail Away*, 'and Joe and I are doing it'. Noel was unsure about the dramatic talents of Jean Fenn and James Hurst, the young male lead: 'They were, after all, engaged for their voices and ... it is madness to expect two singers to play subtle "Noel Coward" love scenes with the right values *and* sing at the same time.' It was decided that Jean Fenn didn't look right, and Lynn Fontanne went to her dressing-room on one occasion, to help. 'She put her hands through her hair and she said, "Do you know, Jean, I couldn't play this part either."' Miss Fenn's hair was cut. But Joe Layton had a more drastic remedy, 'I said, "What would happen if ... we just eliminated [Fenn's] role and gave everything to Stritch?" ... The show was very old-fashioned, and the thing that was working was Elaine Stritch ... every time she went onstage [she] was a sensation.'

---

* The *Sail Away* ship was called the *Coronia*, after the Cunarder *Caronia*, then berthed in New York harbour, where rehearsals were held to give the cast some authentic nautical atmosphere. The *Sail Away* programme credited sixty-six companies for contributions.

The reconstructed *Sail Away* was successful in Philadelphia, and it opened at the Broadhurst Theatre in New York on 3 October, the audience 'chic to the point of nausea'. Noel regarded the star-studded guest list for the after-show party at Sardi's as a personal tribute: 'When I pause to reflect on the number of people who seem genuinely to wish me well from all corners of the world, I am really very proud and pleased.'

Sail Away could have been mistaken for a pre-war musical, were it not for Joe Layton's choreography, which struck a contemporary note. Despite adverse critical opinion, Coward was sure the show was a hit. But soon Don Seawell was reporting a string of complaints: the bad notices had done damage and the production was not the 'smash hit' they hoped; the company was not performing well, and with Joe Layton in Europe it would be difficult to tighten things up. He also told Coward that 'New York theatre-cum-café society is spreading the word that the boys in the show are all pansies and the girls are not attractive enough'.

Coward could not understand what had happened. They'd had full houses in Boston and Philadelphia, why not New York? He blamed the notices and the dreaded theatre parties, but in his diary he admitted that he might be at fault: 'It is perfectly possible that I *am* out of touch with the times. Have I really . . . reached the crucial moment when I should retire from the fray and spend my remaining years sorting out my memories and sentimentalising the past at the expense of the present?'

The past was brought vividly to mind at the beginning of November, when Noel heard of the deaths of Guthrie McClintic and Jack Wilson. McClintic was 'a sweet friend and I shall always miss him'; whereas Wilson had been 'a trouble and a bore to himself and everyone else . . . What a hideous, foolish waste of life! His character was never good . . . Of course I am sad. Of course I feel horrid inside. But not nearly so much as I might have. To me he died years ago.' When John Mills said how sad it was about Wilson's decline into drink and early death, he was surprised to hear Noel's terse reply, 'Well, it was his fault, wasn't it?' Wilson's death caused Coward to consider his own mortality, 'I wonder how long it will be before I make my last exit?' The gloom was compounded. Lorn Loraine, also out in Jamaica, had been diagnosed as having advanced breast cancer in early 1960, and had a mastectomy.

But the living world still beckoned. In New York, he recorded the album of *Sail Away*, a 'disastrous' session initially, but which he hoped would be one of his best records. Other New York business was more fraught. Charles Russell, who had announced in April that he wished to terminate his contract, had changed his mind, and wanted to continue as Coward's American representative, 'and have *first refusal* of all my future products and the right to raise money for them!' Coward regarded Russell's behaviour as irrational and hysterical; Russell could, and did, make the same accusations about Coward.

In London at the end of January auditions began for *Sail Away*, just as the American version was stumbling through its final weeks in New York. Although Coward had made £30,000 personal profit, the show had lost £50,000. Hopes of a 'nice old-age pension' were dashed. Friends and acquaintances saw a certain bitterness in Coward as a result of this further failure, which he must have realised would be the last opportunity to mount such a production. His response as ever was to gather up his bags and sail away, to the next port – or to the next project. In Jamaica he worked on a new comedy, *Three for the Money*, an Irish fantasy of a peer who has to marry off his three daughters to save the family fortunes. It was intended to be 'on a plane just above reality', like *Blithe Spirit*. 'If it comes down to solid ground for a moment it will disintegrate.'

The first Bond film, *Doctor No*, was being made in Jamaica. Coward and Fleming, walking along the beach at Ocho Rios, had to duck the cameras as Ursula Andress emerged from the surf, clad in a white bikini. Coward met Sean Connery, whom he liked a great deal; the film itself was 'enjoyable but, of course, idiotic', and he congratulated himself on not having taken the proffered role of Dr No (Noel had replied, 'No, no, no, a thousand times no!'). In February he flew to San Francisco to begin a holiday: Honolulu ('now crammed with shrill-voiced tourists who make the air hideous with their loud-mouthed arrogance'); then Fiji, quieter and reminiscent of his fictional Samola. The Fijians were 'very attractive and they all wear skirts regardless of gender. As they also go in for "Jackie" [Kennedy] hair-dos this is apt to cause confusion.' Tahiti was 'beautiful and exotic and fascinating and all the things it is supposed to be, or nearly all. What is wrong is "progress"'; even here he heard the rise and fall of 'the eternal nasal twang of the Middle West'.

After the charms of the South Pacific, he stayed with Clifton Webb in Beverly Hills, and met the influential agent 'Swifty' Lazar, whom he already knew and who wanted to take over 'disposal of my properties for movies or television'; in the light of difficulties with Charles Russell,

Coward thought this a 'wise move'. Ed Bigg organised another series of check-ups in Chicago for Noel, who was told he had to stop smoking – an artery in his troubled right leg was already closing up. 'I *don't* want to stop entirely so I think I shall winsomely disregard their advice . . .' He took to smoking menthol cigarettes as a compromise.

In Switzerland Coward had an affecting encounter with Maugham. The elder Master was staying at the Beau Rivage in Lausanne, with Alan Searle, and his nephew Robin, and one afternoon the door to their suite was 'flung open. Willie looked up anxiously, then he smiled with pleasure . . . Noel walked swiftly across . . . and embraced him, "My darling Willie," he cried, "you may *suppose* that I've only come in for five minutes." "That's what I was hoping, Noel," Willie answered. "Well I haven't. I've come for a whole hour. I intend to liven your poor, dreary old life by teaching you a brand new game of patience – not the childish one you play . . ."' Coward set out the cards, and explained the complicated game. 'Suddenly Willie turned to him. "Yer-you know, Noel," he said, "it's very ker-kind of you to invite me to stay in your villa for three months." Noel gazed at him in astonishment. "Now whatever crossed your strange little Chinese mind to suppose that I should issue such an invitation?" he asked. "And may I add that if ever, at some unguarded moment, such an invitation escaped my lips, it is promptly withdrawn. But what makes you imagine that I *should* ask you to stay – and for three months?" "Wer-well it's going to take you three months to teach me this patience," Willie said. "And I'd far rather learn it at your *expense* that at *mine* . . ." He paused. Then he added: "You see, my dear Noel, it may have escaped your attention – but I am in fact a thoroughly stupid man."

'"Escaped my attention!" Noel exclaimed. "*What* did I say to myself when I first clapped eyes on you half a century ago? '*There*,' I said to myself, 'goes a thoroughly stupid man!' And fifty years have only confirmed me in my opinion." Willie laughed. He stretched out his hand for a moment and touched Noel's arm. "Fifty years," he said. "It's a very long time."' But the sentiment of this touching scene would be sharply turned on Maugham in Coward's play *A Song at Twilight*.

Sail Away had opened in Bristol to good notices; the Royal Gala and London opening followed on 21 June, with excellent business, healthy advances – and disappointing reviews. 'Basically, it's a good old-fashioned musical,' said John Higgins in the *Financial Times*, 'colour scenes, and comedy scenes, backdrops of Tangier and the Pantheon, travel jokes, American jokes, and smutty jokes, and a clutch of ship-board romances . . . But open the bright wrappings and what's inside?' Not much in the first half, but 'after the interval, the transformation . . . just about the most enjoyable hour to be found in the West End at the moment'. Other notices were begrudging; even Charles Heriot's report to the Lord Chamberlain had said, 'Mr Coward seems to be straining after an American effect without much sympathy for it, and there is a strong suspicion of laurel-resting about the construction . . . No wonder this show nearly flopped in New York.'

'They hate me very much, these little men', wrote Coward, who found discouraging 'these continual streams of abuse . . . whenever I put anything on the stage'. Their opinion would reach posterity, via the cuttings libraries; the reaction of the audiences would go unrecorded. 'It would be so nice, just for once, to receive a little generosity or at least a little justice, but I fear that there is small likelihood of that happening so long as I continue to entertain the public.'

For some time overtures had been made to Coward regarding a musical version of *The Sleeping Prince*, Rattigan's 1953 romance of a Carpathian prince involved with a chorus girl on a visit to London in 1911. In February 1961, Herman Levin, Broadway producer of *My Fair Lady*, had asked Harry Kurnitz (Hollywood screenwriter and one of Sinatra's 'rat pack') to work on the book, and now invited Coward to write the music and lyrics. The project, which became *The Girl Who Came to Supper*, was Coward's last full score. He did not really want to be involved in another Broadway musical, but as Kurnitz was responsible for the onerous duty of writing the book, the project had some appeal. He loved the play, which was set in his favourite period, pre-First World War England in the London of his childhood, a perfect excuse for unashamed nostalgia. The result was an obvious attempt to reproduce *My Fair Lady*'s runaway success, and to that end, Coward tried to persuade Rex Harrison to play the Prince Regent. But Harrison would not make a decision until he knew whether he would be offered Henry Higgins in the *My Fair Lady* film.

Coward distracted himself with film work, spending four days in Paris, on George Axelrod's *Paris When It Sizzles*. He played a Hungarian film producer (possibly based on Alex Korda) at a fancy-dress party, dressed as Nero in toga, golden laurels and jewellery; the effect was decadent, especially with the tanned and lived-in Coward face. Although the film did not do well, Noel earned $10,000 plus expenses, part of which went to pay for a plastic artery to replace the furred one in his right leg. 'This is a bore,' he told Nancy Mitford, 'because of the two the right one has always been acknowledged to be the prettier.' Additional treatment was suggested: Professor Niehans and his rejuvenating injections of goat or sheep placenta. Coward, quoting Mitford, hoped that it wouldn't be a 'non-U ewe'. Niehans was injecting half of Hollywood with the miracle formula. 'They can't *all* be idiotic!' reasoned Noel, after he and Rebecca West went for the consultation. He announced, 'I have given up smoking and sleeping pills and look forward to a drugless future', and he and West checked into Niehans's clinic to receive their injections.

Negotiations on *The Girl Who Came to Supper* continued, fervid enough almost to overshadow the Cuban missile crisis. In a 'momentous' meeting with Rex Harrison in Paris, the actor turned down Coward's offer. This did not please the Master. Coward's relationship with Harrison had never been easy, partly because he disapproved of his tempestuous private life; the actor was 'guilty' of the most ungentlemanly behaviour to colleagues and to ladies in everyday life. Harrison's subsequent comments about Coward caused outrage. 'I knew him as well as I wanted to know him', said the hooded-eyed actor. 'Noel was a terrible cunt in many ways and I never liked doing his plays because unless you were very careful you ended up sounding just like him . . . I thought he was a lousy actor, personally. He was so mannered and unmanly. He was much better in cabaret, singing his own songs. But as an actor, he was a joke.'

One long-standing hostility ended, however, when Coward took tea with Edith Sitwell in her Hampstead flat: 'How strange that a forty-year feud should finish so gracefully and so suddenly.' John Lehmann reported that Edith forgave Noel because she had become a Roman Catholic and was afraid 'of the violence of her instinct for revenge'. Privately, Coward still found Sitwell's verse indigestible, but sought to 'crush down these thoughts otherwise the dove of peace will shit on me'.

His life remained peripatetic. He had given up residence in Bermuda to become a Swiss citizen, and was now allowed to spend six months a year in England. Just as he sailed for New York, he heard that *Sail Away* was closing after seven months. 'That's that,' he concluded, 'apart from an Australian production, I have seen the last of it.' They arrived in New York on 17 January, but he was not met with the usual joyous welcome. Instead, Coward was handed a writ as he disembarked, served by a lawyer for Charles Russell.

Relations between Coward and Russell had gone speedily downhill over financial matters. When Coward curtailed his contract, Russell questioned his right to do so, and in turn, withheld royalty payments which he was due to pay for summer stock productions he had serviced in the States. Roddy McDowall recalls 'lots of screaming fights'; the fact that the warring parties were living in the same apartment block did not help the situation. Cole Lesley was staying with Russell and Hamilton. 'We used to go and see Noel every morning for coffee', says Russell. '[One morning] Coley said "Are you coming along?" And I said "No, we're not." He said "Why?" And I told Coley to tell Coward to fuck off. "I can't tell him that!" said Coley.'

Writs began to fly, and despite attempts to keep it secret, the newspapers got hold of the story by examining the published court lists. After eighteen months, an out-of-court settlement was made, and the relationship severed. 'It was stupid,' says Russell, 'I didn't want to leave Coward. I could have made him money. He was refusing to allow me to exploit his plays. I said, "If I get richer, then you do too", but he wouldn't listen. He was so pig-headed. He turned everyone against me, after that, spreading poison in London and New York. But Coley and Lorn Loraine knew the truth. Lorn admitted to me that she had been in the same position with Coward, but because she had a family to support she couldn't go off and leave him. I asked Lornie why she put up with it all. She said, "I put up with it because I've got two children, that's why." I could. I was a bachelor, I had no wife and children. I could leave him. And I did.'

With Charles Russell gone, Geoffrey Johnson took over the running of what was in effect Coward's New York office. Soft-spoken, good-looking and diffident, he had originally been an actor and assistant stage manager, and during the production of *Sail Away* had been employed by Charles Russell 'as a kind of assistant', at $100 a week. After the break-up, Cole Lesley asked Johnson to stay on; according to Russell, Lesley had fallen for Johnson, 'He was besotted . . .' Johnson became another indispensable member of the Coward coterie, and privy to Noel's personal life. He soon discovered that Coward was equivocal about the increasingly open displays of homosexuality in New York and elsewhere during the Sixties. When a friend of Noel's took him to Fire Island, a gay vacation spot off Long Island, Coward told Johnson that he 'wasn't very comfortable there. He liked the adulation of the gay crowd there but he really wasn't at ease with the place . . .' Coward wrote that the atmosphere of the place was 'sick-sick-sick. Never in my life have I seen such concentrated, abandoned homosexuality. It is fantastic and difficult to believe. I wished really that I hadn't gone. Thousands of queer young men of all shapes and sizes camping about blatantly and carrying on – in my opinion – appallingly. Then there were all the lesbians glowering at each other . . . I have always been of the opinion that a large group of queer men was unattractive. On Fire Island, it is more than unattractive, it's macabre, sinister, irritating and somehow tragic.' To some this protestation seemed self-hating: Coward as a homosexual unable to come to terms with his sexuality, and disliking its flagrant display in others. Noel would argue that it was all a matter of taste.

Timothy Gray and Hugh Martin, lyricist and composer respectively, had been threatening to do a musical version of *Blithe Spirit*, provisionally entitled *Faster than Sound*. Coward had been apprehensive about the idea, but when they played him the score and sang the lyrics, he was pleasantly surprised. 'Coley and I sat with our mouths open. It is quite brilliant. The music is melodic and delightful, the lyrics really witty, and they have done a complete book outline keeping to my original play and yet making it effective as a musical.' Coward began thinking of a perfect company to bring it to life, and hoped Bob Fosse would choreograph and direct it.

In Jamaica Coward worked on the score of *The Girl Who Came to Supper*, completing four numbers in one morning. 'I am feeling remarkably well. Perhaps, after all, the dear Herr Professor Niehans *has* got something in this "fresh cell" idea. I've had a letter from Rebecca [West]. She also says she's never felt so well in her life!' A new daily routine was established at Firefly: up at seven; letter-writing, then work until one; lunch and a siesta, then painting until seven. After drinks on the terrace, Cole Lesley was sent down to Blue Harbour, leaving Coward to dine alone, listen to opera and go to bed with a book at ten o'clock. 'It's a lovely existence and I adore it more and more.'

29

Dad's Renaissance

Who would have thought the landmarks of the Sixties would include the emergence of Noel Coward as the grand old man of British drama? There he was one morning flipping verbal tiddly-winks with reporters about 'Dad's Renaissance'; the next, he was ... hanging beside Forster, Eliot and the OMs, demonstrably the greatest living English playwright.

Ronald Bryden, *New Statesman*, August 1964

RETURNING to Switzerland, Coward heard welcome, if surprising, news. A modest revival of *Private Lives* in a Hampstead theatre 'has had rave notices! Some critics even praised the play!' James Roose-Evans had recently directed the play at the Pitlochry Festival in Scotland, where its success encouraged him to take it to London. Some vital changes resulted when a friend (who had sat next to Princess Margaret and Tony Snowdon in a restaurant) told Roose-Evans, 'They talk exactly like Elyot and Amanda!' He decided to 'update the play, to take it out of its period, and also to have a young cast'.

Roose-Evans's revival sparked off a re-examination of Coward forty years after his first West End success; his modernisation of *Private Lives* signalled that it was time to look at Coward's work anew. His approach was free of preconceptions. 'It's fatal to start imitating Coward's style. There's a rhythm there, a very strong musical structure – the laughs are built in, into the way you speak the dialogue. But you've got to play it for real people, then the laughs will come.' It was also important to cast young people, 'It's a romance as well'; he recalls tours with actors too old to roll around on the floor.

One problem was getting the production reviewed, partly because the Hampstead Theatre Club was far from the West End nexus. Harold

Hobson's notice would be of inestimable value, and the director wrote him an impassioned letter, asking him to come to the first night. When Hobson's review appeared, the general manager of the theatre rang Roose-Evans in Wales and said, 'Can you come back straightaway? Noel Coward is flying to England for three days, he has dinner with the Queen Mother ... We're laying on a special performance ...' Roose-Evans recalls, 'It was like the arrival of royalty. The audience were all seated by 2.15. At 2.20 this limousine purred up across this bombsite and out stepped [Coward]. All the cameras started clicking and the journalists scribbling. He was in his seat at 2.25, with his programme. And the play began.'

In the first interval, Coward insisted on going into the tiny backstage green room, and announced that he wanted to be photographed with the two leads, Rosemary Martin and Edward de Souza. 'He embraced them and laughed and the cameras all clicked, so then they went triumphantly through that extraordinary *pas de deux* which Act Two is. Then at the end there were shouts for him, and he stepped onstage and took a curtain call with them.' Coward told Peter Bridge, the impresario, 'I want you to bring this in.' Bridge rang Roose-Evans 'and said "If I give you Coral Browne and Ian Carmichael and one or two others, would you do it?" I said "No. The whole point is doing it with young people, and I also owe it to these young actors. They're not names, but they've created this production."' Instead, Michael Codron bought it. 'We ran at least a year ... and the rest is history ... Of course he didn't fly in just to see us,' Roose-Evans conceded, 'dinner with the Queen Mother was just as important!'

Noel wrote that it was 'very well done on the whole but not, I fear, *quite* elegant enough'. He was indeed more concerned with dinner with the Queen Mother, unaware of the ground-breaking nature of the production. But when he learned of the successful transfer to the West End, he realised that those who masqueraded as 'theatre critics' had seen the light: 'What about the notices for *Private Lives*?' he wrote to Joyce Carey. 'Fancy them at last finding out that it is a good play! If Binkie had put it on with a West End cast they'd have torn it to pieces ...'

In May Coward and Lesley went to Australia, where he worked on the Australian production of *Sail Away*, starring Maggie Fitzgibbon, 'really ... excellent and warm and lovable, but of course the brilliance of Stritchie is lacking'. Advance sales were excellent, and by 9 June he was back in the 'blessed, glorious, tropical heat' of Singapore and the

Raffles Hotel, having left Lesley in Australia. He had time to observe, with a writer's eye, some of Singapore's odder characters. A 'heavily tattooed, bearded sailor with a parrot' and his friend called 'Biscuits' ('because his name was Crawford') would populate one short story; another vignette was in the hotel bar: 'I saw this woman, a sort of terrible old thing she was, and with her was this younger woman with thick lens glasses, obviously a travelling companion of some sort. She was flitting around every which way, responding to orders. I kept studying her and wondering about her. I thought she should be wearing contact lenses. I got to wondering what would happen to her if the older woman suddenly died.' The scene surfaced in his story 'Pretty Polly Barlow', in which the death of her aunt leaves Polly a rich girl. Transformed from dowdy shopgirl to *femme fatale*, she falls in love with a sailor, 'a snub-nosed, ginger-headed Yorkshireman'.

He returned to Jamaica, and added more verses to *Not Yet the Dodo* – a word picture of the English middle classes, a dying breed in the reality of the modern age:

> A diminishing few
> A residue
> Of unregenerate characters who
> Despite two wars and the Welfare State
> And incomes sadly inadequate
> Still, summoned by Sunday morning chimes,
> Walk briskly to church to say their prayers
> And later, in faded chintz
> armchairs
> Read of divorces, wars and crimes
> And, shocked by the trend of world affairs
> Compose
> In cosy, post-prandial doze
> Tart letters of protest to *The Times*.

He also edited the book of what had been *Faster than Sound* and was now *High Spirits*. To those who were surprised that he had not written it, he said, 'I simply couldn't do it; after creating a script that worked so well in one form, I couldn't tear it apart and put it back together in another. I don't mind tearing apart and revising drastically a new script of mine that is in the process of being staged for the first time, but I couldn't tamper with *Blithe Spirit*.' He was confident that Martin and Gray had 'done a fine job of giving the play a new form but retaining its spirit and much of the original dialogue. It will be a pleasure to direct it.' Edward Woodward was to play the male lead; Beatrice Lillie, Madame Arcati; Tammy Grimes, Elvira; and among the 'singing-dancing ensemble' was a new actor named Ronnie Walken, later to change his first name to Christopher.

It was a busy summer for a sixty-three-year-old. At the end of August he arrived back in New York to work on *The Girl Who Came to Supper*. The musical was an escape from the sometimes strained modernism of *Sail Away*, although its songs were typical Coward fare, from 'I've Been Invited to a Party', sung by Florence Henderson (as a cross between Eliza Doolittle and a Twenties debutante); to 'Sir or Ma'am', Roderick Cook's advice to the princess on English etiquette; and the somewhat clichéd Cockney singalongs of 'London Is a Little Bit of Alright' sung by the voluminous (in voice and girth) Tessie O'Shea. José Ferrer played the prince, and the sets and costumes were provided by Oliver Smith and Irene Sharaff (Oscar-winning costumier for *The King and I* and *West Side Story*).

Rehearsals were fraught, but Coward stayed in the wings for the sixty-fifth major production he had been involved in since 1920. He would have preferred to have been rehearsing all day, but old age and its effects were being keenly felt; he had just had his last tooth removed, 'so wobbly that it was becoming a menace', and a new dental plate fitted which, 'thank God ... has made no difference whatever to my speech'. (Noel was inordinately proud of his dentures; Rex Harrison and his fourth wife, Rachel Roberts, dining at the 21 in New York, watched Coward commend a new set to his partner by transferring them to his side plate to admire the craftsmanship.) Coward's concern during rehearsals was to keep Layton from 'over-directing' the show. The first runthrough confirmed his fears, 'Too much movement, too many props and everybody overacting like mad and trying to be funny.' Noel lost patience, and in a fit of pique, he let fly at his director and 'flounced out', refusing to go back the next day. 'He really blew up at me', says Layton, admitting that he was trying too hard to 'put his stamp on everything'. Coward thought him 'cursed by a sort of personal insecurity and is afraid of credit being taken away from him. As he is really richly inventive and talented, this is plain silly.' Their relationship suffered as a result; the following year, Coward wrote, 'I have lost faith in his talent.'

The Girl Who Came to Supper opened in Boston 'to a rapturous reception. The next morning rave notices and it is so far quite palpably a smash hit.' According to Layton, it was set to storm Broadway, having been 'very successful out of town. We were coming in like *My Fair Lady*. Then of course tragedy hit. I happened to get a bad case of hepatitis. They had to take the show into New York without me and, even though we were in pretty good shape, all the pins started to shake a little bit. Then we came to New York and Kennedy was assassinated. And you know the original first number of that show? "Long Live the King". And it was staged with assassins all over the theatre, believe it or not.'

It opened on 8 December to a 'glittering, star-spangled audience' and a 'brilliant performance' from the cast. The notices were good, except for the *New York Times*, which thought that 'the glamour and romance seem imposed, as if by an effort of will'. 'Elegant, charming and delightfully cast', said the New York *Morning Telegraph*. Like Rex Harrison, José Ferrer couldn't sing, 'but ... talks fascinatingly and invests the role and the evening with a kind of ripe grandeur, wry and somehow reluctant lubricity ... [Florence] Henderson sings with a voice of gold and wide range ... Irene Browne makes the Queen Mother a delicious flutter-brain and Mr Coward provides the lot of them with a sheaf of songs, including a hilarious and brilliant number in Westminster Abbey for the coronation of George V.'

Coward returned to Jamaica for his sixty-fifth birthday in happy mood. But after Christmas, despite $92,000 worth of business, audiences were dwindling for *The Girl Who Came to Supper*. Joe Layton partly blamed the Kennedy tragedy, 'We opened so soon after, it was really the demise of the show ... I think that broke his heart, because the potential was great.' Noel was in New York in the snowy days of January, watching it inch towards early closure. One consolation was that *High Spirits* seemed to be going well, and he had faith in the cast, 'If Beattie really delivers, which I believe she will, we shall probably have a real smash hit.' But within a week Lillie was driving him mad; she was 'as much like Madame Arcati as I am like Queen Victoria'. Lillie, at seventy years of age (and with a drink problem), was no easier to deal with than she had been thirty-four years previously, in *This Year of Grace!*

Rehearsals were difficult. At one point Coward challenged Tammy Grimes on her pronunciation of 'pretence'. 'You've pronounced it two ways', he complained. 'Well, what's the difference?' asked Grimes. 'One is British and one is definitely American', said Noel. 'Which one is British?' she enquired. 'The correct one!' Coward retorted. Then Graham Payn, who was co-directing, was overtaken by acute pain in his left buttock and thigh, and the company left him in traction. 'This was not only miserable for him 'but highly inconvenient for me to be deprived of my assistant director during the time I needed him most'. They opened in New Haven, 'a nightmare'. Coward wrote, 'Beattie fucked up the whole business in so far as the book was concerned, but managed to make a great success at the expense of the play, the cast and my nerves.' Good notices ensued, and the tour sold out for three weeks in New Haven, and three in Philadelphia, but the stress was getting to Coward. *The Girl Who Came to Supper* closed on 14 March, and he developed a painful stomach ulcer, caused, he said, 'by the ceaseless irritation of Beattie not knowing a word culminating in a hideous scene with John Philip [her husband]'.

When a reporter had asked Coward how old Lillie was, he found the question impertinent, and answered sarcastically, 'She's seventy-five and completely mad!' Unfortunately, two young fans reported the remark to Philip. That night, Coward was sitting in an armchair on the set, delivering his opinion of the performance, when from the darkened wings 'came a strange, high-pitched voice. "That's right, Mr Noel Peirce Coward. You tell 'em, Mr Noel Peirce Coward."' John Philip emerged 'like a Phantom of the Opera', and the cast stood aghast as he launched a verbal attack, telling Noel, 'You're old enough to be my mother', and threatening to 'tie your balls behind your back'. Coward remained calm. Philip stalked off, but as a parting shot, he turned back and shouted, 'Beatrice Lillie loves me!' Noel said quietly, 'Then she *must* be mad.'

Matters did not improve. In Philadelphia, Tammy Grimes suffered from exhaustion and was hospitalised, as was Coward when his ulcer got worse – although the Passevant in Chicago said there was no ulcer. Then, partly because of the friction between Lillie and Coward, and partly because of his illness, the show's producers asked if he minded Gower Champion, fresh from his success in *Hello, Dolly!*, taking over as director. Champion achieved some 'minor miracles', but Coward later spoke bitterly of 'betrayal' by Lillie, and the episode effectively ended their friendship.

The production opened on Broadway on 7 April, and was a success. It ran for 373 performances in New York, becoming one of the sell-out musicals of the season. Tammy Grimes projected the waspish quality Elvira required; Edward Woodward was whimsically phlegmatic as Charles; but Beatrice Lillie stole the show as Arcati. 'Even if *High Spirits* had no other attractions – and it has a stageful – it would be a cause for celebration. It has brought back Beatrice Lillie', said the *New York*

Times; 'a thoroughly satisfying score', the *Journal-American*; 'a brassy spectacular', the *New York News*.

Noel retreated to Jamaica for a rest. The island was much changed since its declaration of independence in 1962; as Ann Fleming told Evelyn Waugh, 'An effort to boost deservedly failing tourist traffic is the inauguration . . . of a Bunny Club . . . for a vast sum you can sit next to an untouchable Bunny and are waited on by footmen. Perhaps the footmen are touchable, more appealing to Chinese Nell.' She explained her remark, 'Noel Coward is known as "Chinese Nell" in this island – rather sinister?'

Coward eschewed the charms of Hugh Heffner's club; he had other concerns. He sanctioned plans to take *High Spirits* to London, possibly with Graham Payn as assistant director, another attempt to find him useful employment. He was beginning to despair of his friend's career; Graham seemed 'quite incapable of doing anything at all. He is, I fear, a born drifter. He just wanders through his life with no impetus and no genuine ambition. I know his theatrical career has been a failure, but there *are* other ploys to go after. He sleeps and sleeps and the days go by. I love him dearly and for ever, but this lack of drive, in any direction, is a bad augury for the future. I am willing and happy to look after him for the rest of my life, but he must do *something*.'

'He tried to educate me,' said Payn, 'tried to make me read better books, which he said was a lost cause because I wouldn't read properly . . .' Payn is defensive about his self-confessed lack of 'star quality'. 'I thought the best thing to do was to get on and work. He tried to say to me, "You can perform with more confidence and more authority on stage. Come on, why do you get so nervous?" I don't know why I got nervous. But I did, and that was no good . . . I think he minded more than I did – I think he longed for me to be a star.' Coward reached the conclusion that 'something must be done'; nothing could be.

High Spirits was still playing to capacity crowds in New York. 'Let's hope it doesn't do that famous "Noel Coward musical nose-dive" after three months.' There were no signs of this, and he could depart for London to enjoy ten days of theatre. In confirmation of the renaissance, Laurence Olivier had plans to produce *Hay Fever* at the National Theatre, putting Coward's work in repertory with Shakespeare, Shaw, Brecht and Chekhov. It was the first time the National had revived the work of a living dramatist. Coward was invited to direct *Hay Fever*, with 'a glorious cast', including Maggie Smith, Robert Stephens, Derek

Jacobi and Lynn Redgrave. He was, he admitted, 'very excited' about the prospect. With Bernstein's Granada Television producing four of his plays (*Present Laughter*, *Blithe Spirit*, *The Vortex* and *Design for Living*) that autumn, and his new collection of short stories (*Pretty Polly Barlow*) about to appear, Coward felt that Beverley Baxter's famous criticism of the Forties – 'Did Noel Coward Survive the War?' – could be consigned to the dustbin of redundant quotes. He was also fully solvent; as a Swiss resident, his earnings were paid into his Crédit Suisse account with a minimal 7.4 per cent tax (as opposed to the 50 per cent company tax he was obliged to pay on monies earned in England).

Life at Les Avants was enlivened by a glamorous, if eccentric encounter. Geoffrey Johnson arrived at Geneva airport, and was impressed that Noel had come to meet him; he was in a state of high excitement. 'You'll never guess who was on the same plane as you', Coward said. 'Garbo. We had a reunion, and she's coming for a drink next week.' The Swedish star, by now almost an obsessive recluse, was staying with the Ahernes, and came to Chalet Coward for drinks. That evening Coward was dining with Adrienne Allen and her guests Phyllis Monkman and Bobbie Andrews, and he persuaded Garbo to join them. Johnson found himself 'in this Mercedes convertible with Garbo and Noel Coward, and he was driving! . . . The sun was setting, and we drove from Les Avants to Glion – it's terrible that road, sheer drops on either side – and he's speeding along, the two of them in the front. I was in the back, and he's talking a mile a minute to her. I thought "We're going to go right over the side of this cliff" . . . I could just see the headlines – "Coward and Garbo Killed in Auto Accident – with Unidentified American".'

When they arrived, Garbo swept through the room with only cursory introductions to the other guests, and went to sit on a porch swing. Phyllis Monkman approached her. 'She screwed up all her courage and said "Miss Garbo, I just wanted to say I saw *Camille* last week in London . . . at a revival and it's brilliant, it's as great as it ever was." Garbo said "No" [covering her face] like Monkman had said something really terrible . . .' Noel witnessed the scene, and marched over, his finger wagging. '"Don't you ever do that to anybody again! You were a great star, and whether you like it or not, you've got to face it" . . . He really laid her flat . . . she was quite shaken.' The next day Coward flew to Rome; the Ahernes and Garbo were also on board. Noel noted that they travelled tourist, 'presumably because La Divina feared recognition in the more sophisticated atmosphere of the first class. She needn't have worried because no one recognised her at all.' Noel, however, was recognised, and was whisked through customs and immigration 'at record speed', leaving Brian Aherne with the luggage and Garbo and Mrs Aherne in the lavatory.

In Rome he visited the Spoleto Festival for 'an orgy of "culture"', seeing Nureyev and Fonteyn in *Raymonda*. Nureyev seemed like 'a curious wild animal, very beguiling and fairly unpredictable'; during dinner he actually bit Coward, 'but it was only on the finger and didn't draw blood'. Alan Helms was also in Spoleto, visiting Luchino Visconti. He introduced Coward to the film director. When Noel had gone, Visconti turned to Helms and said, 'Fascinating man – who was he?' 'Each had understood that the other was famous', says Helms, 'even though . . . neither of them knew what for.'

At Les Avants, he heard news of Ian Fleming's death, 'a horrid but expected sadness. He went on smoking and drinking in spite of all warnings.' His wife Ann, who had never really liked Jamaica, abandoned Goldeneye soon after and returned to London. Life in Jamaica, and the high society of the Forties and Fifties, seemed further away than ever.

At Chalet Coward, he received the imperial presence of Edith Evans. They read through *Hay Fever* together. 'She is, of course, perfectly brilliant. I can't wait to get into rehearsal.' It was an optimistic opinion which (as with so many of Noel's pre-production pronouncements) would be swiftly revised. On the first day of rehearsals, he told the company, 'I'm thrilled and flattered and frankly a little flabbergasted that the National Theatre should have had the curious perceptiveness to choose a very early play of mine, and to give it a cast that could play the Albanian telephone directory.' But as the rehearsals went on, Evans's age became a problem. Coward felt he was 'doomed to sit patient and still, watching elderly actresses forgetting their lines'. Dame Edith was well aware of her predicament, as her companion, Gwen ffrangcon-Davies (then sixty-eight), discovered when they journeyed to Manchester for the opening. Evans was going through her lines, and came to the scene where Judith Bliss defends her flirtatiousness to her children: 'Anyone would think I was eighty the way you go on.' She stopped, and said, 'But I *am* nearly eighty. I'm seventy-six. I can't play this part.'

In Manchester Evans took to her room and refused to leave it. Coward was summoned, and informed Evans that she was 'a disgrace to herself, the theatre *and* Christian Science'. Evans bestirred herself, but the audience invited to the dress rehearsal had to be sent away. Maggie Smith (who thought she should have had the part) stood in as Judith. The stage manager, Diana Boddington, recalled, 'Maggie just sent up Edith's performance something rotten. The mimicry was unbelievably funny. We were all – Noel, Larry, everyone – laughing so much we were lying around on the floor.' Evans 'tottered insecurely' through the opening night on 19 October, 'drying up, mistiming and cutting lots of important lines', but 'the play and the brilliance of the cast got us through'.

Hay Fever opened in London on 27 October. The night was triumphant, and the next day excellent notices confirmed Coward's return to favour. Maggie Smith said it was as though he had never been away, 'There seemed to be no generation gap with Noel, he just seemed to leap right into the Sixties, it didn't seem to make any difference that the play had been written all those years before.' With her Sixties backcombed approximation of a Twenties bob and a modern delivery to match, Maggie Smith was the visual personification of the production; and indeed, in her camp way, threatened to outclass Dame Edith.

Derek Jacobi, playing Simon Bliss, thought Edith Evans 'not the most generous of actresses. She was certainly hideous to us youngsters, giving us notes and summonses and tellings-off and I think to a certain extent Maggie was standing up to her for everyone else in the cast.' This she did by playing 'Baby Love' by the Supremes full volume in the dressing-room next to Evans's, depriving the dame of sleep and making her too tired to cause trouble in the evenings. Jacobi also recalls being summoned by Coward to his Savoy room, there to be asked, 'Tell me one thing. Are you circumcised?' Jacobi replied that he was not. 'Derek, you will always be a fine actor', said the Master, 'but you'll never be a great actor until you are circumcised.' The significance of this escaped Jacobi, he had to admit. 'Freedom, dear,' said Noel, 'freedom!'

After the success of *Hay Fever* came the London opening, on 2 November, of *High Spirits*, with Cicely Courtneidge and Marti Stevens. The audience were 'wildly enthusiastic; all notices horrible'. The *Sunday Telegraph* thought that against the sublime achievement of the original, *High Spirits* was 'grossly over-weighted with conventional songs, derivative dances ... and a series of performances of such brashly confident incongruity ... that the whole caravan soon grinds to a halt in clouds of steam and smoke'. 'The piece is grotesquely unfunny, acted with sledge-hammer clumsiness, and, with its unmemorable music, it is an appalling bore', said the *Sunday Times*. Timothy Gray and Hugh Martin had 'properly bought it', wrote Coward. 'Considering their insensate obstinacy from the very beginning, I cannot feel altogether sorry.' And considering Noel's initial enthusiasm, this was not a generous reaction.

He returned to Les Avants exhausted, and spent the next few days in bed. He received news of the larger world: '*High Spirits* is hobbling along convulsively. *Hay Fever* more and more triumphant. *Pretty Polly Barlow* has so far received one abusive notice from a ghastly young squirt called Julian Jebb in the *Sunday Times* and two other rather patronising ones.'

Coward's latest volume contained three lengthy short stories. 'Pretty Polly Barlow' drew on his Singapore stay; 'Mrs Capper's Birthday' is *This Happy Breed*/'Fumed Oak' territory (a younger Mrs Capper appears in '*Peace in Our Time*'), a meandering observation of an aged cleaning lady; but the best story was one of Coward's most emotive. Noel wrote to Rupert Croft-Cooke, 'I was delighted and touched by your letter about "Me and the Girls". Of course I need hardly tell you it is also one of my favourites. It is based half on life and half on fiction. (The actual prototype is still alive and high kicking!)' A dying gay cabaret entertainer reviews his life from his hospital bed, 'I was never one to go off into a great production about being queer . . . I don't see that it's anybody's business but your own what you do with your old man providing you don't make a bee line for the dear little kiddies, not, I am here to tell you, that quite a lot of the aforesaid dear little kiddies didn't enjoy it tip-top. I was one myself and I know.' (A reference to Noel's own youthful introduction to sex.) The tone prefigured that of Coward's last dramatic works: 'To hell with what might have been', says Banks. 'What *has* been is quite enough for me, and what *will* be will have to be coped with when the time comes.'

The book was not well received; the literary critics, unlike their dramatic counterparts, were not reassessing Coward, and did not appreciate the silken artifice of his slender creations. By Christmas 1964, Coward was complaining that it had 'not one really good notice', so he reviewed it himself. 'I *know* "Me and the Girls" is good, also "Mrs Capper". "Pretty Polly" is less interesting, being more conventional in theme, but it is at moments very funny and eminently readable. The battle, of course, will never end until the grave closes over me, and then! oh dear, the balls that will be written about me.'

*

Coward's sixty-fifth birthday, in December 1965, found him on a return visit to Capri. Gloria Magnus still ran her restaurant on the Piccolo Marina, where he lunched with Payn and Lesley. But out of season Capri was 'not only quiet but moribund', and walking up and down cobbled streets hurt his legs; he felt decrepit and cross. His age had been underlined by the deaths of Edith Sitwell, Cole Porter and Diana Wynyard that year; Churchill was also dying. 'I suppose it's just as well really,' Coward remarked, 'ninety years is a long, long time.'

In London, Coward cast a revival of *Present Laughter*, with Nigel Patrick as Garry Essendine; Phyllis Calvert, Maxine Audley, Richard Briers and Graham Payn were to play his extended family. Noel was still a hard taskmaster. When he saw the finished production, he thought it 'all *apparently* very good but badly gabbled'; after two rehearsals, matters were rectified. Maxine Audley recalled 'the end of Act Two when Joanna and Gary are canoodling on the sofa, getting closer and closer . . . Noel said "No, no . . . watch me Paddy [Nigel Patrick]." And he came up . . . and did the scene with me, and . . . he was much sexier, much more smoochy and tender.' Audley told him so, to which Coward replied, 'I know'.

He returned to Jamaica for the winter, to await the Queen Mother. In a mirror image of *Pomp and Circumstance*, this royal visit, far from being a secret, was 'the talk of the island'. Firefly was vetted by security police, who inspected the tiny black-tiled bathroom at great length, 'and . . . left sadly shaking their heads, which worried us considerably', said Cole Lesley. Her Majesty arrived and was introduced to Coward's favourite cocktail, the potent vodka-based bullshot, of which she had two 'and was delighted'. Lunch, which had threatened to be a disaster when the lobster mousse melted, was rescued by Noel's chilled pea soup and 'cocomania', his version of the local curry, made in a coconut. After lunch she insisted on visiting Blue Harbour, 'which had *not* been frisked, to the security men's horror'. When she drove off, she 'left behind her five gibbering worshippers'.

Coward got on with work. A new collection of stories, *Bon Voyage*, was sold by Curtis Brown to *McCall's* for $12,500, and by mid-March Coward had written the first act of his new play, *A Song at Twilight*, suggested by David Cecil's biography of Max Beerbohm (then living at Rapallo), in which the ageing dandy is visited by Constance Collier. 'I thought how funny it was', wrote Coward. 'There was Constance, Max's old flame, coming to see him again, only now she was still full of vitality and he of course wasn't, so she absolutely exhausted him.' He added, 'My play is more sinister, and there is Maugham in it as well as Max.' By the end of March he had finished it, and was pleased with the result: 'I really think it's a rouser.' He intended to play the lead, Sir Hugo Latymer, and, as companion pieces, he wrote *Shadows of the Evening* and *Come into the Garden, Maud*. The retrospective tone of the trilogy was reflected in real life: Clemence Dane had 'tied a purple nylon scarf round her head, slapped on some lipstick, and sent for Dick [Addinsell] and Victor [Stiebel]' for a farewell party and died the next day. 'Well, that's one more old friend gone.'

In London, Coward began filming for Otto Preminger's *Bunny Lake Is Missing*, starring Laurence Olivier and Anna Massey, in which he played a grubby landlord. He told Roddy McDowall, 'I play an elderly, drunk, queer masochist, and I am in no mood for any wisecracks about typecasting so there.' Dressed like a tramp, he also carried a chihuahua 'crooked in my arm. It just lies there comatose but quivering. I can't stand things that quiver . . . It only has one piece of action . . . it had to wave, but it couldn't do it. I said to it, "You will never make another Lassie."' Much of the filming was done in a garage in West London, and the director did not particularly appeal either: 'a real bully who never let up', said Olivier, 'a heavy-handed egotist [whom] Noel Coward and I didn't like much'. Other duties included a recording of Sheridan's *The Critic*, and a check on *Hay Fever*: 'The cast as good as ever with the exception of Maggie [Smith] who was overplaying.'

He was interviewed by Clive Hirschhorn for the *Sunday Express*, and revealed his dismay at the modern world. He spoke of his ambivalence towards his native land, 'I *am* England, and England is me. We have a love-hate relationship with each other. It's everything I stand for, but day by day the place changes.' He claimed the English had 'such huge chips on their shoulders these days . . . Today everyone here is so damn *rebellious* . . . Take modern youth, for example. All this insufferable long hair . . . Long hair is all very well if it hangs loosely on brocade, or silk or velvet, but it somehow seems all wrong when it's supposed to offset some smelly sports shirt . . . Our system of values is all wrong now. Elegance is a dirty word.' ('I detest the youth of today', Hugo Latymer protests in *A Song at Twilight*. 'They are grubby, undisciplined and ill-mannered. They also make too much noise.') Hirschhorn asked about his reputation. 'I'm an enormously talented man, and there's no use pretending that I'm not', Coward said. 'My name was a household word before I was twenty-five. I have always had a natural facility for entertaining others, and this has never deserted me.' But surely his brand of comedy was out of date? Not at all. 'The lower classes like nothing better than to adore the upper classes ... They *enjoy* striving to be what they aren't, and it doesn't matter whether or not they'll ever reach those dizzy heights. They're *dreamers*, and this keeps them happy. How else can you account for the continuous popularity of my plays amongst people who will never see the inside of a tasteful drawing room?'

The way he expressed himself illustrated how out of touch he was. To maintain that stiff upper lip in the Britain of the mid-Sixties was not only foolhardy, it was virtually impossible. It seemed he was fast becoming a caricature of himself. Or was he just teasing? It was difficult to know; Coward played his part too well. 'Youth always makes too much noise,' Carlotta replies to Latymer's lament, 'their world is more shrill than ours was.' Back at Les Avants, Noel heard news of the Beatles' MBEs, which had war veterans sending their medals back in disgust. 'Some other decoration should have been selected to reward them for their talentless but considerable contributions to the Exchequer.' A week or so later, he saw the noisy youths in concert in Rome. 'The noise was deafening throughout', and he was unable to hear 'a word they sang or a note they played, just one long, ear-splitting din', with the fanatical audience 'like a mass masturbation orgy'.

Coward went backstage to see the group, and was told by Brian Epstein to go to their hotel. There he was told they would not see him, 'because that ass David Lewin had quoted me saying unflattering things about them months ago'. Lewin had interviewed Coward shortly after he had met Lennon and McCartney at one of Alma Cogan's Kensington parties, and had recorded Coward as saying, 'The Beatles, those two I met seemed nice, pleasant young men, quite well behaved and with an amusing way of speaking. Of course, they are totally devoid of talent. There is a great deal of noise. In my day the young were taught to be seen but not heard – which is no bad thing.' Coward insisted their publicist find one of the group, and she returned with Paul McCartney, to whom he explained 'gently but firmly that one did *not* pay much attention to the statements of newspaper reporters. The poor boy was quite amiable and I sent messages of congratulation to his colleagues, although the message I would have liked to send them was that they were bad-mannered little shits.'

His social life remained 'violent'; from the company of a royal queen at Sandringham, where Coward and the Queen Mother sang a duet of

'My Old Man Said Follow the Van', to the tribute of another in cabaret, when Danny La Rue sang a Coward melody, 'beautifully done'. Maxine Audley had suggested they see the show, 'It just so happened that that night they went to John Osborne's *A Patriot for Me*, and I thought, "Oh, God, there's a drag scene in that!" I thought two in one evening might be too much for them. Luckily, for me . . . he'd loathed the John Osborne play, and within five minutes of Danny's show starting he turned to me and said "The perfect antidote!"'

A Patriot for Me, set in *fin-de-siècle* middle Europe and based on the case of the homosexual lower-class Hungarian Jew and spy, Colonel Redl, 'a brilliant man and a fascinating character', had aroused the ire of the censor. To circumvent the Lord Chamberlain, the Royal Court had been turned into a theatre club for the run. The lavish drag scene was a visual climax of the play, when Redl attended a ball full of Viennese homosexuals, its host declaring, 'This is the celebration of the individual against the rest.' But it seemed that Osborne was attacking homosexuality (as weak betrayal), just as he challenged its sway in the West End theatre (particularly the 'gay mafia' of Binkie Beaumont – and, by association, Coward). Noel found it 'muddled, undisciplined writing', with 'interminable scenes and acres of appalling bad taste . . . Osborne has missed all the main points. The "drag" scene is so embarrassing that we could hardly look at the stage.'

Coward summoned the playwright to dinner at his rented flat in Chesham Place. Osborne was 'subjected to a light finger-wagging about my personal and sexual life over a very, very light omelette . . . His second or perhaps third question was "How queer are you?" . . . The fatuous game was afoot, and I played it feebly. "Oh, about 30 per cent." "Really?" he rapped back. "I'm ninety-five." That was it.'

Coward's London trip also had a more narcissistic agenda; he had decided to have his face lifted. After three hours on the operating table, he had a 'claustrophobic panic' when he came round; but after 'lots of heroin' everything was fine, 'underchin jowls now completely gone'. But there was a *frisson* of fear; the surgeon's assistant told him he had 'died' under the anaesthetic. 'My heart stopped beating for forty-five seconds! . . . They had to hit me very hard with their fists, which . . . accounts for the chest pain and panic I suffered when I came round.' Thus revitalised, he returned to Les Avants to finish *Shadows of the Evening*, 'one of the best plays I have ever written', with excellent parts for himself, Irene Worth and Margaret Leighton. But Leighton would take the part only if her husband, Michael Wilding, could come too – a scenario Coward dreaded. Beaumont and Coward decided to ask Lilli Palmer instead.

While staying with the Nivens at Cap Ferrat that summer, Coward called on Somerset Maugham at the Villa Mauresque, where he read *A Song at Twilight* to Robin Maugham, who 'nearly fainted'. 'He was deeply impressed but agitated because people might think it was based on Willie! Actually it isn't, although there are many similarities.' Coward was disingenuous in protesting the obvious comparison; he certainly did not read the play to Maugham (it was perhaps no coincidence that *A Song at Twilight* was performed three months after Maugham's death, on Coward's birthday, 16 December 1965). Had he done so, however, there is little to suggest that Maugham would have understood the implications. According to Coward, Maugham was 'wretchedly, pathetically grateful' for his visit. 'He is living out his last days in a desperate nightmare, poor beast. He barely makes sense and, of course, he *knows* his mind has gone. I managed to cheer him a bit and certainly helped poor Alan [Searle] who is going through hell.'

When Maugham had adopted Searle as his son in an attempt to disinherit his daughter Liza, Coward saw Maugham as 'devoured by retrospective hate of poor Syrie'. Shortly after, Maugham published 'his disgusting autobiography' in an American magazine. 'It really is beneath contempt, and crucifies the wretched Syrie. I don't think I want to see him again.' *Looking Back* had caused outrage among Maugham's friends. He had approached Alexander Frere with plans for Heinemann to publish the book, but when Frere read the manuscript he was shocked at what seemed to him the ramblings of a madman, and thought he owed it to his old friend not to publish. He alerted Doubleday, who also turned it down. Maugham was furious, and disowned Frere as his literary executor. Coward told Garson Kanin,* 'The man who wrote that awful slop is not the man who has been my friend for so many years. Some evil spirit has entered his body.' 'Coward channelled his indignation in the direction of what he did best', said Maugham's biographer, Ted Morgan. 'He did to Maugham what Maugham had done to Hugh Walpole in *Cakes and Ale*, but posthumously.'

A Song at Twilight, like the other two plays in what became known as *A Suite in Three Keys*, is set in the luxurious Beau Rivage hotel at

---

* After Kanin's biography of Spencer Tracy appeared, Coward told Ginette Spanier he dreaded the day when Kanin would pull down from the shelf the file marked 'C'.

Lausanne. The setting is a deluxe limbo peopled by his ageing characters, with the eavesdropping presence of Felix the waiter (a 'startlingly
handsome young man') the constant in all three pieces; he is the
audience to these vignettes of Cowardian drama, with their still incisive
dialogue, dextrously twisting and turning meaning as a composer might
a melody.

Sir Hugo Latymer, an elderly writer, lives with his long-suffering
wife, Hilde, and is nervously awaiting a visit from an old lover, Carlotta.
Latymer is cynical, manipulative and self-concerned; as Carlotta later
comments, 'You are remodelling your public image. The witty, cynical
author of so many best sellers is making way for the Grand Old Man of
Letters.' He has written an autobiography in which he is nice about
nobody, 'the most superlative example of sustained camouflage'. 'Why
the constant implications of heterosexual ardour?' asks Carlotta. 'Why
those self-conscious, almost lascivious references to laughing-eyed dam-
sels with scarlet lips and pointed breasts?' It was a sin of which Coward
was not guilty, and he was drawing attention to the fact. Hilde goes off
to visit Liesel, whom Sir Hugo describes as a 'weather-beaten old
German lesbian',* leaving Latymer and Carlotta to dine alone, served
by Felix. 'He really is most attractive, isn't he?' says Carlotta, 'those
glorious shoulders'. It seems she is trying to trap him into admitting his
desires, and is a prelude to her announcement that she has Latymer's
old love letters to Perry Sheldon, 'the only true love of your life . . .
You've been homosexual all your life, and you know it!'

Carlotta argues against the stigma of homosexuality: 'We are living
in the 1960s, not the 1890s.' The reference to Oscar Wilde is a reminder
of how far Coward had come – from his pre-First World War
experiences, when homosexuals still suffered the backlash of the Wilde
trial, to the permissive Sixties, when his preferences were about to be
legitimised (although not, he contested, accepted). His experience of a
sexually proscriptive society informed his work even now; Morris
Cargill thought Coward was always afraid of legal action: 'What stuck
in his craw was the Oscar Wilde trial. [He might have cited the
Pemberton Billing case, too] . . . He told me once "I'm not going to
court". He was absolutely petrified about that sort of thing . . . That ate
into his soul.'

Carlotta insists that the law 'has become archaic and nonsensical'.
Hugo replies, 'Maybe so, but even when the actual law ceases to exist

---

* Like Mercedes de Acosta, Liesel is a Hollywood scriptwriter.

there will still be a stigma attached to "the love that dare not speak its name" in the minds of millions of people for generations to come. It takes more than a few outspoken books and plays and speeches in Parliament to uproot moral prejudice from the Anglo-Saxon mind.' Coward had objected to *A Patriot for Me*; Osborne had not 'got it right'; *A Song at Twilight* readdressed the question. Yet he was still hiding behind a screen; his protectiveness about his private life even served to hide his intellect, says Cargill. 'I told him, "Noel, your plays are fine, they're first-class. But they're not nearly as good as what you could write" . . . It was a façade . . . this business of "only a talent to amuse" – he was determined that all the world would ever see of him was his plays and his songs. Even when he wrote his autobiographies, he never said anything about himself at all . . . He was a brilliantly clever man, he had a fine mind – but he wasn't showing that to anybody.'

In *A Song at Twilight*, Coward seemed to address Cargill's reservations; there is a sense of his intellect coming out of the closet, an exposition of his innermost feelings, and of what he really could do. Coward told William Marchant, '*A Song at Twilight* is far and away the best-constructed play I have ever written, and when I played it I knew as an actor that as a writer I had served myself very well; there is an almost mathematical precision to it that in no way detracts from the reality of it. It is the first play I have written whose theme was not attacked in at least one quarter as being flimsy or superficial.' Only now, when they least expected it, did he confound the critics' expectations. Of *A Suite in Three Keys*, *The Times* wrote, 'For all their determined glitter and the authentic disclaimers of any purpose beyond entertainment, Noel Coward's plays are among the most earnestly moral works to be found anywhere in modern drama.'

No one who read the play or saw it performed could fail to consider its comments on Coward's sexuality. But his remarks to the contemporary press indicate his unwillingness to apply the play's themes personally; he dodged the issue. 'It is perhaps the most serious play I have ever written', he told Hugh Curnow in an interview in which, for the first and last time, he spoke 'on the record' about a sexuality he shared with his protagonist. 'It is . . . a subject that only lately has come into circulation because only lately have we been able to discuss it openly. And it's very lucky that we can; homosexuality has permeated the whole of history. It's a fascinating subject and must be handled, I think, with taste. A compassionate homosexual play defeats its object if it makes it repellent.' Thus Coward is both Carlotta (espousing acceptance) and Latymer (requiring concealment); at the end of his life and his last play, he remains firmly behind the mask. 'One's real inside self is a private place,' he declared in 1969, 'and should always stay like that. It is no one else's business.'

A Song at Twilight concludes by drawing together the greater themes of Coward's life. Love, rather than sex, is more important, Latymer tells Carlotta; hence the reason for his heartbreaking affair with Perry Sheldon. 'I should have thought that even your cheap magazine mentality would have learnt by now that it is seldom with people's characters that one falls in love.' As with Jack Wilson, Sheldon's alcoholism is seen as part of the reason for the end of the relationship; but here it is blamed on Latymer, as perhaps Gerald Haxton's dissolution reflected on Maugham.*

Some found the portrayal of Latymer's sexuality unconvincing, and Coward's intentions unclear. A later criticism of *A Song at Twilight* by Alan Brien noted that it 'tells us nothing about what it is like to be a homosexual in an unsympathetic society. We learn that Hugo's wife has known all along and that his mistress was never deceived. But what about the rest of his friends, his associates in show business and literature? Did he have only one male lover? If "A Song At Twilight" was not written to demonstrate the strains, the misunderstandings, the comedy and the tragedy of the double life – then what is its purpose?'

Coward might retort that he did not write plays with a message. It is the tone of *A Song at Twilight* which is its most affecting aspect. As with his later short stories, a sense of detachment pervades the trilogy of *A Suite in Three Keys*: Coward is reviewing past lives – his own, those of people he has known; characters in his dramas and those of a greater world. He is the puppetmaster still, and the hotel provides a perfect setting, its rooms echo human frailty and failings, played out as he looks on. Here is the tragedy of Hugo Latymer's life (what Coward might have been); the happier death of George Hilgay (to which Coward looked forward); and the comic characters of the American Conklyns (the objects of Coward's wit). Elsewhere in the ethereal hotel are Amanda and Elyot, on their honeymoon terrace; or Gilda, Leo and

---

* Latymer's letters are evidence of his cruel denial of help to the dying Sheldon. 'Masterpieces of veiled invective', says Carlotta, 'pure gold for your future biographer'. Coward had been alerted to the potential power of correspondence when Maugham wrote him an 'outspoken and moving' letter when Gerald Haxton died. None of Coward's own love letters appear to have survived.

Otto, fighting over each other's affections; or Nicky Lancaster, a dissolute and aged Dorian Gray. *A Suite in Three Keys* is the conclusion of the spectacle of Coward's life, the final exploitation of his art; a coda to the dance, a last attempt to entertain.

Shadows of the Evening also concerns a reunion. The publisher George Hilgay has six months to live, and his former wife and current mistress call a truce to help him. To Hilgay, as to Coward, religion is no panacea, 'I'm quite content to die believing only in life itself...'; and he defies 'treacly compassion': 'I'm going to die – I'm going to die – and, what is more, I'm going to die alone, because everybody dies alone.' The final speech is his, and Coward's, epitaph: 'Every schoolboy has to face the last day of the holidays. That is how I feel now. I still have enough time to recapitulate a few past enjoyments, to revisit the cove where we had the picnic, to swim again into the cave where we found the jellyfish, to swing once more in the wooden swing and to build the last sandcastle.' From a man whose bedside reading remained the works of Nesbit, it is a sharp reminder of his deep nostalgia for his short-lived boyhood. When reviewing Cole Lesley's memoir, Tynan wrote, 'What Mr Lesley shows us in his later chapters is a superbly preserved middle-aged child ... the most pampered, debonair, hard-headed, professional boy on earth. Whether by genetic luck or environmental good judgement, Noel Coward never suffered the imprisonment of maturity.' From infant prodigy to aged artist, the gap of the past closed; Coward seemed to concertina time. It is apposite to repeat Tynan's view that Coward had been Slightly in *Peter Pan* in 1913, and wholly in it ever since.

The last of the trilogy was the slightest. In *Come into the Garden, Maud*, a bourgeois American woman faces social disaster when a dinner party for minor royalty is threatened by a dropped-out guest, and she pleads with a friend to fill the gap. It is an essay on snobbery; while the matron is caught up in petty social dilemmas, her hen-pecked husband is making love to the friend; like the 'hero' of 'Fumed Oak', he rebels against his insufferable wife. This 'light comedy' is the sorbet of the meal, a delicate flourish to complete Coward's final dramatic menu.

30

A Song at Twilight

I have no great social causes. I can't think of any offhand. If I did, they'd be very offhand. But I have done some very valuable things, you know. Changed the face of things completely. Do you realise I stopped the fashion for taking curtain calls after every act? A great revolution. It used to foul up every play.

Noel Coward to Hunter Davies, *Sunday Times*, 28 December 1969

IN September 1965 Noel was back in the South of France, on Sam Spiegel's yacht, with Burt Lancaster and his girlfriend. Coward and Lancaster got on well, despite the film star's joking complaint during the rehearsals for *Night of a Hundred Stars* that Coward pinched his bottom every time they met. On the Riviera, Noel met Graham Sutherland, 'with whom I immediately fell in love. He has promised to paint me next July in Venice.' Sutherland had painted Maugham in 1949, a portrait as harsh as Coward's play; but a similar 'warts and all' oil of Noel never happened.

A conference was arranged to discuss *A Suite in Three Keys* at Binkie Beaumont's house in London, where their chosen director, Glen Byam Shaw, said he wasn't good enough and was frightened by Noel, who would undermine his authority with the actors. He left Coward and Beaumont sitting on the floor 'hissing like schoolgirls in the dorm after lights out, and trying to get Vivian Matalon (whom I have always wanted) on the telephone'. Matalon was at home when the telephone rang at one in the morning. Beaumont requested his presence immediately, and would not explain why. Matalon arrived, 'peered into the room ... and I thought "My God, that face looks vaguely familiar." Binkie said, "Vivian, I'd like you to meet a very old friend of mine, this is", and he got to the N and I realised who it was and I said, "Oh my God."' To which Noel replied, 'Yes, quite right.'

'Will you do me the honour of directing my plays?' Coward asked. His request threw the young director. 'I said ... "Mr Coward, do you want a director, or a stage manager? Because if that's what you want, please don't ask me this. I've been defending you all your years in the wilderness, and I would not want to lose my respect for you." And he looked at me and said, "Dear boy, you have just walked straight into my heart. I need a director. I am absolutely terrified, and I need somebody who's not frightened, as you obviously are not ..."' Matalon's intelligent comments on *A Suite in Three Keys* impressed Coward and, after some rewriting, he set off for a month of isolation and rest in the Seychelles. But at the beginning of November, he fell ill. Severe diarrhoea sent him to hospital, where he was told he had roundworm, but he was vomiting continually and suspected hepatitis. Added to this, he felt 'an undercurrent of evil' in the Seychelles which made him long to get away. He journeyed to Mombasa and Nairobi, where his illness prevented him from enjoying the wildlife and countryside; 'the end of the most disastrous holiday I ever had'. By 6 December he was in Les Avants, 'The weather is vile but I couldn't care less. I have my own comfortable bed and delicious food and peace.' By his sixty-sixth birthday, he was feeling better; not so Somerset Maugham, who died that morning. 'Poor miserable man ... Not very sadly mourned, I fear.'

At Christmas, Vivian Matalon arrived at Les Avants. 'We were supposed to rehearse for two weeks in Switzerland, and then two weeks in London, and then go to Dublin, and then come into the Queen's Theatre. Coward asked me to go out earlier, because he wanted us to get to know each other.' Noel still felt ill, and after a few days said, 'I'm going to go to Italy. There is a doctor there who says he can really cure me'; but when he returned, it was clear that he was no better; in fact, he looked worse. 'He went away as Noel Coward, and he came back as that stooped-over figure ... I took one look at him, and I was really very alarmed. I went down to the village, and I phoned Binkie and I said "Cancel Dublin. He will not make it. He's very ill."'

Cancelling the opening in Dublin was an affront to Noel's professionalism. But Matalon's diagnosis was vindicated when Coward collapsed during one of the rehearsals with Lilli Palmer and Irene Worth, who had arrived at Les Avants. Noel feared he would not be able to open in the play he knew would be his last. 'He called for us to come into his room. He was very matter-of-fact, and he said, very professionally, "I don't think I'm going to be well enough to go on" ...

he asked me to stay behind. He said, "I'm so sorry, I'm so sorry, I've put you all out of work." And then he said, "Oh God, curse my ageing body" and started to cry.'

On 21 January Coward checked into La Source, a clinic in Lausanne, where a urinary infection was diagnosed. He was losing weight rapidly, and was 'hideously depressed and unhappy', knowing there was no chance of opening in London in six weeks' time. As Coward languished in bed, a bill was passed in Parliament (the Sexual Offences Act of 1967) allowing homosexual acts between consenting adults in private. The issues of *A Song at Twilight* became all the more relevant. 'Nothing will convince the bigots, but the blackmailers will be discouraged and fewer haunted, terrified young men will commit suicide.' At the end of February, he decided to 'take a very firm grip both on myself and my circumstances' and, with Mary Baker Eddy's confidence, announced, 'I *know* I am no longer ill and I *know* that the sooner I get out of this hospital and eat proper food and begin to live normally again the white cells will diminish [his white cell count was abnormally high], the sedimentation decrease, and Bob will be my uncle.' The Savoy welcomed its old tenant back to London, and preparations resumed for the plays. Coward had heard news of difficulties with Lilli Palmer; her behaviour throughout the production endangered the success of Coward's last plays, and his friends never forgave her.

Matalon found Palmer 'a truly monstrous person. Not a very good actress . . . absolutely undirectable. Coward was the easiest playwright I have ever worked with in my life . . . Not all that easy as an actor, but he was very professional. If he didn't like something, he would at least try it, and if he didn't like it, he would offer you an alternative . . . But he would do what he was asked to do. Lilli Palmer was . . . unkind to the stage managers and unkind to understudies . . . she never took the trouble to get to know anybody. I think she did ruin *A Song at Twilight*, the play which really meant a lot to me – and I felt meant a lot to Noel – I thought she literally ruined it.'

It soon became obvious that Coward was no longer up to the task. 'His memory just started to go . . . The first extraordinary lapse that happened was in *A Song at Twilight*, [when] Sir Hugo says, "The threat to reveal I have had in the past homosexual tendencies." Carlotta replies, "Homosexual tendencies in the past? You're as queer as a coot and you have been all your life." Latymer says, "That is not true!" And he forgot that section. I thought, "Coward has gone to the trouble to write this play, but when push came to shove, he did not want to stand

on a West End stage and have himself referred to as 'queer as a coot'"
... By the time I had got backstage, somebody had told him, and he
said, "I didn't know I'd cut it." Then he said, "But you know, dear, it
might be better without it."' Matalon suggested a compromise, 'I said,
"How about if we changed it to 'you've been a homosexual all your
life'?" ... He said, "I think that might be better . . ."'*

To Matalon, Coward's honesty stood out. 'The thing he really hated
was hypocrisy. I don't think Coward ever hid his homosexuality, he just
didn't talk about it . . .' Even at sixty-six, love was no stranger, 'Noel
[became] infatuated twice in the period that I knew him . . .' Ben Bagley
recalled a late-flowering passion for a TV repairman (shared with Cole
Porter) in New York; another witness was Peter Wadland, then nineteen:
'Just before *A Suite in Three Keys* came to London, I was sitting in the
William IV pub in Hampstead [a gay haunt] with a friend, and on one of
the opposite seats . . . was a man in a green Tyrolean hat, with a poodle. I
didn't know what Coward looked like then. He looked at me, and asked
me to look after his dog while he went to the toilet. When he came back
he asked if his dog could have one of my crisps. I gave him one, but the
dog wouldn't eat it, and Coward tried to give me the crisps back, which I
thought was disgusting! He said, "Of course, you know who I am?" I
hadn't the foggiest. He said, "I'm the man who wrote *Bitter Sweet*."'

Inevitably, Coward was living in the past. The interviews given for *A
Suite in Three Keys* emphasised how far he was from the modern world.
To the critic Barry Norman, he confided his regrets about the ever-
accelerating changes of the liberal Sixties. 'Man is intrinsically class-
conscious, intrinsically cruel', he said, and, sitting in his pale blue
pyjamas, drawing on a menthol cigarette, he coolly advocated the return
of the death penalty: 'Why should we keep inferior beings in the world?'
If Noel sounded dangerously reactionary at times, he could still summon
up evidence of the talent which enabled one to forgive such remarks; he
refused, even now, to be a meek and mere observer. BBC2 television
aired a fifty-minute interview on 12 March 1966, in which he was
'suavely controversial', *The Times* reported; their correspondent only
wished that the interview 'had been less consistently bland and agreeable. As it was, many of Mr Coward's more arguable assertions went
unchallenged.'

---

* The published version uses the amended line. When Matalon directed the plays in New
York (in 1974, with Jessica Tandy and Hume Cronyn), 'I changed it back to "queer as a
coot", because a heterosexual was playing the role.'

It was as if Coward were unassailable, infallible; a histrionic potentate dispensing wit and wisdom to a world viewed through the wrong end of a telescope. Partly because he knew it was likely to be Noel's last appearance, and partly to counteract rumours that Coward was already dying, Beaumont arranged a widely advertised photocall in the Queen's Theatre. Edward Burrell, the stage manager, watched Noel sit on a sofa in the middle of the stage while theatre staff and other actors queued to pay him homage. 'I have never before seen such bowing and scraping, such unashamed sycophancy', he recalled. 'Most of them called him "Master" and some actually kissed his hand. It was just like an exiled emperor returning home.'

A Song at Twilight opened at the Queen's Theatre on 14 April, and played in repertoire with *Shadows of the Evening* and *Come into the Garden, Maud.* The reaction to what was patently Coward's last stage offering was eulogistic; even the *Daily Express* and the *Evening Standard* produced 'extremely good' notices. 'Fortunately the *Sun* struck a sour note and said "Coward's Return Very Tedious", which convinced me that I hadn't entirely slipped ... To have one of the most radiant successes of my life forty-two years after *The Vortex, and* to have won over those bloody doctors in Switzerland, makes everything – even Lilli – worthwhile.' Even the Lord Chamberlain's office, in the dying years of its reign (the 1968 reform of the Theatre and Obscenity Acts relieved the censor of his duties), delivered a final paean. *A Song at Twilight* – the emergence of his sexual preference into the flashlight of the Sixties – faced no threat from Coward's erstwhile opponents. 'The Old Master in tremendous form', wrote Charles Heriot. 'No one writes better dialogue, even though there is a Mediterranean quality that remains remote from reality ...' William Marchant commented, 'As played by Coward himself, the character bore an astonishing resemblance to Maugham, with an occasional halting stammer and little nervous tics of the mouth ... The possibility that Latymer may die before our eyes without the conflict being brought to a resolution gives *A Song at Twilight* a sense of the greatest urgency that lifts it high above the level of a drawing-room drama.'

Not everyone rendered absolute homage. John Weightman wrote in *Encounter* of Coward's performance, 'He had a way of getting up from his seat and moving jerkily about the stage or fiddling with the drinks tray that said quite clearly, "I must vary things here with a bit of business." More than once he appeared so bored with his lines that he couldn't remember them, and the clear feminine voice of the prompter rang through the hush.' Weightman wondered at such fellow critics as the *Observer*'s Ronald Bryden, who compared 'Mr Coward's three fractious characters and the trio of mutual torturers in Sartre's *Huis Clos*'.

Playing to £10,000 worth of business every week, Coward was encouraged to take *A Suite in Three Keys* across the Atlantic. His name was common currency again, and he appeared on the *Eamonn Andrews Show* on television, with Dudley Moore, Lucille Ball and Cassius Clay. He was now beginning to regret his decision to live abroad, not financially but because he realised the need to be near 'friends, good doctors and the Odeon!' Old age was preying on his mind: 'In only thirteen years' time I shall be eighty! I cannot say that this realisation doesn't depress me a little because it does, but not to an excessive degree for the simple reason that there is *nothing* I can do about it.' He refused to allow creeping age to circumscribe his life. He dined with the Queen Mother, saw Danny La Rue in cabaret, and was taken on an East End pub crawl with Julian Pettifer, where he found 'a great many of both sexes ... extremely attractive'. He recorded spoken verses from his songs on an album with Joan Sutherland, who said, 'I've always loved these songs ... Obviously they're not Bellini, they're Noel Coward, and very good vocal music.' Coward said, 'She sings gloriously and my music sounds wonderful ... there is mercifully very little of me on the disc.'

It was a busy autumn for a man in his late sixties, appearing in a successful stage production and sustaining an active campaign of self-promotion: a television interview with Lord Mountbatten; a launch for the film of *Pretty Polly*, which was about to start shooting in Singapore with Hayley Mills and Trevor Howard; and supper with the Queen, Prince Philip and Princess Anne after they had seen *A Suite in Three Keys*. The run finished with 'tumultuous ... audiences cheering their heads off', and a cast party at Chesham Place. There were also strong hints from Mountbatten that Coward was finally to get his knighthood.

'My life really cannot be described as dull', he wrote in the autumn of 1966. He decamped to Jamaica for the winter, but his stomach bug caused discomfort and he felt ill for hours on end. By early November, he was back at the Passevant, undergoing tests involving a degree of pain. But he was determined to be well, 'if it kills me'. It was widely suspected – although not by Coward – that he had cancer. Patrick Woodcock recalls that after their tests were done, the doctors said, 'We've got marvellous news for you. You've got a kidney stone.' He said, 'I've heard better.'

*

1967 opened with Coward working on a comedy based on *Star Quality* – although less frenetically than before. 'The days slide by', he wrote. 'The urge to get something done in as short a time as possible ... has diminished a bit ...' Friends continued to die at an inconsiderately rapid rate: Clifton Webb, Mary Garden and Dingwall Bateson were the latest cull. Lorn Loraine was suffering 'a sort of physical and mental decline', which was painful to watch. 'For her sake it would be kinder if she could die. This is an intolerable sentence to have to write but I know, miserably, that it is the truth.'

In London, he saw Ian McKellen in Arbuzov's *The Promise*. 'I came away from the theatre bubbling with pleasure.' For the younger generation, Coward was an historical figure, to be parodied, imitated, admired. McKellen recalls auditioning for the Noel Coward part in *Star!*, the Gertrude Lawrence biopic which was about to begin shooting. Photographs were taken of him with his hair slicked back, wearing a dressing gown, and he was called to a film test. 'I arrived on set, spoke some lines, and sang "Parisian Pierrot". When I finished there was spontaneous applause. I thought – and my agent thought – that that was that, I had it. I was told it was between me and Dan Massey. Then the tests were sent out to America, to the producer, and word came back: Noel Coward decided his godson must play him.' But McKellen was rather glad he didn't get the part, 'It wasn't a very good film!' As Julie Andrews's follow-up to *The Sound of Music*, it was given high production values, but failed at the box office. Coward thought Andrews 'talented, charming, efficient and very pretty but *not* very like Gertie. Danny Massey was excellent as me and had the sense to give an impression of me rather than try to imitate me.' Massey had been out to Les Avants to study the part with its original, and had captured Coward in a sort of concentrated pastiche. A friend, Leo Maguire, recalled, 'The whole purpose of the exercise was simply to watch Noel and his mannerisms ... not to make a caricature of him. He told Danny that when he was a young man he would go to bed with anyone – "Oh my dear, goats, parrots, women, men, creatures, anything you like ..." Noel went into some kind of ... seamless witty number, at the end of which Danny said, "Oh Noel, you are wonderful." Noel replied, "Don't talk shop", and carried on.'

That year his volume of four short stories, *Bon Voyage*, was published. Once again they explored a personal geography. In Noel Coward's world, the North of England and the Midlands exist only as jokes; his atlas features only the Home Counties and London; beyond that are Paris and New York (and perhaps Berlin), and the venues of further escape: the Mediterranean, the Far East and South Seas. There is a sense of regret at a lost world, of glamour and travel and excitement, the world thrown open to him in his immensely successful youth. 'Solali' deals with tropical lust, as a bored *mondaine* takes a garden-boy lover, only to be chopped up by his machete when he discovers she has a white boyfriend. 'Mrs Ebony' is a slight study in bereavement, and 'Penny Dreadful' satirises Godfrey Winn, who had made 'a screaming ass of himself' by objecting to row O seats for the first night of *Sail Away*. The eponymous final story revisits the scenario of *Sail Away* itself, as a female writer falls in love while on a South Seas cruise.

These short stories show the dying embers of Coward's talent – sharp, witty and intelligent, but vestiges only of his gifts. The disappointments of recent years, and indeed, the scattered successes, served only to remind him of the heights reached in the pre-war past. The subsequent flares of dramatic and literary success were a pale afterglow. Yet a new generation came to admire him for the very values which might have seemed old-fashioned – the class-ridden themes of his comedies, the elegant wordplay of his dialogue, which could have been Oscar Wilde's to a teenager of the Sixties. It was in this recognition of an historic rather than a contemporary talent that Coward's Las Vegas and New York cabaret recordings became surprise hits on British and American campuses alike. A camp classic, a nostalgic turn, or a lasting genius? He remained a paradox.

Noel's new comedy, *Age Cannot Wither*, was not coming along very well; in fact, it was not coming along at all. 'I've been too agitated by everything.' The deaths of Spencer Tracy and Dorothy Parker, the spectre of Lorn's, and his stomach pain all conspired to an unconducive atmosphere for his aged muse. In London he visited Loraine, now on heroin, who looked 'ghastly but was quite lucid and cheerful'; Vivien Leigh, who had tuberculosis, looking 'pale but lovely, and smoking, which she shouldn't have been doing'; and Laurence Olivier, with cancer of the prostate, 'writhing about on a bed in St Thomas's Hospital'. His friends seemed destined for bleakly dramatic ends. On 8 July Vivien Leigh died suddenly of a haemorrhage, and Noel was asked to read at her memorial service. He refused, afraid he might break down. 'If it could have helped Vivien in any way I would have done anything, but it couldn't because she's gone for ever. I loathe and despise the miserable Christian trappings of death.'

Coward retreated to Paris to see Ginette Spanier and Marlene Dietrich. He told Marlene, 'with an effort at grey comedy, "All I demand from my friends nowadays is that they live through lunch." To which she replied, puzzled, "Why lunch, sweetheart?"' Patrick Woodcock recalls Coward's relationship with Dietrich (both were patients of his) as surprising. 'He was very fond of Marlene. Nobody [was] fond of Marlene, she [was] perfectly odious . . . an extraordinary kind of icon. She was like Danny La Rue, she'd put herself together, and go on. And when she was not on, she'd be absolutely not on. She'd be scrubbing the floor or making some soup . . .' Both Coward and Dietrich rejoiced in a certain prosaic quality, which pointed up their mutual star quality rather than making them more ordinary. 'She and Noel in Paris decided that they were both very old and that they would go for a walk together because they loved Paris but never went out or saw anyone. So they went into the Avenue Montaigne and started to walk and after about a hundred yards they had to sit down because their legs were hurting so much. They got into a café and ordered a drink, and then they staggered home . . . The idea of these two glamorous figures stumbling along the Avenue Montaigne is frightfully funny, I think. And of course he saw how funny it was . . .' Sad and brave, too. Dietrich 'used him, as she used everybody', says Woodcock, but Noel enjoyed pointing out her failings. 'Cease this mental masturbation!' he demanded on one occasion, when Marlene had been singing her own praises too long.

There were still professional challenges. One of them was the part of Caesar in Richard Rodgers's television musical of *Androcles and the Lion*, Shaw's political fable. It was shot in New York and directed by Joe Layton. 'By then [Noel] was getting a little bit of the hardening of the arteries, and his memory was starting to go, but he was a delight, as usual, and so good as an actor.' The rigours of rehearsal and performance were now onerous and Coward 'didn't enjoy any of it . . . However, I was apparently very good.'

That autumn he flew to Sardinia to film his part in *Boom*, with Elizabeth Taylor and Richard Burton. Based on Tennessee Williams's play *The Milk Train Doesn't Stop Here Anymore*, the film was directed by Joseph Losey, 'a dear man. I had a bit of trouble with Tennessee's curiously phrased dialogue, but apart from that everything was halcyon.' Coward's role was that of the Witch of Capri, a patently homosexual character who is carried dinner-suited on to the island to dine alfresco with Taylor, a dying millionairess in a science-fiction headdress of crystalline spikes and a silver tinsel gown. Although the film was panned, the mere appearance of Noel as a sacred monster acting with his latter-day counterparts (and the fact that this was the first occasion on which the word 'fuck' was uttered on screen) gave the picture kudos.

On 21 November, Lorn Loraine died. After the memorial service, supported by Laurence Olivier, Noel 'staggered blindly away' to lunch with Diana Cooper. 'She, of course, knew I was in misery, and why, and was utterly sweet.' Noel, Graham and Cole returned to Switzerland, where Coward found that despite attempts to 'behave beautifully', he gave way to grief. But he summoned up reserves, 'There is no sense in grief, it wastes emotional energy.' And there was little enough of that left.

In the New Year of 1968, Coward challenged his decrepitude by setting off, with Payn and Lesley, on a new Far Eastern tour: Tahiti, Fiji and Kowloon. 'My passion for the tropics remains unimpaired', he wrote, sitting (somewhat stickily) naked on a leatherette chair in Fiji. In Hong Kong, he was invited to fire the noonday gun he had made so famous, 'which made the hell of a noise and scared the liver and lights out of me'; and flew back from Thailand via Beirut. This last holiday was a 'blaze of enjoyment ... I don't suppose I shall ever get over my wanderlust, and I don't particularly want to.'

In August he filmed his final movie role, *The Italian Job*, with Michael Caine, almost unimaginably removed from his first celluloid appearance, more than half a century ago, in D. W. Griffith's *Hearts of the World*. The director was Peter Collinson, an old boy of the Actors' Orphanage. Coward played the criminal mastermind, Mr Bridger, who runs his empire from inside his prison cell, where he is treated like a king. 'Look at him move ... like God', said Collinson to a reporter. The filming was 'great fun', and he enjoyed playing with Caine, whom he found unspoilt. After a television interview with David Frost, happily free of 'snide remarks', Coward returned to Les Avants. To those who did not see him every day, his physical deterioration was marked. Geoffrey Johnson noted that Coward was 'going downhill all the time ... He wouldn't do any of the things the doctors said. He wouldn't stop chain-smoking. He'd make jokes about that, and about eating vegetables...' He was, in fact, acting spoilt, conforming to Tynan's type, regressing to childhood.

He greeted his sixty-ninth birthday from bed, 'looking like an ancient Buddhist priest with a minor attack of jaundice'. He was conscious of the limited time left, as were others. With his seventieth year approaching, BBC television proposed a week of Coward productions to celebrate his life; Hal Burton arrived to discuss it. 'It is not a subject that appeals to me greatly', wrote Noel. 'However, it is inevitable and I must rise above it unless the *angelo di morte* whisks me off in the nick of time.'

By February he and his friends were in Jamaica, but their 'earthly paradise' received a nasty jolt when Graham Payn had a seizure driving down from Firefly; Joyce Carey grabbed the wheel as Fabia Drake turned off the ignition. 'Horribly frightened', they returned to London where Patrick Woodcock diagnosed a minor cerebral haemorrhage. In Switzerland there were visits from Dorothy Dickson, Evelyn Laye and Robin Maugham, who recorded in his diary, 'Switzerland seems littered with spent stars – all trying to radiate some small glow as they recall the past', a *Waiting in the Wings* scene which he found 'infinitely depressing'. Noel stayed in bed all day, conserving his energy 'to sparkle at dinner and tell stories till midnight'. One story told how the Prince of Wales had arrived halfway through the first act of *Private Lives*. 'The Prince put his feet up on the balcony of the circle. Coward sent him a reproof. "He might have been the Prince of Wales", Noel said, "but I was the king of the theatre."'

That title was to be reconfirmed as the pace of life picked up in the second half of 1969. The change was announced by the appearance of the first biography of Coward since Patrick Braybrooke's embarrassingly hagiographic *The Amazing Mr Coward* in 1933. Sheridan Morley's *A Talent to Amuse* was a serious, in-depth look at Coward's public work, but could not go as far as the author wished in its analysis of his private life. Roddy McDowall went to see Noel at the Savoy, where he had the galley proofs of the biography on the bed. 'I said "Oh, it's Sheridan's book. How is it?" Noel said ... "I'm afraid Sherry has to do a bit more work. There are still a few old ladies in Worthing who don't know ..." He meant his homosexuality. He wanted it expurgated ... he was extremely nervous ...' Coward was concerned that even now his public might be put off by his homosexuality. 'I can't afford to offend their prejudice,' he told Morley, 'nor do I really wish to disturb them this late in their lives; if I had a very young audience, I might think differently.' Morley tried to convince Coward otherwise by reminding him that the respected critic T. C. Worsley had 'come out' in his memoirs published in 1966. 'There is one essential difference between me and Cuthbert Worsley', Noel remarked. 'The British public at large would not care if Cuthbert Worsley had slept with mice.'

*

The much trumpeted celebration – wanted or not – of Coward's seventy years was marked by events on both sides of the Atlantic. Washington's National Theater staged a touring production of the now perennial *Private Lives*, with Tammy Grimes and Brian Bedford; and in Britain, the Phoenix Theatre christened its refurbished foyer the Noel Coward Bar, and gave a party to celebrate his birthday. Coward, in grey shantung suit, accepted champagne from the jeroboam proffered by Robert Morley, and smiled at his guests but remained in his seat. The Coward season continued with the BBC's televising of *The Vortex*, *The Marquise* and *This Happy Breed*; the films of *Blithe Spirit* and *Bitter Sweet* were shown; and an *Omnibus* documentary went out on 7 December. Radio programmes included *Private Lives*, and a musical compendium with reminiscences. The National Film Theatre began a season of Coward films with a lecture–discussion at which Noel was interviewed by Richard Attenborough, followed by a screening of *In Which We Serve*. It was a gala occasion, attended by the Prince of Wales, Princess Anne and Earl Mountbatten. The guest of honour arrived with Merle Oberon on his arm – an odd choice when he had so many older friends.

'Holy Week', as Coward dubbed the festival, continued with a birthday lunch at Clarence House given by the Queen Mother, with presents from her ('a crown-encrusted cigarette-box'), the Queen ('an equally crown-encrusted cigarette-case') and Princess Margaret ('some exquisite cufflinks'). On arrival Coward had been handed a letter from the Queen Mother telling him she was ill, and sending her apologies. 'She said, "I'm afraid you'll have to make do with my daughters", and so I thought, "Well, I'll do my best."' The Queen apologised for the similarity of their gifts, suggesting he use one of the boxes for tooth-picks. 'Alas, darling Ma'ams, too late, too late!' he replied. Her Majesty then asked, 'rather casually passing me a salted almond', would he accept Mr Wilson's offer of a knighthood? Coward kissed her hand and said, 'in a rather strangulated voice, "Yes, Ma'am"'. To Esme Wynne-Tyson, oldest of old friends, Noel wrote, 'I am of course delighted to have the knighthood but what moved me most was [that] the Queen . . . gave me the impression that it was I who was conferring the honour on her instead of the other way round.'*

---

* The Home Secretary, Roy Jenkins, had submitted Coward's name to the Honours Committee, asking for his past fiscal offences to be overlooked; Lord Jenkins acknowledges that this was probably the case. It was rumoured that Harold Wilson had not been keen to award the honour because of Coward's sexuality, but was 'overruled' by royalty.

The climax of the celebrations was a Midnight Matinee, held on the stage of the Phoenix Theatre, where *Private Lives* had opened more than thirty years before. 'What was thrilling was that he lived long enough for everything to come full circle', said Roddy McDowall. 'That gala was one of the most moving evenings I have ever spent in my entire life. Anyone who had anything to do with Noel was supposed to appear . . .' At midnight, Noel arrived to watch from his box, where he sat with Merle Oberon and Lynn Fontanne. Gielgud, Irene Worth, Richard Attenborough, Robert Morley, Danny La Rue, Susannah York, Richard Briers and Joyce Grenfell all contributed to the first half, the emotional highpoint of which was Celia Johnson reading Coward's 'I've just come out from England'. The second half was a stage party, with guests such as Edith Evans, Kay Hammond, Adrianne Allen, Gladys Cooper, Evelyn Laye, Cathleen Nesbit and Peggy Wood – all dames of the theatre whom Coward had worked with. Pat Kirkwood, Elisabeth Welch, Jessie Matthews, Cyril Ritchard and Anna Neagle sang and danced a nostalgic tribute.

Then it was time for the Master to take the stage. With his speech of thanks, he accepted, from Richard Attenborough, a book of his lyrics signed by the entire cast. It was four in the morning; Noel stood alone as the one hundred and fifty stars, led by Princess Margaret, gave him a standing ovation.

The following evening, on his birthday proper, there was dinner for three hundred of his closest friends at the Savoy, filmed by the BBC. Coward made his entrance wearing a chocolate-brown evening suit, looking old and hunched, but as soon as the spotlight shone on him, he came to life, galvanised by the audience. Olivier's speech was histrionic, 'My dear Noel, I give you my love', pausing briefly for a break in emotion, then, 'help, Charles Hawtrey, help'; followed by Mountbatten's toast, inviting 'the millions watching' to join him. Coward's reply was a model of restraint: 'For me to say that this is a particularly moving occasion is really too obvious. I'm deeply moved. I'm also very touched because since I was quite a small boy, I've only had two great passions in my life. One was the theatre, and the other was the sea. And tonight I have tributes paid to me by a great sailor and a great actor. I am awfully overcome at this moment, and as you can see, restraining it with splendid fortitude . . .' Despite his age and discernible breathlessness, he remained in absolute control.

To regain energy, Coward returned to Les Avants for Christmas, and, as tradition dictated, took the train up the mountainside to the village of Chateau d'Oex, where David Niven and his family were waiting (under a Union Jack umbrella) with a tray of Bloody Marys. 'We always like to give Noel an interesting welcome', said Niven. On 3 February 1970, accompanied by Joyce Carey and Gladys Calthrop, he made his long-awaited and (to some) long-delayed trip to Buckingham Palace. 'As I advanced', Coward told Nancy Mitford, '. . . the music changed from "Hello Dolly" to "A Life On The Ocean Wave"!' He emerged into the cold February day, in his silk hat and morning dress, a knight of the land. 'The Queen was absolutely charming,' he told waiting reporters, 'she always is. I've known her since she was a little girl.' And he and his two oldest friends swept off to lunch at the Savoy on silverside of beef. It was ironic that his guests for this ultimate acceptance by British society should have been women; many had thought Coward's homosexuality the reason for the tardiness of the honour. It might have been more fitting had he taken Graham Payn and Cole Lesley, but, even now, he had to conform to public mores.

From London, Coward, Payn and Lesley retraced a well-worn path across the Atlantic. When he arrived at Kennedy Airport, the only indication of his age was the wheelchair awaiting him. 'I just use this thing to get me through Customs', he quipped. 'It breaks their hearts to see me this way and they whisk me right through.' They planned to stay for a week, seeing the Tammy Grimes–Brian Bedford *Private Lives*, and other productions, including Tynan's *Oh! Calcutta*. The liberated joys of the latter had little to offer: 'I've seen quite a number of naked people and I don't think it's all that exciting', Noel told a reporter. He left after the first act. (When Coward saw David Storey's play *The Changing Room*, Tynan noted, 'his companion said that the rugby players, when stripped in the bath scene, were not physically very impressive. "No," said Coward, "fifteen acorns are hardly worth the price of admission."')

A dinner was given at the Sherry-Netherland Hotel, where a hundred and fifty guests celebrated Coward's life, among them his leading ladies Hermiones Gingold and Baddeley, Elaine Stritch, Beatrice Lillie and Peggy Wood; Cary Grant, Adele Astaire, Douglas Fairbanks Jnr, Kay Thompson and Joan Crawford. The following evening *Private Lives* was extended by three ovations for Coward, led by the Lunts. 'Considering the way it's done, I'm not all that surprised that it's a hit', he said of the show. 'It's played very beautifully and it is a very funny play.' The accustomed pace of a Coward visit to New York did not slow merely because he was a septuagenarian. The next day he was up bright and early to receive the press, and that night went statewide on ABC television, appearing on *The Dick Cavett Show*. He also taped another interview with David Frost, to whom he spoke of censorship. It was surprising to hear this former victim of the Lord Chamberlain's office claim that censorship was 'nearly always justified. I think it's a very, very good thing indeed.'

Coward, Payn and Lesley left for Jamaica. Here he was cared for by Miguel Fraser, a slight and neat black Jamaican who lived with his common-law wife Imogene in a wooden lodge at the end of Firefly's drive. Miguel recalled that his duties often exceeded those of a normal butler. Noel was fond of Martell brandy and ginger ale, which he drank in the early evening, sitting on his verandah watching the swallows dip into his swimming-pool. 'One day, Master sitting here and he ring the bell for me. I come and he say, "Help me Miguel". I say, "What's the matter Master? you sick?" He say, "No Miguel, I'm drunk". I take him to his bed and undress him. He say, "Ah Miguel, you're better than a mother to a child."'

The rest of the year was spent between New York, Switzerland and London, and ended with a bout of pleurisy. Coward was admitted to St Thomas's Hospital, where he held court to famous names: Mountbatten, Sinatra, Hope, Niven and Olivier. 'Towards the end it did get a bit crowded in there', he told Barry Norman. 'A few stars managed to crawl in, under the wire, though none but the best, of course.'

31

The Party's Over Now

The thrill has gone,
To linger on
Would spoil it anyhow,
Let's creep away from the day
For the party's over now.

Noel Coward, 'The Party's Over Now'

THE last three years of Coward's life were marked by steady
decline, relieved by occasional excitements. 1972 began with a
midnight matinee in honour of the newly knighted Terence
Rattigan. Coward embraced the playwright warmly, and was snapped
in the act by an *Evening Standard* photographer. 'For God's sake,
Noel,' said Rattigan, 'everyone will think we are having an affair.' 'Why
not?' he asked, 'it's perfectly legal, very suitable and, considering our
combined ages, extremely unlikely.' In July, the *Cowardy Custard* revue
opened at the Mermaid Theatre; 'I came out humming the tunes,' was
Noel's review. The next day Coward was presented with an honorary
Doctor of Letters degree by the University of Sussex. Supported by the
pro-chancellor – his protégé Richard Attenborough – he received his
first and last academic qualification. In return, he presented the manuscript of *Quadrille* to the university, together with a signed set of his
complete plays – a deposition which would, in time, be followed by the
rest of his papers.

That year also saw a television documentary by Charles Castle, and a
highly successful revival of *Private Lives* at the Queen's Theatre,
directed by John Gielgud, and starring Maggie Smith and Robert
Stephens. Binkie Beaumont gave a first-night party at his house in Lord
North Street, the last time he and Coward met. Coward was uncharacteristically tongue-tied when asked by a journalist what he thought of

the revival. '"I don't know what to say", he replied, shaking his head. "I was afraid to blub. I think it is right not to say anything sometimes."'

His sequestered Swiss life was not a selfish confinement; when Nancy Mitford wrote a rare letter of complaint about the pain of her terminal cancer, he replied in his now shaky hand, resuming the role of amateur physician, gently admonitory. 'Now listen. There's some stuff, easily obtainable, called IRGAPARYN which worked miracles . . . for Graham when he was in agony with a slipped disc. Perhaps you've already tried it but if not do please have a bash. It has no peculiar side-effects so you won't suddenly go dotty and imagine you're Aimée Semple Mcpherson or the Dowager Empress of China (if you knew Tsu Tsi as *I* know Tsu Tsi). Don't worry about the Irquapryn [sic], I am sending you a box what is laughingly know as "post haste".'

Cecil Beaton visited Les Avants that autumn. Ever critical, he had been told that the house 'might have been brought from Eastbourne'; he thought it had 'no real character, is ugly, is decorated in the typical theatre-folk style, but it is warm and comfortable and it works'. Beaton found Coward 'hunched and crumpled' in a chair, wearing his favourite scarlet Nehru jacket, with brandy, ginger ale and menthol cigarettes to hand; he seemed surprised to see his guest. To Beaton, Noel's decrepitude was absolute; only seventy-two, he was virtually immobile, refusing to take any exercise 'to get the blood pumping to the brain'. Yet Coward had 'aged into a very nice and kind old man', complimenting Beaton again on the work he had done for *Quadrille*. 'He really is a darling, so trim and neat.' Later in the evening he sang songs of his and Cecil's youth, 'in a quiet but musical voice'. It was a touching scene, these two old men reliving the past in songs sung by Vesta Tilley and Albert Chevalier, music-hall stars long forgotten. Coward talked of shows Violet had taken him to – Lily Elsie, Gertie Millar, Maisie Gay – as though the years between had fallen away. The theatre has its own chronology and, just as time was suspended in performance, so it seemed in Coward's life, his beginning and ending barely separated by the years. Beaton noted that although Coward did not like to live in the past, 'like Diana [Cooper, who had come to lunch] he does not enjoy anything he does not understand . . . Luckily I am able to be thrilled by a film (*2001*)* of which I don't know the intention – but not Noel or Diana who are enraged by an abstract painting or many of the present-day playwrights.'

* Stanley Kubrick's *2001: A Space Odyssey*, of whose star Coward commented, 'Keir Dullea, gone tomorrow'.

Beaton was fascinated to learn about his host's finances. 'It is staggering how all the royalties tumble in from over all the world for his plays and songs (the sentimental ones are the chief money skimmers).' Even now new shows sought to exploit Coward's fame. In the States, a Roderick Cook revue, *Oh Coward!* opened successfully, but Geoffrey Johnson recalled problems with such adaptations in the early 1970s. Another Cook tribute, *Noel Coward's Sweet Potato*, played the *Private Lives* balcony scene on roller skates, and there were propositions to revive *Design for Living* using old Coward songs, and *The Vortex* 'musicalised'. Most surreal was an off-Broadway drag version of *Private Lives* 're-set on Fire Island! . . . It wasn't even amusingly camp, it was just terrible . . . We closed it.'

Coward made his final trip to New York in January 1973, en route for Jamaica. On 14 January he arrived at the New Theater for his last public appearance, with the legendary Marlene, friend of forty years, caparisoned in pink Chanel. Noel, by now bent almost double, hung on to her arm; he could not have stood alone. 'We have to get up there', said Dietrich, indicating three flights of stairs. With Geoffrey Johnson and a friend at his elbows, Coward made the painful journey to the top; no easy metaphor this, for nearly seventy years of stage ambition. 'It's going to be all right,' said Dietrich as the cameras flashed, 'we have made it this far, dear love.'

He watched the 119th performance of Cook's *Oh Coward!* Like a drowning man, his past revived before his eyes; the famous numbers which had reverberated through the century – 'A Room with a View', 'I'll See You Again', 'Mrs Worthington', 'Mad Dogs and Englishmen'; and less well-known verses such as 'Land Pastoral', and the confessional 'I'm No Good at Love'. A reporter noted afterwards that, had a bomb exploded, 'NY papers would have had to extend their pages by a dozen apiece to hold the obituaries'. Ironically, their next important obituary would be Coward's.

He stayed in New York a week, and refused to give interviews: 'I haven't got anything left to say.'

On 22 March 1973, word reached Firefly that Binkie Beaumont had died in London. The news visibly upset Coward. 'He'd say "I just can't believe Binkie's dead . . ."', Geoffrey Johnson remembers. It was not that Coward felt this loss more than that of other friends, but that Beaumont's death seemed a harbinger of his own. That Sunday, 25 March, Geoffrey

Johnson, Graham Payn and Cole Lesley went to Firefly for their usual cocktails with Coward. They sat in the enclosed porch as the sun set behind the Blue Mountains. As the friends made to leave, Noel ascended the stairs; he looked down and said, 'Goodnight, my darlings.'

Coward dined alone and went to bed. Miguel Fraser told of his last hours. 'My wife passing by round 6 a.m. and she hear moaning from the bathroom . . . She come get me. First I don't want to go cause he get very mad if he disturbed but she say "Something wrong there". I go to the door and say "Master, Master, let me in . . . but he don't answer so I get a ladder and break the shutter and see Master lying on the bathroom floor. I tell my wife, "Go quick to Blue Harbour and fetch Mr Payn and Mr Lesley." I pick Master up and take him to the bed. He was rubbing at his chest. He open his eyes and say, "Miguel, where's Mr Payn and Mr Lesley?" I say, "They coming, sir", then he reach up and pat me twice on the shoulder and say, "Never mind, Miguel, never mind". I know he's gone. His teeth come out so I put them back, then I come to the balcony. The car arrive with Mr Payn and Mr Lesley . . . I call and say, "Master gone, sir". Mr Lesley say, "Stop it Miguel. Don't say that." I say, "It true sir, Master gone sir". Mr Lesley put his hands on top of his head and he go spinning around on the lawn with tears streaming down.'

At two a.m. British time, Joan Hirst (who had taken over Lorn Loraine's duties) received a call from Cole Lesley, telling her that Noel had died. Lesley was keen that the rest of the Family and other friends should know before they read of it in the newspapers. But, mysteriously, the news had already broken in New York; the next day, it was headlined on both sides of the Atlantic.

Even in death, drama attached to this legendary figure. Much was made of the fact that Coward's body was not brought back to England to be buried; there were accusations that his wish to be buried with his mother at Teddington was being ignored. The truth was rather more bizarre, as Leslie Smith recalls: 'Joan Hirst . . . said that arrangements had been made to bring the body back to the UK . . . Noel claimed that he was domiciled in Switzerland and this was dangerous . . . I asked a QC and a junior to apply their minds to this problem.' By the next morning, Smith had their written opinion, that 'it might be prudent if the body wasn't brought back'; it could have been 'an absolute disaster' from a financial point of view. The question of interring the Master in Switzerland was raised; surely he should rest in some Alpine field? Not if he wanted to stay there. Swiss law said that bodies could stay in the ground for just one hundred years, after which the body was dug up. Noel would have laughed – that his body could be the subject of controversy verging on farce would have amused the author of *Blithe Spirit*.

There was a much better reason for Coward to be buried in Jamaica; as Cole Lesley told a reporter, 'Sir Noel often said to us, "Bury me where I die".' On the evening after his death, Lesley, Payn and Johnson drove up to Firefly to observe the cocktail ritual which the Master's absence seemed to require. There, as the day darkened, Firefly and its memories made them realise this was his rightful resting-place. So on 29 March 1973, Noel Coward's funeral was held on the island which had become his home. Graham Payn and Cole Lesley urged all mourners to wear white; although they had planned a strictly private service, the funeral of such a figure could not but draw attention, and the British high commissioner and a military aide of the governor-general's staff came to represent the British and Jamaican governments. There was a last-minute decision by the bishop of Kingston, the Rt Revd Thomas Clark, to dash across the Blue Mountains to assist the local minister. Eulogies were arriving from around the world, all demanding, by virtue of the fame of their authors, to be read. The minister made a brisk decision to stick to the standard burial service.

The ceremony was simple and solemn. Graham, Cole and Geoffrey Johnson – described by a local reporter as 'the small group of elegant, white-clad men, each wearing . . . the heavy gold-link bracelet favoured by the playwright' – watched as the plain oak coffin was interred in a concrete tomb on the hill at Firefly, overlooking the view Coward had loved. Later, a plain white marble slab was added, with the inscription: SIR NOEL COWARD – 1899–1973.

The Master's immaculate timing was acknowledged. Douglas Watt wrote in the *New Yorker*, 'Coward, with the same nice regard for design that characterized his writings, died while enjoying one of those renewals of popularity which marked a career that, after his string of early stage successes, swung back and forth between almost total neglect . . . and princely favour . . . almost as if he himself were regulating the pendulum.' As he had entered the world in the glorious light of the British Empire, so his life was celebrated in a memorial service held 'by sweet coincidence' on Empire Day. His friends gathered at St Martin-in-the-Fields at noon on 24 May: Earl Mountbatten, the Duke of Kent, the Earl of Snowdon; David Niven, Ralph Richardson, Richard Attenborough and Evelyn Laye; Charles Chaplin, Margaret Leighton, Ava Gardner,

David Frost, Peter Sellers, Liza Minnelli, Rex Harrison and Cecil Beaton. After the strains of Coward's overture for *London Morning* had died away, Psalm 100 was followed by a reading by Laurence Olivier of Coward's verses. A Bach violin sonata was played by Yehudi Menuhin, then Gielgud read Sonnet XXX, 'When to the sessions of sweet silent thought, I summon up remembrance of things past'. John Betjeman, the poet laureate, spoke of St Martin's as a 'beautiful great eighteenth-century theatre of a church . . . it is precise, elegant and well-ordered. Like Noel.' The service ended with 'London Pride'.

The disposal of his estate was precisely indicated in Coward's nine-page will. Despite wild speculation that he had left £10 million, the figure was nearer £275,000. The bulk of the estate went to Graham Payn and Cole Lesley, with an instruction to take advice from Sheridan Morley, Raymond Mander and Joe Mitchenson on the continuing use of Coward's literary and dramatic works. After the deaths of Payn and Lesley, all income from royalties would go to the Actors' Charitable Trust. Les Avants was to be shared by Lesley and Payn; Blue Harbour was left to Cole Lesley (who subsequently sold it), and Firefly to Graham Payn. Payn decided to give the house to the Jamaican Heritage Trust in 1978. For two years after Coward's death, he and Coley went and sat on the hillside, until one evening they realised the 'feeling' had gone; his spirit was no longer there. 'I think he's back here', said Graham in the sitting-room of Chalet Coward.

Miguel and his wife Imogene stayed on to look after the house, regulating what few visitors Firefly had, but through lack of funds the house soon mildewed and decayed; as Coward had observed, Jamaica was 'climatically ruinous to books and pictures and furniture'. The spines hung off his Everyman library, paint peeled from his pictures; an elegant tropical wardrobe of clothes rotted, or was spirited away by souvenir hunters or locals. Photographs faded in the sun, including one of the Queen Mother, her image receding under the strong light. Firefly was subsumed by the late twentieth century, eclipsing the reflection of its former inhabitant. In 1992, Miguel was murdered by a local car-washing mafia, leaving Imogene alone; the place threatened to fall apart. Then in 1993 Chris Blackwell, multimillionaire son of Blanche, stepped in, bought a twenty-five-year lease from the Jamaican Heritage Trust and initiated the renovation of the house. New caretakers were appointed, and Firefly was restored to its former glory.

*

The task of writing the authorised biography was given to James Pope-Hennessy, whom Coward had known since 1943; he had admired his books on Queen Victoria and Queen Mary. Pope-Hennessy had also worked on Coward's *Collected Lyrics*, and Noel had found him 'a dear and so very comfortingly intelligent'. He set about writing an in-depth study of Coward, and interviewed scores of his friends and acquaintances. But Pope-Hennessy was a strange figure who looked 'as if he'd been walking the streets all night'; he was homosexual, and prey to 'rough trade'. Unwisely boasting of the large advance he had received for the book, which he told the *Evening Standard* he had not yet banked, he was found dead in his Ladbroke Grove home with a silk stocking around his throat.

Responsibility for the book fell to Cole Lesley, encouraged by friends to take up the work, despite his lack of experience. He was aided by the discovery at Les Avants of 'Mum's Suitcase', full of memorabilia of Coward's early life assembled by his mother, and which also contained Coward's diaries, kept since 1940. His editors at Jonathan Cape were surprised at the quality of this 'amateur's' work. Published in Britain, in 1976, as *The Life of Noel Coward* (*Remembered Laughter* in the States), it was well received as an affectionate and revealing account of his former master, but not revealing enough, said some. The *New York Times* commented that 'Mr Lesley's massive, authorised biography takes its name from Coward's last poem, and the title is one indication of the book's shortcomings. This is a treasure trove of anecdotes and memorabilia ... But it is not the final or the most complete word ... Mr Lesley is entirely too reticent about Coward's love life, and ... too unrevealing about his artistic process ...'

The reviews were in themselves a critique of Coward's life and work. In an erudite dissection of his career, the playwright Nigel Dennis recalled John Osborne's comment that Coward was 'his own invention, his contribution to the twentieth century ... To be your own enduring invention seems to me to be heroic and essential.' But in Lesley's book, Coward's 'personal shape and invented self are the main things to talk about. The actor overwhelms the playwright ... Mr Lesley is not a critical biographer, and nothing he has to say about Coward's plays can encourage one to believe that he was the Congreve of his day (as Arnold Bennett suggested) and that his work will stand up repeatedly to revival in the manner of Restoration comedies.'

An artist's reputation often reaches its nadir immediately after his or her death, and it seemed that this was happening to Coward; but twenty years later, the plays *are* being revived, and the songs *are* sung. Death has done little to diminish the legend. He has even been assimilated into post-modern critique, his work subject to 'decoding' productions, a sublime if bizarre turn of events for a writer who spent his life fighting critics. Posthumously, he has managed yet another incarnation, 'the fatally damaged celebrity reconstructed rather than ravaged by his critics', as one journalist, Mark Ashurst, wrote.

Kenneth Tynan relished the opportunity to re-examine the legend in his review of Lesley's book. Ever the man of exquisite prose, he thought Lesley unreliable 'on the later, post-war plays, obese with verbiage that the younger Coward would have relentlessly slimmed away',* and regretted the lack of 'new light on the early days of the *Wunderkind*'. Noel's sexuality was a crucial part of his creative persona: 'Coward retained, well into his sixties, the ageless vitality of the talented and prosperous pederast, putting one inevitably in mind of Dorian Gray.' Tynan found it 'little short of miraculous that Coward and others like him managed to survive with such gallant and creative resilience . . . when homosexuality in England was punishable by imprisonment and permanent ostracism. Indeed, I sometimes suspect that Coward's professional persona (theatrical camp overlaid with Empire-building-stiff-upper-lip) was in part a disguise, adopted to put the cops and the public off the true scent.'

In 1980, Cole Lesley died of heart failure, leaving Graham Payn as sole heir to Coward's estate, and in 1982 Payn and Sheridan Morley published Coward's diaries. It is clear that, as a diarist, Coward does not rank with Channon, Nicolson or Woolf. The wit which seemed rapier sharp but not unkind in utterance sometimes went sour on paper. A mood of jealousy pervaded the later entries – a result of post-war failures – as did political naivety. 'It's a bit startling to discover that Coward was a political reactionary', said *Variety*, quoting his opinion of the Suez crisis ('The good old imperialism was a bloody sight wiser and healthier than all this woolly-headed, muddled "all men are equal" humanitarianism which has lost us so much pride and dignity and prestige in the modern world'), and found his judgements on serious theatre 'embarrassing' (he described *Death of a Salesman* as 'turgid meanderings'). Other papers, like the *New York Native*, had complaints

---

* In his programme notes for the National Theatre production of *Hay Fever*, Tynan wrote that 'Coward took the fat off English comic dialogue; he was the Turkish bath in which it slimmed.'

about the lack of intimate detail, while acknowledging that Coward's 'characteristic privacy made sexual revelations impossible'. But despite these strictures, warmth, charm and humanity emerged, and 'even at his angriest, Coward was funnier and more stylish than any comparable humorist'.

Noel's Family was now fragmented and dispersed. Gladys Calthrop moved to Markham Square in Chelsea. Resolutely elegant to the last, she was often seen strolling along the fashionable King's Road, her head as high as ever. She died in 1980, aged eighty-six.

Coward supported Joyce Carey financially, both before and after his death. When he died, she told friends that she too wished to die. But she continued to act on stage and film until the age of ninety. Consistently sought for interviews about Coward, she responded with generosity, whilst keeping her counsel. She died in March 1993.

Cole Lesley was buried at Glion, across the valley from Les Avants, where Graham Payn still lives with his friend Dany Stouvenin, and supervises the extensive, worldwide workings of the Noel Coward Estate. Friends joke that Coward would have been surprised to discover how efficiently he performs this task. He would have been even more surprised that the 'illiterate little sod' published his own memoirs in 1994. Payn travels to each new production, fulfilling his duty to his friend, lover and companion.

Other figures from Coward's life continued well into the 1990s. Jeffrey Amherst lived in Cadogan Place. Diminutive and clear-eyed, he retained the same air of impenetrability which Coward had noted some seventy years previously. He died, aged 93, in March 1993. Exiled from France, Dickie Fellowes-Gordon was discovered living in sheltered housing in Pimlico, and reached her hundredth birthday, still able to sing the ribald verses she and Coward had made up, much to the surprise of the nurses in Westminster Hospital, where she died in 1992. Charles Russell made his fortune as a property developer, having given up the theatre world after his break with Coward, and retired to Sussex. Bert Lister, at the time of writing in 1995, still places daily bets at the bookmakers, and enjoys visits from his son-in-law, the punk rock star Billy Idol.

The official commemoration of Coward's life (in the form of a plaque) was in the Actors' Church, Covent Garden. Westminster Abbey refused to allow a memorial service on the grounds that 'he wasn't a churchgoer'; however, on 28 March 1984, the Abbey invited the Queen Mother to unveil a memorial stone to Coward in Poets' Corner, inscribed with his name and dates and the words, A TALENT TO AMUSE. But the real monument to Noel Coward lies in the immortal cast of his plays, songs, stories and verse: somewhere in the world, even now, Amanda and Elyot are rolling about on the floor, laughing.

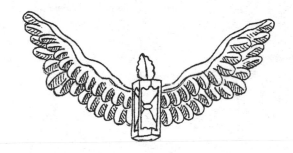

Acknowledgements

This book could not have been written without the encouragement of Hugo Vickers, whose intelligent contributions and practical assistance were, as ever, inestimable. Of the many other people influential in the five years it has taken to retrace Noel Coward's life and work, Graham Payn's benediction has been invaluable. Not only did he answer any question, no matter how frank, but he also allowed me to delve into the depths of 'Mum's suitcase' and the treasure-trove at Les Avants. The English representatives of the Noel Coward Estate were as helpful: Joan Hirst provided archive material and other assistance, and Michael Imison bravely read the unedited script to approve its contents. Jon Wynne-Tyson enlightened me on Coward's relationship with Esme Wynne. Mark Ashurst played chauffeur, tour organiser and researcher with aplomb. I would also like to thank my parents, Leonard and Theresa, my sisters, Christina and Katherine, and my brother Stephen, Peter Goddard, Rob Holden, Claire Eastman, Jane Preston and Neil Tennant for their support.

Further thanks are due to Cheryl Newman, for her help with picture research, and Richard H. Smith, for copying archive prints. John Culme lent hitherto unpublished photographs from Bobbie Andrews's album. The Streatfeild and Bulteel families were generous with information and advice. Karen Nichols of the Combined Theatrical Charities kindly gave me access to Coward's letters to Joyce Carey, and other important material.

Finally, I would like to thank Christopher Sinclair-Stevenson, for the initial inspiration and encouragement; my editor, Roger Cazalet, for elegant, intelligent and patient direction; Biddy Martin, for her sharp editing pencil; and my agent, Gillon Aitken, for his steely defence and commonsense.

The following attempts to be a comprehensive list of the people who

Acknowledgements

have contributed letters, interviews and other assistance. I apologise in advance for any who might have fallen by the wayside, and hope that they do not keep a black book: Toni Allen; the late Earl Amherst; Eloise Armen; the late Maxine Audley; David Baldwin, Serjeant of the Vestry, HM Chapel Royal; Frith Banbury; Lionel Bart; Jeff Begeal; the late Lord Bessborough; Blanche Blackwell; Chris Blackwell; Sir Dirk Bogarde; Joan Booth Wilbraham; Charles Bowden; Michael Bracewell; Eric Braun; Douglas Brown; David Brett; Richard Buckle; Christopher Bulteel; Lynda Lee Burks; Peter Burton; the late Joyce Carey; Morris Cargill; John Carlyle; Theodore S. Chapin, Rodgers & Hammerstein; James Chatfield-Moore; Stephen Citron; Stephen Cole, Rodgers & Hammerstein; Bryan Connon; Audrey Dear; Her Grace the Duchess of Devonshire; Dorothy Dickson; the late Marlene Dietrich; Julian Drinkall; Martin Duberman; the late Edward Duke; Honor Earl; Mary Ellis; Meredith Etherington-Smith; Alan Farley; the late Dorothy Fellowes-Gordon; James Fergusson; the late Robert Flemyng; Michael Foot; Alistair Forbes; Charles Henri Ford; Harold French; Margaret Fulton; Mrs Valentine Gibson; Sir John Gielgud; Clare Goddard; Sam Goonetillake; Caz Gorham; Morton Gottlieb; Helen Grange; Derek Granger; Desmond Gregory; Tammy Grimes; Glynn Griffiths; Norman Hackforth; Broderick Haldane; Jane Harari; Dale Harris; John Harrison; Kitty Carlisle Hart; Tim Hart; Lady Selina Hastings; Sir Anthony Havelock-Allan; Alan Helms; Katharine Hepburn; the late Hon. David Herbert; Vicky Heseltine; Jane Hilary; Peter Hill & the Teddington Society; David Holden; Michael Holden; Horst P. Horst; Michael Imison; Lord Jenkins of Hillhead; Richard Hutto; Geoffrey Johnson; David Keeps; Ian Kelly; Gail Kendall; Michael Keneally; Willy Kerruish; Francis King; Bruce Laffey; Jillian La Vallette-Robins; Joe Layton; the late Nicholas Lawford; James Lees-Milne; the late Susan Lowndes Marques; the late Hon. Lady Lindsay of Dowhill; Bert Lister; Roddy McDowall; Sir Ian McKellen; the late Leo Maguire; Elspeth March; Anna Massey; Daniel Massey; Christopher Matheson; Peter Matz; Roy Moseley; Charlotte Mosley; Roy Nash; Grizel Niven; Patrick O'Connor; Charles Osborne; the late Anthony Pawson; Neville Phillips; John Pringle; Gary Pulsifer; the late Sir Peter Quennell; Kurt B. Reighley; Jean Roberts; Carl Rollyson; James Roose-Evans; Ned Rorem; Steve Ross; Jon Savage; Charles Scatamacchia; LTC Vincent Scatamacchia; James R. Sewell, City Archivist, Corporation of London; Helen Sheehy; Ned Sherrin; Lord Skelmersdale; Leslie Smith; Timothy d'Arch Smith; Enid Spurgin; Philip Streatfeild; Caroline Sutcliffe; Nora Swinburne;

Acknowledgements

Sandy Tatham; Robert Tewdyr Moss; Michael Thornton; Major D. H. Toler, Regimental Headquarters, Coldstream Guards; Elizabeth Vickers; Gore Vidal; Dominic Vlasto; the late Peter Wadland; David Wainwright; Tony Warren; Auberon Waugh; Robert Wennersten; Roy Williams; Diana Windsor Richards; Patrick Woodcock; Lucia and Dan Woods Lindley; Jon and Jennifer Wynne-Tyson.

For permission to publish new material: The Noel Coward Estate; Jon Wynne-Tyson, for the letters, diaries and literary works of Esme Wynne-Tyson; Her Grace the Duchess of Devonshire, for use of Noel Coward's letters to Nancy Mitford; The Combined Theatrical Charities, for use of Noel Coward's letters to Joyce Carey; Diana Marr-Johnson and Peter Burton, for use of Robin Maugham's diaries; the executors of the Literary Estate of Cecil Beaton; and the British Library Department of Manuscripts for papers of the Lord Chamberlain's office.

I would also like to acknowledge the use of material from the following institutions, and thank the curators and librarians involved: Sophie Cant and the Keeper of the Archives, Churchill College, Cambridge; Elizabeth Inglis, Manuscript Librarian, University of Sussex Library; Glenise Matheson, John Tuck and Dr Peter McNiven, The John Rylands University Library, University of Manchester; Gaye Poulton, Random House; Michael Bott, Archivist, University of Reading Library; Wendy Bowersock, Barbara Smith-LaBorde and the Harry C. Ransom Humanities Research Center, University of Texas at Austin; Lori Curtis, Department of Special Collections, MacFarlin Library, University of Tulsa. The staff of the Billy Rose Collection at Lincoln Center, and the staff of the Theatre Museum Study Room, Covent Garden, have supplied countless press cuttings and other source material. The continued existence of their resources is essential to the production of books such as this.

Source Notes

Quotes from Noel Coward's plays, stories, songs and verse are taken from the following published editions:

Play Parade, Heinemann, 1934.
Second Play Parade, Heinemann, 1939.
Play Parade, vols. 3–6, Heinemann, 1950–62.
A Withered Nosegay, Christophers, 1922.
Chelsea Buns, Hutchinson, 1925.
Spangled Unicorn, Hutchinson, 1932.
Pomp and Circumstance, Heinemann, 1960.
The Lyrics of Noel Coward, Tusk/Overlook, New York, 1983.
Collected Verse of Noel Coward, Methuen, 1984.
Noel Coward: The Complete Stories, Methuen, 1985.

Volumes of autobiography by Noel Coward and abbreviations in notes:
Present Indicative (PI), Heinemann, 1937.
Middle East Diary (MED), Heinemann, 1944.
Future Indefinite (FI), Heinemann, 1954.
Past Conditional (PC), Methuen, 1986.

Unpublished Coward material includes:
'Esnomel', 'The Last Chapter' (aka *Ida Collaborates*); 'Woman and Whiskey'; both by permission of Jon Wynne-Tyson.
Noel Coward, *Semi-Monde*; *Volcano*; both by permission of the Noel Coward Estate, as is all other unpublished material by Noel Coward.

Other abbreviations used in notes:
AC: Astley-Cooper, unpublished memoir, in the possession of Jane Harari.
Castle: Charles Castle, *Noel*, W. H. Allen, 1972.
CL: Cole Lesley, *The Life of Noel Coward*, Jonathan Cape, 1976.
D: eds Graham Payn and Sheridan Morley, *The Noel Coward Diaries*, Weidenfeld & Nicolson, 1982.
DFG: interviews with Dorothy Fellowes-Gordon, 5 March–3 August 1991.
EWT diary: Esme Wynne-Tyson, 'Some Biographical Notes'.
EWT interview: discussion, Esme Wynne-Tyson, Jon Wynne-Tyson and Sheridan Morley, 2 April 1967.
HRHC: Harry C. Ransom Humanities Research Center, University of Texas, Austin.
JRL: John Rylands Library, University of Manchester.
LCP: Lord Chamberlain's papers, British Library.

Source Notes

M&M: Raymond Mander and Joe Mitchenson, *Theatrical Companion to Coward*, Macmillan Company, New York, 1957.
NC&F: Cole Lesley, Graham Payne and Sheridan Morley, *Noel Coward and his Friends*, Weidenfeld & Nicolson, 1979.
A Private Life: BBC television documentary, directed by Michael Dean, 1983.
SM: Sheridan Morley, *A Talent to Amuse*, Pavilion Books, 1986.
TM: Theatre Museum, Covent Garden, London.
VC: Violet Coward, unpublished memoir, Noel Coward Estate.

1. Family Album

1 'Oh how fortunate I was . . .', *D*, p. 657.
2 'good family . . .', *PI*, p. 4.
2 'daughter of a family . . .', Philip Warner, *Field Marshal Earl Haig*, Bodley Head, 1991, p. 10.
2 'I believe that a certain . . .', *The Lyrics of Noel Coward*, p. vii.
3 'one of the greatest sinners . . .', Desmond Gregory, *Beneficent Usurpers – A History of the British in Madeira*, Associated University Press, 1988, p. 93.
3 'In what way . . .', NC to Rupert Croft-Cooke, (?1961), HRHC.
3 'was never really fond . . .', VC.
3 'He was good . . .', *PI*, p. 4.
3 'a lovely French girl', VC.
3 'an extra relation called Barbara . . .', *PI*, p. 5.
4 'After a round of gaiety . . .', VC.
4 'comparatively young', *PI*, p. 4.
4 'formerly of the island . . .', H. G. Veitch will (1864), Somerset House.
5 'off my very high forehead . . .', VC.
5 'an extraordinary woman . . .', EWT interview.
5 'That illness . . .', VC.
6 'a trifle sadly . . .', *PI*, p. 5.
6 'After the Display . . .', programme, Crystal Palace 1870, Guildhall Library, City of London.
7 'his compositions . . .', *The Dictionary of National Biography*, (ed. Leslie Stephen), Smith, Elder & Co., 1887, vol. XII, p. 1298.
7 'professional pianist . . . from Australia', *PI*, p. 6.
7 'excelled any woman . . .', Richie Ling, *Globe and Mail*, Toronto, undated.
8 'The Cathedral of the Thames Valley . . .', pamphlet, Teddington Public Library.
8 'furious outbursts', *PI*, p. 5.
8 'highly ambitious . . . London church', Kenneth Ingram, 'Our Thames Valley "Cathedral"', in *The Green Quarterly*, Teddington Public Library.
8 'very enjoyable times . . .', SM, p. 2.
8 'very spruce', *PI*, p. 6.
9 'looking tenacious . . .', *NC&F*, p. 8.
9 'a very shadowy person . . .', EWT interview.
9 'Have a tongue sandwich . . .', CL, p. 185.
9 'unnecessary charm', ibid.
9 'I remember the smell . . .', *Collected Verse of Noel Coward*.
10 'fond of young ladies . . .', Ronald Webber, *R. D. Blackmore of Teddington*, Twickenham Local History Society, 1987.
10 'What a peaceful . . .', CL, p. 2.
10 'so lovely and so clever . . .', VC.
11 'When Queen Victoria died . . .', *Collected Verse of Noel Coward*.

12 'very forward . . . very much spoilt', VC.
12 'born into a generation . . .', *Punch*, 8 July 1953.
12 'highly strung', VC.
12 'economy forced us . . .', *NC&F*, p. 8.
12 'whenever there was anything . . .', VC.
13 'bright red . . .', *PI*, p. 7.
13 'really very naughty', VC.
13 'an action . . .', *PI*, p. 7.
13 'for he was beginning . . .', VC.
13 'Hark to the sound . . .', Lionel Monckton, *A Country Girl*, programme, TM.
14 'large mournful Irish eyes', *PI*, p. 7.
14 'played well and looked hideous', EWT diary, 23 February 1916.
14 'except occasionally from my mother . . .', *Punch*, 22 July 1953.
14 'the sad thing . . .', Castle, p. 18.
14 'kind, pretty, and vain', *PI*, p. 9.
14 'certainly very unpopular . . .', Margaret Fulton, letter to author, 10 February 1993.
15 'didn't much like . . .', ibid.
15 'I had some little boys . . .', *NC&F*, p. 20.
15 'No money . . .', VC.
15 'long chiffon draperies . . .', VC.
16 'pretty rough . . .', David Baldwin, *The Chapel Royal: Ancient and Modern*, Duckworth, 1990, p. 342.
16 'Once during . . .', *PI*, p. 13.
16 'as well as the Almighty . . .', ibid.
16 'I did the whole . . .', interview, Noel Coward and Judy Garland, *Redbook*, November 1961.
17 'didn't make the grade . . .', Baldwin, op. cit., p. 34.
17 'Small poverty . . .', *PI*, p. 14.
17 'romantic desolation', ibid., p. 15.
17 'aggressive gentility', 'Ashes of Roses', in *Star Quality*, Heinemann, 1951, pp. 251–2.
18 'We lived there . . .', *PI*, p. 17.
18 'a milk sop . . .', Enid Spurgin, letter to author, 8 May 1991.
19 'I am still very unhappy . . .', *NC&F*, p. 22.
19 'more full-blooded . . .', *PI*, p. 19.
19 'It was also a pleasant game . . .', ibid., p. 22

2. A Talented Boy

21 'stated that . . .', *PI*, p. 23.
21 'passed out', VC.
21 'It will be . . .', *NC&F*, p. 17.
22 'seemed, with his straight . . .', Michael MacLiammoir, *Enter a Goldfish*, Thames and Hudson, 1977, p. 69.
22 'She said that as Noel . . .', VC.
22 'Tarver, never let me . . .', *PI*, p. 28.
22 'a twinkle . . .', ibid.
23 'who has given up . . .', *Where the Rainbow Ends*, undated cutting.
23 ' "Dorothy . . ." ', *PI*, p. 31.
23 'quite fantastic . . .', Hermione Gingold, *How to Grow Old Disgracefully*, Victor Gollancz, 1989, pp. 32–3.
24 'when he was about twelve . . .', AC.

24 'the atmosphere . . .', *PI*, pp. 44–5

25 'Miss Joan Carroll . . .', *The Times*, 26 June 1912.

25 'and some others . . .', VC.

25 'immersed in a sea . . .', *PI*, p. 39.

26 'not infallible . . .', Coliseum programme, 20 January 1912, TM.

26 'Do you advise . . .', VC.

26 'vivacious child . . .', *PI*, p. 40.

27 'noticeable ears . . .', Harold French, *I Swore I Never Would*, Secker & Warburg, 1970, p. 63.

27 'I did like him . . .', Harold French, interview with author, 27 February 1992.

27 'knew what he wanted . . .', French, op. cit., p. 64.

28 'Not even . . .', Gore Vidal, letter to author.

28 'We used to go . . .', Harold French interview.

28 'faintly bleating voice', *PI*, p. 30.

28 'the only sentimental . . .', EWT interview.

29 'pompous, podgy . . .', *PI*, p. 49.

29 'I was *never* . . .', EWT letter, 23 January 1959.

29 'What wonderful *enemies* . . .', EWT, letter to Sheridan Morley, April 1967.

29 'Can't we arrange . . .', NC, letter to EWT, undated.

29 'a perfectly normal . . .', Jon Wynne-Tyson to author.

29 'borne the convent . . .', EWT interview.

29 'what went on . . .', EWT, letter, 23 January 1959.

29 'egged him on . . .', VC.

29 'beastly little whimsies', *PI*, p. 52.

30 'It had its moments . . .', undated newspaper cutting, NY (?November 1936).

30 'Noel sang . . .', VC.

30 'dizzy with triumph', VC.

31 'clear foreshadowing . . .', MacLiammoir, op. cit., pp. 84–5.

31 'I couldn't have been . . .', *PI*, p. 48.

31 'It is simply . . .', NC, letter to Violet Coward, undated.

31 'talking so gaily', *PI*, p. 57.

32 'a fairly wild life . . .', Philip Streatfeild, letter to author, 18 November 1992.

33 'posed casually . . .', *PI*, p. 49.

33 'blissfully', ibid., p. 52.

33 'It certainly beats . . .', NC, letter to EWT, undated.

33 'My Dear Little Flapper', Aldwyn Smith, letter to NC, undated.

33 'laughed their heads off . . .', CL, p. 26.

33 'Noel was never . . .', EWT interview.

34 'extremely attractive', David Wainwright, letter to author, 10 January 1995.

34 'a common little boy', Mrs Bridge, letter to author, 6 November 1992.

34 'What that particular area . . .', Timothy d'Arch Smith, *Love in Earnest*, Routledge & Kegan Paul, 1970, p. 158.

34 'a young boy . . .', Mrs Bridge, letter, 6 November 1992.

35 'and I don't know . . .', NC, letter to EWT, undated, 1914.

35 'hot and placid', *PI*, p. 54.

35 'beautifully furnished . . .', NC, letter to Violet Coward, undated.

35 'they looked proud . . .', *PI*, p. 54.

35 'stood the boy . . .', Rupert Hart-Davis, *Hugh Walpole*, Macmillan, 1952, p. 116.

36 'Philip is now . . .', NC, letter to Violet Coward, undated.

36 'it was so ridiculously . . .', L. E. O. Charlton, *Charlton*, Faber & Faber, 1931, p. 241.

36 'young officers of the Flying Corps . . .', ibid., pp. 244–5.

37 'having the time . . .', NC, letter to Violet Coward, undated.
37 'loathed military life . . .', EWT interview.
37 'It was heaven . . .', *PI*, p. 56

3. Podge and Stodge

38 'entirely to please . . .', *PI*, p. 57.
38 'groped . . .', Robin Maugham, unpublished diary, 4 August 1969.
38 'I shall never forget . . .', 'Me and the Girls', *Pretty Polly Barlow*, Heinemann, 1964.
38 'dead from the neck up', EWT diary.
39 'made that senseless . . .', AC.
40 'totally unshockable', Tim Hart, interview with author, 8 April 1992.
40 'rather weird friends', Diana Windsor-Richards, interview with author, 15 January 1995.
40 'particularly intellectual . . .', James Lees-Milne, letter to author, 14 November 1992.
40 'Five years . . .', James Lees-Milne, letter to author, 7 November 1992.
40 'a bravely obscene story . . .', Paul Fussell, *The Great War and Modern Memory*, OUP, 1975, p. 297.
41 'His articulate duchesses . . .', Noel Coward, introduction (1967) to H. H. Munro, *The Complete Saki*, Doubleday 1976/ Penguin 1982, p. 70.
41 'full of both . . .', Martin Green, *Children of the Sun*, Basic Books, US, 1976, p 70.
42 'shamelessly borrowed', Saki introduction, p. xiii.
42 'His stories . . .', ibid., p. xiv.
42 'A massive, shapeless lump . . .', James Lees-Milne, *Prophesying Peace*, Chatto & Windus, 1977, p. 135.
42 'draped scarves . . .', *PI*, p. 58.
42 'she took up the chase . . .', Tim Hart, interview with author, 8 April 1992.
42 'dotty', Windsor Richards interview.
42 'enjoyed a sort . . .', AC.
43 'A gentleman . . .', Noel Annan, *Our Age*, Weidenfeld & Nicolson, 1990, p. 20.
43 'frightfully ambitious . . .', EWT interview.
43 'rightfully annoyed . . .', EWT, letter to Sheridan Morley, April 1967.
44 'He died the following year . . .', *PI*, p. 58.
44 'my friend Noel Coward . . .', Philip Streatfeild will, 2 November 1914, Somerset House.
44 'overwrought . . .', G. B. Stern, *A Deputy Was King*, Virago Press, 1988, p. 361.
45 'short but showy', *PI*, p. 60.
45 'went off beautifully', EWT diary, 24 December 1915.
45 'One of the saddest times . . .', VC.
45 'You may never sing . . .', French, op. cit., p. 84.
46 'the rest of . . .', EWT diary, 4–18 January 1916.
46 'had been going the rounds . . .', EWT interview.
46 'nonsense novels . . .', EWT diary, 7–12 February 1916.
47 'He behaved . . .', ibid., 16 February 1916.
47 'poor Noel . . .', ibid., 19 February 1916.
47 'in new suit . . .', ibid., 26 February 1916.
47 'a little *tendresse* . . .', EWT, letter to Sheridan Morley, April 1967.
48 'an almost compulsive thief', Robin Maugham, unpublished diary, 4 August 1969.
48 'and suddenly saw him . . .', EWT interview.
48 'Both dressed . . .', EWT diary, 25 March 1916.

48 'bad house . . .', ibid., 1 May 1916.
48 'two lovely young men', ibid., 2–3 May 1916.
49 'hated being on his own . . .', EWT interview.
49 'We even had baths . . .', *PI*, p. 51.
49 'two subs . . .', EWT diary, 11–18 May 1916.
49 'their unaesthetic eyes', *PI*, p. 64.
49 'black nostalgia . . .', ibid., p. 63.
49 'I wonder if you remember . . .', EWT, letter to NC, 24 February 1960.
50 'He knocked Noel . . .', EWT diary, 29–30 May 1916.
50 'He was a very bad actor . . .', EWT interview.
50 'He went to a call . . .', Earl Amherst, interview with author, 14 January 1991.
50 'the excruciating . . .', *PI*, p. 68.
50 'you mustn't mind . . .', ibid., p. 71.
50 'very tall, skinny . . .', Castle, p. 32.
50 'with the mark of death . . .', *PI*, p. 71.
51 'had rather "stuck-out" ears . . .', Fabia Drake, *Blind Fortune*, William Kimber, 1978, p. 28.
51 'combined the grace . . .', undated cutting.
51 'topping show', EWT diary, 1 January 1917.
51 'that gorgeous spectacle', ibid., 15 January 1917.
51 'a nice sub . . .', ibid., 3 January 1917.
51 'quite an illustrious company . . .', EWT biog.
52 'very casual and grand . . .', *PI*, p. 66–8.
52 'terrifically pacifist . . .', EWT, 'Youth', unpublished manuscript.
53 'from the ungrateful . . .', EWT diary, 16 March 1917.
54 'In one scene . . .', Lillian Gish, *The Movies, Mr Griffith and Me*, Prentice Hall, NY, 1969, p. 200.
54 'a beastly hole', NC, letter to Violet Coward, undated.
54 'the value of "authority" . . .', *PI*, p. 74.
54 'dark enthusiastic American . . .', NC, letter to Violet Coward, undated.
55 'the real start . . .', Castle, p. 4.
55 'illusion of this . . .', *PI*, pp. 73–4.
55 'Nearly mad with excitement . . .', NC, letter to Violet Coward, undated.

4. Rising Star

57 'a gentle, witty . . .', *PI*, p. 78.
57 'The part of . . .', *Talk of the Town*, 23 January 1918.
57 'I was eager . . .', *A Private Life*.
58 'always so very much interested . . .', VC.
58 'savagely goes to tear it up', Esnomel, 'The Last Chapter'.
59 'The Major, while "sitting out" . . .', Ernest A. Bendall, reader's report, 1918, LCP.
59 'There are indeed . . .', SM, p. 38.
60 'fond of bright colours . . .', unpublished notes, Chalet Coward.
61 'thin dividing line . . .', Bryan Forbes, *Ned's Girl*, Elmtree Books/Hamish Hamilton, 1977, p. 11.
61 'evaporated into . . .', *PI*, p. 80.
61 'She was a brave . . .', EWT interview.
62 'appalling impertinence', *PI*, p. 82.
62 'simply didn't want . . .', EWT interview.
62 'several hours of beastliness . . .', *PI*, pp. 86–8.
63 'one long . . .', Castle, p. 35.

63 'My stage life . . .', *PI*, pp. 89–91.
64 'a little bit overdoing it . . .', Castle, p. 35.
64 'knew it was an act . . .', EWT interview.
64 'which resembled an outline . . .', *PI*, p. 92.
64 'a little woman of small build . . .', Ethel Mannin, *Confessions and Impressions*, Jarrolds, p. 117.
65 'a strong pierrotic . . .', *Twentieth-Century Authors* (ed. S. J. Kurnitz & H. Haycraft), NY, 1942, p. 1342.
65 'by sitting wide-eyed . . .', *PI*, pp. 93–4.
66 'We were so terrified . . .', EWT interview.
66 'was getting a bit jealous . . .', Lyndon Tyson, interview with Sheridan Morley and Jon Wynne-Tyson.
66 'we were all shamefully spoiled . . .', EWT biog.
66 'black melancholia', *PI*, p. 95.
67 'a bad novel', ibid., pp. 98–9.
67 'for I am afraid . . .', VC.
67 'that unfortunate taint . . .', *PI*, pp. 105–7.
68 'plaited in a pigtail . . .', Marjorie Watts, *Mrs Sappho – The Life of C. A. Dawson-Scott, Mother of International P.E.N.*, Duckworth, 1987, pp. 76–9.
69 'Now I don't . . .', CL, p. 43.
69 'Maugham gave him . . .', DFG.
69 'pleasant, if not intimate . . .', ibid., p. 112.
70 'dealing in a whimsical vein . . .', ibid., p. 115.
70 'who had written . . .', Mannin, op. cit., pp. 116–19.
72 'being conducted . . .', *The Times*, 30–31 May 1918.
72 'a nice quiet talk . . .', Siegfried Sassoon, *Siegfried's Journey*, Faber & Faber, 1983, p. 83.
73 'Certainly I know him . . .', S. N. Behrman, *Tribulations and Laughter*, Hamish Hamilton, 1972, p. 113.
73 'may possibly have a first . . .', *Sketch*, 9 December 1918.
73 'in a tail coat . . .', *PI*, p. 117.
74 'a large number of actors . . .', *The Times*, 4 December 1918.
74 'disgusting orgies . . .', *The Times*, 14 December 1918.
75 'the drug of the period . . .', Anthony Havelock-Allan, interview with author, 10 July 1991.
75 'Alice: But do . . .', *NC&F*, p. 30.
76 'He had been the greatest interest . . .', AC.
76 'apart from these . . .', *PI*, p. 118.
76 'Noel was engaged . . .', Norah Swinburne, interview with author, 31 July 1991.
77 'I explained with dignity . . .', *PI*, p. 120.
77 'bubbling over with energy . . .', Swinburne interview.
77 'The first and second acts . . .', *PI*, pp. 121–2.
78 'excruciatingly sophisticated . . .', Noel Coward, *Play Parade 3*, introduction, pp. xi–xii.
78 'I flung aside . . .', *PI*, p. 124.
79 'the best anyone has done for years . . .', Maria Albanesi, *Meggie*, Hodder & Stoughton, 1928, p. 106.
79 'one of two understanding . . .', CL, p. 47.
79 'Oh, what a silly girl . . .', ibid., p. 50.

5. The Young Idea

80 'puzzled by the . . .', *PI*, p. 126.
81 'My *dear* . . .', Michael Davidson, *The World, the Flesh and Myself*, Gay Men's Press, London, 1983, p. 134.
81 'no longer oppressed . . .', *PI*, p. 127.
81 'smelling slyly of amber . . .', ibid., p. 173.
81 'two of the dullest . . .', Castle, p. 38.
81 'I played that poor apprentice . . .', *PI*, p. 128.
81 'which contributed richness . . .', ibid., p. 130.
82 'I quite fancied myself . . .', French, op. cit., pp. 187–8.
83 'round the cabarets . . .', *PI*, pp. 132–3.
83 'down to the Lombardy . . .', ibid., p. 133.
83 'wasn't very grand . . .', AC.
84 'I had seen too many . . .', *PI*, p. 134.
84 'One has not far . . .', *Daily News*, 4 May 1920.
84 'When I eventually . . .', *PI*, p. 134.
84 'freshly written . . .', *Daily Mail*, 22 July 1920.
84 'the author, of an age . . .', *The Sportsman*, 22 July 1920.
85 'one of the late Saki's . . .', *Daily Dispatch*, undated.
85 'with renewed vigour . . .', *PI*, p. 136.
85 'One should have liked . . .', *London News*, 11 December 1920.
85 'who appeared to be fighting . . .', *PI*, p. 138.
85 'a landed gentleman . . .', Anthony Havelock-Allan, interview with author, 10 July 1991.
86 'surprisingly good . . .', Patrick Woodcock, interview with author, 18 March 1991.
86 'small of stature. . .', Jeffrey Amherst, *Wandering Abroad*, Secker & Warburg, 1976, p. 200.
86 'in a lovely studio . . .', AC.
86 'I pointed out she had . . .', AC.
87 'a strange relationship . . .', Woodcock interview.
87 'much tawdry glamour . . .', *PI*, p. 139.
87 'I've just re-met . . .', NC, letter to Violet Coward, 13 December 1922.
87 'particularly rowdy night . . .', AC.
87 'By the end of the run . . .', *PI*, pp. 139–40.
88 'It was a large party . . .', Earl Amherst, interview with author, 14 January 1991.
88 'We walked back . . .', Amherst, op. cit., pp. 56–7.
88 'I watched him twinkling . . .', *PI*, p. 140.
88 'He had a very quick brain . . .', Amherst interview.
89 'I suppose it could have been . . .', Amherst, op. cit., p. 57.
89 'loved . . . him', Patricia Frere, interview with author, 22 October 1991.
89 'bursting out . . .', *PI*, p. 140.
89 'in the trouble . . .', Milton Shulman interview, part one, *Sunday Express*, 1961.
91 'Its gigantic sky-signs . . .', *PI*, p. 121.
91 'home of sexual energy . . .', Green, op. cit., p. 236.
91 'as *Polly with a Past* . . .', Amherst, p. 58.
92 'prominent New York families', *Southern Evening Echo*, 14 May 1921.
92 'casually mentioned . . .', Amherst, pp. 62–3.
92 'breathless June morning . . .', *PI*, p. 147.
92 'in high spirits . . .', Amherst, pp. 63–4.
93 'The sky was not yet dark . . .', *PI*, p. 148.
93 'as naughty . . .', Davidson, op. cit., p. 86.

93 'haze of chatter . . .', *PI*, p. 149.
93 'completely lacked . . .', Amherst, p. 65.
95 'rhythmic monotone . . .', *PI*, pp. 152–3.
96 'a bit of a freelancer . . .', Graham Payn, interview with author, 21–22 September 1992.
96 'wary eyes', *PI*, p. 158.
96 'He'd hand me sheets . . .', Jared Brown, *The Fabulous Lunts*, Atheneum, New York, 1986, p. 97n.
96 'very bright', *NC&F*, p. 48.
96 'Who are we to criticize . . .', Noel Coward, *A Withered Nosegay*, pp. 7, 13.
97 'Some of it was funny . . .', *PI*, p. 151.
97 'vaguely bedraggled . . .', ibid., pp. 160–1.
97 'had been consigned . . .', ibid., p. 155.
98 'When she was first running . . .', Amherst interview.
98 'by formulating . . .', *PI*, pp. 156–7.
99 'Whatever she was doing . . .', Helen Hayes, *My Life in Three Acts*, Peter Owen, 1991, p. 34.
99 'rather acrimonious games', *PI*, p. 157.
99 'a ferocity which appalled . . .', Marguerite Courtney, *Laurette*, Limelight, NY, 1984, p. 244.
99 'The Hardly-any-Manners atmosphere . . .', Leslie Howard, *Trivial Fond Records* (ed. Ronald Howard), William Kimber, 1982, p. 58.
99 'shrill arguments', *PI*, p. 157.
99 'Noel had a great deal . . .', Courtney, op. cit., p. 261.
100 'pink, cherubic face . . .', *PI*, p. 165

6. Lord of a Day

102 'unspoiled by anticlimax . . .', *PI*, p. 174.
102 'we called him Nellie . . .', John Dempsey, interview with author, 21 July 1992.
102 'I was in the awkward . . .', *PI*, p. 174.
103 'Too red . . .', CL, p. 67.
103 'darkening country . . .', *PI*, p. 178.
103 'absolutely charming . . .', Noel Streatfeild, *Magic and the Magician*, Ernest Benn, 1958, p. 19.
103 'sweet old lady', Julia Briggs, *A Woman of Passion*, Hutchinson, 1987, p. 388.
104 'We will pay anything . . .', Heinemann edition of 'Lucia' novels, 1968.
104 '30 Oct . . .', Richard Ormrod, *Una Troubridge*, Jonathan Cape, 1984, p. 149.
104 'unlimited sheep', *PI*, p. 177.
105 'a very bitter little comedy . . .', George Street, reader's report, 1922, LCP.
105 'to a little human brutality . . .', *Clarion*, 22 June 1922.
105 'too flippant . . .', M&M, p. 33.
105 'bouncing Michelin figure', *PI*, p. 181.
105 'the young man obviously . . .', Elsa Maxwell, *I Married the World*, Heinemann, 1955, p. 115.
106 'I loved her at once . . .', *PI*, pp. 182–3.
106 'could have made a fortune . . .', DFG.
106 'A tall, stunning girl . . .', Maxwell, op. cit., pp. 58–9.
106 'a faun-like young man . . .', ibid., p. 120.
107 'sat on the floor . . .', ibid., p. 6.
107 'He danced quite well . . .', DFG.
107 'Dickie was so open-handed . . .', Maxwell, op. cit., p. 116.

107 'He did an Italian tart . . .', DFG.

107 'myriads of feuds . . .', *PI*, p. 185.

107 'within the hour . . .', Maxwell, op. cit., pp. 116–17.

108 'What he really meant . . .', *PI*, p. 179.

108 'a clever and amusing comedy . . .', G. S. Street, reader's report, September 1922, LCP.

109 'a dangerous phrase . . .', Beverley Nichols, *All I Could Never Be*, Jonathan Cape, 1949, p. 43.

109 'a delightful friend . . .', John Gielgud, letter to author, 14 November 1991.

109 'a dream of decadent luxury . . .', Bryan Connon, *Beverley Nichols*, Constable, 1991, p. 86.

109 'he squandered . . .', Gielgud letter, 14 November 1991.

109 'divine lunch . . .', NC, letter to Violet Coward, 28 November 1922.

110 'Clothes must avoid . . .', *The Times*, 25 March 1974.

110 'the most elegant place . . .', Caroline Rennolds Millbank, *Couture*, Thames & Hudson, 1985, p. 146.

110 '*Such* a good gesture . . .', NC, letter to Violet Coward, 28 November 1922.

110 'thick snow . . .', ibid., 2 December 1922.

110 'Ned looked better . . .', *PI*, p. 187.

110 'I am to do all the music . . .', NC, letter to Violet Coward, 2 December 1922.

110 '*It's his solely* . . .', ibid., 10 December 1922.

110 '*delighted* – he sat . . .', ibid., 2 December 1922.

111 'a series of cigar-laden . . .', *PI*, p. 188.

111 'to *start* with . . .', NC, letter to Violet Coward, 2 December 1922.

111 'I'm *sure* no daughter . . .', ibid.

111 'It is a promise . . .', NC, interview, *The Times*, undated, 1966.

111 'with the most marvellous . . .', NC, letter to Violet Coward, 5 December 1922.

112 'German is a terribly funny . . .', ibid., 13 December 1922.

112 'gayer than anywhere . . .', ibid., 10 December 1922.

112 'frowsy blonde . . .', Sheridan Morley, *Gertrude Lawrence*, Weidenfeld & Nicolson, 1981, p. 42.

112 'I said of course . . .', NC, letter to Violet Coward, 10 December 1922.

112 'I'm sunburnt and healthy . . .', ibid., 29 December 1922.

113 'the difference was not . . .', *PI*, p. 190

7. Bright Young Thing

114 'usual self-deprecatory speech . . .', *PI*, p. 190.

114 'FIRST NIGHT . . .', *Evening Standard*, 2 February 1923.

114 'contains the first line . . .', *New Yorker*, 24 January 1977.

114 'a compromise between pederasty . . .', Robert Graves and Alan Hodges, *The Long Weekend*, Cardinal, 1991, p. 43.

115 'There is something in the make-up . . .', *Saturday Review*, 17 February 1923.

115 'The play is going quite well . . .', NC, letter to Violet Coward, February 1923.

115 'immaculately dressed . . .', James Lees-Milne, *Caves of Ice*, Chatto & Windus, 1983, p. 182.

115 'a great deal of personal . . .', *PI*, p. 179.

116 'London is outraged . . .', NC, letter to Violet Coward, undated.

116 'one more step . . .', *PI*, p. 191.

116 'smoked far too much . . .', Maria Albanesi, op. cit., p. 98.

116 'She used to mother him . . .', Leslie Smith, interview with author, 17 February 1993.

117 'detestable, gauche and rude . . .', NC, letter to Violet Coward, undated.
117 'I allowed myself . . .', *PI*, p. 194.
117 'chorus mistress . . .', Sam Heppner, *Cockie*, Leslie Frewin, 1969, pp. 150–1.
118 'sat doodling at her piano . . .', James Harding, *Cochran*, Methuen, 1988, p. 112.
118 'Well, dear . . .', *PI*, p. 194.
118 'which has some of the most . . .', Judy Campbell, interview with author, 28 June 1991.
118 'a very tricky and technical . . .', Noel Coward, *Collected Sketches and Lyrics*, Hutchinson, 1931, preface.
118 'There is a good deal more talent . . .', G. S. Street, reader's report, 21 August 1923, LCP.
119 'should never have been allowed . . .', *PI*, p. 197.
119 'Noel and I did a dance . . .', US cutting, undated.
119 'Typical of Gertie's . . .', NC to *New York Herald-Tribune*, undated, 1950.
120 'a few ideas', SM, p. 73.
120 'Hernia is busy . . .', undated cutting.
120 'In 1923, Mr Coward . . .', John Pearson, *Façades*, Macmillan, 1978, p. 391.
120 'even crosser . . .', *PI*, p. 197.
120 'major demon . . .', Pearson, op. cit., p. 397.
120 'this strange managerial juggling . . .', *PI*, p. 197.
121 'like two panthers . . .', Anthony Curtis, *Somerset Maugham*, Weidenfeld & Nicolson, 1977, p. 137.
122 'seated before my mirror . . .', Morley, *Gertrude Lawrence*, op. cit., p. 35.
122 'appetite for sexual adventure . . .', Christopher Warwick, *George and Marina, Duke and Duchess of Kent*, Weidenfeld & Nicolson, 1988, p. 70.
122 'I heard a lot . . .', Peter Williams to author.
122 'Noel and Prince George . . .', Roy Moseley, interview with author, 12 April 1992.
123 'used to tell me . . .', *Evening Standard*, 18 January 1990.
123 'to pick up sailors . . .', Hugo Vickers, *Cecil Beaton*, Weidenfeld & Nicolson, 1985, p. 115.
123 'I've heard so much about Noel . . .', Cecil Beaton, unpublished diary, 8 October 1923; St John's College, Cambridge.
124 'We had great fun . . .', *PI*, p. 202.
124 'tactfully . . . erase', ibid., p. 201.
124 'comfortable greenish apartment . . .', ibid., pp. 204–5.
124 'endowed with a facile . . .', Samuel Hopkins Adams, *Alexander Woollcott*, Hamish Hamilton, 1946, p. 124.
125 'a big thrill . . .', *PI*, pp. 205–6.
125 'It ought to be . . .', SM, pp. 74–5.
125 'into a frenzy . . .', CL, p. 188.
126 'I think he's the only . . .', John Pringle, interview with author, 12 September 1991.
126 'toiled . . . too long . . .', *PI*, pp. 207–11.
126 '. . . I *think* it's going to prove . . .', NC, letter to Violet Coward, 23 July 1924.
127 'an abysmal admission . . .', *PI*, pp. 213–15.

8. The Vortex

128 'During the era . . .', G. B. Stern, *Monogram*, Chapman & Hall, 1936.
129 'Noel Coward put his sexuality . . .', Derek Jarman, *Modern Nature*, Century, 1991, p. 112.
130 'took a serious historic interest . . .', Rebecca West, *Nova* magazine, June 1973.
130 'I doubt it . . .', Milton Shulman interview, part two, *Sunday Express*, 1961.

132 'the celebrity business . . .', Michael Arlen Jnr, *Exiles*, André Deutsch, 1971, p. 7.
132 'Mr Arlen . . .', ibid., p. 70.
132 'the evening seemed . . .', *PI*, pp. 221–3
133 'Mr Coward has been known . . .', G. S. Street, reader's report, 7 November 1924, LCP.
133 'this sort of play . . .', Lord Cromer, 12 November 1924, LCP.
134 'a piece calculated to convey . . .', Sir Douglas Dawson, 13 November 1924, LCP.
134 'I cannot help feeling . . .', H. H. Higgins, 16 November 1924, LCP.
134 'apart from the criminal law . . .', Lord Buckmaster, 19 November 1924, LCP.
134 'that no matter whether . . .', Douglas Dawson to Lord Cromer, 23 November 1924, LCP.
135 'little more than a moral tract . . .', *PI*, p. 227.
135 'The King has read . . .', Lord Stamfordham to Lord Cromer, 22 November 1924, LCP.
135 'sickening silence . . .', *PI*, p. 229.
135 'And now what?', ibid., p. 366.
136 'very exciting', Havelock-Allan interview.
136 'cocaine on the table . . .', Amherst interview.
136 'cocktail-drinking, decadence . . .', *PI*, p. 230.
136 'The public are asking . . .', James Harding, *Gerald du Maurier*, Hodder & Stoughton, 1989, p. 138.
136 'when I was young . . .', Robert Flemyng, interview with author, 8 July 1992.
136 'I suggested . . .', AC.
137 'that flashy Godfrey Winn . . .', Cecil Beaton, unpublished diary, 31 December 1924.
137 'literally shaking . . .', Castle, p. 64.
137 'Darling, could it . . .', CL, p. 332.
138 'big moment . . .', *PI*, pp. 229–30.
138 '[His] room looked . . .', John Gielgud, *Early Stages*, Macmillian, 1939, p. 60.
138 'exclusively to "Us"', *PI*, p. 233.
139 'out of the goodness . . .', ibid., p. 238.
139 'Noel the fortunate . . .', *The Sketch*, 29 April 1925.
139 'I am never out of opium dens . . .', John Lahr, *Coward*, Methuen, 1982, p. 2.
140 'If the part requires one . . .', Milton Shulman interview, part two, *Sunday Express*, 1961.
140 'I took to wearing . . .', *PI*, p. 232.
140 'still inclined . . .', ibid., p. 239.
140 'all sorts of men . . .', Cecil Beaton, *The Glass of Fashion*, Cassell, 1954/1989, p. 153.
140 'started a whole new form . . .', Ginette Spanier, *It Isn't All Mink*, Collins, 1959, p. 35.
141 'clip one's speech . . .', Beaton, *The Glass of Fashion*, p. 153.

9. Society's Hero

142 'And then, there was the sound . . .', Beverley Nichols, *A Case of Human Bondage*, Secker & Warburg, 1966, p. 122.
142 'Don't try to do . . .', Heppner, op. cit., p. 122.
143 'retained his dignity . . .', *PI*, p. 243.
143 'which had begun to sag . . .', Harding, op. cit., p. 118.
143 '"Noel", she screamed . . .', ibid., p. 113.
144 'Continental rages . . .', *PI*, p. 243.

144 'decadent and brilliant . . .', *Morning Post*, 1 May 1925.
144 'It ain't goin' to rain . . .', R. L. Calder, *The Life of W. Somerset Maugham*, Heinemann, 1989, p. 183.
144 'tore off her hat . . .', *PI*, p. 246.
144 'Bellulah Blockhead . . .', Amherst interview.
144 'no sense of struggle . . .', *PI*, p. 246.
145 'brightly written . . .', G. S. Street, reader's report, 27 March 1925, LCP.
145 '. . . I take the view . . .', Lord Cromer, 5 April 1925, LCP.
145 'brilliant and completely assured . . .', *PI*, p. 246.
145 'a better piece of stage-craft . . .', *Punch*, undated (1925).
145 'vulgar, disgusting . . .', *PI*, p. 247.
145 'work themselves up . . .', London Council for the Promotion of Public Morality to Lord Cromer, 8 May 1925, LCP.
145 'Ladies and Gentlemen . . .', Andrew Barrow, *Gossip*, Pan Books, 1980, p. 25.
146 'too many parties . . .', *PI*, p. 247.
146 'On Monday week . . .', NC, letter to Basil Dean, 28 February 1925, JRL.
146 'jog along for ages . . .', *PI*, p. 248.
146 'an English cast . . .', NC, letter to Basil Dean, 28 February 1925, JRL.
146 'walked nervously . . .', *PI*, p. 250.
147 'shiny black hair . . .', *A Private Life*.
148 'in certain circles . . .', Beaton, *The Glass of Fashion*, pp. 152–3.
148 'I think the reason for this . . .', *PI*, p. 208.
148 'You wrote it . . .', ibid., pp. 251–2.
149 'first and last bullfight . . .', NC, letter to Basil Dean, 16 June 1925, JRL.
149 'I'd also like to see . . .', G. B. Stern, letter to Esme Wynne-Tyson, 28 May 1925.
149 'a gay, nervous voyage . . .', *PI*, p. 254.
150 'touchingly poor . . .', Mercedes de Acosta, *Here Lies the Heart*, André Deutsch, 1960, p. 131.
150 'alternated between intellectual . . .', *PI*, p. 253.
150 'Gladys Calthrop had gone off . . .', DFG.
150 'He didn't like their lack . . .', Woodcock interview, 18 March 1991.
150 'I hadn't got a "bob" . . .', *New York Times*, 19 August 1925.
150 'dainty to the point of nausea . . .', *PI*, pp. 254–7.
151 'Never before or since . . .', ibid., p. 263.
151 'the biggest ovation . . .', *New York World*, 18 September 1925.
151 'fine audience, in its entirety . . .', E. W. Osborn, *Evening World*, 17 September 1925.
151 'Brilliantly acted . . .', *New York World*, 17 September 1925.
151 'a good, thrilling, glib . . .', *New York Herald-Tribune*, 17 September 1925.
152 'honor young Mr Coward . . .', *New York World*, 18 September 1925.
152 'offering an insult . . .', *Theatre Review*, 3 October 1925.
152 'the silly people . . .', *New York World*, 17 September 1925.
152 'Fortunately, I remembered . . .', *PI*, p. 264.
152 'Wilson, in a gesture . . .', *New York Times*, 1 August 1937.
153 'Modern Drama . . .', *New York Herald-Tribune*, 4 November 1925.
153 'But since he announces himself . . .', *New York World*, 2 November 1925.
153 'eluded their hordes . . .', *New York World*, 21 December 1925.
153 'brassy blonde . . .', *PI*, p. 265.
154 'In those days . . .', *Redbook*, November 1961.
154 'If not a very good play . . .', G. S. Street, reader's report, 18 December 1924, LCP.
154 'A very intelligent play . . .', Lord Cromer, 20 December 1924, LCP.
154 'Even such an uprising youth . . .', *Denver Post*, 20 December 1925.

155 'preferably three months . . .', *PI*, pp. 273–7.
156 'startled leprechaun . . .', Stephen Citron, *Noel and Cole*, Sinclair-Stevenson, 1992, p. 54.
157 'He has great ideas . . .', NC, letter to Violet Coward, 3 November 1926.
157 'very anxious to do *Semi-Monde* . . .', ibid., 25 November 1926.
158 'a very apposite remark . . .', Nichols, *The Unforgiving Minute*, W. H. Allen, 1978, p. 60.
158 'finer', *New York Times*, undated, 1926.
158 'so that in the event . . .', *PI*, p. 278

10. On with the Dance

159 'Delightful! . . . We all came . . .', Sewell Stokes, *Pilloried!*, Appleton & Carnham, NY, 1929, pp. 17–18.
159 'many plutocratic thrills', *PI*, p. 274.
159 'It felt strange after months . . .', ibid., p. 279.
160 'embraced Christian Science . . .', ibid., p. 248.
160 'and I saw how impossible . . .', EWT diary, 20 September 1927.
160 '. . . I won't come to see you . . .', Ethel Mannin, letter to EWT, 25 January 1930.
160 'relentless superficial humour', 'Quicksand' synopsis, Jennifer Wynne-Tyson.
160 '. . . you always make your characters . . .', NC, undated letter to EWT.
160 'although there is . . .', Jon Wynne-Tyson, interview with author, 24 April 1992.
161 'a very nice person . . .', EWT interview.
161 'served in the box-office . . .', *New York Times*, 1 August 1937.
161 'really was a young businessman . . .', *A Private Life*.
161 'nice looking . . .', DFG.
161 'Jack Wilson was a . . .', Charles Russell, interview with the author.
161 'Having been mistress . . .', CL, pp. 117–18.
162 PERFECTLY SATISFIED . . ., NC, telegram to Basil Dean, 29 April 1926.
162 'I don't know whether I should meet you . . .', Citron, op. cit., p. 51.
163 'indiscriminate sexual experimentation . . .', ibid., p. 59.
163 WHAT MEANING ALTERNATIVE . . ., NC, telegram to Basil Dean, 16 May 1926, JRL.
163 'mobbed by the gallery girls . . .', *PI*, pp. 280–1.
163 'not so good . . .', EWT diary, 9 June 1926.
163 'Mr Noel Coward gets younger . . .', *Sunday Times*, 13 June 1926.
165 'The main intention . . .', G. S. Street, reader's report, 15 September 1926, LCP.
165 'Every character . . .', Douglas Dawson, 26 September 1926, LCP.
166 MY VERY MORAL . . ., *Evening Standard*, 20 October 1926.
166 'lop-sided . . .', *PI*, pp. 283–4.
167 'I don't think it ever occurred . . .', *PI*, pp. 281–2.
167 'unforgettable gallery . . .', Beverley Nichols, *Are They the Same at Home?*, Jonathan Cape, 1927, p. 121.
167 'a lean youth', Margaret Kennedy, *The Constant Nymph*, Heinemann, 1924, p. 4.
168 'whole-heartedly', *PI*, p. 285.
168 'I think I ought to tell you . . .', Gielgud, op. cit., pp. 70–1.
168 'an immediate smashing success . . .', *PI*, p. 287.
169 'Mr Coward has been examined . . .', Dr MacManus, note to Basil Dean, 7 October 1926.
169 'played it successfully . . .', *PI*, p. 288.
169 'made to feel rather small . . .', Gielgud, op. cit., pp. 72–3.
169 'But *did* he write . . .', G. B. Stern, letter to EWT, 28 October 1926.
169 'It's very good . . .', NC, letter to Violet Coward, October 1926.

169 'Colin's outlook . . .', Stern, *A Deputy Was King*, p. 78.
170 'Oh, we were talking . . .', ibid., p. 206.
170 'Colin used to solace . . .', ibid., pp. 278–9
170 'the famous "List" . . .', Edward Holstitus, letters to EWT, 19 January and 28 March 1961.
170 'That's Colin Martial . . .', Stern, *A Deputy Was King*, p. 287.

11. Home Chat

171 'I did hate leaving you . . .', NC and John C. Wilson, letters to Violet Coward, 14 October 1926.
171 'superior and healthy . . .', NC, letter to Violet Coward, 3 November 1926.
172 'obvious influences . . .', *The New Grove Dictionary of Music and Musicians*, Macmillan, 1980, vol. 5, p. 8.
172 'with Noel Coward Inc . . .', NC, letter to Violet Coward, 28 October 1926.
172 'extremely business-like . . .', ibid., 3 November 1926.
172 'unattractive', *PI*, p. 289.
172 'small and red-haired . . .', NC, letter to Violet Coward, 3 November 1926.
172 'a very good cast', ibid., October 1926 and 28 October 1926.
172 'beautifully', ibid., 3 November 1926.
172 'everybody completely mad . . .', ibid., 11 November 1926.
172 'snapped in and out . . .', *PI*, p. 289.
172 'in an enormous house party . . .', NC, letter to Violet Coward, 11 November 1926.
172 'I love being here . . .', ibid., 28 October 1926.
172 'and we're all having grand fun . . .', ibid., 18 November 1926.
173 'I wrote him a note . . .', ibid., 25 November 1926.
173 'The first night was fashionable . . .', *PI*, p. 289.
173 'something very dirty . . .', NC, letter to Violet Coward, 25 November 1926.
173 '. . . if the writing of it was slow . . .', *PI*, p. 290.
173 'primarily satirical . . .', ibid., p. 279.
174 'pleasant little trifles . . .', *New York Times*, 24 November 1926.
174 'irritable and unhappy . . .', NC, letter to Violet Coward, 1 December 1926.
174 'As there are several . . .', ibid., 25 November 1926.
174 'as they all seem so down on me . . .', ibid., 8 December 1926.
174 'to worry about *Fallen Angels* . . .', ibid., 1 December 1926.
174 'nervy', ibid., 14 December 1926.
174 'I began to ache . . .', *PI*, p. 291.
175 'organically', ibid., 14 December 1926.
175 'went quietly . . .', ibid., Christmas Eve 1926.
175 'Noel Coward is on the edge . . .', Diana Cooper, *The Light of Common Day*, Rupert Hart-Davis, 1959, p. 73.
175 'I saw your play . . .', undated cutting.
175 'His voice is amazingly beautiful . . .', Philip Ziegler, *Diana Cooper*, Hamish Hamilton, 1981, p. 144.
176 'with a very forced, gay smile . . .', *PI*, p. 292.
176 'an international celebrity centre . . .', Harold Acton, *More Memoirs of an Aesthete*, Methuen, 1970, p. 14.
176 'very rich and very nice . . .', NC, letter to Violet Coward, undated.
177 'injected into me . . .', *The Complete Saki*, introduction, p. xii.
177 'greedy and predatory', *PI*, p. 304.
177 'both looking much younger . . .', ibid., p. 309.
178 'brought to perfection . . .', *Play Parade* 3, p. xiv.

178 'still cannot write an effective . . .', *Morning Post*, 17 February 1927.
178 'Wasn't *The Marquise* delicious? . . .', G. B. Stern, letter to EWT, undated.
178 'Another satisfied screen author . . .', undated cutting, 1927.
179 'The Count . . .', SM, p. 86.
180 '*Easy Virtue* is the answer . . .', Michael Balcon, *A Lifetime of Films*, Hutchinson, 1969.
180 'almost as prodigious . . .', Gene D. Phillips, *Alfred Hitchcock*, Columbus Books, 1984, p. 27.
180 'It was no doubt wrong . . .', Balcon, op. cit., p. 27.
180 'Wardour Street's ace salesman . . .', Adrian Brunel, *Nice Work*, Forbes Robertson, 1949, pp. 130–1.
181 'epigrams depending . . .', Rachel Low, *The History of British Cinema 1918–1929*, Allen & Unwin, 1971, pp. 169–70.
181 'I'm not interested . . .', *Boston Transcript*, 29 October 1929.
181 'cried out for music . . .', SM, p. 123.
181 'at a ridiculously small price . . .', PI, pp. 309–10.
182 'The house [was] . . . practically . . .', Patricia Frere interview, 22 October 1991.
182 'It was nice . . .', Katharine Hepburn, interview with author, 15 June 1992.
182 'a big jar of French coffee . . .', DFG.
182 'fearfully grand . . .', NC, letter to Violet Coward, undated.
182 'sweet little terrace . . .', ibid., 6 July 1927.
183 'ebony . . .', ibid., undated.
183 'the wrath of . . .', Connon, op. cit., pp. 268–9.
184 'with a hard black hat . . .', PI, p. 311.
185 'This reads like a Noel Coward play . . .', G. S. Street, reader's report, 22 July 1927, LCP.
185 'sinister smoothness', PI, p. 312.
185 'The curtain rose . . .', undated cutting.
185 'with my usual misguided . . .', *Play Parade* 3, p. xiii.
185 'Rotten!', undated cutting.
185 '. . . the gallery was right . . .', *Westminster Gazette*, 26 October 1927.
185 'a thin little play . . .', *Listener*, 12 October 1972.
185 'very slowly directed . . .', *Play Parade* 3, p. xiii.
186 'long string of abuse . . .', G. S. Street, reader's report, 22 July 1927, LCP.
186 'Dear Hubert . . .', Sir George Crichton, letter to Sir Hubert Montgomery, 25 July 1927, LCP.
187 'behaving on the whole . . .', PI, pp. 314–15.
187 'It was understandable . . .', *Evening Standard*, 25 November 1927.
187 'Is it a failure?', PI, p. 315.
187 'Ladies and gentlemen . . .', ibid., pp. 317–18.
188 'by the dispassionate courage . . .', Edward Marsh, *A Number of People*, Heinemann/Hamish Hamilton, 1939, p. 37.
188 'wholly admirable . . .', *Observer*, 27 November 1927.
188 'Just as the third act . . .', *The Sketch*, 7 December 1927.
188 'the most abysmal failure . . .', *Play Parade* 3, pp. x–xi.
188 'My first instinct . . .', PI, p. 319.
188 'quiet, lovely little house . . .', ibid., p. 325.
188 'very simple . . . sleeping . . .', NC, letter to Violet Coward, undated, 1927.
188 'exceedingly upset', PI, p. 325.
189 'marvellous', NC, letter to Violet Coward, undated, 1927.

12. Bitter Sweet

190 'cynical, intelligent dilettante . . .', *PI*, p. 326.
190 CROSSING SUNDAY . . ., NC, telegram to Basil Dean, 29 December 1927, JRL.
190 'a very sophisticated . . .', Castle, pp. 95–6.
190 'constantly breaking . . .', *PI*, p. 326.
190 'After all, if you were . . .', Castle, p. 96.
190 'Noel was in great form . . .', S. N. Behrman, *Tribulations and Laughter*, Hamish Hamilton, 1972, pp. 102–3.
191 'The actors' dressing rooms . . .', ibid., pp. 111–13.
191 'What I have seen of this revue . . .', undated cutting.
192 'the first eight bars . . .', Beverley Nichols, *Telegraph Magazine*, late 1960s.
193 'No, no . . .', Sheilagh Graham and Gerold Frank, *Beloved Infidel*, Cassell, 1958, p. 100.
193 '*This Year of Grace* . . .', *London Mercury*, vol. XVIII.
194 'If he turns his mind . . .', *London Mercury*, vol. XXV.
195 'I can never stay away . . .', *New York World*, 17 June 1928.
195 'the new phenomenon . . .', *PI*, p. 336.
195 'a melodramatic production . . .', Amherst, p. 97.
195 'a man of considerable reputation . . .', Katharine Hepburn, *Me*, Knopf, NY, 1991, p. 157.
195 'was looking for an actor . . .', Jones Harris, interview with author, 13 June 1992.
195 'Not at all . . .', Behrman, op. cit., p. 104.
195 'tore our emotions . . .', *PI*, pp. 336–8.
196 'news of the general fracas . . .', Erik Coward, letter to Violet Coward, 1 July 1928.
197 'new-found "grand" friends . . .', *PI*, p. 339.
197 'There were two houses . . .', Dorothy Dickson, interview with author, 3 July 1991.
198 'a little circle . . .', Frere interview.
198 'very tiresome. His mother . . .', Gielgud interview.
198 'Noel Coward Operated On . . .', *New York Times*, 28 August 1928.
199 'in love with Noel Coward . . .', *A Change of Perspective: The Letters of Virginia Woolf, vol. 3* (ed. Nigel Nicolson), The Hogarth Press, 1977, p. 471.
199 'struck me on the forehead . . .', SM, p. 125.
199 'He is in search . . .', *A Change of Perspective*, p. 478.
199 'Noel very simple and nice . . .', *Harold Nicolson Diaries 1930–1964* (ed. Stanley Olson), Collins, 1980, p. 21.
199 'I have been lunching with Sibyl . . .', *Leave the Letters Till We're Dead: The Letters of Virginia Woolf, vol. 4* (ed. Nigel Nicolson), The Hogarth Press, 1984, p. 523.
200 'I am still hot and glowing . . .', NC, letter to Virginia Woolf, undated, University of Sussex Library.
200 'devilish . . .', *PI*, p. 341.
201 'very charming and gracious . . .', Vickers, op. cit., p. 114.
201 'I do think the play . . .', ibid., p. 51.
201 'showed more aplomb . . .', Cecil Beaton, *Self-Portrait with Friends* (ed. Richard Buckle), Weidenfeld & Nicolson, 1979, pp. 11–12.
201 '. . . I, who usually . . .', NC, letter to Cecil Beaton, undated (? winter 1965).
202 'Every one of us . . .', Heppner, op. cit., p. 147.
202 'then rallied . . .', Harding, op. cit., p. 131.
202 'I submit . . .', *New Yorker*, 24 January 1977.
202 'in grandeur . . .', Amherst, p. 89.
202 '"I'm afraid I'd make . . ."', *Brooklyn Eagle*, 13 January 1929.

202 'I'd rather scrub floors . . .', Evelyn Laye, *Boo, to My Friends*, Hurst & Blackett, 1958, p. 92.
203 'lack of "star" manner . . .', *PI*, p. 350.
203 'on the assurance from Mr Coward . . .', Heppner, op. cit., pp. 264–5.
203 'who had been available . . .', *PI*, p. 350.
204 'terrific risk . . .', Alan Jenkins, *The Twenties*, Heinemann, 1974, p. 202.
204 'People are tired . . .', *Boston Transcript*, 29 October 1929.
204 'there is very little . . .', G. S. Street, reader's report, 19 June 1929, LCP.
204 'riotous . . .', *PI*, pp. 352–3.
205 'the commonplaceness . . .', *Evening Standard*, 19 July 1929.
205 'It would be too bad . . .', *PI*, p. 353.
205 'tongue in cheek', Heppner, op. cit., pp. 151–2.
205 'a thundering good job . . .', *Sunday Times*, 21 July 1929.
205 'Max took a great liking . . .', David Cecil, *Max*, Constable, 1964, p. 422.
206 'open secret', *Guardian*, 23 February 1988.
206 'the "green carnation" young men . . .', G. S. Street, reader's report, 19 June 1929, LCP.
206 'the "Green Carnation" . . .', Lord Cromer, 24 June 1929, LCP.
206 'What kind of person . . .', Stephen Tennant's journal, 17 February 1936, Estate of Stephen Tennant.
206 'the essence of all . . .', Mannin, op. cit., pp. 237–8.
207 'small-minded and foolish', *Daily Sketch*, 18 April 1932.
207 'tortured and all but broke . . .', *Twentieth-Century Authors*, pp. 159–60.
207 'watching the embryo . . .', undated cutting, 1929.
208 'with fire and grace . . .', *PI*, p. 355.
208 'rather neurotic . . .', ibid., p. 365.
208 'turned . . . inside out . . .', ibid., pp. 355–6.
208 'You find it faintly . . .', *Play Parade 1*, Heinemann, 1934, introduction.
208 'strongly elated . . .', *PI*, pp. 355–6.
208 'We saw just part . . .', Peggy Wood, interview with Dale Harris, 1965.
209 'We found him . . .', DFG.
209 'desperately sorry . . .', *PI*, p. 357.
209 'a very good-looking chap . . .', *Guardian*, 23 February 1988.
209 'Noel – who I knew . . .', *Daily Sketch*, 18 April 1932.
209 'the most triumphant success . . .', NC, letter to Violet Coward, 6 November 1929.
209 'ordered a rest . . .', *NC&F*, p. 81.
209 'probably the most distinguished . . .', NC, letter to Violet Coward, undated.
210 'in bland defiance . . .', *New York Times*, 10 November 1929.
210 'Everybody is losing millions . . .', NC, letter to Violet Coward, 6 November 1929.
210 'under a general sense of futility . . .', *PI*, p. 363.
210 'in a blaze of glory . . .', NC, letter to Violet Coward, 20 November 1929.
211 'whirled through . . .', *PI*, pp. 365–9.

13. Private Lives

213 'on a calm opalescent sea . . .', *PI*, p. 369.
213 'but the moment I switched . . .', ibid., p. 373.
213 'egg-bound . . .', Amherst, pp. 117–18.
214 'nasty', NC, letter to Violet Coward, 12 January 1930.
214 'strange . . . and, beneath . . .', *PI*, p. 374.
214 'in a heap . . .', Amherst, p. 119.
214 'a cross between Brussels . . .', NC, letter to Violet Coward, 31 January 1930.

214 'fairly rowdy . . .', *PI*, p. 377.
214 'propped up in bed . . .', Amherst, p. 123.
215 'while jungles and rivers . . .', *Collected Lyrics*, p. 103.
215 'long and demanding', Amherst, p. 127.
215 'I gave a sort of lachrymose . . .', *Listener*, 12 October 1961.
215 'vile libel . . .', Amherst, pp. 127–8.
216 'It's so beastly . . .', NC, letter to Violet Coward, undated.
216 'couldn't wait to get back . . .', Amherst, p. 128.
216 'Jack says I shall *never* . . .', NC, letter to Violet Coward, 20 November 1929.
216 'the "Coward emeralds" . . .', *Chips – The Diaries of Sir Henry Channon* (ed. Robert Rhodes James), Weidenfeld & Nicolson, 1967, p. 419.
217 'Life on board . . .', Amherst, p. 129.
218 'Christians astonish me . . .', Courtney, op. cit., p. 336.
218 'talked about . . .', Peter Parker, *Ackerley*, Constable, 1989.
219 'Mr Coward is afraid . . .', Sean O'Casey, *The Flying Wasp*, Macmillan, 1937, p. 160.
219 'I tore my emotions . . .', *PI*, pp. 390–1.
220 'I have never been so miserable . . .', Violet Coward, letter to Arthur Coward, CL, pp. 130–1.
220 'always one of faint . . .', NC and Judy Garland, *Redbook*, November 1961.
220 'uneasy truce . . .', CL, p. 131.
220 'an astounding sense . . .', *PI*, p. 394.
221 'What fascinates me . . .', Castle, p. 200.
221 'absolutely ridiculous . . .', Elspeth March, interview with author, 3 May 1991.
221 'didn't quite aspire . . .', Gielgud interview.
222 'lightest of light comedies . . .', *Listener*, 7 April 1966.
222 'missed the underlying sadness . . .', *Plays and Players*, undated cutting.
222 'Authors usually write . . .', M&M, p. 4.
223 '"I once wrote a play . . ."', Beverley Nichols, *Are They the Same at Home?*, Jonathan Cape, 1927, p. 106.
223 'Not seldom Mr Coward . . .', *New York Times*, undated cutting, 1926.
223 'wandered in and out . . .', Morley, *Gertrude Lawrence*, p. 79.
224 'Noel adored Larry . . .', CL, pp. 137–8.
224 'nearly passionate involvement . . .', Donald Spoto, *Laurence Olivier*, Harper-Collins, 1991, p. 53.
224 'Are you sure you said no?', Tarquin Olivier, *My Father, Laurence Olivier*, Headline, 1992, p. 256.
224 'He was a great mind-opener . . .', *Observer*, 9 February 1969.
224 'Dear 3381721 . . .', *The Letters of T. E. Lawrence* (ed. David Garnett), Spring Books, 1964, p. 723.
224 'finished product', ibid., p. 702.
225 'this "intimate comedy" . . .' G. S. Street, reader's report, 27 June 1930, LCP.
225 'caution in production . . .', Lord Cromer, 10 July 1930, LCP.
225 'weak and pointless . . .', London Public Morality Council, letter to Lord Chamberlain, 17 October 1930.
225 '. . . I have just had two girls to dinner . . .', Bishop of London, letter to Lord Chamberlain, 18 November 1930, LCP.
225 'Assurance of success . . .', *PI*, p. 394.
225 'full-scale fist-fight', Morley, *Gertrude Lawrence*, pp. 83–4.
225 'Well, you're fired . . .', Laffey, op. cit., p. 113.
226 'who knew the business . . .', *Theatre Arts Monthly*, New York, March 1933.
226 'which might seem in print . . .', *The Times*, 25 September 1930.

226 'as light and shiny as can be . . .', *Observer*, 29 September 1930.
226 'Punctually at the minute . . .', *NC&F*, p. 93.
227 'neurosis and incipient TB . . .', *Observer*, 3 July 1937.
227 'unprofessional', *PI*, pp. 395–6.
228 'Noel used to give . . .', Frere interview.
228 'high excitement', Stern, *Monogram*, p. 70.
229 'something to go silly over', CL, p. 142.
229 'an admirable piece of fluff', *New York World*, 28 January 1931.
229 'has nothing to say . . .', *New York Times*, 28 January 1931.
229 'They are only adults . . .', *New York Review*, undated cutting.
229 'For one thing . . .', NC, letter to Violet Coward, 8 Febuary and March 1931.
229 'rather have a nice cup . . .', ibid., undated.
230 'when business is always bad . . .', ibid.
230 'Darling Jilli . . .', Tarquin Olivier, op. cit., pp. 33–4.

14. Cavalcade

231 'Have you considered . . .', *The Letters of T. E. Lawrence*, p. 696.
231 'no detail of this . . .', SM, p. 153.
231 'awoke at 7.30 . . .', Tarquin Olivier, op. cit., p. 29.
232 'depressing business', *PI*, p. 404.
232 'fair hair . . .', Harding, op. cit., p. 120.
232 'electrify the assembled company', Heppner, op. cit., p. 173.
234 'known to have been stirred . . .', *New York Times*, 31 October 1931.
234 'I was told on all sides . . .', Milton Shulman interview, part five, *Sunday Express*, 1961.
234 'All the pent-up emotion . . .', John Lahr, *Coward the Playwright*, Methuen, 1982, pp. 99–101.
234 'God seemed to be . . .', PC, p. 251.
235 'Noel is getting a Cadillac . . .', Erik Coward, letter to Violet Coward, 14 June 1932.
235 'In spite of the hysterical scene . . .', O'Casey, op. cit., p. 33.
235 'Is this play, or pageant . . .', ibid. pp. 134–8.
235 A PLAY WHICH MAKES ME RAGE, *New Leader*, 29 January 1932.
236 'ought to be a white-hot . . .', Connon, op. cit., pp. 170–1.
236 'a most remarkable race . . .', PC, pp. 251–2.
237 'lofty studio apartment . . .', Amherst, p. 202.
237 'Each time when I'm shaving . . .', Robin Maugham, *The People*, February 1970.
237 'when there were at least . . .', Gielgud, op. cit.
237 'a page out of *Vanity Fair* . . .', Douglas Fairbanks Jnr, *The Salad Days*, Collins, 1988, p. 189.
238 'a party in the enlightened . . .', *New York Times*, 14 September 1980.
238 'became immediately a great favourite . . .', Lord Berners, *The Girls of Radcliff Hall*, privately published.
239 'flew very well . . .', Amherst, pp. 199–200.
239 'turned on her high . . .', ibid., pp. 134–5.
239 'quite terrifying . . .', NC, letter to Violet Coward, Christmas Day 1931.
240 'perfect food', ibid., 21 February 1932.
240 'a couple of fairly libidinous . . .', PC, p. 262.
240 'it really *isn't* very central', NC, letter to Violet Coward, 21 February 1932.
241 'piss-up', PC, pp. 267–73.

242 'greater even . . .', *Halliwell's 8th Film Guide* (ed. John Walker), HarperCollins, 1991, p. 197.
242 'Mr Coward has turned into . . .', *New York Herald-Tribune*, 29 January 1933.
242 'had heard that he and James Cagney . . .', Ned Rorem, interview with author, 12 June 1992.
242 'he had a rough and tumble . . .', Charles Russell, interview with author, 25 September 1992.
242 'work too deuced hard . . .', undated cutting.

15. Design for Living

244 'My mother said . . .', *Sunday Express* magazine, 24 January 1988.
244 'and said, "My mother" . . .', Joe Mitchenson, interview with author, 30 September 1991.
244 'a jaded, sulky . . .', Heppner, op. cit., pp. 178–9.
245 'Mad about the boy . . .', Graham Payn with Barry Day, *My Life with Noel Coward*, Applause Books, 1994, p. 4
245 'Although Noel loved . . .', *New York Post*, 18 December 1981.
245 'this sort of "gala" . . .', H. C. Game, reader's report, 13 August 1932, LCP.
245 'rehabilitated', *Sketch*, 28 September 1932.
245 'in this revue his satirical . . .', *The Times*, 17 September 1932.
246 'a sea voyage . . .', Erik Coward, letter to Violet Coward, undated.
246 'He seemed to have shrunk . . .', *PC*, p. 283.
246 'I also, in a moment . . .', ibid., p. 284.
246 'Auntie [Vida] . . .', DFG.
246 'Everything is so tragic . . .', NC, letter to Violet Coward, undated.
246 'Mr Noel Coward has gone abroad . . .', *The Times*, 28 September 1932.
247 'I'm trying to take your advice . . .', NC, letter to Violet Coward, undated.
247 'disgusted at the size . . .', Philip Ziegler, *Mountbatten*, Collins, 1985, p. 109.
247 'scattering largesse . . .', *New York Herald-Tribune*, 1 December 1932.
247 'bliss . . .', NC, letter to Violet Coward, 10 December 1932.
248 'Somehow, by a sort of underground . . .', undated cutting.
248 'the play is a wow . . .', NC, letter to Erik Coward, undated.
250 'Coward's comic revenge . . .', Lahr, op. cit., p. 83
250 'The house [was] full . . .', Amherst, p. 199.
250 'Oh Darling, a very sad letter . . .', NC, letter to Violet Coward, 10 January 1933.
251 'cut the cackle . . .', *New York Times*, 25 January 1933.
251 'delightful', *PC*, p. 285.
251 'four shabby men', *New York Herald-Tribune*, 17 May 1933.
252 'with piercing blue eyes . . .', *PC*, p. 287.
253 'confused', *Sunday Times*, 19 February 1934.
253 'I have given up . . .', Connon, op. cit., p. 179.
253 'lacked the romantic quality . . .', Heppner, op.cit., p. 173.
254 'I have decided . . .', ibid., pp. 204–5.
254 'taken a malicious pleasure . . .', Harding, op. cit., p. 152.
254 'This is just to tell you . . .', NC, letter to Virginia Woolf, 17 November 1933, University of Sussex.
254 'on a cold foggy night . . .', *The Diaries of Virginia Woolf*, vol. 4 (ed. Anne Olivier Bell), Hogarth Press, 1982, p. 200.
254 '. . . I have to dine with Colefax . . .', *The Sickle Side of the Moon: The Letters of Virginia Woolf*, vol. 5 (ed. Nigel Nicolson), Hogarth Press, 1971, p. 273.
254 'called me Darling . . .', ibid., pp. 276–7.

255 '... Colefax writes ...', ibid., p. 312.
255 'insinuating ...', Woolf, *Diaries, vol.* 4, p. 279.
255 'Talk at dinner ...', ibid., p. 259.
255 'a lunch party ...', Stephen Tennant, journal, 7 October 1935.
255 'in those days Noel was inclined ...', Amherst, p. 215.
256 'I met you ...', *New York Post*, 17 November 1957.

16. Tonight at 8.30

257 'friendly agreement', *New York Times*, 1 August 1937.
257 '"*dis-ah-ster*" ...', Behrman, op. cit., p. 199.
258 'Yes, it was bought ...', undated cutting.
259 'When I went in 1929 ...', Roy Williams, interview with author.
259 'saved him a lot ...', Bert Lister, interview with author, 3 June 1992.
259 'I think Noel must ...', Williams interview.
259 'pretty little pink seals', CL, p. 168.
260 'a partial cleansing', *Halliwell*, op. cit., p. 288.
260 'There's only one line of Coward's ...', SM, p. 180.
260 'an improvement ...', *Halliwell*, p. 288.
260 'The play was trash ...', Martin Bauml Duberman, *Paul Robeson*, Bodley Head, 1989, p. 614.
260 'I had a talk with NC ...', ibid., p. 146.
260 'no evidence ...', Duberman, interview with author.
260 'stopped traffic ...', Duberman, p. 147.
261 'the ill and needy ...', undated cutting.
261 'Dear dainty Darling ...', Brian Hoey, *Mountbatten – The Private Story*, Sidgwick & Jackson, 1994, p. 94.
262 'fainting French Captain ...', CL, p. 166.
262 'in a critical condition ...', undated cutting.
263 'passing dull', *New York Times*, undated cutting.
263 'honestly attempting ...', *Play Parade 6*, Heinemann, 1962, p. ix.
264 'Nonsense! ...', Jared Brown, op. cit., p. 218.
264 'soggy and comatose ...', FI, p. 324.
264 'the public didn't like it ...', DFG.
264 'out of the innocent desire ...', William Marchant, *The Privilege of His Company*, Bobbs-Merrill, Indianapolis/New York, 1975, p. 262.
264 'the kind of thing ...', O'Casey, op. cit., p. 159.
265 'We have got to go very, very easy ...', Lorn Loraine, letter to Violet Coward, April 1935; quoted in Clive Fisher, *Noel Coward*, Weidenfeld & Nicolson, 1992, p. 117.
265 'a holiday from Hollywood ...', Ian Hamilton, *Writers in Hollywood*, Heinemann, 1991, pp. 31–2.
265 'What really induced me ...', undated cutting.
266 'Noel Coward's feminine following ...', undated cutting.
267 'In my private fantasy ...', Alan Jenkins, *Remembering the Thirties*, Heinemann, 1976.
267 'The picture was made quickly ...', FI, pp. 206–7.
267 'unpleasant characters ...', undated cutting.
267 'a singularly adult picture ...', *New York Sun*, undated cutting.
267 'Coward's finest screen performance ...', *The Movie*, Orbis, 1980, p. 2473.
267 'I thought I was very good ...', interview with Harvey Brett, undated cutting.

267 'I act with an incredible swiftness . . .', Marlene Dietrich, *My Life* (trans. Salvator Attansio), Weidenfeld & Nicolson, 1989, p. 138.

268 'kinder, nicer than "normal men"', Steve Bach, *Dietrich*, HarperCollins, 1992, pp. 469–70.

268 'Our relationship repeatedly . . .', Dietrich, op. cit., p. 138.

268 'Marlenah! . . .', Maria Riva, *Marlene Dietrich*, Bloomsbury, 1992, p. 446.

268 'For Dietrich, it was his style . . .', ibid., p. 698.

268 'What is there in it for you? . . .', CL, p. 173.

269 'elliptical patter', Tynan, National Theatre programme.

270 'the best short comedy . . .', M&M, p. 5.

270 'a sly satire . . .', M&M, p. 230.

270 'short play, having a great advantage . . .', ibid., p. 197.

271 'Believe me, Noel . . .', CL, p. 177.

271 'variety of the progamme . . .', *Observer*, 19 January 1936.

271 'theatrical success . . .', *The Times*, 10 January 1936.

271 'second-rate entertainment', *Daily Mail*, 10 January 1936.

271 'I love criticism . . .', 'Let's Do It' programme, Chichester Theatre, 1994.

271 'He signalled for the orchestra . . .', Barbara Ker-Seymer, letter to author, 8 October 1991.

271 EVERYTHING LOVELY . . ., Morley, *Gertrude Lawrence*, p. 121.

271 '"Oh, they *hated* each other . . ."', Russell interview.

272 'What would you say . . .', CL, p. 181.

272 'I remember reading . . .', Vivian Matalon, interview with author, 13 June 1992.

272 'I wish I were dead . . .', CL, p. 193.

272 'He was . . . a vain man', Rebecca West, obituary, 1 April 1972, typescript, McFarlin Library, University of Tulsa.

273 'After dinner, Rubinstein . . .', *Harold Nicolson Diaries 1930–1964* (ed. Stanley Olson), Collins, 1980, p. 99.

273 'Noel, I have a dreadful feeling . . .', CL, p. 182.

273 'gilded', ibid., p. 184.

273 'emphatically not . . .', D, p. 677.

274 'Noel wouldn't even walk . . .', Russell interview.

274 'Alan Webb was his best critic . . .', Gielgud interview.

274 'Short, masculine . . .', Russell interview.

274 'consult your . . . favourite astrologist', *New York Times*, 24 November 1936.

276 '. . . I doubt if he has had . . .', *Observer*, 3 July 1937.

276 'I doubt if Mr Coward . . .', *The Times*, 13 November 1969.

276 'I can't tell you how very much . . .', NC, letter to St John Ervine, undated, HRHC.

276 'When I read a novel . . .', ibid., undated (?1927), HRHC.

276 'glibness was all', *Observer*, 10 July 1937.

277 'almost always shallow . . .', NC&F, p. 127.

277 'Mr Coward, with his frisky . . .', *Sunday Referee*, 8 November 1936.

277 'I've always felt that Mr Coward's . . .', Marie-Jacques Lancaster, *Brian Howard: Portrait of a Failure*, Anthony Blond, 1968, p. 483.

17. To Step Aside

279 'There is a brief reference to fetishism . . .', H. C. Game, reader's report (additional note), 14 May 1938, LCP.

279 'Very *bijou*, my dear', Richard Huggett, *Binkie Beaumont*, Hodder & Stoughton, 1989, p. 75.

279 'Binkie Beaumont could charm . . .', Bert Lister, interview with author, 11 March 1991, p. 58.
280 'took great satisfaction . . .', John Osborne, *Almost a Gentleman*, Faber, 1991
280 'sinister, possibly haunted . . .', Vickers, op. cit., p. 202.
280 'I never went to the theatre . . .', Fritzi Massary, interview with Dale Harris, June 1963.
281 'I will not kiss . . .', DFG
281 'Alan, you're no bloody good . . .', Huggett, op. cit., p. 207.
282 'her quality of beauty . . .', Vickers, op. cit., p. 182.
282 'Telephone conversations . . .', Cecil Beaton, unpublished diary, 1935.
282 '"Who? Me!" . . .', *New York News*, 7 September 1937.
282 'I think he has the best critical . . .', Ward Morehouse, 'Broadway After Dark', undated cutting.
282 'Jack took to drink . . .', DFG.
283 'wasn't of Noel's calibre . . .', Hepburn interview.
283 'I shall keep your twaddly letter . . .', CL, pp. 191–2.
284 'he came always very late . . .', Massey interview with Harris.
284 'Noel was a perfectionist . . .', Linda Gray, letter to Robert Wennersten, 1974.
284 '*Operette* was not one . . .', Alfred Lunt, letter to Robert Wennersten, 28 June 1974.
284 'disappointed in the music . . .', Massey interview with Harris.
284 'a great mistake', CL, pp. 194–5.
284 'whether Mr Coward's tunes . . .', *The Times*, 16 March 1938.
284 'the eminents of College . . .', *The Sketch*, undated.
285 'like an over-ripe plum . . .', PC.
285 'on his uppers . . .', Robin Maugham, *Conversations with Willie*, pp. 45–70.
286 'He cared about the political . . .', Robert Rhodes James, *Bob Boothby*, John Curtis/Hodder & Stoughton, 1991.
286 'So what else is new?', *Daily Mail*, 21 January 1989.
286 'This is the most disgraceful thing . . .', Laffey, op cit., p. 112.
287 'at their best . . .', *New York Times*, 19 January 1939.
288 'still retained unromanticised memories . . .', *Sunday Times*, 22 December 1985.
288 'a real masterpiece . . .', CL, p. 202.
289 'peculiar neatness . . .', *Sunday Times*, 22 December 1985.
290 'Poor Oscar Wilde . . .', D, p. 135.

18. Present Laughter

292 'the play is pure Coward . . .', H. C. Game, reader's report, 11 September 1938, LCP.
292 'an injurious influence', reports submitted by the Public Morality Council, April 1939, LCP.
292 'The Theatre is *not* a pulpit', Major Gwatkin, 19 April 1939, LCP.
293 'barge at each other . . .', O'Casey, op. cit., p. 152.
293 'like piddling on flannel . . .', CL, pp. 204–5.
295 'You never felt . . .', Anna Murray, interview with author.
296 'to see what was . . .', FI, p. 9.
296 'musicians, artists, critics . . .', ibid.
297 'an innocuous little man . . .', ibid., p. 25.
297 'who seemed to have stepped . . .', ibid., pp. 28–9.
298 'There we found a small party . . .', Robert Boothby, *Boothby, a Rebel Remembers*, Hutchinson, 1978, p. 78.

298 'some of my lighter songs', *FI*, p. 51.
298 'He was very depressed . . .', Boothby, op. cit., p. 78.
298 'bungled this moment . . .', *FI*, pp. 56–80.
300 'With a few individual exceptions . . .', *PC*, p. 278.
301 'should surely be cut . . .', G. Dearmer, 12 July 1939, LCP.
301 'I always feel that the British . . .', Sir Alexander Hardinge, 7 September 1942, LCP.
301 'from above to above . . .', Lahr, op. cit., p. 104.
302 'A lot of nonsense . . .', *FI*, p. 65.
302 'What the bloody hell . . .', ibid., p. 77.
302 'It wasn't Coward's cup . . .', *The Spectator*, 17/24 December 1994.
303 'bogus', *FI*, p. 84.
303 'in no uncertain terms . . .', ibid., p. 86.
303 'a ridiculous organisation . . .', Boothby, op. cit., p. 78.
303 'On the whole, I think . . .', undated cutting.
304 'One climbed up a rickety . . .', Amherst, p. 203.
304 'dip your tool . . .', Elspeth March, interview with author, 3 May 1991.
304 'Winifred used to go mad . . .', Judy Campbell, interview with author, 28 June 1991.

19. Could You Please Oblige Us with a Bren Gun?

306 'men of apparent integrity . . .', *FI*, p. 94.
306 'victimised, even more than usual . . .', ibid., p. 101.
306 'hissing unutterable secrets . . .', Milton Shulman interview, part four, *Sunday Express*, 1961.
306 'sauntering along . . .', *FI*, p. 102.
307 'Carefully selected Britishers . . .', Jean Mond, *The Mond Legacy*, Weidenfeld & Nicolson, 1982, p. 28.
307 'to arrange with his agent . . .', *New York Times*, 30 April 1940.
308 'political treacheries . . .', *FI*, p. 123.
308 'general hysteria . . .', ibid., p. 129.
309 'a big hug of praise . . .', Hepburn, op. cit., p. 243.
309 'beyond all logic . . .', *FI*, p. 141.
309 'six-week furlough . . .', *New York Times*, 10 June 1940.
310 'which, in his opinion . . .', William Stevenson, *A Man Called Intrepid*, Charnwood, 1976, p. 97.
310 'confusing talk . . .', ibid., pp. 198–9.
311 'on a mission for Lord Alfred . . .', *New York Times*, 30 July 1940.
311 'I left the school . . .', Roy Williams interview.
312 'celebrity value', Stevenson, op. cit., pp. 199–200.
312 'Commons Questions Coward's Visit . . .', *New York Times*, 7 August 1940.
312 'Mr Noel Coward has gone . . .', Parliamentary Debates, vol. 364, 1939–40, HMS 1940.
313 'What do you think about Noel Coward . . .', Joyce Grenfell, *Darling Ma* (ed. James Roose-Evans), Hodder & Stoughton, 1988, p. 158.
313 'It seems unfortunate . . .', *New York Times*, 9 August 1940.
313 'The actor was bronzed . . .', undated cutting.
314 'who is fast becoming . . .', Dixie Tighe, undated cutting.
314 'Dear Mrs A. Hooray Hooray . . .', SM, p. 214.
314 'Hope you get a warm hand . . .', *Daily Mirror*, 10 October 1987.
315 'something of great importance . . .', *FI*, p. 160.
315 'tough American seaman . . .', ibid., pp. 162–3.

315 'Mayfair witticisms', ibid., pp. 167–8.
315 'a fair, tough young man . . .', ibid., p. 174.
316 'You see – he can't take . . .', ibid., p. 185.
316 'local conflicts . . .', ibid., pp. 192–4.
316 APRIL 2ND . . ., CL, pp. 216–17.
317 'virtually cut . . .', D, p. 355.
317 'You know, dear, the trouble . . .', FI, pp. 198 9.
318 'every hair pinned on end . . .', Philip Hoare, *Serious Pleasures*, Hamish Hamilton, 1990, p. 258.
318 'charm and quality . . .', FI, pp. 201–2.

20. Play Parade

319 'masterstroke of unimaginative stupidity . . .', Morley, *Gertrude Lawrence*.
319 'Spent the morning with Lorn . . .', Noel Coward diary, 22 April 1941.
320 'Disdaining archness . . .', FI, p. 204.
320 'a character takes hold . . .', Cecil Beaton diary, India.
320 '*Blithe Spirit* . . . the only play . . .', Matalon interview, 13 June 1992.
321 'Will you explain . . .', Huggett, op. cit., p. 268.
321 'The audience . . .', FI, p. 205.
321 'Rubbish . . .', Lahr, op. cit., p. 142.
321 'a weary exhibition . . .', D, p. 18.
321 'I thought it was terribly . . .', Gielgud interview.
322 'Should We Laugh . . .', Revd James Colville, *Star*, 18 July 1941.
322 'Christ! It must be tatty . . .', Timothy Morgan-Owen, interview with author.
322 'He got the idea . . .', Havelock-Allan interview.
322 'In my experience . . .', Ziegler, op. cit., p. 122.
323 'out of the 240 men . . .', ibid., p. 127.
323 'About three weeks later . . .', Havelock-Allan interview.
323 'Noel is an expert . . .', *Nova* magazine, June 1973.
324 'three or four . . .', Michael Redgrave, *In My Mind's Eye*, Weidenfeld & Nicolson, 1983, p. 151.
324 'much of Noel's material . . .', Joy Packer, note on NC's letter to Captain Packer, 18 November 1942; Churchill College, Cambridge.
324 'I was astonished . . .', ibid., 11 October 1942.
324 'Of course I could . . .', Caroline Moorehead, *Sidney Bernstein*, Jonathan Cape, 1984, p. 149.
324 'There was a slight silence . . .', Havelock-Allan interview.
325 'Noel and I have never . . .', Cecil Beaton diary, January 1942.
326 'I'm much too old . . .', Havelock-Allan interview.
327 'it is important to remember . . .', Gerald Pratley, *The Cinema of David Lean*, Tanting Press, 1974, p. 26.
328 'Laard Mountbatten', Anne Chisholm and Michael Davie, *Beaverbrook*, Hutchinson, 1992, p. 493.
328 'talked for hours . . .', Kate Fleming, *Celia Johnson*, Weidenfeld & Nicholson, 1991, p. 97.
328 'doing the *Times* crossword . . .', Judy Campbell interview.
328 'After six weeks, he was . . .', Havelock-Allan interview.
328 'extravagant to the point . . .', FI, p. 209.
329 'a gathering of pansies . . .', Charles Ritchie, *The Siren Years*, Macmillan, 1974, p. 125.
330 'a lot of the Hollywood . . .', D, p. 95.

330 'without the Treasury's consent . . .', *New York Times*, 31 October 1942.
330 'Mr Coward testified . . .', *New York Times*, 31 October 1941.
330 'large fine . . .', undated cutting.
331 'The preponderance of naval uniforms . . .', *FI*, p. 231.
331 'escaping being one of . . .', Charles Russell interview.
332 'Noel was finding it . . .', Judy Campbell interview.
332 'You know of course, Noel . . .', *Evening Standard*, 18 January 1990.
332 'I was engaged on a pleasant . . .', *FI*, p. 233.
332 'Don't show him any of your music . . .', Neville Phillips, interview with author, 6 July 1992.
332 'Robb was beautiful . . .', Lister interview.
332 'Robb used to say . . .', Gail Kendall, interview with author, 10 January 1991.
332 'great fun . . .', Campbell interview.
333 'hostile aborigines . . .', *FI*, p. 233.
333 'a first rate play . . .', Cecil Beaton diary.
334 'a perfect piece of escapist froth . . .', Grenfell, op. cit., pp. 292–4.
334 'I was absolutely in love . . .', Campbell interview.
335 'as he was having his bath . . .' *Harold Nicolson Diaries*, p. 283.
335 'I have had a bloody awful . . .', NC, letter to Cecil Beaton, 30 March 1943.
335 'with a fervour . . .', *FI*, p. 236.
335 'secretary-cum-dogsbody', Lister interview, 11 March 1991.
336 'where I considered . . .', *FI*, p. 238.
336 'the second act sees the wittily . . .', *The Times*, 30 April 1943.
336 'Mr Coward keeps firm control . . .', *The Times*, 1 May 1943.
336 'It was very glamorous . . .', Russell interview with author, 28 November 1990.
336 'Noel Coward was very generous . . .', Pratley, op. cit., p. 41.
336 'In the strictest sense . . .', C. A. Lejeune, *Observer*, undated.
337 'It was pleasant to be concerned . . .', *FI*, p. 239.
337 'detached and patronising . . .', Pratley, op. cit., p. 43.

21. Don't Let's Be Beastly

338 'fell automatically . . .', *FI*, p. 243.
338 'The critics might not . . .', private information.
338 'all deeply sunburned . . .', *MED*, pp. 13–14.
339 'that Noel was almost hoarse . . .', Robin Maugham, op. cit., p. 138.
339 'If I were Noel Coward . . .', undated cutting.
339 'appalling taste . . .', *D*, p. 222.
339 'the satire . . . was surely . . .', *MED*, p. 118.
339 'We are bitterly disgusted . . .', undated cutting.
339 'It is cynical, sarcastic . . .', *New York Times*, undated cutting.
339 'most meticulously . . .', *MED*, p. 249.
339 'undeniably a mistake . . .', CL, p. 215.
340 'six foot, youngish . . .', *MED*, pp. 41–5.
340 'far from well . . .', ibid., p. 49.
340 'as I had only had a beer . . .', ibid., p. 53.
340 'bathed in glamorous corruption . . .', Artemis Cooper, *Cairo in the War*, Hamish Hamilton, 1989, p. 250.
340 'run by some colonel . . .', Robert Flemyng, interview with author, 8 July 1992.
341 'If looks could have killed . . .', Artemis Cooper, op. cit., p. 253.
341 'I thought, what an ordeal! . . .', Peter Daubeny, *My World of Theatre*, Jonathan Cape, 1971, p. 29.

341 'performing for the troops . . .', *Redbook*, November 1964.
341 'among those broken . . .', Johannesburg *Star*, 4 April 1944.
341 'I talked to some tough men . . .', *MED*, p. 106.
342 'to confer with the Internal . . .', undated cutting.
342 'almost intolerably shiny . . .', *FI*, p. 270.
342 'The spell was cast . . .', ibid., p. 274.
343 'I wanted to see . . .', Matalon interview.
343 'in a suicidal rage . . .', *FI*, pp. 278–82.
344 'the greatest entrepreneur . . .', Lister interview, 11 March 1991.
344 'best known to you . . .', *Cape Argus*, 19 February 1944.
344 'the crowds melted away . . .', *FI*, p. 287.
345 'She was wearing a dress . . .', Lister interview.
345 'bore the bejesus . . .', SM, p. 245.
345 'he went on and made a right . . .', Lister interview.
345 'I have never been so nervous . . .', *FI*, pp. 290–1.
346 'must have formed a queer impression . . .', *Cape Argus*, February/March 1944.
346 'with some garbled talk . . .', *FI*, p. 293.
346 'tall, slim . . .', Emlyn Williams, *Emlyn*, Bodley Head, 1973, p. 80.
346 'found himself . . . at a party . . .', Roy Moseley, interview with author, 29 April 1992.
347 'before anyone could stop me', *FI*, p. 296.
348 'Noel Coward – In Selections . . .', programme, Palace Theatre, Bulawayo, TM484.
348 'I knew he would not have asked . . .', *FI*, p. 300.
348 'living the life . . .', Lister interview.
349 'an authentic foretaste . . .', *FI*, p. 306.
349 'two thousand coloured troops . . .', ibid., p. 315.
349 'He's too slick . . .', Vickers, op. cit., p. 289.
349 'the Pansies' Parlour . . .', ibid., p. 275.
349 'the more I see . . .', Beaton diary, 1944.
350 'It was in colour . . .', Lees-Milne, op. cit., p. 71.
351 'We all thought . . .', Mary Ellis, interview with author, 6 May 1992.
351 'full page of unqualified abuse . . .', *FI*, p. 324.
351 'oblivious to the fact . . .', *Daily Express*, 1 April 1973.
351 'kick this bum . . .', undated cutting.
352 'a quick drink . . .', *Brooklyn Daily Eagle*, 12 November 1944.
352 'a quite useless member . . .', ibid., 14 November 1944.
352 'If he tries to come back . . .', undated cutting.
352 'for the libel . . .', *New York Herald-Tribune*, 29 November 1944.
352 'I happened to recall . . .', *New York Post*, 5 December 1944.
352 'a tiresome experience . . .', *FI*, p. 325.
353 'I believe him . . .', *D*, p. 25.
353 'film drinking party . . .', Lees-Milne, op. cit., p. 152.
353 'Emerald [Cunard] recounted . . .', ibid., p. 189.
353 'terrible rows . . .', Lister interview, 3 June 1992.
353 'Just photograph it . . .', Alexander Walker, *Fatal Charm*, Weidenfeld & Nicolson, 1992, p. 105.
353 'After the film . . .', Nicholas Wapshott, *Rex Harrison*, Chatto & Windus, 1991, p. 84.
354 'when he's got . . .', Havelock-Allan interview.
354 'the time was right . . .', Pratley, op. cit., p. 49.
354 'There were only four of us . . .', *FI*, p. 328.

354 'There he was . . .', *D*, p. 26.
355 'as in all celebrations . . .', *FI*, p. 328.

22. Peace in Our Time

356 'conjuring trick', Sheridan Morley to author, 22 July 1991.
357 'I was always with aunts . . .', Payn interview, 21–22 September 1992.
357 'our leading *jeune premier* . . .', *The British Theatre Yearbook* (ed. Peter Noble), British Yearbooks, 1946, p. 316.
357 'Soldiers would immediately suspect . . .', Payn interview.
358 'With hair as shiny . . .', Marchant, op. cit., pp. 41–2.
358 'Nobody ever lasted . . .', Lister interview, 11 March 1991.
359 *'coup de foudre* . . .', Frere interview.
359 'the great grand passion . . .', DFG.
359 'He was quick and intelligent . . .', CL, p. 235.
359 'that he wrote "Matelot" . . .', Matalon interview.
359 'the first film which dealt with . . .', Robertson, op. cit., p. 160.
360 'luck, but you won't have any . . .', Pratley, op. cit., p. 52.
360 'by the time we got to shooting . . .', Havelock-Allan interview.
360 'reasonably jaunty . . .', *Three British Screenplays* (ed. Roger Manvell), Methuen, 1950, p. 6.
360 'Not like that . . .', Havelock-Allan interview.
361 'The thing I like best . . .', *File on Coward* (ed. Jacqui Russell), Methuen, 1987, p. 87.
361 'Isn't 'e ever goin' . . .', *Three British Screenplays*, introduction.
362 'Forget about the picture you made . . .', Vivienne Knight, *Trevor Howard*, Muller, Blond & White, 1988, p. 106.
362 'how he evaded fire-watching . . .', *D*, p. 50.
362 'a shoddy lot . . .', ibid., p. 31.
362 'My dear . . .', *FI*, p. 113.
363 'raucous vulgarity . . .', *D*, p. 36.
363 'good for box-office . . .', ibid., p. 38.
363 'lacked wit . . .', *The British Theatre Yearbook*, pp. 173–5.
364 'thrown him out . . .', Russell interview, 24 September 1994.
364 'An evening of enchantment . . .', *D*, p. 41.
365 'in before dinner . . .', Hoare, op. cit., p. 281.
365 'a cute party . . .', *Well Dearie* (ed. William Chappell), Gordon Fraser, 1988, p. 126.
365 'talked about herself . . .', *D*, p. 54.
365 'The Queen thanked me . . .', ibid., p. 56.
366 'They don't forgive lightly . . .', Jon Wynne-Tyson to author.
366 'there can be little doubt . . .', R. L. Calder, *The Life of Somerset Maugham*, Heinemann, 1989, p. 322.
366 'if Winston Churchill has been obstructive . . .', *D*, pp. 19–20.
366 'Noel broke down . . .', Lister interview, 3 June 1992.
366 'We've just had a Cabinet . . .', *Daily Express*, 1 April 1973.
366 'I was told that the King . . .', *Daily Mail*, 29 October 1969.
367 'nervous . . . did his numbers . . .', *D*, p. 57.
367 'everybody fell in love . . .', *Play Parade* 5, p. xxii.
368 '"star grandeur" . . .', Russell interview, 28 November 1990.
368 'a wonderful husband . . .', Lance Hamilton, unpublished memoir.
368 'He has obviously changed . . .', *D*, p. 64.

368 'unhappy stories . . .', ibid., p. 51.
368 'I see clearly . . .', ibid., pp. 64–7.
369 'Doesn't she look pretty . . .', CL, p. 185.
369 '*at last* showing signs . . .', D, p. 69.
369 'either that, or Mary . . .', Payn interview.
369 'Gladys rather took a fancy . . .', Russell interview, 9 January 1991.
369 'really triumphant . . .', D, pp. 71–2.
370 'It was just after the war . . .', Russell interview, 9 January 1991.
370 'if the critics and the public . . .', D, p. 73.
370 'bossed his friends about . . .', Gielgud interview.
371 'whose big chance . . .', D, p. 83.
371 'the most almighty slosh . . .', Johannesburg *Star*, 19 May 1982.
371 'atmosphere of subtle disintegration . . .', *Play Parade* 6, introduction.
372 'Oh Mr Coward, sir! . . .', Kenneth More, *More or Less*, Hodder & Stoughton, 1978, p. 122.
372 'I shan't jump on you . . .', Dirk Bogarde, *Snakes and Ladders*, Chatto & Windus, 1978, p. 237.
372 'a fairly silly holiday audience . . .', D, p. 87.
372 'the applause was like a cannon . . .', Elspeth March, interview with author, 3 May 1991.
372 'to add to the Coward . . .', D, p. 87.
373 'a curious character . . .', ibid., pp. 90–4.
374 'for his kindness in letting them . . .', undated cutting.
375 'Graham better than ever . . .', D, p. 96.
375 'allowed his heart . . .', Banbury interview, 30 April 1991.

23. Island Fling

376 'a great place . . .', Morris Cargill, interview with author, 12 September 1993.
376 'for a brief spell . . .', *The Letters of Ann Fleming* (ed. Mark Amory), Collins, 1985, p. 56.
377 'We are the only heterosexual household . . .', ibid., p. 151.
378 'So far, it all seems . . .', D, pp. 107–9.
378 'did a two-hour . . .', Gore Vidal, letter to author, 18 December 1991.
378 'clapped into a nursing home . . .', D, p. 112.
378 'a sort of glossy figurehead . . .', Woodcock interview.
378 'a middle-aged lady . . .', Leslie Smith, interview with author.
378 'a lesbian row . . .', Frere interview.
378 'Gladys was snarling . . .', D, p. 634.
379 'Joyce Carey and she . . .', Woodcock interview.
379 'the most chic . . .', D, pp. 114–15.
380 'she does not go . . .', ibid., p. 121.
380 'Was ever a mind so mean . . .', Noel Coward, *Collected Verse*.
380 'Good God! . . .', Payn interview, 30 September 1993.
380 'This meant that all those . . .', Lance Hamilton, unpublished memoir.
381 'He didn't have a life . . .', Lister interview.
381 'Coley paints better than I do . . .', Rebecca West, obituary of NC.
381 'give way completely . . .', CL, p. 276.
382 'self-justification . . .', D, p. 152.
382 'quite quite horrid . . .', ibid., pp. 124–5.
382 'Everybody is so *decent* . . .', C. A. Lejeune, *Observer*, undated cutting.
383 'totally stilted . . .', Havelock-Allan interview.

383 'I have never yet . . .', *D*, p. 136.
384 'It would have cost £9000 . . .', Russell interview.
384 '*Fallen Angels* a terrific success . . .', *D*, p. 138.
384 'I am getting sick . . .', ibid.
384 'started off as another . . .', Neville Phillips, interview with author, 6 July 1992.
384 'she would rather be in a flop . . .', *D*, pp. 145–6.
385 'At least it anticipated . . .', *Play Parade 6*, introduction.
385 'The jeers and catcalls . . .', Johannesburg *Star*, 27 April 1982.
385 'Oh Christ! It seems . . .', *D*, p. 153.
385 'after Elsie April . . .', Lister interview, 3 June 1992.
385 'He was very badly paid . . .', Phillips interview.
386 'Dear Noel, so blessed . . .', Gary Carey, *Anita Loos*, Bloomsbury, 1988, p. 226.
386 'bitched the play . . .', *D*, pp. 174–5.
386 'Obviously I could get . . .', ibid., p. 154.
387 'having worked . . .', Amherst, p. 202.
387 'You sit there . . .', SM, p. 267.
387 'a small cluster . . .', *FI*, p. 188.
388 'pre-face', Marchant, op. cit., p. 158.
388 'lovely and . . . at her best . . .', *D*, pp. 165–6.
388 'who was himself resolutely . . .', Peter Quennell, letter to author, 21 October 1991.
389 'it really could be . . .', *D*, p. 157.
389 'Oh, the bliss . . .', ibid., pp. 167–8.
390 '*Relative Values* was . . .', Sewell Stokes, *Without Veils*, Peter Davies, 1953, p. 217.
390 'I did not expect . . .', ibid., p. 14.
390 'very bad-tempered . . .', Campbell interview.
390 'Beaumont knew that it might . . .', Banbury interview, 30 April 1991.
390 'Happily, his latest play . . .', *Sunday Times*, 2 December 1951.
390 'Well, well, what a suprise! . . .', *D*, pp. 180–1.

24. A Bouquet of Violets

392 'his personality almost persuaded . . .', *Sunday Times*, 14 September 1952.
392 'I can't sing . . .', *Observer*, NC interview with John Heilpern, undated, 1969.
392 'came thudding down . . .', *Evening Standard*, 2 July 1953.
393 'triumphant success . . .', *D*, p. 182.
393 'alarmed. Never said so . . .', Dirk Bogarde, letter to author, 1 December 1991.
393 'I don't see why not . . .', private information.
393 'a horrible shock . . .', *D*, p. 188.
393 'he continues to pose . . .', *Letters of Ann Fleming*.
393 'an entirely hysterical affair . . .', Castle, pp. 190–4.
394 'suppressed nervous breakdown . . .', *D*, p. 191.
394 'fattish with white hair . . .', ibid., p. 194.
394 'to have the world . . .', EWT letter, 24 February 1980.
395 'one of the singing . . .', *Tatler*, 21 January 1953.
395 'I am utterly enchanted . . .', *D*, p. 193*n*.
395 'a truly terrifying sight . . .', ibid., p. 197.
395 'looking exactly like an old Baboon . . .', Hoare, op. cit., p. 124.
395 'in an apartment . . .', *D*, p. 197.
395 'Did you hear the one o'clock . . .', Frere interview.
395 'in between phone calls', *D*, p. 198.
395 'We first worked together . . .', Morley, *Gertrude Lawrence*, p. 198.
396 'but no words from the Lunts . . .', *D*, p. 198.

396 'That same day . . .', Peter Quennell, *The Wanton Chase*, Collins, 1980, pp. 147–8.

397 'owing to a recent . . .', D, p. 202.

397 'veteran propagandist', Victor Serge, *Memoirs of a Revolutionary* (trans. Peter Sedgwick), Writers & Readers, NY, 1984, p. xvii.

397 'Coward told him . . .', *The Times*, 24 November 1952.

397 'a complete fabrication . . .', *The Times*, 29 November 1952.

397 'wear your oldest clothes . . .', Skelton, op. cit., pp. 142–3.

397 'The food was awful . . .', John Pringle, interview with author, 12 September 1991.

398 'in watercolours . . .', CL, p. 239.

398 'rather naive . . .', Sheridan Morley, *Out in the Midday Sun: The Paintings of Noel Coward*, Phaidon/Christie's, 1988, p. 8.

398 'Both at the same time . . .', G. B. Stern, *Monogram*, pp. 218–19.

398 'pretty good house . . .', Hepburn interview.

399 'naked on Noel's terrace . . .', Pringle interview.

399 'the working classes were always delighted . . .', Cargill interview.

400 'There is a twelve-minute speech . . .', *Theatre Arts*, September 1953.

400 'I never intend to indulge . . .', D, p. 212.

400 'Revealing no star temperament . . .', Daniel Farson, *Sacred Monsters*, Bloomsbury, 1988, pp. 79–80.

400 'belladonna plasters . . .', D, p. 212.

400 'I told him people were . . .', Russell interview, 25 November 1993.

401 'swarms of people . . .', D, p. 214.

401 'Oh Noel, that was so funny . . .', DFG.

401 'I am really glad . . .', D, p. 214.

401 'He was really remarkable . . .', ibid., p. 209.

401 'enchanting . . .', ibid., p. 218.

402 'My dear, always come . . .', David Lean, interview with Barry Norman, BBC TV, 1990.

403 'Noel sang some of his songs . . .', Nicholas Lawford, diary, 28 March 1954.

403 'On every page . . .', *Sunday Times*, 28 March 1954.

403 'Autobiography written . . .', *Daily Telegraph*, 31 March 1954.

403 'the reason for the book's dullness . . .', *Daily Express*, 2 April 1954.

403 'light-weight championship . . .', Gerard Fay, *Manchester Guardian*, 2 April 1954.

404 'Mary Ellis acted well . . .', D, pp. 233–4.

404 'timing and wit . . .', Mary Ellis, interview with author, 6 May 1992.

404 'In the drawing of the rose . . .', Cole Lesley, letter to Stephen Tennant, 31 May 1954.

404 'the basic melodrama . . .', *Punch*, 16 June 1954.

404 'If one is going to convince . . .', New York *Morning Telegraph*, 3 July 1954.

404 'Everybody was unhappy . . .', Ellis interview.

405 'An obvious success . . .', D, p. 237.

405 'Venus in furs . . .' Bach, op. cit., p. 372.

405 'saloon singing . . .', ibid., p. 367.

406 'the stars belong under a roof . . .', Russell interview.

406 'cosy personal triumph . . .', D, pp. 238–9.

406 'A frail, white-haired figure . . .', *Daily Express*, 1 July 1954.

406 'Fifty-four years of love . . .', D, pp. 239–40.

406 'desolate and suddenly rootless', Charles Castle, *Oliver Messel*, Thames & Hudson, 1986, p. 210.

406 'an escapist holiday . . .', D, pp. 240–3.

25. Live in Las Vegas

408 'amusing, talkative . . .', *D*, p. 249.
408 'used to read to us . . .', Gielgud interview.
408 'What a vain man . . .', Cargill interview, 12 September 1993.
408 'the most perfect house guest . . .', Lance Hamilton, unpublished memoir.
408 'Noel found it very tiresome . . .', Gielgud interview.
409 'I have at least a few months . . .', *D*, p. 250.
409 'I will now propose a toast . . .', NC, 24 November 1956; courtesy Mrs Blanche Blackwell.
410 'Jamaica is a coloured island . . .', *D*, p. 254.
410 'At that time they couldn't . . .', Russell interview.
410 'a bit dull and complacent . . .', *D*, p. 267.
410 'a brisk little Jewish go-getter . . .', ibid., pp. 246–7.
411 'Coward's opening at the Desert Inn . . .', *New York Times* magazine, June 1955.
412 'I have made one of the most sensational . . .', *D*, pp. 267–72.
412 'A certain joke might be . . .', *A Private Life*.
413 'Paramount want me . . .', *D*, pp. 272–6.
414 'It's what they laughingly call . . .', *Daily Mail*, 6 August 1955.
414 'charming to work . . .', *D*, p. 281.
414 'bad character', ibid., p. 283.
415 'Well, we must take . . .', Russell interview, 9 February 1993.
415 'a great performer . . .', *D*, p. 286.
415 'and so is the Thunderbird . . .', Lance Hamilton, unpublished memoir.
416 'One of the directors . . .', Russell interview.
416 'productions of impeccable taste . . .', *D*, p. 286.
416 'invented the concept of cool . . .', *Observer*, 1 April 1973.
416 'but Noel didn't have to worry . . .', Lance Hamilton, unpublished memoir.
416 'There has certainly been . . .', *New York Herald-Tribune*, 26 October 1956.
417 'most Americans who have followed . . .', Mike Graham, undated cutting.
417 'Any sexual activities . . .', *D*, pp. 291–2.
417 'It was a great incentive . . .', Leslie Smith interview, 17 February 1993.
418 'Noel was busy going broke . . .', Cargill interview.
419 'The joke will certainly be on me . . .', *D*, p. 296.
419 '*extremely* tiresome . . .', ibid., p. 301.
419 'unremittingly difficult', *New York Times*, 27 October 1991.
419 'I knew them backwards . . .', Payn interview.
419 'The thing Noel said that hurt me . . .', *New York Times*, 27 October 1991.
419 'We thought Graham was safely . . .', Russell interview.
419 'That's so the men . . .', John J. Sullivan, 'Time Out for Television', 8 January 1956, unsourced cutting.
419 'and injected the damn thing . . .', *D*, p. 304.
420 'very hep . . .', *New York Herald-Tribune*, undated cutting, 1956.
420 'light as thistledown . . .', New York *News*, 16 January 1956.
420 'just about the most emancipated . . .', Philip Minoff, *Cue*, 28 January 1956.
420 'Yes, it is a wrench . . .', *D*, pp. 304–6.
421 'ugly house . . .', Cargill interview.
421 'Isn't it marvellous? . . .', Gielgud interview.
422 'seventeen lorryloads . . .', Payn interview.
422 'hustling and twittering . . .', *Letters of Ann Fleming*, p. 175.
422 'He treated women . . .', Blanche Blackwell, interview with author, 5 July 1993.

423 'You're just an old cunt-teaser . . .', Peter Quennell, letter to author, 21 October 1991.
423 'it wasn't good enough . . .', Russell interview.
424 'it was a case . . .', Smith interview, 17 February 1993.
424 'felt more and more like . . .', *Daily Express*, 19 April 1956.
424 'It hadn't been sold . . .', Smith interview.
424 'From Mr Coward's point of view . . .', undated cutting.
425 'more in sorrow than in anger . . .', *Daily Express*, quoted in *D*, p. 309.
425 'without, I think, impairing . . .', *D*, p. 307.
425 'They didn't like the idea . . .', Russell interview.
425 'It can't be off . . .', *New York Post*, 13 March 1956.
425 'humiliate me as publicly . . .', *D*, p. 313.
425 'People who object . . .', New York *News*, 16 January 1956.
425 'Insiders feel . . .', *World Telegram*, 13 March 1956.
425 'People didn't like him . . .', Russell interview.
425 'Like darling Mum . . .', *D*, pp. 313–16.
426 'to find some less Cowardly . . .', Wapshott, op. cit., p. 172.
426 'Coward spoke the rhymes . . .', New York *Daily Mirror*, April 1956.
426 'Tell me, have you found . . .', videotape, Museum of Television and Radio, New York.
426 'those prehistoric monsters . . .', New York *Daily Mirror*, 4 May 1956.
426 'You could never cook . . .', *TV Guide*, 14 July 1956.
426 'the rapport between us . . .', *D*, p. 319.
426 'frequently touching . . .', undated cuttings.
426 'renouncing my native land . . .', *D*, p. 321.
427 'Of course, I was an improbable . . .', *Evening Standard*, 25 May 1956.
427 'sickeningly vulgar . . .', *D*, pp. 321–3.
428 'What I have been doing . . .', NC, letter to Nancy Mitford, July 1956.
428 'The Island itself . . .', *D*, pp. 325–6.
428 'I must stop now and go back . . .', NC, letter to Nancy Mitford, July 1956.
428 'Just a minute . . .', private information.
428 'I would like to be able . . .', NC, letter to Nancy Mitford, July 1956.

26. Pomp and Circumstance

429 'scandal with local Busta . . .', *D*, p. 125.
429 'violently disliked . . .', ibid., p. 150
429 'I seem, in later years, . . .', ibid., p. 257
430 'madly enthusiastic . . .', ibid., p. 281–2.
430 'The excuse was always . . .', obituary, *Daily Telegraph*.
430 'a roaring success . . .', ibid., p. 315.
430 'an almost perfect example . . .', *Sunday Times*, 29 April 1956.
430 'caused his players . . .', *Sunday Times*, 29 April 1956.
431 'Vivien Leigh has decided . . .', NC, letter to Nancy Mitford, July 1956.
431 'as inevitable as anything . . .', *D*, pp. 330–1.
431 'but then he said he couldn't . . .', Matalon interview.
431 'irritation and tetchiness . . .', *D*, p. 331.
431 'Christ you look old! . . .', John Dempsey, interview with author.
431 'neither of whom . . .', *D*, p. 331.
432 'in a tremendously *hausfrau* mood . . .', ibid., p. 333.
432 '*Nude with Violin* was a very silly play . . .', Gielgud interview.
432 'It's very broad . . .', Ronald Hayman, *John Gielgud*, Heinemann, 1971, p. 195.

432 'firmly scratched . . .', *D*, p. 333.

432 'Criticisms? I haven't read them . . .', *Evening Standard*, 26 September 1956.

432 'This Unhappy Greed . . .', *NC&F*, p. 178.

432 'Sir, Amid the hail . . .', *The Times*, 26 September 1956.

433 'Poor John . . .', *D*, p. 333.

433 'rock'n'roll session . . .', *Evening Standard*, 3 October 1956.

433 'wittily and charmingly . . .', *D*, p. 334.

433 'He couldn't have been . . .', Joe Mitchenson, interview with author, 30 September 1991.

434 'The only thing . . .', *D*, p. 352.

434 'full of praise . . .', ibid., p. 337.

434 'a satirical light comedy . . .', *Play Parade 6*.

434 'persecution mania . . .', M&M, p. 4.

434 'it will sit next door . . .', *D*, p. 337.

434 'I am trying to discipline . . .', ibid., p. 339.

435 'This writing of free verse . . .', ibid., p. 345.

435 'from every angle . . .', ibid., pp. 339–41.

435 'sort of monkey face . . .', Elspeth March interview, 3 May 1991.

435 'there had been some trouble . . .', Lorn Loraine, letter to NC, 10 August 1961.

436 'nothing that was originally promised . . .', *D*, p. 341.

436 'I did not realise . . .', Lorn Loraine, letter to NC, 10 August 1961.

436 'more actual money in the bank . . .', *D*, pp. 345–6.

437 'Noel Coward appeared last night . . .', *Letters of Ann Fleming*, p. 192.

437 'They were subjected . . .', Russell interview.

437 'One can't say NO, NO, NO . . .', *D*, p. 347.

437 'sniffing the sawdust . . .', ibid., p. 352.

438 'Is the bow-tie too loud? . . .', *Daily Mirror*, 5 June 1957.

438 'a curious "welfare state" . . .', *D*, pp. 354–6.

438 'respectfully disagreed . . .', Eddie Fisher, *My Life, My Loves*, W. H. Allen, 1982, p. 95.

438 'an overweening pomposity . . .', *D*, pp. 357–61.

439 'they all said Graham . . .', *The Kenneth Williams Diaries* (ed. Russell Davies), HarperCollins, 1993, p. 139.

439 'just weren't strong . . .', Graham Payn, interview with author, 21–22 September 1992.

439 'I long for him to get . . .', *D*, p. 361.

439 'quite a lot of first-hand accounts . . .', Lorn Loraine, letter to NC, 3 September 1957.

440 'wickedly . . .', *D*, p. 365.

440 'He was . . . upsetting . . .', John Dempsey, interview with author, 21 July 1992.

440 'for polishing . . .', *D*, pp. 365–6.

440 'If I were one who ever had . . .', undated cutting.

440 'the successful homosexual . . .', *New Yorker*, 24 January 1977.

441 'there were six actors . . .', Russell interview.

441 'severely taped eyelids . . .', *New York Herald-Tribune*, 15 November 1957.

441 'I'm made up like Theda Bara . . .', *New York Post*, 21 November 1957.

441 'grim', *D*, p. 366.

442 'It is delightful to have . . .', *New York Herald-Tribune*, 15 November 1957.

442 'The old assurance has gone . . .', *New York Times*, 15 November 1957.

442 'This sent him into . . .', Russell interview.

442 'All the gallant lyrics . . .', *D*, pp. 368–9.

442 'the takings were so low . . .', Russell interview.

443 'told police the actor was . . .', *New York Post*, 3 February 1958.
443 'the months of November . . .', CL, p. 96.
443 'he had just had a boyfriend . . .', Ned Rorem, interview with author, 12 June 1992.
443 'Sometimes we lived those months . . .', CL, p. 96.
444 'I'm tired of the unbrave . . .', D, pp. 378–80.
445 'a total misunderstanding . . .', Marchant, op. cit., p. 53.
445 'You don't like American acting . . .', ibid., pp. 58–9.

27. Prisoner of a Legend

446 'I dream nostalgically . . .', D, p. 387.
446 'not very drunk . . .', ibid., pp. 359–60.
447 '"Ner-now, Noel Coward is coming" . . .', Robin Maugham, *Escape from the Shadows*, p. 230.
447 'ghastly but successful . . .', D, p. 382.
447 'because I even hate walking . . .', *New York Post*, 20 June 1958.
447 'on the turn . . .', D, p. 382.
447 'he was never the same . . .', Gielgud interview.
447 'It's my musical year . . .', *New York Herald-Tribune*, 12 September 1958.
448 'prostitute . . .', D, p. 390.
448 'pointed features . . .', *New York Times*, 4 March 1959.
448 'I said, "I'll do it . . ."', Tammy Grimes, interview with author, 27 September 1992.
448 'He was a wonderful insulter . . .', Roddy McDowall, interview with author, 3 May 1992.
448 'violently', D, p. 392–3.
448 'I don't really mind . . .', ibid., p. 398.
449 'Knowing Carol's reputation . . .', ibid., p. 401.
449 'possibly more helpful . . .', John Osborne, *Almost a Gentleman*, Faber, 1991, p. 133.
449 'Both men were dressed . . .', *New York Herald-Tribune*, 1 March 1959.
449 'at odds about *Lulu* . . .', Roddy McDowall interview.
449 'supreme theatrical redundancy . . .', *New Yorker*, 14 March 1959.
450 'The general consensus . . .', D, p. 405.
450 'Naturally he chose the dates . . .', Alec Guinness, *Blessings in Disguise*, Hamish Hamilton, 1985, pp. 201–2.
450 'Blue Harbour was beautifully run . . .', Lance Hamilton, unpublished memoir.
451 'in a very gilded hotel . . .', Guinness, op. cit., p. 203.
451 'charming, courteous and meticulous . . .', D, p. 406.
451 '"Come in here . . ."', Guinness, op. cit., p. 206.
451 'I have just finished . . .', NC, letter to Nancy Mitford, 8 April 1959.
451 'a squalid little piece . . .', D, pp. 408–9.
451 'John Gielgud was booing . . .', Osborne, op. cit., p. 127.
452 'roomy but fairly hideous . . .', D, p. 410.
452 'On the contrary . . .', Blanche Blackwell, *You* magazine, 21 March 1993.
452 'We have made ourselves . . .', D, p. 411.
452 'Noel wasn't to know . . .', Leslie Smith interview.
453 'a great shine . . .', D, p. 412.
453 'as inconspicuous as a hippopotamus . . .', *Observer*, 3 January 1960.
453 'I *am* very good . . .', D, p. 427.
454 'a succession of varied . . .', *The Times*, 15 July 1959.
454 'He pleaded . . .', *New York Times*, book review, undated cutting, 1982.
454 'lizard tongue . . .', Osborne, op. cit., p. 58.

454 'with a gleam of satisfaction . . .', ibid., p. 135.
454 'suddenly transported . . .', Osborne, op. cit., p. 135.
454 'it failed to do the trick . . .', *The Times*, 26 July 1978.
454 'The trouble is . . .', *Sunday Times*, 2 August 1959.
455 'To do something I wasn't . . .', D, p. 421.
455 'He denies that his creative . . .', *Daily Mail*, 28 November 1959.
455 'She has developed a hard . . .', D, pp. 422–4.
456 'may break up . . .', *Daily Mail*, 2 February 1960.
456 'curiously detached feeling . . .', D, p. 430.
456 'Noel Coward – the prisoner . . .', *Manchester Guardian*, 16 December 1959.
456 'that it was time for me . . .', NC, letter to Charles Russell, 5 February 1960.
457 'a little wobbly . . .', D, pp. 432–3.
457 'at least he does it . . .', Riva, op. cit., p. 446
457 'He asked me to direct . . .', Frith Banbury, interview with author, 30 April 1991.
458 'I'm on to Pinter's wavelength . . .', D, p. 436.
458 'a sort of Cockney Ivy Compton-Burnett . . .', ibid., p. 605.
458 'What he liked . . .', *A Private Life*.
458 'whirled around . . .', *A Private Life*.
458 'badly and greedily', p. 364.
459 'I explained that I had . . .', D, p. 437.
459 'not to be sneezed at . . .', ibid., p. 441.
459 'It's too bad Coward . . .', *Halliwell's*, p. 455.
459 'real blazing row . . .', D, p. 441.
459 'beneath the froth . . .', *Play Parade 6*, introduction.
460 'a resonant metaphor . . .', Lahr, op. cit., pp. 143–6.
460 'There is a heartless sentimentality . . .', C. D. Heriot, reader's report, 22 June 1960, LCP.
460 'I have never read such abuse . . .', D, p. 447.
460 'There is a lot of old shop . . .', *Financial Times*, 8 September 1960.
460 'give a great deal of quiet . . .', *Sunday Times*, 11 September 1960.
460 'This ghastly cold douche . . .', D, pp. 447–9.
461 'Clifton, if you don't stop . . .', Ned Sherrin, *Cutting Edge*, Dent, 1984.
461 'He is a curious creature . . .', D, p. 450.
461 'called me out of the blue . . .', Lionel Bart, letter to author, 7 April 1992.
461 'Noel who? . . .', Hunter Davies, *Independent*, September 1994.
461 'Rattling around loosely . . .', *Saturday Review*, 15 April 1961.
462 'not in the least significant . . .', *New York Post*, 10 June 1956.
462 'He was amiable and gossipy . . .', D, p. 452.
462 'some Jamaican cretin . . .', ibid., p. 456.
462 'touchy about certain things . . .', Blackwell interview, 5 July 1993.
462 'now definitely beyond middle age . . .', D, p. 454.

28. Sail Away

464 'with a well-ordered liver . . .', D, p. 457.
464 'I am bashing away . . .', NC, letter to Lance Hamilton, undated.
464 'brittle, stylised, sophisticated . . .', D, p. 309.
465 'like a pimple on the dome . . .', James Money, *Capri*, Hamish Hamilton, 1986, p. 261.
465 'If I can really pull it off . . .', D, p. 454.
465 'a preposterous piece of work . . .', *Sunday Dispatch*, 30 October 1960.
465 'apparently disastrous . . .', D, p. 448.

466 'my age and experience . . .', *Sunday Times*, 15 January 1961.
466 'Scratch-and-Mumble School . . .', *Sunday Times*, 22 January 1961.
466 'seldom loved or envied . . .', *Sunday Times*, 29 January 1961.
466 'human activity', ibid.
467 'The bridge of a sinking ship . . .', *Observer*, 22 January 1961.
467 'the silly old man . . .', D, pp. 463–4.
467 'Mr Coward, like Miss Dietrich . . .', SM, p. 268.
467 'happily Noel Coward . . .', *Letters of Ann Fleming*, p. 278.
467 'Everybody raved about the score . . .', D, pp. 464–7.
468 'I know Mr Coward's work . . .', *Morning Telegraph*, 10 July 1961.
468 'I don't remember ever having worked . . .', D, pp. 484–5.
468 'Everything is proceeding . . .', D, p. 469.
468 'You look ill . . .', Russell interview.
469 'avant-garde American composer . . .', D, pp. 470–1.
469 'I knew all about him . . .', Ned Rorem interview, 12 June 1992.
469 'We talked there until six . . .', Ned Rorem, letter to author, 9 March 1992.
469 'Later, I mentioned it . . .', Rorem interview.
470 'Brief Encounter!', Ned Rorem, letter to author, 9 March 1992.
470 'blinding, glorious . . .', Dirk Bogarde, letter to author, 1 December 1991.
470 'Garland was the only person . . .', Mitchenson interview.
470 'Not an intellectual occupation . . .', D, pp. 472–3.
471 'had one of the biggest advance . . .', Morton Gottlieb, interview with author, 9 June 1992.
471 'Everything is going so well . . .', D, p. 474.
471 'in walked this tall, gorgeous . . .', *Morning Telegraph*, 11 July 1961.
471 'and Joe and I are doing it . . .', D, p. 476.
471 'She put her hands . . .', Russell interview.
471 'I said "What would happen . . ."', Joe Layton, interview with author, 16 June 1992.
472 'chic to the point . . .', D, p. 480.
472 'New York theatre-cum-café . . .', ibid., p. 483.
472 'a sweet friend . . .', ibid., p. 485.
472 'Well, it was his fault . . .', *A Private Life*.
472 'I wonder how long . . .', D, pp. 486–9.
473 'on a plane just above . . .', ibid., p. 497.
473 'enjoyable but, of course . . .', ibid., p. 518.
473 'now crammed . . .', ibid., pp. 498–9.
473 'disposal of my properties . . .', ibid., p. 502.
474 'flung open . . .', Robin Maugham, *Escape from the Shadows*, pp. 230–1.
474 'Basically, it's a good . . .', *Financial Times*, 22 June 1962.
475 'Mr Coward seems to be straining . . .', C. D. Heriot, reader's report, 27 April 1962, LCP.
475 'They hate me very much . . .', D, p. 508.
476 'This is a bore . . .', NC, letter to Nancy Mitford, September/October 1962.
476 'non-U ewe . . .', CL, p. 422.
476 'They can't *all* be idiotic . . .', D, p. 515.
476 'guilty', obituary, Hugo Vickers, *Independent*, 1 May 1990.
476 'I knew him as well as I wanted . . .', Wapshott, op. cit., p. 325.
476 'How strange . . .', D, p. 518.
476 'of the violence of his instinct . . .', John Lehmann, *A Nest of Tigers*, Macmillan, 1968, p. 100.
476 'crush down these thoughts . . .', D, p. 518.

476 'That's that . . .', ibid., p. 525.
476 'lots of screaming . . .', McDowall interview.
477 'We used to go and see Noel . . .', Russell interview.
477 'as a kind of assistant . . .', Geoffrey Johnson, interview with author, 12 June 1992.
477 'He was besotted . . .', Russell interview.
477 'wasn't very comfortable . . .', Johnson interview.
478 'sick-sick-sick . . .', *D*, pp. 542–3.
478 'Coley and I sat . . .', ibid., pp. 528–9.

29. Dad's Renaissance

479 'has had rave notices! . . .', *D*, p. 533.
479 'They talk exactly like . . .', James Roose-Evans, interview with author, 4 March 1992.
480 'very well done . . .', *D*, p. 533.
480 'What about the notices . . .', NC to Joyce Carey, 19 July 1963.
481 'I saw this woman . . .', John G. Rogers, *New York Herald-Tribune*, 8 December 1963.
481 'I simply couldn't do it . . .', *Newark Evening News*, 8 September 1963.
482 'so wobbly . . .', *D*, pp. 543–5.
482 'He really blew up . . .', Layton interview.
482 'cursed by a sort . . .', *D*, p. 598.
482 'to a rapturous reception . . .', ibid., pp. 546–7.
482 'very successful . . .', Layton interview.
483 'glittering . . .', *D*, p. 550.
483 'the glamour and romance . . .', *New York Times*, 9 December 1963.
483 'Elegant, charming and delightfully cast . . .', *Morning Telegraph*, 10 December 1963.
483 'We opened so soon . . .', Layton interview.
483 'If Beattie really delivers . . .', *D*, p. 557.
483 'You've pronounced it two ways . . .', Laffey, op. cit., pp. 248–9.
483 'This was not only miserable . . .', *D*, p. 558.
484 'a nightmare . . .', Laffey, p. 248.
484 'Beattie fucked up . . .', *D*, p. 559.
484 'She's seventy-five . . .', Laffey, pp. 251–3.
484 'minor miracles', *D*, pp. 560–1.
484 'betrayal . . .', Ben Bagley, interview with author, 15 June 1992.
484 'Even if *High Spirits* . . .', *New York Times*, quoted in *Morning Telegraph*, 9 April 1964.
485 'a thoroughly satisfying score', *Journal-American*, ibid.
485 'a brassy spectacular', *New York News*, ibid.
485 'An effort to boost . . .', *Letters of Ann Fleming*, p. 338.
485 'Noel Coward is known as . . .', ibid., p. 335.
485 'quite incapable of doing anything . . .', *D*, p. 562.
485 'He tried to educate me . . .', *A Private Life*.
485 'something must be done . . .', *D*, p. 589.
485 'Let's hope it doesn't . . .', ibid., p. 564.
486 'You'll never guess . . .', Johnson interview.
486 'presumably because La Divina . . .', *D*, pp. 568–70.
486 'Fascinating man . . .', Alan Helms, interview with author, September 1993.
487 'a horrid but expected sadness . . .', *D*, p. 571.
487 'She is, of course, perfectly brilliant . . .', ibid., p. 573.

487 'I'm thrilled and flattered . . .', Michael Coveney, *Maggie Smith: A Bright Particular Star*, Victor Gollancz, 1992, p. 111.
487 'doomed to sit . . .', D, p. 575.
487 'Anyone would think . . .', Coveney, op. cit., p. 112.
487 'a disgrace to herself . . .', D, p. 577.
488 'Maggie just sent up . . .', Coveney, p. 112–13.
488 'tottered insecurely . . .', D, p. 578.
488 'There seemed to be . . .', *A Private Life*.
488 'not the most generous . . .', Coveney, p. 113.
488 'Tell me one thing . . .', *Independent*, 11 December 1993.
488 'wildly enthusiastic . . .', D, p. 579.
488 'grossly over-weighted . . .', *Sunday Telegraph*, 8 November 1964.
488 'The piece is grotesquely unfunny . . .', *Sunday Times*, 8 November 1964.
489 'properly bought it . . .', D, pp. 579–80.
489 'I was delighted and touched . . .', NC, letter to Rupert Croft-Cooke, 21 December (?1964), HRHC.
489 'not one really good notice . . .', D, pp. 583–4.
490 'I suppose it's just as well . . .', ibid., p. 589.
490 'all *apparently* very good . . .', ibid., p. 599.
490 'the end of Act Two . . .', Maxine Audley, interview with author, 17 September 1991.
490 'the talk of the island . . .', D, p. 592.
490 'and . . . left sadly shaking . . .', CL, p. 441.
490 'and was delighted . . .', D, p. 593.
490 'which had *not* been frisked . . .', CL, pp. 442–3.
490 'I thought how funny . . .', SM, p. 308.
491 'I really think . . .', D, pp. 593–6.
491 'I play an elderly, drunk, queer . . .', NC, letter to Roddy McDowall, 28 March 1965.
491 'a real bully . . .', Spoto, op. cit., p. 287.
491 'The cast as good as ever . . .', D, pp. 599–600.
491 'I *am* England . . .', *Sunday Express*, 23 May 1965.
492 'Some other decoration . . .', D, p. 602.
492 'The Beatles, those two I met . . .', *Daily Mail*, undated cutting.
492 'gently but firmly . . .', D, pp. 602–4.
493 'It just so happened . . .', Audley interview.
493 'a brilliant man . . .', D, p. 605.
493 'This is the celebration . . .', John Osborne, *A Patriot for Me*, Faber, 1965, p. 77.
493 'muddled, undisciplined . . .', D, p. 605.
493 'subjected to a light . . .' *New York Times*, book review, 1982.
493 'claustrophobic panic . . .', D, p. 606.
493 'one of the best plays . . .', ibid., pp. 604–7.
494 'devoured by retrospective hate . . .', ibid., p. 508.
494 'his disgusting autobiography . . .', ibid., p. 511.
494 'The man who wrote that awful slop . . .', SM, p. 302.
494 'Coward channelled . . .', Ted Morgan, *Somerset Maugham*, Jonathan Cape, 1980, p. 606.
495 'What stuck in his craw . . .', Cargill interview, 12 September 1993.
496 '*A Song at Twilight* is far and away . . .', Marchant, op. cit., pp. 262–3.
496 'For all their determined glitter . . .', *The Times*, April 1966.
496 'It is perhaps the most serious . . .', *Sunday Telegraph*, 22 May 1966.
497 'One's real inside self . . .', Hunter Davies, *Sunday Times*, 28 December 1969.

497 'outspoken and moving', Morgan, op. cit., p. 606.
497 'tells us nothing . . .', undated cutting.
498 'What Mr Lesley shows us . . .', *New Yorker*, 24 January 1977.

30. A Song at Twilight

499 'with whom I immediately . . .', *D*, pp. 608–9.
499 'peered into the room . . .', Matalon interview.
500 'an undercurrent of evil', *D*, pp. 615–16.
500 'We were supposed to rehearse . . .', Matalon interview.
501 'hideously depressed . . .', *D*, pp. 622–6.
501 'a truly monstrous person . . .', Matalon interview.
502 'Just before *A Suite* . . .', Peter Wadland, interview with author, 26 November 1991.
502 'Man is intrinsically . . .', *Daily Mail*, undated cutting.
502 'suavely controversial', *The Times*, 14 March 1966.
503 'I have never before . . .', Huggett, op. cit., p. 499.
503 'extremely good . . .', *D*, pp. 629–30.
503 'The Old Master . . .', C. D. Heriot, reader's report, 20 January 1966, LCP.
503 'As played by Coward . . .', Marchant, op. cit., pp. 216–17.
503 'He had a way of getting up . . .', *Encounter*, July 1966.
504 'friends, good doctors . . .', *D*, p. 631.
504 'a great many of both sexes . . .', ibid., p. 633.
504 'I've always loved . . .', *Evening Standard*, 1 May 1965.
504 'She sings gloriously . . .', *D*, pp. 634–8.
504 'We've got marvellous news . . .', Patrick Woodcock, interview with author, 18 March 1991.
505 'The days slide by . . .', *D*, pp. 645–7.
505 'I arrived on set . . .', Ian McKellen to author.
505 'talented, charming, efficient . . .', *D*, p. 667.
505 'The whole purpose . . .', Leo Maguire, interview with author, 17 September 1991.
506 'a screaming ass . . .', *D*, p. 510.
506 'I've been too agitated . . .', *D*, pp. 651–3.
507 'He was very fond of Marlene . . .', Woodcock interview.
507 'Cease this mental masturbation . . .', Hugo Vickers to author.
507 'By then [Noel] . . .', Layton interview.
507 'didn't enjoy any of it . . .', *D*, p. 654.
507 'a dear man . . .', interview with Anthony Haden-Guest, *Sunday Times Magazine*, undated (1968).
508 'staggered blindly away . . .', *D*, p. 657.
508 'My passion for the tropics . . .', ibid., p. 662.
508 'blaze of enjoyment . . .', ibid., p. 664.
508 'Look at him move . . .', *Sunday Times Magazine*, undated (1968).
508 'great fun', *D*, pp. 668–70.
509 'Horribly frightened . . .', *D*, p. 676.
509 'Switzerland seems littered . . .', Robin Maugham diary, 4 August 1969.
509 'I said, "Oh, it's Sheridan's book . . ."', McDowall interview.
509 'I can't afford to offend . . .', *The Times*, 29 October 1994.
509 'There is one essential difference . . .', SM, p. xiv.
510 'a crown-encrusted . . .', *D*, p. 679.
510 'Alas, darling Ma'ams . . .', private information.

510 'rather casually passing me a salted almond . . .', New York *Daily News*, 20 February 1970.

510 'I am of course delighted . . .', NC, letter to Esme Wynne-Tyson, 19 January 1970.

511 'What was thrilling . . .', McDowall interview.

511 'My dear Noel . . .', *A Private Life*.

512 'We always like to give Noel . . .', *Daily Mail*, undated (December 1969).

512 'As I advanced . . .', NC, letter to Nancy Mitford, 10 June 1972.

512 'The Queen was absolutely charming . . .', *Evening News*, 3 February 1970.

512 'I just use this thing . . .', Bernard Drew, unsourced cutting.

512 'I've seen quite a number . . .', *New York Times*, 11 February 1970.

512 'Considering the way it's done . . .', ibid.

513 'nearly always justified . . .', New York *Daily News*, 20 February 1970.

513 'One day, Master sitting here . . .', Susan Ferrier Mackay, 'Noel Coward's Firefly', unpublished article, TM.

513 'Towards the end . . .', *Daily Mail*, 2 December 1970.

31. The Party's Over Now

514 'For God's sake, Noel . . .', *Evening Standard*, undated (January 1972).

514 '"I don't know what to say . . ."', *Evening Standard*, 27 March 1973.

515 'Now listen . . .', NC, letter to Nancy Mitford, 9 January 1972.

515 'might have been brought from Eastbourne . . .', Cecil Beaton diary, 1972.

516 'musicalised', Johnson interview, 12 June 1992.

516 'We have to get up there . . .', *New York Times*, 15 January 1973.

516 'It's going to be all right . . .', *New York Post*, 15 January 1973.

516 'NY papers would have had . . .', *Star-Ledger*, 17 January 1973.

516 'I haven't got anything left . . .', *New York Times*, 15 January 1973.

516 'He'd say . . .', Johnson interview.

517 'My wife passing by . . .', Susan Ferrier Mackay, 'Noel Coward's Firefly'.

517 'Joan Hirst . . . said that . . .', Smith interview, 17 February 1993.

518 'Sir Noel often said . . .', *Daily Telegraph*, 30 March 1973.

518 'Coward, with the same nice regard . . .', *New Yorker*, 3 March 1975.

518 'by sweet coincidence', Laurence Olivier, undated cutting.

519 'beautiful great eighteenth-century theatre . . .', undated cutting.

519 'I think he's back here', Payn interview.

520 'a dear and so very . . .', D, p. 597.

520 'as if he'd been walking . . .', Johnson interview.

520 'Mr Lesley's massive, authorised . . .', *New York Times*, book review, 28 November 1976.

520 'his own invention . . .', unsourced cutting, 20 January 1977.

521 'the fatally damaged celebrity . . .', Mark Ashurst, letter to author, 10 June 1994.

521 'on the later, post-war plays . . .', *New Yorker*, 24 January 1977.

521 'It's a bit startling . . .', *Variety*, 15 December 1982.

522 'characteristic privacy . . .', *New York Native*, 25 November 1985.

522 'he wasn't a churchgoer . . .', Payn interview.

Index

113; cuts NC, 314; in *Relative
Values*, 390
Cooper, Margaret, 56, 57
Cooper, Sally, 442
Co-Optimists, The, 105
Coquette, 195
Corelli, Marie, 72
Cornell, Katherine (1898–1974), 93,
247 &*n*, 251, 304, 441, 451
Courtneidge, Dame Cicely, 50, 51, 488
Courtneidge, Robert, 50, 108
Coward, Amy, family tree; 19
Coward, Arthur Sabin (1856–1937);
family tree; 18, 23, 80, 163, 196,
283; birth and background, 6;
character, 8–9; marries Violet Veitch,
9–10; absence from home, 13; loses
job, 15; again, 61; serves tea, 80;
runs lodging-house, 115–6; 'stupid
old boy', 198; idleness &
bewilderment, 220; dies, 283
Coward, Eric (Erik) (1905–33); family
tree; 17, 24, 216; born, 13; ignored,
25; to Ceylon, 196–7; NC visits
there. 216; illness, 216, 220; criticises
NC, 196, 235; terminal illness, 246;
NC writes to, 248; dies, 250–1
Coward, Ida Barbara *see* Makeham
Coward, James (1824–80); family tree;
6, 7
Coward, James Munro (b. 1854);
family tree; 8
Coward, Katherine Alice (Kitty); family
tree; 7, 50
Coward, Myrrha *see* Alcock
Coward, Sir Noel Peirce (1899–1973):
birth, 1, 10, 11; family background,
family tree, 1–10; admired by family,
11; dressed in skirts, 12; demands
attention, 12; highly strung, 12;
relationship with mother, 12; moves
to Sutton, 13; bites schoolmistress,
13; sings at school concert, 13–14;
plays piano, 14; with Aunt Laura,
14–15; moves to Battersea, 15; toy
theatre, 15; at Chapel Royal School,
16; in Southsea, 17; in Meon, 18;
accidents, 18–19; first dramas, 19; &
clergymen, 20, 38; in *The Goldfish*,
21–2; meets Charles Hawtrey, 22; in
The Great Name, 22–3; in *Where the
Rainbow Ends*, 23–24, 25, 26, 45–6;

moves to Clapham, 24–5; in 'An
Autumn Idyll', 25; first homosexual
experience, 26; in *Hannele*, 26–8;
meets Gertrude Lawrence, 26, 27, 28;
heterosexual experience, 28;
relationship with Esme Wynne-
Tyson, 28–30; 'beastly little
whimsies', 29; in drag, 29–30; in
War in the Air, 30; in *Peter Pan*,
30–1; contracts TB, 31; relationship
with Philip Streatfeild, 32–7, 38–9;
relationship with Mrs Astley Cooper,
39–40, 42–3; & Scott Moncrieff,
40–1; reads Saki, 41–2; & Philip
Streatfeild's death, 44; voice breaks,
45; *Charley's Aunt* tour, 46–50;
communes with nature, 47;
friendship with John Ekins, 47–8;
shop-lifting, 48; 'religious
enlightenment', 49; bad actor, 50; in
The Light Blues, 50; dances at the
Elysee Restaurant, 51; in *The Happy
Family*, 51; writes *Parachutes*, 51; &
John Ekins' death, 52; in *Hearts of
the World*, 53–4; in *Wild Heather*,
54–6; in *The Saving Grace*, 57–8;
meets Ivor Novello, 55–6; writes
with Max Darewski, 55–6; learns
from Hawtrey, 57–8; writes *The Last
Chapter*, 58–9 writes *Women and
Whisky*, 59; short stories and other
juvenilia, 57–60; moves to Ebury
Street, 60–1; called up, 62; in the
army, 62–7; nervous breakdown, 64;
& Sheila Kaye-Smith, 64; & G. B.
Stern, 64–5; & Geoffrey
Holdsworth, 65; leaves army, 67; &
Beatrice Lillie, 67–8; audition
technique, 68; stays with the
Dawson-Scotts, 68-9; in *Oh, Boy*,
70; writes *Cherry Pan*, 70; 'gushing
manner', 70; Pemberton Billing trial,
71–2; & Siegfried Sassoon, 72, 73*n*;
& drugs, 73–6; in *Scandal*, 76;
writes *The Last Trick*, 77; writes *The
Rat Trap*, 77–8; magazine stories, 78;
meets Lorn Macnaughtan (Loraine),
79; and Stewart Forster, 80–3; in *The
Knight of the Burning Pestle*, 81;
writes *I'll Leave It to You*, 82, 84–5;
first visit to Paris, 82–3; to Alassio,
83; 'Puck-like', 85; meets Gladys